THE NEW CAMBRIDGE MODERN HISTORY

ADVISORY COMMITTEE

G. N. CLARK J. R. M. BUTLER J. P. T. BURY

THE LATE E. A. BENIANS

VOLUME VII

THE OLD REGIME

1713-63

THE NEW CAMBRIDGE MODERN HISTORY

VOLUME VII

THE OLD REGIME

1713-63

EDITED BY

J. O. LINDSAY

CAMBRIDGE

AT THE UNIVERSITY PRESS

1957

PUBLISHED BY
THE SYNDICS OF THE CAMBRIDGE UNIVERSITY PRESS

Bentley House, 200 Euston Road, London, N.W. 1
American Branch: 32 East 57th Street, New York 22, N.Y.

Printed in Great Britain at the University Press, Cambridge
(Brooke Crutchley, University Printer)

CONTENTS

CONTENTS

CHAPTER IV

THE VISUAL ARTS AND IMAGINATIVE LITERATURE

By PROFESSOR SIR ALBERT RICHARDSON, *Past President of the Royal Academy*

CHAPTER V

THE ENLIGHTENMENT

By A. COBBAN, *Professor of History, University College, London*

CONTENTS

CHAPTER VI

RELIGION

By R. W. GREAVES, *Reader in History in the University of London*

CONTENTS

CHAPTER VII

MONARCHY AND ADMINISTRATION

1. European practice, by J. O. LINDSAY

2. The English inspiration, by W. R. BROCK, *Fellow of Selwyn College and Lecturer in History in the University of Cambridge*

1. EUROPEAN PRACTICE

2. THE ENGLISH INSPIRATION

CHAPTER VIII

THE ARMED FORCES AND THE ART OF WAR

By the late ERIC ROBSON, *Senior Lecturer in History in the University of Manchester*

CONTENTS

CHAPTER IX

INTERNATIONAL RELATIONS

By J. O. LINDSAY

CONTENTS

CHAPTER X

THE DECLINE OF DIVINE-RIGHT MONARCHY IN FRANCE

By A. COBBAN

CONTENTS

CHAPTER XI

ENGLAND

By W. R. Brock

CONTENTS

CHAPTER XII

THE WESTERN MEDITERRANEAN AND ITALY

By J. O. LINDSAY

CONTENTS

CHAPTER XIII

THE ORGANISATION AND RISE OF PRUSSIA

By W. H. Bruford, *Fellow of St John's College and
Professor of German in the University of Cambridge*

CHAPTER XIV

RUSSIA

By Ian Young, *Lecturer in Slavonic Studies in the University of Cambridge*

CONTENTS

CHAPTER XV

SCANDINAVIA AND THE BALTIC

By R. M. HATTON, *Lecturer in Economic and Political History at the London School of Economics*

CONTENTS

CHAPTER XVI

POLAND UNDER THE SAXON KINGS

By L. R. LEWITTER, *Fellow of Christ's College and Lecturer in Polish in the University of Cambridge*

CHAPTER XVII

THE HABSBURG DOMINIONS

By C. A. MACARTNEY, *Fellow of All Souls, Oxford*

CONTENTS

CHAPTER XVIII

THE WAR OF THE AUSTRIAN SUCCESSION

By MARK A. THOMSON, *Professor of Modern History*
in the University of London

CONTENTS

CHAPTER XIX

THE DIPLOMATIC REVOLUTION

By D. B. HORN, *Professor in History in the University of Edinburgh*

CHAPTER XX

THE SEVEN YEARS WAR

By ERIC ROBSON

xvii

CONTENTS

CONTENTS

CHAPTER XXIII

RIVALRIES IN INDIA

By C. C. DAVIES, *Reader in Indian History in the University of Oxford*

CONTENTS

CHAPTER XXIV

ECONOMIC RELATIONS IN AFRICA AND THE FAR EAST

1. Africa, by J. GALLACHER, *Fellow of Trinity College and Lecturer in History in the University of Cambridge*

2. Asia, by VICTOR PURCELL, *Lecturer in Far Eastern History in the University of Cambridge*

1. AFRICA

2. ASIA

CHAPTER I

INTRODUCTORY SUMMARY

A STUDY of the Old Regime might reasonably be expected to go back as far as 1648 and continue to 1789. The choice of 1713 and 1763 as the limits of the period at once stresses the importance of military, diplomatic and political considerations. But in addition to international diplomacy and domestic politics, which show the emergence of Prussia and Russia in central Europe and the increasing rivalry of France and England in the West and on the high seas, the present study makes an attempt to tell this story in the context of the appropriate economic conditions, governmental institutions, social structure and prevailing ideas, even though these may have developed before 1713 and persisted after 1763

The half-century before 1760 showed an increase in the volume of international trade which might be described as revolutionary: it also showed a change in the relative importance of the chief trading nations (ch. II). The increase in trade already owed something to technological progress, but the chief reason for the spectacular increase in the volume of international trade in the first half of the eighteenth century was the rapid expansion of trade between countries in Europe and settlements in America, Africa and Asia. The re-export of colonial products came to be a very valuable part of the trade of England, France and Holland: it was an essential part of the economic life of Spain and Portugal. The Atlantic trade, especially that with the islands of the Caribbean, was greatly prized in the first half of the eighteenth century, and it naturally became a chronic cause of friction between the four European Powers with colonial possessions in that area. India and, to a lesser extent, south-east Asia provided other areas in which highly valuable trading operations could also be carried on. One outstanding characteristic of the international trade of the early eighteenth century was the failure of the Dutch to maintain their pre-eminent position; by this time France and England had overtaken the Dutch as great trading Powers. A second characteristic of the later eighteenth century was a duel between France and England for commercial and colonial pre-eminence. This rivalry showed itself not only in America and Asia but in the Mediterranean, and in the inter-regional trade of northern and central Europe. This last still accounted for a very large amount of the exports both of France and of England, the German trade after 1713 being even more valuable to English merchants than their highly esteemed trade with Old Spain. In the early part of the century France, with her larger population and finer luxury goods, seemed to English observers to be a very dangerous rival. But France's position had some very serious defects, though they were not apparent to contemporary observers, who failed to notice the weaknesses of the French navy and the fact that France's trade balance was not soundly based on the home manufacture of large quantities of good but cheap commodities, as the prosperity of England was based on hardware and cloth. Contemporaries saw only that France's exports and re-exports exceeded her imports in value, and during most of the eighteenth century this spelt prosperity.

The social conditions existing in Europe in the first half of the eighteenth century (ch. III) showed how the prevailing economic conditions were slowly modifying the kind of society which had existed at the end of the religious wars. Eighteenth-century society was still predominantly aristocratic, even though the position of the aristocrat might vary very much as between the politically powerful nobles of Poland, Sweden, Hungary and England and the politically impotent nobles of France, Denmark or Spain. In Prussia aristocrats had to serve the State, whether in the army or the civil service, and attempts were made to secure similar service in Russia and in parts of the Habsburg Empire. The conditions of the peasantry, who still formed the bulk of the population of Europe, varied considerably: from the free villagers of England, Sweden and some parts of France to the serfs of many parts of central, eastern and southern Europe. One tendency which was clearly evident in the eighteenth century was the growth in the numbers and influence of the urban middle class. As overseas trade expanded, the merchants, especially in England and France, increased in numbers and in wealth; while in central and eastern Europe the ranks of the middle class were swelled by the appointment of increasing numbers of civil servants, especially in the later part of the century.

The visual arts and imaginative literature reflected the conditions of eighteenth-century society and the changes which were taking place in it (ch. IV). Superficially the culture of the age might seem inspired by the art of Augustan Rome, but the men of the early eighteenth century had so much confidence in their own intellectual powers and, particularly in England and France, had evolved such a characteristic form of society, that they were able to evolve examples of town architecture and prose literature which were entirely original and of great beauty. As early as 1730 signs of a romantic interest in medieval architecture began to appear in England and an interest in the Gothic style persisted alongside the appreciation of the classical style for most of the eighteenth century. A romantic tendency also appeared in literature with the publication of *Pamela* in 1741. The novel as a literary form became popular in many countries, especially in western Europe where the numbers of the reading public were increasing. But even more characteristic of the period than the beginnings of an appreciation of the romantic in literature and archi-tecture were the partly classical but largely original developments in literature and town buildings. Journals such as the *Spectator* were charac-teristic of a society in which cities such as London and Paris were thriving centres. The vitality of this urban life was also responsible for another characteristic achievement of the early eighteenth century, especially in England where town houses came to be planned as part of a coherent design in squares and terraces. This English idea of town planning and the kind of house best suited for the purpose was copied to some extent, but many noblemen, as in France, preferred to live in a house standing in its garden, and in central and eastern Europe few towns had developed very much even by the end of the eighteenth century.

As for the ideas which found expression in much of this prose literature of the earlier eighteenth century and which have come to be known as 'the Enlightenment' (ch. v), these were based on a profound admiration for human reason, which by the end of the seventeenth century had achieved such spectacular triumphs in the realms of astronomy and mathematics. The sceptics and rationalists of the eighteenth century were, however, empirical and looked to Bacon rather than to Newton for their inspiration, and it was a period when men tended to abandon mathematics in favour of natural science so that the age which began with Newton found its fullest expression in Buffon. It was an age when scientific ideas were popularised, as Newton's astronomy was popularised by Voltaire in his *Lettres philo-sophiques*. It was also an age of collectors and classifiers, of whom the greatest was probably Linnaeus. Weakness in abstract thought retarded development in chemistry, where advance was blocked by the general belief in the erroneous phlogiston hypothesis. In the first part of the eighteenth century history was rated only second to science in importance, but Vico, one of the greatest of the eighteenth-century historians, was not understood by his contemporaries and had little effect on his own period. Perhaps the most important lines along which thought advanced in the eighteenth century were psychology and the study of society. According to Locke's psychology of sensation, man's character was a blank sheet which was to be filled up by experience. It was hoped that reason would be able to direct the education of future generations and so achieve a degree of progress comparable with the triumphs of the human mind in penetrating the mysteries of astronomy. The attempt to achieve a com-prehensive study of society was less successful. Montesquieu's *De l'esprit des lois* was a splendid failure. The time was not ready for a Newton of the social sciences. The political thought of the Enlightenment was, on the whole, rather shallow. Sceptical and rationalist criticisms were directed against torture, barbarous punishments, the confusion of the laws in many countries. Liberty was advocated as 'natural'. Some of the critics, notably Mably or Helvétius, urged the importance of equality as a political

I-2

principle, but on the whole the critics were very cautious in their discussion of forms of government. In France the critics combined advanced anti-clerical opinions with conservative politics. The economic ideas of the age were generally as conservative as were the political ones.

The position of organised religion in western and central Europe in the first half of the eighteenth century was not strong (ch. VI). In the Roman Catholic Church, the papal throne was occupied by a succession of undistinguished men. In France the Church was torn by a further dispute between the Jansenists and the supporters of the Papacy, particularly the Jesuits, as to the heretical nature of the opinions expressed by Quesnel in his *Le noveau testament en français avec des réflexions morales*. The controversy over the bull *Unigenitus* which condemned 101 of Quesnel's propositions became partly political and for much of the eighteenth century weakened the French Crown (which supported the Bull) and discredited the Roman Catholic Church. Throughout Europe there was a tendency among princes to assert their independence of papal control and this trend found expression not only in the writings of the secular philosophers but in the writings of such authors as Van Espen, Giannone and Hontheim. The Papacy found itself compelled to make practical concessions, as in 1727 to Sardinia, in the Concordats of 1737 and 1750 with Spain, to Portugal in 1740 and to Naples. The eighteenth century also saw the disgrace and expulsion from many countries of the Papacy's old and most effective ally the Jesuits, a movement which culminated in 1773 with the suppression of the Society by the pope himself. In Protestant countries the authority of organized religion was no greater than in Catholic Europe. In the German-speaking world the existence of a multitude of local churches increased the authority of the universities, and the professors brought the ideas of the Enlightenment to bear on ecclesiastical politics. The existence of many small Churches also tended to weaken notions of ecclesiastical authority, and pietism, which found a stronghold at Halle, was, like Enlightenment, anti-clerical. In England the Anglican episcopacy of the eighteenth century tended to be secular in outlook. Appointment and promotion from a poor benefice to a rich one depended on sound Whig principles, and bishops tended to be more interested in politics than in the things of the spirit. The loss of the non-juror clergy was a serious weakness to the Church of England. The Protestant dissenters had been saved from persecution by the accession of George I and, though their numbers declined slightly in the early years of the eighteenth century and their fervour was weakened by the prevailing rationalist temper, they played an important part in the economic and intellectual life of the country. But the real missionary zeal was to be found among the Moravian Brethren, the followers of Wesley and the members of the evangelical revival within the Church of England itself.

The form of government which was normal throughout most European countries in the early eighteenth century was some kind of absolute monarchy (ch. VII). The outstanding example of a brilliant monarchy was that of France where the tradition of Louis XIV still invested the Crown with a great deal of lustre, but to the eighteenth-century observer the king of France, who was bound by the conventions of the constitution, was a less absolute ruler than the kings of Spain, Denmark or Prussia. They, in turn, appeared less autocratic than the tsar of all the Russias who, to eighteenth-century observers, was comparable only to the Grand Seignior. Even when the king's authority was more restricted by the constitution as in England or Sweden, by the Church as in Portugal, or by the nature of his very heterogeneous dominions as in the Holy Roman Empire, there was always the possibility that the Crown might reassert itself, as in the Swedish *coup d'état* of 1772. Even the Crown of Poland could be used to galvanise some semblance of life into that unfortunate country, as was shown after the first partition. While the form of government most usual in Europe remained absolute monarchy as it had been for the past two centuries, changes were taking place from the middle of the seventeenth century until the later part of the eighteenth century which tended to make the government more efficient than it had previously been. At the centre there was a tendency towards increased specialisation and in the provinces steps were taken to make government more effective. The administration of justice in most countries, however, remained a chaotic tangle of ancient customs and local privileges. Except in Prussia the methods of collecting the royal revenue were very ineffective, so that war always threatened most countries with a large deficit. Even the king of Prussia, when he was involved in war, had to rely on foreign subsidies. The Emperor always had to rely on foreign subsidies. The king of France, who ruled one of the largest and richest populations in Europe, was faced with so serious a financial crisis at the end of the century that it culminated in the fall of the monarchy. It was the exceptional good fortune of the king of England that he could obtain money fairly easily and at a low rate of interest.

The armed forces and the nature of eighteenth-century warfare clearly reflected the characteristics of government and the structure of society (ch. VIII). During most of the eighteenth century wars were formal and conventional. They were very different from the 'wars of righteousness and moral purpose' (p. 165) of the sixteenth and seventeenth centuries or the wars of national or ideological fanaticism which became common during the nineteenth century. In the eighteenth century many of the wars were dynastic; it is not by accident that three of them are known as the wars of the Spanish, Polish and Austrian succession respectively. They were fought to gain something specific and ended by exchanges of territory and rectification of frontiers; they were not in any sense total wars, and devastation and bloodshed were kept in check by the observance of laws of war. The fighting was confined as far as possible to small, professional armies and the campaigns consisted largely of siege operations and manœuvring designed to compel the opponents to withdraw. Tactics were rigidly traditional, and during the eighteenth century there was hardly any technical improvement in arms except the substitution of an iron for a wooden ramrod in 1740. Movement was slow and very cramped, for no army could afford to go far from its magazines and ovens. Winter campaigns were almost impossible because of the state of the roads. Armies were made up of the unproductive elements of society— the nobility, who provided the officers, and the vagabonds and criminals who made up the bulk of the rank and file. It was considered thrifty to employ foreign troops since these did not deplete the effective manpower of the country. The troops had little or no enthusiasm for the wars which they fought; they served for pay and for plunder. There was always a serious danger of desertion, so troops were not allowed to live off the countryside but were supplied with rations under the eyes of the officers. Discipline was harsh, for it was essential that the men should fear their officers more than the enemy. Gradually it was found that recruiting, even supplemented by the activities of the press gang, did not supply enough men; in Prussia and Russia experiments were made with some form of conscription, but no form of complete national conscription had emerged during the first part of the eighteenth century. Gradually members of the bourgeoisie began to win their way into the officer class, but this was not usual. The armies and navies of the first part of the eighteenth century were conservative, traditional, expensive playthings carefully husbanded by the kings and used to secure a decision without fighting, if possible, for battles were costly and the rulers of eighteenth-century Europe found it difficult to raise extra revenues.

This reluctance to fight a 'total war', or indeed any war except one with strictly limited and generally dynastic aims, did something to counterbalance the commercial rivalry between France and England which was increasingly evident as a force in international affairs during the eighteenth century (ch. IX). The rivalry was disguised at the beginning of the eighteenth century, because from 1716 to about 1733 the rulers in France and England were both temporarily in a delicate position and allied together. Two areas in which there was danger of conflict provoked by other causes than Anglo-French commercial rivalry were the Mediterranean, where Elizabeth Farnese had galvanised moribund Spain into aggressive activity, and the Baltic, where the decline of Sweden had left the way open for the rise of two new Powers, Russia and Prussia. The peace settlement of Utrecht marked the partial defeat of France and secured several advantages for England, but to call the ensuing half-century a period of English predominance in international affairs[1] is to

[1] As P. Muret does in his *La Prépondérance anglaise* (1937).

6

underestimate the importance of France. When the peace of Europe was threatened by Spanish aggression in 1717, 1718 and again in 1725, the Anglo-French combination proved strong enough to prevent hostilities developing on a grand scale, and France and England were able to persuade the Emperor eventually to make the concessions desired by the queen of Spain in Italy. In the Baltic the long northern war ended in 1721, partly because of the death of Charles XII in 1718 and partly because of the success of Anglo-French diplomacy. Peace persisted in this area until 1733 and its preservation was made considerably easier by the death of Peter the Great in 1725. For about a decade after the death of Peter the Great, Russia ceased to play an important part in the affairs of northern Europe; this was only a temporary eclipse, for one of the outstanding developments of the eighteenth century was the emergence of Russia and Prussia as major Powers. During the War of the Polish Succession a Russian army for the first time penetrated deep into western Europe, and the War of the Austrian Succession was the direct result of an aggressive act by Prussia. The war of 1739–48 was complicated because it became combined with a colonial war between England, Spain and France. By 1739 the domestic conditions in England and France which had made an alliance between the two Crowns desirable in 1716 had completely changed. The war of 1739–48 settled very little, but it clearly marked the emergence of Prussia as a Great Power; and the ability of Prussia to take the diplomatic initiative together with the increasing diplomatic importance of Russia were important causes of the Diplomatic Revolution of 1755–6. The Seven Years War, like the War of the Austrian Succession, was fought partly to settle disputes caused by Prussian ambitions, but it was also an important stage in the conflict of England and France in India and America.

The history of France from the death of Louis XIV to the end of the Seven Years War was really part of a longer period which culminated in the outbreak of the Revolution and was characterised by the gradual decline and failure of absolute monarchy (ch. x). At the end of the reign of Louis XIV the form of absolutism which has become known as the *ancien régime* was still something of a new model of efficient government, combining modern absolutism with the old medieval ideas of divine right. This new kind of monarchy, which had been perfected by Richelieu and Mazarin, was so efficient by comparison with the systems of administration in other parts of Europe that, even after the partial defeats which France had suffered during the War of the Spanish Succession, the French government at the beginning of the eighteenth century was in advance of almost every country in Europe. With her considerable natural resources and her population of about nineteen millions, as compared with twenty millions in the Holy Roman Empire and six millions each in Spain and England, France was still in 1713 potentially the greatest Power in Europe,

7

and she had only been partially defeated because Louis XIV at the end of his reign had pursued a policy which had united the whole of Europe against him. France in the early eighteenth century provided a pattern of government which was widely imitated but, though her prestige was enormous, there were very serious weaknesses in the new absolutism. Even by the end of the eighteenth century France was not completely unified, for within her frontiers there was a great confusion of overlapping areas for administration, justice, taxation, military organization and ecclesiastical affairs. Even the fiscal system was not unified and the country was not a single customs area. Though much local self-government had been extinguished, enough local privileges remained to hamper the royal government considerably. The efficiency of the *intendants* was seriously reduced because the areas they administered were too big, their staffs too small, and their responsibilities too manifold. The efficiency of the royal government was still further reduced because on occasion the *intendants* refused to carry out the orders they received. The central government of eighteenth-century France was carried on, in fact, by a few great ministers. Though there were at least four councils dealing with foreign affairs, home affairs, finance, trade and religion, this did not mean that the individual ministers formed any kind of unified cabinet. Only rarely was there someone with the title of first minister. It was the king who was supposed to be the effective head of the government. It was, therefore, of vital importance to France that the man at the head should be of outstanding ability and prepared to devote a great deal of time and energy to the business of State. Louis XIV had weakened all the institutions which might have shared the responsibilities of government with the Crown, but he had left the clergy, the nobles and the *parlements* enough power to be obstructive. After his death in 1715 power was seized by the regent, who attempted to make good some of the deficiencies in the system of government he had inherited, but the failure of his reform revealed the tenacity of the system elaborated by the cardinals and Louis XIV. The regent also attempted to solve the Crown's serious shortage of money by putting his trust in John Law, but Law's System, after a spectacular success, collapsed in 1720. The experiment did considerably stimulate French trade, but it also caused a redistribution of wealth which resulted in a considerable confusion of classes and so still further undermined the governmental system inherited from Louis XIV. Sound finance was essential to stable government and a pacific foreign policy was essential to sound finance. Fleury realised this, and continued the policy of alliance with England which had been initiated by the regent. Firmly supported by this alliance Fleury was able to restore France's influence in northern and eastern Europe, and by the Treaty of Vienna at the end of the War of the Polish Succession France obtained the eventual reversion of Bar and Lorraine. On Fleury's death in 1743 the control of affairs was resumed by

Louis XV, but he was unsuited to the task. With no strong character directing policy, France was at the mercy of conflicting court factions. Belleisle was the centre of a group that favoured war against Austria in 1740; d'Argenson, who came to the fore in 1743, had little aptitude for executing an effective policy, and between 1748 and 1756 it is difficult to say who was directing French policy. Madame de Pompadour favoured Bernis, who concluded the most startling and unexpected alliance with Austria in 1756, and she also helped Choiseul in his rise to power in 1758. Choiseul was an able minister, but by the time he came to power France had been considerably discredited abroad, and at home the authority of the Crown was being undermined, partly by struggles over religion and partly by the opposition provoked by Machault's attempt to impose a tax of a *vingtième* to restore the finances after the War of the Austrian Succession.

While the eighteenth century saw the gradual collapse of absolute monarchy in France, it saw England under a limited monarchy advance steadily in prosperity and power (ch. XI). In 1713 England did not seem very impressive compared with France. Her population was only about one-third of that of France, and internal communications very were bad. But there were some respects in which England was sounder than France. Local administration might be lax or even corrupt, but England, with her system of counties and boroughs, was not scribbled over with a whole series of different administrative areas. England was also a single customs area, and in 1721 Walpole was able to put through a comprehensive reform of the customs rates, freeing over a hundred goods from export duty and reducing import dues on many raw materials. By comparison with the *intendants* the amateur, voluntary justices of the peace might appear less efficient, but in practice the counties were as well administered as the *généralités*. The system of taxation in England was much more effective than in France. Public confidence in the Government was so strong, especially after the establishment of a sinking fund to pay off the National Debt, that many people began to invest in government stock. The taxes appropriated to supply the Sinking Fund yielded more than had been expected, for trade boomed; and though Walpole, to avoid imposing extra taxes, raided the Sinking Fund in 1727 and again in 1733, public confidence remained unshaken. In no other country in the eighteenth century could money be borrowed so easily or so cheaply. By the mid-eighteenth century the National Debt was eighty times as large as it had been in 1688, but the rate of interest paid by the Government fell to 5 per cent in 1717, 4 per cent in 1727 and 3 per cent in 1749. The governmental system, too, proved to be much more effective than the system in France, though in some respects the two closely resembled each other. As in France, the men who really controlled policy were a few great ministers; unlike France, they met informally and apart from the

9

king to discuss policy. In this inner ring of ministers there was usually one who was recognised by the others as the dominant personality, and he usually had the task of making known the ministers' decision to the king and of trying to persuade him to accept it. This chairman was far from having the same powers as a modern Prime Minister. When he was given this title it was usually by his enemies and as a term of abuse; but the fact remained that in England, unlike France, the ministers largely determined policy by discussion among themselves. A further difference was that the English ministers were not usually men who simply happened to be court favourites. Three-quarters of the eighteenth-century House of Commons might be made up of men elected by boroughs with strangely restricted franchises, or even by pocket boroughs, but Parliament did at least provide some form of representation for the various interests which made up English society, and men who found their way to the front in parliamentary life were usually realistic. The stability and essential soundness of the English system of government was demonstrated by the failure of the Jacobite rising in 1715. The Government was even sound enough to survive the bitter feud between the King and the Prince of Wales, and factious disputes among the Whigs themselves.

Walpole returned to power in time to save the country when the South Sea Bubble broke in 1720, and thereafter until 1742 he directed policy. Like Fleury, Walpole realised that a pacific policy was best suited to the country's needs and his unadventurous administration gave England an era of prosperity such as she had never known before. By 1733, however, Walpole's position was becoming increasingly precarious. The dispute over his proposed excise scheme had sent several Whig peers into opposition, so that for the first time since 1715 there were enough Whigs to form an alternative ministry. In the general election of 1735 Walpole's supporters failed in those constituencies where public opinion still counted. In 1736 Frederick, Prince of Wales, quarrelled bitterly with his father and set up a rival court at Leicester House which became a focus for opposition. Queen Caroline, who had been Walpole's most loyal friend, died in 1737. In 1738 France, by the Treaty of Vienna, seemed to have outwitted England and regained a predominant position in Europe. In 1739 Walpole was compelled to make war on Spain. In 1742 he resigned. His disappearance marked the end of an epoch. 'For twenty years Walpole had just held in check those aspirations natural to a society which was faced with enormous possibilities of commercial expansion.'[1] In the second half of the eighteenth century these ambitions were to be given full reign when foreign policy was directed by Chatham. The War of the Austrian Succession showed comparatively few gains for England, but the Seven Years War won her an empire in India and in America. England's spectacular conquests, her prosperity and comparative stability gave her great prestige, and observers

[1] J. H. Plumb, *England in the Eighteenth Century* (1950), p. 73.

were ready to believe that the English Constitution ensured the preservation of liberty and the acquisition of great wealth.

One area in which the Anglo-French alliance of 1716 had considerable difficulty in preserving peace was the western Mediterranean (ch. XII), where an economically and politically decadent Spain had been revived by the arrival of a Bourbon prince supported by French economic experts, and where Spain's new energy had been used by its new queen, Elizabeth Farnese, to support her claims to Italian territories for her sons. The economic condition of Spain at the accession of Philip V in 1700 had been pitiful. The social composition of the country did not offer much prospect of support for reforming measures. The Church was very powerful, and its influence was all on the side of tradition and conservatism. The nobles were very numerous, owned a great deal of the land, and were exceptionally uncultivated and unpolitical. The bourgeoisie and professional classes were very few. The first three Bourbon kings were not reformers and could certainly not be called enlightened, but they were not extravagant, and they were served by able advisers, who by attention to detail, economy and efficiency managed to increase the royal revenue, build up the navy, revive trade with the Indies and generally improve the condition of Spain. Italy, which from 1700 till 1748 was the chief object of Spanish ambition, presented in the eighteenth century a very diverse appearance. The north and centre seemed to foreign observers a garden full of fine cities in which an energetic artistic life flourished, but the south was one of the poorest and most backward areas in all Europe. Politically, the Papal States remained unaltered during this period, but Milan and Tuscany under the rule of the Habsburgs enjoyed hitherto unfamiliar good government, and so did Parma and Naples under the sons of Elizabeth Farnese. Portugal, preoccupied with religion and richly supplied with bullion from Brazil, was untouched by any reform until the advent of Pombal in 1750.

If increasing commercial and colonial rivalry provided the key to developments in western Europe after 1733, in northern and eastern Europe the developments most important for the future were the emergence of Prussia and Russia as great powers capable of taking the initiative in international affairs; and in these two States the most interesting events were the administrative and financial reforms which laid the foundations of their new position.

Some of the foundations of Prussia's greatness (ch. XIII) had been laid by the Great Elector, but even in 1713, when Frederick William I succeeded to the throne, Prussia was still geographically in fragments, economically backward and weak in manpower. Prussia had a population of a little over 2,000,000; her soil was sandy and her methods of cultivation were primitive; her manufactures, in spite of the efforts of the Great Elector, were still in their infancy and her trade balance was adverse. One of the chief preoccupations of Frederick William I was the army, but to maintain and develop an efficient fighting force he had to raise more money, and his efforts to collect every possible sum due to him either from the royal domains or from the indirect taxes led to a comprehensive reform of the State administration. The royal domain, which in 1710 accounted for between a third of the land and a quarter of all the peasants, was let out on short leases to Crown bailiffs who were so efficiently supervised that the income derived from the domain lands amounted to about as much as was obtained from all the taxes. The main taxes were two: the contribution, which was sometimes as much as 40 per cent of a man's income and which was levied from all peasants except those in the royal domain, and the excise, which was a tax on town dwellers which Frederick William I extended to all towns in his kingdom. To ensure the efficient administration of each town the elected local councils were replaced by salaried officials appointed by the State. To promote the wealth of the towns, trade and industry were regulated on mercantilistic principles and guild regulations were supervised by the State. But even so the trade balance remained adverse. In 1723 Frederick William I simplified the collection of taxes and the administration of the country by combining the two departments which had been responsible for the royal domains and the collection of the war taxes of contribution and excise into a single *General-Ober-Finanz-Kriegs-und-Domänen-Directorium*. This was organised as a committee and took decisions by a majority vote. Under it were local committees in the provinces, and by them each town, royal estate or other rural district was minutely and efficiently supervised. The shortage of manpower he attempted to solve in various ways: he welcomed Protestant refugees from France and Salzburg, he recruited as much as two-thirds of his troops from abroad, he forcibly enlisted peasants at home, and from 1733 introduced a cantonal system to secure replacements of troops killed. The nobles he also made to serve the State by insisting that their sons should serve as 'Junkers' or ensigns in the army. When Frederick II succeeded his father in 1740 he found a full treasury and an efficient army of 72,000 men at a time when the Austrian Habsburgs, ruling a population perhaps three times as large, had only between 80,000 and 100,000 regular troops. Frederick used his resources to take full advantage of the situation presented by the death of the Emperor in the same year to invade Silesia. At the end of Frederick's wars in 1763 Prussia was greatly increased in size; her territory was augmented still further in 1772, when Frederick engineered the first partition of Poland and obtained West Prussia. At home after 1756 Frederick II devoted his attention to making good the physical destruction caused by his wars. He also reformed the administration of justice, a branch of government which Frederick William I had neglected. Frederick II also made attempts to improve the efficiency of the administrative machine which he had inherited from his father. His attempts suggest that though the reforms of Frederick William I had managed to overcome the weaknesses of a small, poor country they had not created a sound form of government.

Developments in Russia (ch. xiv) were comparable to those in Prussia, except that in Russia there had been no ruler comparable to the Great Elector, and when a more effective State machine had been created by Peter the Great he had no immediate successor of genius to play the part of a Frederick II and use the power of the country to win victories and acquire territory. At the beginning of the eighteenth century Russia, like Prussia, was economically backward. Agricultural output was so low and internal communications so bad that before the reforms of Peter the Great the main source of Russia's wealth was not her agriculture and still less her manufactures, which were in their infancy, but the great forests north of a line from St Petersburg to Kazan with their timber, rich furs and salt. Peter's reforms began after the Russian victory over Charles XII at Poltava in 1709, and they were inspired by the determination to increase Russia's military strength. To this end he developed Russia's iron works so that he was able to make Russia self-sufficient as far as munitions were concerned. He also increased the output of cloth, and though even then he was unable to produce enough to supply the needs of the Russian armies, he increased greatly the number of textile factories. He also encouraged the establishment of other factories so that by the end of his reign 200 factories were in operation. The supply of labour for the mines and factories presented little difficulty. Skilled craftsmen were very rare and continued to be so in spite of Peter's efforts to attract foreigners and to train native workmen, but unskilled labour could be obtained fairly easily. In towns, private employers made use of the local poor while the State could conscript orphans, thieves, drunkards, and other undesirables. For enterprises remote from towns Peter obtained unskilled labour by huge drafts of thousands of State peasants. One improvement which was essential before anything else could be achieved was to provide good internal communications. Peter considered making some stone paved roads, but decided that this would be too costly and turned his attention to developing canals instead. In spite of his efforts, however, communications remained bad, and transport costs together with internal customs barriers remained a very great obstacle impeding all economic advance. The one branch of trade which Peter was able to develop successfully was foreign trade via St Petersburg, which increased so rapidly that by 1725 Russian exports were worth twice as much as her imports even though these included some commodities imported from the Middle East and Asia where Russia was able to sell little in return. Peter, having had great difficulty in raising enough revenue to meet his military expenses, revised the system of direct taxation in 1718, substituting a poll tax for the tax on families. He completely reorganised the army, making it a standing force composed of men conscripted on the basis of one man from every twenty peasant households. To ensure the proper collection of taxes Peter completely reorganised the central government, substituting colleges for the welter of overlapping government departments, but his reforms of local government were less successful. He made two attempts, but both broke down and left provincial administration largely in the hands of the military commanders of the regiments quartered at various points. Like Frederick William I of Prussia, Peter did little to improve the administration of justice, though he did issue a criminal code and ordered that both witnesses and accused should be interrogated in person. He abolished the Patriarchate and in 1721 substituted a Synod which continued to govern the Church. His attempt to provide education for the sons of the upper classes and governmental officials failed, as did his attempt to provide books for his people. The effect of Peter's policy on the social structure of Russia was considerable. The fiscal reforms of 1718 increased the numbers of the peasants, who then made up 90 per cent of the population. Peter imposed an additional burden of 40 *kopecks* a year on the 13 per cent of the peasantry who lived in Siberia and who up till that time had paid no feudal dues. It was the 2 per cent of the population that could be reckoned as noble that were most affected by Peter's reforms. He gave legal recognition to the developments that had been taking place during the seventeenth century when he declared all noble estates to be hereditary; at the same time he insisted that all members of the nobility should serve the State, and, departing from old Muscovite custom in his Entail Law of 1714, which compelled landowners to leave their estates to one heir only, he created a landless nobility which had to look to State service for an income. After the death of Peter the Great in 1725, Russia was afflicted by a series of weak rulers, so that she was unable to play an energetic part in foreign affairs and at home the nobles were able to extort concessions from the Crown until they were almost entirely released from the services imposed by Peter the Great. Catherine I, by creating the Supreme Council, gave the nobles more share in the government. Under Peter II the capital was transferred to Moscow and the nobility, in the persons of the Dolgorukys, gained power. In 1730 Anna revoked the Entail Law, and in 1731 she reduced the amount of military service required of the nobility. On the death of Anna a series of palace revolutions ended in 1744 when Elizabeth, the last surviving daughter of Peter the Great, seized power with the help of the Priobrazhensky regiment. Russia was thought sufficiently formidable to be of very real interest to France and England, France trying unsuccessfully to secure her alliance in 1742 and England in 1756. On the whole, Russian policy after the death of Peter the Great tended to be one of alliance with Austria until the death of Elizabeth in 1762 gave the throne to a devoted admirer of Frederick the Great in the person of Peter III, who ended the war against Prussia and left for Catherine II, when she ascended the throne in 1762, a situation in which Russia could at last pursue an independent policy which allowed her to make full use of the strength built up by what had remained of the reforms of Peter the Great.

One of the areas in which the emergence of Prussia and Russia as Great Powers first made itself apparent was the Baltic (ch. xv). The end of the Great Northern War in 1721 established an equilibrium between the two Scandinavian Powers of Denmark (which then included Norway) and Sweden (which then ruled Finland), but it also relegated them to the position of secondary Powers. One of the chief problems confronting both Denmark and Sweden at the end of the Great Northern War was that the dukes of Holstein-Gottorp had claims to the Crown of Sweden and to territories coveted by the Danish rulers. Danish policy from 1721 till 1773 was directed to getting the Danish claims to the whole of Slesvig and the ducal parts of Holstein finally and universally recognised. The problem was made much more difficult because the dukes of Holstein-Gottorp could sometimes count on strong support from Russia and looked at times as if they might strengthen themselves by obtaining the throne of Sweden. On the death of Charles XII in 1718 without a male heir, one possible claimant was the duke of Holstein-Gottorp, the son of Charles's elder sister and the son-in-law of Peter the Great. Charles Frederick failed to secure the Swedish throne, but this did not mean that the Holstein-Gottorp claims ceased to be a political reality. The Holstein party in the Diet was so strong in 1723 that it was able to secure a considerable present of money for Charles Frederick and the title of Royal Highness, which showed that he was not excluded from the succession. Between 1723-6 Danish statesmen feared that Peter the Great, who had a grudge against the king of Denmark, might support Charles Frederick in war to regain his possessions in Slesvig and Holstein and that the Holstein party in Sweden might still be strong enough to get Charles Frederick recognised as heir apparent. The danger passed. In 1726 the Holstein party in Sweden was broken, and after the Tsaritsa Catherine I followed her husband to the grave in 1727, Russia ceased to support Charles Frederick. Till 1738 Count Horn and his party, which was nicknamed the 'Night Caps' because of its sleepy and unadventurous policy, remained in control in Sweden, and the Baltic was relatively peaceful, but in 1738 Horn was superseded by the warlike party of the Hats who, in alliance with France, plunged into the War of the Austrian Succession against Russia in hopes of recovering some of the Swedish possessions lost in 1721. Sweden was heavily defeated and the Hats only saved themselves from losing power in 1742-3 by diverting attention in Sweden to the problem of the succession. A strong candidate was Charles Peter Ulrich of Holstein-Gottorp, a great-nephew of Charles XII and nephew of the new Tsaritsa Elizabeth. The Hats hoped that by supporting the claims of the young duke of Holstein-Gottorp they might please his aunt and induce her to make favourable concessions to

Sweden. Charles Peter Ulrich's candidature was popular in Sweden but, before the Swedes could officially invite him to become heir apparent, the Tsaritsa Elizabeth had recognised him as her own heir in Russia, since through his mother he was grandson of Peter the Great. The Tsaritsa Elizabeth, as a price for restoring Finland, conquered in the recent disastrous campaign, forced the Swedes to recognise as the heir apparent yet another member of the Holstein-Gottorp family, Adolphus Frederick, who was the heir to Charles Peter Ulrich who at that time had no issue. For a time 12,000 Russian troops occupied Sweden to support Adolphus Frederick and Russian ships were attached to the Swedish navy, ostensibly to prevent any attempt to upset the succession arrangements by Denmark, which was terrified of the growing powers of the Holstein-Gottorps. In 1762 Charles Peter Ulrich became tsar and immediately made peace with Prussia in order to turn his forces against Denmark, but before he could actually commence hostilities he had been deposed and his successor Catherine II, having no personal interest in her husband's claims in Slesvig and Holstein, was prepared to agree that when her son Paul came of age he should make over his claims to the Crown of Denmark. In Sweden, too, Russian influence declined after 1743, for Adolphus Frederick married the sister of Frederick the Great and gradually drew away from Russia. During the Seven Years War a Swedish attack on Prussia was a failure and brought about the fall of the Hats in 1764–5. It left Sweden weak and so much exposed to Russian and other foreign influence that in 1768 it looked as if she might well be partitioned between her stronger neighbours. By 1772 it was clear that Sweden and Denmark had sunk to the level of second-rate Powers.

In Poland (ch. xvi) the effect of the emergence of Russia and Prussia during the eighteenth century was even more obvious than it was in the Baltic and had more tragic consequences. From 1679 to 1763 Poland was ruled by Saxon kings of the House of Wettin. For the first twenty years of this period Augustus II had been confronted by a considerable body of his subjects who actively supported a rival king in the person of Stanislas Leszczyński. Only Russian help enabled Augustus to return to Poland in 1709 when Russian prestige had been greatly increased by the victory of Peter the Great over Charles XII at Poltava, and Russian help again (in 1717) enabled him to reach an agreement with his rebellious subjects. In return, Russia occupied Courland on the extinction of the ducal family and also refused to hand over Livonia. The king of Poland struggled to get free from his position of subservience to Russia and even in 1719 concluded a treaty with the Emperor to compel Russia to evacuate Mecklenburg, but the Polish nobles refused to support this policy because they feared it might involve them in a war against Russia. The Russian court maintained a policy of keeping Poland weak. In 1720 Russia and Prussia agreed to safeguard Poland's political institutions, that is to prevent internal reform that might restore Poland's strength. This agreement was renewed in 1726, 1729, 1730, 1732, 1740, 1743 and 1762. Russia also allied with the Emperor in 1726 to prevent the Wettin family from establishing too firm a hold on the Polish throne. However, when in 1733 Augustus II died and the candidature of Stanislas Leszczyński was again supported by France, Russia again played the part she had played in 1709 and 1717, and helped to establish the Saxon Augustus III on the throne. Under Augustus III only one Diet out of fifteen was not exploded and Polish political life presented the spectacle of the two greatest families seeking outside support: the Potockis looking to France and Prussia, and the Czartoryskis looking to the Empire and Russia. During the Seven Years War Polish soil was continuously occupied by foreign troops. Both Prussia and Russia cast covetous eyes on the territories of the distracted republic, and the one hope for Poland was hostility between these two countries. The alliance between them in 1762 and the death of Augustus III in 1763 spelt the doom of Poland, which under the Saxon kings had enjoyed an illusory prosperity (at least for the nobility), bad leadership, intellectual stagnation and political anarchy.

The third area in which the rise of Russia and Prussia had a very considerable influence was in the dominions ruled over by the Habsburg family (ch. XVII), and here the impact of the new Powers, and especially of Prussia, was to begin the disintegration of the Habsburg Empire. The Habsburg dominions were particularly susceptible to the influence of their increasingly powerful neighbours because in the first half of the eighteenth century the Emperor had no male heir. Until 1720 the Emperor Charles VI was preoccupied with establishing himself firmly within his own dominions, in face of the Turkish menace and after the great international conflagrations which had been caused by the War of the Spanish Succession. In 1712, by the Peace of Szatmár, the Emperor was able to re-establish his authority in Hungary; in 1718, by the Peace of Passarowitz, he gained considerable territories from Turkey, including the Banat and Belgrade itself; and by 1720 the prolonged hostilities over the Spanish Succession were at an end. After 1720 the guiding principle of the foreign policy of Charles VI was to secure that his possessions should pass to his daughter. No woman could wear the crown of the Holy Roman Empire, but it was within the power of Charles VI to determine the successor in his hereditary possessions in Austria and Bohemia; and although on the extinction of the Habsburg male line Hungary would have had the right to elect a new ruler, it was the Hungarian Diet which first announced its readiness to elect as queen of Hungary the Austrian archduchess who should inherit the hereditary lands of Austria and Bohemia. Thereafter Charles VI painfully pursuaded most of the European Powers to recognise his daughter as his heir. In 1733 the Empire became involved in the War of the Polish Succession in which Charles's candidate triumphed, but the war was chiefly important because of its effects in Italy, where Charles had to cede Naples and Sicily to Spain, though he recovered Parma and Piacenza and secured Tuscany for his son-in-law, who in return ceded his hereditary possessions in Lorraine to France. Towards the end of his life Charles's position was weakened first by the death of his only really able general, Prince Eugene, in 1736, then by a disastrous war against the Turks which, when it ended in 1739, deprived Austria of everything she had won in 1718 except the Banat. The next year Charles VI died. Bavaria at once challenged the right of Maria Theresa to inherit her father's possessions. Prussia offered help to resist Bavaria, but claimed Silesia in return. The War of the Austrian Succession, which began in 1740, confirmed Prussia's claim to Silesia, but left Maria Theresa in possession of her father's other territories. From the conclusion of peace in 1748 to 1756 she pursued a policy of domestic reform inspired by fear of a renewed assault from Prussia. She reformed the army, increased the yield from taxes and improved the system of administration: all with the intention of being able to offer more effective opposition to Prussia. Many of the reforms themselves were imitated from Prussia. Maria Theresa's foreign policy was also directed to recovering Silesia, and it was to put herself into a better position to achieve this aim that she changed her old system of alliances with the Maritime Powers and in 1756 allied with France.

Three great episodes in the history of Europe in the eighteenth century involve so many of the Great Powers that they cannot be adequately treated in the history of any one of them, and are so complex that they need to be studied in greater detail than is possible in a general survey of international relations. These are the War of the Austrian Succession (ch. XVIII), the Diplomatic Revolution (ch. XIX) and the Seven Years War (ch. XX). They show clearly the reluctance of the Great Powers to engage in war except for a limited objective or to conduct war except in terms of manœuvre and siege. They also show the extent to which European diplomacy was increasingly influenced by the emergence of Russia and Prussia, and they show the way in which the colonial and commercial rivalry of France and Britain became more acute as the second half of the century approached. The War of the Austrian Succession, lasting from 1740 to 1748, was in fact a series of wars fought for limited objectives. Frederick II of Prussia made war on Austria to secure specific territory in Silesia, twice betraying his allies and finally breaking off hostilities in 1742 when he was given those territories in absolute sovereignty; he only resumed hostilities during 1744–5 because his control of Silesia was threatened by Austria's successes against her other enemies. The elector of Bavaria fought Austria to secure his position as Emperor, to which dignity he had been elected by all the votes cast in 1742. He also fought to increase his territories, for the Emperor needed considerable resources of his own if his rule were to be effective. For a time France supported

Bavaria and Prussia, but only as an auxiliary; she did not declare war on Austria until 1744. In the same way England was an auxiliary and only became a principal when France declared war on her in 1744. Hanover remained neutral until 1744. At the same time as Prussia and Bavaria were fighting for their limited objectives in central Europe, Spain fought Austria in the Mediterranean to gain more possessions in Italy for the sons of Elizabeth Farnese, and from 1739 England had been at war with Spain over conflicting ambitions in America and the West Indies. Frederick II's victories in 1745 won him the title of 'Great', and the peace settlement of Aix-la-Chapelle in 1748 allowed him to retain Silesia, though Maria Theresa retained the rest of the Habsburg inheritance and her husband was recognised as Emperor. Spain acquired Parma and Piacenza for Don Philip, Don Carlos having already been given Naples and Sicily in return for Spain's help in the War of the Polish Succession. France gained no territory by the peace, but in 1748 her rulers had good reason to be satisfied with her situation. The Habsburgs were weakened by the successes of Prussia, and the alliance between Austria, the Dutch and Britain had been badly strained. British statesmen had reason for concern. British colonial rivalry with France was becoming more acute, and the Anglo-French alliance which had existed between 1716 and 1731 had broken down completely. Britain's old ally Holland had proved a very lukewarm supporter and Austria was so pre-occupied with the question of Silesia as to be deaf to almost every other consideration.

The second major international episode which involved so many Powers that it must be described by itself is the Diplomatic Revolution of 1755–6. This again closely illustrates several of the developments which characterise the eighteenth century. The rise of Prussia meant that England now had an alternative to Austria as an ally against France. It also meant that Austria's primary enemy was no longer France but Prussia. The rise of Russia meant that the diplomacy of that Power could upset the balance of existing alliances. The situation in 1755 made it clear that France and England had become increasingly preoccupied with their commercial and colonial rivalries, and events since 1748 had shown the increasing ineffectiveness of French policy under a weak king and a divided ministry. The way for the reversal of alliances was prepared at the end of the War of the Austrian Succession, when Prussia had been disgusted with the weakness of the French court, France had been irritated by Prussia's assumption that Berlin was the equal of Versailles, England had been dissatisfied with Austria, and Austria had been resentful of England's preoccupation with colonial affairs. As early as 1749 Kaunitz had wanted to cultivate the friendship of France, and though in 1750 his mission to Paris failed to achieve an understanding between the two courts, he did not abandon the idea. At the end of 1754, when England and France became involved in hostilities in North America, England tried to get Austria to guarantee effective military help in Germany. Austria demanded stiff terms which England was reluctant to accept, and in 1755 Kaunitz proposed to renew the attempt to secure an alliance with France. Negotiations were opened in Paris with the Abbé Bernis, but they hung fire. What gave the Austro-French negotiations impetus was the outcome of English diplomatic activity in the north. In September 1755 Britain concluded a subsidy treaty with Russia. This was only an extension of the Anglo-Russian understanding of 1742 and had been warmly advocated by Maria Theresa as likely to strengthen the Austro-Russian agreement of 1746, but it had the effect of disrupting the existing system of alliances. When Frederick II heard of the Anglo-Russian Convention he, in January 1756, concluded the Treaty of Westminster with England. He hoped by this to neutralise Germany, and he also hoped that his ally France would not think his agreement with England was contrary to the engagements he had contracted with France. In this Frederick miscalculated. The French court was furious, and in May 1756 concluded the Treaty of Versailles with Austria. Ironically, Russia, when she saw how the system of alliances had altered, remained loyal to Austria and did not continue in alliance with England, though it was the Anglo-Russian Convention which had begun the revolution. One fact about the European situation which was brought out clearly by the Diplomatic Revolution was the almost complete separation between east and west. The two basic rivalries were between England and France (in the colonies and in trade) and between Austria and Prussia (for Silesia and ultimately for supremacy in eastern Europe). These were the rivalries before 1755, and they remained the rivalries after the revolution. That the two rivals in colonial affairs could exchange allies among the Powers of central and eastern Europe showed how completely independent were the interests of the western Powers and those of central Europe.

The Seven Years War seemed the direct outcome of the Diplomatic Revolution, and it constituted the third great international episode of the mid-eighteenth century transcending the separate histories of individual countries. Frederick II began the war by invading Saxony in 1756. He claimed that this was only to forestall aggressive action against him by Austria and Russia, but it had the effect of stiffening the alliances against him. Austria and France concluded a further treaty in May 1757, and Austria and Russia another treaty eighteen days later. In October 1757 the Saxon army capitulated. Austria invoked the help of France and Russia, promised under their treaties. A French army attacked Hanover and forced the duke of Cumberland to capitulate at Klosterseven in September 1757. The Russians invaded East Prussia, but, alarmed by a false rumour that the tsaritsa had died, withdrew again. The Swedes attacked Frederick in Pomerania. Frederick lost the battle of Kolin to the Austrians, who occupied Berlin; but before the end of the year he had defeated the French and the army of the Empire at Rossbach, and the Austrians at Leuthen, by which victory he recovered Silesia. During the winter of 1757–8 Frederick got the Swedes out of Prussian Pomerania. In 1758 the Army of Observation was increased and given a much greater British subsidy, enabling it to contain the French forces, so that for the rest of the war the main continental battles were to be fought between Prussia and her two chief rivals in eastern Europe, Austria and Russia. In 1758 Frederick held and defeated the Russians at Zorndorf, but was able to reach no decision against the Austrians in Silesia and Saxony. By 1759 the strain on Prussia was beginning to tell. Frederick was able to put only 100,000 troops into the field and was not able to take the offensive. The Austrians failed to take advantage of this situation, but the Russians took Frankfurt-am-Oder and defeated Frederick at Kunersdorf, though they too failed to follow up their victory. Choiseul, who came into power in France in 1759, decided to concentrate on the war against Great Britain. He reduced the French subsidy to Austria by half, but his elaborately prepared schemes for invading Great Britain collapsed after the British naval victories of Lagos and Quiberon Bay. Even though Frederick the Great was still able to raise an army of 100,000 men in 1760, the initiative remained with his enemies. The Austrians invaded Silesia and won the battle of Landshut in June 1760; in August they were defeated at Liegnitz. In October the Austrians and Russians occupied Berlin, but Frederick's victory at Torgau showed that he retained tactical mastery even in a strategic stalemate. In the west, the war had degenerated into the same kind of stalemate. Overseas, France's success in persuading Spain to take an active part in the war from January 1762 only resulted in heavy loss of Spanish territories to England. The death of the Tsaritsa Elizabeth in January 1762 saved Frederick, for her heir reversed her policy, not only suspending hostilities against Frederick but seeking an alliance with him. In November 1762 France and England concluded peace preliminaries and their example was followed by Prussia and Austria in February 1763. In Europe the military stalemate was reflected in the peace terms, which restored the *status quo ante bellum*. In fact, the extent to which Frederick had been defeated was suggested by the fact that even to regain the *status quo ante bellum* on the Continent of Europe, Prussia's ally Britain had to relinquish many of her colonial conquests. England certainly did not take full advantage of her position to secure a peace which effectively weakened France. The Seven Years War left the duel for domination still to be fought between England and France.

In the world outside Europe the Anglo-French commercial and colonial rivalry played a decisive part, but this only became dominant during the Seven Years War. The first fifty years of the eighteenth century were marked in the English colonies on the American mainland (ch. XXI, pt. 2) by steady growth. Though only one new colony, Georgia, was established in this period from 1713 to 1755, the area occupied doubled and between 1715 and 1750 the population trebled. About 61,000 Ulster Scots and 222,000 Germans settled in the English colonies, and the descendants of original settlers pressed inland. After 1730 South Carolina men pressed inland in search of more land to grow rice, and the introduction of indigo in 1742 helped the expansion of Georgia. As the tobacco planters of Virginia and Maryland found their land becoming exhausted, they, too, pressed inland. The spread of settlement into the back country created friction between these remoter areas and the older established coast. There were complaints that merchants of the coastal area monopolised trade. The farmers up-country suffered considerably because of currency and credit difficulties and the Currency Act of 1751 left them with a sense of injustice. The back-country settlers were not adequately represented in the political life of the various colonies, and as the century progressed a society gradually grew up which was impatient of control either from the older settlements or from England. The French colonies showed less vigour than the English ones, and in 1744 while there were 100,000 English colonists the French in North America numbered only 50,000. But though the economic foundations of the French colonies were too narrow, the colonies were planned with a brilliant eye for strategy, and by the middle of the eighteenth century it seemed possible that the French chain of settlements from the St Lawrence via the Great Lakes and the Ohio to the Mississippi and the Gulf of Mexico might check the further westward expansion of the English colonists, and might even sweep them into the sea. Most of the great Spanish empire (ch. XXI, pt. 1)—weakly defended, economically unsound and, even in spite of the reforms of the Bourbon kings, badly administered—remained remote from the colonial struggles of the eighteenth century. There was some expansion in the frontiers, largely through the work of missionaries such as the Jesuits, the Capuchins and the Franciscans. More new mines were opened and more new towns founded than at any other time since the sixteenth century. But, as in the English colonies, an increasing gulf developed between the Creoles and the Spaniards, and the Creole merchants developed a sense of grievance. Brazil in this period showed a spectacular development and its administration was centralised with success by Pombal.

Actual conflict between England and France in North America (ch. XXII, pt. 2) was avoided for some time, partly because of the size of the wilderness separating the settlements of the two Powers—especially in the south—and partly by the neutrality of the six Indian nations in the north and the reluctance of the French and the New Yorkers to interrupt the fur trade. Even during the War of the Austrian Succession, North America was not a major theatre of war. Louisbourg in Cape Breton was captured by British colonists in 1745, but at the peace of 1748 it was restored in return for Madras. It was on the Ohio that the Anglo-French conflict really became acute in 1754, and the British decision to back the Virginians with troops from England showed that the mainland colonies had now come to be recognised as of prime importance to the whole colonial system. The campaign which won Canada destroyed the French empire in North America.

The colonial conflict with Spain was concentrated in the Caribbean (ch. XXII, pt. I). This conflict was partly between Spain and all the other Powers who coveted a share in the trade of the Spanish empire, and in this the English enjoyed an apparent but not a real advantage after 1713, because an English company had been granted the privilege of supplying slaves to the Spanish empire. It was partly between the various Maritime Powers to decide which should profit by Spain's weakness. This resolved itself into a duel between France and England, but though the Anglo-French war spread to the West Indies in 1744, the main forces of both Powers were engaged elsewhere. The fighting in the West Indies was merely a rehearsal for the Seven Years War, and the Peace of Aix-la-Chapelle in 1748 settled nothing of importance in the West Indies. A third aspect of the struggle became apparent during the Seven Years War when the English Government made every effort to occupy as many of the unsettled West Indian islands as possible in addition to conquering the French islands of Guadaloupe and Martinique in 1759 and 1762 respectively, and Spanish Havana in 1762. By the time of the Peace of 1763, however, Bute had succeeded Pitt, and in his desire to conclude a hasty peace he restored Guadaloupe, Martinique and St Lucia, thus inaugurating a period during which Britain tended to ignore the importance of the West Indies and to neglect her possessions there.

In India (ch. XXIII) the period from the death of the Emperor Aurangzeb in 1707 to the defeat of his titular successor by the British in 1764 was marked by the disintegration of the Mogul Empire until conditions developed favouring the extension of the power of the French and British, the rivalry between these two European Powers ending in the triumph of Britain. The power of the Mogul Empire was undermined by the failure of the Emperors to continue Akbar's policy of religious toleration and moderate taxation. It was also weakened by bad communications, by the presence of rival aristocratic factions at court and by the absence of any settled rule of succession. For two years after the death of Aurangzeb in 1707 his sons disputed the throne, and between 1712 and 1719 five puppet Emperors ruled at Delhi. As was natural, provincial governors asserted their independence. The weakness of the Mogul Emperors also provided an opportunity for the emergence of the Hindu Marathas, whose authority spread across central India from their capital of Satara, about a hundred miles south of Bombay on the west, to within two hundred miles of Calcutta on the east. Between 1742 and 1747 the Marathas harassed Bengal and in 1751 the governor of that province had to agree to pay them tribute. In 1740 they had struck south-east at the Carnatic, where England and France occupied such important trading stations as Madras and Pondicherry. It was in this situation of disintegrating central authority and growing Maratha menace that the English and French East India Companies heard in 1744 that their respective countries were at war. But in India the war of 1744–8 was of little importance and the Peace of Aix-la-Chapelle left the relative strength of English and French in India unchanged. After 1748 an unofficial war developed between the English and the French Companies when they interfered in support of rival candidates in the Deccan. A similar struggle developed in support of rival claimants in the Carnatic. In the Deccan Bussy succeeded in establishing the French claimant to the throne. The English authorities in London proposed to ally with the Marathas to oust Bussy, but the local English officials in Bombay refused to support this plan, so that Clive was free to strike in Bengal when in 1756 the new nawab, Siraj-ud-daulah, attacked the English settlement at Calcutta and imprisoned the survivors in the Black Hole. Clive's victory at Plassey in 1757 gave the English control of Bengal, one of the richest provinces of India, and gave them resources which helped them to defeat the French on the south-east coast. During this time the Marathas extended their power in the north-west, but were gradually driven south by the Afghan leader Ahmad Shah Durrani who between 1747 and 1769 led no less than ten invasions into India, capturing Delhi in 1757 and defeating the Marathas at Pampat in 1761. The Afghans did not take advantage of their victory, but it had given the English time to consolidate their power in Bengal. An attempt by the Mogul Emperor and his *nawab-wazir* of Oudh to overthrow British power in Bengal was decisively crushed in 1764. Henceforward the English were undisputed rulers of Bengal.

Africa (ch. xxiv, pt. 1) was so remote from Europe in the early eighteenth century that even the growing colonial rivalry between England and France was felt only faintly, and the increasing commercial rivalry of the two Powers was less important than the rivalries between chartered national companies and private interlopers. The main area of commercial activity in Africa in the eighteenth century was the West Coast, stretching some 3500 miles from Senegal in the north to Angola in the south. The development of colonies in America increased the importance of the slave trade, and as sugar prices in the West Indies rose between 1740 and 1770 so the trade in slaves from West Africa flourished. Even in good times the slave trade could be dangerous and as it involved a long interval before any return could be expected on capital invested, nearly all the nations which engaged in it organised the traders in chartered companies. These companies had to maintain fortified posts in West Africa, and during the eighteenth century they lost ground to the private traders or interlopers who did not have the expense of maintaining forts and could experiment and explore as they thought best. Among the various European nations trading to West Africa the Brandenburgers did so little trade that they sold out in 1717. The Danes encountered recurrent difficulties, partly because their market in the West Indies was so restricted. The Portuguese were able to carry on a considerable trade and the demand increased with the development of mines in Brazil, but even so they were handicapped by lack of capital. The French slave trade satisfied neither the West Indian planters nor the Government in Paris. Sometimes the annual export of slaves by the company was only 500 and in the 1720's Senegal was being maintained at an annual loss. War with England from 1744 to 1748 and again from 1756 to 1763 knocked the bottom out of the trade of the private merchants, though in peace-time it was fairly prosperous. The Dutch were in a much stronger position than the Portuguese or the French. Their islands of St Eustatius and Curaçao in the West Indies provided a useful entrepôt from which they were prepared to sell to all buyers. They had the capital and the business experience to develop a thriving trade, but even so by 1750 the Dutch slave trade had been overtaken by the English. The Royal African Company was the official body conducting the English slave trade till 1750, but it had lost its monopoly in 1698, and the interlopers from Bristol and Liverpool came to carry more slaves than the Company. Even the South Sea Company tended to buy its slaves in the West Indies, thus favouring the private merchants. After 1750 English trade with Africa boomed. Lancashire cottons superseded Indian products, and between 1750 and 1775 English exports to Africa increased by 400 per cent. The private merchants were able to experiment with new markets where slaves could be bought more cheaply and by 1771 half the slaves exported by the English came from the bights of Benin and Beafia. But in spite of this considerable trade with West Africa there was little attempt by the Europeans to penetrate into the interior. Partly this was because the merchants were interested in trade and the climate did not attract settlers. Partly it was because European penetration inland was checked by the emergence of strong tribes such as the Dahomey and the Ashanti. Far removed from the West Coast was the small Dutch settlement at the Cape. Here the amount of trade was almost negligible, but there was considerable expansion inland until 1779, when the Boers came in contact with the Xosa. In East Africa the Portuguese bases in Mozambique had declined in importance after the Portuguese had lost most of their East Indian trade to the Dutch. There was some trade with the Arabs and in 1768 the French annexed Madagascar.

The Far East (ch. xxiv, pt. 2) was for the most part so remote from Europe in the eighteenth century that even the commercial rivalries had hardly any repercussions. Only the Philippines felt some breath of Anglo-Spanish hostilities, for during the War of Jenkins' Ear Anson captured the galleon which traded between Manila and Mexico laden with tea, teak, spices, raw silks and other produce from the Far East. In 1762 the English actually conquered Manila and held it till the end of the war. Otherwise the history of the Philippines in the eighteenth century is one of controversy with Spain as to whether the Acapulco galleon should import manufactured Chinese silk to Mexico since this drained so much silver from the Spanish colonies. The other recurrent problem was what to do with the large number of Chinese in the Philippines, and the answer was too often expulsion or even massacre. The Netherlands East Indies in 1740 also saw a massacre of about 10,000 Chinese out of a total Chinese population of 80,000. Apart from this episode, the eighteenth century was a period when, in spite of paying an annual dividend of 18 per cent, the Dutch East India Company from 1724 to 1725 was beginning to operate at a loss. However, the prosperity of the East Indies was saved by the spectacular growth in the production of coffee. The first 100 pounds of coffee were harvested in 1711, and by 1723 the crop was twelve million pounds. At first the directors of the Dutch East India Company were quite unable to manage this enormous crop. Efforts were made to limit production, but eventually coffee was accepted as a form of tribute and had a beneficial effect on the cultivation of the Dutch East Indies. For the rest of the eighteenth century coffee was the foundation of their prosperity. European efforts to develop trade connections with China in the eighteenth century were not very successful. The Europeans wanted Chinese silk, porcelain, lacquer and tea as well as such luxuries as fans and screens, but the Chinese wanted nothing in return except silver. The English gained a footing in Canton in 1699 and by 1720 their trade had developed so considerably that the Chinese authorities thought it worth while to clap on a tax of 4 per cent which was eventually increased to 16 per cent. Such restrictions were put on foreign trade that in 1734 only one English ship came to Canton and one to Amoy. In 1736 only ten European ships traded with Canton. The English tried to open up trade with Amoy and Ningpo, but in 1757 an imperial edict restricted all foreign trade to Canton. In the eighteenth century China was outside the sphere of European politics almost as much as Japan. The intense activity which was taking place in France and England, Prussia and Russia, Austria and Spain was felt more and more faintly until westward of the Mississippi, in the interior of Africa, in much of the Middle East and in the Great Empire of China its influence was imperceptible. By the mid-eighteenth century the world had not become a single political unit.

CHAPTER II

THE GROWTH OF OVERSEAS COMMERCE AND EUROPEAN MANUFACTURE

THE half century which ended at the Treaty of Utrecht had been a formative and decisive period in the history of world trade. An analysis of the structure of seaborne commerce in the mid-seventeenth century would have revealed that it was preponderantly European in character and that a large part of the total volume was handled by the Dutch. The prosperity of Amsterdam derived primarily from the exchange of bulk commodities from northern Europe—timber, naval stores, and corn—against the produce of southern and western Europe—the salt of Biscay, the wool and silver of Spain, the herrings caught by Dutch fishermen off the British coasts, the wines and textiles of the Mediterranean. On the firm foundation of these bulk trades the Dutch had built up a vast entrepôt trade, served by a merchant fleet which was calculated in one contemporary estimate to be double that of England and nine times that of France.[1] To this entrepôt were drawn other commodities—the cloths of England and France in particular—as well as an increasing flow of colonial wares—the spices brought from the East by the Dutch East India Company, and the tobacco, sugar and dyes of the Caribbean. Throughout the century an economic organisation was steadily built up to deal with the unprecedented scope and variety of the entrepôt trade. The Bourse, a central banking system, and a money-market together constituted its financial apparatus. The merchants themselves were divided into broad groups corresponding to the nature of their operations. The so-called 'Second-Hand' merchants specialised in dealings in imported goods which they stored until they were sold, sorted and graded them, or arranged for them to be processed or refined by local industries. The importing merchants formed a second group, while yet a third group was responsible for distributing goods to their final markets. A fourth group, the commission traders, handled goods for foreign account, some of which passed directly from the area of purchase to the area of sale without even coming to Amsterdam. In 1700 the whole of this organisation remained intact, though there was already a clear tendency for financial operations—discounting, banking, acceptance credit operations and foreign loans—to supplement and even replace active trading. The Dutch economy, highly precarious by nature, was under steady economic and political pressure

---

[1] The estimate of Sir William Petty, quoted by C. E. Fayle, *A Short History of the World's Shipping Industry*, p. 175. The figures cannot be much more than an intelligent guess, but Mr Fayle remarks that Petty's proportions may not be far wrong.

from European rivals, and from France and England in particular. It is these pressures, applied with increasing consistency from 1660 onwards, which give a special character to the first half of the eighteenth century in European economic history. For it became steadily more evident that the real direction of economic expansion was westwards, and a prime object of both English and French policy from 1660 to 1763 was to obtain as large a share as possible in the new colonial trades. It was evident too that shipping and the ability to protect that shipping were essential to these policies. The wars of the late seventeenth century had disclosed the serious strategic weaknesses of the Dutch position. More than any other European power the Dutch depended on overseas trade. Their large industries —cloth-making, brewing, sugar refining, shipbuilding, and oil milling—all relied on imported materials. The life of the people was dependent on imported corn. Yet the Dutch sea lanes to the Baltic and through the English Channel were open to attack from the English naval bases, while their land frontiers were vulnerable to the French armies. All these circumstances, combined with a relatively small population, dictated a policy of caution and limited ambitions. The essential problems of the United Provinces were nowhere more strikingly illustrated than in their opinions on international law at sea which they maintained throughout the greater part of the eighteenth century. Strategic and naval weakness could be mitigated if not concealed by the policy of 'free ships, free goods', the doctrine that a neutral should be free to carry for belligerents in war time.[1] By such stratagems the Dutch aimed at, and to a large extent succeeded in, maintaining their share of the world's carrying trade. But it was not in their power to maintain predominance in the rapidly expanding international trade of the eighteenth century.

Rapid commercial expansion, especially in the colonial trades, and the Anglo-French struggle for primacy are the main themes of the period from the Treaty of Utrecht to the Treaty of Paris. Dangerously faulty as the so-called 'statistics' of trade are for the period, there can be no doubt as to the fact of expansion, though there is a good deal as to the dimensions. The recorded value of British exports in 1720 was about £8,000,000; by 1763 it stood at about £15,000,000. In the same period, the tonnage of shipping cleared from British ports rose from about 450,000 tons to some 650,000 tons. A large proportion of this tonnage was British by 1763— perhaps half a million tons, or about six times the tonnage of a century earlier. British tonnage probably represented about one-third of that of all Europe. The expansion of French overseas trade was no less remarkable, though the growth of the French merchant fleet was a good deal less rapid than that of the British. The recorded value of French exports in 1716 was about 120 million *livres*; by 1789 it had risen to over 500 million

---

[1] Although it was not achieved during the seventeenth century, the case for a pacific or neutral policy was forcefully argued in the so-called *Maxims* of De Witt (1662).

livres and included a considerable proportion of colonial re-exports. Thus, long before the inception of those profounder changes which are conveniently termed 'industrial revolution', it is evident that world commerce and shipping had undergone a change of scale which might itself be regarded as revolutionary. The increase in trade had stimulated the growth of new centres of trade and industry and of new mercantile classes; it had introduced new commodities into society, and changed the flow of world trade and the economic balance between nations. In both England and France these changes were associated in men's minds with the policies later described as 'mercantilist'—the conscious pursuit of commerce (as distinct from agriculture) as a means of national enrichment. Foreign trade above all was valued for this end. In practice the object was to expand exports, and diminish all imports except those essential to life and employment. In particular, a high degree of importance was attached to those branches of trade which were supposed to attract a net influx of bullion. A careful watch was therefore kept on the balance of trade, wherein lay the evidence of progress or regress. Since 1696 England had had an office supervised by the Inspector General of Imports and Exports for this purpose. From 1726 France followed suit, though it was not until 1756 that the figures were arranged into general tables, and only in 1781 did Necker create a comparable office to supervise the general balance of trade.

The increased volume and variety of goods which entered into international trade already owed something to technological progress. The number of industrial patents taken out in England was rising by 1750 and this increase was accompanied by a significant growth of popular interest in technical improvement. Societies to promote industrial improvement sprang up in London, Birmingham and Manchester, and had their counterparts in Paris and Hamburg. Not all the inventions had practical consequences in industrial production, and those which did often had to await modification and improvement for some time before they could be applied on a commercial scale. But some effect there was. The use of coal in industry, though relatively unimportant by the standards of a later age, was yet sufficiently widespread to make its increased production significant. One of the brakes on production, at least in England, was removed with the invention of Newcomen's atmospheric engine in 1708. From the midland coalfields, its use spread to the north and by 1765 there were about 100 engines at work in the Tyne area. It now became possible to work the deeper seams which flooding had previously put out of reach. The increased output of coal was particularly important to the iron industry, for from 1709 onwards the Quaker ironmasters of Shropshire were slowly developing a coke smelting process for the production of pig iron. The new process spread only slowly, but there was in these years a gradual shift of furnaces from the forests to the coalfields. It was, however, in the manufacture of iron goods, in the making of tools, implements, chains, locks and nails, rather than in the production of iron itself, that mineral fuel was most important. Above all, the demand for munitions during the Seven Years War encouraged the iron masters to expand their works, and John Roebuck's works at Carron, established in January 1760, have been described as the 'portent of a new type of undertaking'.[1]

Of more immediate importance than strictly new inventions was the transfer of existing technical knowledge from place to place, and from small groups of industrialists and artisans to much wider circles. A great many such transfers went on in the first half of the eighteenth century and much industrial change may be traced to this process. The European textile industries remained organised on the 'domestic' basis, but there were important changes in the kinds of product turned out. Stimulated by the demand of more sophisticated urban markets on the one hand, and of tropical markets on the other, the textile industries shifted their emphasis to newer and lighter fabrics. The necessary technical knowledge was borrowed from those who had it already: sometimes they were near at hand, sometimes they were at the other end of the earth. In the English cloth industry, the smoother 'worsteds' tended to oust the rougher, thicker woollens, and manufacture became increasingly concentrated in Yorkshire. Expert artisans from Norwich were borrowed to assist in the process. Again, somewhere between 1700 and 1750, English manufacturers seem finally to have overtaken the Dutch in the arts of dyeing and finishing cloth. The older system of exporting cloths 'in the white' to Holland was still in force, but increasingly the final processes, which were the key to the control of the markets, passed into English hands. English apprentices ceased to go to Holland as part of their recognised scheme of training. In other textile industries similar exchanges took place. French Huguenots brought valuable skill to the silk-weaving industry at Spitalfields, to the lace industry of Buckingham and Hertfordshire, and to the Irish and Scottish linen manufacture (as well as to the glass and metal industries of the midlands, and to the paper industry of Hampshire). Conversely, Lancashire emigrants were active in France. John Kay, the inventor of the flying shuttle, who had probably suffered from popular prejudice against his inventions in England, fled over the Channel, while John Holker played an important part in the development of the French cotton industry and was finally appointed Inspector of Foreign Manufactures by Trudaine in 1754. The methods of the Italian silk-throwing industry were slowly introduced into France and about 1716 the Lombes brought them to England. Such were a few of the European exchanges: but other techniques travelled even longer distances, notably methods of textile printing. The imitation of Indian chintz by printing either on white calico or linen arrived more or less simultaneously in France, Holland and

[1] T. S. Ashton, *The Industrial Revolution*, 1948, p. 65.

England. By 1744 the English calico-printers had perfected the work to a point at which they could threaten the re-export trade in the original article. Oriental influences were strong throughout Europe's textile industries. Rouen, the most progressive centre of the French cotton industry, specialised in striped fabrics known as *siamoises*; the Dutch made *nicconnees* and other copies of Indian striped goods; Lancashire had by 1720 a large trade in cotton-linen checks influenced by Indian example, while Glasgow weavers were making *bengals* in the 1740's. The pottery industry, scarcely less than the cotton industry, drew its designs from oriental patterns. Delft, the most important centre of the ceramic industry in northern Europe in this period, copied Chinese wares in blue and white porcelain, and its lead was followed by the English makers at Bow, Chelsea and Worcester and by the French industry at Nevers and elsewhere. European customers everywhere paid tribute to the old civilisations of East and West in their tastes.

These innovations did not in themselves imply any revolutionary change in industrial organisation, though the importance of the new designs and fashions as a factor in the conquest of markets is difficult to exaggerate. Most of the industries affected continued to work on traditional handicraft lines, or some variant of the 'domestic' system. There were exceptions, of course. The power-driven silk-throwing factory of the Lombes at Derby employed several hundred hands. Matthew Boulton's iron works at Soho, near Birmingham, employed seven hundred people and a considerable amount of mechanical equipment. Wedgwood's Burslem factory was built in 1759. The van Robais factory at Abbeville had many of the characteristics of the modern factory, and the so-called *grande industrie* controlled a limited field of the French cotton industry. But these were as yet exceptions to the general rule: the typical industrial unit everywhere remained small. In France official regulation, in Holland fiscal policy, worked against the development of the larger unit. Even in England there was fierce resistance from the artisans to the introduction of new machinery which threatened to save labour as well as to expand output. Everywhere industrial change was slow and often painful.

On the available evidence it is difficult to indicate with any precision the sources from which the capital for the industrial expansion was obtained. One writer has spoken of 'the role of Negro slavery and the slave trade in providing the capital which financed the Industrial Revolution in England'.[1] But this is to ignore a good deal of evidence that the planters themselves were as often as not embarrassed by a shortage of money. Professor Pares has shown that the planter of sugar and tobacco was not infrequently indebted to his English factor. And since England herself was still on balance a capital-importing country, the planter sometimes had to resort

[1] Eric Williams, *Capitalism and Slavery* (1944), ch. VII.

to the Dutch money-lender. It is therefore a matter of doubt how far the capital needs of the colonial traders themselves left any large surplus for the financing of industry. There were of course cases where importing and exporting merchants gave manufacturers credit for three or more months and paid for their output week by week. Many early industrial enterprises in Lancashire were financed in this way, by a flow of capital inwards from commerce to industry. There were equally other cases, and they may have been numerous, where a successful business supplied its capital needs out of its own profits. Elsewhere banks and private lenders assisted industrialists by loans and mortgages, often out of the profits of land and farming. Until the problem has been more closely examined, it must be left at this: that industrial expansion was financed from a variety of sources and that it seems unlikely that the pocket of the planter or the nabob was the most important of them.

Throughout the period 1713 to 1763 the overall expansion of British foreign trade went hand-in-hand with a mercantilist policy of regulation. The foundation of her policy was the Navigation Code established by the Acts of 1660, 1662, and 1663 and supplemented by the further Acts of 1673 and 1696. The Acts were especially directed towards the colonial trades; their object was to canalise trade between Britain and her colonial territories, reserving the purchase of valuable colonial produce to British buyers and reserving colonial markets to British manufactures: in a word, to fashion by conscious effort a commercial position for Britain similar to that which Holland had apparently acquired by a process of organic development. The precise relationship between the Acts and the expansion which accompanied them must remain a matter of doubt. Our knowledge of the facts is too partial and insecure to allow of dogmatism. To some extent it would seem that the Acts, which especially limited the participation of foreign shipping in British trade, sacrificed the interests of European trade to those of colonial trade. Yet it is clear that there was a general belief in their efficacy amongst practical men which was only partially shaken by the fundamental criticisms which began to be voiced in the 1740's. It is nevertheless evident that there were at least two other major factors which must be considered along with legislative factors in any explanation of British economic expansion. One was the industrial expansion which took place before the age of the great inventions and was in large measure independent of the Navigation Acts, though closely associated with a paternal policy of bounties, subsidies and protective tariffs. The output of the coal industry, for example, was already expanding rapidly in the seventeenth century. Between 1700 and 1760 it more than doubled, from about three million tons a year to perhaps six million tons. In spite of severe foreign competition, the condition of the metal industries was full of promise. Metal wares, nails especially, paper and pottery, featured regularly on the lists of exports. There was some, though not much, export of the newer silk and linen goods. From about 1700 the cotton industries of Lancashire added their weight to the list of exports, especially to Africa and the colonies, while the woollen and worsted exports, hard pressed by foreign competition since the Restoration, began to grow again after 1720. Most striking of all was the growth of the re-export trade in colonial goods. The 'enumerated' commodities reserved for British buyers—sugar, tobacco, cotton, and West Indian dyestuffs—together with Indian spices and textiles, China tea and Mocca coffee, were its foundation. In 1724 more than four million pounds of tobacco came to the Clyde and more than three-quarters of this was re-exported. It was indeed in the development of the west-coast ports of Bristol, Liverpool and Glasgow that the changing emphasis of British overseas trade may best be seen. In each of these ports the period witnessed a rapid growth of population and rapid profit making for the great shipowners, sugar refiners, tobacco merchants and slave traders. The day had passed when the exports of British cloth to Europe dominated British trade. The new Atlantic trades had given rise to a demand for bulk shipping unknown in the seventeenth century. England by 1750 not only rivalled but had easily surpassed her Dutch rivals, and her prosperity and strength were firmly based on a growing variety of local manufactures in a way the Dutch primacy had never been. The new colonial trades should not be allowed to obscure entirely the continuing importance of the inter-regional trades of Europe, yet their importance to Britain is manifest. By 1763 trade between England and the Americas may well have employed as much as a third of her total shipping engaged in overseas trade.

To industrial growth at home and conscious legislative effort must be added a third factor. The Western Approaches were relatively safe and open to British Atlantic trade. Thus far, Britain had a strategic advantage shared only perhaps by the western ports of France: but trade was indivisible. In the Caribbean, naval strength was necessary to protect Britain's colonial shipping, while the markets for British re-exports in the Baltic and Mediterranean were under constant threat. A strong navy and an organised system of naval bases was therefore indispensable to the protection of a growing seaborne commerce. Without it, the Navigation Acts would have been a dead letter and the colonial territories in standing danger of attack.

The unprecedented expansion of French overseas trade in the same period seemed likewise to be a tribute to the efficacy of economic regulation and mercantilist policy; for here, even more than in England, the period 1660 to 1763 saw the regimentation of trade and industry on strictly mercantilist principles. It was natural that French independence of Dutch services should be one of the principal aims of French mercantilism, and Colbert's attack on the Dutch with the two-fold weapon of high tariffs and exclusive trading companies formed the French equivalent of the English Navigation Acts. Colbertism was not immediately or entirely destructive of Dutch participation in French trade—in 1726 French merchants were still complaining bitterly of Dutch competition, and perhaps something like a quarter of French foreign trade was still in Dutch hands—but it was subject to vexatious and unpredictable interference.

Colbert's companies—the Company of the North, the Levant Company, the Senegal Company, and the East and West Indian Companies—seem to have done little to foster French overseas trade, and Louis XIV's wars reduced most of them to near bankruptcy. But the years following the Treaty of Utrecht saw a distinct revival. It was an integral part of the 'system' of John Law to reorganise the companies under the supervision of the *Compagnie des Indes*. Law's company was liquidated after the spectacular collapse of his 'system', but was reconstituted in 1722–3. There seems little doubt that this reorganisation provided a stimulus enabling French trade to overcome the problems created for it by the terms of the Treaty of Utrecht, which had yielded Gibraltar and Minorca, as well as Nova Scotia and Newfoundland to Great Britain. The revival of trade continued until, round about 1740, France was enjoying a phase of unprecedented prosperity in her foreign trade.

Like English overseas trade, the French was in some measure based on the growth of home industry. Throughout the period the French luxury industries—gobelins and furniture stuffs, hosiery, ribbons, lace, silks, threads, mirrors, and porcelains—were carefully supervised and subsidised. The French cloth industry likewise received official support, especially where it manufactured for export (for example, the Levant), yet French woollen textiles remained, in general, inferior to English, and in fact unprivileged cloth manufactures played an increasing part even in the export trade. It was principally in those industries to which the Government directed least attention—the iron and coal industries, the cheaper cloth and cotton industries of Normandy, hardware and glass—that the most striking developments took place. These were the source of exports which fed the transatlantic trades.

Superficially the structure of French eighteenth-century trade resembled not a little that of her English rival. While European, Levant and Eastern trade occupied an important place in the system, it was again the Atlantic trades which occupied pride of place. By the middle of the century the French possessions in the West Indies and America may have accounted for about a quarter of the total value of French overseas trade. The Labrador fisheries, retained in 1713, were frequented by fishermen from St Malo. La Rochelle was the importing centre for the fur trade, but it was above all the tobacco trade of Louisiana and the sugar, coffee and (after 1750) indigo trades of the West Indies which were the foundations of the prosperity of Bordeaux and Nantes in the eighteenth century. When Arthur Young visited these ports in 1787, their commerce, wealth and magnificence 'greatly surpassed' his expectations. Liverpool, he observed, must not be named 'in competition with Bordeaux'. Between 1722 and 1782 the merchant fleet of Bordeaux rose from 120 to 300 ships. Its trade, largely with the Antilles, represented a quarter of the total maritime trade of France, and was the basis for a wide range of local industries—distilling, refining, and shipbuilding. With its colonies of Dutch, German and Irish merchants it was one of the most cosmopolitan and prosperous of French cities. Second only to Bordeaux was Nantes, with its strong connections with the Spanish and colonial trades. Yet the influence of the trade with the Antilles was not limited to the western ports. Marseilles, primarily the centre of the Levant and Mediterranean trade, received immense stimulus from the re-export to those areas of West Indian produce, particularly sugar and coffee.

There is every reason to suppose that until a date well after the Peace of Paris the output of certain of the large French industries—cotton and iron especially—was greater than that of rival industries in England. Indeed, with a French population three to four times the size of the English, it would be surprising if this were not so. Nevertheless, over the whole range of her foreign trade, France does not appear to have achieved the balance which characterised English trade. The figures of trade (though of limited statistical value) show that England's exports consistently reached a greater value than her imports in the period 1713–63. The balance of French trade on the other hand seems to have turned against her. If there were no supporting evidence, it would be rash to draw any firm conclusions from the customs figures, but a suspicion that behind the imposing façade all was not well with the French economy is borne out by other facts. There is some evidence that France failed to supply either the exports, the ships or the necessary credit system which were essential if trade between France and her colonies was to flow smoothly and without interruption. The French West Indian sugar colonies in particular demanded supplies of slaves, manufactures and food which France was less well placed to supply than Britain, Holland or the North American colonies. In the absence of sufficient credits from France, imports of French manufactures to the colonies languished from time to time. The shortage of French shipping left vast quantities of sugar and indigo dammed up in the West Indies. Meanwhile ships were leaving Nantes in ballast for lack of cargoes. These difficulties were rendered especially acute during the War of the Austrian Succession and the Seven Years War, but they were probably symptomatic of a fundamental lack of balance in the French economy, which encouraged smugglers at all times (especially in the French Antilles) and let in the ever-present Dutch shipowner in time of war. The perennial shortage of slaves for the French West Indian plantations was not the least serious aspect of this dis-equilibrium in the French colonial economy. It was in wartime that the real weakness of France—at sea—

was most apparent. The roots of her naval deficiency lay deep in French history, in the long dynastic struggles in which most of the emphasis had been placed on land warfare and in the relative economic self-sufficiency of large sections of France which bred indifference to naval matters. The neglect was neither absolute nor continuous. Choiseul had bargained hard and not unsuccessfully in 1762 to keep those colonies and trades which would support shipping, but there was something in the Abbé Raynal's criticism at the end of the century that the long story of naval reverses had failed to teach French governments wisdom. The only remedy lay in encouraging 'the mercantile branch of the navy'. It was, that alone 'which can form men inured to the hardships of climates, to the fatigues of labour, and to the danger of storms'. A Navigation Act might not be as suitable to France as to England, but it behoved France to make regulations which would enable its subjects 'to share those benefits with the Swedes, the Danes and the Dutch, who come and take from them even in their own harbours'.[1]

Any lingering anxieties over rivalry from Holland faded rapidly in English minds before the suspicion that the French had recovered far more quickly than they should have done from the economic and military disasters of Louis XIV's wars. The knowledge that the pacific policy of Fleury aimed at the steady recovery and extension of French commerce and industry turned that suspicion into an obsession by the 1740's. Thus one writer was made aware of the complexities of economic planning by the revelation that the prohibition of Irish cloth exports undertaken in the interests of English manufacturers was in fact driving Irish wool into the French market, thereby giving France the raw material for a cheap and saleable export and 'as this increased, that of Britain declined'. Hence, too, from quarters where French naval weakness was perceived, a crop of suggestions that the best (and perhaps the only) way to call a halt to French recovery was by a war. Thus the author of *Common Sense* (1738) held that 'A rising trade may be ruined by a war; a sinking trade has a chance to revive by it'. While another in 1745 argued that '...our Commerce, in general, will flourish more under a vigorous and well-managed naval war, than under any peace, which should allow an open intercourse with those two nations' (i.e. France and Spain).

In all the main areas of world trade, Anglo-French rivalry is the dominant theme of the period. Nowhere was it more persistent than in the West Indies, in this period the heart of an Atlantic system of trade which embraced also the mainland colonies from Spanish America to Newfoundland in the north, took in the West African slave trade, and formed a prime source of wealth to western European ports from Cadiz in the south to Glasgow in the north. Within this Atlantic theatre, the largest

[1] G. T. F. Raynal, *A Philosophical and Political History of the Settlements and Trade of the Europeans in the East and West Indies* (London, 1798), vol. IV, p. 466.

volume of trade was probably carried on by direct routes which crossed from coast to coast, but a proportion went by triangular and quadrangular routes, and indeed by round voyages of every description. A 'regular' ship on the direct run from Liverpool to Jamaica might with luck do two trips a year, but a slaver which called in to sell cheap textiles in exchange for slaves on the West African coast, passed on to the West Indies to sell the slaves and buy sugar, tobacco, indigo, and a little cotton, might only do one journey a year. Other ships, the equivalents of the modern 'tramp', seeking cargoes and profits where they could find them, might be away from their home port, be it Bordeaux, Amsterdam, or Glasgow, for several years. Most of the Atlantic ships were of medium size (three or four hundred tonners) half-way between the big East Indiamen and the smaller 150 tonner which was common in the Narrow Seas.

On one thing English and French writers seem to have agreed in the first half of the eighteenth century: the immense value of the Atlantic trade, and within that trade the special desirability of the West Indian trade. They were slower to appreciate the commercial potentialities of the North American colonies with their rapidly growing populations. West Indian products—sugar, tobacco, cotton, indigo and dyewoods—had been the first commodities to be 'enumerated' under the Navigation Acts; while the West Indian colonists with their slave dependents represented a solid demand for British goods until the middle of the eighteenth century. The idea that 'every Englishman in Barbadoes or Jamaica creates employment for four men at home'[1] died hard. Conversely, the north and middle colonies fitted far less neatly into the old colonial system. The colonists of New England employed less shipping, consumed fewer English manufactures and produced less desirable goods. Their trade was less with England than with the Mediterranean, the Azores and the West Indies, British and foreign, where they sold their lumber, provisions, horses, cattle and fish. With the proceeds of these trades, it was true, the northern colonists were able to buy British manufactures, but that did not wholly allay English suspicions that these colonies of settlement were by nature competitive with England. Hence a series of Acts designed to restrict North American industrial tendencies. But the most unsatisfactory feature of the northern colonists was their obstinate predilection for trade with the foreign West Indian colonies. The Treaty of Utrecht, apart from depriving the French of half of St Christopher's, allowed them to retain their West Indian possessions. Martinique, Guadeloupe and St Domingo could all produce sugar more cheaply than Barbados or Jamaica. Likewise the Dutch in Curaçao and St Eustatius had access to supplies (their own as well as smuggled French supplies) which undersold the British. Here were the flames of a family conflict which were constantly fanned by

[1] Josiah Child, *A New Discourse of Trade* (1698), quoted by R. Pares, 'Economic Factors in the History of Empire' (*Economic History Review*, May 1937), p. 125.

a powerful group of West Indian interests which did not lack strong parliamentary support. One method of dealing with the problem was to try to obstruct the colonists' trade with the foreign West Indies by imposing a crushing duty on foreign sugar, molasses and rum imported to the mainland colonies. Such was the object of the Molasses Act (1733), though fortunately for the colonists it proved impossible to enforce the high duties. Another method was to encourage the production of American commodities which could be sold directly to Britain. This, if it had proved practicable, would have conformed exactly with the idea of the colonial function in mercantilist theory. It was, for example, notorious that the Baltic supply of naval stores, timber, and Swedish iron, vital to the British shipbuilding and small-arms industries and therefore of vital importance in the national defence, were not only highly vulnerable to attack but were at best a drain on the treasure of the State. The Baltic balance of payments was persistently unfavourable to Britain. There was much to recommend a policy of supplementing or, if possible, replacing British imports from the Baltic by imports from America. But progress was slow and disappointing. By 1721 considerable quantities of tar and pitch were forthcoming, with corresponding relief to the Baltic balance of payments, but the New Englanders obstinately preferred to sell their boards, planks, pipe staves, beams and clapboard to the West Indies. Contractors employed by the surveyors to fell trees for the navy were driven off or ducked in the rivers by the loggers. Production of iron from Virginia and Maryland remained only a fraction of Swedish and Russian imports. Unsatisfactory as these failures were to English mercantilists, they were perhaps less odious than the colonists' 'pernicious and unwarrantable' action in the Seven Years War, when, under cover of the flag of truce, North American ships chartered to exchange prisoners of war poured provisions into the starving French West Indies.

The various sources of wealth and profit offered by the transatlantic colonies thus became a chronic cause of friction between the four major European Powers which had interests in the Caribbean. Old Spain, desperately clinging to the remains of her original empire, looked to New Spain to produce the bullion with which her own purchases in Europe were still sustained. Yet the size of the Spanish convoys was always small, and the unsatisfied needs of the Spanish empire constantly attracted the attentions of smugglers, especially English and Dutch. England had, it was true, rights of legitimate trade as a result of the War of the Spanish Succession. These included the *asiento* (the right to supply slaves to the Spanish empire) and the right to send one ship a year to Portobello. Yet these concessions were too meagre to satisfy the ambitions of the English merchants. Legal trade was supplemented by illegal, and the ostensible cause of the War of 1739 with England was Spanish interference with the British smugglers.

Again, though wider political issues were involved, economic rivalry in the West Indies contributed in some measure to the friction which culminated in the Anglo-French wars. Both sides had strong vested interests in sugar production. England saw in the war of 1744 an opportunity to ruin the French sugar colonies and eliminate their competition in the European market. The French West Indian interests likewise saw an opportunity to ruin a rival and enlarge France's share of the Spanish colonial market for manufactured goods. Similar considerations entered into the policies of both Powers in the Seven Years War, although the West Indian issue was increasingly overshadowed by political and military issues elsewhere, notably the question of Canada. By the mid-century, indeed, British opinion on the relative importance of the different colonial areas was changing. The West Indies had been, after all, something of a disappointment, for disease kept the white population more or less stationary, while in the continental colonies further north, the growth of population promised to create valuable markets for British exports. The balance of trade with the northern colonies, previously unprofitable to the mother country, was supposed to be turning in her favour after the middle of the century. When peace finally came in 1763, therefore, France was allowed to keep her sugar islands, although the record of the war in the West Indies was one of reverses suffered at the hands of greatly superior British naval power and the complete disruption of French West Indian trade. Trade at Nantes and Bordeaux had come to a complete standstill. It might be true that the French economy as a whole could withstand attack by blockade, but eighteenth-century wars were not 'total' wars; and the pockets and luxuries of a sufficient number of Frenchmen had been affected by the colonial blockade to give Britain valuable bargaining counters in 1763.

The value of naval power in relation to trade was shown on a smaller scale in the operations against Dutch West Indian Islands in 1757 and 1758. Like the English, the Dutch derived handsome profits from smuggling into the Spanish colonies from their West Indian entrepôts. In wartime, their services to the French Islands, starved of supplies by the shortage of French shipping and the British blockade, were indispensable. To the British it was equally vital that these neutral services to a belligerent should be stopped and for two years the Royal Navy seized Dutch ships wholesale. The lesson of the West Indies seemed, in fact, to be that trade and sea power were in the eighteenth, as in the seventeenth, century but two sides of the same coin.

The second great theatre of trade and trade war was India and southeast Asia. And the same three Powers which had intruded upon the Spanish empire in the Caribbean had seized upon the disintegrating inheritance of the Portuguese in the East. During the seventeenth century one major development had taken place in the struggle for Asiatic trade.

The Dutch had driven the English out of the Spice Islands. The last English foothold, Poleroon, had been lost in the Second Dutch War, and the disputes at Bantam forced them to retire to Bencoolen in 1682. Thus the trading interests of the English became concentrated on the mainland, round the factories at Surat, Bombay, Madras and Calcutta. Each of the three latter Presidencies had its satellite settlements tapping the trade of large interior regions. The period 1709 to 1750 was a period of steady prosperity for the English East India Company. Its imports and exports doubled in value, and from eleven ships a year at the beginning of the period, its fleet grew to twenty, and those bigger, by the mid-century. Deprived of a large part of the spice-producing areas, the Company's trade changed in character. In the eighteenth century the cargoes from India included an increasing proportion of those Indian textiles whose competition disturbed so profoundly the English woollen interests at home. Tea from China and coffee from the Red Sea ports were less controversial, while the increasing imports of saltpetre had a strategic as well as an economic value. The East, in fact, provided many commodities which Europe needed. The fundamental problem of the trade remained one of payment, for India was not a good market for European exports. Throughout the seventeenth century, there had been vigorous if fruitless opposition to the export of silver which was the method adopted by the Company to meet its obligations in India. In the eighteenth century the proportion of silver in the exports to India continued to rise, and the continuing demand helped to keep alive the notion that the object of economic, and on occasion strategic, policy should be the winning of precious metal. Not until the coming of cheap cotton goods from Lancashire in the nineteenth century was an economic solution of the payment problem forthcoming. Meanwhile, the nature of British intervention was slowly changing. From the Restoration period onwards, the East India Company was not only a trading monopoly but a political and judicial power. Earlier than its rivals, the English Company grasped the fact that the only firm basis of European power in India was naval and military strength.

The centre of Dutch power lay in the archipelago, its administrative centre at Batavia. Originally the Dutch Company had been organised as a firm of shipowners and merchants, deriving its profits from its monopoly of the spice trade and by competitive trading in Persia, India and Japan. Batavia was conceived as an eastern entrepôt and the problem of payments for the exports from India was partially solved by means of local profits from the Asiatic trade itself. On the mainland, the Dutch stepped into the place of the Portuguese on the Malabar Coast and in Ceylon. There were Dutch factories at Surat and Bengal. On the Coromandel Coast they were at pains to organize the local textile industry. The produce of all these areas, together with copper bought in Japan and tea and textiles from China, was sent to the Archipelago to pay for the exports of spices. During the eighteenth century, a change came over the character of Dutch trade in the East. The Company changed from a commercial to an agricultural enterprise. New crops came to the fore in the islands. Sugar—only a ballast cargo till 1700—found a profitable market in Europe, though quantities remained small by comparison with West Indian shipments, while coffee began to rival spices by the middle of the century. There was some cultivation of cotton and indigo. Yet by 1750 it was clear that all was not well with the Dutch enterprise. As rival Powers began to extend their authority over the native States in India, Dutch trade with the mainland dwindled. In spite of heavy charges for administration and fortification, Dutch power in India declined, and their navy was allowed to fall in decay. The last desperate attempt to enforce their power in the Hoogli expedition in 1759 only served to reveal their essential weakness.

With the Dutch limited, to all intents and purposes, to the Archipelago, the struggle for economic supremacy in India became an Anglo-French duel. The French had been latecomers to India. Colbert's Company had made little progress, and even the acquisition of Pondicherry as a base only brought a temporary revival. The real growth of French power dates from Law's reorganisation of colonial trade under the *Compagnie des Indes* in 1719. The new Company held exclusive privileges of trade from the west coast of Africa round the Cape to the Red Sea, the islands of the Indian Ocean, India itself and the Farther East. Under Lenoir (governor until 1735) and Dumas (governor until 1742) progress was rapid and an annual convoy of thirty ships was supplying the French market with Indian textiles, China tea and Mocca coffee. So far the objectives of French policy seem to have remained purely commercial. Such forts as were erected were to protect trade. Then with Dupleix came a new conception and policy—to acquire territorial possessions as a basis for both trade and empire; in practice, to use Pondicherry as a base from which to establish French power over all southern India. Once again, it was primarily failure to grasp the importance of sea power which led to Dupleix's defeat at the hands of Clive and Coote. In 1761 the French were left 'without a foot of ground in India',[1] and relieved of their rivalry, the English Company passed on to enjoy a period of prosperity from its expanding trade and revenues.

In yet a third area, the Mediterranean and Levant, the rivalry lay mainly between the English and the French. The Levant trade was in many ways a less controversial matter than the Indian. It provided a valuable market for European cloth exports, while the raw silks and cottons imported were increasingly important as the raw materials for expanding home industries. The French cotton industry especially seems to have relied heavily on the Levant product, though it was apt to be dirty, full of knots and altogether inferior to the best produce of the French

[1] *Cambridge History of the British Empire* (1929), vol. IV, *British India*, p. 164.

Antilles. From this Levant trade the Dutch, who had occupied a leading position in the seventeenth century, seem to have been largely eliminated by the mid-eighteenth century. Their trade, necessarily suspended during the Anglo-French wars, failed to re-establish itself after 1713, mainly because Dutch woollens were unable to compete with the cheap French cloths of Languedoc and Provence. France was geographically in a strong position to dominate the Levant from Marseilles, while friendly relations with Turkey gave the French traders special privileges at Constantinople and Smyrna. These advantages were supplemented by other forms of assistance. The political expenses of the consular establishment were borne by the French Government, and not by the Company; while liberal credits were given to the Marseilles exporters to bridge the gap between the departure of their ships to the Levant and the final payment for their exports. Such were some of the advantages which enabled France to retain first place in the trade to the Levant and the Barbary Coast.

There remained the central, and even more complex, network of inter-regional trade in Europe. It is easy to underestimate its importance when viewed alongside the more spectacular colonial trade. Yet economic activity remained overwhelmingly European: inter-regional trade in the eighteenth century was still chiefly a matter of exchanging European goods—Baltic corn and timber, English cloth and metal wares, French cloths, brandies and wines, Spanish wool and Portuguese wine. The newer trades in colonial goods stimulated the demand for shipping in the ports of western Europe, and created valuable re-export business. But at any rate in the first half of the eighteenth century it seems likely that their most important function was to act as a 'leaven' to the older trades, easing the problem of international payments by varying the commodities available for purchase and sale.[1] During the seventeenth century a great deal of the trade and shipping had been controlled by the Dutch. Even in the eighteenth century the Dutch held tenaciously to their position. The Amsterdam corn trade with the Baltic remained considerable, though it was smaller by 1750 than it had been a hundred years earlier. There were fewer Dutch ships in the Baltic, and more English, Swedish, Danish, Danzig and Lübeck ships. The sources of Dutch weakness were threefold. First, Holland lacked the natural resources which would have enabled her to establish local industries, and such industries as did survive (for example, the Leyden cloth industry) were not helped by a tariff policy which put protection of local industries below the free flow of goods as an object of economic policy. A thorough inquiry into the problem in 1751 produced proposals which would have resulted in lower fiscal duties and more effective protective duties, but the inevitable conflict between the merchant and industrialists prevented any action. Secondly, as 'broker and carrier of Europe' she was peculiarly vulnerable to the mercantilist policies of

[1] See below, p. 44.

contemporary Europe, which aimed at reducing visible and invisible imports from other countries. French and English tariffs, the English Navigation Laws, and similar measures adopted by smaller countries like Sweden, struck at the Dutch position as European middleman. So, by 1730, West Country merchants in England were buying hessians direct from Hamburg, which they had previously bought through Amsterdam. Others who had marketed their cloth exports through Dutch firms were shipping goods directly to Germany and Spain. By the middle of the century the North German ports, Bremen, Altona, but above all Hamburg, were proving formidable competitors to Amsterdam. In 1750 it was reported that three times as much sugar, coffee and indigo was shipped for Hamburg from France as for Amsterdam, while the London firm which wrote in 1762 that it had lately made it 'a principal part' of its business to buy West Indian articles 'for the Marketts of Hambro and Bremen' was probably no isolated case. Direct routes were in many trades beginning to replace the older route that had for long lain through Holland. And those tendencies were strengthened by the progress in the technique of merchant shipbuilding. The 'flyboat' was no longer a Dutch monopoly. By the middle of the eighteenth century there was little to choose between British, French and Dutch merchant ships in point of cheap freights. Finally, the Dutch were in no position to maintain any real primacy in the Atlantic trades. Although they kept a foothold in the French West Indian trade (St Eustatius was the smuggling entrepôt of the West Indies), they had little success in diverting the growing stream of colonial goods from the British colonies, which was almost wholly focussed on England. The sugar was refined and the tobacco cut and packed in Liverpool or Glasgow, the raw cotton cleaned, spun, woven in Lancashire, the indigo and logwoods consumed in the woollen industries of Yorkshire. Thus the control of colonial trade reinforced the tendency for the central market of European trade to shift westwards from Holland to England. Not all was lost. Bulk cargoes, chiefly coal and corn, continued to go from the east-coast ports to Amsterdam and Rotterdam, and throughout this period Holland was the largest single market for English cloth. A considerable proportion of the products of the French Antilles continued to come to Amsterdam, and the supplies of sugar, coffee, tobacco and cotton from the Dutch companies themselves remained considerable. But the Dutch share in the total foreign trade of England and of Europe as a whole had shrunk appreciably by 1763.

Although the Dutch share in the active trade of Europe was less in the eighteenth than it had been in the seventeenth century, there is little doubt that a large proportion of world trade continued to be financed from Holland. One of the principal problems facing European merchants in this experimental period of foreign trade was the problem of payments. The difficulty lay partly in the limited number of commodities available for export. The case of English trade with the Baltic and India is a good example. Neither of these areas could absorb a sufficient quantity of England's principal export—cloth—to pay for the desirable (and, in the case of the Baltic strategically vital) commodities which England needed to buy. Payment had therefore to be made in bullion, supplies of which had in turn to be derived from areas of trade where the reverse position obtained. This problem may help to explain the emphasis placed by seventeenth-century theorists on bullion, an emphasis which by no means wholly disappeared in the eighteenth century. The problem was eased to some extent by the coming of colonial commodities in bulk in the eighteenth century. You could sell tobacco and sugar where you could not sell cloth. But this did not wholly or immediately dispose of the problem. In this period it was partially solved by the growing use of the bill on Amsterdam. The Dutch merchant who had become accustomed to make advances of cash to foreign sellers moved easily into the discount and acceptance business. European traders everywhere were in the habit of arranging with Amsterdam houses to accept and pay bills drawn on them by other foreign merchants selling to them. The bill on Amsterdam was to the eighteenth century what the bill on London was to become to the nineteenth century. From the bill business the Dutch went on to foreign loan business. The balances from a century of active trade and shipping, the relatively easy profits to be had from financial operations and the growing difficulties of active trade all combined to give an increasing financial complexion to Dutch economic activity. By 1763 the Dutch had lent money to Sweden, France, Poland, Prussia, Denmark, Bavaria, Spain and many other States. Since the seventeenth century they had been lending to England and in the period after 1739 it was the British funds which principally occupied the attention of Dutch investors—institutions with funds to spare, admirals, lawyers, widows and orphans as well as a large class of professional speculators. The last three years of the Seven Years War in particular saw a large expansion of Dutch capital in England, and by 1763 their holding represented a significant proportion of the total English National Debt. This phenomenon seems to indicate that the apparently favourable English balance of payments was illusory. The national outgoings (for example, the interest on existing foreign debts, the upkeep of foreign embassies, the expenses of Grand Tours in Europe and above all the cost of a great navy and army) eliminated such favourable balances on visible trade as may have existed, and left England a debtor nation—indebted in particular to Holland. In addition, Amsterdam remained a centre of European marine insurance business, and though by punctuality and probity London was already offering serious competition in this line of business, it remained the bugbear of English insurance houses that any relaxation of vigilance on their part would certainly throw the insurance business into the hands of the Dutch.

The relationship between foreign trade and the interest of the State varied from country to country. In general it remained true that the essential basis of society was in most parts of Europe still agrarian. Holland was the obvious exception to the rule. Here the employment of a large proportion of the working population and the fortunes of capitalists depended on an uninterrupted flow of raw materials from all parts of the world. Even the nation's food was largely imported from the Baltic. These facts help to explain the apparent timidity of Dutch foreign and economic policy in the eighteenth century. With a small population, poor resources, vulnerable lines of communication, Dutch statesmen were in no position to pursue adventurous policies. In other countries foreign trade did not impinge so directly on national interests: yet its pursuit and protection was in many countries an obsession with statesmen and the achievement of a favourable balance of trade a prime aim of policy. The explanation of the seeming paradox must lie in the close relationship between governments and strong groups with vested interests in foreign trade, as for example those of the East and West Indian merchants, as well as in the fiscal interests of the governments themselves. More than that, a trade stoppage might produce unemployment and danger to public order in particular areas, or even a threat to national security. In England, Jamaican cotton was increasingly used in the Lancashire cotton industry. West Indian dyes were essential for the treatment of dark cloths in Yorkshire and the West Country; Swedish iron was essential to the sword makers and gunsmiths of Birmingham. Raw silk from Smyrna and Leghorn was necessary for the silk spinners of the English midlands and the weavers of Spitalfields. Above all, imported timber was necessary to merchant and especially naval shipbuilding. Markets had also to be considered: the market for midland nails in the American colonies, the great market for Yorkshire worsteds in Germany, and the scarcely less vital West Country trade to Spain and to Italy, where the nuns were 'vail'd with fine Kersies and Long Ells'.[1] Considerations of this kind go far to explain the attention devoted by British governments in the period to naval power, and the continued association of prosperity and power. In the Baltic, where Sweden or Russia might threaten our timber supplies, it was the naval task to ensure that there was no *Dominium Maris Baltici*. In the Mediterranean, the Levant trade might be threatened (as in 1725) by Spain and the Empire from Sicily, by France from Toulon and Marseilles, by the Barbary pirates from North Africa. Hence the importance of naval bases like Gibraltar and Minorca which were 'in a more convenient situation to give them Disturbance'.[2] It is difficult to accuse English statesmen of over-estimating the protective value of naval power. It is more arguable that they sometimes overvalued its offensive power. The assumption, widely

---

[1] Defoe, *A Plan of the English Commerce* (1728), p. 185.

[2] Thomas Shaw, D.D., F.R.S., *Travels or Observations* (Oxford, 1738), p. 318.

held, that Spain could be reduced to terms by stopping the treasure fleet from New Spain proved optimistic, while a recent historian has put on record his opinion that the Seven Years War demonstrates 'the impotence of blockade and colonial conquests to break the will of France'.[1] Within a few years after the Peace of Paris the colonial trade of Bordeaux rose to unprecedented dimensions. Yet, in the wider plan, the extinction of French sea power and the reduction of her colonies and trade played its part. In spite of enemy successes on the Continent, sufficient injury had been done to powerful interests in France to enable Britain to drive a hard bargain in 1763.

So far as the practical application of economic theories was concerned, the historian of this period can record little deviation from the classical mercantilist position. In the minds of statesmen, foreign trade and shipping remained the object of their exertions and the source of national welfare. 'Our trade depends upon a proper exertion of our maritime strength: that trade and maritime force depend upon each other...the riches, which are the true resources of the country, depend upon commerce.' That was the essence of what was called 'Pitt's System' and there was little to choose between the ideas of Pitt in 1760 and those of Sir George Downing and the authors of the Navigation Act a hundred years earlier. To determine the health of the nation, men looked to the balance of trade just as they had done a century earlier. More than that, they were apt to quote figures of exports and imports gathered more or less at random from writers of the previous century as though nothing had changed. Why economic thought should have been so static it is not easy to say; but one consideration certainly was the assumption, fundamental to mercantilist writers, that the total volume of trade available to be shared was itself fixed and unchanging. Matthew Decker, an anglicised Dutchman and a writer of wide practical commercial experience, whose views have often been held to be a source for Adam Smith, could write in his *Essay on the Causes of the Decline of the Foreign Trade*: 'Therefore if the Exports of *Britain* exceed its Imports, Foreigners must pay the Balance in Treasure and the Nation grow Rich. But if the imports of Britain exceed its Exports, we must pay Foreigners the Balance in Treasure and the Nation grow Poor.' The words are practically a paraphrase of Thomas Mun's, and, half a century after Decker, Necker set up an office to enable him to judge the state of French trade by the same criterion. In Spain the fiscal system had for centuries run contrary to the fundamental tenets of mercantilism, taxing heavily raw material imports and manufactured exports and encouraging manufactured imports and raw material exports, and it is in this period that the two most popular economists, Uztariz and Ulloa, began to emphasise the importance of industry and the export trade after the manner of orthodox mercantilists. Everywhere, the attitude

[1] Pares, *War and Trade in the West Indies* (1936), p. 392.

of practical men towards colonies remained substantially unchanged. Colonies served, as a Bristol merchant had put in it 1717, 'to take off our product and manufactures, supply us with commodities which may either be wrought up here or exported again, or prevent fetching things of the same nature from other places for our home consumption, employ our poor and encourage our navigation'.[1]

Yet even amongst practical men, signs were not lacking of dissatisfaction with certain aspects of the existing systems of trade. Thus Decker, whose theme was the decline of foreign trade, looked forward as well as backwards. For if he accepted the importance of the favourable trade balance, he rejected the machinery of regulation by which mercantilists normally sought to achieve it. He attacked not only the customs system, the National Debt, and 'ill-judged laws', but the whole system of monopolies and the Navigation Acts. Attacks of this kind on the Navigation Acts were not immediately effective and it is doubtful how far his opinions were popularly held. Even the energetic Dean Tucker was not converted from orthodox views on the value of colonial possessions until the Stamp Act controversy of 1765. It was indeed difficult for observers who saw several hundred ships a year leaving the west-coast ports with cargoes of textiles, and returning with cargoes of colonial goods, and could watch the growing wealth of Liverpool (or for Frenchmen the growing wealth of Bordeaux), not to assume that these things were causally linked with a benevolent system of commercial regulation. In another direction, however, the attacks of Decker and others may have been more effective. The 'first monopoly' singled out for attack was 'Companies with exclusive charters, namely *East India*, *South Sea* and *Turkey* Companies' which 'prevent the increasing the vent of our Manufactures abroad'. Their exclusive charters, Decker alleged, debarred Englishmen 'from a Free Trade to three quarters of the known World', for their policies led to deliberate restriction on the growth of shipping. There were 'greater numbers of Ship Tonnage employed in the Trade to the free Port of *Leghorn* only than by the three chartered companies all together'.[2] Here Decker was on a more popular platform, and it is perhaps significant that the years about the mid-century saw considerable relaxations in the company system by which English foreign trade was conducted. There were more capitalists wealthy enough to finance voyages individually than there had been a century earlier. The risks of foreign trade, though still considerable, had been diminished by the spread of diplomatic offices, by the efficiency and strength of the Royal Navy, and by the development of marine insurance. All these developments reduced the need for the Chartered Company, at

[1] John Cary, *An Essay towards Regulating the Trade and Employing the Poor of this Kingdom* (1717), quoted by J. F. Rees, *Cambridge History of the British Empire* (1929), vol. I, ch. XX, p. 566.
[2] Decker, pp. 43–7.

any rate in many areas of trade. Of the great Joint Stock Companies, the East India and the Hudson's Bay Company survived, largely because in the last analysis it was recognised that these trades needed the protection which only a company with permanent and collective financial resources could provide. The third, the African Company, was wound up and turned into a regulated company comprising all the merchants trading to Africa in 1750. The other regulated companies—the Eastland and Muscovy and the Merchant Adventurers—had been opened up after the Revolution of 1688. Then, in 1753, a Bill was passed which threw open the Levant Company and brought it into line with the new fashion. Even in France there had been sporadic attacks on monopolies and commercial restrictions in the Council of Commerce since the beginning of the century, and after 1750 the Council's deliberations showed growing liberal tendencies; in 1759 the new spirit was manifested in the decision to allow the import of Indian cottons. Meanwhile the followers of Vincent de Gournay (1712–59) popularised the phrase *laissez-faire, laissez-passer*. The fifties were thus a transitional stage between monopoly and freedom of trade, but the assumption remained that overseas trade must be 'ordered'.

Such changes were perceptible but small. They hardly indicated that the edifice of mercantilism was about to fall: indeed, it was to survive the century. Yet it is precisely in this period that the theorists were preparing an attack on the very foundation of the mercantile system which were in time to bring it down in ruins. In England a succession of thinkers—Locke, North and Hume; in France, Richard Cantillon and François Quesnay, the leader of the Physiocrats, were formulating a theoretical indictment of the mercantile system. Their approach differed from that of writers such as Decker in its relative freedom from immediately practical preoccupations. Their criticism sprang rather from intellectual dissatisfaction with the unsatisfactory analytical apparatus of the mercantilists, and their achievement was to fashion a more universal (if often less practical) conception of economic theory and analysis. Cantillon's *Essai* (1755) contained a full treatment of the central questions of value, wages and price and the relations between foreign trade, exchange rates and price levels superior to that of any previous writer. Hume, though less original, made his mark on later thought, not least by an attack on the mercantilist conception of the balance of trade, worked out on the basis of the quantity theory of money. Some of these ideas were reproduced in France in the writings of the Physiocrats, for whom commerce had only a subsidiary economic function, that of distribution. They demonstrate the extreme lengths to which the most advanced contemporary theory had gone in shifting the emphasis from the functions of exchange (where the mercantilists had put it) to the function of production. It was in the sphere of production that they found the power of creating wealth and possibly a surplus for accumulation. Here was a mode of thought which at the very least diverted men's gaze from commerce and at most might destroy the elaborate mechanism of economic nationalism carefully built up over a period of at least two centuries. It is nevertheless easy to exaggerate the contemporary importance of the new approach. Hume might declare in 1752: 'Not only as a man but also as a British subject, I pray for the flourishing commerce of Germany, Spain, Italy and even France itself.' But it was to be a long time before many were found to share his faith. On the philosophical plane alone, a full synthesis of the theoretical and practical implications of the new thought had to await the publication of the *Wealth of Nations*. Pitt's 'System' was more attuned to the climate of popular opinion than the economic philosophy of Hume or the anti-imperialism of Tucker.

It was characteristic of the later phases of the Old Regime that its rulers should look largely to the past, but its thinkers somewhat to the future. For the age itself was compound of the old and the new. The foundations of European society remained agrarian and mercantile. Industrial development was local and uneven. Older industries like the Leyden cloth industry in Holland and the Devonshire serge industry in England were in decay, Newer industries, like the cheap textiles of southern France, the worsted manufacture of Yorkshire, the silk and cotton industries of north and midland England were in the ascendant. Some technological change there was, especially in metallurgy, but in industry as a whole there were few signs of any far-reaching change in the organisation of production itself. Industrial interests were sufficiently organised politically to challenge governments on the issues that affected them, and they did so successfully both in France and England over the import of competing Indian textiles. Yet it is significant that they considered that their interests, like those of the merchants, lay in measures of protection and restriction and not of economic freedom. Such moves as were made towards greater economic freedom derived more from the changing relationships between commerce and industry rather than from a change in the internal organisation of production. More people were affected in 1763 than in 1713 by commerce with countries other than their own. More employers and employees were concerned with raw materials obtained abroad and with the opening up of foreign and colonial markets. They were therefore increasingly inclined to question the principles of ossified regulated economies which often seemed to lack flexibility, sometimes ran counter to common sense and fair dealing, and increasingly appeared to hinder rather than promote trade and employment.

CHAPTER III

THE SOCIAL CLASSES AND THE FOUNDATIONS OF THE STATES

EARLY eighteenth-century society, as mirrored by Saint Simon and Lord Harvey, by the family papers of the Russells or the Wyndhams, by the correspondence of the duke of Berwick or Lady Mary Wortley Montagu, seemed predominantly aristocratic and French. This impression is supported by castles in Sweden and palaces in and around Vienna, by portraits and libraries and famous collections of porcelain in England and in Russia. However, the impression is rather different if one considers Fleet Street, Liverpool and Bristol rather than St James's, Welbeck and Woburn; Rennes and Marseilles rather than Versailles; or Hamburg and Frankfurt-am-Main rather than Potsdam, Karlsruhe and Mannheim. It then appears that, even in the first half of the eighteenth century, economic forces were already in operation which tended to make the urban middle class increasingly numerous and powerful, and that French ideas and fashions were already being challenged from England, the German cities and even from the non-European world.

The social prestige of the aristocrats in the early eighteenth century was, however, undoubtedly very great. In most countries high office in the army, at court and in the diplomatic service was filled almost exclusively by members of that order. In most of Europe the aristocrats were marked off from the third estate by the right to display armorial bearings, as for example on the panels of their carriages, or, as in Spain, carved conspicuously over the main entrance to a town house. In most countries, though here the practice in England was peculiar, all descendants of aristocrats were still further differentiated from other people by the hereditary use of a title. The right to such a title usually involved a grant of nobility from the Crown, and the king's right to ennoble commoners was sharply watched and vigorously restricted, as for example by the Swedish Constitution of 1720 though, in fact, between 1719 and 1792 about 624 families were ennobled in Sweden as compared with 144 creations made between 1702 and 1783 in England. Much of the power of the aristocrats was based on wealth and in the first half of the eighteenth century this wealth was still most often in the form of land. In Spain a few great nobles such as Infantado, Medina Sidonia or Osuna held such enormous estates that the heads of these families could not be ignored politically even when personally they might have very mediocre capacities. The nobles in several countries had worked out roughly comparable methods of keeping together great landed estates. Whether by a system of *mayorazgo* as in Spain, or of *Fideikommiss* as in Austria, or of strict entail as in England, land passed intact from father to eldest son. The *Tatler* denounced the practice as monstrous,[1] but it remained very popular. Even if some individual members of the aristocracy lacked wealth and had to have suits made from the family tapestry, as did M. de Louvois, they still enjoyed very considerable privileges. In many parts of continental Europe nobles, simply by virtue of their rank, were exempt from taxation, could exercise jurisdiction over their tenants and were still entitled to various feudal payments and often to services. Whether it was the world of such a minor English country gentleman as Sir Roger de Coverley, as it is reflected in the pages of the *Spectator*, or of a great noble such as Luynes or Saint Simon, whether it was observed by another noble such as the duc de Richelieu or from below by Beaumarchais or by Gay, eighteenth-century society appeared to be dominated by the fine gentleman. The peasant was his tenant, sometimes his serf. Urban craftsmen embroidered his waist-coats or inlaid his furniture. Even painters of genius like Reynolds or Gainsborough were glad to execute his commissions while it was the exception for a man of letters to be as independent as Pope and dispense with noble patronage.

At first sight the predominantly aristocratic character of early eighteenth-century society was reinforced by the very considerable power and prestige of the Roman Catholic Church for, although the parish priests were some-times recruited from the ranks of the peasantry or the urban craftsman, the higher positions in the Church were nearly always filled by members of the nobility. One place where high office in the Church was open to men of humble origin was Spain, but this was not usual in most countries. In France, Spain and Naples the clergy, the members of religious orders and the hangers-on who found some employment connected with the Church accounted for about 2 per cent of the population. In Portugal the per-centage seems to have been much higher. The clergy were exempt from most of the ordinary taxes. They enjoyed tithes and dues of many kinds. They largely monopolised education. In politics their influence was usually on the side of the Crown and of conservatism. The Protestant clergy, whether in Scandinavia, northern Germany, Holland or the British Isles, enjoyed a less exalted social position than many of the Roman Catholics, but in general their influence was as steadily on the side of the established order. Only the Methodists took a lively interest in the con-dition of the poor and even they, though deeply concerned to save the souls of the poor from damnation, were not much concerned to improve their social or economic conditions or to rouse them to claim any political power.

Yet to say that the early eighteenth century was 'aristocratic' is to give the period a misleading uniformity; in spite of considerable similarities the

[1] The *Tatler*, no. 223, 12 September 1710.

aristocrats of different countries differed very markedly from one another. The rural noble of Russia (ch. XIV) was very different from the court aristocrat of France (ch. X). The bureaucratic or military nobility of Prussia (ch. XIII) or Sweden (ch. XV) presented a sharp contrast to the leisured absentee landlords of Spain (ch. XII). In Prussia, and to some extent also in Hungary (ch. XVII) and Sweden, many nobles were practical farmers cultivating their estates for profit; in England most of the land was leased to tenants, but the English landlord had a tradition of keeping in close touch with country affairs through his bailiff; in Spain, Denmark and much of France, many nobles lived almost permanently at court, visited their estates seldom and took little personal interest in farming problems so long as the feudal payments were made to them regularly. Not only did the connection between the nobles and their estates vary considerably between one district and another, but their powers over their peasants also varied very widely; in Poland and Hungary the powers of the aristocrat on his estate were very considerable; in Sweden and England they were less than almost anywhere else in Europe.

The difference in the relations between the noble and the peasants who cultivated the soil vividly illustrates the difference between one part of Europe and another. The English landlords in the eighteenth century, except for a home farm, did not generally cultivate the bulk of their estates themselves. They leased their land to tenant farmers and lived off the rents. These were very profitable, for during the seventeenth century English agriculture had experienced a period of prosperity, only temporarily interrupted by the Civil War, and farm rents had increased very considerably. The large tenant farmer also prospered during the eighteenth century. If he had been lucky enough to get his farm on a long lease, he was sometimes able to make 14 or 18 per cent on the capital he had invested in his farm. He could live in comfort and even in luxury. He could even indulge a taste for cleanliness, and his wife and daughters seldom had to do hard work. But while the great landlord and the large tenant farmer prospered the small, independent yeoman, who, at the end of the seventeenth century, had made up as much as one-seventh of the population, slowly declined. He lacked the capital to compete with his wealthy neighbours or to imitate their technical improvements. He had no game rights even on his own land. The Poor Rate was a very heavy burden on him and after 1750, when the movement for enclosures revived, the yeoman's position became much worse. Corn prices began to fluctuate and he could not afford to hold up his crops to wait for a favourable price as the capitalist farmers could. The yeoman sank into the ranks of the wage earners. The agricultural wage earners in England during the first half of the eighteenth century had been fairly prosperous. Wheaten bread had replaced rye on their tables, they ate cheese almost daily and meat often, they drank beer and sometimes even tea, but towards the middle of the century conditions became worse. The official assessment of wages tended to keep them low. The system of subsidising a married man's income out of the Poor Rate indirectly undermined the market price of all labour. The concentration of industry in the towns of the north and midlands removed one source of peasant income and the enclosure of common land in the later eighteenth century was a serious threat to the wage earner. At first the improved methods of cultivation had offered employment to the wage earner, but by the middle of the century agricultural methods had so much improved that it was possible to economise on labour. Some of the great landlords preferred to evict their cottagers and rely for labour on men from a neighbouring village. By the end of the eighteenth century an iron age was beginning for agricultural workers in England though the pressure on them was not so much political or even social as economic.

In France peasant families made up about 80% of the population. Rather less than one-twentieth of the peasants actually owned their land, just under a quarter were tenant farmers while perhaps a half were *métayers*, who had to give half the produce of the land to their lord, under a quarter were landless labourers and about one twentieth serfs. By the end of the eighteenth century in France the landlords were not particularly oppressive, but the peasant had a heavy burden of money payments to make. He had to pay tithe to the Church, he had to pay the State taxes of *taille*, *vingtième*, *décime* and *capitation* as well as the tax on salt. In addition to this he had to pay various feudal dues to his lord. The peasant who was not a free landowner had to pay to use the lord's mill, wine press and bakery. He had either to perform so many days' work each week for the lord or make a money payment in lieu.

In central and eastern Europe most of the peasants were unfree, though even in these districts conditions varied considerably as between one country and another. In Hungary the land was cultivated by peasants who were essentially unfree, though some were much more prosperous than others. In 1514 the feudal dues which a peasant owed his lord had been settled at one gold florin annually, one day's work a week, one chicken a month and two geese a year. In addition ten peasants had to supply one fatted hog each year. Moreover, the lord had a right to one-ninth and the Church to one-tenth of the harvest and of the vintage. In 1548 the peasant had been compelled to give two days' work every week during harvest, haymaking and vintage. In 1557 the State had begun to impose taxes on the peasants in addition to the feudal dues they owed to their local lords. These taxes tended to increase during the centuries. By the eighteenth century the peasants of Hungary were still paying these feudal dues, performing weekly work, contributing a share of their harvest to their lord and carrying the major burden of the State taxes. As the Hungarian peasant was exclusively under the jurisdiction of the feudal lord and could not appear as witness against a noble, his position was difficult. However, the tendency developed of writing down the dues which each peasant owed his lord. It has been claimed that the Hungarian peasants were better off than were the peasants in some other parts of the Habsburg dominions, in some of the German States and even in some parts of France. The chief disadvantage which the Hungarian peasant had suffered was that the scale of dues was taken as being a minimum. When Maria Theresa in 1767 issued the Urbarium, regulating feudal dues and the numbers of days that a peasant could be required to work for his lord, she made the generally accepted figures a maximum that could be exacted. The conditions of the peasantry in Moravia, Bohemia and Silesia were, according to the Council of State in Vienna, even worse than those in Hungary, as were those of Denmark whose status was more like that usual in East Germany than in the rest of Scandinavia. In Prussia, in other German districts east of the Elbe and in Bavaria, where the peasants made up three-quarters of the population, the condition of the serfs was also bad. In East Prussia a peasant might be expected to work at least three days a week for his lord and in some cases the number might be raised to five or six. Some peasants had only the late evening or night hours in which to cultivate their own land. In most of the districts east of the Elbe the landlords had combined rights of jurisdiction with ownership of land and were thus in a very strong position in relation to their peasants. The peasants were simply 'left' in possession of some land, the terms of tenure being left vague, so that, though the peasant could not leave the estate without the permission of the lord, he could be turned out of his house and off his land without any chance of redress. In western Germany, on the contrary, the peasant's status was more like that in the less oppressive parts of France. He often paid a money due, restrictions on his personal freedom had disappeared, and he held his land on an hereditary basis so that his son might reasonably expect to inherit. His lord exercised jurisdiction over him in minor cases only, and when actual work was exacted it was sometimes as little as fourteen days in a year. In Poland (ch. XIV) the condition of the seven or eight million serfs was very miserable. Fifty-five years of war before 1717 had caused appalling damage. The population had decreased and an increase in the number of days' work required from the serf each week had not solved the difficulty. In the first half of the eighteenth century the number of days' work required each week was three. The peasant's other dues also increased. He was bound to the soil and subject to the jurisdiction of his lord who, until 1768, retained the right of life and death. In Russia (ch. XIV) the position of the serf was comparable to that of the serf in Poland. About 60 per cent of all the peasants were serfs on estates belonging to private owners. They either did two or three days' work a week for their lord or paid an annual levy which might vary from fifty *kopecks* to two *roubles*. The amount of money was fixed by the landlord and could be increased arbitrarily. Landlords could sell a serf with or without his land and even apart from his family. Landlords were also responsible for collecting the poll tax from their serfs. The 15 per cent of the peasants who lived on Church land were said to be worse off than those who had secular landlords. 'State peasants' were rather better off than the others, for they paid a very light money due of forty *kopecks*. In general, in those countries where State services were exacted from the nobility the demands of the nobles on their serfs were also heavy as in Prussia and Russia; when the nobles enjoyed considerable political power, as in Poland and Hungary, there too they were able to impose heavy burdens on their serfs.

Political importance of the aristocrats varied as much between one country and another as did their power over the peasantry. In some, though individual aristocrats usually filled the great offices of State, commanded the armed forces and served as ambassadors, the political power of the nobility was negligible. This was the case in France, where perhaps as few as 4000 noble families actually shared in the life of the court and a few individuals got offices and pensions, but where the Estates-General had not met since 1614 and where the business of local government was largely in the hands of paid officials of the Crown. In Spain the nobles, who made up about 5 per cent of the population, were in much the same situation. The *Cortes*, though it very occasionally met, had almost no power. As in France, many Spanish noblemen absented themselves from their estates and lived as hangers-on at court. The Danish nobility also tended to leave their estates and congregate in Copenhagen, as did many of these nobles in the small German States. In the courts of the small German princes the nobles had very little effective political power, but they enjoyed great social prestige. Greater importance was attached to noble birth as a prerequisite for admission to court society in Germany than was the case in France, and even in the late eighteenth century elaborate devices had to be thought out before the bourgeois Goethe could be received to play cards with the young duchess of Weimar. Moreover, in the stiffly ceremonious small German courts the number of paid posts was very numerous. In the Saxon State Calendar in 1733 the list of offices covered fifty-three pages. In most courts there were amusements provided by the prince, hunting, operas, receptions, balls, according to the taste of the prince and his consort. There was gambling and drinking. There was plenty of opportunity for love-making and gossip and petty political intrigue which kept a great many nobles in expensive, sometimes highly cultivated, but always politically ineffective attendance at court in France, Spain, the two Sicilies, Denmark and many small German courts.

In contrast to this politically ineffective court nobility, the nobility of Prussia and Russia was expected to spend a lifetime in the service of the State. In Prussia many of the nobles were so poor that they had to seek employment either as officers in the army or as civil servants. Frederick William I and Frederick II insisted that the members of the Prussian aristocracy should serve the State and a tradition grew up among the nobility by which public service became the natural career of an aristocrat and was looked on as an honour. The same ideal that the nobility must serve the State had inspired the reforms of Peter the Great, but the Russians proved less co-operative than the Prussians. In 1714 Peter declared that all estates were to be classed as hereditary, but at the same time he altered the old Muscovite system of inheritance, substituting instead a system of entail which meant that only the eldest son inherited land and that younger sons must seek employment. In 1722 Peter classified all posts whether military or civil into fourteen grades and announced that even nobles must begin at the bottom grade and work up. After Peter's death these drastic social reforms were modified. In 1730 the Entail Law was rescinded and young nobles were allowed to begin their State service in a special Cadet Corps of nobles. In 1736 the duration for which nobles had to serve the State was reduced to twenty-five years, and though this was not immediately put into operation because of the Turkish war it was confirmed and given effect in 1742. Even during the 1730's Russian noblemen had managed to evade the strict obligation of State service by resorting to various devices, such as inscribing the name of a baby on the muster roll of a Guard Regiment so that by the time the boy was 25 he had technically completed his term of compulsory service. In 1762 the nobles obtained from Peter III permission to leave the service at any time.

In Hungary the nobility enjoyed a degree of local administrative and judicial authority and even of political power which was comparable, not with the State service of Prussia or Russia or the courtly futility of France and Spain, but with the conditions of Sweden or England. In Hungary, even after the reforms of Maria Theresa, the nobility and gentry occupied a peculiarly strong position. Hungarian society was a society of nobles. The nobles were a far larger proportion of the population than was the case in France or England. In 1787 it was estimated that in Hungary, which had a population only a quarter the size of France, the number of noble families was about three times as great. In 1741 the army made up of the Hungarian nobility had been the mainstay of the Habsburg dynasty. In a country where over a long period the Crown had been worn by a foreign prince, where the towns were largely inhabited by foreigners and where the Church had been shaken by heresy, the nobility had provided the most real expression of Hungarian national unity. In Hungary no one who was not noble could own land, and the Hungarian nobility owned enormous estates which had been increased by lands granted from territories reconquered from the Turks. Some Hungarian nobles such as Count Gabor, Prince Esterhazy, the Grassalkovics,

Palffy and others were immensely rich and in 1741 it was established that Hungarian nobles need pay nothing in tax. As in other countries nobles filled the great offices of State and in Hungary, as in France, they filled high office in the Church as well. They were all personally members of the national assembly, and they filled the highest administrative posts throughout the provinces of Hungary. Gradually under Maria Theresa the powers of the great nobles began to decline, but until the end of the eighteenth century they remained very considerable, and even the poorer members of the aristocracy, the gentry, who lived in the provinces and remained largely untouched by French manners and fashions, vigorously administered justice and jealously protected the customs and rights of their districts. In Poland the eighteenth century was so much the age of the aristocrat that the Polish Constitution of that time is known as an 'aristocratic democracy'. It might with more justice have been called 'aristocratic anarchy' but, though the anarchy terminated in the annihilation of Poland, in the half century before 1772 the Polish nobility enjoyed a golden age. It has been estimated that the number of Polish gentry in the eighteenth century was somewhere in the region of one and a half millions, of whom twenty or thirty were really great magnates. The Polish nobility attended the Diets and controlled the policy of the kingdom. They dominated the provinces, electing the tax collectors and in effect administering the local districts, for the paid State officials were few and those who existed had little power. By comparison with the unbridled powers of the Polish nobility the Swedish aristocrats, even after the absolutism of the Crown had been curtailed by the Constitution of 1720, seemed much more limited, yet for just over fifty years they controlled the political life of their country. Between 1720 and 1772 control of Swedish policy was in the hands of the four Estates, and the nobles who composed the First Estate exercised a determining influence. It has been estimated that there were something like 2000 noble families in Sweden and Finland in the first half of the eighteenth century. The noble heads of families, or the representative chosen as substitute for someone himself unable to attend, did not have to seek election for each meeting of the Diet but attended regularly. In the very powerful Secret Committee of the Estates there were fifty nobles as against twenty-five clergy and twenty-five burghers. Only on occasions of special gravity were twenty-five peasants invited to join the Committee, so as a rule the nobles made up half the Committee. Of seats in the Royal Council the nobles had a complete monopoly. Though the nobility had gradually to cede some of their privileges during the eighteenth century, it was not until 1809 that office was open to members of all the Estates, and as late as 1762 the nobility refused to recognise any family which had been ennobled without the consent of the First Estate. In 1723 the nobility agreed to allow inter-marriage between members of different Estates, recognised the right of non-nobles to own noble land and to hold minor office in the administration and in the armed forces, but this was only because Sweden happened to be confronted with a serious crisis in her foreign policy. For some time to come the nobles successfully defended their considerable immunity from taxation. In England the nobility and gentry, though their victory in 1688 had not humiliated the Crown to quite the same extent as the victory won by the Swedish nobles in 1720, dominated the political, administrative and social life certainly till 1832 and perhaps till much later. The nobility made up one house of the legislature and the other was composed largely of gentry. High office in the State and in the armed forces was normally filled by noblemen. In the country districts the nobility and gentry administered justice and regulated the affairs of their county and parish as Justices of the Peace. But though in some respects the political, judicial and administrative power of the English aristocracy presented some features comparable with the powers of the nobility in Hungary and even in Poland, the extent to which the nobility and bourgeoisie tended to intermix made the social conditions in England appear 150 years in advance of those in central and eastern Europe.

Not only did social conditions vary very considerably as between one country and another; even within one country economic and civil changes were creating a multiplicity of social groups until the structure of society came to present a picture of almost infinite complexity and was far from being anything so simple as predominantly aristocratic (ch. x).

Through these delicate and complex changes in the character of society in the early eighteenth century one tendency emerges in most parts of Europe. In the prosperous trading countries of western Europe, particularly Holland, England and France, a mercantile middle class became increasingly numerous and powerful, and in the increasingly efficient autocracies of central and eastern Europe, particularly in Prussia and the Habsburg dominions, emerged a middle class made up of civil servants. Everywhere the eighteenth century saw the emergence of an upper middle class rooted in the professions such as the Army, the Navy, the Church and the Law, but the growth of an increasingly important middle class was very noticeable in England.

Perhaps because no large standing army had developed in England, as such armies had in France, Prussia, Austria and Russia by the middle of the eighteenth century, English society showed no sign of sharp divisions related to military grades. Primogeniture and entail survived in England as in many continental countries, but in England only the eldest son inherited his father's title so that in a few generations even the descendants of dukes had no title at all. This peaceful interpenetration of one class by another produced a similarity of interest which was strongly reinforced by the fact that in the Lower House of the legislature the gentry and the representatives of the towns, even if they were not gentry, sat together. As early as 1726 Defoe pointed out that it was no disgrace for gentlemen to go into commerce, or any impropriety in a merchant entering the ranks of the nobility:

in short trade in England makes gentlemen, and has peopled this nation with gentlemen; for the tradesman's children, or at least their grand children, come to be as good gentlemen, statesmen, Parliament men, privy counsellors, judges, bishops and noblemen, as those of the highest birth and the most ancient families.[1]

and Jack Anvill, transformed into Sir John Envill, appeared in the *Spectator* as an example of just this kind of self-made man 'bent on making a family'. A county M.P. and a baronet, whose ancestors had sat in parliament in the fourteenth century, could marry the daughter of a city iron master. Men who had made money in brewing might buy estates, as many did in Hertfordshire, or as wool manufacturers did in the west or as iron masters did in the midlands. English mining and industry were also booming, even at the beginning of the eighteenth century. The Revocation of the Edict of Nantes sent many French Huguenots to seek refuge in England, where they considerably encouraged such industries as glass and paper-making, hat-making and the manufacture of silk. A Prussian writer, Bonet, testified to the prosperity and comfort of English life in the eighteenth century, where meat was the staple diet and bread and vegetables were looked on only as a relish. The long internal peace which England had enjoyed had encouraged this prosperous growth, and much of the wealth made by trade or manufacture was invested in land. To some extent noble status continued to be based on the possession of land, but in England, as 'no subject of the king was debarred from holding land', even the land-holding aristocracy came gradually to include some men who had made fortunes first and then invested in land. Not only did the wealthy manufacturer buy an estate but some aristocrats farmed their estates with a keen commercial sense. It has been pointed out that in England alone were landed estates described in terms of their rental. Jethro Tull, a gentleman farmer in Berkshire, published his book on horse-hoeing in 1733, and between 1733 and 1738 Lord Townshend demonstrated that improved methods of cultivation could be profitable. From 1760 Robert Bakewell, of Leicestershire, showed what profits could be made by stock breeding and at the end of the century Coke of Norfolk, and even King George III himself, showed the practical interest of the aristocracy in profitable husbandry.

Before this time the upper middle class had flourished in other parts of Europe, particularly in small urban societies. The Italian cities, especially the republics of Venice and Genoa, had such a class, so had the cities of Switzerland. The wealthier German towns such as Hamburg, Frankfurt-am-Main and Leipzig had maintained a proud patriciate and this class

---

[1] D. Defoe, *The complete English Tradesman* (1726), pp. 376-7.

had been the backbone of the United Netherlands in the seventeenth century. The Dutch patricians were the merchants who had their grave portraits painted as administrators of poor relief or as leading officials of a guild, who gave its name to the Heerengracht in Amsterdam and who built along it the stately houses fitted with paintings by Ellenger, Delius or Moucheron, with elaborate stucco decorations in the manner of Marot, ornate and magnificent staircases, spacious rooms, gardens and summer houses. In the Swiss towns and in the free German cities a commercial patriciate had also emerged at an early date, so well educated that in the seventeenth century half the population of Zürich could read and write, and so cosmopolitan that Leipzig was spoken of as 'little Paris'. Basle was able to support an ancient university. Italian refugees formed a considerable proportion of the patriciate of Zürich and Basle, while Hamburg was not only a most important port, but a refuge for exiled Protestants and Jews, was the home of a flourishing opera and had the first German coffee house and the first weekly journal on the pattern of the *Spectator*. In Leipzig, where fairs were held three times every year, thousands of merchants congregated and the turn-over could be measured in hundreds of thousands of pounds; it was one of the first places where concerts were organised for the enjoyment of members of the middle class instead of being exclusive to a prince and his aristocratic guests. Even Frankfurt-am-Main, though it had lost some of its financial business to Amsterdam and much of its book trade to Leipzig, contained many patrician families, such as the Bethmanns and the Rothschilds, and became a home for Jews exiled from Augsburg, Ulm and Nürnberg. The patricians, such as those who made up the societies known as the Limpurger and Frauensteiner in Frankfurt, considered themselves the equals of the imperial nobility. This pride was based on 'inherited wealth', traditions of civil service, legal privileges and a high standard of living.[1] An important part of this urban patriciate of the German and Dutch towns had been the Jews. Amsterdam, Hamburg and Frankfurt-am-Main had particularly flourishing and influential Jewish colonies. In the Frankfurt ghetto lived about 300 Jews and a newcomer was only accepted if he had a capital of 1000 *gulden* and could pay fees over 70 *gulden*. Every three years a Jew had to pay 12½ *gulden* for a renewal of his permit to reside in the Frankfurt Judengasse. Merchants and professional men, as soon as they had made a fortune, were eager to gain admission to the ranks of the aristocracy. All the learned professions were not, however, as respectable socially in the mid-eighteenth century as they were to become in the England of two centuries later. Clergymen might sometimes be younger sons of the nobility and gentry, but they might also be clever men who had risen from poor homes, and the village parson or family chaplain might often be treated as something very like a domestic. Barristers had a good

[1] W. H. Bruford, *Germany in the Eighteenth Century* (1935), p. 195.

social standing, but attorneys were looked on by gentlemen as social inferiors. Doctors did not enjoy a very high status. Authors and men of letters generally, though their position in England struck Voltaire as much better than the position of his friends in France, did not rank high unless they started with the advantage of gentle birth or a private fortune, or alternatively attained great eminence. The situation was somewhat similar in France. Some of the most prosperous members of the French bourgeoisie were the tax collectors and financiers. The lawyers were, perhaps, less rich, but they enjoyed greater social prestige. Doctors were moderately wealthy, but not very numerous and did not enjoy great social esteem. Members of such professions as those of apothecary, bookseller and printer were moderately wealthy. Merchants and manufacturers such as those who sold wine or cloth were sometimes very wealthy, but in France they found it less easy than in England to end their days as country gentlemen. In the German States, as distinct from the free imperial cities, the gulf between the social classes was much greater than in France. Members of the middle class had different forms of address from those appropriate for the nobility, and though Von Loen in 1752 grumbled that the young women who sold herrings in Breslau were now called *gnädiges Fräulein*, as late as 1816 a German newspaper reported that post offices in a north German town had been instructed not to deliver letters addressed to middle-class girls if the title *Fräulein* had been used. The German bourgeois tended to live very simply in old-fashioned houses, dressing in long-wearing black and brown clothes, ruling their families and apprentices with a strict discipline and exacting from them the degree of deference which the merchants had to observe towards the aristocracy. In the eighteenth century most German towns were still suffering from the effects of the Thirty Years War and of the decline in importance of the spice trade which had reduced the medieval importance of such south German towns as Ulm, Nürnberg and Augsburg. Some towns such as Hamburg, Leipzig and Frankfurt-am-Main were relatively prosperous, but in most of the German States the towns were in the sleepy state that made Hume comment in 1748 that if a citizen of Nürnberg had been better lodged than the king of Scots then the king must have lived in very wretched style. If the German merchants were generally much less numerous and a less influential class than the merchants of England, the members of the learned professions were correspondingly lower in the social scale than their English counterparts. Even the trained lawyers who gained employment in the hundreds of independent territories or semi-independent counties or estates of imperial knights were treated with very little ceremony or even consideration by their masters, and many were so poorly paid that they can have earned little more than skilled artisans. Doctors of medicine could be sure of a comfortable income, but they remained few in number in the eighteenth century, and surgeons were still classed as skilled artisans. Schoolmasters were usually very badly paid and enjoyed no social prestige. Protestant pastors were often of humble origin and very poor. Yet in spite of all this the German middle class was numerous enough and energetic enough for the towns to be the cradle of the German literary revival of the late eighteenth century. In Hungary, on the other hand, the towns were not centres of wealth, and the learned professions were largely recruited from the nobility. Hungarian merchants such as the Turzos, Henchels or Hallers, as soon as they succeeded in making a fortune, at once set about acquiring noble status. Members of the legal profession in Hungary were all noble. Very few Hungarians became doctors and in 1747 Count Joseph Esterhazy had to be sent to Pozsony because there was no good doctor in Pest. To some extent the urban middle class in Pest was made up of orthodox Greeks who not only had no hope of ever gaining aristocratic status but could not even buy house property in the town where they traded or form part of the town council. In many towns the merchants were Germans who would have liked to join forces with the Habsburgs to reduce the privileges of the nobles and the Church, but the urban middle class, which by the end of the eighteenth century numbered in Hungary only about 300,000, lacked the strength to play any decisive part in the history of Hungary. In Poland the towns were in an even more pitiable state than were those in Hungary. Warsaw had a population of over 100,000 in 1772, but only four others had more than 20,000 inhabitants. The towns were financially ruined by the unfair competition of the local gentry who, though they might not engage in trade, paid no export duty and might import goods duty-free for their own consumption. Trade and industry, except for woollen manufacture in the towns of Greater Poland, were so wretched that craftsmen took to agriculture and left small-scale trade to the Jews, so that any indigenous middle class in Poland was very small and impoverished. In Russia the merchants made up about 3 per cent of the total population and, though many of them clung to their traditional costume and habits and heartily disliked the reforms and innovations introduced by Peter the Great, it is a fact that Peter did everything in his power to develop industry and trade and to raise the status of the merchants who before his time had been to some extent social outcasts.

In eastern Europe the upper middle class, in so far as it emerged at all during the eighteenth century, was swelled not so much by prosperous merchants or manufacturers as by the increasing number of civil servants. The best known of these bureaucrats were the servants of the king of Prussia, though by the time of Frederick II they made up only one in every 450 of the population. The appointment of these men was less influenced by patronage than was the case in England, Hanover or Saxony, nor could it be purchased as office could be in France. Promotion was given to the official with the longest experience. The pay was proverbially bad, and though the Prussian bureaucrats were efficient they had very little scope to use their own initiative. But nevertheless, during the eighteenth century the bureaucrats who made up the seventeen provincial boards did, in effect, govern Prussia, and even though decision had to be by majority vote, the president of each board had very considerable influence and his judgment sometimes carried even more weight than that of his fellow bureaucrats at the capital. Even at the end of the reign of the redoubtable and omnicompetent Frederick II the administrative officials of Prussia already exercised very considerable authority, so that Prussia could be recognised as in process of developing into a 'civil service state'. The emergence of a full-time, professional civil service in the Habsburg dominions was hastened by the military successes achieved by the bureaucratic State of Prussia after 1740. Inspired partly by the civil service of Prussia, Maria Theresa set up District Officers in her own provinces. By the time of Leopold II the Austrian provincial administrators were entitled to pension graded according to the length of their service. If a man had served for forty years, his pension was equal to his full salary. Widows were granted pensions and were allowed an additional allowance for each dependent child. In 1776 a candidate for office in the Austrian provincial bureau had to have studied cameral science at the university. The profession was becoming recognised as a career with its own special qualifications. Not till 1813 was the status of the Austrian civil servant regulated in relation to the army officer and the imperial noble not in the civil service, but by then the civil service in the Habsburg dominions, as in Prussia, had become an important part of society, providing much of the educated and cultured element that in western Europe was provided by the wealthy merchants and manufacturers. The growth of this upper middle class, whether in England and France or in Prussia and the Habsburg dominions, was a characteristic of the early eighteenth century, more significant for future political developments than the superficial appearance of the domination of society by court and aristocracy.

Another important feature of eighteenth-century society was the extent to which it was becoming influenced by countries other than France. Ever since the sixteenth-century Renaissance, Italy had exerted a great influence on European art and architecture and this was still true even in the eighteenth century (ch. IV). In the seventeenth century the influence of Italy had been challenged by that of France. The political prestige of France under Louis XIV and the social prestige of his court had popularised French fashions in dress and manners. The elegance and purity of the French language and the excellence of the literature of the age of Racine, Corneille, La Fontaine and Molière had ousted German as the language of polite society in most of the German courts. But just in the early eighteenth century, when the influence of French civilisation seemed at its height, at least two new influences were becoming powerful in European society. One was the scientific and literary influence of England (ch. IV), the other was German music. Ever since the sixteenth century Italians had been supreme in the world of music. In the eighteenth century Cremona continued to produce the best violins in Europe, and Italians were recognised as some of the best instrumentalists and singers. Italians were in charge of the music at many German courts. Italy was the country where opera had first been evolved as an art and other countries first learned to like opera in its Italian form, but in the eighteenth century music in other countries began to rival that of Italy. France, where at the end of the seventeenth century the foremost composer had been the Italian-born Lully, saw the foundation of the *opéra comique* in 1715, the emergence in 1723 of J.-P. Rameau, soon to become a composer of European reputation, and the establishment of '*concerts spirituels*' in 1725 which ensured musical performances on the twenty-four days of the year when for religious reasons operatic performances were impossible. But the musical development in the German States and in the Holy Roman Empire was much more spectacular. Almost every German prince maintained his private orchestra. The Emperor Charles VI spent 20,000 *gulden* a year on his music. Dr Burney on his travels in 1772 remarked on the high level of performance even among young children in the Austrian dominions. Many princes could themselves play an instrument in a court concert of chamber music. The highly developed musical tradition of the Lutheran Church combined with the patronage of many small courts to produce a very large output of compositions, some of which were of outstanding quality. In religious music such forms as chorale, cantata, passion music and oratorio flourished, especially when developed by the two great contemporaries Bach and Handel, both born in 1685 and beginning their careers in the first years of the eighteenth century. In secular music, with the growth and elaboration of the orchestra and the technical developments of such keyboard instruments as the organ, the harpsichord and the clavichord, it was possible for the fugue to attain a complete development at the hands of Bach comparable with the perfection of the oratorio by Handel. Opera, though it became smothered by over-elaborate conventions from which it had to be freed in the second half of the eighteenth century by Gluck, was universally popular. Vienna was one of the first German towns where opera had been established, and from 1716, when Caldara became the assistant of Fux, Viennese operatic performances began to acquire a European reputation which did not depend on the fact that sometimes members of the imperial family took part in the production. In Berlin, opera flourished under the patronage of the queen between 1703 and 1705, and was revived again under Frederick the Great, when it enjoyed a particularly brilliant period. In Dresden Italian opera seems to have been introduced about 1717, and in 1772 Burney thought Dresden rivalled Berlin as the most flourishing musical centre in the German states. In Munich opera had been introduced in 1689 and was warmly encouraged by the duke, who met the heavy expenses by a tax on playing cards. One characteristic common to the musical life of all the princely capitals was that the concerts and operatic performances were private entertainments given by a prince for his guests. A contemporary noted with surprise that in England the concerts in Vauxhall Gardens were open to anyone who cared to pay a fee. In the German cities the only music that could be heard easily by anyone except aristocrats with the *entrée* to court circles was what might be performed in church. In Leipzig, however, in 1743 a mixed body of sixteen nobles and citizens founded an institution called the 'Grand Concert'. This flourished and, though it was interrupted for a time by the Seven Years War, was resumed in 1763 and became the ancestor of the 'Gewandhaus Concerts'. Hamburg was another place where music was probably a less exclusively aristocratic preserve, and can even claim to have been the cradle of German opera, for there in 1678 the first opera in German was produced, and in the early eighteenth century, when Handel was for a time an accompanist and Mattheson sang, played, wrote and quarrelled there, it became one of the most famous of German musical centres. Erfurt, Weimar, Stuttgart, Salzburg all contributed musicians of note during the first half of the eighteenth century, but perhaps Mannheim deserves special mention as the home of a school which in the early eighteenth century faintly foreshadowed some of the characteristics which were to make the Vienna school internationally famous at the end of the century. Stamitz (until 1757) and Holzbauer (from 1753) worked at Mannheim to achieve hitherto unrealised differences of expression by giving more importance to the conductor, and developed orchestral playing to such a pitch that Burney in 1772 spoke of the electoral band of Mannheim as 'an army of generals'. By the time of Haydn, Mozart and Beethoven the contribution of German musicians to the civilization of Europe was of first-class importance.

Europe was also receiving many influences from countries beyond the seas. It was not only Chinese porcelain, silk and tea, Indian gauzes and muslins, colonial chocolate, rice, sugar and tobacco that were revolutionising European habits. The use which such writers as Montesquieu, Voltaire or Defoe made of a Persian or Chinaman or noble savage to point a criticism of European conditions was indication of how much the impact of other civilisations was affecting European ways of thought. The effect of colonial and Asiatic trade on the merchants and manufacturers of Europe was equally great and did much to prepare the way for the social changes which took place with the development of the Industrial Revolution.

CHAPTER IV

THE VISUAL ARTS AND IMAGINATIVE LITERATURE

IN matters of taste the period 1715–63 is only part of a longer period beginning in the late seventeenth century and ending with the triumph of the romantic spirit during the eighteenth century. During the whole age men prided themselves on their appreciation of the classical art of Augustan Rome, yet they had so much self-confidence in their own intellectual powers and had, specially in England and France, evolved such a characteristic form of society that while paying sincere lip service to the classic ideals they evolved examples of town architecture, of essay and of novel, which were entirely original and of great beauty.

In architecture the predominant influence throughout Europe during the first half of the eighteenth century was that of classical Rome as reinterpreted by the Italian architects of the Renaissance. But in France and England, and indeed in northern Europe generally, that influence was transmitted in a rather different form from the one it assumed in Italy and southern or Roman Catholic Europe. In Italy the style which persisted during the first half of the eighteenth century was the baroque which developed in Rome early in the seventeenth century. It had found expression in the work of such architects as Maderno (d. 1629), Bernini (d. 1680), Borromini (d. 1667) and Curtoni (d. 1669), and the finest examples are perhaps the Palazzo Barberini designed by Carlo Maderno and built by Borromini and Bernini, the church of St Carlo alle Quattro Fontane designed by Borromini who built the front at the very end of his life, the Scala Regia in the Vatican designed by Bernini in 1665 and the chapel of St Teresa in the church of Santa Maria della Vittoria designed by Bernini in 1646. This art went back to Michelangelo and through him to classical antiquity, but its character was very different from the gravity associated with the architecture of classical Rome. The works of the baroque architects had an astonishing vitality. There was wild extravagance, luxurious detail, and a lack of restraint that was positively voluptuous. Façades were full of movement; interiors, where ovals tended to supersede the more formal and static circle, gave an impression of swaying, dancing rhythm. This was the architecture which inspired such an astonishing expression of religious emotion as the Trasparente executed in Toledo cathedral by Tomé in 1732, the church of St John Nepomuck built in Munich between 1733 and 1750 to the design of the Asams, or the church of the Vierzehnheiligen built between 1743 and

1772 by Neumann. In these churches the effects were dramatic in the extreme. The lighting was sometimes, as in Toledo, positively theatrical. The effect of life-size figures such as that of a silver St George riding straight out of an altar piece, angels in high relief, the use of brilliant colours such as the white, gold and pink of the Vierzehnheiligen can be to intensify the emotions immensely. When these effects are combined with a freedom and boldness of design and a use of space that is almost magical, the effect can be intoxicating. At Klosterneuburg, St Florian and Melk, all on the Danube; at Dresden, where Poppelmann designed the Zwinger as part of the royal palace; at Warzburg and at Bruchsal, with its baroque staircase, the immense vitality and emotional force of this supposedly 'classical' style was demonstrated. It was sensational and even violent. It did not appeal to the taste of England or of France, and by the beginning of the eighteenth century Paris had become the vital centre of European art. French architects, though like Italians they sought inspiration in the work of classical Rome, expressed the result not in the voluptuous violence of baroque but in the restrained elegance of Perrault's Louvre front of 1665 and the almost contemporary country palace design by Le Vau at Vaux le Vicomte. The most characteristic example of this French version of the classical style was the royal palace of Versailles extended for Louis XIV by Hardouin-Mansart. The palace was a monument to the power, magnificence and dignity of the greatest king in late seventeenth-century Europe. Its proportions were huge: from north to south it extended over a quarter of a mile. The famous Hall of Mirrors was 240 ft. long and 43 ft. high. It was imposing, formal, overpowering and oppressive. The park façade produced an impression of uniformity that bordered on the monotonous. The great length was almost unrelieved. Even the skyline was a monotonous straight line, for the roof was masked by a balustrade. The huge palace was surrounded by gardens of astonishing size laid out by Le Notre and completed in 1688. These by their apparent infinity outshone even the long and stately vistas of such Italian gardens as those of the Villa Este or of Caprarola. French baroque might be less violent than the baroque of Italy or Austria, but it was a sumptuous style boastfully expressive of political triumphs.

After the death of Louis XIV French architectural style was modified to make it less formal and more elegant. The substyles of Louis Quinze, whether Watteau, Rocaille or Pompadour, were all versions of Italian baroque. These styles owed a good deal more than did the earlier French 'classical' architecture to Italian baroque work, particularly to that of Borromini, Juvari and Guarini. Beginning as interior decoration, this essentially curvilinear style aimed at vivacious elegance. In developing French taste in this direction the work of two Italians, Meissonier and Servandoni, is important. Meissonier's designs include the decoration of rooms, the design of silver, gold plate and porcelain. He made designs for elevations in which curvatures are prominent. He modelled his designs in such a way that assymetrical compositions appear perfectly balanced. Ground plans were modified to include curved and angular features as well as circular and even elliptical *salons*—a curved *salon* was found specially convenient as the setting for a conversational evening. Some of Watteau's decorative panels, especially those which border on fantasy, epitomise the charm of this style. But though there was plenty of lively experiment in internal design and decoration, the methods of the earlier 'classical' architects, especially the elevations they had favoured for public and private buildings, were by no means disregarded. The most striking examples of French design in the eighteenth century are those of Boffrand and Here de Corny; at Nancy, Here de Corny completed the lay-out of the new town including the Place du Gouvernement with the enclosing wrought-iron screens. The tendency of the French architects as the eighteenth century progressed was towards severity of elevation and greater freedom of embellishment. By 1760 this had produced a style which was not unlike the reticent classical style which had been practised by architects in England throughout the eighteenth century. So great was the influence of the classical spirit in architecture that it assisted the development of a style which, by the end of the century, had become universally European.

In eighteenth-century England architects sought their inspiration from classical Rome, but by way of the cold formality of Palladio (d. 1580) rather than from the baroque extravagances of the architects working in Rome in the eighteenth century itself. In the early seventeenth century Inigo Jones had already sought inspiration from Palladio when he designed the Queen's House at Greenwich in 1616 and the Whitehall Banqueting Hall between 1619 and 1622. He had described his work as 'solid, proportionable to the rules, masculine, unaffected'. For a time this severe style went out of favour. Sir Christopher Wren (d. 1723) borrowed freely from the Italian baroque of Borromini when designing the west towers of St Paul's Cathedral; Vanbrugh (d. 1726), in his immense palace of Blenheim and in the dome dominating the whole design of Castle Howard, had also shown a tendency towards Italian baroque, and so had Nicholas Hawksmoor (d. 1736), but after the death of Sir Christopher Wren English architecture passed once more under the influence of Palladian severity and simplicity. As early as 1716 Lord Burlington had published an edition of Palladio's writings. In 1730 he followed this up by issuing Palladio's restorations of ancient buildings. These illustrated books influenced many English architects. The Palladian manner became the style for great country houses and for public buildings. Churches built in this style include St Alfege Greenwich, St George Bloomsbury, Christ Church Spitalfields, St George-in-the-East, St Anne Limehouse, St Mary Woolnoth. All these were by Hawksmoor. James Gibbs designed St Martin-in-the-Fields and St Mary-le-Strand; John James, St George Hanover Square; and George Dance the elder the church at Shoreditch. New buildings at Oxford and Cambridge were also built in the Palladian manner. James Gibbs designed both the Radcliffe Camera at Oxford and the Cambridge Senate House. The characteristic feature of this English style was the elimination of superfluous detail, even sculpture was banished from the elevations. As the English architects became more familiar with the style, they were able to abandon the exact compositions and details of the sixteenth-century Italian masters. By 1760 the English 'classical' manner was well developed, as may be seen from the elevation of Stone Buildings, Lincoln's Inn, designed by Sir Robert Taylor in 1756, or the façades of Woburn and Wrotham Park, designed by Flitcroft and by Ware in 1748 and 1750. It is also apparent in the early works of Sir William Chambers (d. 1795) and in the later buildings designed by John Carr of York (d. 1807). This style led naturally to the neo-classicism associated with the name of Adam (d. 1792), but even when the influence of Rome and Greece seemed paramount in England as early as the 1740's there were signs of a revived interest in the Gothic manner.

An inclination towards romantic medievalism in architecture became apparent as early as 1730 when Browne Willis published his description of Lincoln Cathedral. The movement was fostered by the founding of the *Gentleman's Magazine* in 1731, for thereafter country gentlemen and antiquaries had a periodical which was prepared to publish facts connected with medieval history. Towards the middle of the eighteenth century many architects, including Isaac Ware and Batty Langley, were introducing Gothic features into their designs. Two volumes dealing with the royal and ecclesiastical antiquities of France collected by the French antiquary Bernard de Montfaucon were translated into English and published with illustrations in London in 1750. Judging from the scope of this fine work it is probable that it influenced English collectors. It remained for Horace Walpole to embattle the parapets of the small cottage at Strawberry Hill for public interest in Gothic architecture to increase.

An interest in the Gothic manner persisted in England side by side with an appreciation of 'classical' qualities for most of the second half of the eighteenth century, but in so far as English and French architecture influenced taste in northern Europe it was exclusively in the direction of the classical. The one-story palace of Sans Souci built at Potsdam in 1745 after designs by Dietrichs was clearly inspired by French rococo and contained interiors after the manner of Boffrand. In Austria Fischer von Erlach (d. 1738) combined French motifs with others from Italian baroque. In Germany Paul Decker (d. 1713) was known as the German Le Pautre and did much to popularise French designs by his great *Architectura Civilis*. It was largely due to Decker that after 1710 an independent style flourished in Germany. Of this version of baroque the most successful example is probably the Frauenkirche at Dresden, designed by George Baehr in 1726-34. The influence of French rococo spread to Poland, where the delicate Łazienki Palace in Warsaw was a particularly attractive example of this influence. In Russia the influence of France alternated with that of Italy in the vast palaces and public buildings that were erected from the time of Peter the Great onwards; under Peter the designs of Zemzoff (d. 1720) and Le Blond (d. 1714) showed the influence of France. Under the Empress Elizabeth I the Italian influence was predominant, and Tsarskoe Selo was designed in 1752 by the Italian architect Carlo Rastrelli (d. 1770) who in 1754 built the Winter Palace and became Professor of the Academy of Fine Arts. Under Catherine the Great buildings showed the influence of French taste and even of British, particularly as many of the designs were by the Scotsman Cameron (d. 1812).

One of the original achievements of north-western European and more particularly of English architecture in the eighteenth century was the arrangement of groups of houses into squares and terraces, crescents and streets which gave to cities such as London and Bath a peculiar charm. Inigo Jones, in the early seventeenth century, made designs for town houses as part of a coherent whole. Inspired by the design of the Place Royale or des Vosges in Paris (1604), Jones, with his design for Covent Garden 'piazza', set the fashion for regularly designed London squares. As London was developed towards the north and west in the eighteenth century the town was laid out in orderly squares and streets made up of the individual town house, this remained characteristic until the end of the Victorian era. It is worth noting that whereas in England the nobleman or man of property lived in such a terrace house, the French aristocrat lived much more spaciously in a detached hotel with its garden, its magnificent *cour d'honneur* screened from the street, its grand staircase and its suites of rooms. The difference between the English and French town house may perhaps be explained because whereas the English nobleman only came up to town for a short visit to attend parliament, to transact business or to give his wife and daughters a season at court, the French noble made Paris, if not Versailles itself, his permanent home. The difference in social habits is reflected in the magnificence of the English country houses erected or rebuilt in the eighteenth century while in France the amount of mansion building in that period is of very little importance.

Just as in the eighteenth century the new squares and terraces provided some of the most original and successful examples of western European architecture, so town life, especially the life of London and Paris, provided the atmosphere which encouraged what was most original and characteristic in contemporary literature. In 1657 the first coffee house in London had been prosecuted as a nuisance: by the end of the War of the Spanish

Succession there were over 3000. Berkeley, writing in 1732, gave an ironical picture of the role played in society by these coffee houses:

'I'll undertake, a lad of fourteen, bred in the modern way, shall make a better figure, and be more considered in any drawing room or assembly of polite people, than one of four and twenty, who hath lain by a long time at school or college. He shall say better things, and in better manner, and be more liked by good judges.' 'Where doth he pick up all this improvement?' 'Where our grave ancestors would never have looked for it, in a drawing room, a coffee house, a chocolate house, at the tavern or groom-porter's. In these and the like fashionable places of resort, it is the custom of polite persons to speak freely on all subjects, religious, moral and political.'[1]

Addison, according to Pope, spent five or six hours a day lounging at Buttons's, Pope went to Wills's as a boy to look at Dryden. In such a tavern met 'The Club' founded by Johnson and Reynolds in 1764.

By the beginning of the eighteenth century in England the society of which the coffee houses were symbolic provided a reading public which made possible original and unprecedented developments in the world of literature. In 1695 Press censorship in England had been abolished. The political controversies of the preceding fifteen years had developed among the better class of Londoners a habit of reading pamphlets. Between 1688 and 1694 as many as thirty new journals had made their appearance; with the final abolition of the censorship, newspapers sprang up. As early as 1690 Dunton had tried the experiment of publishing a paper which dealt with non-political topics, and which he called the *Athenian Mercury*. In 1704 Defoe followed suit with a weekly *Review* containing a literary section. When the *Review* had been running nine months a gentleman from Norwich wrote, 'I had read it to several gentlemen...in the chief coffee house here where we have it as oft as it comes out and is approved as the politest paper we have to entertain us with. I had some difficulty to prevail with the Master of the house to take it in but now he finds I advised him well there being no paper more desired.'[2] In 1708 Richard Steele, who had been editor of the official *London Gazette* since 1707, brought out the *Tatler* which devoted far less attention than did the *Review* to political news. After the eighty-third number politics disappeared from the *Tatler* completely. In 1711 Addison, who had already been collaborating with Steele on the *Tatler*, combined with his friend to produce the even more ambitious *Spectator*. This was to be a daily paper, yet the editor took a great risk when he expressly announced that it would not deal with politics. 'As, on the one side, my paper has not in it a single word of news, a reflection on politics, nor a stroke of party; so, on the other, there are no fashionable touches of infidelity, no obscene ideas, no satires upon

---

[1] G. Berkeley, *Alciphron or the Minute Philosopher* (1732). *The Works of George Berkely*, ed. A. A. Luce and T. E. Jessup (1950), vol. III, p. 48.
[2] Quoted by A. Beljame, *Men of Letters and the English Public in the Eighteenth Century* (1948), p. 259 n.

the priesthood, marriage and the like popular topics of ridicule; no private scandals, nor anything that may tend to the defamation of particular persons, families or societies.'[1] Addison's daring experiment might have collapsed; in fact it proved one of the most successful ventures in eighteenth-century letters, for he managed to appeal to a reading public which no previous author had discovered. Beyond the court, the party politicians, polemical clergy and argumentative fellows of colleges Addison discovered a great body of readers in many different sections of society and in all parts of England. Who they were may be guessed from the members who made up the famous Club which was supposed to provide the copy for the *Spectator*.[2] Sir Roger de Coverley was a Worcestershire gentleman who came sometimes to London, another member was a lawyer with more interest in the theatre than in law, Sir Andrew Freeport was much interested in trade and commerce, Captain Sentry was a retired army officer, the Church was represented by a clergyman 'of general learning, great sanctity of life and the most exact good breeding'. Will Honeycomb, who always kept himself up to date in matters of elegance and fashion, provided copy which might be expected to appeal specially to the ladies. Addison was at special pains to interest the ladies and declared that he would try to increase the number of those multitudes of a more elevated life and conversation for whom the great scene of business was not simply the toilet and whose principal employment was not the right adjusting of their hair.

The particular merit of this new journalism was its natural treatment of contemporary life. Witty, penetrating observation of contemporary society and of familiar characters had been the secret of the great literature which had been produced in France forty years earlier. La Rochefoucauld's *Maximes* produced first in 1665, the letters of Mme de Sévigné, La Fontaine's *Fables*, the comedies written by Molière from 1689, even the great tragedies written by Racine between 1667 and 1677, though treating themes from classical or biblical history, presented characters whose ideas and language were those of the Louvre, Saint Germain or Versailles. Yet neither in France nor in England were writers fully aware of the outstanding merit of their descriptions of contemporary life. Just as the architects sought to imitate the achievements of classical Rome so men of letters, as they had done in the sixteenth century, admired the masterpieces of Homer, Virgil and the other writers of Greece and Rome. In 1674 Boileau had given expression to this veneration of antiquity in his *Art poétique* in which he set up Homer, Virgil and Horace as the great masters of literary style and declared that they had given perfect expression to eternal truths which must be models for all subsequent ages.

[1] *Spectator*, no. 262. For a discussion of the emergence of the newspapers and literary periodicals see A. Beljame, *Men of Letters...in the Eighteenth Century* (1948).
[2] These descriptions of the members of the Club are given in *Spectator*, no. 2.

Admittedly this view of literature had been sharply challenged as early as 1687 when Perrault in his *Poème sur le siècle de Louis le Grand* had claimed that the seventeenth century could show works of art worthy of the Age of Pericles or of Augustus. The battle between the ancients and moderns had gone on and such men as Fontenelle and Fénelon had championed the claims of the moderns, but in fact classical literature formed the basis of every gentleman's education whether he studied at Eton or at the College of Louis le Grand. The dictionary produced by the French Academy in 1694 favoured traditional, classical language, poets such as J.-B. Rousseau wrote odes according to the classical rules laid down by Boileau, and by 1725 Pope had made a considerable fortune by translating the *Iliad* and the *Odyssey*. Yet even so it is misleading to suppose that the greatness of the early eighteenth-century literature consisted in its similarity to the literature of ancient Greece. Pope's Agamemnon wears a full-bottomed wig and expresses the opinions of a man bred up with the ideas on reason and nature that might have been heard in Wills's coffee house or a Twickenham garden.

Gentlemen might subscribe to a new translation of Homer, but other kinds of poetry were more eagerly read. Both in England and France the character of the poetry produced in the first half of the eighteenth century was largely determined by the kind of society in which that poetry was to be read and discussed. In England the most usual gathering where new work was heard was the coffee house or club and such an atmosphere was not congenial to lyric poetry. In France the most usual gathering was the *salon* which again was unfavourable to the lyric. Both in England and France the poetry most generally esteemed was satire. Pope's *Rape of the Lock* and his *Dunciad* delighted a society which valued wit and verbal dexterity. In France, Voltaire's short poetical squibs were equally appreciated.

The taste for satire explained the popularity of many prose works both in England and France which ridiculed and exposed the weaknesses of contemporary society. Montesquieu's *Lettres Persanes* contained much serious criticism of contemporary France as did Swift's *Gulliver's Travels* which appeared in 1726. One curious feature of the literature of the early eighteenth century was that much of it was set in some remote country. Voltaire set *Zaire* in a Moslem background, *Alzire* was set in Peru. In 1704 Galland had translated the *Thousand and One Nights*. Turks, Chinamen, Persians, even Ghengis Khan himself, appeared in the shops of the French booksellers. In England Defore scored a great triumph with his story of Robinson Crusoe, published in 1729. It has been suggested that the popularity of these books supposedly about the remoter parts of the world was to be explained by the interest in overseas expansion which was apparent particularly in London and the other English ports.

Certainly there was a lively interest in the contemporary world and in human nature as it was known in St James's or the Rue St Honoré. There might be a great deal of emphasis on the observance of the conventions. In reply to an inquirer who asked what qualities a man required in order to be a good poet the *Spectator* replied that he must be very well bred, and the maxims of Lord Chesterfield were widely accepted; but the conventions to be observed were essentially those of Versailles or St James's, not those of Periclean Athens or of Augustan Rome. The attitude of mind of the reading public was that implicit in Pope's *Essay on Man* or in Voltaire's *Philosophical Dictionary*. Great store might be set on wit and on a knowledge of the world, but even more fundamental was the belief in man's own reason. The literature of the age was redolent of self-confidence. Even more than the classics nature was considered to be the supreme standard. Pope thought the business of the poet was to reveal nature but 'nature methodised', by which he and his contemporaries meant that it was the business of the author to present as elegantly and wittily as possible the kind of life which was normal in the eighteenth century.

But if this was to be done, some new literary genre would have to be developed. The essay had shown itself a most flexible and delightful instrument, but after Addison it lost much of its freshness. Poetry, though it might be used by Pope for a neat and pointed satire, was too artificial. The stage which might in another age have served as the vehicle for contemporary satire was in England almost entirely moribund. After the Restoration English comedy, though sometimes most witty, was often extremely lewd. Indeed, Ravenscroft declared 'A Bawdy Play was never counted Dull'[1] and another suggested that one of the staple jests had been 'to hear young Girls talk Bawdy'.[2] Indeed, the plays had become so notoriously improper that in 1698 Jeremy Collier, a non-juror divine, published *A Short View of the Immorality and Profaneness of the English Stage*. This very well-documented and intensely sincere denunciation had great effect, more particularly because it was made by an extreme Anglican Tory whose opinions could not be discounted as those of a Whig or a Puritan. The dramatists replied with some spirit, but Collier routed them and for ten years he poured out pamphlets renewing his criticisms until by the beginning of the eighteenth century the dramatists voluntarily began to reform their works. As Vanbrugh put it in the Prologue to *The False Friend*:

To gain Your Favour, we your rules obey
And Treat you with a moral piece to-day:
So moral, we're afraid 't will damn the play.[3]

Vanbrugh's fear was to some extent justified. The stage became more decent, but lost much of its vitality and charm. Until the end of the century,

---

[1] E. Ravenscroft, *Prologue to Dame Dobson* (1684).

[2] *A Lenten Prologue refused by the Players* (1682), attributed to T. Shadwell. Young girls had often been expected to recite conspicuously immoral epilogues.

[3] J. Vanbrugh, *The False Friend* (1702).

when Sheridan emerged, English comedy languished. Tragedy, in spite of the efforts of Addison, was lifeless, rigid, formal and bound by the chains forged by Aristotle and Boileau. In France the situation was much the same. There drama, like serious poetry, was largely out of favour in a society which believed with Fénelon that art must be at once truthful and useful. Those who were seriously interested in the philosophical and mathematical discoveries that had culminated with Newton dismissed poetry as childish nonsense and found fault with tragedy because it 'proved' nothing.

Some part of Paris society preferred to read prose works such as Voltaire's histories of Charles XII, Louis XIV or Louis XV, or such serious books as Voltaire's *Lettres philosophiques* or Montesquieu's *De l'esprit des lois,* but there were large sections of the greatly increased reading public, especially in England, which did not subscribe to Fénelon's utilitarian conception of literature. These people wanted to be amused and yet edified by something more solid than the essays of the *Spectator* or of the *Gentleman's Magazine.* The needs of this large section of the reading public were met in 1741 when Samuel Richardson, a homely middle-class London printer, already well past middle age, produced *Pamela.* Setting out to provide a moral lesson, he produced a work of art and took the public in England and France by storm. In 1747–8 Richardson produced *Clarissa,* a masterpiece of characterisation. In 1753–4 he wrote *Sir Charles Grandeson.* The novel as a literary form was in process of development. Henry Fielding followed where Richardson had shown the way. As early as 1743 he had produced three volumes of miscellanies. In 1749 appeared his *History of Tom Jones, a Foundling* which is now recognised as the first English novel to show artistic unity. Smollet's *Roderick Random* came out in 1748. This was a novel of adventure rather on the lines made familiar by Defoe, but Smollet gave the form a new unity and vitality. In 1751 appeared his *Peregrine Pickle.* All Smollet's novels are faithful accounts of low life. His last novel, *Humphrey Clinker,* showed him to be an accomplished humorist. The importance of the English novel of the mid-eighteenth century cannot be overestimated. Among other things it showed an increasing interest in the life of the lower classes such as induced Hogarth to take many of his subjects from the London pavements, and had already led John Gay to write the libretto of his *Beggar's Opera* round such characters as highwaymen, fences, turnkeys and women of the town. The time had arrived when familiar scenes in various walks of life could be described and examined, and the novel provided the exact vehicle for this operation.

The novel developed also in France, and this tendency was much encouraged by the success of the English novelists, this being one of the periods in history when French writers followed a lead from England and when English science and political institutions were already much admired in France. Some rather primitive novels had, however, already appeared in France before the successes of Richardson, Fielding and Smollet. In 1698 Fénelon had published his philosophical novel *Télémaque*. Le Sage, who had as early as 1709 written a play, *Turcaret*, dealing with a self-made man, in 1735 produced a picaresque novel of adventure, *Gil Blas*, which, though the action was supposed to take place in Spain, fairly obviously portrayed conditions in Paris. Between 1736 and 1741 Marivaux, who had begun his literary career with a parody of Homer, turned to a naturalistic and contemporary subject and produced his *Vie de Marianne* which was chiefly remarkable for its analysis of character. In 1731 Prévost wrote his *Manon Lescaut* which had a good deal in common with Richardson's *Clarissa* and was from the first an outstanding success which influenced the development of the novel in Germany, Denmark and Holland. Prévost also translated *Clarissa* and helped to extend the influence of the English novel in France. *Clarissa* is supposed to have inspired J.-J. Rousseau when in 1756 he wrote *Julie ou la nouvelle Héloïse*. Rousseau did not visit England till 1762, but before that date he had clearly recognised the genius of such English writers as Defoe and Richardson. After the success of Le Sage, Prévost, Marivaux and Rousseau the sequence of imaginative novels was increased by many writers who imitated these recognized masters.

When the novels written by Richardson, Prévost and Rousseau are compared with the papers of the *Spectator* or the satirical poems of Pope, or even the tales of Voltaire, they reveal a great increase in sensibility. Even when Montesquieu was writing the *Lettres Persannes* in 1721 to demonstrate that it was possible to combine serious observations with wit, there were hints of an increasing readiness to recognise the importance of the emotions. 'Sensibility' soon became as important in a gentleman as reason. The same fine ladies and wits who prided themselves on their philosophic spirit were ready to faint with emotion at the touching spectacles presented to them in the novels. In England there were hints of this increased emphasis on the emotions well before the middle of the century. In 1726, two years before the *Dunciad*, Thomson published his poem on *Winter*. In this there was a great deal of moralizing, but Thomson believed that poetry should be animated not only by moral reflections but by sublime ones as well, and his conception of the sublime and its relation to terror was closely akin to the ideas expressed by Burke in his *Inquiry* in 1756. Thomson came from the Border Country which was destined to be a source of romantic poetry. From these regions came Allan Ramsay, James Hogg and Sir Walter Scott. A sentimental tenderness for, and veneration of, nature was part of the north-country ballad tradition which had begun with Dunbar, and this streak was clearly evident even in the early works of Thomson. Four years after the publication of *Winter*, Thomson published the collected *Seasons* and very shortly after this, in 1727, Shenstone published the first version of a pastoral poem of village life called *The Schoolmistress*. In this Shenstone was consciously trying to imitate Spenser, especially the 'peculiar tenderness of sentiment' which he found characteristic of all Spenser's work. Professor Butt has pointed out the similarity in tone between Shenstone's treatment of this village dame school and that of George Morland's paintings of country scenes almost forty years later.[1] When Shenstone and Thomson were writing, Wesley was just embarking, in 1738, on his career as a religious reformer. In 1742 Young's *Night Thoughts* continued to move away from the satirical and reasonable towards the 'sublime' and 'affecting', even if his poem was sometimes sentidious and even dull. In 1746 Warton produced a volume of odes which he prefaced with the opinion that 'the fashion of moralizing in verse had been carried too far', and soundly declared that the chief faculties of the poet were 'invention' and 'imagination'; Collins, who published a volume of odes in 1747, was inspired by a similar revolt against 'didactic poetry' and the 'essays on moral subjects' which had hitherto satisfied the public. All these works gave clear signs of a growing interest in the emotions such as had characterised the works of the novelists. This tendency was further strengthened by the publication by Percy in 1756 of the *Relique of Ancient English Poetry*. Percy, writing to Warton just before the publication of this collection, had expressed the view that the public 'requires some new species [of poetry] to quicken its pall'd appetite'. The ballads so carefully collected by Percy 'absolutely redeemed', as Wordsworth thought, English poetry just as the novels which culminated in the *Nouvelle Héloïse* seemed to Hazlitt the great essence of romantic sentiment. It is clear that the romantic movement in literature was making itself felt both in England and France as early as the 1730's and 1740's of the eighteenth century.

In painting and sculpture the same kind of development was apparent as in the other arts; admiration of the classical and gradual creation of something completely contemporary and natural which in turn developed into something romantic. As in the other arts there was an inheritance of Greek and Roman tradition. Many painters of the early eighteenth century remembered the 'academic' manner of Nicolas Poussin (1594–1665) and the dreamlike, sublime landscapes of Claude Lorraine (1600–82). They still admired the 'classical beauty' which had been the aim of Carracci (1560–1609) and they were prepared to paint mythological scenes such as had inspired Rubens (1577–1640), but with an academic, conventional classicism almost reminiscent of Reni (1575–1642).

In painting, one development from this rather formal classicism was in the direction of baroque violence and emotion. In Italy Gaulli (1639–1709) painted ceilings alive with saints and angels, giving the spectator the idea that he was looking straight into the vault of heaven. Such ceilings were familiar in many palaces and noble houses all over Europe. Not

[1] J. Butt, *The Augustan Age* (1950), p. 101.

77

only were ceilings decorated with mythological groups. Great pictures were painted to cover the huge expanses of wall and made a sumptuous background for audiences, halls and banquets. As late as 1757 the Venetian Tiepolo (1696–1770) was painting such a decorative fresco as Cleopatra's Banquet.

The influence of Italy on painters was still enormous in the first half of the eighteenth century, but after the death of Louis XIV in 1715 developments took place in France which produced some works of great charm. The emergence of this new style can be dated from the death of Le Brun (1619–90) when a change came over patrons and artists alike. Mythological allegories were superseded by less conventional and much more dainty fantasies in which brilliantly dressed figures in more or less contemporary costume moved within softly tinted scenes set for the most part in landscapes that were based on realities of French scenery. Watteau (1684–1721) was the leader of the new manner. He was a fantasist. When he dealt with mythological scenes, it was in the lightest possible manner. In decorative panels he sometimes painted monkeys in human dress. But for all his idealisation of country life and the unreality of his *fêtes galantes*, he was a very close student of nature. His shepherds and shepherdesses might wear satin and do nothing but dance minuets, but his satins are real and his figures give an impression of life that is very different from the conventionality which had characterised the work of Le Brun. Lancret (1690–1743) and Pater (1695–1736) followed Watteau's lead, and, though the work of Coypel, Antoine, Noel and Nicholas shows that Le Brun's influence was still alive, the outstanding feature of the painting of the period is one of delicacy, gaiety and even of frivolity. Boucher (1702–70) managed to catch the popular taste exactly. His mythological pictures lacked seriousness and his country scenes were simply a delightful background for figures in fancy dress. His style was voluptuous and a triumph of brilliant colouring. French portraiture, in the Age of Louis XV, reflected the same frivolity and magnificent elegance. Jean Raoul de Largillière (d. 1746) indulged a taste for dressing his sitters in theatrical costumes, Nattier (d. 1766) painted Henriette of France as Flora, thereby inspiring Tocque (d. 1772) and Van Loo (d. 1771). Quentin de la Tour (d. 1778) revived the taste in France for chalk drawings of a delightful grace and delicacy. After a time there was a slight reaction against the *scènes galantes* in favour of pictures depicting morality and virtue, the best of these were painted by Greuze (1725–1805), but his pictures were still elegant and somewhat idealised as were those of Fragonard (1732–1806), who linked the period of rococo elegance with the later period of voluptuous sensibility.

French sculpture retained more respect for academic traditions than did painting or other arts of decoration. Boucharden's celebrated fountain in the Rue Grevelle made in 1739 is an example of the austere taste then prevailing in sculpture. The bronze statue of Peter the Great which Falconet (d. 1766) made for St Petersburg also shows a return to the classical. Though in his other busts Falconet tried to make real portraits, the tendency in sculpture seemed in the direction of a return to classical simplicity.

In England the tradition in painting had been rather less formal and classical than had been the case in France or even in Italy. Vandyke (1599–1641), Sir Peter Lely (d. 1680) and Sir Godfrey Kneller (d. 1723) had produced portraits showing the influence of the Netherlands school, which had developed a virtuosity in the rendering of different materials. Vandyke had been a pupil of Rubens and had learnt from him how to paint texture whether of silk, velvet, lace or human flesh, and the taste for technically accomplished, elegant portraits persisted in England. Cultivated Englishmen admired the masterpieces of Italy, Spain and France. Claude's paintings induced many English gentlemen to remodel their parks into landscape gardens. Sir Joshua Reynolds (1732–92) had been to Italy and believed that an artist should try to emulate the draughtsmanship and colouring of the great painters of the Italian Renaissance. Yet in spite of his theories Reynolds painted pictures of an amazing freshness and naturalness. Even more natural and unacademic was the work of Gainsborough (1717–88), whose interest in painting direct from nature and whose reluctance to idealise or conventionalise what he saw are reminiscent of the early seventeenth-century Caravaggio, of the seventeenth-century Dutchmen such as Vermeer or Franz Hals, or perhaps of the seventeenth-century Velasquez.

The tendency to paint in a realistic manner and honestly to record scenes from real life was most clearly evident in the works of three men, the English Hogarth (1697–1764), the French Chardin (1699–1779) and the Dutch Cornelis Troost (1697–1750). Hogarth broke with the tradition of painting elegant, aristocratic portraits and produced pictures which told a story and usually conveyed a moral. These pictures, designed to teach the results of sin, appealed to the English public which tended to require art to have some use. Engravings of his pictures were especially popular but Hogarth was more than a moralist. He painted the street scenes of London, he painted all sorts of people from fine ladies callously observing lunatics in Bedlam to wretched drabs lying dead drunk in Gin Lane. The contrast between his portraits of the Shrimp Girl or of Mr Justice Welch and the usual elegant, academic work of the school of Poussin or of Tiepolo could not have been more complete. Chardin, like Hogarth, occupied himself with commonplace situations and painted ordinary people with a realism that owed something to Jan Steen and perhaps more to Vermeer. Cornelis Troost combined something of the fantasy of Watteau with the acute observation and unfaltering realism of Hogarth. Some of his pictures, like those of Hogarth, make a sequence, as for instance those which record the successive stages in a convivial evening which begins with a party of sedate Dutchmen in one of the patrician houses along the Kaesergracht or Heerengracht in Amsterdam, smoking their clay pipes by candlelight while a servant uncorks the bottles. The title of this picture in *Nemo loquebatur*, that of the last in the series is *Ibant qui poterant, qui non potuere cadebant*. The pictures bear comparison with Hogarth's *Mariage à la Mode*. His illustrations of scenes from Dutch comedies are admirable records of Dutch manners and customs, of costumes and furniture and character.

Yet the few men who theorised about art in the first half of the eighteenth century failed to appreciate what was original in their own time. The problem which concerned them, as it concerned the architects and artists of the early eighteenth century, was not so much to explore the philosophical nature of beauty as to improve and refine taste. Their success is manifested in the court circle as it is in the façades of the buildings of cities and provincial towns. It is seen in the ballrooms and the salons of the nobility as it is in the little apartments of the upper and middle bourgeoisie. Every architect, every painter, every sculptor endeavoured to give expression to the principles of beauty which conformed to accepted and prevalent fashion. If the national tendencies prescribed certain forms, if custom demanded the perpetuation of these forms, then there was no alternative for the executants but to come into line. The main question which had to be answered by artists who enjoyed the confidence of the ruling classes was that of taste. In 1713 Addison produced eleven essays in the *Spectator* on 'Pleasures of the Imagination'. The fourth of these compared the works of Nature with those of Art. Number five dealt with architecture and number six with statuary, painting and music. The English painter Richardson attempted an analysis of painting and tried to explain theories of invention and composition. His views were much esteemed by Sir Joshua Reynolds. Hogarth too in 1753 wrote an essay, 'The analysis of Beauty', but by comparison with the work of Fresnoy or Roger de Piles on painting it is very slight. An example of the eighteenth-century attitude to aesthetics is d'Alembert's lecture to the Academy in 1757, when his subject was 'Reflections on the use and abuse of philosophy in matters that are properly related to Taste'. In the course of his lecture he said: 'Taste, though far from being generally possessed, yet is by no means an arbitrary thing.' He added to this a definition of Taste as 'the faculty of distinguishing in the works of art, the various qualities which are adopted to excite pleasure or disgust in minds that are susceptible of delicate sentiments and perceptions'. Voltaire, Montesquieu, and the Scotsman, Alexander Gerard, were others who wrote on taste, but they said little of value.

In general there was a dearth of philosophical books on the subject of the Arts; instead, the tendency was to produce books of illustrations with a short explanatory text, but these illustrated compilations dealing with architecture, decoration and painting were of great importance in forming taste. In 1710 appeared *Gentlemen's Recreations*, an illustrated volume divided into three parts which became a work of reference for the landed gentry. The bias was generally towards classical antiquity, but there was some information about contemporary work. The designs of Fischer von Erlach for palaces in Vienna and of the German Paul Decker had a considerable influence on English taste. In 1710 Daniel Marot published a series of decorative designs forming a volume of 260 plates. The designs of Decker had a certain similarity to those of Marot. Both were essentially French and derived from the school of Versailles. They had a considerable influence on the followers of Lord Burlington, particularly William Kent, Henry Flitcroft and Isaac Ware. In particular Decker's book *Architectura Civilis* greatly influenced the taste of Sir Robert Walpole when he was building Houghton Hall, Norfolk.

From 1700 the demand for illustrated books on architecture steadily increased. In England these began with translation from the French and the publication of pocket guide books. John James of Greenwich, for example, translated a book on gardening with plates by Van der Gucht. The finest architectural volume of the time, however, was produced in 1728 by James Gibbs. The illustrations shown in this book determined the character of many buildings in the American colonies. *Britannia Illustrata*, published by J. Kip in 1701, showed the grandeur of English country palaces. Kip also published *Nouveau Théâtre de la Grande Bretagne* in 1724. These plates gave views of cities, royal palaces, seaports and cathedrals, with views of seats in England and Scotland. For the first time architects in France were made aware of a grand style of architecture in England. Meanwhile the issue of small guides for the use of builders and craftsmen continued unabated. Colin Campbell's *Vitruvius Britannicus* gave illustrations of public and private buildings, a series continued by John Wolfe and James Gandon. The most prolific architect author was Isaac Ware, whose chief work, *The Complete Body of Architecture*, appeared in folio form in 1755. A far more important publication, *A Treatise on...Civil Architecture* by Sir William Chambers, appeared in 1759. Prior to this Chambers had published designs of Chinese buildings, furniture, dresses, etc. in 1751. There is little to prove that Chambers intended his dissertation on Chinese art to be taken seriously. Regarding the treatise on civic architecture it is clear that Chambers attempted to bring the basic principles of classic architecture into line with post-Renaissance thought. His aims are aptly epitomised in the perfect composition and detail which distinguishes Somerset House, London. From 1710 to 1760 books on architecture published in England dealt with the various moods of the Palladian manner, which had come to be regarded as part of English taste. Not only was this period one of ideals based on tradition, but it was seen that the classic style of antiquity was not fully understood. This led to very careful investigation of the ruins of Rome and later of Athens by architects.

Parallel to the English illustrated books dealing with the decorative arts was the more sustained output in France. Here the objective was to increase the scope of designers while modifying the established style. Illustrations now formed the chief part of the authoritative books dealing with architecture, decoration and the crafts. There is little in the story of the arts that is so fascinating or so encouraging as the number of books published in Paris giving actual compositions and details of buildings. Not only are these books fine in themselves, but the engravings are of the highest quality. In the series of illustrations published by Jombert, architecture is presented in such a way that architects and craftsmen in other countries found it easy to follow the designs. The planning of houses and apartments as well as the lighter forms of decoration which can be attributed to social changes, form part of all the important architectural books published in France between the years 1720 and 1760. One leading exponent of post-Renaissance architecture of this epoch was Jacques-François Blondel (1705–79), who had in early life undertaken engraving, following in the steps of his father, Jean-François Blondel. He continued a volume entitled *Architecture Française* begun by Jean Marot, until eight volumes were completed. Another important publication, the edition of d'Aviler's *Cours*, published in 1738, contains many plates engraved by Blondel. Blondel's greatest work and the one which had the most lasting influence on post-Renaissance buildings was published in Paris between the years 1771 and 1777. Blondel's account is limited to describing each of the buildings illustrated.

The publication of fantastic Italian compositions by Giuseppe Bibiena[1] and Giovanni Battista Piranesi coincided with the demand for architectural composition. These two artists were endowed with creative skill which they demonstrated in a series of engravings and etchings. Previously in the seventeenth century the landscape painters Claude Gelle and Nicolas Poussin had popularised scenes in which they depicted the ruins of classical temples. But it was the influence of Claude's landscape paintings that determined the character of English pictures of scenery. At a later date Ghilsolfi and Pannini, inspired by Claude's compositions, continued this form of pictorial art. This in turn led Italian draughtsmen to show the pictorial aspect of classical designs, combined with the elements of seventeenth-century Baroque, which produced the vigorous system followed during the post-Renaissance period. In the compositions of Bibiena and Juvara are the inherent forms which in turn gave rise to new motifs. The expansion of the phase of post-Renaissance architecture was both rapid and striking. Piranesi's remarkable skill as a composer of

[1] Folio volume of designs entitled *Architetture e Prospettive* (Vienna, 1740).

classical elements can be attributed to the spirit which inspired the invention of fantasies. Piranesi's more important plates were published between the years 1748 and 1765. These include *Opere Varie di Architectura*, and *Le Antichità Romane*. The influence of Piranesi's etchings was widespread among architects, decorators and furniture designers. This influence can be seen in the work of Sir William Chambers, Robert Adam, Robert Mylne and many others. It is found in the design of contemporary marble fireplaces and in some of the furniture designed and made by the Chippendales. The versatility of this Italian draughtsman, his power of selection no less than his extraordinary skill as an assembler of motifs, was only equalled by the rapidity with which he met the demand for his work. It was from this source that many European architects gained their ideas of classical elements which they could adapt to contemporary designs.

The brilliant and elegant French painting of the Age of Louis XV owed a great deal of its popularity to the engravers such as Gravelot, Eisen, and Moreau le Jeune, who reproduced the works of famous artists. Eisen in particular became famous for his ornamental designs, particularly for his treatment of rococo frames and garlands of laurel. In many directions a style of decoration was developed which proved very well suited to furniture and silver work as well as to larger schemes such as the embellishment of whole buildings. Various kinds of craftsmen, iron workers and carvers adopted the new style which evolved at an opportune moment. Its more intimate moods showed charming qualities, typically French. It became widely popular in almost every part of Europe apart from England and Italy, and it appealed to the Teuton and Slav by its playful charm no less than by its delicacy.

Illustrations at long last had made the complexities of classical design universally intelligible in every country north of the Alps. What had been accomplished for architecture, however, could not be made to apply with equal force to painting and sculpture. It was seen that visits to galleries were more important than were descriptions or even illustrations in books. Travel was still essential not only for patrons but for artists, and in the eighteenth century it was still natural, as a preliminary to further investigation, to visit Rome. All over Europe in the palaces of kings or the great houses of the nobility the influence of Italy and of classical antiquity was apparent.

In England the royal palaces of St James's, Hampton Court and Kensington, formed the chief art centres where works by Italian artists were numerous. In France the same was true of the palace of Versailles; in Spain of La Granja; in Holland of Het Loo; in Germany of Charlottenberg and Potsdam; in Austria of Nymphenburg and Schönbrunn. In Sweden, the palaces of Stockholm and Drottningholm; in Poland, Łazienki; in Russia, Peterhof, Tsarskoe Selo and Pavlovsk all proclaimed the influence of Italian baroque. On Italian soil, the magnificent palace of

Caserta, built as late as between 1752 and 1774, showed the same characteristics. But the age which saw the building of great houses in versions of the Italian baroque also saw the erection of town squares and terraces in a manner essentially original. The squares and crescents, the realistic paintings of Hogarth, Chardin and Troost, the journalism of the *Spectator* and the novels of Richardson and Prévost were works of original genius peculiar to the eighteenth century and gave more than a hint of the growing importance of an urban middle class.

CHAPTER V

THE ENLIGHTENMENT

THE eighteenth century was to be the age of the Enlightenment, but already before the seventeenth century had closed the prototypes of all the weapons in its armoury had been created and tested. Of the new thought of the seventeenth century Paul Hazard has written, 'Total, imperious and profound, it prepared in its turn, even before the seventeenth century was completed, almost the whole of the eighteenth century.'[1] The great battle of ideas took place before 1715, and even before 1700.

Religion was the main citadel of orthodox thought, and the grand strategy of the attack on it had already been laid down by the English deists before 1715. A handful of extremists, such as Anthony Collins, moved beyond deism and repudiated religion altogether; but the latitudinarian divines of the Church of England had themselves gone so far towards the acceptance of rational religion that the deistic controversy died down in England for lack of opposition. Meanwhile the deistic and free-thinking writings of England were being introduced into France, where they were to acquire a new lease of life. Though French writers in the first half of the century handled the subject of religion with caution, their treatment concealed a more deep-seated hostility than existed across the Channel. When deism emerged into the open in France with the writings of Voltaire and the *Encyclopédistes*, it had lost its theological associations and become a loose formula, merely retained as a sanction for politics and morals, and a defence against the charge of atheism. It provided a means of reconciling what was agreed to be the social need for religion with the claims of reason. Triumphant in England and France, deism spread to the educated classes of other countries of Europe, and was in due course to reach a wide American public with Benjamin Franklin. But for all its diffusion, the conquest was a barren one; deism in the eighteenth century had lost its vitality and significance. It became a stagnant pool in England. In Europe, outside France, it petered away into a trickle in the marshes of orthodoxy; and in France it proved to be a mere tributary poured into the main stream of French scepticism. It muddied but did not divert the current of infidelity which had already in the seventeenth century dug a deeper if narrower channel.

Contemporaries of ours lived under Louis XIV, said Diderot, and the influence of these early fathers of scepticism was summed up in the work of Bayle. Among his followers in the eighteenth century first, naturally,

[1] P. Hazard, *La Crise de la conscience européenne* (1935).

85

came those whom Mornet signalises as '*les maîtres cachés*',[1] of whose writings, circulated in manuscript copies, as many as one hundred and two different treatises have been discovered. The most notorious among them, the *Testament* of the curé Meslier, turned the deistic argument from design against the Author of Nature himself by showing the evils that he had permitted in this world. Acknowledged and published works did not go much beyond the ingenuous observations of Montesquieu's Persian visitors to France, or the surprise innocently expressed in Boulainvillier's *Vie de Mahomet*, published posthumously in 1730, that a false religion should have produced such remarkable results.

The middle of the century was marked by the end of the period of preparation. Such works as Diderot's *Pensées philosophiques* and *Lettre sur les aveugles*, Toussaint's *Les Mœurs*, La Mettrie's *L'homme machine*, Montesquieu's *De l'esprit des lois* and Buffon's *Histoire naturelle* presented barely veiled or open challenges to orthodox thought, and in 1751 appeared the first volume of the *Encyclopédie*, in which lip-service was paid to orthodoxy in articles dealing directly with religious subjects, while infidel ideas were hidden by Diderot under such innocuous titles as *Agnus scythius* or *Aius Locutius*. The Church, more concerned with the dispute with the Jansenists than with the danger from irreligion, was at first not alarmed. The realisation of the progress of irreligious ideas came suddenly when it was discovered that a thesis presented to the Sorbonne in 1751 by the abbé Prades and accepted unanimously by the examiners contained a concise statement of the sensational psychology and the theory of natural religion, and incidentally destroyed the significance of the New Testament miracles. Clergy and university turned on the serpent in their bosom; Prades was censured and the approval of his thesis withdrawn. The episode revealed the extent to which the unnoticed permeation of religious thought by heretical ideas had progressed and provided the stimulus for a belated attempt to impose a severer censorship. Before the wave of repression had made much progress Malesherbes became *directeur de la librairie*, and under his benevolent eye, and the patronage of Madame de Pompadour, the propaganda of the *philosophes* was resumed, and unofficially, or sometimes even officially, protected. In the following decade with Helvétius, Diderot, Voltaire and d'Holbach, the great guns of the anti-Christian offensive were uncovered, while a barrage of lesser writers was popping off continually. The attack, supported by a strong wave of anti-clericalism, was particularly concentrated against the Jesuits and was inspired mainly by practical and not theoretical considerations. Its noblest motive was a hatred of the cruelties perpetrated in the name of religion, its positive creed was toleration. At the same time the opponents of religion did not conceive the possibility of leaving the people in matters of religion entirely to their own devices. Religion was ceasing to be re-

[1] D. Mornet, *Les Origines intellectuelles de la Révolution française* (1933), pp. 27–8.

garded as the foundation of the social order, at least by advanced opinion, but Gallican tradition in France was so strong that no great revolution in ideas was involved in conceiving of the Church as a kind of cement to the State. To speak of 'civil and ecclesiastical government', said Voltaire, is an absurdity; one should say civil government and ecclesiastical regulations, 'and none of these regulations ought to be made except by the civil power'.[1]

Similar Erastian ideas prevailed in England. Hoadley, the chief advocate of latitudinarianism in the Church of England, criticised the sacerdotal claims of the Church of which he was a bishop on the ground that they set up a State within a State; while the fundamental article of Warburton's *Alliance* was 'that the Church shall apply all its Influence in the service of the State; and that the State shall support and protect the Church'.[2] In Germany the opposition to the claims of the Church came from the prince prelates themselves, anxious to assert their independence of Rome. Later in the century Johann Nikolaus Hontheim, the coadjutor of the archbishop of Trèves, writing under the name of Febronius, expressed the grievances of the Catholic German States against the Papacy and gave his name to the movement called Febronianism. Thus, although throughout Europe the forces of religious intolerance were being beaten back, an acute observer might have noticed that the victory for freedom of thought was only being achieved with the aid of the political authorities, and that the decline in the power of the Church was accompanied by an extension of the claims of the State.

Moreover, religion was not to be replaced by philosophy. The sceptical literature which poured out so prolifically in the eighteenth century has for the most part only the intellectual value of brilliant propaganda. The so-called *philosophes* were one of the most unmetaphysical schools of thinkers that has ever existed. Spinoza was admittedly a name to conjure with among them, but they made no attempt to rescue his philosophy from the discredit into which it had fallen as a result of orthodox attacks and Spinozism became a mere synonym for criticism of the Bible. Voltaire above all had a practical man's impatience with all thought which did not derive from empirical facts and lead to conclusions with a direct bearing on practical actions. He had no sympathy with the writers who had contributed to what he called '*le roman de l'âme*'. In the same spirit Condillac, in his *Traité des systèmes* of 1749, headed one chapter, '*De l'inutilité des systèmes abstraits*'. The attack on metaphysical thought was an appeal to the common sense of the generality, to *bon sens* as the criterion of philosophic truth. On a more respectable intellectual level it represented a new stage in the old conflict between empiricism and rationalism. Against *a priori* thought the so-called Age of Reason appealed to nature, by

[1] Voltaire, *Idées républicaines* (1762) (*Œuvres complètes*, 1877–85, vol. XXIV, p. 415).
[2] Warburton, *The Alliance between Church and State* (1736), p. 68; translated into French, 1742.

87

which it meant the facts of experience. It set up physics in opposition to metaphysics, and believed that every question that was worth asking could be answered by discovering the right facts. The age of religion and metaphysics was over; science was the new evangel.

The history of science does not, of course, begin in the eighteenth century, nor does the period of the greatest advance in scientific thought coincide with the age of the Enlightenment. One achievement of the eighteenth century was not so much in making fundamental new discoveries as in extending the knowledge of discoveries that had already been made to a wider circle than before. The ordinary educated man could still understand scientific techniques and explanations, except in the higher branches of mathematics, without being a specialist. Experimental demonstrations could be performed and scientific theories comprehended in the fashionable *salon*. The *beau monde* mixed with the scientists; men of letters like Voltaire and women of society like Madame du Châtelet had their private laboratories and made serious contributions to the progress of science. Literary journals afforded increasing space to reviews of scientific writings. Buffon proved that a work of science could also be a literary success. Christian Wolff introduced science to the Germans, writing for the first time on such a subject in their own language. Even the universities were influenced by the intellectual movement of the day. Between 1702 and 1750 chairs were founded at Cambridge in anatomy, astronomy, botany, chemistry, geology, geometry and experimental philosophy. Marvels still survived, of course; mermaids, basilisks and wonders of all kinds were not the least savoured elements in would-be scientific treatises, but even theological motivation contributed to the popularisation of science. 'The existence of God proved by the Marvels of Nature' was a common theme, the most successful of many such attempts to combine religion with science, the Abbé Pluche's *Spectacle de la Nature* going through at least eighteen editions and being translated into English, Italian, Spanish and German.

The popularisers perhaps only deserve to be relegated to the apocrypha of the scientific bible. The prophet of the new dispensation, whose genius transformed science from the obscurity of apparently random experimentation into a rational subject with its own comprehensible laws, was Isaac Newton. In England Newtonian ideas carried all before them. On the other hand there was a strong resistance to them in France. Descartes with his *tourbillons*, which had only just conquered the learned world, stood in the way of an immediate acceptance of Newton's ideas, though the support which Newtonian physics gave to deism by providing an apparent cosmological proof of God aided their acceptance. Fontenelle, whose war against superstition begins before Louis XIV's reign was half through and was to be continued almost to the middle of the eighteenth century, remained a convinced Cartesian to the end of his life.

The influence of Maupertuis, however, weighed heavily on the side of Newtonian principles, as did that of Voltaire. Their triumph was practically complete in France by the middle of the century, when d'Argens, who in the first edition of *La philosophie du bon sens* in 1737 had made only a passing reference to Newton, in a later version of 1746 could write of '*la fureur de l'attraction*'. From England and France Newtonian science spread to the rest of Europe. Antonio Conti, who passed many years in Paris and visited Newton in England, took back to Venice and Padua instruments with which he repeated Newton's experiments. The progress of the scientific spirit in Italy was marked by the publication in 1744 of Galileo's *Dialogo*, with a papal licence, though on condition that it was prefaced by the sentence of the Holy Office and Galileo's retraction. In 1757 the Holy Office decided not to enforce any longer the decrees against books which taught the movement of the earth. Newton, indeed, had carried scientific thought so far forward that a century was required to assimilate and work out the implications of his ideas. In England the worship of Newton may even be said to have stood in the way of the progress of mathematical thought until the nineteenth century, though important discoveries were added by the astronomers royal, Edmund Halley and James Bradley. On the Continent there was a more important theoretical development of Newton's principles by such mathematicians as the Bernoulli family and Leonard Euler of Basel, Lagrange of Turin and d'Alembert in France.

Newton had shown the uniformity of nature and set men searching for nature's laws, but the abstract and theoretical form—to say nothing of the difficulty—of mathematics set a strict limit to the number of those who could voyage in the seas of thought that he had explored. The true bent of the eighteenth century was towards empiricism and Voltaire looked behind Newton to Bacon as its founder. There was a tendency, therefore, to turn from mathematics to the natural sciences. Buffon, in a preface to a translation of the Englishman Hales's *Vegetable Statics*, proclaimed the need 'continually to collect experimental evidence and shun, if possible, the whole spirit of systematising'. Mathematical truths, he declared in the introduction to his *Histoire naturelle* in 1749, are truths of definition and therefore abstract, whereas physical truths are founded on fact; and French scientists fully accepted the teaching of the Dutch scientist P. van Musschenbroek, that observation and experiment are the only foundation of physics. Buffon himself carried out the doctrine of empiricism imperfectly, for he attempted to grasp the whole world of nature in a great speculative system. Réaumur's careful observations on insects, published between 1734 and 1742, embody a truer application of scientific method. Yet Buffon provided in his person an example of devotion to science, and the prestige which he gained from the enormous success of his *Histoire naturelle*, even if it were due more to his literary than to his scientific skill, cast a lustre on natural science from which even those who criticised his methods benefited. He set his mark on what was to be a new age of discovery. Scientists, antiquarians and the fashionable world began collecting like mad. Buffon himself presided over the magnificent *Jardin des Plantes* and *Cabinet du Roi*. Along with the collectors went the classifiers, as the model for all of whom may stand the Swedish botanist, Linnaeus, whose monumental labour saved botanists from being swamped under the mass of new material which his own energy and inspiration did so much to bring forth. The price paid was that for a time classification came to be an end in itself and rather superficial generalisations often took the place of scientific experiment.

Theory, in fact, still tended to hold experimental science back, but the practical interests, which scientists shared with *philosophes*, stimulated its progress. In the field of botanical studies interest was directed towards agricultural, and especially horticultural practice. Valuable work was done on pollination and hybridisation. A similar interest in industrial processes, such as distillation, influenced the experiments of the early chemists, particularly those on the effect of heat. The progress of chemical science was, however, still hampered by the mystical atmosphere which continued to surround it. The greatest chemist of the first half of the eighteenth century, Stahl, professor at Halle and later at Berlin, is best known for his theory of phlogiston, though this was only one among his chemical theories. With considerable insight he grasped the similarity between the burning of combustibles and the calcination of metals. He attributed this similarity to the presence of an inflammable principle, which he called phlogiston, which in the process of burning was released and dissipated into the air, in spite of the known fact of the increase in the weight of calcined metals, which was irreconcilable with this theory. No alternative explanation was found until a later generation abandoned the idea of phlogiston. The Dutch chemist Boerhave's useful treatise, *Elementa Chemiae* (1732), also showed the lack of new chemical ideas; and though a notable advance was made by the Scottish chemist, Joseph Black, with his discovery of fixed air in 1755, chemistry was not to have its Newton until the time of Lavoisier. Electricity and magnetism were in an even more rudimentary state. Little more can be said than that interest had been aroused in simple electrical phenomena, but no serious hypothesis for their explanation had yet been put forward. In medicine, though the establishment of a clinical tradition at Leiden and subsequently at other schools of medicine helped to improve practice, the dominance of practical interests was itself a barrier to scientific progress. Of great importance was the development of more accurate scientific instruments, often stimulated by practical needs, for the Enlightenment was associated with a revolution in material conditions as well as in ideas. The Age of Reason was also the Age of Invention.

The scientific development that has so far been outlined did not for the most part conflict openly with orthodox modes of thought. Geological speculation was more liable to arouse resistance on religious grounds, for even an elementary study of rock formations tended to produce ideas on the history of the earth which were difficult to reconcile with the version presented in the book of Genesis. The study of astronomy had already predisposed scientists to suspect that the world might be somewhat older than the 4000 years recorded in the Bible. Buffon cautiously pointed out the long periods of time which must have been needed to produce the present stratification of the rocks, to account for which, as well as for the fossils, it was evident that ages of oceanic submersion had to be hypothesised in place of the short if dramatic episode associated with Noah. The narrow line that still divided scientific theory from fanciful speculation may be illustrated by the deductions drawn from the marine hypothesis by de Maillet in his *Telliamed*, published in 1748 but in manuscript circulation some time before. He saw the implication that land forms of life must have evolved from those whose habitat was the ocean, and from this leapt to the idea that the link, obviously, had been provided by mermen and mermaids (about whose terminations he exhibited a certain scientific scepticism) who at some point in the polar regions quitted their watery home and became the ancestors of the human race. Even such an errant fancy throws light on the ways of thought of the eighteenth century. It exhibits the transference of the ancient idea of the Chain of Being, the principle of the continuity of all created things in an unbroken hierarchy from lowest to highest, from philosophy into the field of biology. To try to discover in the eighteenth century more than the beginnings of the theory of evolution would be premature, but the idea was there in embryo and the search for missing links in the chain of evolution had begun. Diderot, in his *Pensées sur l'interprétation de la nature*, questioned the existence of a barrier between dead and living matter, believing that the spontaneous generation of life from dead matter had been demonstrated in the famous experiment of Needham in 1748. The fallacy of the experiment was demonstrated by the Abbé Spallanzoni of Naples in 1760. The studies of the polyp by Baker (1743) and by the Genevese Abraham Trembley (1744), suggested that these creatures formed the link between plants and animals. Despite such speculations, however, in biology, as in practically every other scientific field, this was a period of diffusion and of tentative exploration of new territory rather than of fundamental advance. It was an interlude between the Age of Newton and the Age of Lavoisier.

The most important new development of the scientific mind in the eighteenth century was the application of the scientific analysis to man himself, which meant in the first place to individual psychology, and then to social life. The Enlightenment believed, in the words of Hume, that the study of man could and should be based on observation and experiment and that, as d'Alembert put it in the article *Expérimental* in the *Encylopédie*, the study of man as a social animal, including his morals and history, was a proper subject for experimental philosophy. In practice there proved to be a big gap between the psychology of the eighteenth century, based on rationalist and individualistic presuppositions, and the achievement of a science of society. The one great attempt at a systematic treatise on social science, Montesquieu's *De l'esprit des lois*, started from history and not psychology. Even so, it must be reckoned from this point of view a magnificent failure. Montesquieu attempted to skip the work of a couple of centuries in scientific jurisprudence, economics, human geography and anthropology. The time was not yet ripe, if it ever was to be, for a Newton of the social sciences. Montesquieu's aims were far higher than his achievement. He was trying to analyse the laws operating in social life, to build up politics, morals, religion, economics, with all their inter-relations, into a vast sociological synthesis, to reduce to scientific terms the social behaviour of man, not, he said, to pass judgment on it. The task was far beyond the possibilities of his day. Moreover, whatever he might protest, behind the social scientist in Montesquieu there was a moralist, who was aware that the moral disinterestedness of the scientist is difficult for the student of human institutions. The dilemma of the social sciences, which emerges for the first time clearly in Montesquieu, is exemplified in his use of the key-word of the age, *Nature*. Thus, slavery, he said, is against nature; but in some countries there is a natural reason for it. Nature is here evidently two different things. It is *la nature des choses*, the way in which things work; but it is also the way in which they *ought* to work. The same ambiguity is evident in his use of the words *droit* and *devoir*. *Droit*—right—is based on eternal law, but it is also related to the conditions of each particular society; *devoir* is what ought to be, but it is also what must be. The result was that curious combination of empirical evidence with ethical presuppositions which was characteristic of the social thought of the Enlightenment.

In the social sciences the first half of the eighteenth century was a period of preparation rather than of positive achievement. The economic writings of Berkeley and Hume prepared the way for the later English economists, as did those of Melon, Dutot and Forbonnais for the Physiocrats in France. Neo-mercantilist ideas were put forward in Spain, by Ulloa and Uztáriz. The Neapolitan disciple of Vico, the Abbé Galiani, basing himself on Locke, produced a remarkably clear analysis of the theory of value, and the Franco-English banker Richard Cantillon, of Irish origin, was the author of a treatise on commerce which has led some historians of economic thought to regard him as the greatest of the precursors of Adam Smith. The new science of economics was also to be influenced by the economic and political theories associated with the Physiocratic school in France and the Cameralists in Germany; but the more important developments of physiocratic and neo-cameralist economic thought were only to come in the latter half of the century.

In the eighteenth century the social sciences, like the natural sciences, were still in the collecting stage. All facts, or supposed facts, were welcome, and in the intellectual hierarchy of the Enlightenment history came second only to science. The great work of historical documentation begun by seventeenth-century scholars was continued, and an increasing number of laymen turned their attention to historical erudition. The historical pyrrhonism of La Mothe le Vayer and Bayle had prepared the way for critical scholarship. History was henceforth to be not a mere interpretation of man's life and destiny but, in the words of Lenglet du Fresnoy, 'an exact and sincere narrative of events, supported by the evidence of one's own eyes, by certain and indubitable documents, by the evidence of persons worthy of credence'.[1] There were signs, especially in the histories of the greater writers, such as Voltaire, Hume and Robertson, of the appearance of a gap between historical scholars and men of letters who wrote history: that this gap could be bridged was shown by Gibbon, who combined the interpretative history of a Voltaire with the learning of a Benedictine and presented ideas and erudition in an elegant and conscious literary garb.

The historians of the Enlightenment inevitably based their work on the current rationalist and individualist presuppositions; and since there are many things that cannot reasonably be understood in these terms they sometimes seem to reduce history to little more than a mere series of dynastic accidents. The straightforward narrative of facts proved a means not of avoiding preconceived prejudices but merely of taking them for granted. History, moreover, became a weapon in the war against religion. Religious apologists themselves accepted the challenge to historical testimony and based their own case on it. More ingenuously, the French Jesuit, Jean Hardouin, tried to turn the point of historical scepticism against the sceptics by flatly denying the authenticity of all documents purporting to date from before the fourteenth century, except the Vulgate and a limited number of classical texts, the result being to leave the tradition of the Church as the only court of appeal. Another French Jesuit, Isaac Berruyer, hoped by rewriting the Bible in a contemporary style to produce a work 'at the same time edifying and agreeable'.[2] English apologists more soberly attempted to confirm revelation by historical evidence. Thus Sherlock, in his *Trial of the Witnesses* (1729), submitted the evidence for miracles to critical examination, naturally with more favourable conclusions than Hume was to reach in his famous *Essay on Miracles*.

---

[1] P. N. Lenglet du Fresnoy, *L'histoire justifiée contre les romans* (1735), p. 24; cf. his *Méthode pour étudier l'histoire* (1713).

[2] *Histoire du peuple de Dieu* (1728–58), vol. I, p. xxvii; cf. La Baume Desdossat's *Christiade* (1753).

The religious interpretation of human history was not one that could easily be reconciled with the ideas of the eighteenth century. Perhaps influenced by the Leibnizian conception of universal continuity, the *philosophes* objected as much on historical as on scientific grounds to the theory of a catastrophic breach in the operation of the universal laws which controlled the destiny of the human race. They clung to an *a priori* belief in the existence of a single line of historical development. Though they were determined to dethrone the Hebrews from the central position attributed to them in sacred history, they still kept unconsciously to biblical modes of thought and assumed the necessity for a single point of origin for the progress of mankind. Instead of Palestine, with its deplorable biblical associations, they placed the cradle of human history in Egypt. From Egypt civilisation passed to the Greeks and Romans, but with the victory of the Moderns in their contest with the Ancients there was no longer any temptation to regard the classical world as the peak of human achievement. The regrettable dominance of religious ideas in the Middle Ages, it is true, rather spoilt the picture of steady, uninterrupted progress. Only Turgot, interested in medieval technical developments, ventured to qualify the general condemnation. But after the ages of Gothic darkness the human mind took up again the torch of progress, which was to burn ever more brightly until it came to full illumination in the *siècle des lumières*.

Except by Turgot, the historical philosophy of the *Encyclopédistes* was never developed beyond a rather rudimentary collection of vague general notions, until it culminated at the end of the century in Condorcet's theory of universal progress. There was, however, one profounder historical philosopher living at the time. The school of Naples, which contributed a series of notable thinkers to the eighteenth century, produced one of the greatest of all in Giambattista Vico, the first edition of whose *Principi d'una Scienza Nuova* was published in 1725. Vico is one of those thinkers whose greatness is such that it cannot be summed up in any brief account. Besides, he is a chronological error who does not belong to his own century. The Neapolitan jurist Gravina, who died in 1718, in his historical treatment of jurisprudence may be regarded as a predecessor of Vico, who was influenced also by Grotius' dream of a universal *ius gentium*, but essentially he stands alone. His ancestry is to be found, if anywhere, in Platonic thought, and especially in the Platonists of the Renaissance. His starting point, like that of Locke and Hume, is opposition to Descartes, but it leads him in a contrary direction from theirs. He asks the questions that his generation was asking; the *Scienza Nuova* is a theory of the mind, a history of humanity and a social science. But his answers could hardly be more different from those given by his contemporaries. Although an attempt has been made to present Vico as essentially a conservative and Catholic thinker, and though he calls himself *defensor*

94

ecclesiae, he is fundamentally divorced from orthodox thought, for his God is one who is immanent in man, operating through natural causes and not transcendent. His New Science is essentially a philosophy of history, but not in any sense which the Enlightenment could apprehend. Vico, in the words of Croce, was 'neither more nor less than the nineteenth century in germ'.[1] There is no evidence that anyone in his own generation, and few if any in his own century, understood more than isolated fragments of his thought.

The eighteenth century, then, was the age of science and history, the age of the triumph of the empirical fact. Let us not underestimate the importance of the victory that this involved for the human mind, even if it was won over its own theoretical genius. Men were now, in all fields, observing rather than imagining. But the human mind cannot live on facts alone. A study of the writings of the Enlightenment on the social sciences and history soon reveals, behind the apparent determination to seize on objective facts and base the argument on these alone, the existence of theoretical presuppositions. These were not, of course, philosophical or religious. Where we find the *a priori* element hidden at the heart of empiricism is in the conception of human nature. For the basis of the ideas of the eighteenth century it is necessary to look at its psychological theories. The *philosophes* would not have admitted that their pyschological theories were other than scientific. They assumed that the laws of individual psychology were also those that operated in the progress of civilisation— the proposition on which d'Alembert's *Discours préliminaire* to the *Encyclopédie* was founded—and that these laws had been revealed in Locke's *Essay concerning Humane Understanding*. Locke's belief that all our ideas are the product of sensation dominated eighteenth-century psychological theory as completely as the Newtonian theory of gravitation dominated its physics. Its most authoritative exposition was the Abbé Condillac's *Traité sur les sensations* (1754) with its famous analogy of a statue, organised within like a man but encased in marble, which as it is gradually given senses so develops the powers of its mind. The principle of the sensational psychology was the belief that, in the words of Helvétius, 'Everything in man can be reduced to sensation.'[2] It went even beyond Locke, for where he had attributed to the mind an ill-defined power of reflection, his eighteenth-century disciples explained the development of all complex ideas out of simple ones by the automatic process of association.

From the sensational psychology to a fully developed theory of materialism was only a short step. The possibility of taking that step had already been envisaged in Locke's discussion with Stillingfleet concerning whether a material being could think, which was continued in the debate

---

[1] Croce, *The Philosophy of Giambattista Vico*, trans. B. G. Collingwood (1910), ch. xx.
[2] Helvétius, *De l'esprit* (1758), Discours I, ch. I (*Œuvres complètes*, 1795, vol. I, p. 135).

between Clarke and Leibniz. Voltaire had cautiously suggested in his *Lettres philosophiques* that perhaps thought might be a function of matter. Later, when he wrote the article *Âme* in the *Dictionnaire philosophique*, his mockery suggests that he did not regard at least the problem as a very material one. The controversy became involved with that over the *âme des bêtes*. Descartes had pronounced animals mere automata without sensation. The sceptics of the eighteenth century seized on the opposite idea that animals had souls—or at least minds—like men, as a weapon in their war against religion. 'That the *âme des bêtes* is a proof that matter can acquire the faculty of thought', so d'Argens headed one of his chapters. It followed that, if there were no fundamental difference between men and animals, if the soul were not an independent entity added by divine creation to a mechanical universe, then the Cartesian dualism which had been accepted by the Jesuits in the eighteenth century and made into the basis of Christian apologetics was wholly undermined. By the middle of the century the bolder spirits had followed the Curé Meslier and the marquis d'Argens in proclaiming a completely materialist doctrine. David Hartley, an English prophet of determinism and universal happiness, best known for his development of the psychological theory of association, reconciled materialism with deism in his *Observation on Man* in 1749 by arguing that God had endowed matter with the capacity for thought. La Mettrie saw no necessity for introducing God into the argument. Form and motion, he said, are the essence of matter: it has the capacity for sensation in itself, and therefore for thought.

The sensational psychology, whether pushed openly to the extreme of materialism or not, made rapid progress in France. When a systematic statement of it appeared with Helvétius' *De l'esprit* in 1758, Diderot could write, 'Ten years earlier this work would have been quite new; but today the spirit of philosophy has made such progress that there is little that is new to be found in it.'[1] The attempt of the *philosophes* to reduce the human mind to a mere arrangement of sense-impressions may strike us as crude and even unscientific. The profounder thought of Hume penetrated beyond the simple dogmatism of the French materialists. 'That which we call a *mind*', he said, 'is nothing but a heap or collection of different perceptions, united together by certain relations, and supposed, though falsely, to be endowed with a perfect simplicity and inentity.'[2] But Hume's treatise, in his own words, 'fell dead-born from the press'. The dogmatic thinkers of the eighteenth century were not prepared for such an uncomfortable extension of the sceptical spirit. The importance of their psychological theory did not lie in its scientific value but in the practical corollaries that were drawn from it in the field of society and *mœurs*.

[1] Diderot, *Réflexions sur le livre de l'esprit par M. Helvétius* (*Œuvres complètes*, 1875–7, vol. II, p. 273).
[2] *Treatise on Human Nature*, bk I, part IV, § 2.

Here also Locke had anticipated the *philosophes*. His pleasure-pain analysis of the motives of human action, associated with rationalism, individualism, and the bias towards materialism, made possible the development of an advanced form of hedonistic thought. Self-love became the chief of virtues. *Luxe*, denounced by preachers and theologians since the commencement of the Christian era, was held up for admiration, as in Voltaire's *Mondain*—

> J'aime le luxe et même la mollesse,
> Tous les plaisirs, les arts de toute espèce,
> La propreté, le gout, les ornements:
> Tout honnête homme a de tels sentiments.[1]

Nature made even our vices serve good ends. It could, in the words of Pope, 'Build on wants, and on defects of mind, The joy, the peace, the glory of mankind'.[2] 'Private Vices, Public Benefits', declared the subtitle to the much admired *Fable of the Bees*,[3] in which, like Voltaire, Pope, Saint-Lambert and many others, Mandeville put the hedonistic morality into verse. The English politician Soame Jenyns sums up the prevailing hedonism in its ultimate form:

To say truth, Happiness is the only thing of real value in existence; neither riches, nor power, nor wisdom, nor learning, nor strength, nor beauty, nor virtue, nor religion, nor even life itself, being of any importance but as they contribute to its production. All these are in themselves neither Good nor Evil; Happiness alone is their great end, and they desirable only as they tend to promote it.[4]

Finally, it must be emphasised that the pleasures in the hedonistic scale were primarily physical. Toussaint and Duclos, recognised and popular moralists, expressed in moderate language the view put more crudely by La Mettrie and Morelly, that obedience to the passions was the basis of morality.

The hedonist psychology effected a drastic reorientation in moral ideas. It deprived revealed religion of any relevance to moral truth and by its denial of innate ideas opened the door to the questioning of all traditional morals. 'There is no moral idea which is innate,' declared Diderot, 'and the knowledge of good and evil derives, like all other knowledge, from our bodily faculties.'[5] A whole library of eighteenth-century works upholding happiness, *bonheur* or utility as the criterion of morality could be collected. Utilitarianism was the science not only of the moralist but also of the legislator. All laws, declared Helvétius, must be related to the

---

[1] Voltaire, *Le Mondain* (1736) (*Œuvres*, vol. x, pp. 83–4).
[2] Pope, *Essay on Man*, II.
[3] Mandeville, *The Grumbling Hive: or, Knaves Turn'd Honest* (1705); *The Fable of the Bees: or, Private Vices Publick Benefits*, Part I (1714); revised and enlarged many times subsequently.
[4] Soame Jenyns, *A Free Enquiry into the Nature and Origin of Evil* (1757), p. 46.
[5] Diderot, *Suite de l'apologie de l'abbé de Prades* (1752) (*Œuvres*, vol. I, p. 470).

single principle of public utility, 'a principle which includes the whole of morals and legislation'.[1]

Individualist and rationalist utilitarianism, however, represents only one side of eighteenth-century moral theory, and it did not answer every question. Above all it left unsolved the problem of the reconciliation of individual hedonism with the interests of society. The dilemma could be evaded, as in the *Essay on Man* or the *Fable of the Bees*, by assuming that it did not exist. It could be treated more seriously by postulating the existence in the human mind of a spirit of humanity, or *bienfaisance*, to use a word invented by Saint-Pierre. The most selfish of doctrines concerning human nature became in this way the foster-mother of benevolence and humanitarianism. For an age with such a reputation for immorality, the eighteenth century exhibited a remarkable obsession with ethical questions. The moralising tone and glorification of bourgeois virtues which appeared in England with Addison and Steele spread subsequently to France. Even Gil Blas and Tom Jones were to decide, though not until the last pages of their respective histories, to settle down to middle-class morality, and Pamela in the defence of her virtue was found more alluring than any other heroine in the loss of hers. The source of this social and moralistic form of utilitarianism is to be found particularly in Shaftesbury's *Characteristics of Men, Manners, Opinions, Times* (1711), wherein interest and virtue were reconciled and universal harmony established by the postulate of a moral sense. For Shaftesbury this moral sense was a rational faculty, but Hume carried the argument, as he did others, a stage further than his contemporaries. 'The approbation of moral qualities most certainly is not derived from reason, or any comparison of ideas,' he wrote, 'but proceeds entirely from a moral taste.'[2] Francis Hutcheson, in his *System of Moral Philosophy* (1755), attempted to combine Shaftesbury's moral sense with the assertion of an objective standard of public utility. Adam Smith, on the other hand, writing his *Theory of Moral Sentiments* in 1759, took the innate moral sense, which he termed sympathy, as itself the standard of morality, and thus reduced utility to a subordinate position, which was equivalent to solving the problem of social ethics by an evocation of the natural goodness of man—a faith which was to receive its fullest expression in Rousseau.

A contrary trend in moral theory—though this is not to say that the existence of the contradiction was generally appreciated—developed largely from Bayle, for whom morality was the law of reason, and therefore opposed to the passions. His view was very much that expressed by Pope, 'Two principles in human nature reign; Self-love, to urge, and reason, to restrain.'[3] On this basis, however, it was clear that some

---

[1] *De l'esprit*, Discours II, ch. XVII (*Œuvres*, vol. II, p. 323).
[2] *Treatise on Human Nature*, book III, Part iii, §1.
[3] *Essay on Man*, II.

reinforcement for reason might have to be provided by the social order and public law, which raised the problem of discovering the appropriate moral laws to be enforced by society. As they had rejected theological teaching and innate moral ideas, the *philosophes* could only hope to discover a basis for these in the nature of man and his circumstances. Since institutions were regarded as of human and not of divine origin, the necessity for an experimental and inductive science of morals seemed to follow. Montesquieu's attempt to establish what might be called a sociological morality has already been referred to. He took the essential first step in the declaration, 'It is not Fortune that governs the world; that is proved in the history of the Romans....There are general causes, either moral or physical, which operate....In a word, the dominant trend carries with it all particular incidents.'[1] Where Voltaire saw a concatenation of little causes changing the destiny of man, Montesquieu looked beyond these to the great forces operating in the life of society, which he tried to grasp in general causes or laws. But his scientific analysis and his search for an objective social morality conflict with rather than complement one another. The final trend of his thought was towards the justification of whatever customs existed in any country. 'To recall men to ancient maxims is ordinarily to bring them back to virtue.'[2] The men of the Enlightenment more often reached the opposite conclusion, but in their search for the laws of human nature and the moral foundations of society it cannot be said that they achieved great theoretical success. Yet as their interests were above all practical, it was appropriate that the fruits of their efforts should grow on the tree of practice. Out of the soil they tilled sprang the humanitarian movement and all the reforms in law and society that it brought with it.

The Enlightenment was more interested in moral and social than in specifically political problems. In political thinking, indeed, the first half of the eighteenth century was an interlude between the age of Hobbes, Grotius and Locke, and that of Rousseau and Burke, and was marked by no thinkers of comparable stature. Generalisation about the political thinking of the period is difficult, for each country followed its own traditions. In England Locke, in Germany Grotius and Pufendorf, and in France the rival traditions of the absolute monarchy and the Fronde, were dominant.

While English and French political thinking was moving on to more positive and utilitarian ideas on government, in Germany the natural law school of thought continued to flourish. The most prolific and highly esteemed of the successors of Pufendorf and Leibniz was Christian Wolff, who aimed to reduce all knowledge to a system, and for the first half of

[1] Montesquieu, *Considérations sur les causes de la grandeur des Romains et de leur décadence* (1734), ch. XVIII (*Œuvres*, 1822, vol. II, pp. 307–8).
[2] Montesquieu, *De l'esprit des lois*, v. 7 (*Œuvres*, vol. II, p. 228).

the eighteenth century produced an average of over one book a year. Not an original thinker, Wolff drew his ideas from Leibniz and from the English and French thinkers of the previous century. His thought was an amalgam of rationalist and utilitarian ideas with those of positive religion, set in a framework of Natural Law. In politics, with equal inconsistency, he combined an advance towards the idea of popular sovereignty with a retreat in the direction of upholding the duty of total submission to the ruler. His ideas illustrate the manner in which the Enlightenment entered Germany and was purged of all its more significant political and social ingredients on the way. Christian Thomasius (1655–1728), also a follower of Pufendorf, was another light in the same now rather obscure galaxy.

Outside Germany the school of Natural Law jurists was represented by the Neapolitan Gianvincenzo Gravina, the Dane Martin Hubner, in France by Barbeyrac and A. Y. Goguet, and by the Genevese J.-J. Burlamaqui. Barbeyrac and Burlamaqui deserve rather more than a passing mention, for they represent a significant development beyond the ideas of the Natural Law jurists of the previous century. Barbeyrac is often regarded as the mere translator of Grotius and Pufendorf, but in his notes he reveals himself as a disciple of Locke and an admirer of the English Constitution. In opposition to Grotius and Pufendorf, he maintains the right of disobedience to the sovereign on moral grounds and the possibility of the divisibility of sovereignty. Burlamaqui's model is the Constitution of his native city of Geneva—a mixed government in which aristocracy is tempered by democracy, and power limited by being divided, as well as by the existence of fundamental laws. Barbeyrac, Burlamaqui, and with them the international lawyer Vattel, break away from the absolutism of Grotius and Pufendorf, largely under the influence of Locke. For them not only does the sovereign hold power on condition of governing in the interest of the people, but if that power is abused the people have the right of resistance. This last stage in the development of the school of Natural Law represents the culmination of the theoretical struggle against the twin doctrines of Divine Right and Absolutism. It was, perhaps, not so much significant in itself as because it provided the intellectual soil out of which the democratic movements of the latter part of the century were to grow. These writers were also the immediate precursors of the political theory of Rousseau, which in the light of their writings seems much more a logical development of the school of Natural Law and much less a completely new creation than has been supposed.

The new wave of political ideas, however, was only to acquire practical significance at a much later date, and meanwhile utilitarianism was undermining the hold of the Natural Law jurists outside Germany. Their ideas only regained contemporary significance when they returned to the field in which they had achieved their greatest triumph in the previous century with Grotius. In the development of international law the great figure of the period was the Swiss Vattel. Apart from Vattel, who as a practical diplomat tried to link his theories with actual practice, the Natural Law school had lost touch with reality. The conclusions of the German jurists on questions of practical politics were similar to those of the cameralists, whose writings helped to provide a theoretical justification for benevolent despotism. Older constitutional ideas of the rights of the Estates and of the people, which still survived in some of the German States early in the eighteenth century, were undermined and destroyed both by practical developments and by juristic condemnation of the division of power.

In England and France opinion was moving in the opposite direction. English political thought, it is true, hardly advanced beyond Locke, though the framework of Natural Law and contract was gradually dropped. Francis Hutcheson clung to the traditional ideas, but Hume abandoned the contractual theory: we obey government, he held, not because of any hypothetical contractual promise but because otherwise society could not continue to exist. The only other theoretical development worthy of remark in the reigns of the first two Georges was the forsaking of the principle of Divine Right by the Tories themselves. Bolingbroke proclaimed that 'a divine right to govern ill, is an absurdity',[1] and Hume echoed the same verdict.

In France the absolute monarchy reached its apogee in the reign of Louis XIV. A Jacobite disciple of Fénelon, A. M. Ramsay, in his *Essai sur le gouvernement civil* (1719), is one of the last notable advocates of Divine Right. The last phase of the Grand Monarch's reign had witnessed the beginning of an aristocratic reaction, associated with the names of Fénelon, Boulainvillier and Saint-Simon; but the *philosophes* themselves had no alternative to suggest to monarchy, nor indeed did they really want one. The combination of advanced anti-clerical opinions with moderate and even conservative political ones is characteristic of the Enlightenment. On the whole the *Encyclopédistes* were little interested in politics. The one section of opinion in eighteenth-century France which was really politically minded was the small but powerful corporation of the *parlements*, inheriting the tradition of the Fronde and proclaiming the doctrine of a fundamental law upheld by the intermediate bodies in the State, that is by themselves.

The great transformation in the political atmosphere in France which occurred during the eighteenth century was not the result of conscious political theorising but of a combination of many different causes operating on a governmental structure which was unequal to new demands. Among these causes one of the most important in the earlier part of the century was the example of England. The prestige accruing to England from its successful Revolution of 1688, its defeat of Louis XIV and its

[1] Bolingbroke, *On the Idea of a Patriot King* (1738) (*Works*, 1841, vol. II, p. 379).

scientific progress turned the eyes of Frenchmen across the Channel. Refugee Huguenots like Rapin-Thoyras and Abel Boyer prepared the ground for Voltaire's *Lettres philosophiques* and for Montesquieu. Montesquieu's *De l'esprit des lois* has already been discussed as a sociological treatise. It was also the one great political classic of the first half of the eighteenth century. Montesquieu's achievement was to sum up, at a critical stage in the development of European thought, the tradition of power checking power and authority limiting authority. It was a tradition which had its roots deep in the past, but one which needed restatement in the age of enlightened despotism. To enshrine in a single book the basic ideas of liberty and law was a great historic achievement. *De l'esprit des lois* is far from being a perfect book. Its later chapters contain much mere academic magpie-collecting of insignificant facts. But where Montesquieu has something of significance to say he says it greatly. The lapidary conciseness of his style at its best made it a fitting medium for the expression in memorable form of great political truths; and not the least of his virtues was his ever-present sense of the importance of moderation. 'Political liberty is only found in moderate governments.'[1] 'The excess even of reason is not always desirable.'[2] He was a systematiser who was not the victim of his own system, a theorist who knew the limitations of theory.

In the second half of the century the English model was to lose much of its attractiveness in France, except for sections of the *noblesse*. A more permanent influence was that of the classics, which stimulated the literary cult of a vaguely republican ideal. Rhetorical exercises on the republican virtues of Rome and Sparta and the vices of the emperors seen through the eyes of Tacitus were commonplace. Montesquieu himself derived his ideas partly from classical sources, especially his definition of 'virtue', which itself became classical. 'What I call *virtue* in the republic is the love of the patrie, that is to say the love of equality.'[3] Such a definition was an implied criticism of existing institutions and at least a theoretical justification of republicanism, the antithesis to which, however, was despotism, not monarchy. As de Jaucourt wrote in the *Encyclopédie*, 'There is no *patrie* under the yoke of despotism.' Although they were careful to draw a distinction between a monarchy such as existed in France and despotism, the denunciation of despotism, allied with the undermining of the religious basis of society, was dangerous to a divine-right monarchy. Even a former minister like d'Argenson could write, in 1747,

Will anyone dare to propose an advance in the direction of republican government? I see no aptitude in the people for it. The nobility, the great lords, the tribunals,

[1] *De l'esprit des lois*, XI, 4 (*Œuvres*, vol. III, p. 6).
[2] *Ibid.* XI, 6 (*Œuvres*, vol. III, p. 28).
[3] *Avertissement*, ed. of 1749 (*Œuvres*, vol. II, p. 3). The article 'République', contributed to the *Encyclopédie* by de Jaucourt, is derived almost entirely from Montesquieu.

accustomed as they are to servitude, have never turned their thoughts toward it, and have no inclinations of that kind. Still, these ideas are coming, and a habit is readily formed among the French.[1]

However, only in the conflict between the *par lements* and the Crown did there appear as yet any serious clash of power. In Europe, outside France, even such theoretical and implicit rather than explicit questioning of the political order is hardly to be found.

The main trend of thought on economic matters was equally moderate and cautious and went to strengthen the tendencies making for an increased emphasis on individual property rights. The continuance of the controversy over the legitimacy of usury showed that in France economic thinking was still largely a branch of morals. There was less speculation in England on this question. Locke's theory was interpreted in terms of a general justification of the property system, though a cautious qualification was suggested by Francis Hutcheson, who held, 'That property, and that chiefly in lands, is the natural foundation upon which power must rest; though it gives not any just right to power',[2] and Robert Wallace, who saw in the establishment of property 'one great source, not only of those calamities, but of those vices, which have been so sensibly felt, and so largely complained of in every age'.[3] On the other hand, Thomas Rutherford, in his *Institutes of Natural Law* (1754), challenged Locke's theory of the origin of all property rights in labour, and laid great stress on the rights of prescription; while Hume, who provided a connecting link from Harrington and Locke to Burke, further strengthened the conception of property rights by rejecting the rationalist explanation. 'If it often happens', he wrote, 'that the title of first possession becomes obscure through time, and that it is impossible to determine many controversies which may arise concerning it; in that case, long possession or *prescription* naturally takes its place, and gives a person a sufficient property in anything he enjoys.'[4]

French speculation on economic questions was more adventurous, though in the earlier part of the century equalitarian ideas were manifested only in the shape of Utopian fancies, such as appeared in Fénelon's *Télémaque*, Montesquieu's history of the Troglodytes, or in accounts of imaginary voyages. Narratives by genuine travellers and missionaries encouraged a tendency to provide such Utopias with a local habitat in the South Seas or other remote paradise. Sometimes, as in Gay's *Polly*, the Utopian state of nature was a literary gesture; sometimes, as in Diderot's *Supplément au voyage de Bougainville*, written in 1772, it was crudely

[1] D'Argenson, *Journal*, ed. Rathery, 27 December 1747 (vol. v, p. 142) and June 1754 (vol. VIII, p. 315).
[2] F. Hutcheson, *System of Moral Philosophy* (1755), vol. II, p. 245.
[3] R. Wallace, *Various Prospects of Mankind, Nature and Providence* (1761), p. 109. He provides an answer to his own arguments, however, in terms of the effect of population pressure later to be used by Malthus (*ibid.* pp. 114–25).
[4] Hume, *Treatise on Human Nature*, book III, Part ii, §3.

amoralistic; sometimes, as in Rousseau, it was an idealisation of the simple life of the countryside, free from the corruption of great cities. But whatever form it took, 'back to nature' was always an implied criticism of existing society. It is rarely to be equated with mere primitivism and especially not in Rousseau.

One or two French writers, even in the earlier part of the century, went beyond this literary cult of nature. The Curé Meslier's *Testament* has achieved fame among the clandestine literature of the first half of the century as the only manuscript which to the attack on religion added a violent criticism of the social and political order. In 1755 Morelly's *Code de la Nature* expounded the ideal of community of property, but though he doubtless meant it in earnest there is no evidence that anyone else took his views seriously. The eighteenth century was used to the expression of similar ideas in the writings of the classics. The virtues of Plato's Republic, of Solon, Lycurgus, and the Gracchi, were a literary commonplace which meant even less than the similar echoes of classical republicanism until Rousseau by his literary genius put the emotional force of moral indignation behind what had been for the most part a mere literary fashion or an exhibition of eccentricity. At the same time, it would be an exaggeration to attribute even to Rousseau's *Discours de l'inégalité* anything more than a literary influence at the time when it was written.

The social and political criticism which was latent in the ideas inherited from the seventeenth century did not cut very deep into the prevailing optimism of the Enlightenment. Archbishop King's proof of the necessity of evil in a world of imperfection amounted to little more than a rather shallow justification of things as they are. The optimistic spirit obtained a wide diffusion in the memorable verse of Pope, and orthodox religious writers in all countries tried unsuccessfully to refute the equally mellifluous doctrines and poetry of the *Essay on Man*. Pope's optimism found a disciple in the young Voltaire. 'I dare to take the side of humanity against this sublime misanthrope',[1] he wrote in a fragment on Pascal; though the mere fact that he thought Pascal worthy of refutation was significant. The earthquake at Lisbon in 1755, followed by the bloodshed of the Seven Years War, shook Voltaire out of an already tenuous attachment to optimism. The next year he wrote his poem on *Le désastre de Lisbonne*, and in 1759, with *Candide*, the full stream of his bitterness and disillusionment was turned, by way of Doctor Pangloss, on the 'best of possible worlds' theory of Leibniz and his disciple Christian Wolff. '"What is optimism?" asked Cacambo. "Alas," said Candide, "it is the mania for pretending that all is well when all is ill."' Men, Voltaire came to believe, are mostly wicked and stupid: the only reasonable verdict on all the evil of

---

[1] *Remarques sur les pensées de Pascal* (1728) (*Œuvres*, vol. XXII, p. 28). Even in *Zadig*, 1747–8, where Voltaire sees men as 'insects devouring one another on a little heap of mud', his conclusion is not truly pessimistic.

this world is that we cannot understand the reason for it, and it is best not to try. Almost alone of his generation Voltaire looked into the tragic depths. Not quite alone perhaps: though their adventures are more of the mind than of the body, and are narrated in a more urbane and contemplative fashion, the conclusion reached by Dr Johnson's *Rasselas* and his fellow travellers—'Of these wishes that they had formed they well know that none could be obtained'—and their final return to the place whence they had set out, teach a lesson not very different from that drawn at the end of *Candide*. Voltaire's real greatness lay in the fact that he was so much more than the mere mocking Pococurante of Carlyle's foolish caricature. He saw that behind Leibnizian optimism there was a tacit justification of the existence of evil; and the conclusion of his pessimism was not resignation, but rather the need to concentrate on dealing with local and particular ills in the hope of diminishing the sum of universal evil. In his belief in the possibility of practical reform he still remained one with the optimistic spirit of his age.

The precursor and prototype of an age of reformers was the abbé de Saint-Pierre, member of the *club de l'Entresol*, deist and utilitarian, who held that social ills were the result of ignorance or prejudice, and that with the elimination of these a continuous progress towards increasing happiness lay before man. His innumerable projects, ranging from the famous plan for perpetual peace, through schemes to improve education, suppress the Barbary pirates, make books and sermons more useful, reform spelling, diminish the number of law-suits, and construct roads which would be serviceable in winter, down to his favourite scheme for an improved arm-chair, may seem pathetic illusions, though many of them are now accomplished facts; but by way of Saint-Pierre, though it mocked at him, the eighteenth century was to come to Bentham, whose ideas France was more prepared to recognise in theory, though England more ready to apply in practice. So we arrive at that idea of the progress of mankind which was the formal expression of the optimism of the Enlightenment. Perfection, wrote Formey, is that state of harmony in which we are led by nature and by the 'law written in our own hearts'.[1] In its ultimate form of perfectibility the idea of progress was only to reach full bloom with Condorcet in the shadow of the guillotine.

There is one important problem that has so far not been discussed in this chapter. The significance for the development of European thought of the ideas of the Enlightenment cannot be doubted, but by what means and to what extent were they diffused? The initial impetus in most respects came from England, where the stage of popularisation had already been reached by the end of the seventeenth century, but the true home of the Enlightenment was to be France. The new ideas were diffused in France by

[1] J. H. S. Formey, 'Essai sur la Perfection', in *Mélanges philosophiques* (1754), vol. II, pp. 105-6.

various agencies, and first by word of mouth, in *salons* such as those of Mme de Lambert, Mme de Tencin, Mme du Deffand, Mme Geoffrin and Mlle de l'Espinasse; or again in meetings such as those of the *club de l'Entresol*, which, after its discussions had acquired some notoriety, was brought to an end by Fleury in 1731. Another centre of discussion was the group of sceptics round the comte de Boulainvillier, which met in the houses of d'Argenson or of the duc de Noailles, or at the *Académie des Inscriptions*, of which one of its members, Mirabaud, was perpetual secretary. This was one of the sources of the clandestine literature, the diffusion of which had already begun before the death of Louis XIV, which reached its height between 1710 and 1740, declined as the censorship became milder after 1740, and practically came to an end after 1750 when the effective censorship of published works broke down. Though Paris was the home of the Enlightenment, in the French provinces literary academies were rapidly springing up. There were about twenty before 1748, and some forty by 1770. Their members came at first almost exclusively from the privileged orders, and in the earlier part of the century the exercises which they encouraged were mainly literary and strictly orthodox in tendency. From the middle of the century, however, scientific interests increased and bourgeois entered their ranks. Between 1725 and 1730, also, the first lodges of Freemasons were founded in France by refugee Jacobites. Freemasonry became popular among the aristocracy and easily survived the mild efforts at repression by Church and State. Though their activities were social rather than intellectual, the Masonic lodges provided an environment in which vaguely deistic and philanthropic ideas could grow.

The spread of the new ideas can also be traced in the journals, which were increasing in numbers and changing their character during this period. Desfontaines, in his *Nouvelles littéraires* founded in 1721, developed a new genre, the literary review aiming by *comptes-rendus* to keep its readers abreast of the latest developments in literature and thought. The older *Mercure de France* and the Jesuit *Journal de Trévoux* followed more cautiously along the new lines. The important change, in this as in every field, comes about 1750, after which many new journals appear with a less strictly orthodox bias. Another medium for the diffusion of ideas was the scientific dictionaries and more general encyclopaedias, such as had appeared in English, German and Italian even before the more famous French *Encyclopédie*. After the publicity acquired as a result of the case of the Abbé Prades, the *Encyclopédie* was seen as a compendium of the new ideas, and its contributors regarded, as indeed they saw themselves, as the propagandists of a new faith.

From France the new ideas gradually spread to the rest of Europe. It was a cosmopolitan age and Paris was only the greatest of the centres of an international culture. Foreigners, above all from the German-speaking countries, continued to come to the great Dutch universities, and J. Leclerc's *Gazette de Hollande* carried news of the world of learning to all Europe. Gottsched has been described as making Leipzig 'a little Paris'. Hamburg formed the channel through which English ideas entered Germany direct. In Italy, literary societies of one kind or another existed in many cities and Scipione Maffei imitated the French reviews in his *Giornale* (1710–37), followed by the *Osservazioni letterarie* (1737–40), mainly scientific in its interests. Scientific academies, emulating the Royal Society at London, appeared at Berlin (1701), St Petersburg (1724), Upsala (1710), Stockholm (1739), and Copenhagen (1743). The despots of Prussia and Russia called to their courts men of science and letters from the West. Scientific activities appeared in Spain under the stimulus of the ministers of Ferdinand VI and Charles III. From Europe the Enlightenment spread to the English colonies in America and found one of its most characteristic and influential disciples in Benjamin Franklin. Paris, of course, remained the Mecca of the *philosophes* of all nations. Manuscript letters giving news of the French world of letters were circulated by the German baron Grimm from 1753, for the political hegemony that France had lost had been succeeded by an intellectual hegemony and French replaced Latin as the language of the world of letters and diplomacy. Frederick II, ordering in 1743 that the Memoirs of the Academy of Sciences of Berlin should be published in French, gave as his reason that it was the universal language.

Towards Paris flowed an unending stream of foreign visitors. Its *salons* were the university of Europe, for fashionable society provided the medium through which the ideas of the *siècle des lumières* were spread. Schools and universities, at least during the earlier part of the century, remained wedded to older ways of thought. The *philosophes*, as disciples of Locke, were fully aware of the power of education, but their influence only affected traditional education slowly. The foundation of a new university at Göttingen in 1734, the reform of teaching at Halle under the influence of Christian Wolff, and rather later at Leipzig, the establishment of universities at St Petersburg (1747) and Moscow (1755), represent conquests for the new spirit. Across the Atlantic the foundation of an important group of colleges showed that academic learning was taking firm root in the New World. The older universities, however, were slipping back. Louvain was sterilised under Jesuit influence; nothing of note emerged from the University of Paris; the universities of Italy and Spain were for the most part in complete decadence; and Oxford and Cambridge in the eighteenth century could hardly be described as centres of intellectual activity.

The effort by the schools of Port-Royal to make the vernacular the principal medium of education in France came to an end under the persecution of Louis XIV. Rollin, in 1726, puts forward with patent caution the suggestion that half-an-hour every day, or perhaps every other day, might be devoted to the study of the mother tongue, but even late in the eighteenth century French played very little part in formal education. Cartesianism was accepted in the teaching of the French Jesuit colleges about 1730 and together with scholasticism it presented a formidable barrier to the introduction of the ways of thought of the Enlightenment. In the *Traité des Études* (1726–8) of Rollin, a former rector of the University of Paris, and in *De ratione discendi et docendi* (1711) by the Jesuit father Joseph de Jouvency, all the traditions of seventeenth-century education survive. True, in the 1750's and 1760's a new spirit was appearing, but just as the actual educational practice of our period belongs to an earlier age, so these new influences require to be studied when they begin to have some positive effects, in the following generation. Until 1762 the Jesuits dominated school education in France and theologians controlled the universities; and if this is true of France, how much more of the rest of Europe, except where the equally traditional influence of the jurists rivalled that of the theological faculties. In England the many dissenting academies provided an alternative to the traditional education controlled by the Anglican Church but they only became an influential factor in the second half of the eighteenth century. The chairs of experimental science and history founded at Oxford and Cambridge bear witness to the influence of the new spirit, but they had little effect in the general intellectual stagnation of public schools and universities, which is in part responsible for the common preference of the upper classes for private tutors for their sons; a similar use of *précepteurs* prevailed in France.

To obtain a balanced picture of the intellectual world of the time, as this glance at its educational systems reminds us, we must see the great, exciting and dangerous new developments against the background of a profoundly conservative intellectual environment. Religion was still the dominating influence over the minds of the vast majority. Devotional works formed the largest class of publications in all countries. A picture of the English reading public as devoted to the philosophical treatises of Hume, or of the literary output of France as monopolised by the *philosophes*, would be completely misleading. Voltaire and the *philosophes* may have lasted better, but at the time the *Journal de Trévoux*, the *Année Littéraire* of Voltaire's great enemy Fréron, the anti-philosophical literature of such writers as Palissot, did not occupy the inferior place that they are now given in histories of thought and literature. Outside France the preponderance of orthodox opinion was even greater. It is evident, of course, that religious apologists were increasingly on the defensive. In England Bishop Butler, who in his *Analogy of Religion* (1736) attempted to prove the case for religion from the facts of the moral experience of the individual, was perhaps the most successful among the critics of the deists. In France, the Jesuit Order, which had been the bulwark of the Church in the previous century, showed itself less prepared to stand up against the attack of the infidels than against that of the Protestants. The *Mémoires de Trévoux* do not betray any consciousness of the dangerous progress of infidelity before the middle of the century. Indeed, the emphasis of Jesuit teaching on the Redemption and a tendency to pass lightly over the idea of Original Sin provided an intellectual atmosphere in which optimistic and naturalistic views could flourish. The Cartesian dualism which the Jesuits had accepted assisted them to draw a dividing line between natural law or reason and supernatural truth. It was thus possible to accept many of the new ideas as true in the world of nature while maintaining the existence of a parallel but quite separate world of grace. The trouble was that the scope of the former was constantly expanding at the expense of the latter. The weakness of the Jesuits was that they assumed the possibility of a compromise between the spirit of the *siècle des lumières* and the ideas of religion. Their apologetics might have been more effective if they could have transferred the debate back to their own ground, but although devotional works appeared in large numbers, mystical tendencies were at a discount in the French Church. Fénelon's *Œuvres spirituelles* went through fifteen editions between 1716 and 1752, but he had few disciples. A more uncompromising attitude was to be found among the Jansenists, but despite the perseverance of the editors of the clandestine *Nouvelles ecclésiastiques* they did not succeed in giving permanence to the declining doctrines of Port-Royal. French Jansenism in the eighteenth century was a source of popular enthusiasm and political passion rather than of profound religious thought, though a more purely religious form was taken by the small Jansenist movement which developed in Italy.

In the Protestant countries mystical tendencies were stronger. Law's *Serious Call* (1728) rejected the claims of reason and proclaimed a universe ruled by a mysterious God, who spoke to men not through the traditions of a worldly Church, but through the profound intuitions of the human heart. A more popular emotional and subjective conception of religion was propagated by Wesley, himself influenced by the German mystics. The pietists of seventeenth-century Germany were followed by Count Nikolaus Ludwig von Zinzendorf, founder of the Moravian Brethren, and an emotional religiosity was represented by Johann Georg Hamann and in Klopstock's poetry. Emanuel Swedenborg, after experiencing conversion in 1754, became the prophet of a new apocalyptic religion which found ardent disciples. Jonathan Edwards revived an austere and mystical Calvinism in America. None of these movements contributed to the history of ideas more than can be summed up in a few sentences, nor indeed did they intend to. They are of significance as evidence, even in the hey-day of *lumières*, that this plateau of intellectualism was not likely to provide a permanent resting-place for the human mind.

The Enlightenment did not satisfy—of course it did not intend to satisfy—the religious emotion. It had equally little to say that would content the metaphysician. Duclos wrote a revealing phrase when he declared that he was not claiming to speak as 'a subtle metaphysician', but 'as a philosopher, who only relies on reason, and only proceeds by reasoning'.[1] The fashionable philosophy in Britain was the common-sense teaching of Hutcheson and Reid. True, on the eve of the Age of Enlightenment two philosophers of a different kind—Leibniz and Berkeley—had been writing. For Leibniz reason had been something far different from the rationalism, or empiricism, of the Age of Reason. Berkeley, in the effort to escape from the rigorous necessitarianism of a mechanistic universe, came to the view that mind was the only reality. 'All these bodies', he wrote, 'which compose the mighty frame of the world have not any substance without a mind—their *being* is to be *perceived*, or *known*.'[2] The American Samuel Johnson was the one important follower of Berkeleyan idealism, though Jonathan Edwards reached for himself a doctrine of idealism which parallels the views of Berkeley.

Berkeley's philosophy took its place on the road leading away from Locke; but it was a road which bifurcated in two directions: one branch was to lead to Kant, and the other more directly to Hume. The conclusion that Hume drew from the sensational psychology was that we can only know the appearances of things; the chain of causation by which we link together observed phenomena is a condition of the operation of our own minds and incapable of philosophic proof. But this is not the place to attempt a summary of the ideas of the one great philosopher of the period, nor is it necessary, for the thought of Berkeley and Hume aroused little echo in their own day. The Neapolitan Vico, as has been said, was not to be discovered even by small groups before the nineteenth century. What passed for philosophy in Germany was merely a kind of abstract juristic thought. Among the French *philosophes* we may single out Condillac as possessed of real philosophic understanding, and in a sense also Diderot, whose *Lettres sur les Aveugles* (1749) was at bottom as dangerous to the positivism of the *philosophes* as was the analysis of Hume; but there was no contemporary reaction to Diderot's relativism or to the other brilliant anticipations in which his thought looks into the future. Most of his manuscripts, indeed, were only published long after his death.

The rare philosophical thinkers, like the mystical writers, were at least a sign that the triumphs of the Enlightenment had not entirely eliminated other ways of thought. There were even more evident signs in the field of imaginative literature that the Age of Reason would be only of limited duration. A conflict was appearing in the hey-day of rationalism

[1] C. P. Duclos, *Considérations sur les mœurs de ce siècle* (1750), ed. F. C. Green (1939), p. 49.
[2] Berkeley, *Essay towards a new theory of Vision* (1709).

between sense and sensibility, which was to be fought out in terms of changing ideas of nature. Nature was the key to the thought of the eighteenth century, but it was a key which opened more than one door. Gradually, as the variety and apparent irrationality of the social pattern that human nature could evoke became increasingly known, nature became less clearly identifiable with reason. Knowledge of Eastern civilisations encouraged a cult of exoticism. The *Thousand and One Nights* had been translated into French early in the century. Egypt challenged the renown of Greece and Rome. Above all China haunted the imagination of the Enlightenment. The cult of primitivism became stronger when the travellers of the eighteenth century, like the missionaries of the previous century, brought back accounts of peaceful and unspoilt primitive peoples. Sometimes more imaginative writers even brought back in fancy a sample savage and pictured the reactions of the simple and virtuous natural man to a corrupt and insincere civilisation. 'Back to nature' in fact came to mean something more than was suggested earlier in this chapter. It even conquered the orthodox theologians, for the Molinist theology of the Jesuits, so strongly opposed by the Augustinian Jansenists, taught that man was good by nature. Here were some of the sources on which Rousseau drew for the attack on the corruptions of society, in his two discourses. The *bon sauvage* was an accepted idea before he wrote, and the element in his thought was neither original nor consistently followed, but it was an ingredient in that potent compound of ideas which, presented through the medium of his literary genius, swept the rational eighteenth century off its feet and into the new and fathomless waters which were to drown the dry lands of reason. But with this we pass beyond the Enlightenment to the dawn of a new age in the intellectual history of Europe.

Summarized baldly the picture of the Enlightenment is somehow not impressive. Still less is it if we remember that the light of the *siècle des lumières* did not enlighten all the world, or even all the Western world, at once. Only a small educated minority was affected in any country. Round the centres where its rays had been cast, from Edinburgh to Naples, and from Paris to Königsberg, there was a penumbra of shade and beyond that total darkness. In Italy, and even more in Spain, the new ideas only gained a slight and precarious foothold. Did the *Aufklärung* ever really become translated into German? What random shafts penetrated into the Byzantine dreams of Russia and the Slav world, just beginning to emerge from thraldom to Tatar and Turk? For all these limitations on its diffusion there are doubtless social and political causes, as well as explanations appertaining to the intellectual sphere. It is hardly an accident that the ideas of the Enlightenment spread and took root only where there were middle classes in the possession of appreciable economic and political liberties, and where the political and ecclesiastical machinery for the control of thought had broken down or was in the process of breaking down.

The relation between such social conditions and the progress of ideas is, however, a highly speculative subject, and even the existence of such a relationship was hardly suspected at the time. A noble faith in reason closed the eyes of the men of the eighteenth century to the restricted scope and conditional nature of their triumphs. They failed to notice that even in the limited geographical area in which its influence was felt the Enlightenment was accompanied by the first signs of religious revival and by the rise of a sentimental literature in the early writings of the pre-Romantics. Yet for all its innate weaknesses, its limited scope and the rising challenge of a world which did not bow to its conception of reason or acknowledge its universal laws, the Enlightenment began a movement the impact of which on the history of the world it is difficult to overestimate. Its theoretical defects were compensated by its practical strength. The latter does not form the theme of this chapter. If it did, there would be a story to tell of the triumph of empiricism and the scientific spirit, of a great ethical advance and the rise of a humanitarian movement such as the world had never known, of the beginning of a progressive elimination of systems of organised cruelty in which the civilised upholders of law and religion had fought for the perpetuation of the barbarous tortures and superstitions. The *philosophes*, by the second half of the century, could be well content with the promise of positive achievements. They were equally content with their intellectual victory. 'This century', Voltaire wrote to Helvétius in 1760, 'begins to see the triumph of reason.'[1] He meant of the spirit of humanity and scientific empiricism, but he spoke too soon. The Enlightenment had still to win its greatest victories: two centuries later its work was still not completed. But forces it had not guessed at were already rising in its midst to challenge its belief and perhaps to make its very victory in the end look something like defeat.

[1] Voltaire, *Œuvres*, vol. XLI, p. 41.

CHAPTER VI

RELIGION

THE War of the Spanish Succession and the Peace of 1713 showed how negligible in the common political concerns of Europe the Papacy had become. In Sicily and Sardinia territories which the popes had long claimed as their fiefs were disposed of without reference to Rome. The Treaty of Utrecht registered a great increase in the power of Britain, head of the Protestant interest. Every growth in the strength of Prussia meant extra weight on the Protestant side. The extinction of the Spanish Habsburgs was in its political consequences unfavourable to the Holy See. The Most Catholic King, the Most Christian King, the Holy Roman Emperor, even the Most Faithful King of Portugal, decorated with this title only in 1748, seemed to have but cupboard love for their Church. They were all interested that no one should be made pope who might be too independent, or under hostile influence.

In these circumstances, another Gregory VII, or another Innocent III, was hardly to be expected. Clement XI (1700–21) was 'timorous and undecided'.[1] Innocent XIII (1721–4) owed his election partly to his great age, as the princes were determined that the long pontificate of Clement XI should not be repeated by another begun by a young man. Old, ill, and difficult of access, so far from emulating his thirteenth-century namesake, he maintained only a respectable level of diplomatic competence. The pious Orsini, the Dominican Benedict XIII (1724–30), was an austere and exacting ritualist, but administratively gullible and incompetent. Clement XII (1730–40), a Corsini, an experienced curial administrator and good with money, had first to undo much that Benedict XIII had done, whom he as a cardinal had steadily opposed; or that Benedict XIII had permitted to be done, by corrupt favourites like the cardinal Coscia, who paid for his misdeeds until the next conclave with seven years in the Castel Sant' Angelo. Unfortunately Clement XII was blind for most of his reign, and for much of it bedridden. Prospero Lambertini, Benedict XIV (1740–58), lively, witty, wise, and lovable, eminently learned, admired by Protestants, was thought by many to concede too much to the spirit of the times. Clement XIII (1758–69), the Venetian Carlo Rezonnico, according to Gibbon 'neither possessed the wit of his predecessor Lambertini, nor the virtues of his successor Ganganelli'.[2] The hostile Cordara, historian of the Jesuits whom the next Clement was so reluctantly to suppress, thought him lacking in confidence and weakened by indulgence.

---

[1] L. Pastor, *History of the Popes* (E.T.), vol. XXXIII, p. 534.
[2] *Autobiography* (World's Classics edition), p. 159.

These pontiffs were faced with formidable problems. The Enlightenment promoted secular monarchy, but was hostile to monarchy in the Church. The popes were subject to terrible pressures from parties in the curia: the *zelanti* who were sticklers for ecclesiastical rights, the *regalisti* who were the agents of princes, and the men who worked for a reform on lines commonly designated Jansenist. Henry VIII of England could not altogether be forgotten. Thus the popes could hardly be more liberal than curial traditions would permit, or intransigent against princes. All they could do was to avoid compromising the claims of their see, whatever the concessions they had to make in practical politics.

Louis XIV had in 1693 abandoned the Gallican principles of 1682, and so opened the way to an alliance with Rome. A fruit of this alliance was the bull *Unigenitus*, extorted out of a temporising Clement XI, expressed in terms agreed by the king's Jesuit confessor Le Tellier, and promulgated on 8 September 1713. It began the second phase of the Jansenist controversy. *Unigenitus* condemned a hundred and one propositions taken from the book of Pasquier Quesnel (1634–1719), *Le nouveau testament en français avec des réflexions morales*. The edition used was published at Paris in 1699, with a text modified by Noailles, then bishop of Chalons, later archbishop of Paris. It was widely read in France, and well known in England. Clement XI had in 1708 already condemned the book, but this condemnation had not been received in France, because of unacceptable references to the Inquisition.

The errors condemned concerned chiefly grace and nature, free will and moral discipline, and ecclesiastical authority. Quesnel was held to propound errors that had been already condemned in the *Augustinus* of Jansen, bishop of Ypres (1585–1638). These were the doctrines of irresistible efficacious grace, and the irreversible predestination of individuals to heaven and hell, so set forth as to exclude any genuine co-operation of the human will, to undervalue the natural human virtues and the natural reason, and to involve a discipline of penance which was morbidly rigorous, and made the yoke of the gospel heavy and not light. Language in Quesnel's book which appeared to define the Church as consisting of those predestined to salvation, known only to God, might be taken to destroy the visible Church and to make insignificant the authority of its pastors. The notion that Church authority resided first in the whole body, and should be exercised (particularly in excommunication) with general consent recalled the conciliarism of Jean Gerson. As expounded by Gerson's seventeenth-century editor, the Paris syndic Edmond Richer, it was used to assert the claims of the presbyterate to consultation in government, and to a jurisdiction inherent in their orders independently of episcopal authority. The ninety-first proposition to be condemned touched on an old sore spot, in maintaining that fear of unjust excommunication should be no deterrent to duty. It seemed to be aimed in the interest of princes at a useful engine of

Church discipline. When Quesnel's book treated as necessary things the reading of the scriptures in the vernacular by the laity, and their participation with the priest in public worship as a common prayer, present customs seemed impugned, and present authority. Being written in biblical and patristic terms, the book excited the dislike of the Jesuits, great upholders of scholastic divinity, and of an infallibility, a universal ordinary jurisdiction, and an indirect power in the see of Peter.

Although the bull had been carefully drawn up so as to avoid offending Gallican susceptibilities, the *Parlement* of Paris registered it only with reservations. The assembly of the French clergy accepted it only in terms which implied that the bishops were co-judges of the faith with Holy See; which protected the similar Dominican and Thomist doctrines of grace (Augustinian, but allowing a genuine freedom to the will); and which made the condemnation of the ninety-first proposition as little likely as possible to undermine the obedience of subjects to princes. Noailles and eight other bishops affirmed episcopal rights. 'We only ask that no occasion be given to the court of Rome to think that we act merely as simple executants of its decrees.'[1] As between pope and bishops Jansen had been ultramontane. The opponents of *Unigenitus* thought otherwise. In 1718 the theological faculty of Caen dismissed papal infallibility as a 'frivolous claim'.[2]

The death of Louis XIV on 1 September 1715 promised policies less rigid. A significant nomination was that of Jacques Bénigne Bossuet, the 'little Bossuet', nephew of the great bishop of Meaux, as bishop of Troyes. Jesuit influence for years had kept him from the episcopate. When Clement XI tried to hold up his consecration, and that of several others, in order to force compliance with the bull, the regent under the influence of Jansenist advisers made threats which smacked of schism. Above all, in March 1717 the bishops of Senez, Montpellier, Boulogne, and Mirepoix published in the Sorbonne their appeal against *Unigenitus* to a general council. Noailles next year added his protest. The French clergy were thus divided into 'appelants' and 'constitutionaries'. The appelants had the support of the *parlements*, and were strong in the theological faculties. The constitutionaries had generally the court behind them, and most of the bishops. Especially after Clement XI in 1718 had denounced the appelants in *Monita pastoralia*, William Wake, archbishop of Canterbury, thought he saw a chance to detach the French Church, or a substantial part of it, from the Roman obedience. His correspondence chiefly with L. E. Du Pin, a great 'Jansenist' scholar, came to nothing, because of the timidity of the archbishop of Paris and the lukewarmness of the court; not to speak of Wake's dislike of Du Pin's observations in his *Commonitorium* on the Thirty-nine Articles. The regent, failing in conciliation, forbade appeals

[1] *Dictionnaire de Théologie catholique*, vol. xv (part ii, 1950), col. 2067.
[2] L. Pastor, *History of the Popes* (E.T.), vol. xxxiii, pp. 300–1.

by a declaration of August 1720, which was registered only in a *lit de justice*. In 1725, for all that Benedict XIII was a Dominican, the Roman council designated *Unigenitus* as a rule of faith, in a phrase which was declared by the dissident party to have been dishonestly interpolated by the secretary to the council at the behest of the Jesuits. In 1726 Louis XV suddenly replaced as chief minister the duc de Bourbon, friendly to the appelants, by Fleury, bishop of Fréjus, hostile to all nonconformity. Next year in a national council held at Embrun, presided over by the local archbishop (Benedict XIV's great friend Tencin), the one appelant bishop who was not an aristocrat, Soanen bishop of Senez, was reduced to lay communion, and exiled to the remote and windswept abbey of Chaise-Dieu, where he died of old age in 1740. This council condemned also the vindication of Anglican orders which had been composed with Wake's aid, as part of his effort for an Anglo-French reunion, by Le Courayer, of the abbey of St Geneviève in Paris. In 1728 Noailles submitted. He died in May 1729. By the end of 1729 only three appelant bishops remained. As they died they were replaced by ardent constitutionaries.

As the French episcopate became quickly and overwhelmingly constitutionary, and as Fleury purged the religious orders and theological faculties, the clerical opposition to *Unigenitus* appeared more as a rebellion of disobedient clerics against their bishops, *Richériste* rather than in a strict sense Jansenist, fortified by works of learning which developed in a presbyterian direction Richer's maxim that the episcopate is no more than a certain eminence or dignity, but not an order different from the priesthood. Their ideas were spread by the *Nouvelles Ecclésiastiques*, which authority failed to suppress. Miracles were claimed, chiefly at the tomb of the deacon Pâris, which if true in John Wesley's opinion 'struck at the root of the whole papal authority as wrought in direct opposition to the famous bull *Unigenitus*'.[1] The miracles of Pâris were condemned by Vintimille, archbishop of Paris, with the help of a report prepared by a priest who later became a functionary of the *Parlement*, a Gallican but constitutionary. The neurotic excesses of the convulsionaries[2] discredited and divided the party.

The last great conflict was begun when Christophe de Beaumont, archbishop of Paris (1746–81), adopting a device which Noailles had used against the Jesuits, ordained that clerics should exact from dying persons a *billet de confession*, so making recourse to a constitutionary priest a condition of the last sacraments. This placed the clergy between two fires. They were denounced by their bishops if they did not comply, and coerced with imprisonment, exile, and loss of goods by the *parlements* if they did.

Seeing that the French bishops were linked closely with the French court, obedience to whose policies was a condition of preferment, and

---

[1] *Letters of John Wesley*, vol. IV (1931), p. 348.
[2] For some particulars of the convulsionaries see E. Larisse, *Histoire de France* (1909), vol. VIII, part 2, pp. 115–16.

that the nominations of Louis XIV's successors were uniformly of aristocratic persons, it was only to be expected that opposition in the lower clergy should find support in the secular opposition to the court in the *parlements*. Many of the *avocats* had been educated by the Oratory, educational rivals of the Jesuits, and suspect of Jansenism. They shared that dislike of an aristocratic prelacy which in the discontented clergy showed itself in *Richériste* notions of Church government. On numerous occasions, as against the bishops, the *parlementaires* of Paris asserted the duty of the Crown as *évêque du dehors* with their advice so to regulate the clerical exercise of spiritual functions as to safeguard public peace and Gallican liberties. In France, no less than elsewhere, the will of the prince was decisive. Benedict XIV was anxious to stop the strife. In 1756, in the brief *Ex omnibus*, in terms suggested by the French court and approved by Jansenisers in the curia, he refrained from describing *Unigenitus* expressly as a rule of faith, and withheld approval from the refusal of sacraments as that had been used of late. Although the *Parlement* of Paris disliked this brief, it was to the advantage of their side. It robbed *Unigenitus* of its effectiveness.

This emasculating of *Unigenitus* was the more remarkable because the court of France was more in harmony with Rome than were most others. *Unigenitus* had not merely condemned a particular doctrine of grace but a whole programme of reform, which was in its tendencies anti-curial, and in its morality puritanical; and which was founded in an appeal to scripture and the ancient fathers. This appeal was an historical one to antiquity as opposed to tradition and present usage. Some Jesuit writers, in the spirit of Richard Simon the Oratorian (1638–1712), made the uncertainty of historical evidence a ground for resting everything on Church tradition. In a modernistic fashion they opposed truths of faith to truths of fact. 'The vast volumes and ostentatious quotations of rash reformers', wrote the Jesuit Berruyer in a book condemned at Rome, 'will never avail against the force of prescription. It is in the teaching of the Roman Church, and in its *present teaching*...that the religion of Christ must be found.'[1] On the other hand the predestinarianism of the Jansenists was a religious counterpart to the secular fatalism of such as Holbach. Their denigration of the natural reason, which went with their unfashionable denial of natural religion, would have consisted equally well with the glorification of the passions which was the fashion in Encyclopaedist circles, where no religion was professed but a natural or a 'civil' one. The Jansenist idea of the will as passive before irresistible grace corresponded with the passivity of the mind in the epistemology of the sensationalist philosophers. It fell therefore to Jesuits like Bergier and other orthodox men to defend reason and moral freedom against both religious and secular attack. Jansenists

[1] *Histoire du people de Dieu*, cited in R. R. Palmer, *Catholics and Unbelievers in eighteenth-century France* (1929), pp. 70–1.

and *philosophes* agreed in contempt for the Middle Ages. The 'rash reformers' also by their upholding the rights of princes fitted in well with the Erastian bent of the Enlightenment.

The appeal to antiquity was part of a whole movement of scholarship, in which most of the greatest works were in no sense Jansenist. From the days of the great Mabillon (1632–1707), the Benedictines of the Congregation of St Maur had made their house and great library at St Germain-des-près a Mecca for scholars. Edward Gibbon recalled in his Autobiography that at Magdalen College Oxford the library shelves 'groaned under the weight of the Benedictine folios, of the editions of the Fathers, and of the collections of the Middle Ages, which have issued from the single abbey of St Germain des Prez at Paris'. In Paris also at the Oratory, and at St Geneviève, were learned industrious men. Among the Paris Jesuits Hardouin maintained a meticulous documentary criticism. The Maurist Montfaucon (1655–1741) in his Greek palaeography provided New Testament scholars with a fundamental tool. There was an interchange of scholarship which transcended the barrier of Papist and Protestant. Richard Bentley, J. J. Wettstein, Theodore Küster and other Protestant scholars found here a friendly helpfulness. The Maurists Martène and Durand, the one an upholder and the other an opponent of *Unigenitus*, together made foraging journeys for ancient liturgical material. Richard Bentley sent material from English sources to the liturgist Pierre Le Brun of the Oratory. The historical works of the Jansenist L. E. Du Pin (1657–1719), and the Gallican Claude Fleury (1640–1719) were soon influential amongst the scholars of Britain and the Continent.

These researches strongly suggested simplification in breviary and missal. Cardinal Tomassi (1649–1713), whom Benedict XIV would gladly have canonised, like the great Muratori (1672–1750), Gibbon's 'guide and master in the history of Italy' (whom Benedict XIV protected), a man of views anything but ultramontane, produced a breviary for private use entirely out of scripture, even putting *pater noster* for the collects.[1] Benedict XIV himself, in the spirit of Erasmus or Quignon, expressed in 1743 a wish for a drastic reform of the breviary in terms of scripture and the ancient fathers, because historical criticism had made so many things incredible that earlier generations had been able to take as undoubted. French bishops in particular (but not they alone) multiplied diocesan service books, 'sometimes excellent in their sober scholarship, but often absurd in their pseudo-classic Latinity'.[2] In the missal of Bossuet of Troyes there was a drastic removal of medieval ceremonies. Vintimille, who was no Jansenist, employed on his Paris breviary (1738) Mésenguy, author of a catechism condemned at Rome, and for the hymns Charles

[1] J. Wickham Legg, *The Reformed Breviary of Cardinal Tomassi* (1904).
[2] A. Fortescue, *The Mass* (ed. 1937), p. 210; in general, *Dictionnaire d'Archéologie chrétienne et de la Liturgie*, vol. IX, part II (1930), H. Leclercq, 'Liturgies Néo-Gallicanes'.

Coffin, who in 1749 was denied the last sacraments as an obstinate refuser of *Unigenitus*. Individual priests like Jubé of Asnières had ceremonies all their own, and an audible canon. By 1791, of the 130 French dioceses, eighty had given up the Roman liturgy for rites and ceremonies of local authority. These sometimes embodied principles of public worship which *Unigenitus* appeared to deprecate. They might be taken as expressing a certain diocesan independence towards Rome on the part of bishops who though driven into a closer alliance with the Papacy by their troubles with Jansenists were still not ultramontane. They kept a Gallicanism which Benedict XIV sought to combat as a source of weakness in the church by his *De Synodo Diocesana* (1748, 1755). In this book he turned a device of government which appelants favoured as a means of decentralised ecclesiastical aristocracy into a support for an autocratic rule centralised at Rome.

Episcopal independence towards the Papacy and the rights of Christian princes in their local churches were two ancient themes of contention closely connected in the eighteenth century as they had been in the fourteenth. The Papacy being weak, the princes had no need of the Enlightenment in their traditional game of twisting the pope's tail, but they found it useful. In small but significant ways secular influences prevailed. The canonisation of Bellarmine had to be indefinitely postponed. Benedict XIV had to connive at the *de facto* suppression in France of the feast of St Gregory VII the office for which used language which was disagreeably Hildebrandine. Moreover, the cause of the princes was served by writings of great ability, argued in terms not obviously of the new philosophy but for the most part traditionally ecclesiastical. In 1722 there was published at the Hague, and quickly available in English, the treatise in which Paolo Sarpi (1552–1623) had upheld for the republic of Venice *the Rights of Princes* against unjust papal excommunication and interdict. Zeegers van Espen (1646–1728), the great canonist of Louvain, professor at the college of Adrian VI, father of what was sometimes called the 'new' canon law, defended the claim of the rebellious chapter of Utrecht that in that country the right of choice of a bishop devolved to the chapter, and denied the right of the Papacy (asserted there by the Jesuits) to abolish bishoprics at will. In his *Jus Universum Ecclesiasticum* he denied that the pope was universal ordinary, criticised present claims as resting on the dubious foundations of the forged decretals, and allowed only a certain primacy of authority. He thought it proper that a royal *placet* should give authority for the execution of Church laws. He upheld the right of the clergy to appeal to the secular ruler against tyrannous acts by their ecclesiastical superiors. This notion applied to Van Espen himself, until a change of government in the Austrian Netherlands brought in a regent who strongly upheld *Unigenitus*, so that in 1727 he fled to Holland, where he died the next year.

More specifically addressed to the laity was the work of a Neapolitan lawyer, Pietro Giannone (1676–1748), *The Civil History of the Kingdom of Naples* (1723). This book won the admiration of Muratori. It was counted by Gibbon as one that had 'remotely contributed to form the historian of the Roman Empire'.[1] A half-pay captain, J. Ogilvie, translated it into English in 1729–31 (the first translation of it into another language), as being useful against the Papacy for showing 'how that Monster of a Spiritual Monarchy, an *Imperium in Imperio*, was conceiv'd, brought forth, and nourish'd till it came to full maturity'.[2] Giannone wrote as a layman against clerical power and as a Neapolitan patriot resenting the interference of a foreign ecclesiastical prince. In Naples medieval clericalism flourished exceedingly, fortified by that claim to a papal suzerainty which had been so pointedly ignored in the peace of 1713. Giannone was but the most important of a group of Neapolitan anti-curialists who, quite apart from the general intellectual movement, were sufficiently provoked by an excess in their own country of clerical persons, wealth, and privilege. They stand fully in the long Italian tradition of anti-papal and anti-clerical polemics. It was in the same tradition that Giannone addressed his book to the Emperor, but unfortunate for him because by identifying him with the Austrian party in Naples it lost him the protection of the Bourbons.

As a lawyer Giannone was primarily concerned that the two authorities, ecclesiastical and secular, should each stick to its own sphere. His criticism of Marsiglio of Padua and John of Paris that they gave too much to the secular power, attributing to it a jurisdiction rightly belonging to the Church; his comment that it was against common sense to do as they did in England, give sovereignty over the Church to a king or queen; and his generally respectful language about the Holy See have led to the suggestion that he was orthodox, and a clerical. In fact, drawing upon current scholarship (so far as to be accused of plagiarism), upon authorities fashionable in reforming circles, he used the appeal to antiquity in the interest of princes and laymen. He looked back to the days before the great medieval prelates, when only princes exercised a coercive *jurisdictio*, but never ecclesiastics. He explained the authority of the Roman see wholly in terms of historical development. For him as a Neapolitan the most monstrous overstepping of due limits was the papal suzerainty over Naples, a right of investiture gained by vigilance and cunning. In fact, his cry that ecclesiastics should keep to spiritual matters had been for centuries the cry of anti-clericals of all nations, not least the Italians. Thus he exalted the secular ruler, and would have him closely superintend ecclesiastical laws. In his *Profession of Faith*, published at Vienna in 1731, he pretended with a savage irony to claim world dominion for the Roman bishop. In the *Triregno*, published only after his death, he praised the

[1] *Autobiography* (World's Classics edition), p. 76.   [2] E.T. by J. Ogilvie (1729), preface.

evangelical simplicity of early days, before the superintendence exercised by a simple leader of a presbytery had become the dominance of a bishop; before an admixture of heathen philosophy and pagan observances had turned the Christian religion into a heathen one; and before the Roman pontiff by his canon law had made it an engine of priestcraft. He died a prisoner in the citadel of Turin. According to the protonotary apostolic of that place, his death was edifying. With tears he repented his attacks on Church and clergy.

The starting point of Nicholas von Hontheim (1701–90), auxiliary bishop of Trêves, was different. His book, *De statu ecclesiae et legitima potestae Romani pontificis* by Justinus Febronius (1763), was, according to its title, *composed with a view to the reunion of dissenting Christians*. For it he expected to be denounced as another Sarpi, de Dominis, or Richer. Distinctly in the style of the Council of Basle he addressed himself to princes, bishops, and doctors of universities. He believed that the Roman primacy was of divine institution, and the centre of unity, but that it was not the primacy that had driven Protestants out, only its abuse. To bring them back, the primacy must therefore be restricted within the limits of primitive practice; a primacy merely, not a domination. This meant (an old, old story) restoring to bishops and princes rights which had been usurped by popes. Like Van Espen, under whose influence he had come at Louvain; with a view of the relative authority of scripture and tradition more Anglican than Tridentine; and sharing with Luther an intense dislike of scholasticism, he recognised in the Papacy only a primacy of honour. For him there was no infallibility but a limited one in the whole body of the Church. The conciliar doctrine of the council above the pope was thus reinforced by Hontheim, who frequently cited Gerson, and preferred Aeneas Sylvius to Pius II. Even more than the rights of bishops he asserted those of princes in the external ordering of their local churches. Bellarmine's distinction of indirect from direct power he scorned as mere word play. He went so far as to justify a temporary withdrawal by a catholic prince of obedience from the pope, in matters of human and not of divine law, where the grievance was grave and universal, and where other means had failed of redress. Such a withdrawal was not from the see, but only from its occupant. This was indeed not an uncommon doctrine, and certainly provided justification for procedures not unusual. There was hardly any device which princes had used to vex popes which he did not justify, including English *praemunire*. Vehemently hating the Roman curia, he appealed for a union of princes to put down curial pretensions. It is not surprising that within a year this book was on the Index. Its influence spread rapidly over Europe.

Febronius and Giannone did not stand alone. Febronius completed the work of a school of reforming divines long influential in Germany. The canon law of Febronius suited the anti-clerical, anti-Jesuit policies of the Austrian minister Kaunitz. In Naples Giannone had influential disciples. Three years after Clement XII had, under Spanish pressure, conceded to the Bourbon Charles III the investiture of Naples, Benedict XIV agreed to a concordat whose terms seemed inspired by Giannone's principles, put into practice by Tanucci, who admired him. There was even granted a supreme court of ecclesiastical appeal, half clerical, half lay. This agreement did not bring peace, so that Tanucci, himself quite a devout person, admired by St Alphonsus Liguori, continued fighting the curia. In other places similar agreements were made, where Giannone's influence cannot have been great, and before 'Febronius' had written. To Sardinia in 1727 Benedict XIII had made concessions so great that Clement XII had in 1731 revoked them, only for Benedict XIV ten years later to concede even more, including the title to the king of Vicar of the Holy See, and the nomination to all ecclesiastical benefices. In 1740 the king of Portugal received the patronage of all sees and abbeys. In 1737 and 1753 Spanish concordats gave great powers to the Spanish king, who aimed at as complete a control of the Church in the peninsula as he had always had in the colonies. By the later agreement, practically all the important patronage formerly enjoyed by Rome passed to the Crown.

Febronius wrote, not like Giannone as a patriot and a nationalist, but in the universal terms of a churchman, advocating a general Gallicanism. Joseph II was said to have been his best pupil. That prince certainly preferred Febronian clergymen to ultramontane, but he was more subject to secular influences than ecclesiastical, and cared less for the rights of bishops than did the auxiliary of Trêves, who after experience of the Emperor was moved in 1778, and after some vacillation again in 1788, to recant his Febronianism. He thus made occasion for that indefatigable polemist for the Roman see, the Jesuit Zaccaria, to make in 1779 a collection of recantations by learned catholics; precedents for this, the most pleasing of all, including Richer, Du Pin, Noailles, Giannone, Montesquieu, and Helvétius. He was not able to include Voltaire's. The recantation of De Dominis was relegated to an appendix, as insincere and followed by relapse. Hontheim was less happy about his recantations than the Jesuit. Owing in part to Jansenising influences at Rome Zaccaria was not able to publish the book till 1791.

Van Espen, Giannone, Febronius, and others like them, exaggerated the power, influence, cleverness, and riches of the Jesuits. As European politics had become secularised, the political importance formerly enjoyed by the Jesuits as the court confessors of Europe had sensibly diminished since the middle of the seventeenth century. They were not able to prevent their royal penitents from pursuing policies which shocked the popes more than the activities of Protestants. *Unigenitus* was counted against them as in France a focus of disorder, even in 1757 of attempted regicide. There was a strong party in Rome itself, without which the campaign against them might not have ended in their destruction. Above all, against the enmity of the European princes, even without their countenance, they could not prevail.

Already, before *Unigenitus*, they had had a setback. In 1704 Clement XI had hoped to end a long controversy by condemning the policy which the Jesuits had followed in their Chinese mission. In 1715 he renewed this condemnation. In 1742 Benedict XIV definitively confirmed it. In China the Jesuits had permitted the use by their converts of certain Chinese terms for the Godhead, some of which by these rulings were disallowed. They had permitted also the use of the traditional ceremonies, of venera-tion of ancestors and of Confucius (an important part of Chinese civilisa-tion). These also the Papacy prohibited. This prohibition Benedict XIV justified as being 'by virtue of the first of the ten commandments', but the Chinese Emperor (who liked the Jesuits) had solemnly affirmed that the ceremonies were merely civic. The two legacies *a latere* of the cardinals Tournon and Mezzabarba only angered the Emperor. Right or wrong (Leibniz thought wrong), the papal policy meant the ruin of the Jesuit effort to convert the governing class of the Chinese empire. Persecution quickly reduced the Chinese Christians to a remnant of the poor and illiterate. Apart from the delicacy of the theological problem of the Chinese rites, the campaign against them was undoubtedly influenced by the rivalry of the secular clergy and other orders (especially Dominicans and Franciscans), by Jansenists who denounced the rites as idolatrous, and by the dislike of the Portuguese for independent religious activity touching upon their ecclesiastical *padronado*. The Jesuits' similar con-cessions to their Malabar converts were similarly condemned.

Nor were the Jesuits worldly wise enough to avoid antagonising their most deadly foe Carvalho, better known by his later title of Pombal (1689–1782), minister of the new king of Portugal, Joseph I (1750–76). The boundary treaty of 1750 between Spain and Portugal, whereby a large tract of Paraguay passed from Spanish to Portuguese rule, involved the Jesuits because they had there their most celebrated mission. They gathered their native converts into villages, the 'reductions' of Paraguay, where, shielded by priestly oversight from contact with colonists, they made the commodities by whose sale the work was financed. When the Jesuits resisted the forcible transplantation of entire villages the worst construc-tion was put on their actions. A native revolt was put down to their intrigues. Their great mission preacher, the Italian Malagrida (1689–1761), provocatively ascribed the Lisbon earthquake to divine disapproval of the new government of Portugal. All these iniquities Pombal explained in a *Brief Relation* (1758), quickly translated into other languages and spread through Europe, which presented the Jesuits as masters of a mighty republic, exploiting the native Indians as slaves, and aiming at world dominion. The reductions of Paraguay could easily be made repugnant to the men of the Enlightenment and the 'new' canon law, both as being a State within a State and as investing in priestly persons secular and even military authority. Moreover, they controlled a large labour supply which others coveted. Although the *Brief Relation* was burnt by the hangmen of Spain, it was well-tuned propaganda. Spanish disapproval only confirmed Pombal in the belief that the Jesuits intrigued in Spain against his colonial policy. A brief was secured from Benedict XIV in 1758 investing powers of visitation and reform of the Portuguese Jesuits in Pombal's relative Saldanda, patriarch of Lisbon, who anyhow as a metropolitan disliked Jesuit independence of ordinary jurisdiction, and favoured the policy of transferring the pastoral care of the natives from religious to seculars. By these means the Jesuits' 'illegal' commerce was forbidden. In a land where only eight years before they had controlled the Government they were almost in the twinkling of an eye stripped of their privileges.

On 3 September 1758 what looked like an attempt to assassinate Joseph I enabled Pombal to implicate in treason not only hostile nobles but Malagrida and other Jesuits, who had at least been politically indiscreet. Pombal demanded of Rome that these clerics equally with the lay suspects should be tried by a new State court of conscience, and not by a Church court. He further required that for the future any clerics suspect of treason should be amenable to this new court. Clement XII, disliking so remarkable an invasion of clerical immunity, in *Exponi nobis* of August 1759 tried a compromise by agreeing for the present, but not for the future.

By a decree of 3 September 1759, a day advisedly chosen, the Jesuits were expelled from Portugal. In June 1760 the nuncio Accaiuoli was put in an impossible position and expelled. For ten years there was a withdrawal of Portuguese obedience from the pope, 'the usual method', as the Portuguese canonist Figureido explained, 'by which the sovereign Majesty of Catholic princes (without offence to religion or the Primacy of Peter) has been accustomed to resent the injuries and slights of the Roman court'.[1] The Portuguese Government's *Exposition of Facts and Motives which decided its Conduct*, from Pombal's pen, in tart and angry language asserted the rights of princes, which had in particular been outraged by the nuncio's idea that Malagrida and his clerical accomplices should be tried by a special legatine commission. 'Was it imagined...there existed in this Kingdom neither monarchy, nor a monarch independent of a superior in temporal affairs...no ministers, no tribunals of justice?'[2] In 1761 Malagrida was tried by the Portuguese Inquisition, now fully under State control, and barbarously executed. The bishop of Coimbra in 1770

[1] A. P. Figuereido, *Tentativa Theologica, Episcopal Rights and Ultramontane Usurpations* (ed. E. H. Landon with introd. by J. M. Neale, 1847), p. 25.
[2] Conde de Carnota (John Smith), *The Marquis of Pombal* (1871), pp. 131–61.

was imprisoned for denouncing 'Febronius' and other writings. In 1766 and 1769 the right of the Portuguese metropolitan to confirm and consecrate bishops named by the king without reference to the pope was defended by Figuereido with arguments which, like those of Febronius, drew on the conciliarists. In 1767 there was published at Lisbon by royal authority, perhaps in part written by Pombal, Seabra de Silva's *Chronological Deduction*. This was a comprehensive indictment of the Jesuits, and quite a compendium of eighteenth-century anti-papalism, with Giannonistic views of Church history. It was propaganda aimed at the Jesuits' total destruction. When in 1767 Clement XIII attempted a reconciliation with Portugal, he was told he could not have it except he wholly suppressed the Jesuits. On this all the Bourbon courts were now agreed.

The sensational proceedings of the Portuguese Government encouraged the Jesuits' enemies everywhere, especially in France. These enemies were the more dangerous because the Jesuits did not always show firmness before them. In 1757 the attempt of Damien upon Louis XV aroused such a fury of anti-Jesuitical rage amongst the *parlementaires* that the Paris Jesuits renounced tyrannicide and indirect power, and accepted the Gallican articles. The *Parlement* of Paris moreover set themselves up as guardians of Christian truth. They attacked first the modernism of the Abbé Prades, condemned as well by the Jesuits, and then the *Histoire du Peuple de Dieu* of the Jesuits Hardouin and Berruyer, which was used as showing that the Jesuits set themselves above even the authority of the church. Their final misfortune came from the too great financial initiative of Lavalette, superior of their mission in Martinique. Unable to recover debts he owed, his creditors sought to recover from the French Jesuits, who unwisely appealed to lawyers in the *Parlement*, the secular rallying point of Jansenist opposition. There in 1761, on the motion of the Abbé Choiseul, demand was made for their constitution to be submitted for inspection. This resulted in the judgment that they had no legal existence in France but were at best only tolerated, and that, as it stood, their constitution was inconsistent with the maxims of the realm, or indeed of any well-ordered polity. The majority of the French bishops publicly testified their admiration for the Jesuits, but 'at the price of admissions and declarations which impaired the dignity of the Holy See'.[1] For all the acceptance by the French Jesuits of the Gallican principles, the one concession could not be got from Ricci, the General of the Society in Rome, by which they might in France have been saved, namely that the general's authority might in that country be exercised by a vicar-general there resident, the only way in which the objection could be met that a powerful body of clerics was tied to an unquestioning obedience to an authority outside the realm. The general was not Jesuitical enough to dissemble with a policy

[1] L. Pastor, *History of the Popes* (E.T.), vol. xxxvi, p. 419.

of *reculer pour mieux sauter*. Finally by a royal decree read in the *Parlement* on 1 December 1764 the Jesuit society in France was suppressed. The *Apostolici pascendi* of 7 January 1765 in which Clement XIII declared the constitution of the Society excellent did not prevent their being suppressed in Spain and Naples in 1767, and in Parma in 1768, and their final dissolution in 1773 by the unfortunate Clement XIV, the unwilling victim of Bourbon bullying.

The suppression of the Jesuits was more a triumph of statecraft than of religion. The religious ideas of their enemies took no root, whereas for example such popular devotion as that to the Sacred Heart, which they had encouraged and their critics condemned, became well established. The new missionary colleges at Rome, and the new religious orders, such as the Christian Brothers (1680), the Passionists (1727), the Redemptorists (1732), were loyal to the Papacy. On the other hand the suppression of the Jesuits was a severe blow to foreign missions. Perhaps also, by their intellectual bent, as ready to argue with the philosophic enemy on some common ground, they were in France at least 'the one group which might have found some means of reconciling traditional authority with eighteenth-century belief'.[1] No doubt they paid now for their earlier triumphs, which they had hardly used gently. They fell as standing for papal authority and clerical intervention in politics. Their enemies were not generally irreligious men, bent on making the world atheist or encyclopaedistic, but Christian persons who made too much perhaps of the authority of the Christian prince in spiritual matters. They did this in a not unnatural reaction against those (of whom Benedict XIV did not appear to be one) who treated as necessary to the faith clerical immunities and privileges which were more consistent with medieval governance than with the modern State.

'The only thing that makes Protestantism considerable in Christendom', remarked the fashionable high-church preacher Dr Robert South, 'is the Church of England.'[2] Archbishops of Canterbury seemed to be more heeded by continental Protestants than the popes were by the princes of their own obedience. Like the popes, the archbishops of Canterbury, *alterius orbis papae*, were good men and friends of learning. In William Wake (1657–1737) the see of Canterbury was adorned from 1716 to 1737 by an ecclesiastical statesman of European vision, who was in the opinion of an observer from Geneva 'a prelate worthy of apostolic times'.[3] For all that the Church of England retained an antiquated organisation, and a medieval system of courts, and in spite of the gulf between rich pluralists and poor curates, Wake had no doubt that this Church was the best constituted in the world. As he put it in the Introduction of his *Genuine*

[1] R. R. Palmer, *Catholics and Unbelievers in eighteenth-century France*, p. 129.
[2] Cited by H. H. Henson, *The Church of England* (1939), p. 128.
[3] *Correspondance de Jacques Serces* (ed. F. Gardy, 1952), vol. I, p. 2.

Epistles of Apostolical Fathers (1693), the ways of the Primitive Church were 'so exactly agreeable to the present doctrine and discipline of the Church of England as by law established, that no one who allows the one can reasonably make any exceptions against the other'. He was perfectly sure of his position as a catholic bishop. He had a pontifical sense of the dignity of his primatial see. 'Let the Divine Right of...Episcopacy be preserved', he had written in 1703 (before he became a bishop), 'which our Fathers have taken care with so much Zeal and Piety to support.'[1] On the other hand he disliked clerical assemblies and the ordinary run of high churchmen, vigorously detested popery, and forcefully upheld the rights in the Church of the Christian prince. He wholeheartedly accepted the common assumption that the Church of England shared with foreign Protestants the 'same religion'. He was ready (as were most Englishmen) to come to their aid when persecution fell on them as it did on the Calvinists of France. He strove for unity among and with them, as strengthening the common cause against Rome.

John Potter his successor (1737–47) was no less satisfied that the Church of England since the Reformation, like 'other ancient churches before it' had 'at once maintained their own inherent rights and the just prerogative of the civil magistrate'.[2] Thomas Herring, who was translated from York to Canterbury after Potter's death; munificent, conscientious, courtly, eloquent, and latitudinarian; a loyal Whig (most useful in Yorkshire at the '45); and thought by some to be deistically inclined, was in Horace Walpole's opinion, 'a harmless good man, inclined to much moderation, and of little zeal for the tinsel of religion'.[3] More completely of the eighteenth century than his two predecessors at Canterbury, he paid less attention than they did to ecclesiastical polity. After a year's primacy of Matthew Hutton (1757–8), who was also translated from York, Thomas Secker, formerly of Oxford, reigned at Canterbury till 1768. He suffered great difficulties with the accession of George III, whose advisers ostentatiously omitted to consult him 'about the disposal of anything or the character of any person'.[4]

Even more than the episcopates of France, Spain, and Portugal, that of England was closely bound to the secular government by royal nominations and by translations from poorer to richer sees as rewards for good conduct. As a rule government could count on a score of votes in the Lords, where the bishops 'all clung together to advance any proposition that has a court air'.[5] On the other hand, their compliance had limits. That learned man, Walpole's 'Wolsey', 'Pope Gibson', bishop of London, quarrelled with him when legislation about mortmain and Quakers' tithe

[1] W. Wake, *State of the Church and Clergy of England* (1703), p. 118.
[2] J. Potter, *A Discourse of Church Government* (1707, ed. 1838), p. v.
[3] H. Walpole, *Memoirs of George II* (1846), vol. I, p. 148.
[4] N. Sykes, *Church and State in England in the eighteenth century* (1934), p. 47.
[5] *Egmont Diary* (Hist. MSS. Com. 1920), vol. I, p. 153.

was pressed, in a spirit of Whig anti-clericalism, which was detrimental to the Church. The silencing of the convocations in 1717 prevented the Church of England from being distracted by such chronic conflict between the bishops and the second order as was for decades the bane of Church life in France; and threatened to break out in England also. In 1741 Walpole agreed to the convocation's sitting to do business, and the lower house took the opportunity to flout the authority of the upper. Wake himself had noted the virtual presbyterianism of the rebellious party in the reign of Anne, and its likeness to the positions Richer had taken out of Gerson.

In Great Britain the Hanover succession had been accepted as a security against popery. It had happened in time to save the Protestant Dissenters of England from destructive legislation aimed against them by the hotter Tories in the Schism and Occasional Conformity Acts. The Dissenters were not numerous, but they were not negligible. They appear to have declined somewhat in the first years of the regime, perhaps as Archbishop Wake suggested, precisely because they were tolerated, perhaps because the theological Calvinism for which historically they stood seemed extinct, and because their fervour was weakened by rationalism. They counted out of all proportion to their numbers in the technological and scientific developments of the time. As the English universities were Church preserves, the Dissenters developed in their academies, at Northampton, Warrington, Hackney and other places, curricula more diversified than could be got at Oxford and Cambridge, including modern history, languages and the natural sciences, more suited perhaps to the modern world than the traditional grammar education. Furnished with men of distinguished calibre, like the delightful and eclectic Philip Doddridge, the earnest Isaac Watts, the amateur statistician Richard Price, and the polymath Joseph Priestley, they perhaps depended too much on personalities. They suffered too from being uncertain whether to be seminaries for ministers or academies for laymen. From them came some of the most important Anglicans of the age—Joseph Butler, bishop of Durham, Secker, archbishop of Canterbury, Samuel Wesley senior, and T. R. Malthus. The Dissenters made another important contribution to English religion in their vernacular hymns, precedents for those of the Methodists.

Although the English Dissenters were not vexed by such persecutions as harassed the Protestants of France, the Palatinate, Hungary and Salzburg, they were subject to irritating disabilities and harassments. In 1727 the ministers of the Presbyterian, Independent, and Baptist congregations in and around London formed themselves into the 'General Body of Protestant Dissenting Ministers of the Three Denominations'. Five years later came the parallel lay organisation, the 'Protestant dissenters' Deputies', consisting of two members chosen annually from each congregation of the three denominations, originally within ten, later twelve, miles of London. With a very circumspect wisdom the deputies defended their aggrieved brethren all over the country against invasions, great and small, of their civil rights. The Dissenters naturally hoped that a Whig government might repeal the Test and Corporation Acts of Charles II, but the most they got was the repeal in 1718 (now opposed by Archbishop Wake) of the Occasional Conformity and Schism Acts; the *regium donum* from 1723 of a royal bounty for ministers' widows; the Act for quieting corporations of 1718; and from 1727 the almost annual Indemnity Acts. The Government's fear of antagonising the Church interest meant that Sir Robert Walpole could only tell Dr Chandler in 1739 that the time for repealing the religious tests would be never. The deputies won their most signal triumph in the sheriff of London's case, provoked by the practice of the City corporation of naming as sheriffs rich Dissenters who refused to qualify by an occasional conformity, and then fining them handsomely for refusing office. In 1767, on appeal to the Lords, the Dissenters who refused to pay were upheld.

In England, as on the Continent, the relations of Church and State reflected a prevailing Erastianism. In 1734 Lord Hardwicke as Lord Chancellor laid down in *Middleton* v. *Croft* an important judgment that canon law applied to laymen only as ratified by parliament, with arguments about the place of the clergy in the State that squared fully with those that Archbishop Wake had used as a younger man against Francis Atterbury's claims for convocation, in which a convocation appeared, not at all as a law-making body sharing in sovereignty, but 'truly as no more than an Ecclesiastical Council... to Advise, and Assist the King in matters pertaining to the Church'.[1] Hardwicke's marriage act of 1753, for all that it made the English clergy monopolists of marriage (and excluded the dissenting ministers), was an invasion by the secular power of ground traditionally ecclesiastical, yet the bishops took it with what Horace Walpole regarded as a laudable equanimity.

An organised dissent, legally tolerated, made necessary some change in the theory of the Establishment from Tudor principles. On behalf of the non-jurors, those frequently learned men who had refused allegiance to William of Orange in 1689 and abjuration of the Stuart pretenders in 1702, Charles Leslie (1650–1722), an eminent enemy of Erastianism, Deism, and Latitudinarianism, had in his *Case of the Regale and the Pontificate* (1700) made fun of the existing Establishment as making the gentry deists and the common people Muggletonians. He strongly asserted the spiritual independence of the Church. At the opposite extreme Benjamin Hoadley (1676–1761), at this time bishop of Bangor, followed up his *Preservative against the Principles and Practices of the Non-jurors* (1716) with a discourse in 1717 that so emphatically asserted that Christ's kingdom was not of this world as to render unnecessary the visible Church, priesthood, creeds,

---

[1] Philip Yorke, *Life of Lord Chancellor Hardwicke*, vol. I (1913), pp. 121–3; W. Wake, *The Authority of Christian Princes over their Ecclesiastical Synods asserted* (1697), pp. 284–5.

and sacraments, and utterly to dissipate the apostolic authority of bishops. These opinions so provoked the lower clergy that the convocations of 1717 were suspended because of their anti-Bangorian clamour. A middle view of the Establishment, more generally acceptable, was given by William Warburton, bishop of Gloucester (1710–79), in his *Alliance of Church and State* (1736). This appealed to the political arguments of John Locke, rather than to the high doctrine of the Church to be found in Richard Hooker. Warburton neither reduced the visible Church to invisibility nor condemned the State connection, but held Church and State together in an alliance of two societies, with 'the aim of the State...*Utility*; and the aim of the Church...*Truth*'; and the church receiving protection from the State by a test law. Although a bishop, Warburton justified the establishment of a presbyterian body in Scotland, as of an episcopal one in England, by the argument that 'if there be more than one at the time of the Convention, the State allies itself with the largest of these Societies'.[1]

Learned men in Germany had to consider these questions against the different background of a multitude of local Churches, each with the local prince exercising the rights of a *summus episcopus* in his own *Landeskirche*, Churches moreover of two distinct religious confessions, Lutheran and Reformed. The old principle of *cujus regio ejus religio* was so far broken down that in the domains of Prussia a family of Reformed traditions ruled over subjects of both confessions, and in Brandenburg over a people overwhelmingly Lutheran. During the eighteenth century the Protestant States of Saxony, Würtemberg and Hesse passed under Roman Catholic rulers. After 1740 Frederick II of Prussia had Catholic Silesia. Throughout the century Protestants were persecuted in the Palatinate. When the prince bishop of Salzburg in 1728 expelled his Protestant subjects, English churchmen, using the machinery of S.P.C.K., helped to settle many of them, and of the persecuted 'palatines', in General Oglethorpe's new colony of Georgia. One of the consequences of a multitude of local Churches was the greater influence of universities, whose professors of law were particularly active in bringing the ideas of the Enlightenment to bear on problems of ecclesiastical polity. There being so many small *Landeskirchen* also explained in part why doctrine about the Church was weaker, and notions of ecclesiastical authority less firm than in the works of the English prelates Gibson, Wake, Potter, and even Warburton. Pufendorf's maxim (used indeed by Febronius) that the Church was in no way to be treated as a kind of State expressed a common and influential assumption. Christian Thomasius (1655–1728), one of the foundation professors at Halle, came indeed to deny the very notion of ecclesiastical government, as one incompatible with the rights of the prince. C. M. Pfaff (1686–1760), the pietistic chancellor of Tübingen, in his *Origines Juris Ecclesiastici* (1719,

---

[1] J. M. Creed and J. S. Boys Smith, *Religious Thought in the Eighteenth Century* (1934), pp. 269–73.

and later), made an effort to 'safeguard the spiritual rights of the Church without destroying the Establishment basis of the *Landeskirchen*',[1] but he still regarded the Church as simply a society within the State, a *collegium* founded by a pact mutually agreed by its members, and in its framing and subsequent observance subject to the *inspectio* of the civil magistrate. Marriage discipline he emphatically assigned to the civil power, as he did all Church laws, *jura sacra absoluta*, involving coercion. Thus, although he gave good advice how the magistrate should use his ecclesiastical powers moderately, there was in fact in his 'collegial system' no real mitigation of that Erastianism which had been inherited, by the Lutheran Churches especially, from the Reformation.

Pietism and the rationalistic enlightenment were alike in that they also told against clericalism. They rejected scholastic divinity. Both operated to weaken the external authority of a visible Church. Philip Jakob Spener (1635–1705) aimed to replace a dry Lutheran 'orthodoxism' by a religion of the heart. The Pietists appealed to Luther's earlier ideas of ecclesiastical democracy, and even justified conventicles. Spener formed his converts into *collegia pietatis* for mutual edification and Bible study. He laid great emphasis on conscious conversion, not necessarily instantaneous. His pupil, August Herman Francke (1633–1727), whose name, said John Wesley, 'is indeed as precious ointment',[2] made the new university at Halle a metropolis of pietism. He established there a great orphanage. He was a great promoter of translations of the Bible. From Halle came the first impulse to Protestant missions overseas. The Pietists produced also a popular religious literature, and in Francke's son-in-law, A. Frey-lingshausen (1670–1727), their own hymn writer. Pietists were not quite the only people, but they were the most important group, whose influence in some measure corrected the religious shallowness of the rationalism which in Germany was to overshadow pietism even at Halle. They also made the rationalist triumph easier by a religious individualism, and, in such men as Gottfried Arnold (1666–1714), by a distinct indifference to orthodoxy, which were hardly compatible with a firm churchmanship.

'Rationalism', said Mark Pattison in a justly celebrated essay, was in England in the first half of the eighteenth century 'a habit of thought ruling all minds'.[3] The orthodox no less than the heretic appealed to reason, not to authority or to feeling. Locke's *Letters on Toleration* (1685, 1689) treated the Church as merely a voluntary association within the State. His *Reasonableness of Christianity, as delivered in the Scriptures* (1695) prepared the way for his deistical disciples, John Toland who found *Christianity not mysterious* (1696), and Matthew Tindal who found it *as old as Creation, and the Gospel a republication of the Religion of Nature* (1730). Alongside the naturalism derived from Newton and Locke was a

---

[1] A. L. Drummond, *German Protestantism since Luther* (1951), p. 242.
[2] *Journal*, 24 July 1738.　　　　[3] *Essays and Reviews* (1851), p. 257.

new biblical scholarship, which was turned by persons of sometimes less deep erudition to serve the purposes of a 'critical' deism. Richard Bentley, an orthodox churchman, aimed to carry on the textual criticism of John Mill (?1644–1707), and to construct a New Testament text as that had been known to Origen. At the same time on the Continent and known to him, John James Wettstein (1693–1754) published in 1730 an epoch-making *Prolegomena*, and in 1751 from his refuge in the Remonstrants' seminary at Amsterdam a cautious Greek Testament text with annotations and variants. At Tübingen in 1742 J. A. Bengel (1687–1742), professor at Berlin, made an important departure by classifying the manuscript authorities in families. His *Gnomon* (1742) was the basis of John Wesley's *Notes on the New Testament* (1754).

To nervous churchmen, as Bentley lamented to Wake and to the 'Arian' Samuel Clarke, support seemed to be given by these studies to dangerous positions. The proved inauthenticity of the 'Johannine comma' was used by Clarke and his disciples. In his *Scripture Doctrine of the Trinity* (1718) he accepted as biblical only the co-eternity of the Son of God, and not the consubstantiality as set forth in the Nicene and Athanasian creeds, which he wished to see removed from the public liturgy. The superficial Anthony Collins was inspired by Mill's 30,000 variants (most of them unimportant) in 1713 to write a flippant essay on free-thinking. The greatest of the critical deists, Conyers Middleton (1683–1750), by denying the ecclesiastical miracles, seemed to threaten also the biblical, and as well by a certain maturity of judgment prepared the way for the historical criticism of the nineteenth century. Even Roman Catholics, placing all reliance in the Church, might benefit by the undermining of the Bible, which was widely held to be the religion of Protestants. By the middle of the century this impulse was waning in England, as pietistic influences were magnified. As pietism waxed in England, it declined in Germany. Rationalistic criticism triumphed there 'on a scale unthought of in England'.[1] In particular Christian Wolff (1677–1754), professor of mathematics and physics at Halle, seemed so strongly to emphasise Natural Religion, as almost to make it sufficient, a position which Pufendorf had carefully repudiated. Wolff's successor at Halle, J. S. Semler (1725–91), devotionally pietist, was not so much a philosopher as a biblical critic. He came to hold with Samuel Clarke that the Nicene Christology was a departure from Revealed Religion. Wolff's disciple Reimarus (1694–1768), professor of oriental languages at Hamburg, came almost to reject the very idea of Revelation. The contentious papers of Reimarus on the Resurrection and on 'the Aim of Jesus and his Disciples' were published later by Lessing, who was not at this time known for theological criticism. There were other men, more orthodox, working in the same field, such as J. A. Ernesti (1707–81), J. D. Michaelis (1717–91) and J. S. Eichhorn

[1] A. L. Drummond, *German Protestantism*, p. 91.

(1752–1827). Eichhorn, Michaelis's pupil, drawing upon the *Conjectures* of the Frenchman Jean Astruc about the books of Moses, and lectures of the Oxford professor Robert Lowth on Hebrew poetry (both works published in 1753), produced in 1781 the first comprehensive criticism of the Old Testament literature. Dr Pusey, who sat under him in 1826, thought his criticism acute, but accompanied by great religious insensitivity.

Erastianism, pietism, and rationalism were reflected in their different ways in various projects, in England and on the Continent, for Christian reunion. In England the idea of a comprehension of the orthodox Dissenters within the Establishment received some countenance, though no effective support, from Archbishop Herring.

Men's minds are now calmed [wrote a pseudonymous Anglican cleric in 1753] and disposed to listen to the Voice of Reason; the sad Distinctions of High and Low Church are laid aside; Those of the Established Church show more Kindness and Condescension to the Dissenters than they formerly did; and the Dissenters are more moderate in their Reflections upon the Church: so that there seems to be such a happy temper among us, so well inclined to give Ear to Truth and Reason, as by God's grace may reunite the Generality of our Dissenters.[1]

For this end, this writer, while Trinitarian in divinity, was prepared to alter the common prayer in (its present form 'too long, tedious, and full of repetitions'). He would expunge the *Quicunque* and the descent into hell; abolish the Lenten fast as absurd and superstitious; purge the catechism of the mystery-mongering inherited in his view from Bucer; and adapt the communion office to 'the opinion of *Zuinglius*', which he said, 'is most certainly the true one, and as such most generally received by the present Members of our Church'.[2] Besides the liturgies proposed to aid a comprehension were others compiled in the interests of a Clarkeian divinity. With this end John Jones, a friend of Doddridge, founded a Catholic Christianity Society. That remarkable man William Whiston used an 'arianised' liturgy in his oratory at Tonbridge. Samuel Clarke left behind an annoted prayer book which was used by Theophilus Lindsey (1723–1808) in preparing a liturgy for use in the Essex Street Chapel, where he hoped to inaugurate after his secession from the Establishment in 1772 a reformed Church of England. Clarke's influence was wider spread among the Presbyterians than in the Church. At a celebrated meeting of the Dissenters at Salters' Hill in 1719 those who favoured his doctrines split from their more orthodox brethren. Like the once Anglican Lindsey after them, they moved generally to a more explicit unitarianism.

Archbishop Wake was busy in 1718 not only with the Gallican Church but also with 'transactions of moment to the foreign Protestants'.[3] In

[1] *A New Form of Common Prayer* (1753).
[2] J. H. Lupton, *Archbishop Wake and the Project of Union between Gallican and Anglican Churches* (1896), p. 91.
[3] For Wake's project, N. Sykes, *Life and Times of Archbishop Wake* (1957).

accordance with an opinion very general in the Church of England, he made a sharp distinction between the non-episcopal foreign Protestants who dissented from the errors of Rome, and the English nonconformists who designedly had rejected the authority of a pure and apostolic part of the Catholic Church. He was willing and ready to give to orthodox foreign Protestants a valid episcopal succession if they were willing to receive what some of their writers insisted had been unwillingly relinquished by their reformers in the sixteenth century. In Europe the weakening of doctrinal rigidity offered hope of reuniting Lutheran and Reformed. Three Swiss theologians, J. A. Turretini (1671–1737) of Geneva, Samuel Werenfels (1657–1740) of Basel, and J. F. Ostervald (1653–1747) of Neuchâtel worked for a union on the basis of a 'reasonable orthodoxy',[1] such as they considered to be exemplified in the Church of England. Turretini, of great authority in the Church of Geneva, succeeded in bringing about there the abandonment of subscription to the Helvetic Consensus, which involved amongst other things profession of belief in the inspiration of the smallest jot and tittle of the scriptures. George I of England and Frederick William I of Prussia had to intervene in 1722 to prevent its being re-imposed. Turretini persuaded Wake in 1718 to write his epistle advocating to the theologians of Switzerland the English habits of agreement to differ on non-essentials, and of refusal to burden the consciences of the faithful with unnecessary articles of belief. These he presented as indispensable conditions of Protestant union. Englishmen had indeed often great confidence in their ecclesiastical position. Jacques Serçes found in 1720 some difficulty in convincing the incumbent of St Albans that there might be some obstacles in the way of Canterbury's episcopalising Geneva. Hope of a reunion seemed to be fortified by the interest of some among the Reformed in ancient liturgies, even borrowing from the Roman mass. English churchmen heard with interest of the liturgy used by Ostervald at Neuchâtel, which drew considerably on their own incomparable prayer book.

For several years Archbishop Wake was concerned also in the project of an Anglo-Prussian church union, which was initiated by Frederick William I, and enthusiastically promoted by the Moravian bishop Daniel Ernst Jablonski. Difficulties of all sorts frustrated this union, perhaps most of all unwillingness in the Hanoverian entourage of George I. Frederick William I, like his predecessor Frederick I, saw in the Church of England such an one as he would like to have at home. The bicentenary of the Reformation in 1717 (like its tercentenary in 1817), along with intense Protestant feeling against *Unigenitus*, gave a fillip to Protestant unionism in Germany. There moreover the influence of the king of Prussia was naturally very great. The Wurtemberg pietist Pfaff was an active

---

[1] M. Schmidt, 'Ecumenical Activity on the Continent of Europe in the Seventeenth and Eighteenth Centuries', in Rouse and Neill, *History of the Ecumenical Movement*.

propagandist for this cause. He gave a great deal of attention to such interesting problems as those of episcopal succession. He published at Halle in 1723 a collection of reunion essays. This *pax Tubingenensis* an old friend, now turned hostile, scornfully derided as *pax, tuba, ignis, ensis*. Propaganda failing, the king tried to bring a union of the confessions in his own lands by the use of his territorial supremacy, by centralised administrative action through a developing bureaucracy for Church affairs, in regulating public worship and the training of ministers. After fruitlessly trying to confine candidates for the ministry to universities in his own dominions, he had to be content with a compulsory two years at Halle. He tried by decree to assimilate the religious practice of the Lutherans to that of the Reformed by eliminating so fast as he could such vestiges of medievalism as altars, candles, monstrances, confessionals and chasubles. Although he marched with the times in this, for pietism and the Enlightenment were his allies in this work of liturgical destruction, he was not wholly successful. Even a visitation of 1736 could not wholly eradicate the old usages inherited from Luther himself. They were to be observed by John Wesley, just outside Prussian territory, when he visited Saxony two years later. Under Frederick II, who was sceptically tolerant, this form of royal pressure by the *summus episcopus* was removed.

Quite apart from the conservatism of the simple worshipper, which was a brake upon change in all the Churches, the Church of England had in the common prayer a liturgy orthodox and scriptural, which was by now well established in the affections of churchmen, and fortified by such widely read expositions as Wheatly's *Rational Illustration*, and by popular companions like Robert Nelson's *Festivals and Fasts*, to which Dr Johnson in 1776 attributed 'the greatest sale of any book ever printed in England—except the Bible'. Nelson's book, like *The Whole Duty of Man*, fully emphasised the ordinary duties of life as parts of religion, and inculcated reverence for Church and Sacraments. Both the *Rational Illustration* and the *Whole Duty of Man* recommended a proper use of private confession. Written for more leisured as well as learned persons, Joseph Bingham's massive *Antiquities of the Christian Church* (1708–22) achieved a European reputation. Although its author accused foreign liturgists of 'varnishing over the novel practices of the Romish church' with a face of antiquity, the motive was not altogether absent from his own work of justifying the contemporary usages of the Church of England. The classical ideals of piety were far from forgotten. There were even a few who dreamt of a restored monasticism. Amongst the non-jurors, as with many of the high churchmen, the Eucharistic presence and sacrifice were strongly asserted. The usages of the 1549 prayer book, which the learned George Hickes used in his chapel, split the non-jurors into two parties. In 1718 a non-juring liturgy was published, which like Thomas Deacon's prayers of 1734 reflected the influence of eastern rites. Inside the Establishment there was a hearty prejudice against transubstantiation as contrary to reason and law. The balanced and subtle doctrine of Waterland, avoiding alike popery and Zwinglianism, was that most widely held. Communions were infrequent, rarely more than monthly even in populous places; infrequent, it was sometimes said, that they 'might be observed the more religiously and solemnly'.[1]

Orthodox apologists in England rose handsomely to the challenges presented by deism. Thomas Sherlock's defence of the resurrection narratives was an immediate success. Waterland's defence of the Trinity was more convincing than either the elder Sherlock's effort to the same end, or than Warburton's treatment of the Old Testament books in the too ingenious *Divine Legation of Moses* (1738–41). Inevitably criticism was made of the rationalists' assumption of the total adequacy of the human reason, as was done by Law and Berkeley, and with the gravest circumspection by Joseph Butler, bishop of Durham. In particular Butler emphasised the supremacy of conscience over reason. In his *Analogy of Religion Natural and Revealed to the Constitution and Course of Nature* (1736) he set out to show that Christianity was at least as credible as the Natural Religion of the deists. As a good high churchman, he urged the necessity of a visible Church, with 'an instituted Method of Instruction, and an instituted form of external Religion'.[2]

In spite of the piety of many churchmen; and of much philanthropic work; and of pious benefactions for charity schools, apprenticeships, and hospitals, the Church of England was hampered by an inflexible organisation in the necessary task of ministering to new concentrations of industrial workers in areas where formerly people had been more scarce. The grave and rational cool piety which as a rule it inculcated was hardly adequate in ostensible emotional drive to rescue the lost sheep of the Lord from often brutish barbarism and heathendom. It was deficient in missionary impulse. The warmth of German pietism was brought to bear on English life by the Moravian brethren, chiefly by their kindling of the early Methodists. In 1722 the Count Ludwig von Zinzendorf, a godson of Spener and a pupil of Francke, welcomed on his estate at Bertholdsdorf in Saxony a company of the persecuted Bohemian brethren looking for a home. There they built up their settlement of Herrnhut, the Lord's hill. Zinzendorf soon became their ecclesiastical dictator. The Moravian community subjected its members to the closest supervision, so that even Plato's guardians would hardly have found their marriage discipline loose. 'Except in the power of withdrawing from the community', remarked Robert Southey, 'there was as little personal liberty in Herrnhut as in a convent, and less than in a Jesuit Reduction.'[3] Quite apart from their theological peculiarities, it was

---

[1] *A New Form of Common Prayer* (1753).
[2] Creed and Boys Smith, *Religious Thought in the Eighteenth Century*, pp. 104–28.
[3] *Life of John Wesley* (1925), vol. I, p. 143.

this close organisation, combined with a reserve which was held to cover deceitfulness, and the personal autocracy of the count, that led to their being attacked on the characteristic eighteenth-century ground that their existence was (like that of the Jesuits) incompatible with a well-ordered civil polity. They were indeed at one point expelled from Saxony. 'Matters concerning the interior state of their Affairs are so contrived', wrote a Prussian court cleric, 'as evidently shews, their leaders are gradually sapping the Foundation of the civil Government of any Country they may settle in, and establishing an Empire within an Empire.'[1] The count intended no more than that this *unitas fratrum* should comprise pious sodalities, *ecclesiolae in ecclesia* on Spener's model, within existing Churches, organised for each denomination in a separate *tropus* or type. Had this worked, there might have been here a means of Protestant union, but as it happened, the Moravians could not be contained within the *Landeskirche*. The establishment of a Moravian liturgy in 1727; the consecration of Zinzendorf as a Moravian bishop in 1737; and his near bankruptcy, which his great munificence brought upon him, by making necessary a specifically financial organisation for the brethren, were factors in the separation. The Moravians were the greatest Protestant missionaries of the time. In Greenland and Labrador they organised their native converts into missionary settlements rather like those of the Jesuits in Paraguay. By the end of the century they had missionaries in every continent.

Their influence in England was singularly remarkable in giving a new direction to John Wesley. The Wesley brothers were the sons of remarkable parents, former Dissenters, now strictly of the high church. The Oxford 'holy club', started by Charles in 1729, was active in pious works of a traditional high church character—fastings, frequenting the sacraments, and the corporal works of mercy. Altogether they behaved with a religious singularity noticeable in a worldly university. These men were putting into practice the ideas of William Law's brilliant and severe book, *A Serious Call to a Devout and Holy Life*. When John Wesley returned to England in 1738, after the failure of his mission to Georgia, where he had antagonised the settlers by an excessive high church rubricalness and a mishandled love affair, he found that the name of 'Methodist' had been made famous by another member of the old 'holy club', George Whitefield, who by his extraordinary eloquence in the preaching of 'vital religion' won the attention of that remarkable lady Selina, countess of Huntingdon. In 1739 he made an important precedent by preaching in the open air. On his journey to Georgia John Wesley had fallen under the spell of a company of Moravians, whose piety had deeply impressed him by its reality and warmth. On his return he learned from Peter Boehler that he had never had that saving faith that gives consciousness of dominion over sin, and

[1] H. Rimius, *A Candid Narrative of…the Herrenhuters…*(1723), p. 3.

that therefore he had been hitherto only 'almost a Christian'. In this sense he was converted at a meeting in Aldersgate in the city of London on 24 May 1738, when he felt his heart 'strangely warmed'. Under the influence of this great experience he preached on 11 June 1738 a remarkable sermon before the university of Oxford proclaiming the nature of saving faith, as 'not barely a speculative, rational thing, a cold lifeless assent, a train of ideas in the head, but also a disposition of the heart'. Although Wesley claimed that Methodism was no more than 'Church of Englandism felt', his characteristic doctrine thus came to life under Moravian influence. He became a member of the first 'Anglican-Moravian-Methodist' society in England, founded in Fetter Lane on 1 May 1738. The same year he made pilgrimage to Herrnhut.

The years 1739–42 saw the separation of Methodism from the Moravians, and the split amongst the Methodists between Calvinists and Arminians. The breach with the Moravians was virtually complete with the starting of the Methodist society at the Foundry, in July 1740. The causes of this separation lay partly in the characters of Zinzendorf and Wesley; partly in disagreement about the strange convulsions which seized some hearers at Wesley's sermons; partly by Wesley's intense dislike of the doctrine of *stillness* taught by some of the brethren, which made of no account the means of grace; and partly by Moravian dislike of Wesley's teaching on Christian perfection. In 1741 Wesley's following broke with Whitefield's about predestination and particular election. The leaders were afterwards reconciled.

The first rules which Wesley drew up for the Methodist societies, published in February 1743, were simply directions for a religious society, not for a new denomination. They recommended attendance at the parish church. Yet in spite of Wesley's repeated desire that the Methodists should remain within the Church of England, by the time he died in 1791 they were virtually a separate body. It was not simply that the clergy of the Establishment were hostile to 'vital religion'. Wesley, in a lifetime of immense pastoral activity, in the course of great journeys all over the British Isles, and by a vast correspondence, had been the leader in creating a great, flexible, and effective organisation. The class system, begun at Bristol in 1724, was not only a useful way to collect money, but a splendid device for pastoral oversight. Class leaders had a training in responsibility which increased their self-respect, as much as invidious social distinctions inside the parish churches often wounded it. The organisation was completed by the starting in 1744 of the annual conference of ministers and lay preachers, in whom were later to be vested all Methodist properties; and in 1747 by the grouping of societies into circuits. Here indeed was rather an *ecclesia*, than an *ecclesiola in ecclesia*. Secondly, the Methodists had their own customs. Their love-feasts, their watch-night services, some of their hymns, their organisation of bands savoured of their Moravian antecedents. Field preaching, and organised itineracy, were momentous innovations. Thirdly, there was, as Wesley himself perceived, a weakening in his own churchmanship. Lord King's account of the early Church persuaded him he could ordain no less than Archbishop Potter. Stillingfleet's *Irenicum* destroyed his episcopalianism. 'Who would have believed five and twenty years ago...that I should have consented to preach in a Scots kirk?'[1] Naturally therefore when it seemed that the issue might lie between sacrificing his lay preachers, who were indispensably necessary to a great pastoral work, and keeping the Methodists in the Church, he was disposed to treat the question as one merely of expediency. Possibly also with Wesley as with the pietists, the exclusive emphasis laid on the dispositions of the heart made for a low view of Church order. Wesley's connivance at lay administration of sacraments; his calling on a Greek bishop to give ordination to lay preachers in 1763; his own laying of hands on men to serve in America in 1784; and his consent to accept in 1787, as Lady Huntingdon had done in 1779, the protection of the Toleration Act for ministrations outside the parish churches, all made for separation.

Independent of the Methodist movement, but influenced by it, was the evangelical awakening in the Church of England. This was in large measure the fruit of fresh recourse by devout churchmen to biblical founts of Christian doctrine. Many of them had heeded the *Serious Call* of William Law. If in the earlier days evangelical divines like Berridge at Everton (1755–93) seemed disposed after John Wesley's manner to take the world for their parish, the Church evangelicals as a rule rated highly the obligation of obedience to Church order. They joined a high sacramentalism to a strong emphasis on conversion experience, not always without strain, for occasionally some might feel that *Church-man* and *Gospel-man* fitted hardly together. They rejected Wesley's doctrines of Christian perfection, and leaned in their treatment of grace and nature to a 'Calvinism' for which they urged the support of Anglican formularies, and of the Reformation divines to whom they appealed more than did the Methodists. As a rule, they were ready to co-operate with Dissenters in a fashion abhorrent to high churchmen, though not often to go as far as the converted slave trader, the hymn-writer John Newton, curate at Olney (1764–80), who cancelled in 1765 one of his own week-day prayer-meetings in order to sit under the local Independent minister. Walker at Truro (1746–61), and Fletcher at Madeley (1760–85) (with the strictest regard for ecclesiastical regularity); the elder Venn first as curate at Clapham (1754–9) and later as vicar at Huddersfield and rector at Yelling (with at times a less strict regard for order than he came afterwards to think proper); Romaine in his lectureship in the city (1749–95), were essentially great parish priests, who did not set up to be universal missionaries. The work of the Church evangelicals, unlike that of the Methodists, was strongest in the middle

[1] *Journal*, 20 April 1753.

class. The conversion in 1754 of John Thornton, a London merchant, brought to the support of the evangelical cause one of that company of devoted, generous and influential laymen who made one of its great glories. For the evangelicals, as for the Methodists, the Moravians and the Pietists, as even for Rousseau's deistical Savoyard vicar, religion was primarily of the heart, rather than rationalistic or drily orthodox. In this warmth of heart-devotion was one of the great driving forces for the marvellous Christian expansions of the next century.

CHAPTER VII

MONARCHY AND ADMINISTRATION

THE mid-eighteenth century was a period when much thought was devoted to the nature of government. Probably the best known of the commentators was Montesquieu, who produced his *De l'esprit des lois* in 1748; but the same kind of problem occupied many other writers, including Bielfeld, who produced his *Institutions politiques* between 1759 and 1774, d'Argenson, who wrote his *Considérations sur le gouvernement ancien et présent de la France* in 1765, and F. K. von Moser who discussed the duties of a prince in his *Der Herr und der Diener* in 1759. Yet the problems which interested these contemporaries are not always those which seem most important to later observers, who have to consider the political and administrative developments which have taken place in Europe since 1789. To the modern observer the most characteristic features of the governmental institutions of the period 1713–65 are the very general acceptance of more or less absolute monarchy, the increasing administrative specialisation at the centre and the increasing effectiveness of governmental control in the provinces.

The inspiration behind the very generally held eighteenth-century idea of monarchy was still the belief that kings ruled by a right derived from God himself. This view had found expression in the sixteenth century, when Bodin had described the king as the image of God on earth, and in the seventeenth century, when the *Parlement* of Paris assured Louis XIV that the seat of His Majesty represented the throne of the living God, and that the orders of the kingdom rendered honour and respect to him as to a living divinity, or when Bossuet had declared that princes were sanctified by their charge as being representatives of the divine majesty appointed by Providence to carry out its purposes. It was still familiar and acceptable in most of Europe until 1789. Even the *Encyclopédistes*, though they did not hesitate to question the authority of the Church, did not, for the most part, criticise the excellence of monarchy as a form of government.

The powers which it was generally thought ought to belong to a monarch were based on the principles of Roman law. A monarch should be independent of any other authority, and no person or institution should be in a position to call him to account. He must be able to make law. His power must be so great that no one would dare to disobey him. The extent of his power must be to the very limits of his realm. In cases of urgency he had the right to make use of property belonging to any of his subjects; for example, he might order a house to be demolished in time of siege or fire, or private stores of corn to be opened in time of famine. These were the essential characteristics of sovereignty; from them it followed that in practice a king could declare war and make peace, conclude alliances, send and receive ambassadors, levy taxes, administer justice and appoint subordinate officials. Monarchy was not necessarily hereditary. Indeed, the Polish Crown had long been elective and in the eighteenth century the Swedish Diet made good its claim to determine the succession, but in both countries the royal power was so weak that elsewhere in Europe it was generally accepted that if a monarchy was to be strong it should be hereditary. In the eighteenth century the coronation and anointing of a king had come to be of little importance as a confirmation of his authority. The king of Prussia did not require to have his authority confirmed by coronation, and one sign of the growth of the power of the monarchy in France was that the kings took less and less trouble to arrange for a rapid coronation. Even a long minority like that of Louis XV did not perceptibly weaken the institution of monarchy in France, while in Spain the monarchy survived though Philip V was incapacitated by long fits of melancholia. In Portugal the Braganzas of the eighteenth century were indolent and stupid, in the Austrian dominions the succession of Maria Theresa was contested during eight years of war, in Russia direct heirs failed, in England the succession passed to a foreign royal family ignorant of English customs and of the English language, yet in all these countries the institution of monarchy survived. To an eighteenth-century observer it seemed natural that a flourishing country should have a monarchical constitution.

Yet as between one country and another the institution of monarchy differed very considerably. To a modern observer the similarities are generally more obvious than the differences, but to observers of the mid-eighteenth century there were perceptible and important shades of difference as, for example, between absolute monarchy and despotism. To some contemporaries the king of France, in spite of the extravagant praise of Bossuet, appeared much less despotic than some other rulers. Bielfeld thought the French king was so limited by law and custom that he could not be described as despotic, and this opinion was supported by d'Argenson. To observers writing in the mid-eighteenth century the power of the king of Spain seemed theoretically greater than that of the king of France. In the days of Charles II the power of the king had been restricted by a multiplicity of councils, but the Bourbons had reduced the power of these institutions, and the authority of the king of Spain in the mid-eighteenth century was in theory limitless. On his accession he simply proclaimed himself: he had no need of a solemn coronation. In practice the Estates of the realm only met to render homage or to receive royal orders. Bielfeld believed that no people in Europe was so much at the command of their ruler. Yet the kings of Denmark and Prussia were as absolutely powerful in theory and their power was more real in fact.

Since the *coup d'état* of 1660 the Crown in Denmark had been an absolutism and in Prussia the ruler had grown steadily more absolute since the Great Elector had defeated his diets and forced them to guarantee a regular sum in taxes. In Denmark, Prussia and Spain the king legislated according to his good pleasure. His authority was not restricted by parliament, law courts, nobility or any other intermediary authority. In Prussia the king succeeded as soon as his predecessor was dead; he had no need of coronation or anointing. The people and the army swore an oath of loyalty. All these rulers were answerable for their conduct to God alone.

To the eighteenth-century observer there was, however, a distinction between the regimes of Prussia, Denmark or Spain, even though these might be classified as 'completely monarchic', and the despotism of Russia which some foreigners thought could be compared only with the rule of the Grand Turk. The tsar seemed to govern as despotically as had the king of Assyria, and he seemed able to do as he wished with the lives and the goods of his subjects, who obeyed him like slaves. The theoretical distinction between the tsar, for example, and the absolute monarch of Prussia does not seem so clear to a modern observer. Bielfeld had apparently never been to Russia, but seems to have been particularly shocked by the brutality of the punishments enforced there. When he wrote in the late 1750's the memory of the violence of Peter the Great was still vivid, the enlightened views of Catherine II were still to come and the stability of the government of the Empress Elizabeth had done nothing to overcome the prejudice which saw the Russian autocrat as essentially different from the absolute monarch who ruled in several European states.

A clearer distinction than that which contemporaries saw between the tsar and the kings of Prussia, Denmark and Spain divided all these absolute rulers from those whose power was more or less controlled by some authority within their kingdom. The Bourbon king of the Two Sicilies, though it seemed possible to d'Argenson that he might try to establish a despotism of the most absolute kind, had to summon the Diet whenever he wanted additional money. The king of Portugal was restrained by a powerful Church and by the fact that in matters of supreme importance he had to consult the Estates of the realm. The succession was also laid down by the pragmatic sanction made at Lamega in 1641, and financially the king of Portugal had to be content with taxes granted in 1697, though this restriction had little practical value at a time when Brazil was supplying large quantities of gold and diamonds. In Sweden the power of the Crown was much more effectively restricted after the death of Charles XII in 1718, when the Diet was able to assert its control. The monarchy was not only declared elective but the Diet chose between two rival candidates, and, when the newly elected Queen Ulrika Eleanora proved too autocratic, was able to obtain her abdication and elect her more pliable husband who had no hereditary claim. By the Constitution of 1720 the Swedish Diet was to be summoned every three years, and without its consent there was to be no change in the fineness of the coinage, no war declared or peace concluded, and no new law passed. The situation in England had something in common with that in Sweden. In England the Crown was hereditary and there was no written constitution comparable to the Swedish instrument of 1720, but when the hereditary ruler fled into exile in 1688 the Crown had been transferred first to the female line and then to a remote collateral descendant, rather than to the son of the exiled king. The Act of Settlement did not state quite so explicitly as the Swedish Constitution of 1720 the limits on the royal power, but taken in conjunction with the practice of the preceding half century it meant in fact that no new taxes could be imposed without the consent of the elected representatives of the country, that no changes were to be made in the Protestant form of religion as established by law, and that no new law could be passed. The essential difference between England and Sweden was that in Sweden the Constitution was overthrown in 1772 and absolutism restored, whereas in England George III's attempt to reassert the power of the Crown after 1760 showed that parliament was too strongly entrenched to be controlled by a king trying to rule in the manner familiar in most of the great States of Europe. The limitations on the power of the king of Poland were so extreme as to make that country a unique and tragic example of bad government. For the most part, in mid-eighteenth-century Europe strong government was synonymous with monarchy and successful monarchy was often synonymous with military victories. Much of the ruler's time was devoted to territorial aggrandisement, but in order to do this it was necessary to collect taxes and ensure an adequate flow of military supplies. From these two unpromising roots sprang those improvements in the institutions of central and local government which made the monarchs of the eighteenth century more effective than any previous rulers.

One tendency in the administrative machinery of the early eighteenth century was a widespread increase in specialisation at the centre. This movement had begun long before 1700, and was apparent in some countries as early as the sixteenth century. Indeed, by the late seventeenth century the process was almost complete in some countries, and in the eighteenth century the experiments in Sweden and France were imitated in Spain, Russia, Prussia and the Habsburg dominions. The development usually took the form of the creation of something like modern ministries. The clearest and most efficient reforms in the direction of specialisation were those which had taken place in Sweden, where the central administration had been fundamentally reorganised as early as the reign of Gustavus Adolphus. He had gradually transformed the great hereditary offices of State into specialised departments organised as 'colleges' or boards; in 1614 the

Exchequer had been reformed in this way and by 1618 was working well; from 1618 the Chancery was gradually reorganised and financial business was removed from it; the marshal's office was turned into a department in 1620 and that of the admiral in 1632; the reforms were given final legal expression in 1634. Thereafter the central administration of Sweden consisted of five boards dealing respectively with finance, the royal correspondence, defence, foreign affairs and justice. The head of each department sat in the Council of State.

The influence of the Swedish reforms on the development of Russian institutions was considerable, for when Peter the Great began to think of improving the Russian institutions, he studied the Swedish system in some detail; the projects of reform drawn up in 1715 were clearly based on the Swedish division of functions and the Swedish regulations for the various 'colleges' (ch. XIV). Peter had inherited a tangle of institutions whose overlapping produced chaos, delay and peculation. In 1718 he substituted for the numerous old *prikazi* a few specialised departments. Of the new departments those for foreign affairs, war, admiralty and justice, which last alone absorbed seven of the old *prikazi*, were obviously copied from Sweden. The Russian system differed from the Swedish model in the creation of three separate departments to deal with finance: one for State revenue, another for income and expenditure and a third known as the Pay Office. There was also a department for mines and manufactures and another for trade. Some overlapping still remained, but the new 'college' marked a great advance in specialisation on the old *prikaz*. Within each department the organization was also simplified. In future, each department dealt with business from every part of the tsar's dominions and not from one district only—as had often been the case with the *prikazi*.

In France (ch. x), where some degree of specialisation had been achieved as early as the sixteenth century, an attempt by the regent to take this process a stage further by setting up councils for war, the navy, and commerce in addition to the existing departments for foreign, financial and domestic affairs, failed. After the collapse of Law's financial schemes the new councils disappeared, and France reverted to the institutions which had evolved gradually under Henry IV and Richelieu and which had been used by Louis XIV. It was an indication of the relative unimportance of domestic questions in the eighteenth century that whereas the *Conseil d'Etat*, which dealt with foreign affairs, met five times in a fortnight, the *Conseil de Dépêches*, handling domestic questions, met only once during the same period. Further administrative specialisation was achieved by the development of the office of Secretary of State. This office had emerged as early as the reign of Henry II and had acquired its name by 1557, but it then meant little more than secretary to the king. Under Henry IV there were four secretaries, each of whom dealt with business from a different part of France, but even then some degree of specialisation was beginning to appear, for foreign affairs tended to be the responsibility of one secretary. Under Richelieu not only were foreign affairs handled by one secretary, but from 1630–43 matters which could be classified as military tended to be concentrated into the hands of another. Under Louis XIV the specialisation remained only partial, each of the four secretaries still being responsible for one-quarter of the interior. Under Louis XV the work was more clearly divided, one secretary being responsible for foreign affairs, a second for war, a third for the navy (though this included questions affecting colonies and commerce) and the fourth for the branch of affairs known as the *maison du roi*, which covered much that would normally be the concern of a Minister of the Interior together with questions affecting religion. But even so the specialisation at the centre was not quite complete, for questions of finance, agriculture, industry and communications were the concern of the Controller General of Finance, and there was also a *Garde des sceaux* and a Chancellor. The chancellor held office for life, but the other ministers were appointed and dismissed at the king's pleasure. They did not form a ministry, but were simply the individual servants of the king. Even when, as in the time of Fleury, there was someone who might be called a chief minister he did not in theory choose his colleagues, though he might influence the king's choice. He did not control them, nor did they work as a team.

In England (ch. XI) the central governmental institutions showed some similarities to those developing in Sweden and France, and the tendency towards specialisation had gone a long way. The administration was essentially the province of the Crown, but the strength of the English parliament ensured that great offices were usually held by men eminent in one or other House of the legislature. The number of offices was considerable. Some, like those of Lord Chancellor, Lord Treasurer, Lord Privy Seal and Lord High Admiral, had originated in offices closely associated with the royal household, while others, such as the Secretaries of State, the Secretary at War and the Post-Master General, had been of more recent origin. Some of these offices, as for example those of the Treasurer and Admiral, were assigned to boards, others were held by individuals. As in France, the ministers were still looked on as the servants of the king. They were chosen by him and dismissed by him. Though most of them were members of the policy-forming committee, which came to be called the Cabinet, membership of this body was open to some of the household offices, and sometimes to the Lord Chief Justice and to the archbishop of Canterbury. There was little feeling of solidarity among the ministers who sat together in the cabinet at any one time. One or two strong personalities might sometimes impose some sort of unity on the other ministers, but in the eighteenth century the English ministries and cabinet had more in common with the 'colleges' and Council of State in contemporary Sweden than with the political institutions of modern England.

In Spain (ch. XII) the advent of the Bourbons initiated institutional changes almost as fundamental as those made in Russia at about the same time by Peter the Great, except that the older institutions of government persisted in Spain as the *prikazi* in Russia did not, although Philip V imitated French institutions as Peter had imitated those of Sweden and Denmark. In Habsburg Spain the government had been carried on by a mass of councils of which the most important had been the Council of State, which advised the king on foreign affairs. In addition there had been a Council of War composed of the same members as the Council of State but with the addition of some generals or other military experts. There had also been a Council of the Inquisition. Some councils dealt with the affairs of the Spanish dominions; these included the Council of Aragon, the Council of Italy, the Council of Flanders and the Council of the Indies, and for a time the Council of Portugal. Many Councils dealt exclusively with affairs in Castile, as for example the Council of the Military Orders, the Council of the Cruzada, the Council of the Hermandad and the great Council of Castile itself. The competence of the Council of Castile was prodigious. It issued laws in the name of the king; its judicial sentences and its advice to the king had the force of law; it received the king's will and transmitted the seals to his successor; as a court of law it heard the most serious cases both civil and criminal; it could hear cases involving an official and could even hear appeals against a judgment given by an *Audiencia*; it tried cases of treason and *lèse majesté*. Even in ecclesiastical affairs it had great authority. It allowed bulls and apostolic briefs to circulate in Spain; it administered the goods of vacant bishoprics; it was responsible for monasteries and hospitals; it issued diplomas to teachers and supervised instruction at the universities. It was responsible for trade, agriculture, corn supplies, livestock, afforestation, mines, roads, bridges and municipal finance. One of its subordinate institutions was the *Sala de alcaldes de casa y corte* which was responsible for the maintenance of good order in Madrid itself. Not only did the spheres of these various bodies overlap geographically, but they dealt indiscriminately with business of various kinds, legislative, administrative and judicial, conducting nearly all their business in writing with proverbial slowness. Philip V tried to clear a way for efficient and speedy administration through this jungle of councils, but in spite of his efforts, and those of his successors, there were in 1816 even more councils than when the Bourbons had come into power. What Philip was able to do to reform Spanish administration was to appoint ministers rather like the French secretaries of state, each handling a special section of governmental business. From the Habsburgs Philip V inherited only one official who could in any sense be called a secretary of state. In 1705 he appointed a second to deal with war and finance. In 1714 two more were appointed, one to deal with ecclesiastical affairs and justice, the other for the Indies and the navy. Finance was the responsibility of a controller general. In 1717 an attempt was made to reduce the number of ministers to three, but this did not last long. Until the middle of the century the number of ministers was four, and after the reform of 1754 and 1755 it was five, for the official in charge of finances was then raised to the position of minister.

In Prussia (ch. XIII) the administration had first to be unified before the work could be specialised. Even by the beginning of the eighteenth century much of Prussia was still administered directly by the king almost as though it were a private estate. The domain lands of the king of Prussia accounted for between one-third and one-quarter of all the peasants. These domain lands were farmed by royal bailiffs, *Beamten*, and their work was supervised by finance committees. The rest of Prussia was administered by another body of officials who were responsible for collecting the war tax. In country districts these officials were known as *Landräte*, in towns as *Steuerräte*. The methods by which the tax was collected varied as between town and country, but the work of both *Landräte* and *Steuerräte* came under the supervision of a war committee in each district. In Berlin there was a supreme Finance and Domain Commission which was responsible for the work of the *Beamten* on the royal domains and a War Commission supervising the collection of the war tax in the other parts of Prussia. In 1723 Frederick William I combined the two systems, unifying the finance committee and the war committee in each province and creating in Berlin a single supreme authority called the *General-Ober-Finanz-Kriegs-und-Domänen-Directorium*. Unification had been achieved, but specialisation had hardly begun. This General Directory was a curious confusion. Each of its four departments was, as it were, one-quarter of a Ministry of the Interior. The first department dealt with East Prussia and Pomerania, the second with Brandenburg and Magdeburg, the third with Cleves, Guelders, Mark and East Friesland, and the fourth with Halberstadt, Minden and Ravensberg. Each department dealt with all kinds of business arising within its geographical area, and the General Directory itself handled all kinds of business except foreign affairs and justice. Frederick II was often sharply critical of the lumbering procedure of this unspecialised General Directory. In 1741 he created an entirely specialised ministry for commerce; in 1746 he created another for the army. Both had some relation to the machinery of the General Directory, but the ministry set up in 1742 to deal with Silesia had none. Frederick the Great did not complete the specialisation of the central Government of Prussia; he rather increased the confusion by setting up new departments without abolishing the old, and occasionally he even added to the confusion by going over the heads of all the central authorities and dealing with the provincial administration direct. The central institutions of the Prussian administration were most unsatisfactory. They worked while there was an indefatigable autocrat of genius to hold the different institutions together, but only twenty years after the death of Frederick II the Prussian State was in the dust, and Stein was penning a bitter memoir[1] pointing out the fatal weakness of the administrative institutions.

The central government of the Habsburg hereditary dominions showed the same tendency towards centralisation as did Prussia, for Maria Theresa had the benefit of Prussia's example and was able to learn by the experiments of the Hohenzollerns. After 1748 Maria Theresa put through a series of reforms to increase her military strength and achieved on paper in a decade all that had been going on in France since the time of Richelieu or even of Henri IV, or in Prussia since the time of Frederick William I. At the core of the Austrian system of government during the later eighteenth and nineteenth centuries was the *Staatsrat* or Council of State. This was composed of officials and its purpose was only to advise. It made the government of the Habsburg dominions a bureaucratic absolutism rather than a personal one such as was the case in the Prussia of Frederick II. Internal and financial affairs were controlled by a *Directorium in publicis et cameralibus* whose competence was made to embrace not only the Austrian lands but also the lands of the Bohemian Crown. This institution was clearly copied from that in Prussia, as was the special *Kommerzdirektorium* set up to foster trade. An institution already existed to deal with war; this was overhauled and improved and its authority was extended to cover all parts of the Habsburg lands. The *Staatskanzlei*, or foreign office, was also reorganised in 1753. In addition to all this, judicial business was separated from administration and a new supreme court was set up to handle cases from all parts of Austria and Bohemia. From having been one of the most backward of States, the Habsburg dominions under Maria Theresa emerged with one of the most clearly specialised systems of administration in Europe.

Throughout Europe the developments in central government during the first part of the eighteenth century varied. Some countries such as France or Spain relied on individual ministers, others, especially those of eastern Europe, relied on departmental boards. Some countries were much less centralised than others and had to achieve administrative unity as a preliminary to any other administrative reform. In Sweden and England the situation was complicated by the existence of a vigorous elected legislature. But underlying the local variations can generally be seen a powerful Crown assisted by one or sometimes several councils, and making its will effective through departments whose competence tended to become more clearly defined. The machine was on the whole effective, but it was very different from the system of cabinet government which emerged in the nineteenth century, and the similarity of some of the titles should not disguise the very real differences.

[1] The text of this memoir is printed in J. Seeley's *Life and Times of Stein* (1878), vol. I, pp. 267 *et seq.*

The central administrative institutions of most European monarchies in the early eighteenth century were slowly developing in the direction of increased specialisation, but the financial arrangements of nearly all the countries were chaotic. A comparison of conditions in France, Spain and Prussia will make this plain. In most monarchies the king still owned territories from which in the past he had drawn revenues which had been expected to meet his expenses. In France these royal domains had ceased to be of any practical value; in Spain they were a real liability, but in Prussia, thanks to the careful administration of Frederick William I, they produced almost as much as all the taxes. From very early times it had become clear that a king could not maintain armed forces and meet the other expenses of the State from the income of the royal domains alone, so taxes had been agreed between him and the representatives of his subjects. By the eighteenth century many of these taxes were more or less permanent. The taxes consisted of a very large number of different imposts. There was usually some form of customs duty levied on goods imported into the kingdom. The value of the duty might vary very considerably according to whether the importer was a native of the kingdom, whether he belonged to a nation which had concluded a commercial treaty, or whether he was simply a foreigner with no special privileges. Sometimes duties were a percentage of the value of the commodity, but it was extremely difficult to know what the duty ought to be, and at most ports there was a great deal of smuggling. Another form of tax very common in the eighteenth century was some form of royal monopoly. Often the king had a monopoly of the sale of tobacco, or playing cards, or stamped paper necessary for legal documents, or salt. In France a tax, the *gabelle*, was collected from each household for salt which it was estimated the family ought to consume each year. It was much resented, but it was a tax by no means peculiar to France. In Spain indirect taxes on the sale of commodities had luxuriated into a financial jungle. In addition to the *alcabala*, which was a tax of 10 per cent on every sale, there was another form of excise known as the *cientos*, there was the *alcabala de alta mar*, an excise charged on goods sold at sea which brought in more than the ordinary *alcabala*. There was the *milliones*, an additional tax on meat, wine, vinegar, oil, candles and soap which had been imposed as an exceptional tax under Philip II for six years and which at the end of each six years had been renewed. There was a similar tax on various other commodities. The *quinto y milliones de nieve* was a tax imposed on ice and snow used to cool drinks or keep food fresh. There was a tax on brandy, though it yielded a relatively small sum. There were taxes on *sosa y barilla*, on sugar and on silk. In Prussia the Excise ('*Accise*') was collected from towns and was at once an indirect tax on food and drink and a tax on each individual, on his occupation and on his premises. It has been said that the Excise was the foundation of the Prussian civil service; in Spain, certainly, it was one chronic cause of poverty, and there was some reason for the fear that inspired an eighteenth-century caricaturist to show Walpole's excise scheme as involving servitude and humiliation. The British lion was shown harnessed to a wagon in which Walpole rode on a barrel of dutiable liquor. The lion had had his tail docked, his ribs showed through his mangy hide, he was wearing wooden shoes and he was bridled so that a soldier, who rode a unicorn, might drive him. The cartoon was labelled 'Excise and Servitude'. Though Walpole's scheme might never have undermined English liberties, the eighteenth-century observer might well consider the experience of other countries and be suspicious.

In the conditions of the eighteenth century direct taxes were very difficult to collect. It was almost beyond the powers of a monarchy of the *ancien régime* to make regular assessments of the wealth of its subjects. In an age when money was not normally invested in a bank it was almost impossible to assess movable wealth. Different districts claimed varying exemptions and the different social estates also claimed degrees of exemption. Even in Prussia the nobles, except those of East Prussia, claimed exemption from the direct tax known as the contribution, and in any case the Prussian tax was collected on the basis of an assessment long out of date. In France the direct tax, or *taille*, was, in fact, generally assessed on land, but here again the assessment was long out of date; there were considerable divergencies between one district and another, the *pays d'états* paying at a lower rate than the *pays d'élection*; the privileged orders of nobles and clergy were exempt. The other direct taxes, the *capitation*, imposed in 1695, and the *dixième*, imposed in 1705, were no more uniform than the *taille*. In Spain the direct taxes were peculiar in that they affected both the nobles and the clergy: such had been the financial desperation of the Spanish kings that not even the two privileged orders had managed to evade tax. The clergy paid a proportion of their tithes, the *tercias reales*, which had been granted to the king in 1219 and had been made a permanent tax in 1501, and the *excusado* which had been granted by the pope in 1571 but only became a permanent tax in 1757. They also paid a tax which had been granted to the king in 1561 for five years to defray naval expenses and which had been renewed. Bishops paid the king half their first year's income from a new see, and contributed a very large sum to be used for pensions. The king enjoyed the income of benefices in the Indies left vacant by the death of the incumbent and received the movable property of bishops who died in office. The clergy contributed a tax known as a Crusading tax. They also paid the *alcabala* and *milliones*, though at a rather lower rate than did the laity, but did not have to pay on the sale of produce from ecclesiastical estates. The nobles since the time of Philip IV had paid a contribution instead of doing military service; they also paid a tax on ennoblement and a similar tax was paid by office holders on promotion.

The monarchs of the *ancien régime* tried desperately to raise money. If they did not tithe mint and rue the king of Spain taxed grass and snow. Yet the king of Prussia was the only monarch in continental Europe who managed to balance his budget. The others had to resort to loans and, in general, royal credit was so poor that the kings had to pay very high rates of interest. At the end of the century the credit of the French king, who ruled one of the largest and richest populations in Europe, was so bad that a financial crisis developed which ended in the fall of the monarchy. Prussia built up a treasure by a rigorous efficiency in collecting taxes and farming the royal estates, but when involved in war she still required foreign subsidies. One object of the reforms of Maria Theresa was to make her government independent of such subsidies from England. Against this background the establishment of the Bank of England and the creation of a Sinking Fund in England in 1717 acquire a special interest. The personal credit of Charles II had been shown to be valueless when the Exchequer was closed in 1672. William III had had to offer an interest-rate of 14 per cent to raise a loan to finance the War of the Grand Alliance. The Government of England had not had a reputation for good economy, yet with fewer subjects than the king of France, the Austrian Habsburg or the king of Spain, the king of England was able to mobilise a greater proportion of his resources for war than could any of those great monarchs. After the establishment of the Sinking Fund had shown that the English Government, unlike the French, regarded a debt incurred in time of war as binding and not to be repudiated, English credit improved, whereas the personal credit of the French royal house did not.

If the finances of the European monarchies of the early eighteenth century were a labyrinth of temporary expedients devised without any co-ordinating plan and indefinitely continued, the administration of justice was in equal confusion. The root of the problem was that over very large parts of Europe nobles still exercised some feudal rights of justice over their peasants. Where possible the monarch tried, as did Maria Theresa, to establish the tradition that a sentence in a manorial court had to be confirmed by a representative of the imperial Government, and this Bielfeld believed to be the ideal. Until a comparatively late stage the administration of justice, even in the capital, had been combined with executive functions. It was one of the reforms of Maria Theresa to separate the two—at least at the centre of government. In France justice was administered by the lawyers in the provincial *parlements*. In the first half of the eighteenth century there was great confusion as to what the law was. In France Roman law prevailed in the south and customary law in the north. It was not until the time of the Enlightened Despots (and in this matter Napoleon counts as the last and most enlightened of them all) that laws were codified and simplified. In many countries, even in France itself, torture was used to try to obtain from condemned criminals the names of their accomplices. Bielfeld was only one of many observers who deplored this practice. Spain had its great collection of laws and a magnificent system of law courts, both at home and in the Indies, but the procedure was interminably slow.

The finances might be confused and uncertain and the administration of justice a tangle of unco-ordinated institutions, some of them still feudal in character, but during the eighteenth century monarchical government in Europe was undoubtedly becoming more efficient. Not only was there increased specialisation at the centre of the administration; there was also increasing effectiveness at the extremities. The development of a professional civil service during this century was one of the most enduring achievements of the *ancien régime*. The symbol of this new efficiency was the *intendant*, whose office had grown up in France since the time of the wars of religion. The office seems to have been originated to meet the extraordinary conditions created by the civil war. From 1560 onwards trained lawyers, *maîtres des requêtes*, were sent occasionally to some part of France to investigate a particular difficulty. The practice was dropped at the end of the wars, but Richelieu revived it again as an emergency measure. Mazarin continued the practice, although it aroused some opposition, and by the time Louis XIV took over personal control of political affairs, *intendants* were not only general in all the provinces of France but had ceased to be temporary visitors charged with a particular mission, and had become regular, permanent administrative officials. In 1689 an *intendant* was appointed to the province of Brittany, the last province of France to receive such a representative of the central authority. By the eighteenth century it could be said that the prosperity or ruin of France was in the hands of thirty *intendants*. They were appointed either by the Controller General of Finances or, if they were to work in a frontier province, by the Minister of War. The area for which each *intendant* was responsible was roughly the same as that of one of the old *généralités*, of which there had been thirty-four. Within his area the *intendant's* scope was very wide. He superintended recruiting for the army, he dispensed justice, he apportioned the *taille* and was responsible for collecting direct taxes; he regulated trade, industry and agriculture; he emitted orders from the *Conseil des Dépêches* affecting administration. Sometimes it was he who, in fact, drafted legislation; sometimes his advice was invited by the central Government; sometimes he took the initiative and submitted a memorandum. By the eighteenth century these *intendants* were men of considerable position. They had all had enough money to buy themselves the post of *maître des requêtes*, and even if they provoked the anger of the central authority and were dismissed from their intendancy they could always return to their practice of the law. Sometimes the *intendants* came from old and honourable families. They were usually men of about thirty and in the eighteenth century this was not young; men had become secretaries of state at the age of twenty-five. Sometimes the *intendants* felt strong enough to resist the central Government. One *intendant* refused for four years to answer an inquiry from the central Government as to why he had issued a particular *ordonnance* and when he did reply it was only to say that he had been entitled to act as he had. Another *intendant* openly expressed regret at having to implement a royal order. A third regularly included a sum in his account which was as regularly queried. But though the *intendants* sometimes showed a considerable spirit of independence towards the central Government the fact remained that they were the king's salaried servants. They made administration their profession, and though communications were slow and local privileges and customs strong, the presence in the provinces of the *intendants* with their secretaries and assistants made the Government of the late seventeenth and the eighteenth century more effective than monarchical government had ever been before .The same system was eventually, after a generation, introduced in Spain. These military *intendants* had proved useful during the War of the Spanish Succession, and in 1718 Philip V tried the experiment of appointing a military *intendant* in each province. This attempt proved unsuccessful, and had to be countermanded, but in 1749 the office of *intendant* was once more introduced and this time the reform was permanent. In Spain there was a special class of military *intendant* who was better paid than the civilian official. The military *intendants* were appointed in frontier districts such as Estremadura or Valencia, in an outpost of Spanish authority such as Majorca, in Aragon and even in Castile itself. The other seventeen posts were filled by civil *intendants* whose functions embraced a very wide field. Until 1766 in theory, and probably until the end of the *ancien régime* in fact, they had judicial powers in the exercise of which they were helped by two experts, one in civil and the other in criminal law. They were responsible for drawing up the lists of men eligible for military service and for drawing lots to see which individuals should actually perform it. They were responsible for the upkeep of barracks and magazines. They were supposed to study the economic conditions of their provinces and to prepare reports on how the economic resources of the province could be improved. They were also required to produce maps of their provinces showing exactly which lands belonged to the Crown, which to the nobles, the Church and the Military Orders. In 1749 the king of Spain suppressed the farming of royal revenues, and the responsibility for collecting taxes was one of the earliest duties of the re-established office of *intendant*. In the business of assessing and collecting taxes the *intendant* had the help of various specialised officials such as those concerned with provincial taxes and with the monopolies of salt and tobacco. But even with the help of specialists and of subordinates who administered smaller territorial divisions within each province, the business which the Spanish *intendant* was supposed to do was prodigious. As Campomanes said, the instructions drawn up for the *intendants* were very fine, but they were about as far from reality as the dreams of Plato or of Sir Thomas More.

In Prussia, Sweden and Denmark the system of provincial administration as it had developed by the middle of the eighteenth century differed from the French and Spanish system in that the work was carried on not by one man but by a board which deliberated and took decisions by a majority vote; but it resembled the French system in that it marked a great increase in effective control over the economy and justice of the different parts of the country. In Brandenburg-Prussia the increased efficiency in the administration began in the time of the Great Elector, who had divided his dominions into small administrative units known as *Kreise*. As in so much else, Frederick William I completed the work of the Great Elector by setting up a series of seventeen provincial boards covering all the *Kreise* which made up the sprawling State of Prussia. A provincial board had twenty or thirty members, one of whom might be responsible for one or two rural *Kreise*, another might control some cities, another might be responsible for some farms belonging to the royal domain. Generally one official would check the work of another. Decisions were taken by majority vote, but the opinion of the minority was also forwarded to the General Directory. The competence of these provincial boards was enormous. They collected the taxes and the income from the royal domains; they fostered industrialisation; they promoted internal colonisation. On the whole the officials were not well paid and *travailler pour le roi de Prusse* became synonymous with working for a pittance. There was very little scope for initiative: each member of the board was checked by his colleagues and they were all closely restricted by the written regulations issued by the king on almost every possible point, but the system of government by local boards had several considerable merits. In Prussia the bureaucracy was exceptionally efficient: its methods of accountancy were better than those of many merchants. The Prussian administration was also singularly free from the evils of patronage which were rampant in such countries as England, Hanover and Saxony, and from purchase, which was sometimes a cause of inefficiency in France. In Prussia many noble families were so poor that their sons were glad to enter the provincial administration in the hope of acquiring the prestige of a president of one of the seventeen provincial boards.

The nature of this eighteenth-century provincial civil service is clearly to be seen in the emergence of such a body in the Austrian Lands of the Habsburgs. The institution which Maria Theresa had taken as the basis of her reforms to improve the efficiency of her administration in the provinces was that of district officer, or *Kreishauptmann*, which had existed in the lands belonging to the Bohemian Crown since the late thirteenth century. Originally these officials had been local nobles, and as late as 1526 they had been an essential part of the power of the local Estates of Bohemia and Silesia. Gradually the office had passed increasingly under the control of the Crown, partly because of the increase in royal authority as a result of the Counter-Reformation and still more because of the eclipse of the power of the Bohemian Estates after the battle of the White Mountain in 1620. After 1620 the district officers were no longer elected by the provincial Estates: they were appointed by the Emperor as king of Bohemia. In 1669 the institution was overhauled, rates of pay were improved and the servants of the district officers were given regular status. In 1748 the Bohemian institution of district officer was introduced in Styria, Carinthia and Carniola; in 1753 it was set up in Lower Austria and in 1754 in Tyrol. When the reforms of Maria Theresa were complete, there were forty-seven districts in her Austrian and Bohemian provinces. The number of district officers serving the Habsburgs is comparable to the thirty *intendants* who held in their hands the welfare or the misery of France. By comparison, the twenty-four *intendants* in Spain seem very few, though the seventeen provincial boards of Prussia were probably adequate because of the large number of officials on each board and the relatively small extent of the territories of the king of Prussia. The staff of an Austrian district officer was often very small; for example, in Moravia in 1760 there were in addition to the district officer himself two or three commissioners, a secretary, a few clerks and some messengers. By comparison with the small staff the responsibilities of the district officer, like those of the *intendant*, were legion. When the office was established in the Austrian provinces in 1748 the functions laid down were to supervise the quartering and provisioning of troops and to see that the peasants were kept in 'a proper state of taxability'. To these responsibilities were later added supervision of vagabonds, forests and hospitals. In 1765 the district officer was put in charge of police, schools, religion, communications and commerce. In 1769 all sentences by manorial courts had to be confirmed by a district officer. In 1770 his functions were described as being 'to fulfill her Majesty's orders reliably, to keep good order and to look after every thing concerning the public welfare'. The fact that it was possible to require an official to 'look after every thing' was an indication of the increase in the scope of royal government which had taken place since the middle of the seventeenth century. The development of the office of district officer in the later eighteenth century was also symptomatic of the changes that were taking place within the governmental machine. In 1781 rights of pension were recognised according to length of service. Complaints at the slowness of promotion suggest that men had come to look on the provincial administration as a permanent profession. That members of this profession were developing a corporate sense is suggested by quarrels over questions of precedence between civil administrators and officers of the army. From as early as 1776 candidates for office in the administration of the Habsburg empire had to show evidence of having studied the science of administration and politics known as *Kameralwissenschaft*.

By contrast with the efficiency of the civil service built up in Bohemia and Austria the Habsburgs had much more difficulty in getting their orders carried out in Hungary. The difficulty confronting the Crown came not from the parliament, which was a mere shadow, but from the impossibility of creating an effective civil service. In each county of Hungary there was a *föispán*, or high sheriff, but he was a very different person from the district officer in the hereditary Austrian provinces. According to instructions issued in 1752 and repeated in 1768 the business of these high sheriffs was to preserve the Catholic faith and advance sound learning. They were required to make returns of the number of people in their county and of their religion; they were to keep roads in repair, maintain prisons, take care of orphans and keep the local archives; they were to see that royal orders were put into effect. The instructions were in the tone of those issued with excellent effect to the civil servants in the German and Bohemian provinces of the Habsburgs, but in Hungary they were less effective. The *föispán* often was a great noble living in his castle. The post could be hereditary in a great family or by custom associated with the see of a particular bishop. The *föispán* was a Hungarian magnate by no means enthusiastic in his duty to a monarch whom he looked on as a foreigner. He did not show himself particularly zealous to carry out the reforms ordered from Vienna, and he was more interested in preserving the liberties of the Hungarian nobility than in building up a more effective kind of absolutism. The Hungarian gentlemen who administered justice in the country districts were more like the J.P.'s of England than any body of officials in France, Prussia or even nearby Austria. The only officials who were effective instruments of royal authority in Hungary were the paid subordinates who collected the customs or the salt tax. Hardly one-tenth of these were Hungarians and, in general, employment as a paid bureaucrat was despised by the Hungarian gentry. Monarchical absolutism extended to Hungary, partly because the crown of St Stephen was worn by a Habsburg who was already the head of an effective administrative machine in the other half of his dominions, but it was a less efficient absolutism than the system which operated in Austria and Bohemia, which could rely on the willing and intelligent service of men trained in the principles of cameralism.

The J.P.'s of England had more than a little in common with the *Tablibiro* of Hungary. The J.P. of the eighteenth century was a local nobleman or gentleman who voluntarily helped to dispense justice and to administer his locality. His powers were considerable. He was concerned with revenue, the armed forces, trade, poor relief, food supply, prices, wages and many other things. In 1700 J.P.s were empowered to build and maintain prisons. In 1744 they were empowered to confine lunatics, though it was not till 1774 that they got power to licence and control asylums. After 1766 they were specifically responsible for the maintenance of highways. In 1739 they were empowered to levy a general rate. Yet though the J.P. performed many of the functions of the French *intendant*, the Prussian *Landrat*, or the Habsburg *Kreishauptmann*, in theory his position was very different. At a time when in most of continental Europe the power of the State was increasing, in England the idea of State control had never had less meaning. All administration was looked on as the mere fulfilment of duties imposed by common or statute law. The justices obtained their position because they were prominent local gentlemen. They held office for life, and received no payment. They gained experience which might be useful if they were elected to serve as members of parliament, but their business was to carry out the law, and not to obey the central Government.

It was symptomatic of the great increase in the efficiency of government in most parts of continental Europe from the late seventeenth and early eighteenth centuries that this period saw the elaboration of a theory of administration by the cameralistic writers in the German-speaking part of Europe. Forerunners of this school of political thought can be discerned in such writers as Osse and Obrecht, who were preoccupied with currency problems of sixteenth-century Saxony. As administrative technique was improved, first in Austria by the Emperor Maximilian I, and then in the second half of the sixteenth century in Bavaria, Saxony and Brandenburg, a body of paid, professional officials, trained in Roman law and devoting their whole time to the business of administration, emerged and came to be known as the cameralists of the bureaus. They were, in fact, the 'back-room boys' of the new absolutisms of the sixteenth century, and they differed from the contemporary mercantilists who served the rulers of England, by being preoccupied not so much with problems of commerce as with problems of administration. In the seventeenth century, when Leopold I consciously set out to imitate the reforms of his cousin Louis XIV, another school of cameralist writers developed in Austria. Of these the best known were Becker, von Hornigke, von Schröder and Seckendorf. In 1727 chairs for the study of cameral science were created at Halle and Frankfurt-am-Oder, and, though neither of the first two professors, Gasser or Dithmar, was of any great eminence, the influence of the chairs was considerable, for generations of young Germans learnt cameralistic principles. Darjes was a cameralistic thinker who much influenced Frederick II, and Sonnenfells played an important part in the administrative reforms of Maria Theresa. The principles of cameralism were, in the middle of the eighteenth century, set out most clearly by Justi. He declared that of all types of government monarchy was the best, that the success of a monarch was the true happiness of the State, and that to attain this should be the object of all government. He then went on to say that the business of the ruler must be to preserve and increase the resources of the State, to apply these resources so as to achieve his triumph, and finally to ensure the safety of his State. The way in which administrative technique could increase the State's resources and how these could be applied most effectually to achieve the triumph of the monarch were the study of young men who hoped to become officials, whether of the Habsburgs, the Hohenzollerns, the Wittelsbachs or the Wettins.

The effect of these studies and of the system of administration, which developed in the German-speaking States, was to create a type of government peculiar, in the nineteenth century, to eastern Europe, and known as the Civil Service State. It was immensely efficient, its officials were honest and devoted, but it was a society in which the political virtues were different from those of France (where an *intendant* could and did resist and criticise the central Government), and very different indeed from those of England, where most of the administrative and judicial functions, which in France, or Prussia, Spain or the Habsburg dominions were in the hands of paid professional civil servants, were done voluntarily by private gentlemen—some of whom were as eccentric as Sir Roger de Coverley and some as intractable as Squire Sullen.

This then was the monarchical system of government which was usual in most of the great countries of Europe in the eighteenth century. It was characterised by a king with more or less absolute powers at the centre surrounded at court by counsellors who were becoming increasingly expert in their particular branches of administration, and served in the provinces by a corps of civil servants who were becoming increasingly professional. There were some exceptions to this pattern but, with one exception, their political records were not such as to make their systems of government appear as serious rivals to that of centralised, absolutist, well-served monarchy. Indeed, Frederick II was expressing a common opinion when he said that Sweden, which had since 1718 been transformed in fact from a monarchy into a republic, was naturally declining in power. Both Montesquieu and Rousseau supposed that it was natural for republics to govern small territories. Even the record of the United Provinces did not shake the eighteenth-century belief that the characteristic function of a monarchy was war and aggrandisement and the characteristic state of a republic peace and moderation, for the Dutch had won their greatest successes when their political system had most nearly resembled the monarchical, and since the House of Orange had taken a less prominent share in their government their prestige in Europe had declined. The other republics, such as Genoa, Venice and Switzerland, were by the eighteenth century very inconsiderable politically. There remained one State which did not conform to the monarchic and bureaucratic pattern familiar in Europe from Portugal to Russia and from Norway to Naples: that was Poland.

The Polish system of government was by the eighteenth century a notorious example of inefficiency. The Crown was elective, and at each election was limited by further concessions. The authority of the Crown was challenged by the Diet made up of the Estates. The central Government still bore an obvious resemblance to a medieval arrangement of officers. There was a body of seven counsellors who attended the king for six months at a time, but this could hardly bear comparison with the councils of France or the General Directory of Prussia. In the provinces the king could appoint a *starosta*, or sheriff, to promulgate royal orders, collect taxes, preserve order and perform some judicial duties, but the *starosta's* authority was much less than that of the local assembly of magnates, even as the authority of the king was continually hampered by the sessions of biennial parliaments. The ineffectiveness of Polish policy completely discredited the form of government in the eyes of eighteenth-century observers. A writer such as Bielfeld, commenting on the Polish Constitution before the catastrophe of the partitions had demonstrated its utter weakness, affirmed that the governmental machinery seemed to observe some rules and that the State seemed very regularly contrived, but admitted that the government of Poland could be nothing but 'confused and tumultuous' and a 'perpetual anarchy'. D'Argenson was even more outspoken in his criticism of a system of government which left Poland defenceless and hopelessly weak.

One problem of government which much interested politically-minded observers of the early eighteenth century was posed by England. In Sweden the elected Diet had, since 1718, made good its claim to control the king, but Sweden had thereafter declined as a Power. Poland, where the Diet could block any unpopular royal policy, was a by-word for weakness and anarchy, but England, though the parliament shared the government with the king, was steadily increasing in wealth and prestige. At the end of the seventeenth century the English were not regarded as models of political wisdom, yet these turbulent and seditious people had proved themselves the most formidable opponents of Louis XIV, were fast becoming the world's greatest colonial Power, increased yearly in wealth and nourished such geniuses as Locke and Newton. Locke's *Essay concerning Humane Understanding*, published in 1690 and immediately translated into French, had a formative influence upon the thought of a generation which hovered between traditional Christian metaphysic and the outright scepticism of Bayle; Newton's European reputation was achieved more slowly, but at no distant time he would be hailed as the prophet who had revealed the harmony of rational law behind the mysterious and chaotic face of nature. The time could not be long delayed when men would ask whether there might not be some link between these achievements and the political institutions of the country which produced them. In a more superficial way curiosity was stimulated by the influence of British party politics upon European affairs during the War of the Spanish Succession, and by the arrival, after 1714, of a new crop of Jacobite exiles who had, nevertheless, accepted the principles of limited monarchy.

Locke's political writings had been ignored abroad while his philosophy was welcomed, and European ideas upon English history and institutions had been moulded by extreme monarchist interpretations, of which Bossuet's funeral oration upon Henrietta of England was perhaps the finest example. The barrier of language was a formidable obstacle to any real understanding, and unquestioning acceptance of absolutist dogma had blinded travellers to any merit which might exist beneath the violent and complex surface of British politics; but after 1685 there were those—the Huguenot exiles—who wrote in French for a European public and were animated by a propagandist zeal against the regime of Louis XIV. One of the most distinguished was Paul de Rapin-Thoyras, who published in 1717 a *Dissertation upon the Whigs and Tories* and in 1723 the first two volumes of a monumental *History of England*, which was to be for many years a standard work upon both sides of the Channel. The significance of Rapin-Thoyras's work lay not only in its scope, but also in its interpretation. He saw English history as a record of conflict between liberty and despotism, in which the contemporary party struggle was the latest and perhaps the last chapter, and which had culminated in a 'mixed monarchy' preserving in a civilised age liberties derived from the remote past. In the 1720's there was therefore already a considerable interest in English institutions, a growing belief that the British people enjoyed an elusive quality called liberty, and a demand for an answer to the question 'what is it like to live in a free country?' It was this question which Voltaire was enabled, by his exile in England, to answer in a masterly way.

At first sight the *Lettres philosophiques* appeared a haphazard collection of impressions by an intelligent observer; they were, in fact, carefully chosen to illustrate significant aspects of English life, and the omissions are as important as the text. The banal splendours of George II's coronation were ignored, but the prestige of scientific genius was shown by a description of Newton's funeral. The British aristocracy were described not by the magnificence of their country houses, but by their encouragement of inoculation for smallpox and their patronage of literature. The theory and limitations of religious toleration were not discussed, but the reality of toleration was demonstrated by the long account of life with a Quaker family. Nothing could have been better calculated to satisfy curiosity about the real nature of English life, and, by implication, to reproach the conventions of contemporary France. In one respect, however, some readers must have found the *Lettres* inadequate; though Voltaire drew attention to some of the effects of free government—

proportional taxation, no legal immunities, no seigneurial justice—his comments upon the form of government were superficial and poorly informed. Europe had to wait until 1748 and the *De l'esprit des lois* for a formal analysis of the British system.

In England, which he visited shortly after Voltaire, Montesquieu was probably converted from an unrealistic regret for the decay of republican virtue to an appreciation of what could be done for liberty in a 'mixed monarchy'. He also owed much to English writers, especially to Locke and to Bolingbroke. Unlike Voltaire, Montesquieu was not concerned to describe but to analyse, and he felt himself entitled to omit many of the qualifications which he knew to exist. He was certainly aware of the corrupt influence of the executive upon the legislature, and he placed his main faith for the future of English liberty upon the good sense of the middle classes. 'It is not for me', he wrote, 'to discover whether the English enjoy this liberty or not. It is enough for me to say that it is established by their laws and I go no further.' He found the distinctive characteristic of English law to be the recognition that the powers of government were of three distinct kinds—executive, legislative, and judicial —and that they ought to be separately exercised by different persons. The fact that this was not always adhered to in practice does not really affect his argument, for, if the Lord Chancellor was both minister and judge or if a magistrate both executed the law and punished malefactors, different codes were observed in exercising the two functions. Montesquieu did, however, weaken his account by failing to give a satisfactory account of the judicature, and by attempting, unsuccessfully, to identify the separation of legal powers with the political separation between King, Lords, and Commons. It is also true that his disciples seized upon the main features of his analysis to support a highly idealised picture of English government.

Locke was the mainspring of Montesquieu's theory of the separation of powers, and from the same source English writers adopted the notion of the separation of powers and 'checks and balances' as the distinguishing characteristic of their constitution. Blackstone presented this picture, though in a more refined and perhaps more realistic form, while a host of writers at home and abroad agreed that the main object of this complex balance of power was the preservation of liberty. It was this which gave Britain a position not unlike that of Russia in the third and fourth decades of the twentieth century as the promised land of an influential intelligentsia. While Rousseau was to criticise the false concept of English liberty, the lessons of English constitutionalism were written deep into the intellectual beliefs of Europe; they influenced both rationalist critics of the *ancien régime* and the constitutional claims of the *Parlement* of Paris enunciated on the eve of the Revolution; they emerged as decisive influences upon the Constitution of the United States and upon the experiments in constitutional monarchy of revolutionary France.

CHAPTER VIII

THE ARMED FORCES AND THE ART OF WAR

THIS picture of the art of war and the social foundations of the armed forces in the eighteenth century has been drawn from a study of the conditions in England, France, and Prussia: conditions in the Austrian, Russian and other armies, though different in detail, were not different in essence.

A note of leisure characterised eighteenth-century warfare, both on land and at sea, until the Revolutionary wars, first of America, then of France, introduced a sense of energy such as the preceding years had never known, and began that ideological warfare characteristic of the nineteenth and twentieth centuries. Whereas in modern times the function of generals is to win campaigns by decisive battles, in the eighteenth century few would have questioned a saying of the great duke of Alva, quoted with approval by Lord Hardwicke to the duke of Newcastle in September 1760: 'It is the business of a general always to get the better of his enemy, but not always to fight, and if he can do his business without fighting, so much the better.'[1]

At sea, Clarendon's views in his verdict on Blake, written in the preceding century, also still held good. Blake, according to Clarendon, was 'the first man that declin'd the old track... and despised those rules which had been long in practice, to keep his ship and his men out of danger; which had been held in former times a point of great ability and circumspection; as if the principal art requisite in the captain of a ship had been to be sure to come home again'.[2] Armies and navies were expensive necessities for the limited resources of eighteenth-century governments; military forces and ships represented a heavy investment in time and money, and if lost in action could not be easily replaced.

The art of war recognised this. Unalterable precedent was the keynote of most eighteenth-century warfare—a pedantic regard for what were becoming petrified military rules and conventions. Although the highly trained but relatively small armies grew gradually in size as population increased, and although methods of transport and communication improved, the Powers, when at war with one another, relied more and more upon defensive fortifications and siegecraft; their basic strategy and tactics continued with little change until the end of the century. On land, there was formal fencing instead of fighting, conventional manœuvring instead of seeking decision by battle. At sea, the century is characterised

[1] Sir J. S. Corbett, *England in the Seven Years War* (London, 1918), vol. II, p. 95.
[2] Michael Lewis, *The Navy of Britain* (London, 1948), p. 228.

by the dead hand of the British Permanent Fighting Instructions, coupled with the sacrosanct doctrine of the maintenance of the line of battle. 'A line of battle', runs *A Narrative of the Proceedings of his Majesty's Fleet* (1744), 'is the basis and formulation of all discipline in sea fights, as is universally practised by all the nations that are masters of any power at sea. It has had the test of long experience, and stood before the stroke of time, pure and unaltered, handed down by our predecessors.'[1] The French navy, according to Ramatuelle in his *Tactique navale*, 'has always preferred the glory of assuring or preserving a conquest to that more brilliant perhaps, but actually less real, of taking some ships, and therein has approached more nearly the true end that has been proposed in war'.[2] Contests between forces were to be discouraged; indeed, it was almost a mishap to fall in with a hostile force. Action was avoided wherever it was possible honourably so to do, and particularly at sea. Two hostile forces rarely joined in battle unless they could oppose an equal number of ships of the same class. Until the Battle of the Nile (1798), where all thirteen British line-of-battleships took a relatively equal share, there had nearly always been a number of unengaged ships in naval clashes, vessels which suffered no casualties, and only exchanged passing shots. Drawn in two parallel lines, rival fleets manœuvred with a view to direct engagement in a series of single combats, making a sea battle a gun duel pure and simple. As late as 1794, it was considered 'rascally' when French battleships fired on frigates not taking part in the direct engagement, the breaking of careful rules and established precedent.

Wars were conducted as economically as possible; circumspection and defence prevailed over audacity and offence. Preservation of a force was the first object, the results of its action secondary. A commander like General Braddock exemplified the system that produced and trained him —traditional, methodical, and inflexible—a man lacking originality of mind, who would not fail to do everything the regulations prescribed, but would certainly do nothing more. Admiral Byng, more alive to the difficulties of a task than resolute to overcome them, a man who met failures half way, though personally brave, was further harassed off Minorca (1756) by the conviction that he must preserve his line of battle, and must justify each signal by the Permanent Instructions. The duke of Cumberland, fighting a set piece battle at Hastenbeck (1757), was pinned down by the rigidity of his plan; the correctness of his scheme was in fact its weakness. Wolfe criticised Lord Loudoun in North America for imperilling his force by adhering 'so literally and strictly to the 1–2–3 firings by the impracticable chequer'.[3] Insufficient allowance for unavoidable contingencies, and leaving nothing to that incalculable element in war,

---

[1] *A Narrative of the Proceedings of His Majesty's Fleet* (London, 1744), p. 48.
[2] A. T. Mahan, *The Influence of sea power upon history* (10th ed., London), p. 287.
[3] Hist. MSS. Comm. *Stopford Sackville MSS.* vol. ii, p. 257.

chance, was precisely what the formalised art of war overlooked: 'defeat and victory', it was written in 1776, 'depend much upon the chapter of accidents and fortuitous causes that admit not of regular reasoning upon, and numberless events that can neither be guarded against nor foreseen'.[1]

The defensive nature of warfare was further promoted by the belief that the function of a navy was primarily trade protection, direct or indirect, more especially in this age of competition for mercantile empire. As soon as the mercantile marine became a recognised burden on the navy, the main lines of commerce became also the main lines of naval strategy, the crossings of trade routes its focal points. Even when new feelings were stirring, the War of American Independence continued the inconclusive naval contests, 'the heading off of an enemy from some objective towards which his approach was most usually half hearted',[2] fought, apart from the frigate duels, close to some convoy route. Trafalgar (1805) was perhaps the last great naval battle entered with the pomp and ceremony of eighteenth-century circumstance. The manner was still that of the approach to the duel, but the intention, annihilation, vastly different.

In theory and in practice, eighteenth-century wars were wars of limited liability—about something concrete, rather than the earlier wars of righteousness and moral purpose—clashes between rulers, between dynastic States in limited wars fought with limited means for limited objectives, which ended with the drawing up of a balance sheet. They were a natural revulsion from the horrors of the Thirty Years War, where fanaticism and moral indignation had multiplied the number of atrocities. Though there were great wars, devastation and unnecessary bloodshed were kept in check by strict adherence to the rules, customs, and laws, of war, the accepted code of the eighteenth-century war-game. To the benevolent despots, war, like peace, could be planned, The art of war prescribed elaborate rules of strategy, siegecraft, capitulations, military honours, treatment of prisoners, and the rights of civilians. Clear distinction was made between armed forces and civilians in military operations. While in strict law the entire enemy population was subject to attack, approved usage generally exempted civilians—who, after all, provided the resources for the game to be played. That game was left to the professionals, who were a self-contained service apart from the general population, with a separate organisation, discipline, law, and professional standard. A good government in this age was one that demanded little of its subjects, which regarded them as useful, worthy, and productive assets to the State, and which in wartime interfered as little as possible with civilian life. Frederick the Great's ideal was that, when he was engaged in war, the civilian population should not be aware that a state of war existed—a brave combination of the order and stability of bureaucratised monarchy with the

[1] Hist. MSS. Comm., *Laing MSS*, vol. ii, p. 492.
[2] David Mathew, *The Naval Heritage*, p. 114.

disciplined and conventionalised warfare of professional armies. As for the English, their view was that they should man the navy, serve on board merchantmen, conquer enemy colonies, and keep the workshops humming to increase the national wealth, that someone else should do most of the soldiering, and that European allies should be subsidised to take the field against a common enemy. By such means, the civilian population achieved a security quite unknown in the previous century of wars of general devastation. This also had an important effect on the social structure of the armed forces, which were drawn from the economically unproductive elements of society. A clear attempt was made to distinguish between the political and economic life of the State.

War had lost its imaginative idealism, and had become formalised both in initiation and in waging. It was mainly concerned with the balance of power—wars were between dynasties, not between peoples. Royal war and royal marriage were the two procedures through which conveyances of the private estates of dynasties, or parts of them, were effected from one dynasty to another. The names of the three chief wars of the first half of the century, the wars of Spanish, Polish and Austrian Succession, suggest that war only occurred when matrimonial arrangements had failed, or become inextricably confused. Defence predominated over offence; victory was seldom pushed to the complete destruction of the beaten force. Operations were precise, rational, mechanical—because of the lack of mobility, arising from the badness of the roads, the slowness of communication, the difficulty of winter campaigning, and the problem of supply in enemy territory, and also because of the social composition and military structure of the armies. For these reasons, small countries could still survive against large. Such narrowly political wars admitted of compromise, of arranging compensation. If the result produced a more unsatisfactory balance and disposition of forces than before, sides could be changed—even at times in the middle of a war.

Balance was the most marked characteristic of the eighteenth century; battles which were destructive, and upset balance, were for that reason not sought. Instead, there was preference for operations against fortresses, magazines, supply-lines, key positions—a learned warfare in which ingenuity in manœuvre was more prized than impetuosity in combat. War of position prevailed over war of movement, a strategy of small successive advantages over that of annihilation. Wars were long, but not intense.

Until the Revolutionary wars changed the character of warfare, the number of sieges exceeded that of battles. The possession of a hostile fortress was of greater positive value than the results of the average field victory, since apart from its immediate benefits it served as a bargaining counter at the making of peace. Fortresses were built along the well-defined geographical routes of invasion, which were also the historical routes, and citizens of large cities and towns still valued walls against an enemy. Fortified cities on a frontier exposed to sudden attack, and those in the interior whose populations were of questionable loyalty, were strengthened by the ruler with citadels garrisoned with State troops, secure against an attack from without or a revolt from within. The commander of such a fortress was given definite written instructions, setting out clearly the nature of the defence required in the event of a siege. If the commander surrendered prematurely, he was liable to trial before a military tribunal. The revised instructions to fortress commanders issued by Louis XIV in 1705 remained in force in the French army until 1792, requiring the commander to repulse only one assault on the body of a fortress after a breach had been made. Honour was then satisfied, although it was to the interest of all invaded States that fortified places should resist as long as possible; a prolonged defence both weakened the hostile army, and also gave time for the arrival of help, or the preparation of the next counter-move.

When artillery made a breach in fortress walls practicable for an assaulting army to enter, and when the third parallel of attack had been completed, bringing the attacking infantry within 100 yards of the breach, the fortress commander was frequently summoned with the threat that, if he did not surrender before the assault took place, no quarter would be granted the garrison, the town would be thrown open to looting, and he would be put to death. The commander of a fortress who held out need-lessly when honourable terms were offered, and nothing could be gained by prolonging the defence, was treated with the severity of the law of war —he was not correctly playing the game. If a place capitulated before the assault, soldiers were not entitled to sack, and could expect only a gratification from their commander raised by forced contributions on the town. If a place was taken by assault, it was customary to abandon it to the soldiers for a stated number of hours or days, making provision to protect the life and honour of the inhabitants. 'Such is, in this case, the right of the soldier, authorised by usage.'[1]

When a fortress surrendered, the garrison was expected to have in store at least two days' supplies of rations and ammunition, and not to have destroyed the works, and in spite of these supplies the defenders were reckoned to have been reduced to the last extremity, with no hope of prolonging the siege. The reason was that at the close of a siege, if the defence was destitute of all means of sustenance, the attacking force was in no position to furnish the necessary additional supplies.

A siege was an affair of artillery, assisted by infantry. The besieging guns opened fire initially from the first parallel, a trench about 600 yards from the hostile works, and parallel to the front attacked. Approach trenches

[1] Count Turpin de Crissé, *Commentaires sur les mémoirs de Montecuculi* (Paris, 1769), vol. II, p. 272.

were then constructed from this parallel to within 400 yards of the fortress, where the second parallel was built. Other approach trenches next carried the attack to within 100 yards of the hostile works, where the third parallel was built, and here were sited the breaching batteries of the heaviest guns. When the first parallel was completed, the days of open trenches began. On the opening of the trenches of the first parallel, a formality that could not be dispensed with took place—the troops marched in, with drums beating and flags flying. Reaching their posts in the parallel, they placed their colours on the parapet as a challenge to the enemy—as late as 1781, on the completion of the first parallel before Yorktown, Lafayette with his light infantry divisions did this in strict accord with European practice. Although the British seem to have given up this custom in the War of the Spanish Succession, because of the losses from hostile artillery, the French continued to follow it throughout the eighteenth century. At Yorktown, Lieutenant-Colonel Alexander Hamilton even went one better—he directed his light infantry battalion to mount to the very top of the parapet, where they executed a manual of arms. British gunners were so astonished at this performance that they actually ceased firing.

Surrender of a fortress was equally a matter of great formality. The honours of war were granted by a besieging army to a garrison which surrendered after valiantly defending itself. Terms of capitulation prescribed the exact details of the exit. When the evacuation began, the drums, fifes and horns of the garrison played a march of the enemy as they came out, in return for receiving the honours of war, and to show that they were not humiliated to the point where they could not exchange compliments with the victor. Throughout the century, it was always held that a fortress must be taken, and taken by siege rather than by *coup de main*. There was no question of by-passing these strongholds, of leaving them behind by sweeping operations.

Just as the art of war was reflected in the social structure of the armed forces, so the social structure in part determined the art of war. Partly to maintain effective discipline in armies, large magazines were built, from which troops could be regularly and adequately supplied in war. To allow troops to forage freely over the countryside for supplies would have encouraged wholesale desertion. Before a campaign, great stores were collected at points near a frontier, and from these, armies in the field were supplied. Two or three days forward from the magazines, ovens were built, where the flour, brought by mule train, was baked into loaves for issue to the troops. This practice limited the mobility of an army, fettered to a chain of magazines. No army could safely advance beyond five days' march from its supply base, or fifteen miles from a navigable river. Similarly, swift and scattered movements, such as the pursuit of a routed opponent, were rarely possible for armies composed of individuals and nationalities of all sorts. Such movement would dislocate the planned order of the military machine, and give too many opportunities of desertion. When Frederick the Great had to draw on his brother's army for fresh drafts to repair his losses at Hochkirch (1758), he stipulated that no Silesian battalions should be sent; as they knew every quarter of their native province, the temptation to disappear might be too great.

The column and close-order formations of the parade ground were the actual tactical formations and movements employed on the battlefield; this explains in part the rigid, exacting discipline, and constant drill. 'Unless every man is trained beforehand in peacetime for that which he will have to accomplish in war', wrote Frederick in 1752, 'one has nothing but people who bear the name of a business without knowing how to practise it.' The problem of infantry tactics in the eighteenth century was to find the forms and evolutions best suited to the use of the flintlock and the bayonet. In order to fire, it was necessary that the men should stand side by side. But the weapon took time to load—if a line was to be always ready to fire, or to be able to keep up a continuous fire, it was necessary to have several rows of men, one behind the other, called ranks, so that when one rank was firing, the others could be loading. The Prussian army was the first to dispense with a fourth rank, but three ranks remained normal throughout the latter part of the century. This formation enabled a given number of troops to produce the greatest volume of fire from what still remained an unreliable weapon—Frederick once ordered his men to aim nine paces in front of an advancing foe, trusting to the kick of the muskets to bring the muzzle into proper alignment.

The formation of such a line required precise and accurate movements, and was very slow—'in the tactics of thirty years ago and of some armies today', wrote Guibert, in his *Essai général de Tactique* (1772), 'the movements for forming a line of battle were so slow and complicated that they took hours. The line had to be formed at a safe distance from the enemy, and once the formation had been taken up it was dangerous to attempt to change it.' Drill was aimed both at accustoming men to load and fire quickly, and at enabling the line to be formed with promptitude and accuracy—marching in open columns of platoons (seventy or eighty men in three files) to form line on a given straight line. During the formation of line, the troops were defenceless; when formed, the flanks were the weak point, with little or no power of resistance. To obviate attacks at these points, commanders sought to form line at the head of an open slope with their flanks resting on obstacles such as marshes or cliffs. Line tactics were the main cause of the heavy casualties of eighteenth-century wars. Rather than attack the front of the line, attempts were made to attack the flanks, or even the rear, of the formation. The defence against this was a further line facing to the flank, or rear, and ultimately the square—a line facing in every direction. If the flanks and rear could be

protected by obstacles, there was little to fear, even from a superior force
—hence the insistence on geographical knowledge, to find a position
which the assailant could not without great risk attack in front.

At sea, there was the same formality, though never the same drill—
tactical exercises designed to implement the principles of the Fighting
Instructions were carried out in the British fleet, but systematic training
developed only gradually, depending upon the energy, initiative, or
indolence of individual flag officers. The accepted formation of a British
fleet, as it prepared for battle, was single line ahead. Rooke's Fighting
Instructions of 1703, which lasted until 1783, were based on those of
Russell, issued in 1691, and were the tactical bible of the eighteenth
century. Both had arisen from defensive circumstances, but remained
unaltered when circumstances had changed. What had been particular
orders by one man in charge indicating what he was likely to do, or order
his subordinates to do, in a set of circumstances, ceased to be those of
an admiral commanding any particular fleet, but Permanent Fighting
Instructions—standing orders, emanating from a higher authority, as
binding on the admirals themselves as on everyone else in the fleet. And
the sacrosanct twist given to the Instructions by the trial of Admiral
Matthews (1744) not only discouraged revision born of experience, but
seemed to make all striving after revision an offence. Moreover, just as
poor communications immobilised land warfare, so an inadequate signalling system at sea prevented an enterprising admiral from passing on
to his subordinates any new instructions not in the Permanent List (and so
linked to a signal). A commander-in-chief might break most other commandments, and hope to survive, but if he broke the parallel, conterminous,
inviolable line, the odds were that he broke himself. No British fleet
inflicted a wholehearted defeat upon any enemy in any stand-up fight
between Barfleur (1692) and The Saints (1782). Just as pursuit was almost
impossible by land, by sea it was discountenanced. Articles 21 of the
Instructions laid down that none of the ships of a fleet should pursue any
small number of the enemy's ships before the main body of their fleet had
been disabled or had run. The aim became entirely defensive—neither to
break the enemy's line, nor allow him to break one's own. Hence the
duel nature of naval warfare. Given equal, or nearly equal, fleets, the
eighteenth century naval system was incapable of producing victory, when
both sides played to the same set of rules. With a really good fleet, and
able commanders within the limits set by the line, the results remained
tactically indecisive, and completely unproductive.

In the eighteenth century, it was practically impossible to fight a winter
campaign in Europe. Swampy or frost-bound roads stopped the movement of guns and heavy supply transport; thus supplies could not be
maintained. As soon as bad weather came, armies went into winter
quarters. At sea, convoys came home in the autumn, battle fleets were

recalled to port, and refitted for the next fighting season. The loss of the *Victory* in the War of Austrian Succession, and of the *Association*, forty years earlier, both victims of October weather in the outer Channel, reinforced the belief that it was unwise to keep the great ships at sea after September. In West Indian waters, scene of much eighteenth-century naval warfare, there was also a respite. The constant factor there was the trade wind blowing down on the Windward Islands from a little to the north of east. From May to October the wind veered round almost to the east, and the last three months of that period, the hurricane season, precluded naval operations. The main fleets moved north then, up the eastern seaboard of the American mainland—a factor of prime importance in the War of American Independence.

'The military science may almost be called mechanical', wrote an old officer towards the end of the century.[1] Formalised warfare required little imagination and initiative of officers. Frederick the Great wrote of French officers in 1758: 'Their officers have learnt a military jargon, but they are simply parrots who have learnt to whistle a march and know nothing else.'[2] Their commander, Broglie, writing after the Seven Years War, ascribed the principal cause of the mistakes which he had seen committed to the officers, complete ignorance of the duties and of essential military detail. In six years of fighting in that war, the French armies were commanded by six generals, of whom only Broglie knew his business; for his efficiency, his command was divided, and he was then dismissed and exiled. Sub-commanders had a negligible part to play—it was observed of the French Army in 1760 that 'sometimes even the general officers directing the columns do not know to what points the staff officers are guiding them, as they are not permitted except in certain cases to open their routes'.[3] There was a weakness even in the engineers, who had a prominent part to play in defensive and siege operations—Major General Studholme Hodgson, preparing for the expedition against Belleisle (1761), wrote that he 'also desired more engineers, and that some of them may have seen service: the six I now have are unacquainted with the practical part of their profession. I dare say they made a good figure at the academy, but I think them very unequal to the conducting of a siege'.[4] As all armies were of one model, and fire and shock were well balanced, genius, when in command, dominated the field, and inspired subordinate mediocrities—this largely accounts for the decisive battles of the century.

Frederick the Great embodied the utmost in military achievement that was possible in Europe in the conditions prevailing before the French

[1] *Cautions and advices to officers of the Army*, by an old officer (Perth, 1795), p. 31.
[2] R. Lodge, *Great Britain and Prussia in the Eighteenth Century* (Oxford, 1923), p. 140, note 2.
[3] H. S. Wilkinson, *The French Army before Napoleon* (1915), p. 46.
[4] Thomas Keppel, *The Life of Augustus, Viscount Keppel* (London, 1842), vol. I, p. 316.

Revolution when citizen replaced professional armies, and aggressive, mobile, combative strategy replaced the slow strategy of statecraft. Moreover, his victories were due quite as much to his swift judgment and resource, which enabled him to surprise the enemy, as to the formations and evolutions of his forces, which he inherited. His military works— *Principes généraux de la Guerre*, (1746), *Testament politique* (1752), *Testament militaire* (1768) and *Eléments de castramétrie et de tactique* (1771) illustrate both facets. At first, Frederick preferred 'short and lively' war—'It does not suit us in the least to spin things out. A long-drawn-out war would imperceptibly destroy our admirable discipline; it would depopulate the land and drain our resources.' If a war was long, it should be one of low intensity in the expenditure of men and material. For this belief, the governing conditions of eighteenth-century war could equally well be applied—the limited resources of a State, the dependence on fixed magazines prepared beforehand, soldiers, who, however well drilled, had little inward conviction to sustain them in time of trouble. In those early years, Frederick believed the aim of warfare was not the occupation or defence of a piece of territory, but the destruction of the forces of the enemy. The best method for the efficient conduct of a great war was to take the offensive resolutely on enemy soil, and force the other side to subordinate its movements to one's own. His main strategic purpose was always this—to force an enemy to move. If compelled to fall back on the defensive, it should be given all the appearance of an offensive war—mobile, cunning, active—'a trick to flatter the vanity of the enemy and thus tempt them to make mistakes of which the general will be able to take advantage'. As Frederick wrote in 1759, 'I have so many enemies that I have no choice but to attack...I have only kept going by attacking whenever I can and by scoring little advantages which add up.' A commander should never attempt to prevail on all sides at once, but only at one well-chosen point, the result of which decided that of all the others.

Later, after hard experience of the realities of warfare, Frederick's advocacy changed. Forts were 'mighty nails which hold a ruler's province together'. Dispositions for battle should be drawn from the rules of besieging positions. The outcome of full-size battles depended too much upon change and chance, the opposite of system and calculation. 'Most generals in love with battle, resort to this expedient for want of other resources. Far from being considered a merit in them, this is usually thought a sign of the sterility of their talents.' 'To win a battle', he wrote in 1768, 'means to compel your opponent to yield you his position.' Increasingly, he argued for a war of position, the accumulation of small gains by complex manœuvre, leisurely and slow in its main outlines, though never so in tactics.

Although his strategical thinking remained within the limits of the war of position, Frederick differed from all his contemporaries in his tactical application. He never favoured passivity in operations, and was always interested in surprise. His concept was of an active challenging defence, based on fixed fortifications, but freely assaulting enemy positions and detachments. The conditions of warfare made him dubious of the gains to be expected from participation in it: 'armaments and military discipline being much the same throughout Europe, and alliances as a rule producing an equality of force between belligerent parties', Frederick wrote in 1775, 'all that princes can expect from the greatest advantages at present is to acquire, by accumulation of successes, either some small city on the frontier, or some territory which will not pay interest on the expenses of war, and whose population does not even approach the number of citizens who perished in the campaigns'. Under Frederick's direction, to a certain extent, the Prussian army with a vigorous discipline, aggressiveness, and new strategic ideas, broke through the defensive technique of the eighteenth century—but because a successful army clings to the forms in which it has been victorious, the formations and evolutions of Frederick continued to be employed by the Prussian army in an age to which they became less and less suited—until the catastrophe of 1806.

Great Britain consciously adopted a policy of naval superiority, and relied upon control of the seas as her main instrument of warfare. Factors involved in this decision were the increasing importance of commerce, the vulnerability of the British Isles to blockade, and their immunity from land attack. By control of the seas, sieges and campaigns in Europe could be assisted by naval blockade, which would also withhold supplies from enemy forces. But on occasions British land forces had to fight on the Continent, and the art of war practised there had generally disastrous results when Great Britain had to undertake land operations at first in, and then against, her American colonies.

Henry Bouquet, who commanded a battalion of the newly formed Royal American Regiment in the Seven Years War, summed up the position in his memorandum on 'Indian warfare' in 1763:

It may be taken for granted . . . 1st that their general maxim is to surround their enemy, 2nd that they fight in extended order and never in a compact body, 3rd that when attacked they never stand their ground, but immediately give way to return to the charge when the attack ceases. These principles being admitted, it follows 1st that the troops destined to engage . . . must be lightly clothed, armed, and accoutred; 2nd that having no resistance to encounter in the attack or defence they are not to be drawn up in close order—a formation which would only expose them to needless loss; 3rd, that all their evolutions must be performed with great rapidity, and the men enabled by constant practice to pursue the enemy closely when put to flight, and not to give him time to rally.[1]

This clearly required a different art of war, the evolution of new formations, particularly that of light infantry. Though the British improvised

[1] Lewis Butler, *The Annals of the King's Royal Rifle Corps*, 2 vols. (London, 1913), vol. I, pp. 159–60.

much, they never went as far as was necessary, inhibited by their European background: Light Infantry, dispersed and individualistic, did not fit into the eighteenth-century European pattern, and European habits died hard.

Tactics were also affected by the same European dead hand—the lack of co-ordinated campaigns; the siege rather than the *coup de main*. But by the War of American Independence the times were changing. Sergeant Lamb described the nature of hostilities on the American Continent as 'a sort of implacable ardour and revenge, which happily are a good deal unknown in the prosecution of war in general'.[1] The rules of the eighteenth-century warfare on land were clearly breaking down.

At sea, in the Battle of the Saints (1782), Rodney, breaking his own and the enemy's line, broke all the formal rules; he won the first clear-cut victory in a stand-up naval fight since 1692. Five ships, including the opposing Admiral's flagship, were taken by him, whilst his subordinate, Hood, took two more. It was apparent by that date that rigid adherence to the line never won battles, but that the chase often did. This realisation did not mean that all order should be abolished in fleet tactics, especially in the approach, but it did make possible a judicious combination of line and chase.

To sum up: in the eighteenth century, wars were conducted with moderation. With the casting out of religious fanaticism, the evil of war was reduced to a minimum never approached before or since. This period of relatively civilised warfare was ended by the treatment meted out to the Loyalists by the victorious colonists at the conclusion of the War of American Independence, and then by the French Revolutionary wars. War, which had ceased in the seventeenth century to be a weapon of religious fanaticism, became an instrument of nationalist fanaticism. Armament development was almost stationary—the sole improvement in infantry arms was the substitution of an iron for a wooden ramrod by Leopold of Anhalt Dessau in 1740. The middle years of the century saw a more rapid increase in the use of artillery, in proportion to other arms, than any other period between the sixteenth and twentieth centuries. Armies were limited in size—and no organised permanent divisions emerged until almost the end of the period; armies were still a single mass forming an unbroken front in battle. Success depended on skill of generalship rather than on force of arms, quality rather than quantity, and battles depended on manœuvre rather than on destruction. The masses of the people were excluded from war, and protected against its ravages by rules and conventions. Eighteenth-century war has been described as a sport of kings, rather than the issue between peoples which it has since become. The royal participants, conscious of their responsibilities, and knowing quite well the degree of licence that their subjects would tolerate, kept their

[1] R. Lamb, *Memoir of his own life* (Dublin, 1811), p. 175.

activities within bounds. Their armies were not recruited by conscription; they did not live off the country they occupied, nor did they destroy the works of peace. They observed the rules of their military game, set themselves moderate objectives, and refused to impose crushing terms on defeated opponents, conscious that their own turn might come next. The game should not disturb the general state of happiness, the system of arts and laws and manners which were the peculiar pride of the eighteenth century. In short, the art of war reflected in another facet the stabilised complacency which was so common in that period.

The States of Europe in the eighteenth century were States in which social classes were sharply defined—superior and inferior groups based on birth, inherited privilege, and property. A feudal aristocracy and nobility, whose loyalty could be relied on, commanded the fleets and officered the armies. The history of that nobility was a military history, their principal and proper occupation military service, their rewards the honours and the perquisites of victory. True feudal military service still continued on the Croat military frontier, and with the Cossacks. The bulk of the population, the rising bourgeois and the peasants, were generally exempt from the activities of war, being left to get on with their business, the increase of the resources of the State, the raising of agricultural, industrial, and financial wealth to a maximum level. So great was the distinction between economic and military activity that these classes usually acquiesced in whatever peace might be imposed. The age of patriotism and nationalism was not yet come; provided they could retain their property, they were little concerned if the territory on which they lived had a new sovereign. The professional military forces were drawn from elements outside the productive classes of society—the officers from the nobility above, the soldiers and sailors from the unemployed, vagabonds, and beggars below. This only further reflected the attempt of eighteenth-century rulers to achieve that balance characteristic of the age by the best use of all available manpower. To use foreigners to do one's fighting was likewise statecraft—that might conceivably upset the balance of a rival whilst helping to maintain one's own. Only in England was there no military aristocracy as such, for there the social gulf between classes was not so marked; there was never an impassable gulf between the upper and middle classes. By her commercial wealth, Great Britain was also in a better position to hire soldiers to do land fighting, and to pay subsidies to European allies.

All eighteenth-century armies lacked homogeneity, and formed an amalgam of national and foreign elements (who comprised between one-quarter and two-thirds of all armies). Their fighting quality was often mediocre, and only a savage discipline, it was believed, could hold together men who were inspired by no great or common ideal. Soldiers enlisted for long terms, and fought, not to die for a cause, but to make a living.

Generally the economic and social outcasts of a State, they were looked on by other more fortunate classes with either a complete lack of interest, or at best a general feeling of contempt, and were hedged round by elaborate rules to prevent desertion, the nightmare of all commanders of that age. The system of recruitment precluded all chance of amenities, and operated in a vicious circle. How, for example, could shore leave be given to men obtained by the press gang? Some form of common purpose had to be created to make efficient forces of such motley bodies—by the imposition of order from outside and above, 'that order, discipline and astonishing precision which', as Frederick the Great wrote, 'made these troops like the works of a watch, the wheels of which by artful gearing produce an exact and regular movement'.[1] Eighteenth-century commanders believed discipline to be the soul of an army—it made small numbers formidable, procured success to the otherwise weak, and esteem to all. Thinking was no part of the duty of soldiers—this was left to the officers. The rank and file of that age required a tight hand—there could be no reasoning with mostly uneducated men. Only by making the profession of soldier and sailor more attractive, by granting better pay, and by giving all the amenities that were feasible, could changes come.

Even when, as in the British forces, the social gulf between classes was not so marked, an observer in 1765 commented that anyone who saw a regiment of foot drawn up 'might think the officers and soldiers mighty sociable; just so is the company at Soho Square—all together, yet all distinct'.[2] Officers generally forbore to inquire and inspect how the men were actually served and this was thought to be a frequent reason of desertion. (It seems established that punishments, though severe, had little effect on the desertion rate.) The troops and the seamen were simple, blunt, matter-of-fact men, the greater part of whose attention was fixed on the basic matters of food and pay—in which very mundane matters officers seem to have taken very little interest. There were few officers like Wellington, who, on first entering the army in 1787, had a private soldier weighed in his clothes only, and then in full marching order. If a single officer was hurt, he was named in the casualty list: not so the common soldiers, who were lumped by numbers. There was a psychological as well as a practical gulf between officers and men. As Sir William Monson had put it: 'the seamen are stubborn or perverse when they perceive their commander is ignorant of the discipline of the sea, and cannot speak to them in their own language'.[3]

Because of the social classes from which the troops and lower-deck men were drawn, almost all the literary evidence dealing with their life and

---

[1] Pierre Gaxotte, *Frederick the Great* (London, 1941), p. 216.
[2] A. M. W. Stirling (ed.), *Annals of a Yorkshire House*, 2 vols. (London, 1911), vol. I, p. 319.
[3] M. A. Lewis, *Navy of Britain*, p. 296.

outlook comes from the officers; the whole service is seen through their often not impartial eyes. If letters and diaries written by the men do exist, it is of the highest importance for a true picture of army and naval life in the eighteenth century that they be brought to light. The gulf between the ranks explains why the element of mutiny simmering in the British navy, as in the *Invincible* at Portsmouth in 1780, did nothing to prepare naval officers of rank, or the Admiralty, for the events of 1797. Most of the old high school in naval and military affairs tended to ignore the individual, and described him, if at all, in scathing terms. Mutual confidence was the real answer to imperfect discipline. Lacking this mutual confidence, reliance was rather placed on constant activity and severe discipline. Men's minds had to be kept on their business. Kempenfelt's remarks were characteristic of the age: 'men must be constantly employed to keep them orderly'; 'the only way to keep large bodies of men in order is by dividing and subdividing them, with officers over each to inspect into and regulate their conduct, to discipline and form them'.[1] All this placed too great a reliance on the supposed zeal of many officers. Some of the conditions of the rank and file may be excused—through the ignorance of what constituted a reasonable diet, the impossibility of preserving food by air exclusion, the difficulty diagnosing many imperfectly understood diseases. Even so, the complacency of the age entered too much.

Some attempts were made to bridge this gulf between officers and men, and to create a mutual confidence. Burgoyne's code of instructions for the guidance of his officers in the 16th Dragoon Regiment insisted on a knowledge of every article that concerned a horse; the ability to accoutre and bridle a horse until each officer was thoroughly acquainted with the use of each strap and buckle. The officers were not to swear at the men, and were to treat them as thinking beings, using an occasional joke in talking to them. Burgoyne declared himself opposed to the Prussian method of 'training men like spaniels by the stick'.[2] But those who criticised the Prussian system forgot that it had something else besides discipline. Major-General Joseph Yorke, in his report on the Prussian army, July 1758, made the following points: notwithstanding his sensitiveness to cold, Frederick the Great 'never gets into a coach but constantly marches on horseback with his infantry, begins his march with them, and leads them into camp or quarters....He formerly used to encamp with the army....He and Marshal Keith are the only officers of the army who are lodged, the rest all encamp'. The King was 'very attentive to have his soldiers well furnished with everything necessary and I really think, the whole considered, that they are better in that service than in any other, provided they can accustom themselves to the confinement of never

---

[1] J. K. Laughton (ed.), *Letters and Papers of Charles, Lord Barham, 1758–1813*, Navy Records Society, vols. XXXII, XXXVIII, XXXIX, 3 vols. (London, 1907–11), vol. I, pp. 299, 306.
[2] F. J. Hudleston, *Gentleman Johnny Burgoyne* (London, 1928).

177

stirring out of sight of their officers without an under-officer with them'. The troops received clothing every year, for both summer and winter use, and were never without bread. Frederick 'never fatigues them unnecessarily, so that, when they have once learned their exercise, which they do quicker there than anywhere else, they have nothing to do but their ordinary duty, as he never exercises or reviews them in the field, after the first month of the campaign is over, unless by way of punishment, when he remarks any relaxation of their discipline'. Yorke concluded that Frederick 'has with reason the confidence of his troops, for they are sure to see him always with them; and upon a march he mixes in the ranks and converses freely with the men, and learns their private histories. Besides, no detachment of any consequence, not even of a thousand men, goes out from camp which he does not accompany'. For consideration of small details, Yorke cited the fact that Prussian soldiers never carried their tent poles, which went with the tents upon horses.

Several inconveniences are avoided by this, such as the soldiers fastening their poles to their fire-locks and being upon any surprise embarrassed to handle their arms; and in case of a retreat before an enemy after an action, the men are not obliged to lie without cover upon the ground for want of tent poles to pitch their tents, which is, and must always be, the case with us, whenever we lose a field of battle, as the men must throw down their poles whenever they are to engage.[1]

In the British navy, a man like Lord Howe was an exception—the men remembered how he used to go below after an action, and talk to the wounded, sitting by the side of their cradles, and ordering his own food and wines to be given to them. By the end of the century, there had developed a certain regimental pride. A ship, in a naval man's life, because of the fleeting association between them, rarely played the part that a regiment played in that of the soldier. Nevertheless, when at sea for long periods in necessarily cramped surroundings (the *Victory* was 186 ft. long, of 2162 tons burden, with not far short of 1000 officers and men on board) an *esprit de corps* was bound to arise in such a closed community, with little to do outside their professional interests. From the long blockades of the Revolutionary and Napoleonic wars, there came a new humanising influence. After the 1797 mutinies, there may have been more vigilance, but there was also a new care on the quarterdeck, an individual care for the members of a ship's company, particularly marked in Nelson.

It was becoming generally apparent that voluntary enrolments, and the other methods used, no longer produced sufficient men, even for the limited wars of the eighteenth century. Tentative gropings for some equitable form of national service had begun—Prussia, Russia, and France early tried a form of conscription; Austria and Spain followed their example after the Seven Years War. Even in England, the militia

[1] B.M. Add. MSS., Hardwicke 9, f. 261. Reprinted in P. C. Yorke, *The Life and Correspondence of Philip Yorke, Lord Chancellor Hardwicke*, 3 vols. (London, 1913), vol. III.

bill of 1757 proposed to choose sixty thousand men by lot from the parish lists, and to train them once a week (twenty-eight days in all) from April to October, over a three years period of service, whilst Pitt's proposals would have gone even further. In naval service, the French '*Inscription maritime*' and the British 'press gang' were the heralds of wider systems to come. Only limited peasant and artisan groups were subject at the beginning to conscription; changes in the nature of war, and in the national attitude to it, were necessary before the full realisation and accomplishment of national service. Similarly, although the upper ranks of the officers were the preserve of aristocracy, the number of middle class officers was on the increase, especially in those countries where commissions were sold—a development which brought no marked increase in the efficiency of eighteenth-century armies.

Prussia, with a population twelfth among the States of Europe in 1740, had a peace-time army of 80,000, compared with France and Austria, with ten times greater populations, but armies of only 160,000 and 100,000 respectively. No other army was more flexible, none could strike more quickly—it was mobile as well as expert in trained manœuvre, well organised and thoroughly trained in one regular uniform drill. Frederick the Great believed that, to have an army, a king of Prussia must hold a firm balance between classes in the State, and between economic production and military power. A rigid class structure was essential to both the army and the State. He must preserve the nobility by prohibiting the sale of noble lands to peasants or townsmen. Peasants were too ignorant to become officers, whilst to have bourgeois officers was, he considered, the first step toward the decline and fall of the army. He placed great reliance on the spirit and efficiency of the officers, drawn mainly from rural nobility, not permitted to take service elsewhere. Officers must lead their men into danger; since honour had no effect on the troops, they must fear their officers more than any danger. Each of the noble families gave one son, who served in cadet companies between the ages of twelve and eighteen, and then went to their regiments. Major-General Joseph Yorke noticed that captains were obliged to keep a table for their subalterns, by which means 'the young officers were constantly under the eye of their superiors, have no pretence for absenting themselves, and have nothing to attend to but their duty; whilst quarrels, caballing, and all other inconveniences of too many young men messing together are avoided, of which I have myself seen many bad effects in other armies'.

Equally, the peasant families must be protected. Their lands must not be absorbed by either nobles or bourgeois—only men not indispensable in agriculture should be recruited. Peasants and townsmen were most useful as producers—'useful hardworking people', Frederick wrote in 1768, 'should be guarded as the apple of one's eye, and in war-time recruits should be levied in one's own country only when the bitterest necessity compels'. Half the army or more might be filled with non-Prussian professionals, prisoners of war, or deserters from foreign armies—entire battalions were composed of deserters from the Austrian army. Recruiting on enemy territory was an integral part of Prussian policy. In 1742 one-third of the Prussian army was native, in 1750 one-half, in 1763 two-thirds. The whole Prussian army in 1761 comprised $4\frac{2}{3}$ per cent of the population (as compared with $1\frac{1}{3}$ per cent of the French population). There was a fixed minimum of one-third natives in the Prussian army, raised by compulsory military service. The kingdom was divided into cantons, each canton being responsible for a regiment, and large enough to recruit the regiment three times. (A regiment of infantry comprised 5000 muskets, of cavalry 1800 horse.) Male children were reported to the local authority by the baptising minister, and were at the disposal of the army between the ages of eighteen and forty, with the exception of only sons, sons of widows, master craftsmen, theological students, peasants on isolated farms or with large families.

Exact discipline and continuous service were considered essential to shape such an army into an instrument of a single mind and will, so allowing full scope to Frederick's art of generalship. He placed no reliance on courage, loyalty, or group spirit in his troops. They could neither be trusted as individuals, nor in detached parties, nor out of sight of their officers. This unreliability was a potent reason against the division of the army in the field. There were most elaborate rules to prevent desertion. Troops should not camp near large woods; their rear and flank should be watched by Hussars, night operations should be avoided wherever possible. When going to forage or bathe, the troops must be led in files by an officer. In the Prussian army, there was an average of one officer to thirty-seven men. Yorke commented on this.

The only very superior point of discipline I observed among the Prussians, which I had not seen elsewhere, was that, whenever the army marched through a small town and that by any embarras any part of the line was obliged to halt in the town, I never saw a soldier quit his rank, though I have seen a halt last above an hour at a time. It is true that the same regulation is established in all other services; but this is the only one I have yet seen where it is rigidly observed.[1]

No detachments were ever made in the Prussian army by men of different regiments, he reported, but 'always by whole corps or in proportion from one corps, as the numbers are demanded, so that the officers are always with their own men'. His conclusion was that 'the service is certainly done with exactness, but with less life and gaiety than anywhere I have yet seen. A pensive attention to their duty is the prevailing turn...the machine is created, subsists and is put in motion solely by the genius of the Prince that presides over it'. If Frederick slipped, all slipped. Despite this care,

[1] P. C. York, *The Life and Correspondence of Philip Yorke, Earl of Hardwicke* (1913), vol. III, pp. 222 *et seq.*

there was more desertion from the Prussian army than from any other in Europe. Burgoyne reported to Lord Chatham in 1766 that the Prussian army was 'more harassed with precautionary guards against their own soldiers deserting than against the enemy, and, after an unsuccessful action, the number missing usually trebles the number to be accounted for by death or capture'. At times then, the main function of the officers was to prevent desertion, to fight the enemy a secondary consideration. Thus, despite its discipline and its flexibility, from its very structure, the Prussian army was rarely able to deal annihilating blows. The same iron discipline was instilled to overcome the nervous tension of action. If an enemy fled, the victorious line must remain in position—plundering the dead or wounded was forbidden on pain of death. 'If a soldier during an action looks about as if to flee, or so much as sets foot outside the line', Frederick ordered in 1745, 'the non-commissioned officer standing behind him will run him through with his bayonet and kill him on the spot.' Eighteenth-century soldiers, themselves blunt men, might well be expected to appreciate orders such as this rather than pious unobserved regulations.

At the beginning of the century, the French army had been the most perfect military instrument in Europe. By the Seven Years War, it was never able to gain a decisive victory over the troops of Hanover, Hesse, and Brunswick. This decline was largely caused not only by the inadequate financial resources allotted to it, and by an excessive veneration for hallowed, once successful traditions, but also by the weaknesses of its social composition. There was a succession of incompetent generals, bound to the court, and a bitter struggle between aristocratic and bourgeois officers. By 1750 one-third of the infantry officers were men of middle-class origin, who had acquired their commissions by purchase, or had risen from the ranks. However efficient they might be, it was not merit, but birth and money which determined the appointments to senior military positions, which were held by men with little military education, and no inducement to develop it. As late as 1781, a royal decree provided that every candidate for a commission must satisfy the court genealogists that he was possessed of sixteen quarters of nobility. By 1787 there were five distinct classes of officers: the great nobles; nobles eligible to be presented to the king, requiring proof of nobility dating back centuries; nobles possessed of sixteen quarters of nobility, but not of the court circle (the country gentlemen of France); bourgeois officers; and lastly, men risen from the ranks who had secured their commissions before the door was shut in the face of the rising middle classes in 1781. From the first two classes were drawn the holders of senior ranks, colonels and upwards. A court noble might become a general at the age of thirty-nine, and would require to have had service with the troops for eight years and five months. Other nobles would not possibly reach the rank until they were fifty-eight, after thirty-one years' service. The third class provided the majority of the officers. Those drawn from the last two groups never rose higher than lieutenant, could not command a company, and retired with a small pension—a system which was perpetuated in the 1787 Army Council promotion regulations.

The French army, with one officer to every fifteen men, was more over-officered even than the Prussian army, but for a very different reason; although discipline entered, the main cause was that now nobles were no longer created for commissions, but commissions were created for the nobility. Many were rarely present with their troops, did not know their men, never possessed their confidence. Their large baggage, and numerous servants, further reduced the army's mobility. These very numerous officers were an embarrassment—to give the more senior officers something to do, command had to be rotated—with marshals and generals commanding in turn, hence the absence of cohesion and continuity. Of a total army strength of 170,000 in 1775, 60,000 were officers whose pay and pensions absorbed more than half the army budget and of whom only one-sixth were doing duty with their regiments. For some 200 regiments, there were 1100 colonels and 1200 generals. By 1789, in a nearly doubled strength, the officer establishment had been reduced to 9578, of whom 6633 were noblemen. French officers were indeed gentlemen. This reduction was mainly due to Choiseul, who cut down by nearly one-half the number of officers for whom pay and pension were provided. He compelled colonels in actual command of regiments to spend a part of a year with them, and instituted periodical manœuvres for the training of young officers. Recruiting, instead of being left to the captains of companies, was brought under the Minister of War; in place of the 'farming' of regiments and companies, a regular system of accounting and administration was begun.

The organisation of the French army reflected this aristocratic basis. There were household troops, doing duty at the royal palaces, French and Swiss Guards. Then came the line regiments, bearing the titles of great noblemen who had originally raised them, or of the provinces of France. One-quarter of the regiments were foreigners, the remainder being made up of the less fortunate poorer classes, idlers and unemployed. The diversion from Flushing against north-east England in support of Hoche's invasion of Ireland in 1796 failed because of its composition. A force of prisoners and deserters, including Prussians, Austrians, Hungarians, Poles, Russians, Italians, Croats, Dutchmen, Swiss, Turks, and even English, refused duty at the point of embarkation, deserted in hundreds, and roamed round the countryside, a menace to the population, until they were rounded up by the civil police. The troops for the main expedition, the Directory wrote to Hoche, 19 June 1796, should be 'such that it can purge France of many dangerous individuals'.[1] Provision was made for a

[1] E. H. Stuart Jones, *An Invasion that failed* (Oxford, 1950), pp. 88.

militia by ballot among the French rural population, but it was only occasionally assembled for very elementary training.

French naval officers were as aristocratic as those of the army, and even more exclusive, since no naval commission was sold. The comte d'Estaign (1729–94), who commanded the fleet in American and West Indian waters from 1778 to 1781, despite his brilliance, was never highly regarded by most French naval officers: an old musketeer, and not a professional sailor, he was considered to be an 'outsider'. Merchant marine officers were taken in only for the duration of war—there was no avenue of a naval career for them as there was in the British navy. There was a rigid, almost feudal, division between fighting, preserve of an exclusive aristocracy, and seamanship, making the warship go. Even so, French naval officers were better equipped than the British to handle their ships. Whereas naval construction as a profession only began in England in 1810 with the School of Naval Architecture at Portsmouth, and whereas most reliance in the British navy was placed in experience, oldest and wisest of instructors, at the Académie de Marine in the eighteenth century mathematics, hydrography, astronomy, navigation, instrument construction, and naval architecture were all represented in the curriculum. In the middle of the century, Admiral Charles Knowles believed a French ship of fifty-two guns to be near as good as an English one of seventy; it was in the French navy that signalling reforms were first developed.

A system of naval conscription, 'Inscripton maritime', had existed in France since 1689—the first great naval power which experimented to build up a force of regular naval personnel. All sailors of maritime provinces were divided into three, four and five classes—each class serving one year out of four, five or ten, according to the number of seamen in the province. While one class was drafted for the navy, the others were free to serve in the merchant marine. Called up in rotation, they received half pay when not needed, but remained at the disposal of the navy for their entire lives. Belated similar schemes were suggested to the British parliament in 1771, and again in 1786. The main ideas were to limit the period of service in the British navy, after which immunity could be claimed; to give pensions, higher pay, and increased prize money to those men who served on a national register of seamen; and to prevent the cut-throat competition for personnel between the State and merchant shipping in time of war. The French system had to be supplemented by pressing, because of the evasion of the national service for better pay in merchant shipping; pressing also embraced peasants, who had never seen the sea, and foreigners. Clearly, the problem to be solved in the finding of naval personnel, in both England and France, was financial.

The British army depended for its recruits on volunteers enlisted by regimental officers; on criminals and debtors released from prison on condition that they joined the army—three regiments in the War of

American Independence were composed entirely of such reprieved criminals; and (by Acts passed between 1739 and 1763) on paupers from parishes on payment of bounties to the parish authorities, 'any sturdy beggar, any fortune teller, any idle, unknown, or suspected fellow in a parish that cannot give an account of himself'. Only those of the first group could rise far. Nor was that class very numerous. Thomas Pitt, introducing a bill in 1750 to limit the period of enlistment, thought that 'a man's listing in the army can never proceed from prudence or discretion or from a deliberate act of the mind; for no man in his right senses would ever bind himself for life to serve another man', whilst Lord Barrington declared in the same debate that idleness, extravagance, and dissoluteness were the causes that sent most common men into the army.

As the army was normally kept on low establishment, in time of threats of foreign invasions or emergencies it was necessary to borrow troops from the Irish establishment, to hire from German principalities, or to subsidise other nations to do the fighting. At the time of his resignation, the elder Pitt had over 200,000 men under arms in a total population (England, Scotland and Wales) of less than eight million; despite the enormous increases in the British forces, £3,091,000 was voted in 1761 for the Prussian subsidy, and the payment of German troops in the Army of Observation. Much work still requires to be done on this subject of expansion of the British army in time of war, for example, by analysis of an Army List in a normal year of peace, and its comparison with a similar list in time of war, to consider whether the same (and which) classes met such great extensions.[1]

Ships in the Royal navy were manned by volunteers, attracted by the reputation of the captain of a vessel for taking prizes, or of being tolerably easy to serve under; by the children of poor or destitute parents, orphans, waifs and strays—between 1756–1815 the Marine Society passed 31,000 boys into the fleet; by impressed men; by foreigners; and, at the end of the century, by debtors, rogues, and vagabonds on a quota from each county and seaport, according to its size and population. Here again, volunteers were few. In Dr Johnson's opinion, no man would be a sailor who had contrivance enough to get himself into a jail, for being in a ship was being in a jail with the added chance of being drowned—hence perhaps the development of jail delivery to the fleet: 'a man who went to sea for pleasure', wrote a contemporary, 'would be likely to go to hell for a pastime'.[2] But once in the navy, every man seems to have been judged on his merits; where he came from did not matter when classing as an able or ordinary seaman. If prize money and patriotism were the chief incentives which made men enter the navy, the existence of the press gang

---

[1] See, for example, E. Robson, 'The Raising of a Regiment in the War of American Independence', *Journal of the Society for Army Historical Research*, vol. XXVII, pp. 107–115.
[2] H. C. Wilkinson, *Bermuda in the old Empire 1684–1784* (London, 1950), p. 119.

made up for any deficiency in patriotism in war-time. The press gang was a bad, inequitable system of conscription which fell particularly on the seaports, and on incoming merchant ships. In time of peace, England maintained only one-fifth of the men in the navy that were needed in an emergency. Pressing was done by ship's officers with a naval party, and at the end of the century, under stress of the Revolutionary and Napoleonic wars, by an official impress service. The navy relied on the system because, without raising naval pay, it was impossible to attract sufficient personnel —the navy offered less rewards than privateers, and imposed more hardship than the merchant service. The navy could not, or would not, keep its men by offering them advantages; pressing thus became a necessary, though an objectionable custom, objectionable because it interfered seriously with the chief aim of eighteenth-century statecraft, trade. To maintain commerce, rules were laid down to mitigate the inconveniences of pressing. Outward-bound shipping was spared as much as possible. The Navigation Acts were amended in war-time to allow employment of foreign seamen up to three-quarters of the crew: the 1775 Act not only suspended the manning clauses and the three-quarter rule, but allowed all foreigners who had served on board any British ship for two years to be called British seamen. The press gang thus secured men with experience of the sea, but who preferred merchant service pay and discipline, or landsmen who lived near, or had unwarily ventured into, harbourside districts. In the eighteenth century, few of the town dwellers of Great Britain had ever seen either the sea, or a line-of-battle ship: the civil enthusiasm for the navy is a later development, fostered by the growth of English watering places, and the annual holiday by the sea. For those who wished to go to sea, the merchant navy offered superior terms—its pay rose in war time, there was less danger, less overcrowding, and better conditions—1512 naval seamen were killed in the battles of the Seven Years War, but 133,708 died of disease, or were missing. In the navy, rates of pay remained unchanged between 1651 and 1797—the able seamen receiving 22s. 6d. a month, the ordinary 19s. (compared with 50s. to 60s. in merchant ships). Wages were not paid until they were six months overdue (six months after arrival in a home port) and often longer. No efficient provision existed until 1758 for transferring to his dependents any portion of the sum owing to a seaman. When they were paid, until 1825, it was by a ticket cashable only at the Pay Office on Tower Hill, London. Not until a commission was over could the men go ashore, and not until just before the Crimean War did any contract last longer than a ship's commission, with no security of re-employment.

The British army was the only one in Europe where the purchase and sale of commissions was universal, founded on regular and fixed principles. Advancement in the army was made easy for those whose way was smoothed by wealth, or influence, or interest. There were few limitations on this practice, save in the artillery; the talents or inclinations of the officers themselves were unimportant; there was no question of serving a specified period in one rank before being promoted to the next. Purchase recognised no barrier of orderly progress through successive ranks; older officers, of proved ability, but with empty purses, were often brushed aside for younger, wealthier men of no experience whatsoever. This prevented the real asset of a promotion system—the spur to the attainment of real merit—taking effect. Patronage and the premature vesting of interest contributed to produce indifference and stagnation in the ranks of officers who considered their careers as pre-ordained or hopeless.

The practice of purchase was liable to many abuses, and there were already many who saw its weaknesses. After 1760, attempts were made to reform and regulate purchase. As a result, fixed prices were approved, which were not to be exceeded; and an established procedure for the purchase of commissions was laid down. Attempts were made to deal with the abuse of exchanges, and the holding of commissions by infants; consideration was given to the protection of officers serving overseas from influence used in favour of others at home, and also to officers without any influence whatsoever. These regulations made some little headway against the potent force of influence in army promotion, but despite the growing criticism of its evils, the purchase system was not abolished until the inglorious events of nineteenth-century wars revealed its complete inadequacy, and led to a long overdue reform. Whatever those evils, purchase did prevent the high appointments of the British army being a preserve of the aristocracy, though it reflected the property-owning basis of society—the landowners and the country gentlemen. George Washington of America equally believed that none but gentlemen ought to hold rank in the army.

Interest was a potent force in army promotion in the eighteenth century. The duke of Cumberland, a royal son, commanded an allied army in 1745 at the age of twenty-four; Wolfe, a second-lieutenant at the age of fifteen, was a lieutenant-colonel at twenty-three, and backed by the interest of an all-powerful minister, was a major-general at thirty-two. Wellington, entering the army in 1787 at the age of seventeen, through the influence of his brother Richard, was a lieutenant by the end of that year. As his mother wrote, 'in six months he has got two steps in the army and appointed aide-de-camp'. He was a lieutenant-colonel at twenty-four, major-general at thirty-two, and lieutenant-general, commanding the expeditionary force which made his reputation, at the age of forty.

Purchase and interest had an important effect on the quality of army officers. Since money and powerful relations or acquaintances could always procure them what they wanted, there was no inducement for officers to apply themselves to the knowledge of their often undesired profession. It was not so much the want of genius, as the want of application, which characterised British officers, and explained why so many of their campaigns were 'damned near things': if put to the test and pushed back to the wall, the British were usually successful, but they rarely made an effort without great provocation. The effective practical result thus differed little from that produced by the aristocratic recruitments of European armies, described by Burgoyne in comments on the general officers of the Austrian army in 1765: 'Some are superannuated; others owe their preferment (and have no other pretensions to it) to family rank and court intrigue; many have risen by gradual seniority, without faults, and without merits, whom it would be unjust to put by, yet whom the State can never employ for great purposes.' By the end of the century, great purposes were on foot; sheer necessity, a new art of war, brought about radical changes in the composition of European military forces.

In the British navy, there was no purchase of officers' commissions. 'The Royal Navy, in its final form, was officered by men qualified in seamanship, who give their lives to the Crown's naval service, which conferred status, offered no security of employment, provided but small remuneration, and was an honourable career in a great nation.'[1] These officers were drawn from the aristocracy and the gentry—from the ruling families, or connected with them by marriage, or capable of procuring their interest; from the middling classes—sons of smaller landowners, of clergy, of lawyers, who advanced themselves by efficiency and keenness; and from the merchant service—though this class was lessening. Cook, Campbell, and Benbow reached the quarter-deck of a man-of-war, but were possessed of exceptional ability, or blessed with exceptional good fortune; hampered by lack of social standing, this latter class of officers was usually promoted too late in life to rise very high. Promotion from the deck produced a small number of officers.

Although such a man as Hyde Parker had little family or political influence, and Kempenfelt and Jervis none, almost all the great flag officers possessed some initial advantage, or its equivalent, the early patronage of men of rank, to hasten their advancement. Parents belonging to the wide circle of the governing class regarded command of a man-of-war as the equivalent of a regiment; they prudently provided for their children in both arms of the service. Officers who possessed no interest thus rarely reached the quarter-deck of flagships—they remained the middle-aged junior officers by whose labours other men made their reputations. It was these junior officers, from midshipmen to lieutenant, who were employed between the wars, whilst the leaders came to sea from long periods on half-pay. Adam Duncan, victor at Camperdown (1797), had won his reputation in the Seven Years War; between 1764 and 1795, when he was appointed Commander-in-Chief in the North Sea, at the age of sixty-four,

[1] D. Mathew, *The Naval Heritage* (1944), p. 13.

Duncan had only two years' sea service. Admiral Lord Hawke, of a prosperous London merchant stock, originating from the Cornish parish of St Clether, had no connection with the sea, and did not become a post-captain until 1734, at the age of twenty-nine. But he flourished with the support of his uncle, Martin Bladen, M.P. for Portsmouth, and a Commissioner of Trade and Plantations. The Hoods, Alexander and Sir Samuel, entered the navy in 1741, being taken in by a naval captain, Thomas Smith, who had been entertained by their father. Smith was a natural son of Sir Thomas Lyttelton, and the Lytteltons were first cousins of the Grenvilles. Samuel Hood further favoured his own cause by marrying a daughter of the commissioner of Portsmouth dockyard. As late as 1815, when the flagship was fitting out for the Leeward Islands station, Admiral Sir John Harvey took one nephew as flag lieutenant, whilst his sister's sons were first and junior lieutenants, provoking from the senior naval Lord, at the admiral's request for the last, the tart comment, 'Uncle and two nephews, Father, Son and Holy Ghost, it must not be'.[1] On the other hand, Kempenfelt, son of a Swedish father and an English mother, did not reach post rank until he was thirty-nine, whilst the mother of Bartholomew James opposed his entry in the navy from 'the want of interest to secure situations that would lead to the channel of promotion'.[2]

No other navy possessed a rank, that of post-captain, an officer in command of a ship of a certain rate, which separated those who obtained it so completely from their juniors—it was a real dividing line between these captains and the lieutenants from among whom they were recruited; the real mark of the organised naval hierarchy. Post-captain was a rank which could be attained early in life during time of war, because of the new constructions as well as the vessels captured. Keppel achieved the rank at nineteen, Howe and Cornwallis at twenty, Rodney at twenty-three during the Seven Years War. On attaining post rank, each officer was bound to work slowly up the captains list before he could become an admiral. The life of the senior naval officer was thus governed by considerations of promotion, and of half-pay. The British navy, in its employment of senior officers, worked on a part-time basis—it paid its employees fully only when it actually used them. The senior ranks spent the greater part of their time ashore without employment, but were retained on half pay. Before 1737 there was no such thing as retirement, and only a disguised form after that date. 'No commissioned officer could retire from the service without also retiring from the earth.' This explains much eighteenth-century practice: the poverty of many senior naval officers, and hence the constant criticism that they preferred prize money to naval

[1] D. Mathew, The *Naval Heritage* (1944), p. 190.
[2] J. K. Laughton (ed.), *Journal of Rear-Admiral Bartholomew James, 1752–1828*, Navy Records Society, vol. VI (London, 1906), p. 4.

188

battles; and the numbers that entered parliament until 1805, when Barham ordered leave of absence from the fleet to be refused to officers who wished it for the prosecution of parliamentary duties. Hawke was put into the Portsmouth seat vacated by his uncle, and held it for almost thirty years: Rodney was member for five different constituencies between 1751 and 1782. Samuel Barrington took thirty-one years to work from bottom to top of the captains' list, whilst Nelson, who entered the navy aged twelve, was a lieutenant at seventeen, commander at twenty, captain one year later, and rear-admiral at thirty-nine. Had he lived, it has been computed he would only have reached the rank of admiral in 1844. Nelson's career typifies the requisites of eighteenth-century advancement—interest (his uncle was Comptroller of the Navy 1770–9), ability, and sufficient war in which to engage steadily.

The number of officers employed was strictly dependent upon establishment, and ship-building programmes in time of war. Until the end of the century, an officer was given a new commission to each ship he joined, appointing him to as exact a post on board as possible—there was as yet no question of being an officer in the fleet. There were several methods of recruiting the social classes which composed naval officers. A small group, 'King's Letter Boys', chosen by the Admiralty, were trained from 1733 at the Naval Academy in Portsmouth Dockyard. These were intended to be 'sons of noblemen and gentlemen', between the ages of thirteen and sixteen, paying £15 yearly towards their keep, no more than forty in number. By 1773 there were only fifteen such candidates; in that year twenty-five places were retained for that class, and fifteen sons of officers were invited to be educated at the public expense. The Admiralty had therefore really failed to attract those who anyway received advancement by entering the service through influence. A similar scheme was inaugurated in 1779 by Jonas Hanway's 'maritime School at Chelsea', a private concern, backed by interested naval officers, to provide their sons with a preliminary training both for the Naval Academy and for life at sea. Then came the 'Captain's Servants'. Until 1794 a captain could take four servants per one hundred ship's company to sea with them. They normally chose their own relatives or youths of their own class. Parson Woodforde's nephew, William, desirous of going to sea in 1778 was sent to London to show himself to a captain of a ship. An admiral and commander-in-chief was allowed as many as fifty 'servants', and from this class came such commanders as the Hoods, Howe, and Duncan.

Qualifications were laid down. By the rule of 1731 the age of entry for captain's servants was fixed at over thirteen, unless the son of an officer, when the minimum age was eleven. A servant could not be rated midshipman until he had given four years' service and was 'in all respects qualified for it'. For lieutenants, there was a minimum age limit of twenty, a certificate of good conduct and ability, a practical examination controlled after 1728 by the Navy Board, and six years at sea, of which one should have been spent as a midshipman, and two as a volunteer. Here again, regulations did not always withstand interest—Nelson not only entered the navy at the age of twelve, but was a lieutenant before twenty, whilst Collingwood's first lieutenant at Trafalgar, John Clavell, born in 1778, had been entered on a ship's books at the age of one, though he only went on board in 1792. The examinations at the Academy seem to have been purely formal—but if the system of 'Captain's Servants' be judged by its results, the officers so recruited and trained had a deep professional knowledge and experience. Leadership and management of man, the making of decisions, the exercise of judgment, come not from formal training and education, but from experience. When the formal tactical system was relaxed after 1782, and independence in action was restored to the commander on the spot, those commanders justified the confidence which Great Britain placed in the social structure which produced them.

CHAPTER IX

INTERNATIONAL RELATIONS

IN 1713 and 1714 eleven separate treaties of peace almost brought the War of the Spanish Succession to an end. They left the Emperor and the king of Spain still at war, but large-scale hostilities were over and most of the belligerents had been able to reach a satisfactory settlement. The Spanish possessions were divided. Philip V, the grandson of Louis XIV, was recognised as king of Spain in spite of the disapproval of the Protestant Powers and of the Emperor; but he had to resign his claims to the throne of France, and he was not allowed to inherit the empire of Charles II in its entirety. Philip V received Spain and Spanish America, but the Netherlands, Milan, Naples, Mantua, Sardinia and the Spanish ports in Tuscany went to the Emperor Charles VI. Sicily went for a few years to the duke of Savoy.

In addition many other problems besides the division of the territories of the Spanish Habsburgs were settled by the peace treaties of 1713–14. In the treaty concluded between England and France the claim of the Hanoverians to the throne of England was also recognised. Implicitly this gave recognition to the theory of civil contract, and this concept was given further validity by the provisions that the arrangements for the successions to the thrones of France and of Spain were to be officially registered by the *Parlement* and by the *Cortes* respectively. The French diplomats warned their English colleagues that such an attempt to regulate the succession was not valid in French law; that the right to rule was derived from God, and that, should the death of the infant French prince leave the throne vacant, Philip V could not be bound by his renunciation but must mount the throne to which God had called him; but they did, at last, accept the provisions in public law which professed to regulate the succession by man-made agreements.

Another provision of the peace treaties which was to have considerable influence on international relations during the next thirty years was the establishment of 'barriers' along the frontiers of France. In the Austrian Netherlands the Dutch, by the Treaty of November 1715, acquired the right to garrison Namur, Tournai, Menin, Ypres and other places. In Italy the duke of Savoy in 1713 gained Exilles, Fenestrelle and some other places towards the Alps, and Allesandria, part of Montferrat, Valenza, Vigevano and other places in the south and east so that he might bar the way into Italy against France or the way into Liguria against the Austrian Habsburgs. These advantages were secured partly by the astute diplomacy of the duke of Savoy, but this was made more effective by the support of

England. Small districts on the Rhine were obtained by various German princes who had supported the Emperor in the recent war. By the treaties of Rastadt and Baden in 1714, Brandenburg-Prussia got part of Gelders. Bavaria recovered the Palatinate and the elector of Cologne was restored to his electorate. These German princes might be expected to check any attempt at renewed French aggression, but also to act as a counterbalance to the emperor. Yet they were not strong enough to act independently of English support

England further benefited from the settlement in that, as a result of the war, she emerged with additional naval bases that were to be of great value to her trade. She retained her hold of Gibraltar and Minorca, and her position in the Mediterranean was further strengthened by the settlement which gave Naples and Reggio to the Emperor but balanced this by giving Messina and Palermo to the duke of Savoy. The approaches to the Mediterranean were protected by the alliance with Portugal which England had concluded in 1703. In the north, England's position was strengthened by her connection with Hanover and by her alliance with Denmark. While England had thus improved her own position, that of France was weakened by the terms of the Treaty of Utrecht which laid down that the naval base at Dunkirk was to be destroyed, and that that of Mardyk was also to be rendered useless for warlike purposes.

England also benefited very considerably from a series of commercial treaties which were either concluded as part of the peace settlement or had already been made to cement alliances during the war. The earliest and most successful of these treaties was that of 1703 with Portugal. Agreements with the Low Countries followed in 1709 and 1713 and in 1713 three other treaties were concluded with Savoy, Spain and France. It is not necessary to see the designs of the 'interloper' as inspiring a secret English policy, comparable with the secret policies of the regent, Dubois and Elizabeth Farnese, to admit that even before the advent of the duke of Newcastle, who was so very sensitive to popular and mercantile opinion, English governments were always eager to express a political or military success in terms of commercial advantages.

Immediately after the Peace Settlement of Utrecht it seemed as if the alliances of the European powers would re-form along familiar lines. Admittedly relations between England and her allies, the Dutch and the Emperor, had been badly strained by what the allies regarded as England's desertion of them in 1712, but very soon after the conclusion of the peace treaties it appeared that France was not going to carry out the terms, and this immediately put new life into the Anglo-Imperial-Dutch alliance. The terms which Louis XIV seemed determined to evade were those stipulating the demolition of Dunkirk as a naval base. In face of this renewed threat England busied herself to reconcile her old allies, who were at loggerheads over the arrangement that the Dutch were to garrison fortresses in the southern Netherlands which, under the Peace Settlement, had passed to Austria. After some considerable difficulties the differences between the Emperor, the Dutch and England were overcome and the Barrier Treaty was concluded in November 1715.

However, by the time that the Barrier Treaty was concluded, the whole international situation had been radically altered by political and personal changes at the court of Versailles. In September 1715 Louis XIV died. His successor was his great-grandson, a delicate child of only five. According to Louis' will the control of France should have been shared between his bastard son, the duke of Maine, and his legitimate nephew, the duke of Orleans. Maine was to have had guardianship of the young Louis XV and command of the household troops, and Orleans the title of regent, but his activities would have been limited by a council having control of patronage. Orleans would not tolerate this. He won over the colonels of the household troops, the princes of the blood, the politicians and the *parlement*. Immediately after Louis XIV's death Orleans claimed command of the household troops, the right to nominate and dismiss members of the Council of Regency, and control of patronage. Maine left the way free by refusing to accept guardianship of the young king if he could not also command the household troops.

But though Orleans had managed to establish himself as supreme in France, his position was not strong. Philip V remained an implacable enemy. Both men were preoccupied with the problem of the succession to the French throne should Louis XV die, and in the eighteenth century, when it was thought better to have one child who had survived the small-pox than two who had not yet had the disease, the chances of a sickly child growing up to manhood were very slight. Philip V had the better dynastic title to the French throne, and was not unduly embarrassed by the fact that in the Peace Settlement of 1713 he had renounced this claim. He was jealous of Orleans who had served bravely in Italy and Spain, and had gained considerable popularity. There were even fears that Orleans might have designs on the Crown of Spain, and Philip V was alarmed by stories that the duke, who was among other things an amateur chemist, had been responsible for the deaths of the father, mother and elder brother of Louis XV, and had designs on the lives of the Spanish Bourbons, though he had renounced his claims to the Spanish throne in favour of the house of Savoy should Philip die without issue. Before the death of Louis XIV the rivals had been reconciled, but Philip V continued to brood on his wrongs, and when Louis XIV actually died the Spanish ambassador at the court of France, Cellamare, was supposed to lodge a protest and claim the regency for his master. In fact he was taken by surprise and the protest was not made in 1715, but it was obvious that Philip V remained an unreconciled enemy, and as those sections of the French court which disapproved of the regent and sympathised with the bastards of Louis XIV tended to rely on Spain for help, it was imperative that the regent should find some other Power which might be prepared to give him friendly support.

The regent might seek an understanding with the Emperor, who at that time was still at war with Spain, or he might try to come to an understanding with England. There were peculiar conditions in England which made it seem more promising to try to come to an understanding with that country rather than with Austria. In 1714 the Hanoverian George had succeeded Anne. The 1715 elections had returned the Whigs in sufficient strength to enable them to attack such Tories as Bolingbroke, Ormonde and Oxford. This Whig policy provoked the Jacobite rising of 1715, and even though the rising failed and the Hanoverian king and his Whig ministers remained in power, the Whigs were only a minority, of about seventy, of the great landed families in alliance with the London merchants. England was still predominantly agricultural and the rural districts were largely Tory in sympathy. James III remained a serious menace, and there was always the possibility that he might change his faith and so enormously increase his prospects of success in England. From a French point of view George I's position seemed sufficiently vulnerable to make it probable that he might not rebuff an overture to establish a closer understanding with France.

The originator of this scheme was the Abbé Dubois, formerly tutor to the duc d'Orléans. In 1716 Dubois was sent in disguise to The Hague to have most secret conversations with Earl Stanhope, then Secretary of State for the Southern Department and in effect in control of English foreign policy. Dubois felt that his master's whole future hung on the success of his mission: Stanhope was much less anxious for an agreement. Dubois was next sent to Hanover to continue the negotiations, but at first he could make very little headway. He was at a serious disadvantage, for the point he was really trying to gain was a guarantee from England to recognise the duc d'Orléans as the next heir to the French throne in the event of the death of Louis XV. He could not ask for this directly, and had to content himself with asking for a general guarantee of the whole settlement achieved at Utrecht.

Stanhope could not agree to Dubois' demands, for at that time the Dutch had not recognised the duke of Savoy as king of Sicily, and the Emperor was still theoretically at war with the king of Spain. Moreover, England did not urgently feel the need of a French alliance. The Jacobite rising of 1715 had failed, although Orléans had winked at the embarkation of men and supplies from France, and England's international position was rather stronger than it had been in 1713: in November 1715 she had concluded the Barrier Treaty with the Emperor and the Dutch, and whereas the French ambassador in Spain had failed to reach an understanding with Philip V, England, courted by the new Spanish minister

Alberoni, had succeeded in 1715 in concluding a commercial treaty with Spain to overcome a series of minor difficulties which had made the commercial treaty of 1713 very disappointing in practice.

It was only after September 1716 that the English court became more eager to come to an agreement with France, and the reason for this change in temper was the development of events in northern Europe. There the second Northern War, which had begun in 1700, was still raging, and in the autumn of 1716 Peter the Great gave signs of becoming a menace to the interests of Hanover. He quartered his troops in Mecklenburg and, at the same time, seemed to become less interested in attacking Sweden. When in 1716 Brandenburg-Prussia joined Russia, it seemed not unlikely that these powers might prevail on France to join them. George I, as ruler of Hanover, was eager for Swedish territory on the southern coast of the Baltic, and was ready to come to an understanding with France because of that court's traditional influence in Sweden. In 1716 the Anglo-French treaty so eagerly desired by Dubois was concluded, and in January 1717 it was joined by the Dutch.

The value of the alliance to England was great. France had as yet lost little of the great prestige she had acquired under Louis XIV, her diplomatists were the most experienced and the ablest in Europe, and her influence with Germany and the northern Powers supplied that in which England was deficient. The immediate results of the alliance were that France prevailed on the tsar to withdraw his troops from Mecklenburg, and on Charles XII of Sweden to recall his envoy Goertz, who had been suspected of encouraging Jacobite plans in the Hague. The alliance continued even after the death of the regent in 1723 and the rise to power of Walpole in 1721. It persisted till the 1730's and during that time English policy generally directed the action of the alliance. The regent and Dubois relied on Stanhope even against French opposition, and the duke of Bourbon and Fleury were not the men to oppose Walpole and Townshend.

England and France had concluded their alliance in the hope that this would help to stabilise the international situation and so reduce the risks of either George I or the regent finding his precarious position made even more dangerous by the renewal of a general war, or the outbreak of a serious international crisis involving his particular country. But for some time after the conclusion of the Anglo-French alliance the international situation remained very unsettled. The main centres of disturbance at this time were two: the Baltic, where Sweden and Russia were still at war, and the Mediterranean, where Spain had been left after 1713 a dissatisfied Power. From time to time the two theatres of war were combined when a Spanish statesman tried to gain help for his country's plans by courting Sweden or even Russia. England's policy was to end the war in the north, since, whether Sweden or Russia was victorious, each threatened the possessions and interests of Hanover. England also wanted to establish a lasting peace in the Mediterranean so that her merchants might enjoy their trade with Spain, Italy and the Levant. French policy was inspired by slightly different purposes. In the Baltic France wished to preserve her traditional ally, Sweden, and in the Mediterranean she was fairly well disposed towards Bourbon Spain. But, on the whole, England and France in the years immediately following their alliance of 1717 managed to co-operate fairly harmoniously.

The first serious tension developed in the Baltic, where the policy of Sweden looked for a time as if it might destroy the new Anglo-French alliance. Swedish foreign policy was directed at this time by Count Goertz, who had entered the service of Charles XII as recently as 1714. He wished to make peace with Russia by ceding her the Baltic provinces she had already captured and he further hoped to revive the traditional alliance with France. The Hanoverian ambitions of George I to acquire from Sweden the secularised bishoprics of Bremen and Verden had made England an enemy. This suspicion of England led Goertz to encourage Jacobite plots. But though English relations with Sweden were bad, English relations with Russia were becoming far less cordial than they had been in October 1715, when George I as elector of Hanover had actually concluded an alliance with Peter the Great, agreeing to help him in his war against Sweden if, in return, he would guarantee the right of Hanover to Bremen and Verden. The occupation of Mecklenburg by Russian troops in 1716 had been one reason for George's decision to ally with France, and Hanoverian policy as well as English became steadily cooler towards Russia as the building of St Petersburg, the control of Riga and Reval, the efforts of the tsar to promote Russia's trade in the Baltic, and the realisation that the Russian fleet was a good one, all tended to make clear that Russia was a potential menace in the Baltic. In 1716 and 1717 Peter the Great tried hard to win France as an ally. It was no wonder that Stanhope worked steadily to prevent Russia winning too complete a victory over Sweden when he was virtually in control of English foreign policy after April 1717.

The second crisis, which soon became involved with the first, developed in the Mediterranean, where the policy of the new queen of Spain threatened to involve Europe in another general war. Elizabeth Farnese was very conscious that she was only the second wife of Philip V of Spain. By his first wife Philip had had two sons, and though one died very early and the other was to die without issue in 1759 no one would have supposed it probable that a son of Elizabeth Farnese would ever rule Spain. The queen was therefore determined to secure for her sons considerable territories outside Spain. The possessions of her family, the Farnese, seemed very attractive objectives. A smash and grab raid in Italy was made easier because the king of Spain was still technically at war with the Emperor and had not as yet acquiesced in the loss of the territories which had formerly belonged to the Spanish crown. Alberoni, the Farnese envoy whose influence Elizabeth had made predominant in Spain in 1716, had done what he could to build up Spanish resources. In August 1717 Spain was in a position to send two squadrons to Sardinia and by October the island had been won from the Emperor. There was a real danger that this incident would develop into a full-scale war. In August 1717 the Emperor had gained some successes in his war against the Turks and so felt more free to devote his attention to the Spanish threat to his possessions in Italy. In England the Whigs were eager to support the Emperor, even if this meant again sacrificing English commercial interests by declaring war on Spain. Even in France, where many members of the Council of Regency were very reluctant to fight a grandson of Louis XIV, Dubois was prepared to overcome this reluctance, since he wanted to secure the recognition of the regent's claims by the Emperor.

In June 1718 Elizabeth Farnese urged Alberoni to make his second move and send the most powerful Spanish squadron since Lepanto to attack Sicily, a strong-point obviously indispensable to any Power that aimed at dominating the western Mediterranean. In preparation for this, Alberoni had exerted all his diplomatic skill to build up a combination that could be relied on to hamper and distract the forces of his opponents. He encouraged Francis Rákóczi to stir up civil war in Hungary, he urged the Turks to continue their war against the Emperor, he resumed Spain's correspondence with the enemies of the regent inside France, he revived Jacobite intrigues in Holland and he negotiated with both Sweden and Russia in the hope that they might be prevailed on to accommodate their differences and both torment the elector of Hanover.

For a time some of these schemes looked quite hopeful. Peter the Great had succeeded in concluding a treaty with France in August 1717, and though on the French side this had been only an empty politeness its object had been declared to be the restoration of peace in the north. In 1718 Sweden and Russia even conducted conversations on the Aaland Islands to see if peace terms could not be agreed. But Alberoni's grand project soon began to disintegrate. In 1717 England arrested the Swedish envoy in London and the Dutch arrested Goertz himself. The conversations on the Åland Islands came to nothing, and finally in December 1718 Charles XII was killed and in March 1719 Goertz was executed. A Jacobite rising planned for 1719 failed, as did a rising that had been hoped for in Brittany. In the Mediterranean Alberoni's policy was equally unsuccessful. In spite of his urgent advice, the Turks made peace with the Emperor at Passarowitz in July 1718, thus leaving Charles VI free to concentrate on resisting Spanish aggression in Italy. On 7 August 1718 England, France and the Emperor concluded an alliance on the basis of the English 'plan' for pacifying southern Europe, though this plan had been rejected by the Emperor in November 1716. This plan aimed at

establishing peace on a sure footing by persuading the Emperor to renounce his claim to the Spanish throne if, in return, Philip V would
renounce his claims to what had been Spanish possessions in Italy; this
did not involve the abandonment of the claims of Elizabeth Farnese's
eldest son to Parma, Piacenza, Tuscany and the Presidios. Savoy was to
give the Emperor Sicily and receive Sardinia in exchange: in return the
Emperor was to confirm the claim of the house of Savoy to the Spanish
throne should the Bourbon line fail. The Emperor was, moreover, to
recognise the respective claims of George I and the regent to the thrones
of England and of France. In a secret clause Britain and France agreed to
press Spain and Savoy to cede Sicily to the Emperor. This treaty of 1718
nominally included the United Netherlands, and, though the Netherlands
played little real part, the Alliance was known as Quadruple. Four days
after this treaty had been signed, the English fleet soundly defeated the
Spaniards off Cape Passaro. In December 1718 Dubois, by revealing the
conspiracy of the Spanish ambassador Cellamare, was able to make Spain
appear obviously the aggressor and was thus able to overcome strong
French reluctance to make war on a king who was a Bourbon. A French
army invaded Spain in 1719 and achieved such success that by December
1719 Philip V was ready to discuss peace terms and to dismiss Alberoni.
In January 1720 Philip V, as a result of English pressure, acceded to the
Quadruple Alliance and in June 1720 he again renounced all claims to the
French throne. All the outstanding points in dispute were left to be
settled by a congress which was to meet in Cambrai in October, but for
the moment peace had been restored in the south.

In the north the crisis was not so easily resolved, though here, as in the
Mediterranean, the existence of the Anglo-French alliance strengthened
the resources of both St James's and Versailles. The death of Charles XII in
December 1718 fundamentally altered the whole situation in the Baltic.
Power in Sweden passed to the aristocracy, which was vigorously anti-
Russian and therefore disposed to listen to the advice proffered by the
English and French diplomats that the tentative negotiations which
Sweden had begun with Russia should be broken off. The re-formation of
a vigorous coalition of Powers against Russia seemed likely to take place
in the near future. In February 1719 the Emperor authorised a Hanoverian
force to occupy Mecklenburg. But while this was still in the air Russia
took vigorous action. In July 1719 she invaded Sweden and in September
broke off the negotiations which had been going on in the Åland Islands.
This only hastened the formation of an anti-Russian coalition. In August
1719 Prussia concluded an agreement with Great Britain. In November
Denmark ended hostilities against Sweden, and in the same month the
Treaty of Stockholm marked an agreement between Sweden and Hanover
by which Sweden ceded Bremen and Verden. In January 1720 another
Treaty of Stockholm signalised the agreement between Sweden and Prussia,

Sweden ceding Stettin and part of Pomerania in return for two million *écus*. In June and July treaties marked the satisfactory conclusion of eight months' negotiating between Sweden and Denmark, by which Denmark renounced her claims to Rügen and Wismar and the Swedes their claim to a share in the Sound dues. An impressive coalition had been built up against Russia, but it was not enough to bring about the end of hostilities in the north. The German princes were very unreliable, Saxony and Brandenburg tended to turn away from Great Britain and to lean once more towards the tsar. The Emperor began to be anxious at the prolonged occupation of Mecklenburg by Hanoverian troops. The English decision to make use of Norris's squadron in the Baltic only brought failure. Norris's ships could not pursue Russian craft into the Gulf of Finland, and they failed to prevent a Russian invasion of Sweden in 1721. The king of Sweden was on the point of reopening the separate negotiations with Russia which had been broken off in 1719. Russia invoked her alliance of 1717 with France and it was French diplomacy which managed to achieve the Treaty of Nystadt in September 1721, ending at last the Northern War. The Anglo-French alliance had achieved two resounding successes. In the south the two Powers had forced Spain to abandon her attempt to overthrow the Utrecht peace settlement. In the north they had reconciled Sweden with her neighbours and had finally ended the war which had been troubling the Baltic since 1700, thereby ending, for the moment, Swedish and Russian threats to territories occupied by German princes. The Emperor retained the territories assigned him at Utrecht; in England, George I was seated rather more steadily on the throne; in France, the reins of government were more firmly in the hands of the regent. By 1721 the Anglo-French alliance seemed to have been a success.

Unfortunately the solution of outstanding disputes which in 1721 appeared to be under way nearly foundered; a satisfactory solution was only reached in 1729.

Trouble developed first in the Congress of Cambrai, which was discussing the outstanding causes of dispute affecting the south of Europe and the Empire. Spain and the Emperor both had reason to be still dissatisfied with England and France. Spain had two main grievances: the British occupation of Gibraltar and the Emperor's failure to allow a Spanish prince to occupy the Farnese possessions in Italy. As far back as Stanhope's visit to Madrid in January 1720, Spain had reclaimed Gibraltar. Stanhope had not been able to give a categorical refusal. Instead he had promised to return the place within a year, but in January 1721 he had died. The most that Spain had been able to extract from England had been a letter from George I promising to make use of the first favourable opportunity to bring the question before parliament. But this had been in May 1721 and the favourable opportunity showed no sign of ever presenting itself. As for the Spanish claims in Italy, Philip V and his wife saw no practical results accruing from their accession to the Quadruple Alliance of 1718. In 1719 the Emperor had actually negotiated with Victor Amadeus to put a Piedmontese candidate on the throne of Tuscany, and in 1720 Charles VI had been supporting the claims of a Bavarian to this Grand Duchy. The Emperor had just as little reason to be satisfied. He knew that the British politicians were deeply divided over the policy they should pursue towards the empire. Stanhope, Sunderland and Carteret had tended to sympathise with Charles VI and to look favourably on his attempts to win support for his Pragmatic Sanction. Townshend, the Hanoverians and King George I disliked any attempt by the Emperor to win support for the Pragmatic Sanction, for they saw in this a dangerous increase in Roman Catholic power in Germany. Charles VI, impatient of having to depend on subsidies from the Maritime Powers, was eager to increase his own revenue and, with this in mind, decided in December 1722 to make use of his newly acquired territories in the Netherlands by establishing a trading company to operate from Ostend.

Relations between England and France and the disgruntled Powers of Spain and the Empire were not improved by the changes in office which took place in 1723 and 1724. In August 1723 Dubois died, to be followed four months later by the duc d'Orléans. This did not, however, seriously disturb the good relations which had been established with Great Britain. The duc de Bourbon remained loyal to Britain, and Cardinal Fleury, less warlike than some of the English ministers, did not at first pursue a policy independent of Britain when he took over the direction of French foreign policy in 1726. In fact, he restrained Morville, the Secretary of State, who would have preferred more independence. In Spain changes of personalities had a restraining effect, at least for a short time. In January 1724 Philip V abdicated, but the young son who succeeded him had little time to gather up the reins of policy, still less to guide Spanish diplomacy in any particular direction, for he died in August 1724. It was the changes in Britain which had the most marked effect on the development of international relations. In April 1724 Carteret fell from power and his influence was replaced by that of the duke of Newcastle. Already in October 1723 Britain had passed an act against the Ostend Company and in the same month had concluded a treaty with Prussia. The advent of Newcastle to power, as Secretary of State for the Southern Department, intensified this tendency in British policy towards hostility to the Empire.

Already the negotiations which had begun at Cambrai in 1721 had proved very slow and difficult; in 1724 they became even more delicate. The Dutch wished to bring the question of the Ostend Company before the congress, and in April 1724 Spain urged Great Britain to press for the suppression of the Company. French diplomacy managed to get the question evaded, but the Emperor realised his danger and was convinced that no reliance could be put on the English and Dutch allies with whom he had concluded the Quadruple Alliance of 1718. Just at this time Spain became very sceptical of getting any effective help from England or France under the Triple Alliance of June 1721. In June 1724 Spain was pressing for the restitution of Gibraltar, but England and France merely referred the question to the Congress of Cambrai. Spain was also impatient to get effective help in the introduction of Don Carlos into Parma and Tuscany. His claims had been recognised by the treaty of 1718, but the Emperor had shown no eagerness to see this clause of the treaty made effective. He was supposed to have advised Antony of Parma to marry and produce heirs. A rumour was spread by Bavarian relations of Violante Beatrix, daughter-in-law of the Grand Duke Cosimo III of Tuscany, that if the Medici male line in Tuscany should end the Emperor would send in troops and dispose of Florence and Siena in the interests of the Bavarians who were, for the moment, on good terms with Vienna. On the death of Grand Duke Cosimo III in 1723 there were further rumours that Victor Amadeus of Savoy would marry his daughter Anne Marie. The situation was becoming more acute, since the new grand duke, Giovanni Gaston, was unlikely to have any heir and was drinking himself steadily to death. In January 1724 the Emperor had gone some way towards placating Spain by giving Don Carlos letters of investiture to Parma and Tuscany, but he showed no willingness to allow Don Carlos to take possession and was flatly opposed to the dispatch of Spanish troops to guarantee his claim to the territories in the event of the death of either the duke or the grand duke. In June 1724 Spain urged England and France to press the Emperor to allow Don Carlos to go immediately to Italy, but here again His Catholic Majesty could get no satisfaction from his allies of 1721. In despair and exasperation Spain decided to try the effect of seeking an agreement with the Emperor.

A secret envoy, Ripperda, was sent to Vienna in November 1724 and his negotiations began in January 1725. The reconciliation of the Emperor and Spain was made easier by a snub administered to Spain by France. In February 1725 the Infanta, who had been in France as the fiancée of Louis XV, was returned to Spain, and Louis married the Polish Marie Leszczyńska. By March 1725 a treaty of peace between the Emperor and the king of Spain was ready for signature. In April followed a treaty of commerce and in the same month the Emperor agreed that one of his daughters should marry one of the sons of Elizabeth Farnese. 'The wedding bells of Austria and Spain were the passing bells for England and France.' The Congress of Cambrai broke up in confusion.

English opinion, as expressed by Townshend, was resolutely opposed to returning Gibraltar to Spain, and in September 1725 the Austro-Spanish alliance was checked by the Alliance of Hanover between England, France and Prussia. Prussia withdrew in 1726 and resumed her traditional loyalty to the Emperor, but other Powers such as Sweden and Denmark joined the alliance and by 1727 Europe was organised into two armed camps. In 1727 Spain declared war, but the Hanoverian alliance was so imposing that the Emperor showed great reluctance to support his ally. That a general war was arrested was largely due to the pacific policy of France, where Fleury had succeeded the duke of Bourbon in 1726. Fleury managed to mediate between England and the Emperor, and peace preliminaries were signed at Paris in May 1727. In March 1728 Spain yielded to diplomatic pressure from France and the Maritime Powers. The attempt to gain her ends by negotiating directly with the Emperor had failed, and the extent of this failure was brought home to Spain vividly in February 1729, when the Emperor refused to give her any assurance on the proposed marriage alliance between the Spanish Bourbons and the Habsburgs. Elizabeth Farnese in disgust turned once more to France and England. English ships which had been seized in the Indies were to be returned, the siege of Gibraltar was to be raised and the privileges enjoyed by English merchants trading in Spain were to be restored. France agreed that Spain should send 6000 Spanish troops to Italy to guarantee Don Carlos's succession to Parma and Tuscany. The Treaty of Seville, signed in November 1729, was faithfully and effectively observed by England and France.

The Emperor threatened to invade Tuscany if Spanish troops were brought in, and the grand duke of Tuscany was not cordial towards the Spanish claimant, but in 1730 the grand duke was prevailed on to recognise Don Carlos as his heir and to make public proclamation to this effect. In January 1731 the duke of Parma died and the Emperor sent troops to occupy the duchy as an imperial fief. For a time the chanceries were kept in suspense by the widowed duchess, who thought herself to be pregnant; diplomatic dispatches contained reports of such certain signs of pregnancy as a craving for chocolate; but in the end the duchess was proved to have been mistaken. In March 1731 Great Britain, by the Treaty of Vienna, recognised the Pragmatic Sanction, which had begun to occupy a place of paramount importance in the Emperor's diplomacy. In return Charles VI withdrew his troops from Parma and allowed the Spanish garrisons to occupy not only Parma but also Tuscany. In July the grand duke of Tuscany joined the Treaty of Seville. In October 6000 Spanish troops landed at Leghorn. In December they were followed by Don Carlos, who in October 1732 formally took over the Duchy of Parma. Once again it seemed that the peace of Europe had been assured and guaranteed by the Anglo-French alliance.

In the north-east of Europe from 1721 to the eve of 1733 the peace was also preserved, except for a few short crises, and here again the credit went to the Anglo-French alliance. Immediately after the conclusion of the Peace of Nystadt in 1721 the most urgent crisis was created by the ambitions of Charles Frederick of Holstein, whose claims to Slesvig had been disregarded in favour of Denmark in 1720 and whose claims to the Swedish throne were rather better than those of his aunt Ulrika (ch. xv). Charles Frederick was supported by Peter the Great, who would have found a Russian protégé on the Swedish throne most useful. This Russian help became more energetic after May 1725, when Charles Frederick married the tsar's daughter. This menace to the tranquility of Sweden and Denmark declined however after 1727, when Peter's widow Catherine followed her husband to the grave.

The north-east was more widely disturbed by the complete oversetting of the whole European system of existing alliances when Ripperda achieved a *rapprochement* between Spain and the Empire in 1725. Even before this volte-face in Spanish diplomacy, the Emperor, disillusioned with the treatment he had received from England and France at the Congress of Cambrai, had cast about to come to some better understanding with Sweden or Russia, or perhaps with both. In an attempt to check this possible extension of imperial influence England, under the influence of Townshend, took vigorous action and sent a squadron to the Baltic under Admiral Mayer in 1726. This commander proved more successful than the unhappy Norris in 1721. Sweden was much impressed, and in March 1727 joined the Anglo-French alliance of Hanover. Denmark followed in April. The energetic English policy in the Baltic had, however, one most unfortunate result. Russia, thoroughly alarmed, and seeing in the naval demonstration of 1726 another example of the attempt in 1716 to rival her dominant influence in the Baltic, joined the Austro-Spanish alliance in August 1726. Even after Spain had deserted the Emperor and returned to an understanding with France and England, Russia remained the ally of the Habsburgs.

In fact the diplomatic development in the period 1713–40, which seems in the light of later history to have been the most important for the future, was something which escaped contemporary observers until at least 1733. The formative influence was provided not by the ambitions and audacities of Elizabeth Farnese which, for all the anxiety they caused, did not achieve more than a minor transfer of territory in Italy. What was to be far more important for the future of Europe was the emergence of Russia and Prussia as Great Powers. These two States had been the real victors in the Northern War, but for the next twenty years neither felt itself in a position to pursue an independent policy and to take the diplomatic initiative. After the death of Peter the Great in 1725 Russia had a series of short reigns—Catherine I (1725–7), Peter II (1727–30), Anna (1730–40), Ivan VI (1740–1)—which, together with the characters of her rulers, rendered her incapable of playing a consistently effective part in international affairs. Prussia under Frederick William I built up her resources but did not launch out and take the initiative. In the seventeenth century,

when Sweden was menacing all the territories of North Germany, Brandenburg had inclined towards an anti-French policy, partly because France
was the patron of Sweden and partly because the great elector had been
grievously shocked by the religious intolerance of Louis XIV. In the wars
of 1688–97 and 1702–13 Brandenburg-Prussia had continued this anti-
French policy and had fought on the side of the Emperor, the Dutch and
England. In 1726 Frederick William waveringly joined the Anglo-French
alliance of Hanover, but in 1728 he withdrew and reverted to his alliance
with the Emperor. It was profoundly significant for the later development of the German people that Prussia got very little profit from this
period of loyalty to the Emperor. She was snubbed over Mecklenburg in
1733, her interests in Poland were ignored in 1732, and in 1738 her claims
to Jülich and Berg were disregarded. But in 1732 the potential importance of both Prussia and Russia was not obvious to contemporary
observers. The importance of Russia was the first to be revealed and this
took place during the War of the Polish Succession.

The diplomatic origins of the War of the Polish Succession went back at
least to the short-lived Austro-Spanish alliance negotiated by Ripperda in
1725. France, in an attempt to counteract the Austro-Spanish treaties of
1725, had revived her traditional policy of building up an anti-imperial
coalition among the princes of the Holy Roman Empire and had concentrated particularly on Bavaria and the Evangelical Union. Friction
between Austria and France had been further increased in 1726 when
Austria had concluded an alliance with Russia, for this constituted a
direct threat to French influence in Sweden and Turkey as well as checking
France's traditional anti-imperial policy. The effect of the Austro-Russian
alliance began to appear in 1727, when Russia felt herself strong enough
to occupy Courland, and in 1728 when Prussia decided to abandon her
association with France and England and return to her traditional loyalty
to Austria. Walpole's general reluctance to see England involved again in
European disputes and his understanding with the Emperor by the Treaty
of Vienna in 1731 left France isolated in her attempts to dominate affairs
in central and eastern Europe just at a time when the question of the
succession in Poland was likely to become acute. In January 1732 France
sustained yet another rebuff when the Diet of the Empire recognised the
Pragmatic Sanction. France countered this by herself concluding a treaty
with Augustus II of Poland in May 1732 and by persuading Bavaria to
enter into an alliance with Poland in July 1732. But though France was
ready to make use of Augustus II to try to shake the control which the
Emperor, in alliance with Russia, was exercising over Poland, the French
had no intention of supporting Augustus's designs for making the Polish
Crown hereditary in the Wettin family. France hoped to see Stanislas
Leszczyński, father-in-law of Louis XV, elected when Augustus II died.

In September 1732 Austria, Russia and Prussia concluded the Treaty of Loewenwolde to put a Portuguese prince on the Polish throne, but when in February 1733 Augustus II died, Austria and Russia agreed to recognise his son Augustus III. Prussia, left in the cold, allowed Stanislas Leszczyński to pass through to Poland. France strengthened her position by a series of treaties concluded in 1733. In September she entered into an alliance with Sardinia, in November she concluded an alliance with Bavaria and a treaty by which the Dutch guaranteed to pursue a policy of neutrality. In November also France concluded with Spain the Treaty of the Escorial, by which Elizabeth Farnese secured a guarantee of Parma and Tuscany for Don Carlos, together with whatever other territories might be conquered in Italy.

England's policy throughout the war was to refuse to be entangled. At the end of 1734 Walpole could boast to Queen Caroline that though 50,000 men had been killed in Europe in one year, not one of them was an Englishman. Twice in that year Walpole had refused to give help to the Emperor under the 1731 Treaty of Vienna, and in 1735 he was to do so again. It was feared that the Emperor might denounce the treaty of 1731 and there was an even more serious danger that he would come to an understanding with France.

In 1735 the war ended, and in November 1738 another Treaty of Vienna agreed the terms of a settlement. Augustus III was to be king of Poland but Stanislas Leszczyński renounced the throne 'voluntarily and for the sake of peace', which implied that his election had been legal. As compensation for the loss of Poland Stanislas was given Lorraine and Bar which on his death were to go to his daughter, the wife of Louis XV. Spain was rewarded for her decision to support France by the transfer of Naples and Sicily to Don Carlos, but for the moment this accession of territory was counterbalanced by the loss of the long-disputed Tuscany which went to the duke of Lorraine.

It was noticeable that in this war for the first time a Russian army penetrated deep into Europe, reaching the Neckar. Within four years, at the end of the Russian war against Turkey in 1739, Fleury uttered a warning: 'Russia in respect of the equilibrium of the north has mounted to too high a degree of power and its union with the House of Austria is extremely dangerous.'[1] This comment was the more interesting because in the war of 1735–9 against Turkey, Russia had not been spectacularly successful. She had fought in concert with her ally Austria, but after some initial military successes neither Russia nor Austria had been able to win any decisive victories. In 1736 the Turks had made peace with Persia, thus freeing their hands to grapple more effectively in the Balkans. In 1737 France had begun to mediate, and the treaties of Belgrade signed

---

[1] Fleury in secret instructions to la Chétardie, French ambassador to St Petersburg, quoted in the *Cambridge Modern History* (1909), vol. VI, p. 308.

in September 1739 marked a decline from the Austrian successes recorded in the Treaty of Passarowitz in 1718; but still Russia seemed too powerful.

But the crisis which in 1739–40 engulfed nearly all the European Powers in war was not provoked by Russia. Partly it was brought about by the other newly emerged Great Power, Prussia, but partly it was the result of a chronic state of friction between England and Spain, which developed into war in 1739 against the wishes of the responsible statesmen of both countries.

The war between England and Spain broke out largely because of disputes over British ships prized in the West Indies because they were suspected of smuggling. This illicit trade was carried on by interlopers and had been common in Spanish America for many years. The geography of the West Indies favoured such a trade, for the prevailing winds and currents made it usual for ships, whether bound for British colonies on the American mainland or even home to Europe, to pass close to the southern shores of Hispaniola and Cuba and then to go north through the Bahama Channel. Between 1670 and 1700 the activities of British and Dutch smugglers had been tolerated by the Spanish authorities. After 1713 the British smugglers found that the reforming energy of the new Bourbon dynasty in Spain had stiffened the efforts of the Spanish colonial authorities to check foreign smuggling. The two wars between England and Spain which broke out in 1718 and 1727 provoked a crop of disputes over ships illegally prized for smuggling, and until 1731 political relations between England and Spain were bad and depredations were frequent. But from 1731, when England did effectively help to get Don Carlos into Italy, the Spanish authorities showed themselves active in checking illegal interference with British trade. From 1733 to 1735, while Spain was at war with the Emperor in support of Stanislas Leszczyński's claims to the Crown of Poland, English traders in the West Indies were treated with some consideration for fear that England might join in the European war against Spain. Even after 1735 the English were still well treated because Spain was so thoroughly angry with France for having concluded a separate peace treaty with the Emperor. But though the illicit trade of the British might be tolerated by the Spanish Government for political reasons, it exasperated the Spanish colonial governors, who saw foreigners blatantly arriving in a convoy of as many as thirty ships at once to gather salt from one island, carrying provisions and dry goods very generally, trading so regularly for Spanish mules that not a day passed without some ship putting in to a Spanish island for these animals, and on occasion actually burning a Spanish guard ship. The governors of Spanish colonies found it difficult to induce men to fit out coastguard ships. The governor of Puerto Rico was eloquent in his reports of the barbarous conduct of British and

Dutch smugglers towards Spanish coastguards and of his own difficulties in 'prevailing' on local men to fit out as privateers. In 1737, however, the activities of the foreign smugglers were so notorious that the Spanish colonial governors induced their colonists to fit out a few more privateers and in the course of the year these took about a dozen English ships.

It is noteworthy that in all this dispute over illicit trade there was no official complaint against the South Sea Company. Admittedly the Company's servants smuggled. The supercargoes and other members of the crews of the annual ships had smuggled. In 1725 the *Prince Frederick* had been accompanied by a sloop full of additional goods. In 1730 the *Prince William* had taken in an extra cargo to fill the place left by fuel and provisions consumed on the voyage. In 1725 the *Royal George* was so heavily laden that it was said she could not have used her guns had she been attacked. This was well known to the Spanish ministers, but they believed that this smuggling in the annual ships was less than what was carried on by the servants of the Company under cover of the negro trade. The Company's factors in the Spanish ports were sometimes dangerously reckless in their illicit trade, and masters of the negro sloops often carried provisions and liquor or casks of blue paint under the ballast. But the smuggling by these masters was carefully kept within bounds by the Company's agents at Jamaica and, though the Board of Directors itself had connived at the false measurement of two permission ships, the Company, with a representative of the king of Spain among the directors, could not afford to be indiscreet. The attitude of the Company was that there was nothing immoral about some private trade, but that nothing should be taken to the Indies which competed with the official trade of the Company or in such quantities as to irritate the Spanish authorities. About 1737 the agent of the Company in Jamaica reported that the Spanish authorities were enforcing new and severe regulations, but the Company's illicit trade did not become involved in the diplomatic dispute which this new rigour produced.

In the autumn of 1737 the merchants of London, Bristol, Liverpool and other centres of the American trade petitioned parliament for a redress of their grievances caused by the seizure of ships in the West Indies. That the Spanish Government at this time had no wish to pick a quarrel with England was shown by the exceptionally conciliatory answer made when the British complaints were officially brought to their notice. It was genuinely difficult to decide the justice of the claim. Five of the ships reclaimed would seem to have been captured by pirates and not by regular *guarda costas* at all, six had been involved in very suspicious activities, three had only been attacked and not seized. The conciliatory attitude of the Spanish Government was clearly revealed in an official opinion given early in 1738 by the Council of the Indies to the effect that 'even if some suspicion of illicit trade remain, the prevention of illicit trade should never make Spanish officials lose sight of the need of good harmony with the other Powers of Europe'.[1] Unfortunately for the preservation of this good harmony the conciliatory Spanish answers were not made in time to prevent further demonstrations of merchants and Walpole's political opponents in March 1738, when public opinion was further inflamed by learning that British sailors from ships prized in the Indies had been in chains in a Cadiz prison, herded with robbers and felons and fed 'on nothing but bad biscuit and *bacalao* (salt cod)'.[2]

But in spite of the popular clamour the responsible ministers both in England and Spain did their best to avoid war. The duke of Newcastle sent a stern note to Spain, but its effect was modified by a separate letter from Walpole. Walpole was almost certainly behind a proposal that £200,000 should be paid by the king of Spain in settlement of all the claims and that of this £60,000 would be provided by the British Government. But to appease the popular outcry a squadron was sent to the Mediterranean under Admiral Haddock. This irritated the Spanish ministers, who refused to pay more than £95,000. This lower sum was eventually accepted, but a new and unexpected difficulty then appeared. The king of Spain wanted to pay the sum through the South Sea Company, which owed him a regular sum every year for the duty on the negroes imported into America, and which was in the habit of using this money to pay salaries of Spanish officials or even ordinary bills. In addition to this regular sum owed by the Company to the king it had recently been agreed that the Company owed the king £68,000, being his share in the profits of the annual ship the *Royal Caroline* and the difference between the import duty on the negroes paid in new silver reals and the sale-price of the negroes paid in old silver reals. In 1738 the Company refused to pay the £68,000, much less to advance the king the balance necessary to make up the £95,000, unless they were given by Spain satisfactory orders for the restoration of their effects which had been seized on the outbreak of war in 1718 and 1727. In vain the Spanish envoy in London took it upon himself to declare that if the Company refused to pay then the king of Spain would pay the money in some other way, and the Spanish court issued orders for restoring the Company's property seized in 1718 and 1727. The governors of the South Sea Company found four objections to the orders on whose complete acceptability hung the continuation of peace. In a last attempt to preserve the peace Walpole suggested drawing up a new treaty which should contain no reference to the possibility of annulling the *asiento* should the South Sea Company refuse to pay the £95,000 for the king of Spain. The new convention was concluded in January 1739, but was accompanied by a Spanish declaration that it had only been signed on condition that the

---

[1] Consulte of 6 May 1738. Seville, Archivo de Indias, Indif. Gen. Legajo. 1597.
[2] The complaints of the sailors were carefully examined by the British Consul at Cadiz in a letter he wrote to the duke of Newcastle 13 May 1738, P.R.O., S.P.F., Sp. 222.

South Sea Company paid at least the £68,000 which it admitted to be owing to the king of Spain.

The Company refused to pay. In March 1739 the popular outcry against Spain was so loud that Admiral Haddock who, in February, had been ordered to return to England was now ordered to remain where he was. Newcastle was moved by fear of the opposition and of public opinion, Walpole by fear that France intended to act in concert with Spain. In October 1739 England and Spain were at war.

France's policy was much less friendly than Spain could have wished. In an attempt to distract Elizabeth Farnese from Italy, Fleury inflamed the nationalist sentiments of the Spanish ambassador at the court of Versailles, yet when the crisis became acute he urged Spain to pay the £95,000 if the British fleet were withdrawn from Gibraltar. In October 1739 a marriage was arranged between the Infant Don Philip and a French princess, but France refused to enter into a closer alliance with Spain without commercial concessions in America. In August 1740 a French fleet was ordered to the West Indies to check British aggression, but Fleury refused to go on with the negotiations for a political or commercial treaty. But in October 1740 the Emperor Charles VI died; the Anglo-Spanish War was now caught up in the War of the Austrian Succession in which France and Spain were to fight against Austria. Their troops were not very successful and in 1743 Spain, though prepared to treat with Sardinia, was prevented from doing so by Sardinia's concluding a treaty with Maria Theresa. In intense anger Spain concluded the Treaty of Fontainebleau with France in October 1743. But this second family compact was to be no more an enduring principle of Spanish or French policy than the first in 1733.

The Anglo-Spanish War was extended to most of the Powers of Europe by the action of Prussia after the death of the Emperor Charles VI in October 1740. Since the death of Frederick William of Prussia in May 1740, England had been trying to persuade the new king of Prussia to enter an alliance to stir up trouble for France on the Continent. But Frederick II had been too astute to be made into a catspaw of English policy, and with the death of the Emperor the whole situation in central and eastern Germany and northern Italy altered. Sardinia was preparing for war to improve her position in north Italy at the expense of the Empire. The elector of Bavaria was eager to make good his claims to the miperial throne. Spain was eager to make use of any opportunity that might be presented by imperial weakness in northern Italy to obtain additional possessions for Don Philip which she had failed to get in 1735. France hesitated, first recognising Maria Theresa as heiress of Charles VI, and then qualifying this action by pointing out that to recognise the Pragmatic Sanction was not the same thing as to support Maria Theresa's husband in his candidature for the imperial crown. England was also hesitant:

some of her ministers favoured a renewal of the alliance with Austria, others deprecated any further entanglement in the affairs of Europe, and when in June 1741 it was decided to support Austria, the opponents of this policy insisted on reopening conversations with Prussia. In the midst of this confusion Frederick II realised clearly what policy would be most valuable to Prussia. Abandoning his attempts to recover Berg and Cleves, in December 1740 he invaded Silesia.

France became involved in the Austro-Prussian struggle largely against the will of Fleury. The cardinal was growing very old and other statesmen had the ear of Louis XV. His policy of reaching an understanding with Austria as a basis for a stable peace in Europe was swept away by the impetuous anti-Austrian programme of Belleisle and of those other Frenchmen who still believed in the tradition of an anti-Austrian 'Westphalian' policy. In December 1740 France entered into tentative negotiations with Frederick only to find that he wanted more than a purely defensive agreement. By June 1741 France had concluded a Prussian alliance. In July she had agreed to give armed help to Bavaria. In August she encouraged Sweden to attack Russia (ch. xviii).

Gradually the turmoil of the War of the Austrian Succession and of Jenkins' Ear settled into an uneasy peace. Ever since the end of 1744, when d'Argenson had become responsible for the direction of foreign affairs in France, there had been a possibility of ending hostilities. When in 1745 France and Spain won victories in the Netherlands, at Fontenoy, and in northern Italy, against the Austrians and Sardinians, both the Dutch and Sardinians began to approach France with overtures of peace. For a time peace negotiations were held up because Maria Theresa still hoped to recover Silesia by force of arms, but after her troops had been defeated by Prussia she was prepared to conclude the Treaty of Dresden in December 1745, thus ending the war with Prussia. Still the war in the west dragged on. In May 1746 a project of peace was actually sent to England by France, but the death of the king of Spain in July and some victories by the Austrian and Sardinian forces in northern Italy revived English hopes, and it was only after France had declared war on the Dutch and inflicted an unmistakable defeat on English forces in the Austrian Netherlands that discussions at Aix-la-Chapelle became really serious.

In 1748 France finally concluded peace with England rather than with Austria, because of the two England was thought more likely to fight on alone than was Austria. The treaty brought no triumph to any Power. The situation in Spain was left much as it had been in 1739, though a change of ministers gave better prospects of a further explosion being avoided. In Italy, Parma, Piacenza and Guastilla went to Don Philip while Don Carlos retained Naples and Sicily. The colonial disputes between England and France were left unsettled. Cape Breton was exchanged for Madras.

In the Empire the title of Emperor went to the husband of Maria Theresa, but Silesia had been ceded to Frederick II by the Treaty of Dresden. The two Powers which emerged triumphant were Prussia and Russia. Prussia had shown the value of her army and the genius of her king. Russia had heavily defeated Sweden and conquered Finland, which was only recovered by Sweden in return for accepting a Russian nominee as heir to the Swedish throne. Russia had maintained what was in effect a protectorate over Poland. Never had she stood so high as at the end of the war in 1748. One of the most important influences on the future of Europe was friendliness or hostility between these two Great Powers. By 1769 Frederick II was to express a lively fear of Russia and to point out how dangerous she might become.

The reversal of alliances (ch. xix) which startled the diplomats of Europe in 1756, was largely brought about by the very existence of Russia as an effective Great Power and was actively manipulated by Prussia.

In the Seven Years War (ch. xx) one of the chief protagonists was the king of Prussia, and the peace concluded in 1763 was brought about, at least partly, by a *coup d'état* in Russia. By a curious freak the negotiations which preceded the peace treaties of 1763 were characterised by an intermingling of Spanish policy with the policies of Prussia, Russia and the Habsburgs, reminiscent of the dreams of Alberoni or the theatrical transformation scenes of Ripperda, but in the period 1759–63 the son of Elizabeth Farnese was no more able to determine the outcome of negotiations than his mother had been between 1717 and 1732. In 1763 as in 1718 the Great Powers were still England, France and the Habsburgs, though there had now unmistakably been added to their number Russia and Prussia.

In 1759 the military situation on the European mainland was so serious for England and her Prussian ally that Pitt had to agree to open negotiations for peace. Even Brunswick's victory at Minden in August and Wolfe's victory at Quebec in September could not outweigh Prussia's further military disasters in November. In December 1759 England and Prussia approached the representatives of France, Russia and Austria at the Hague. Peace negotiations went on until April 1760 but came to nothing, partly because Choiseul declared his intentions of negotiating with the help of the good offices of Spain, where Charles III, the elder son of Elizabeth Farnese, had succeeded his almost Anglophile half-brother in 1759. Pitt haughtily rejected the Spanish attempt at mediation and the whole negotiation came to nothing.

The war dragged on during 1760, and though French and Russian troops won successes in Europe, English forces in America and India gained Montreal and Arcot and, in January 1761, Pondicherry. When, in June 1760, the Spanish ambassador at the Court of St James had attempted to get satisfaction from England about various grievances, such as the illicit cutting of wood at Honduras, Pitt proved very unaccommodating, and in January 1761 Grimaldi was sent to Versailles to negotiate a defensive alliance between France and Spain. Early in 1761 Kaunitz was advocating a general peace conference and Choiseul had agreed, on condition that during the conference, and even before, the belligerents might exchange envoys and carry on negotiations independently of the congress. From March to June 1761, while negotiations were going on for a Franco-Spanish alliance, other negotiations were also going on between France and England to reach an agreement on peace terms. In June there was an equal chance of an agreement being reached between England and France, but in August 1761 the *pacte de famille* was concluded between France and Spain. Spain agreed that if peace had not been concluded between England and France by 1 May 1762 she would declare war on England. Louis XV agreed to include Spain's claims to satisfaction in his negotiations with England, though this was to have a fatal effect on the Anglo-French peace talks, even though English policy had become much less belligerent after the death of George II in October 1760 and the entry of Bute into office in March 1761. In October 1761 Pitt, who wanted to prosecute the war vigorously, was defeated and left the cabinet, but this did not prevent England from declaring war on Spain in January 1762.

In the month that England declared war on Spain occurred an event which brought the end of the war in Europe much nearer. The tsaritsa Elizabeth died and her heir, Peter III, son of Charles Frederick of Holstein-Gottorp, speedily reversed Russian policy. He was a great admirer of Frederick of Prussia, and he wanted to be free of the war against Prussia so that he might assert the claims of his family to the ducal parts of Slesvig and Holstein and avenge the wrongs which his family had suffered at the hands of the Oldenburgs. He also had claims to the throne of Sweden (ch. xv). In May 1762 the new tsar concluded peace with Frederick II; and in the same month Sweden, alarmed lest the tsar might try to assert his claims to the Swedish throne, also made peace with Prussia so as to leave herself free for any emergency in the Baltic. In June 1762 the tsar entered into an offensive alliance with Frederick II and in August Russian troops were helping the Prussians to win the battle of Reichenbach. In July 1762 the tsar was deposed by his wife Catherine and shortly afterwards murdered, but though the new tsaritsa withdrew Russian troops from the campaign she did not break the treaty of May 1762. In October 1763 Frederick won further victories, but though the events of 1762 had transformed Prussia's prospects they did not encourage Frederick or his English allies enough to make them want to prolong the war.

In England enthusiasm for the war was at a low ebb even by 1760, by which time it was thought that England had gained her objectives in America and India. When the French peace terms under discussion in

1761 were divulged by the French a considerable section of public opinion regretted their rejection. Bute, opposed to the belligerent policy of Pitt was eager to reach an agreement with France and Spain. He had even put pressure on Frederick II to buy peace by a surrender of territory, so that the temporary improvement in Frederick's situation on the accession of Peter III to the throne of Russia appeared almost as a defeat for the policy of Prussia's nominal ally England. For domestic political reasons Bute was very eager to make peace in the West, and to do so he was prepared to be more accommodating than England had been in the Hague negotiations in 1759–60. Bute no longer insisted on Frederick II's adherence to the agreement and he was even prepared to consider the grievances of Spain. In February 1762 Martinique fell to an English squadron and England was in a favourable position to reopen peace negotiations. In the same month a Spanish army invaded Portugal but made such poor progress that the campaign had little effect on the Anglo-French negotiations. In September 1762 it was learnt in England that an English squadron had captured Havana. This produced wild enthusiasm in England and suddenly revived interest in the war, but Bute, for political reasons, was determined to reach a settlement. Parliament was postponed from 8 November till 25 November and Bute was able to present the House with terms of peace concluded at Fontainebleau on November 3. In eastern Europe the military success of Frederick II in 1762, combined with the changed policy of Russia, determined Maria Theresa to seek peace and in February 1763 Austria and Saxony concluded peace with Prussia. By the treaty concluded at Paris in 1763 England gained considerable territories in India and in America, but by the Treaty of Hubertusburg Prussia failed to gain the Saxon territory which had been the political objective of the war. 1763 marked a decline in the prestige of France (but Bute's policy prevented the influence of England from increasing to a corresponding extent). Spain, even under the vigorous leadership of Charles III, still had little influence in the affairs of Europe, but Prussia emerged from the negotiations an unmistakably Great Power, and Russia could affect the whole balance of power in eastern and central Europe.

CHAPTER X

THE DECLINE OF DIVINE-RIGHT MONARCHY IN FRANCE

URING the period extending from the sixteenth to the eighteenth century monarchy in most of the States of western and central Europe represented a compromise between medieval and modern conceptions of government; medieval ideas of the divine sanction of kingship were combined with an increasingly absolute form of rule. This phase in the history of European polity reached the completest development possible within its own limits in France. In his capacity as a Divine-Right monarch, Louis XIV embodied a tradition that went back to the *rois thaumaturges*; but the rays that darted from the *roi soleil* were not the effulgence of a setting sun. The new absolutism, allied to the old Divine Right, had given the French monarchy a renewed and more vigorous life. It must be remembered that the effete and decadent system of 1789, the *ancien régime* of the historians, only a century before was the new deal of Louis XIV and Colbert. At the close of the seventeenth century, by the efficiency of its administrative and governmental structure, France was in advance of every other country in Europe. True, Louis XIV did not leave his country at the height of her greatness. He outlived his own glory both at home and abroad and bequeathed more problems than solutions to his successors. In France distress and discontent were widespread before he died; and in Europe, during his long reign, Louis had first used and then abused the power with which the cardinals had endowed France, until the Treaty of Utrecht registered his defeat and opened what has been called, though hardly with justice, the age of 'the English preponderance'. This is the customary picture, but there is a good deal of exaggeration in it. The truth is that the partial defeat of Louis XIV's ambitions had only been brought about by the combined forces of Europe: and despite much internal unrest, France was still by reason of its population and natural resources potentially far stronger than any other Power. All that was needed to restore her to her natural preponderance was a return to a foreign policy which would not unite the rest of Europe against her, and the restoration of the machine of government to the efficiency it had known under the great ministers bequeathed by Mazarin to the *roi soleil*.

The other great Divine-Right monarchies, Austria and Spain, and the lesser principalities of Germany and Italy, in their different ways echoed the pattern of French history. But it was in France that the great edifice that towered over Europe was erected in the seventeenth century, and it was in France that the principle of Divine Right was to receive its death-blow. It is justifiable, therefore, to study the decline of Divine-Right monarchy primarily in France, and to concentrate our attention on an examination of its nature and functioning there. Its interpretation has passed through various phases. Royalists in the nineteenth century, conscious of the long arm of the Ministry of the Interior reaching out through the prefects to control the political and administrative life of the country, looked back to the Bourbon monarchy as the golden age of freedom from the domination of a centralised bureaucracy. This view, though it was not abandoned, became much more difficult to uphold after de Tocqueville had shown that centralisation was far from being an invention of the Revolution, and that before 1789 the *intendants* held France in *tutelle*, as the prefects did after 1799. Taine followed de Tocqueville and even pushed the argument to excess: monarchical centralisation, he declared, had reduced the population of France to 'une poussière humaine'. More detailed historical research has modified both these views, and the picture of the government of France that has emerged is far more complex than either suggests.

In the first place, to be effective a centralised bureaucracy requires a country divided into coherent and exclusive administrative units. To see such units in the France of the *ancien régime* it would be necessary to concentrate attention on the *généralités*, some thirty in number, over which the *intendants* presided; but the *généralités*, organised in the first place for the collection of taxes, though in the course of time coming to be used for many other administrative purposes, were far from being the only administrative divisions. A closer inspection of France under the *ancien régime* reveals a complex structure of overlapping divisions more like a medieval mosaic than the simple slabs of colour with which the territorial divisions of the modern administrative State can be painted.

France itself was not a solid block of territory. Independent enclaves, such as Avignon and the Venaissin, Dombes, Mulhouse, Henrichemont, Orange and many others, survived within its frontiers. Apart from these the country was still riddled with exceptional jurisdictions. The Duchy of Bouillon, for example, counted in law as a separate sovereign State. The Clermontois, with 40,000 inhabitants, belonged to the prince de Condé, who collected and kept all the taxes imposed there. The Boulonnais had its own separate army, commanded by the gentlemen of the province. Many of the provincial *états* had been suppressed, but those of Brittany and Languedoc retained important powers which formed an effective brake on the *intendants*, while those of Provence and Burgundy possessed minor rights. Side by side with the *généralités*, but entirely different in area and boundaries, were the jurisdictions of the *parlements*, the ecclesiastical dioceses, and the thirty-nine military *gouvernements*, though by the eighteenth century these last had been robbed of most of their importance.

Even in its fiscal system the monarchy had not achieved administrative unity. The provinces which possessed *états* had the theoretic right of taxing themselves, which meant at least the right of putting obstacles in the way of the *Contrôle générale* and escaping with a lighter burden than the rest of the country. The *gabelle*, or salt tax, varied from the *pays de grande gabelle*, through the *pays de petite gabelle* and the *pays rédimés* to the *pays exempts*, and the price of salt varied correspondingly, from a half to twelve or thirteen sous a *livre*. The use of *papier timbré*, with corresponding payment of tax, was not required in Hainault, Cambrésis and Alsace. France was not even a single customs unit. The *cinq grosses fermes* had one tariff; the *provinces réputées étrangères*—Brittany, Flanders, Artois and several others—each had its own particular tariff; the *provinces d'étranger effectif*—Alsace, Franche-Comté and the Trois-Evéchés—formed another group; and the free ports, including Dunkirk and Marseilles, could trade freely with foreign countries, but with the rest of France only on paying customs dues.

When we look at the lower organs of government we see a different picture. The old sub-divisions of *sénéchaussées* and *bailliages* had lost practically all their administrative significance, though they were revived for use in the election of the *États généraux* in 1789. The institutions which had given the people a share in local government were those which had suffered most from the encroachment of the *intendants*. In the smaller communes the close supervision of the *intendants* had turned the *syndic perpétuel* into an agent of the Government. In the latter years of Louis XIV a series of edicts made municipal offices saleable. Though they subsequently escaped to some extent from royal nomination, they remained in the possession of small local patriciates. The relics of local self-government were thus largely extinguished in France by the eighteenth century; but there were still innumerable local privileges, which constituted a network of restrictions, rights and customs in which the most energetic of *intendants* found himself cabined and confined. Moreover, the sanctity of property was barely second to the sanctity of the king, and most of the exceptions and privileges, including that of office-holding, partook of the nature of property.

The *intendant*, though the local agent of the greatest bureaucracy in Europe, was thus far from possessing arbitrary power. His role was not the proclamation of ruthless dictates to be obeyed unquestioningly by a servile populace, but rather, in the words of Turgot's biographer, a commitment to 'a perpetual drudgery in administrative bad habits, to a wearisome tidying of endless lumber'.[1] Every move he made brought him into conflict with the privileges of one class or another. If he was an administrative giant, he was one who was pinned down by innumerable miniscule claims and customs as effectively as Gulliver by the tiny ropes of

[1] D. Dakin, *Turgot and the Ancien Régime in France* (1939), p. 27.

the Lilliputians. Moreover, the large area of most *généralités* made their close supervision difficult, especially as the potential scope of the *intendant's* interests was practically co-extensive with the whole field of public life. Primarily a financial officer, he also supervised the practice of religion, exercised important judicial and police functions, regulated trade and industry, and even shared the military authority of the commandant, who had taken the place of the military governor and whose co-operation was necessary for the smooth running of local affairs, especially in time of crisis. With all these powers, the *intendant* never possessed adequate machinery for their continual and effective exercise. At the head of the bureau of the *intendance* there was a *subdélégué général*, and under him a varying number of *subdélégués*, who were often charged with incompetence and corruption. On the principle that those who receive the kicks are most likely to be doing the real work, it might be suggested that the *intendants* may have been given some of the credit which should have gone to their subordinate officials. It will not be possible to give any general verdict on the *intendants* of the eighteenth century until there are many more studies of their activities, but the absence of *intendants* from their *généralités* for lengthy periods, which was far from rare in the latter part of the century, suggests that they were not altogether indispensable to the functioning of the official machine. An *intendant* of the efficiency and conscientiousness of Turgot was not unique, but equally he was not necessarily typical.

While the administration of the *intendants* was hampered by a network of privileges and exceptions, the authority of the central Government was restricted by the independence of the *intendants*, who were quite capable, if for any reason they disliked an instruction, of simply ignoring it. In the case of continued opposition to its orders by an official the central Government had no remedy but to transfer him, or to dismiss him, and it was rarely prepared to go as far as this. At the same time, the strength of even an able and energetic *intendant* depended in the last resort on the extent to which the central Government was able and willing to support him.

This government was in theory a government of councils. The *conseil d'en haut*, sometimes called *conseil secret* or *conseil d'état*, which decided the great questions of national policy, especially those of foreign affairs, was composed of those who received a personal invitation from the king. Apart from the Secretary for Foreign Affairs, the Secretaries of State and the Controller-General were not necessarily included in its membership. They sat, however, in the *conseil des dépêches*, which supervised the whole of the internal administration and heard appeals against the judicial decisions of the *parlements*. The *conseil des finances*, established in 1661 after the fall of Fouquet and the suppression of the *surintendance*, dealt with financial questions. Its functions were difficult to distinguish from those of the *conseil des dépêches* and in fact the two councils probably often sat as one. The *conseil privé* or *conseil des partis*, composed of *conseillers d'état* and *maîtres des requêtes*, represented the supreme judicial authority of the king. At intervals there was a *conseil de commerce*, periodically suffering eclipse. Finally, the *conseil de conscience*, which had been concerned chiefly with the granting of benefices, in the eighteenth century became reduced to the king's confessor. This elaborate structure of councils, however, was far from representing the real government of the country. In appearance a government of councils, in fact it was much more a government of individuals. The Secretaries of State and the Controller-General were the effective heads of the administrative services, and the decisions that were taken were nearly always their personal decisions.

First in rank among the great officers of State was the *Chancelier*, the head of the judicial system of France, and the embodiment of eternal justice, as a sign of which he alone never wore mourning for the death of the king. He was the last of the great life officers of the Crown. For that very reason all his effective powers had been transferred to the *Garde des sceaux*, appointed and dismissed at will by the king. Only when he also held the latter office did the *Chancelier* exercise the right of sealing the king's declarations and edicts, and incidentally drawing the great income that accrued in fees, so that it was said, 'Chancelier sans les sceaux est apothicair esans sucre'. Along with the *Garde des sceaux*, the Secretaries of State and the Controller-General constituted the real government of France. Throughout most of the eighteenth century there were four secretaries, one for Foreign Affairs, a second for War, a third for Marine with colonies and commerce, and a fourth for the *maison du roi*, including also the supervision of the affairs of the clergy and of the *religion prétendue réformée*, of the interior provinces, police and passports and, above the *lieutenant de police*, responsibility for Paris, except during the years 1749–57, when Paris was under the authority of the comte d'Argenson. The secretary for the *maison du roi* was sometimes called the *ministre de Paris*. From an administrative point of view the Controller-General was the most important member of the Government. He was in charge of finance, agriculture, industry and communications; hardly any aspect of internal administration escaped him, except in those fields where the Secretary for the *maison du roi* exercised a rival authority.

These ministers must not be regarded as forming a united team. Each was individually appointed and dismissed by the king, and the tradition was for rivals rather than allies to be chosen, as Louis XIV had made use of Louvois and Colbert. The rivalry of the ministers was intensified by a more permanent rivalry between their bureaus, for which the lack of definition in their functions provided ample scope. There was usually no titular head of the ministry. Dubois was *premier ministre* in 1722–3 and Orleans took the office for himself in the last few months of his life. The duc de Bourbon, another prince of the blood, succeeded him, but held office for only two years. Fleury then became the head of the Government in effect but never took the title of *premier ministre*. His term of office, except towards the end when his authority was being challenged, was the one period between the death of the regent and the Revolution when the *ancien régime* knew something like unified control. Choiseul was never *premier ministre* and exercised his authority by the accumulation of separate offices. Under Louis XVI, to anticipate, the head of the *conseil des finances* seems to have been regarded as the leading minister, but only Loménie de Brienne again obtained the title of *premier ministre*, in 1787–8.

The absence of a *premier ministre* was fully in the logic of the *ancien régime*. The king himself was regarded as providing the necessary unity in the conduct of affairs of State, and he was equally head of the army, the judiciary, and the Church. The royal Councils met and made their recommendations, at least theoretically, in the king's presence, and their decisions were his decisions. His will, formally declared, was the law of the land. By his personal *lettres closes*, which did not go through the chancellery, he could issue orders, judicial or administrative, deciding the fate of any individual in the country. The famous *lettres de cachet* were one example of these. It is no exaggeration to say that the whole Law and Constitution of France dwelt in the bosom of the king. It was a personal government, not an administrative system. The king held his authority as an individual and delegated it in turn to individuals; each subordinate official was endowed with a share of the royal *bon plaisir* and therefore with a degree of personal independence. Absolutism in fact was qualified by indiscipline: the king, or his ministers in his name, could command anything, but they could not guarantee that their commands would be obeyed.

None the less, the king was the State in every sense. Absolute and divine, the monarchy was also paternal: the king was the father of his people, living constantly in the presence and before the eyes of his loving subjects. The corporate life of France was concentrated in his person and at his court, which Louis XIV had deliberately organised as a public spectacle; and if it was a costly one, at least he gave the people a good show for their money. He opened the Tuileries and the gardens at Versailles to the public, despite the defacing of statues, damage to flowers and plants and promiscuous nuisances that were involved; in 1789 Arthur Young comments on the ragged beggars, men looking like galley-slaves, ranging about the palace of Versailles and even penetrating into the king's bedroom. It was to provide the proper order and decorum for a court that was on permanent public exhibition that Louis XIV drew up the complicated and rigorous system of etiquette which regulated every moment of its life, from the most intimate occasions reserved for the highest *noblesse* to the *grand couvert* when all the world might see the king and queen dine in the midst of their courtiers.

Both in its formal and in its governmental functions, therefore, the Louis-quatorzian monarchy called for a king who could play the part laid down for him by the *grand monarque*. The ruler who succeeded him, and reigned as boy and man from 1715 to 1774, was far from equal to these exacting demands. Even with a much stronger king than Louis XV, however, there would have remained an inherent contradiction in the system of government created by Louis XIV. On the one hand it was a centralised bureaucracy, controlled by a Grand Bureaucrat, whose own position was unchallengable because it was based on a thousand years of history and upheld by right divine. But the central figure of the whole machine, who provided the source of power, from which every subordinate power derived its impetus, was himself a man, living in a determined environment and not existing in a vacuum. That environment was provided by the court and the court *noblesse*. Under Louis XIV government had not been immune from the influence of court intrigues; under a weaker successor it was to be dominated by them, and the State was to veer uneasily in contrary directions as one court faction or another obtained control.

By completing the elimination of all rival authorities from the Government Louis XIV had put on the monarchy the burden of total responsibility, but at the same time without endowing it with total power. He had gone either too far or else not far enough. Apart from the *parlements*, all the bodies that might have shared its responsibility had been robbed of their authority, but he had left the higher orders of the State—clergy, *noblesse* and *parlements*—sufficient independence to oppose the will of the king, hamper the work of the bureaucracy and stand in the way of efficient government. France was in fact still far from being a modern State. The legal system, in spite of the codes of Louis XIV, remained chaotic. The administration of the *intendants*, as has been said, was tied down by a network of privileges. The formal structure of economic life was still medieval. All jobs went by purchase or favour and the irresponsible influence of corruption and favouritism pervaded the Government from top to bottom.

The weaknesses in Louis XIV's System were already becoming manifest in the later years of his reign, when dissatisfaction was widespread. A school of reformers, including Vauban, Fénelon, Boulainvillier and Saint-Simon, believed in the possibility of undoing the work of Louis XIV and calling back the *noblesse* to a share in the actual government. Their hope of finding in the young duc de Bourgogne a reforming king was frustrated by his death, but on the accession of the child Louis XV, the regent, Philip of Orleans, brought the same ideas to power with him. Orleans, cultured and able, had been kept in the background by Louis XIV and suffered from his reputation for dissipation. His first task was to dispose of the rival claims of the royal bastards, and to free himself from the control of the Council set up by Louis XIV. By seizing exclusive power the regent prevented almost inevitable governmental chaos from developing. The will of Louis XIV was overthrown in the famous session of the *Parlement* of Paris, of which Saint-Simon has given such a dramatic if inaccurate account.[1] The price paid was the restoration of the *parlement's* right of remonstrance, and though it is true that this was to be the beginning of much trouble for the monarchy, it is hardly fair to blame the regent for not foreseeing the weakness of his successor. Indeed, given that weakness, it is reasonable to suppose that the *parlements* would have reasserted themselves whether the regent had formally revived their rights or not. It is equally unjust to interpret his actions as mere self-interested opportunism. The changes in the structure of the government which he introduced have been presented as a mere device for winning support for his ambition to succeed the sickly boy-king on the throne. It is difficult to reconcile this interpretation with his willingness to share his authority with newly created councils, intended to replace the Secretaries of State, to which most of the notables of the kingdom, including even the regent's personal opponents, were called. Orleans' new Polysynodie consisted of six councils, each of ten members, including both nobles and royal officials, entrusted with the supervision of the departments of war, navy, finance, commerce, home and foreign affairs. Time was to show whether this attempt to undo the work of Louis XIV would succeed. Meanwhile there was an immediate crisis to be faced if a new Fronde was not to develop. The regent dealt with it by an energetic reversal of the policy of the late king.

The most pressing problem, not for the first or last time in France, was presented by the condition of the finances, which had been left in so desperate a situation that Orleans even contemplated summoning the *États généraux* to cope with the problem. The Council of Finances resorted to a partial repudiation of the debt, called in the more recently coined *louis d'or* and *écus* and reissued them over-stamped for twenty and five *livres* respectively, instead of sixteen and four, and established a court to examine the transactions of the financiers, scale down their claims and order punishment or restitution where necessary. The *parlementaires* who constituted this court flung themselves into the traditional task with their accustomed disregard for petty trifles of justice; but little positive result was achieved. However, the other measures had eased the financial situation of the Crown, and a pacific foreign policy enabled military expenses to be reduced. Only a radical reform of the system of taxation could have put the finances on a sound basis, and hoping as he did to restore the privileged orders to a share in the government of France it was difficult for the regent to remedy the deficiencies of Louis XIV's system by such a measure.

The main direct tax was the *taille*, for which the *brevet* was drawn up

---

[1] Saint-Simon, *Mémoires* (ed. A. de Boislisle, 1879–1928), vol. xxix, pp. 12–32, and Appendix 1, pp. 467–97.

each year by the *conseil des finances*. It was then divided between the *généralités*, and sub-divided by the *intendants* in the *pays d'élections* and by the *États* in the *pays d'États*. In the latter, which were mostly *pays de taille réelle*, the tax was in general based on land, and wealth other than land escaped. Moreover, the tax registers were old and out of date. The *pays d'États* therefore were taxed more lightly than the *pays d'élection*, where the *taille* was generally a *taille personnelle*, based on the assumed total wealth of the individual taxpayer. It was collected on arbitrarily drawn-up assessments by collectors, chosen from among the *taillables* and often incompetent for the task. The privileged orders were of course exempt, as were many of the towns. Other towns compounded for the *taille* at a fixed rate, and most of the rest had converted it into a simple addition to their *octroi*. Two attempts had been made under Louis XIV to create a tax which would fall on all classes without exception, the *capitation*, established in 1695, and the *dixième*, in 1710; but the clergy bought exemption from both, the *noblesse* and the towns obtained exemption or avoided payment, and these taxes became merely an additional imposition on the *taillables*. The burden of the indirect taxes fell with similar inequity. The *gabelle* varied from district to district, *seigneurs* paid at a reduced rate and the religious orders and officers of justice and finance were exempt. The varying rate of the *traites*, the internal and external customs dues, has already been mentioned. The *don gratuit*, paid by the clergy as a body, was small in relation to their taxable capacity. Finally, to complete the picture, there were the *aides*—excise dues on various commodities, royal *octrois*—the taxes imposed on gold and silver, leather, playing-cards and other articles (*marque des fers, du cuir*, etc.), the tobacco monopoly, the *droits de contrôle* and *droit de timbre*, imposed on all legal transactions, receipts and so on, and the *domaine corporel*, deriving from the royal estates, which was now of little importance. These indirect taxes were collected by *fermiers*, who brought the right for a fixed sum and made what profit they could. Money was also raised by lotteries, by the sale of offices and by payments from their holders. In the last resort the king could fall back on loans, either direct or, when the royal credit was at a low ebb, raised on the credit of other authorities, such as the Hôtel de Ville of Paris and the provincial Estates; he could also issue paper money, secured on the credit of such bodies as the Farmers General and usually current at a rate below its face value. To complete this picture of financial disorder, it would be necessary to describe the multifarious organs of control struggling to reduce chaos to order, or at least to produce some representation of it that could be put down on paper. At the head of the whole lack of system was a frequently changed Controller General, whose inextricably confused budgets ran one year into another, who could just make ends meet in peace-time, but who was invariably reduced to desperate expedients in time of war.

Searching for a more permanent remedy than bankruptcy for the endemic financial ills of France, the regent lent an ear to the proposals of a former acquaintance, the Scottish financier, John Law. The power of credit, which had long been known by the Dutch, was now being revealed to England and France. Unfortunately their early experiments with its magic were only to be performed by apprentice sorcerers. However, Law explained his theory of credit, which was not unfounded, to the regent, and in 1716 was authorised to set up a private bank. This was successful, and it was followed in 1717 by the establishment of the Company of the Occident with a monopoly of the trade with Louisiana. In 1719 it became the Company of the Indies and was given control of the whole foreign trade of France. In 1718 and 1719 Law also obtained first the farm of the indirect taxes, and then—a revolutionary step—the collection of the direct taxes and the right of issuing paper money. He was now ready to deal with the problem of the royal debt: in 1719 the *rentes* on the State were suppressed and declared payable in shares of the Company. Finally, in January 1720 Law, who had become a naturalised French citizen and a Roman Catholic, was appointed Controller General. The whole economic life of France was now in his hands, and he used his colossal power to introduce reforms in every sphere. Saint-Simon, usually no kindly critic of his contemporaries and hardly disposed by nature to admire a foreign adventurer, describes him as 'without avarice or roguery and unspoilt by the extreme of good fortune'.[1] But the incredible success of the System, added to the optimistic temperament of a gambler, had led Law to erect his colossal financial superstructure on the most exiguous of foundations in actual trade. When the inevitable crash came, after a gallant but hopeless struggle to save something from the wreck, he had to abandon his efforts. He fled the country in December 1720.

What was the balance-sheet of the System? In appearance everything was restored as it had been before the meteoric Scotsman turned the State upside down. The mass of paper money was reduced to manageable proportions by drastic reductions in its face value. Most of Law's reforms disappeared with him. One particularly unfortunate result of the collapse of the System was to confirm the French in their distrust of credit institutions and particularly of the idea of a national bank. The size of the debt was reduced by the liquidation, but only to about the level it had stood at before Law's operations, and at the price of a renewed bankruptcy. On the other hand, the stimulus given to economic life by the System was not entirely lost. Commerce and industry profited, and the great roads and canals planned by Law were not all abandoned. Lorient, the headquarters of the Company of the Indies, slowly grew in importance, as did Nouvelle-Orléans, founded in America. Overseas trade had received a considerable impetus and attention had been directed to the

[1] Saint-Simon, vol. xxxviii, p. 76.

possibilities of the colonies. In France landowners who were lucky enough to profit in the early stages of the System and get out in time had been able to free their land from debt. While many families had been ruined, others had risen from poverty to riches. The redistribution of wealth and the consequent confusion of classes which resulted from the crash was its most marked result. The financiers, whom Law had temporarily eclipsed, returned in greater strength than before, at their head the Pâris brothers, the ablest of whom, Pâris-Duverney, supervised the liquidation of the System and under the duc de Bourbon (1723–6) was in effect, though not in name, Controller-General. A generation of *nouveaux riches* emerged out of the crash of the System.

Not only in respect of finance did the regent's experiments fail. The system of government by councils also collapsed. The regency proved, if proof were needed, that the work of the cardinals and Louis XIV could not be undone. Yet while France returned to the political habits and institutions that had been fixed on her by the Grand Monarch, their insufficiencies became the more marked as French society continued to develop while its institutions remained stationary.

In foreign policy Orleans and his minister Dubois had been more successful (ch. IX), but the domestic policy of the regency must be written down as a failure and one that was all the more significant in that it could hardly be attributed to the personal weaknesses of the regent himself. He was an intelligent and strong ruler, who saw the need for a new beginning in France. He was not afraid of drastic measures and he chose ruthless and able ministers like Law and Dubois to assist him. It is arguable that he saved France from the disaster of a new Fronde and he certainly prevented the governmental chaos which was the normal accompaniment of a regency. He was responsible for the only fundamental attempt to reform the structure of government in France, between Louis XIV and the Revolution, that went beyond paper plans, such as those drawn up later by d'Argenson. The cause of such a resounding failure must be sought not in Orleans's defects of character but in the inherent contradictions of the system of government laid down by Louis XIV, which were to become steadily more apparent in the course of the next century.

After the death of the regent in 1723 it was natural that the duc de Bourbon, as the next in line among the princes of the blood, should take charge of the Government. He was argely dominated by his mistress, Mme de Prie, and his incompetence was soon manifested. In 1726 the young king's former tutor, the aged Cardinal Fleury, who had Louis' entire confidence, felt strong enough to bring about Bourbon's downfall. Fleury ruled France from 1726 to 1743. This fact was a breach—though it was only to be a temporary one—with the system of Louis XIV, who had never been willing to put his entire confidence in any single minister and in his greatest days had played off one against another and kept the supreme direction of policy in his own hands. Fleury was the successor, not of Louis XIV and Colbert, but of Richelieu and Mazarin, and not unworthy of the heritage. He was *premier ministre* without the title; in terms of a court instead of a parliament he was a French Walpole, holding power by the confidence of the king, his own personal ability and his capacity for managing men. Like Walpole's, his authority was never unchallenged; it was at its height between 1732 and 1737, when he worked in close alliance with Chauvelin as *Garde des sceaux* and Minister for Foreign Affairs. With the implicit trust of the king he was able to build for himself a place above the coteries of the court. While Fleury remained in power the rivalries of the factions did not control French policy. The smouldering fires of the new Jansenist controversy (see p. 229), if they were not extinguished, were at least damped down. Again like Walpole, he was no innovator. France needed, he believed, a period of repose. He gave it that and it was not wasted. In d'Aguesseau, from 1717 to 1751, France had a great Chancellor, who, even during the periods when the seals were not in his hands, continued his task of codification and law reform. Philibert Orry, Controller-General from 1730 to 1745, was a hard-working, conscientious and vigorous official, a great administrator if not a reformer, under whom the finances were reduced to such order as the *ancien régime* permitted, and whose methods were successful in maintaining financial stability so long as the moderate foreign policy of Fleury prevented any excessive demands from being imposed on them.

If finance was the key to successful government in France, foreign policy was the key to successful finance, and Fleury devoted his greatest efforts to the maintenance of a peaceful but not a weak foreign policy. In particular the charge that he neglected the navy had been shown to be unjustified. His fundamental aim was to prevent the recreation of the general European coalition against France which Louis XIV had brought upon himself. He therefore continued Dubois' policy of alliance with England. Secure on this side, he was able to rebuild French influence in the north and the east of Europe, and to achieve in 1738, by the Treaty of Vienna, after the War of the Polish Succession, the attribution of the duchies of Bar and Lorraine to Stanislas, and after him to his daughter, the queen of France and her children.

Although Fleury remained nominally at the head of affairs, control had begun to slip out of his hands by 1740. The increasing independence of the king led him to listen to rival advisers at court, and the cardinal could only retain his position by yielding to the new influences and accepting policies of which he fundamentally disapproved. When he died, in January 1743, Louis determined to appoint no successor and to return to the system of Louis XIV. The king was no longer to be, like Louis XIII, the 'illustrious slave' of a great minister, but, like Louis XIV, himself to preside over the *conseil d'en haut* and assume personal responsibility for

French policy. This decision must not be put down merely to the whim of the king: it was a necessary condition of the System of Louis XIV, which had been held in suspense because of the peculiar personal relationship existing between Louis XV and his old tutor, a situation which was not likely to be repeated. A king who ruled as well as reigned was essential to the proper functioning of the *ancien régime*: monarchy by Divine Right, which still retained much of the medieval element of personal government, could not be reconciled with a *roi fainéant*.

Now was to be seen what would happen when Divine Right descended from a Louis XIV to a Louis XV. Not that the traditional picture of Louis XV is altogether to be accepted. The real problem of the *ancien régime* has been concealed by the deliberate denigrations of his character in the memoirs or pseudo-memoirs of gossiping bourgeois, factious courtiers and dismissed ministers. The great-grandson of the *roi soleil* began with many apparent advantages. He was a pretty boy, who grew up amid the affections of the nation, the second *bien-aimé* of France, on whom countless hopes were lavished. His cold dignity and *voix enrouée* marked the man accustomed to command. He moved through the complicated routine of court life with grace. The story of his ignorance and lack of education is a myth. He was intelligent and had a remarkable memory. The origin of the fatal weakness in his character is doubtless only to be sought in the mysterious recesses of the human personality, but whatever innate defects there were, they were intensified by his early upbringing under Villeroy, who forced the boy-king into a premature and hated publicity. Here was one factor for which Louis XIV had not allowed: the education of a court, surrounded by courtiers, was the worst possible preparation for a king who had to rule as well as reign. Louis XV was bored with the duties of a king even before he properly came to exercise them, and he turned to the two things which were ever varied even when they were always the same, hunting and women. The days when the king did not hunt, it was said, 'le roi ne fait rien aujourd'hui', and a long procession of royal mistresses, among whom only the Pompadour and Mme du Barry knew more than a transient favour, helped to keep boredom at bay. But these pursuits did not give Louis permanent satisfaction. There was a religious sense in him which turned into a morbid obsession with death, slightly tempered by a conviction that God could not damn a king of France. His worst vice was the fatal incapacity for decision which paralysed the machine of State at its very centre, and arose perhaps in part from his pervading boredom and distaste for the labours involved in conducting the business of the State. Yet he clung stubbornly to his royal prerogatives and the position he had inherited from Louis XIV. After Fleury he gave his whole confidence to no one, but reverted to the policy of playing off one minister or court faction against another. This was to erect ministerial instability into a principle of government. Still worse, Louis could not refrain from intriguing against his own ministers. He had a natural taste for the back-stairs, which was manifested in his foreign policy by the *secret du roi* and equally in the *département de l'interception*, that section of the Ministry of Foreign Affairs (transferred after the fall of Choiseul to the *Contrôle générale*) where letters were opened and those of interest copied for the private delectation of the king.

Under such a ruler, the struggles of court factions emerged as the real structure of government in France. Favourites and mistresses competed for influence over the king. Transient alliances were perpetually being formed and dissolved among the coteries at Versailles. Women made and unmade the alliances of court faction. Intrigue was the politics of the *ancien régime*, and intrigue led back, behind Louis XIV, to the spirit of the Fronde. Taine has summed up the situation in one of his scintillating epigrams, 'Désœuvrer une aristocratie, c'est la rendre frondeuse'.[1]

The aberrations in the domestic and foreign policy of France during the eighteenth century are only really to be understood in the light of a more detailed analysis of the court factions than has yet been made. Only a few brief indications can be attempted here. The dominant element in foreign policy during the first part of the reign of Louis XV was dynastic intrigue. The hope of succeeding the sickly Louis XV on the throne was the motive of the *secret du régent*. Opposition gathered round the party of the old court, supported by the royal bastards, but the regent and Dubois were able to keep it in check and even to make use of the implication of the duke and duchess of Maine in the pro-Spanish conspiracy of Cellamare (1718) to further their policy. The three years between the fall of Dubois and the ascendancy of Fleury (1723–6), during which the duc de Bourbon was nominally in charge of France, and Mme de Prie effectively in charge of him, witnessed the struggle of various influences for the control of foreign policy. It was ended in 1726 by the victory of Fleury, who knew how to remain in control of his own foreign policy, though dynastic ambitions played their part in the War of the Polish Succession, out of which arose in turn the *secret du roi*. When, in 1737, Chauvelin began to develop a different line of policy from that of Fleury, and to intrigue with the duc de Bourbon, he disappeared from the scene. But by 1740, after the death of Charles VI of Austria had precipitated an international crisis, Fleury was no longer master of the situation. The cardinal evidently could not live for ever and a new and dazzling star had appeared above the horizon, to whom courtiers began to think it might be worth while to hitch their wagon. The comte de Belleisle became the centre of the party that favoured war with Austria, and Fleury, against his better judgment, had to yield. When he died in 1743, by the king's decision he was to have

[1] Taine, *Les Origines de la France contemporaine: l'ancien régime* (14th ed. 1885), p. 371.

no successor and he unwillingly left France committed to a war with no clear idea what it was for.

The marquis d'Argenson, who became Minister of Foreign Affairs in 1743, was a man more apt for drawing up bold plans than for executing them; but even if his ideas had been more practical they would have stood little chance of success, for Louis XV was simultaneously listening to half-a-dozen contrary views. The failure of d'Argenson's schemes, to which Louis XV had only accorded a half-hearted support, led to the fall of the minister in 1747, and the military successes of Maurice de Saxe enabled France to achieve in 1748 a compromise peace. For the next ten years it is difficult to say who was in charge of French policy. The king's secret diplomacy, in which his chief agents were the comte de Broglie and the prince de Conti, occupied much of his attention. The prevailing influence in the French court was now Madame de Pompadour, who ceased to be the king's mistress only to become his chief *confidante*. Though doubtless not in a position to decide policy herself, she was often able to determine who would decide it; the Abbé de Bernis, who was largely instrumental in the negotiation of the Franco-Austrian treaty of 1756, was her protégé, and when his calculations had been shown to be mistaken, her influence helped Choiseul to become Minister of Foreign Affairs, in December 1758. With the support of important elements in the court in addition to the Pompadour, and by his own astute and determined character, he was the first minister since Fleury to have effective control of French policy. But by now the general weakness and confusion in the government of France had so reduced her strength that even a minister as capable and energetic as Choiseul could not avert defeat. The causes of the failure of French foreign policy were many, but though there were such contributory factors as the diversion of the Austrian alliance from its proper ends, the difficulty of waging war on land and sea at once, or the decline of France's eastern allies, the ultimate cause must be sought in the weakness and disunity of the Government, and this can be traced to the personal defects of Louis XV as the activating agent in the machine of State. 'La foiblesse trompe tous les calculs de la politique', wrote the comte de Ségur later. 'Placez un homme de génie sur le plus petit trône de l'Europe, et de princes foibles sur tous les autres, il les dominera et fera une révolution totale.'[1]

The same weakness was manifested in the internal government of France; and whereas foreign policy was directed by the influence of court factions which could easily have been controlled by a strong king, or a minister with the king's full confidence, domestic policy was exposed to more powerful pressures. Certainly the monarchy was never openly attacked, but it was steadily being undermined in its very foundations—its religious sanction and its financial resources. For convenience the two

[1] L. P. Ségur, *Politique de tous les cabinets de l'Europe* (1802), vol. 1, p. 253.

struggles over religion and finance may be taken separately, though it must be remembered that they were in fact being waged simultaneously.

A monarchy by Divine Right implied a general acceptance of the religious basis of society, and a Church which was equal to its role in the State. Unfortunately the Church in eighteenth-century France was in no condition to face the attacks delivered from opposite quarters by Jansenists and *philosophes*. Its greatest weakness was that it could not face its enemies as a united body. The upper clergy, who monopolised the greater part of the revenues of the Church, were almost exclusively drawn from the higher ranks of society: there was no room in the episcopate, as there had been even under Louis XIV, for a Bossuet or a Mabillon. The higher ecclesiastical offices were often practically the hereditary property of great families. That prince de Rohan, whose desire for the favour of Marie-Antoinette was to be so fatal to them both, was Bishop *in partibus* of Campe at the age of 26, and in due course succeeded his uncle as Bishop of Strasburg, Grand Almoner of France, Abbot of St Vaast, Provisor of the Sorbonne and Cardinal. In striking contrast to the wealth of the higher clergy was the poverty of the *curés* and *vicaires*, hardly passing rich on the remnant of their endowments left them. This, the *portion congrue*, fixed at 300 *livres* a year for *curés* in 1686, was raised to 500 *livres* in 1768, while *vicaires* at the same time were allocated a minimum of 200 *livres*, paltry sums which the parish priests supplemented as best they could by fees extracted from their reluctant parishioners.

While they existed in poverty, however, the lesser clergy had one advantage over their successors in the nineteenth century. The *vicaires* were mostly *vicaires perpétuels*, and, like the *curés*, were therefore much less dependent on the episcopate than the parish priests of the following century. Thus, at the same time the parish clergy had strong grounds for discontent and considerable freedom for expressing it. Their restiveness took the form of the movement known as *richérisme*, after Edmé Richer, who, in a work published in 1611, had taught that the Church was a constitutional monarchy rather than an absolutism. Sovereignty in the Church belonged, he held, to the whole body of the clergy, including the parish priests. *Richérisme* became important when religious discontent was added to the material causes of resentment, for the French Church in the eighteenth century was spiritually at a low ebb. Especially among the higher clergy, laxity in religion and morals was widespread. Unorthodox ideas were welcomed by the regulars even more freely than by the secular clergy, while orthodox theology could produce no adequate intellectual counter to the brilliant propaganda of the *philosophes*.

Such religious enthusiasm as appeared in the eighteenth-century Church was mostly diverted into the heterodox channel of Jansenism. Louis XIV and the Jesuits had extinguished Port-Royal, but in completing their victory over the old Jansenism a new one had unwittingly been started by the famous bull *Unigenitus* of 1713. The Bull condemned as Jansenist 101 propositions in a devotional work written by Quesnel in 1671, *Réflexions morales sur le nouveau Testament*. Former bulls in the Jansenist controversy had been addressed mainly to theologians. This one chose for condemnation a widely read devotional work, which had been publicly recommended by the archbishop of Paris. The latter fact was perhaps the reason why it was singled out for condemnation; it was an indirect way of attacking the independence of the archbishop of Paris and through him the Gallican tradition of the Church in France. The Bull at once provoked a public outcry. The *parlements* for the first time for many years resisted the will of Louis XIV and refused to register the king's order compelling the bishops to accept the Bull. They were supported by a considerable section of opinion inside the Church as well as outside. Louis XIV had begun an active persecution of those opposed to the Bull when he died in the midst of the controversy he had aroused, leaving the nation divided between *acceptants* and *refusants*, the former, according to Voltaire, being the 100 bishops who had adhered, together with the Jesuits and the Capucins, the latter the entire nation.

The regent began by reversing the policy of Louis XIV. He freed those who had been imprisoned for opposition to the Bull, made the archbishop of Paris, Noailles, President of the Council for Ecclesiastical Affairs, dismissed the Jesuit le Tellier and gave Louis XV a non-Jesuit confessor, the Abbé Fleury. Who could have guessed the last was to be in the long run the most important of the steps he took at the time, and the only one with permanent results? Orleans had as little success in his efforts to stifle the religious controversy as in his plans for solving all the other problems bequeathed by Louis XIV. Moreover, though the flames of the new Jansenism had been lit almost accidentally by Louis XIV, the materials that were burning were amply combustible. The Jesuits had many enemies, especially among the *parlements*, which were traditional upholders of the liberties of the Gallican Church against Rome. The regent's attempt at a compromise solution therefore brought him into conflict with the *Parlement* of Paris, from which he emerged successful in 1720. The struggle broke out again in 1726, but the bishops who were committed to the neo-Jansenist party were now weakening. The archbishop of Paris, Noailles, accepted the bull *Unigenitus* shortly before his death in 1729.

But while it was losing its support among the episcopate, the new Jansenism had made many converts in the ranks of the lower clergy. The efforts of the bishops to enforce discipline on their clergy brought them into conflict also with the *parlements*, which restated the principles of Gallicanism in a declaration of 1731, proclaiming that 'The temporal power is independent of all other powers, to it alone belongs the task of coercing the subjects of the King, and the Ministers of the Church are accountable to the *Parlement*, under the authority of the Monarch, for the exercise of their jurisdiction'.[1] This declaration was quashed on the following day by the king, who had been brought up to hate Jansenism, while the queen was so completely in the hands of the Jesuits that she was nicknamed 'Unigenita'. The restoration of discipline in the Church was evidently desirable, but it is striking evidence of the inherent contradictions in the system inherited from Louis XIV that it should have been necessary to seek to restore order by attempting to crush the party which was asserting the rights of the Crown over the Church. The difficulties of the Government were increased by the growth of popular agitation, stimulated by an outbreak of miracles at the tomb of the Jansenist deacon Pâris, who had died several years earlier in the odour of sanctity. Crowds gathered round the cemetery where he was buried and *convulsionnaires* indulged in scenes of wild religious frenzy. The *Parlement* of Paris, which was not yet as confident in its defiance of royal authority as it was to become later, itself became alarmed, the cemetery was closed to the public, and Fleury's combination of moderation with firmness secured temporary appeasement.

When the agitation broke out again it really took the form of Richérism rather than Jansenism. As well as embodying the resentment of the lower clergy against the aristocratic monopolists of higher offices and revenues, this movement was now putting forward a claim on behalf of the laity to a greater share in the conduct of the affairs of the Church. Faced with this spirit of rebellion in the ranks of the clergy, the episcopate attempted stronger disciplinary measures, the lead being taken by the virtuous but not very intelligent archbishop of Paris, Christophe de Beaumont, who ordered the clergy to refuse the sacraments to those who could not produce a *billet de confession* signed by a priest who had accepted the bull *Unigenitus*. This brought the *parlements*, which claimed a right of supervision over the religious field, back into the conflict, to take punitive action against those priests who obeyed the archbishop.

The new Jansenist controversy flared up about 1750, just at the time when the Government was engaged in a determined effort to compel the Church to accept new taxes created by Machault (see p. 234). Instead of seizing the opportunity to bring additional pressure to bear on the hierarchy, the king, under the influence of the *dévot* party at court, took its side against the *parlements*. To strengthen his alliance with the Church he even abandoned Machault's financial proposals, though to be sure the *parlements* had no objection to this, and were indeed well satisfied to have the onus of blocking financial reform fall upon the clergy instead of themselves. They did not on that account moderate their opposition to the religious policy of the monarchy. The *Parlement* of Paris issued the *Grandes Remonstrances* on 9 April 1753, asserting its claim to be the

[1] Isambert, Decrusy et Taillandier, *Recueil général des anciennes lois françaises* (1830), vol. XXI, p. 366.

repository and rightful defender of the fundamental laws of the kingdom, and to resist even the king if necessary in the performance of its duty. A royal order exiling the leaders of the *parlement* from Paris followed. The legal profession as a whole went on strike in sympathy and held up all legal processes. The *parlements* of the provinces seconded that of Paris by copying its procedure. The population of the capital was in a turmoil. D'Argenson believed that France was moving in the direction of another Fronde, but the king once again gave way and a compromise was negotiated in 1754 in the form of a rather absurd *loi du silence* which naturally was not obeyed. However, the demand for *billets de confession* was abandoned by the Church in France after the issue of the papal Encyclical *Ex omnibus* of 1756. Jansenist enthusiasm among the clergy was also diminishing, though *richérist* tendencies did not altogether disappear and were to emerge again as an important factor in the early stages of the Revolution.

The role of Jansenism in the eighteenth century has received much attention; the story of the Huguenots, who were now a local and not a national problem, is usually passed over in silence. Dispersed and crushed by the persecutions of Louis XIV, discredited in national opinion by identification with the Camisard revolt, the Huguenots might have seemed unlikely to present any further problem for France. The law according to Louis XIV was that there were no non-catholics in France: all subjects of the French Crown were under the canon law and refusal to submit to the order of the Church was equivalent to rebellion against the king. In fact, however, the persecution of the Huguenots gradually abated in the early years of the eighteenth century, and the central Government would easily have contented itself with a few gestures of outward conformity on their part. However, the bishops in the south of France, where the Huguenots were most numerous, laid down almost prohibitive conditions for the marriage and baptism of Protestants, and the efforts of the Government to secure a less rigid policy failed. The laws against Protestants remained very severe: their assemblies for religious worship were prohibited under penalty of the galleys for men and imprisonment for women; to travel abroad for the purpose of securing marriage or baptism by Protestant rites was punishable by heavy fines; and preachers who were caught were liable to be hanged. It must not be thought that these laws were inoperative, but their incidence depended upon the zeal with which the *intendants* put them into application. The result was that the fate of the Protestants turned largely on local caprice. 'Today they profited from the indulgence of an *intendant*, who might tomorrow be replaced by a ruthless successor.'[1] Their worst persecutors were the *parlements* of Bordeaux and Toulouse, not so much perhaps out of religious zeal, as from a desire to assert their claim to supervise religious discipline as against the bishops and the

[1] J. Dedieu, *Histoire politique des protestants français (1715–1794)* (1925), vol. I, p. 215.

intendants. Hangings, torturing, imprisonment and the galleys on the one hand, sporadic resistance or flight across the frontiers on the other, make up a sorry story of yet another failure by the ministers of Louis XV to cope efficiently with a problem bequeathed to them by Louis XIV.

After the middle decade of the century the persecution of the Protestants, like the Jansenist struggle, began to die down. The initiative was passing to the enemies of the Church. The *dévot* party, which had been supported by the queen and the dauphin, was losing influence at Court, and under the patronage of Mme de Pompadour the anti-religious propaganda of the *philosophes* found protection and encouragement. While the forces of religion were engaged in internecine warfare, intellectual anarchy had been spreading. The advocates of the new ideas were not for the most part intentionally attacking the social and political order, but the rise of a critical and scientific spirit was necessarily dangerous and the attack on religion was an implicit threat to a monarchy founded on Divine Right.

Meanwhile the *parlements*, though the neo-Jansenist struggle proper had died down, continued their feud against the Jesuits, who could no longer rely on the monarchy to defend them. The Society of Jesus, which had exercised an important influence in building up the absolute authority of the monarchy, now found the instrument it had helped to create turned against itself. Sooner or later it was bound to be seen that the existence of a society owing allegiance to an external power was incompatible with absolute monarchy. Other Catholic Powers led the way in the campaign against the Jesuits. In France the Society provided the opportunity for its enemies when Père Lavalette, Superior of the Mission in the French West Indies, who had engaged in extensive commercial operations, found himself ruined by the effects of the Seven Years War. Proceedings in bankruptcy were brought against the whole Society in France, and the *Parlement* of Paris not reluctantly condemned it to pay Lavalette's debts. The *Parlement* then proceeded to set up a commission to examine the statutes of the Society, and in due course announced that they were incompatible with allegiance to the king. Personally Louis was still favourable to the Jesuits, but it is significant of the weakening of the monarchy that his efforts to protect them could now do no more than delay their fate. By a decree of August 1762 the *Parlement* of Paris ordered the abolition of the Society of Jesus in France and the sequestration of its property, on the ground that the doctrines of the Society were 'perverse, destructive of all principles of religion, and even of honesty, injurious to Christian morality, pernicious to civil society, seditious, hostile to the rights of the nation and the power of the king'.

The weakness of the monarchy before the increasing aggressions of the *parlements* was equally manifest in the field of finance. The great struggle took place when Machault was Controller-General (1745–54). The expenses of the War of the Austrian Succession had once more reduced the royal finances to a desperate condition. Machault determined to utilise the following period of peace to put through a fundamental reform, the essential feature of which was the introduction of a new tax, the *vingtième*, to be imposed without exception on all sources of income and on all classes, including *noblesse* and clergy. The opposition of the *parlements* was over-ridden, but it was one thing to decree a tax and another thing to collect it. The *noblesse* did their utmost to avoid payment and the *États* of Languedoc and Brittany resisted the application of the tax. But as has been observed above, the opposition that was to prove fatal to Machault's plan came from the clergy. The king gave way to the pressure of the *dévot* party at court, whereas in the case of the Jesuits a decade later he was to yield to the opposite faction. The dilemma of the Crown was that whether its decision was for or against the Church, the result was likely to be equally dangerous to the monarchy: the principle of Divine Right implied an identity of interests between Church and State which it was difficult to maintain permanently in practice. Where the identity broke down, either the king had to sacrifice the interests of the monarchy to the Church, as he did in supporting the extreme anti-Jansenist policy or in allowing the opposition of the clergy to dictate the financial policy of the State, or else, as in tolerating the *philosophes* and yielding to the condemnation of the Jesuits by the *parlements*, he had to suffer the religious basis of the monarchy to be undermined.

After Machault, under a series of weak Controllers-General, the *parlements*, whose co-operation was indispensable for the success of the loans and for the application of the petty financial expedients to which the Controllers had recourse, were practically masters of the situation. The provincial *parlements* emulated the *Parlement* of Paris by launching attacks on the *intendants*, which almost reached the point of civil war in the conflict between the *Parlement* of Rennes and d'Aiguillon in Brittany. Only in the last years of his reign, between 1770 and 1774, faced with total bankruptcy, did Louis XV make one more attempt to put the royal finances into order, and as a necessary first step to deprive the *parlements* of their powers of obstruction. He found two able ministers in Maupeou and Terray, but though they did their work ruthlessly and successfully, when Louis died in 1774 the *parlements* were recalled by his young successor, and all that Maupeou had achieved was a temporary alleviation of the financial situation by an enforced bankruptcy.

The financial distress of the French monarchy was, however, not the fundamental problem, though it was a symptom of the increasing dislocation of the *ancien régime*. The root cause lay in the fact that Louis XIV and his ministers had created a social and institutional structure which was essentially static just at a time when society itself was beginning to change at a faster rate than ever before. It became increasingly difficult to reconcile the simplified Louis-quatorzian pattern of society with the facts. Under Louis XIV French society had been conceived as a pyramid. At its base was a peasantry in the countryside and an urban population of merchants and craftsmen. The function of all these was to provide the economic foundations of society and to pay the taxes by which the State was financed; in return they looked to the king for protection in their traditional rights. This was the concrete meaning of the old alliance between king and people, and it had not been altogether a one-sided bargain. The peasants, or at least a large number of them, had come to be recognised as proprietors of their farms. The crafts were organised in guilds in the towns and given a monopoly. The bourgeois were themselves a privileged class, for they were protected from competition by the exclusion of the *noblesse* from trade under penalty of losing their rank in society. At a higher level in the social scale, law and administration were provided by a *noblesse de robe*. Finally, the *noblesse de l'épée*, while it had been deprived of the political power which might be dangerous to the monarchy, retained its privileges in respect of taxation and in return provided the officers of the army and the personnel of the court; it was, in the language of Burke, the 'Corinthian capital of polished society'.

These were the assumptions on which the *ancien régime* was based. A short examination of the facts will show how far removed they were from reality. In the first place, the division of the nation into *noblesse*, *noblesse de robe*, clergy, bourgeois and peasants was a simplification which concealed the real complexity of French society. Each class had in fact its own internal divisions, which prevented it from being a coherent unit. At least nine major divisions have been traced in the *noblesse*. The greatest cleavage was that which existed between the *noblesse de cour* and the provincial nobility. The latter ranged from the wealthy country gentleman to the poverty-stricken Breton noble, who might be the cultivator of a few ancestral acres; most of them never saw Versailles, and many could not even afford to compete with the bourgeoisie in the social life of the provincial capitals. Only in defence of their own exemption from taxation or rights of collecting seigneurial dues did they act as a united class. The division in the clergy between the wealthy and aristocratic upper clergy and the poor parish priests has already been described. The *noblesse de robe*, in so far as it was more than a legal fiction, was split into two sections, bitterly hostile to one another. The *parlementaires* proper, members of the sovereign courts, were, as has been shown, the most persevering opponents of royal authority. On the other hand, the Controllers-General and sometimes other ministers, the *intendants* and important officials, drawn only in part from the old families of the *robe*, were naturally identified with the interests of the royal administration. While the members of the *parlements* provided legal sanctions for the financial exactions of

the *seigneurs* from the peasantry, and often indeed possessed such seigneurial rights themselves, the *intendants*, on the other hand, as collectors of
royal taxation, were interested in protecting the rural communities from
seigneurial demands. This was not the least among the causes of the bitter
conflicts between *parlements* and *intendants*.

The structure of the unprivileged classes was equally complex. The very
term 'unprivileged' is itself a misnomer. A wealthy bourgeois patriciate,
often with hereditary title to municipal office, formed what has been called
a *noblesse de cloche*. Lower down the social scale, the members of the
guilds or corporations were largely an hereditary class, into which the
ordinary *compagnons* had practically no prospect of penetrating. The
Farmers-General, the wealthy bankers and financiers, and all those
sometimes described as *bourgeois vivant noblement*, were distinct from the
industrial entrepreneurs or smaller merchants. This financial class constituted the dominant element in economic society. Great fortunes were
gained in the wars of Louis XIV and financial dynasties were built up
which took full advantage of the speculative mania of the second decade
of the century. With the consolidation of the *ferme générale*, which in the
first half of the century realised enormous profits for the Farmers General,
the financiers reached their apogee shortly after the turn of the century,
when they were powerful enough to be described as a state within the
State. There were few doors in eighteenth-century France which were not
open to wealth. The daughters and nieces of the financiers married into
the ranks of the *noblesse*, or aspired higher like Mme de Prie, mistress of
the duc de Bourbon, or Mme le Normant d'Étioles, daughter of a clerk of
Pâris-Duverney who, as marquise de Pompadour and *maîtresse-en-titre*,
was able to perform valuable services to her financial entourage. The
principle of venality opened even the ranks of the officer class to the
roturier; up to the time of Choiseul a captaincy was a piece of property
purchasable in the market. The purchase of the office of *secrétaire du roi*
was a common route to nobility. The financiers could also afford to tie up
sufficient capital to purchase the office of *maître des requêtes* for their
offspring, in preparation for their subsequent nomination to the post of
intendant, for the tasks of which, so largely financial in nature, they were
often well prepared. In this way a new aristocracy was rising, as its
predecessors had risen in the past, to challenge the monopoly of the
noblesse de la robe et de l'épée.

To sum up, then, the actual structure of French society was much more
complex than the traditional simple division into three Estates allowed for.
De Tocqueville long ago compared it to 'those supposed simple bodies in
which modern chemistry has revealed more and more separate parts in
proportion as it examines them more closely'.[1] The trouble with French
society was that it was a sum of disunities which did not add up to social

---

[1] De Tocqueville, *L'ancien régime*, liv. II, ch. 9.

unity, and the conflict of interests was not the less because the period was one of marked economic progress. The economy of France being pre-eminently an agricultural one, the source of this economic progress may have lain in the increased returns of agriculture; though, because of increasing pressure of population, the rise in agricultural prices brought little benefit to the mass of the rural population, apart from the more pros-perous *laboureurs*, who were enabled to enlarge their holdings, and the *fermiers*, who gained from the fact that the rise in rents only slowly followed the rise in prices. On the other hand the towns were now entering a phase of great prosperity. Under Fleury's careful administration the bases of economic progress were soundly laid. The perpetual fluctuations in the value of the *écu* and the *louis d'or* were brought to an end by the stabilisa-tion of the currency in 1726, at the rate of 24 *livres* to the *louis d'or*, which aided internal trade; but the development of overseas commerce was more important. Out of the trade with the French West Indies, ports like Bordeaux and Nantes, the latter the headquarters of the slavers, flourished and grew great. French trade practically doubled between 1715 and 1740, and again doubled between then and 1763, and with its growth the merchant class of the ports began to rival the wealth of the financiers. Industry also was developing, aided by the flow of profits from agriculture and commerce, and by a small but influential stream of immigration from across the Channel. The most famous of the immigrant manufacturers, the Jacobite Holker, who came to France after the Rebellion of 1745 and established a textile manufactory with royal warrant in a suburb of Rouen in 1752, was so successful that in 1755 he was appointed Inspector-General of Manufactures. Technical invention, if not as extensively applied as in England, made great progress, with the encouragement of the *Académie des sciences*.

Capitalist industry found its most extensive field for exploitation in mining. The development of industrial activity in France in the eighteenth century came at a time when the great forests were already being thinned and seemed threatened with total destruction if the supply of fuel was to continue to be drawn mainly from them. The rudimentary and chaotic conditions of mining offered no hope of coping with the shortage of fuel. To deal with this situation the Controller-General Orry issued in 1744 his great *arrêt*, taking back into the hands of the king the sole right of granting concessions for mining and establishing a code for the conduct of the industry, including rules for the safeguarding of workers. The department of mines, which formed a branch of the *Contrôle générale* up to 1764, exercised a continuous and close supervision of the industry. Though a host of small, primitive workings escaped effective control, much larger mines were now sunk. The greatest of these, that of Anzin, developed its annual production from 55 tons in 1720 to 310,000 in 1790. Another growing industry was shipbuilding, especially in the ports of Nantes and

Bordeaux. Internal communications were improved by the labours of Orry, who organised the *corvée* in 1738. The increase in wealth in the towns found its outward expression in the great outburst of building which created the fine eighteenth-century quarters of Paris and the provincial cities.

This picture of economic progress is, however, not the full story. Here, as in every branch of the social and political structure of France, there were inherent contradictions, which date back to the reign of Louis XIV. The organisation of French industry, like that of French society as a whole, had been given a rigid form on the eve of the great age of change by Colbert, with his *manufactures royales*, trading companies and *métiers jurés*. It might even be said that the guild system in France reached its height in the eighteenth century. At Poitiers, where there had been eighteen guilds in the fourteenth century, there were forty-two in the eighteenth century. These industrial guilds, which were largely hereditary and under the hierarchical control of a limited class of masters, were themselves supervised by the royal *lieutenants de police*, except in towns where the municipalities had bought this office for themselves. Central control was in the hands of the Director-General of Buildings, Arts, Academies and Manufactures, who exercised his power through the *intendants* and a body of inspectors of doubtful competence. Petty regulations of all kinds were imposed on industry, and inventions suppressed by the joint action of the corporations and royal inspectors. Against this obstacle improvements in industrial technique could make only slow progress. Moreover, the domestic industry, which was widespread in the countryside, was by its very nature largely uninfluenced by new methods. Factories of any size were exceptional and nearly all of them were either royal manufactures or establishments set up with a privilege from the Crown. For the most part industry was still carried on by craftsmen, one master usually working with a few journeymen. The latter were completely under the control of the privileged masters; Colbert's edict of 1673, which had attempted to generalise the system of corporations, prohibited journeymen's associations. This did not prevent them from organising themselves clandestinely, and even, under the pressure of rising prices, occasionally taking joint action in the effort to improve their conditions. A royal decree of 1749 forbade all *compagnons* to form any combination with one another for the purpose of influencing the employment or dismissal of workers. *Compagnonnages*, however, appeared in certain trades, such as those of the masons, carpenters, smiths, in which the *tour de France* was customary. In these circumstances strikes (or *coalitions* as they were called) were rare, though not entirely absent. The most violent were those which developed among the silk-workers of Lyons, always restive. In their rising of 1744 *maîtres-ouvriers* and *compagnons* joined forces against the merchants who controlled the silk industry.

A local victory was followed by the arrival of royal troops at Lyons in the following year and the torture and execution, or condemnation to the galleys, of the leaders of the movement. As this episode showed, the difference in social conditions between the small masters and the *compagnons* was usually not sufficient to produce much sense of class difference. The chief conflict of interest between them arose where the *compagnons* tried to set up as independent masters on their own. The corporations engaged in incessant activity against this practice, but a safety-valve was provided by the existence of privileged areas—in Paris, Saint-German-des-Prés, the faubourg Saint-Antoine and two or three other smaller areas where the restrictions of the corporations did not operate, while in the smaller towns and the countryside, of course, organisation in corporations was not possible. Here police regulations took their place, but in the second half of the century the authorities encouraged the spread in the countryside of industries which were restricted by guild privileges in the towns. From the middle of the century enlightened opinion was turning against the corporations, stimulated by the rise of physiocratic thought, though the attack on the corporations only achieved governmental recognition with Turgot and did not finally triumph until the Revolution. The system of privileged corporations was doubtless one of the reasons why the industrial revolution, for which the technical knowledge was there, made little progress in France in the eighteenth century, but it was not the only one.

Another element in the situation was the fact that the bourgeoisie of the eighteenth century was in the main a financial and official class, not a commercial and industrial one. What it desired was a change in status, not in economic conditions, which indeed suited it very well. With the Revolution it was to defeat the privileged orders and substitute itself for them as the dominant factor in the State. If the monarchy could at the same time have freed itself from the incubus of the privileged orders it might have contrived to preside over an evolution instead of a revolution, but to do this it would have had to change its nature. The traditions of the Divine-Right monarchy, the personalities of the monarchs, the influence of the court, the social force still embodied in the privileged orders, forbade such a solution. The inherent incapacity of the monarchy of Louis XIV to preside over the translation into institutional form of the changed conditions of French society was destined to bring about its fall, and all the factors in the problem were evident before the reign of Louis XV had come to its end.

Elsewhere Divine-Right monarchy was equally in its decline, but the forces which could give it the *coup de grâce* were far weaker than in France. In Spain the Bourbon monarchy represented an advance on the regime of the later Habsburgs and the country was too backward for the small, weak bourgeoisie to play a role comparable to that of the *tiers état* in France in

1789. In the Austrian domains the population was largely rural and the forces which undermined the monarchy in France were absent. In Prussia and Sardinia the conditions were again very different from those in France. Finally, in England the Divine-Right monarchy of the Stuarts had met with destruction before it knew fulfilment. Nowhere, outside France, did monarchy as it had been incarnated in Louis XIV find its peer; and in no other monarchy was there more than a pale reflection of the social and intellectual evolution which accompanied the decline of Divine-Right monarchy in France.

CHAPTER XI

ENGLAND

IN 1714 some six million people lived in England and Wales and though this fact was unknown to contemporaries their number was increasing more rapidly than in any previous period. More than half the people and considerably more than half their wealth were found south of a line from Worcester to the Wash and almost one-quarter probably lived in London and the adjacent counties. According to the predilections of the observer England might be viewed as a rural paradise disfigured by a rank growth at the centre or as a small world of wit and wisdom surrounded by rural barbarism. Bristol and Norwich might boast commercial institutions which rivalled those of London, but financial control was passing to the metropolis, and one had to go north of the border to find at Edinburgh a culture comparable to that of London. Moreover, London was not only the national capital but also the metropolis of an imperial domain of islands, trading posts and coastal settlements scattered over the face of the world. The interests of her merchants ranged from the fur of the North American wilderness to the tea of Canton, from slaves, sugar and spices to textiles, hardware and nails. London merchants, together with those of Bristol and the lesser trading ports, were concerned with the export of British manufactures, with the import of many luxuries and some necessities, and with a world-wide carrying trade; but the greatest single source of wealth was the re-export of colonial and Indian goods to Europe. The entrepôt trade bore a special responsibility in fostering commercial techniques of an advanced type and the credit facilities, distributive organisation, and economic specialisation of the British merchants played an ever increasing part in the development of the world's trade and economic resources. It is not therefore surprising that eighteenth-century Englishmen overvalued the benefits of foreign trade, undervalued the importance of home production other than that of exportable goods, considered the restriction of home consumption an object of commercial policy, and sustained a complex system of regulatory laws designed to secure for Englishmen the maximum benefits from the colonial and carrying trades. The balance of trade was the barometer of prosperity, and prosperity was the first element in national strength.

With an almost feverish energy Englishmen accumulated those great capital reserves which were destined to play so dominant a role in world history. Plentiful money combined with internal security to produce cheap money. Private investment was for the time being attracted mainly to the further expansion of trade, to the purchase and improvement of land,

and to domestic building, but the greatest beneficiary of cheap money was the State, which was able to use private savings for public purposes on a scale unmatched in any other country. Although the National Debt, which had been about £1,000,000 in 1688, rose to near £80,000,000 by the middle of the century, the rate of interest on government securities fell to 5 per cent in 1717, to 4 per cent in 1727, and to 3 per cent in 1749. No other country could hope to borrow so much so cheaply and this significant fact goes far to explain England's success in war and colonial acquisition. Government borrowing was not yet directly from the public at large, but from a few wealthy individuals and from incorporated companies headed by the Bank of England; but a growing number of influential men were acquiring a vested interest in stable government and national expansion. The readiness to entrust private savings to public funds was largely a by-product of constitutional government: the arbitrary power to cancel obligations was a thing of the past, the debt was guaranteed by parliament which also appropriated expenditure and audited public accounts, and the narrow basis of parliamentary representation assured propertied men that their money was in safe hands.

The economic geography of England was still determined largely by the sea and by navigable rivers. While dairy produce and vegetables could be brought to consumer markets from the immediate neighbourhood, heavy goods could be carried long distances only by water. London received her coal from Newcastle, her grain from the east-coast ports, and her building stone from Portland and other places where it could be quarried near the sea. Economic unification had lagged behind political unification, and ports which sent ships to distant parts of the world extended their economic influence over a comparatively small hinterland and took in many of their supplies by water. Of the great consumer trades only that in livestock used long overland routes and every year thousands of cattle and sheep were driven from their breeding grounds in Scotland and Wales to rich midland pastures and thence on the hoof to London markets. Much industrial production, perhaps the greater part of it, was carried on solely for local markets. Woollen cloth, the great export industry, had developed mainly within easy reach of the greater ports, and it was not inclination or special skill which led midland areas to concentrate upon light easily portable goods but the plain facts of geography. Stockings from Nottinghamshire and Leicestershire, 'toys' and nails from the Birmingham district, cutlery from Sheffield, and hats from many districts were all goods able to travel on the primitive transport over the abominable roads of early eighteenth-century England. The iron industry depended upon the import of smelted Swedish ore because the timber which supplied the charcoal for smelting was either exhausted or remote from native iron.

In spite of the limitations placed upon the economy by poor inland communications, English exports were large and important. The great cloth trade was supplemented by many other items, ranging from the nails made by poorly skilled and wretchedly paid labour in the midlands to the watches and luxury clothing made by the skilled craftsmen of London. These manufactures went a good way toward the purchase of the eastern and colonial luxuries and to that of certain necessities for England's economic existence. England was short of timber, and had very little tar, pitch, hemp or manufactured cordage (the naval stores which figure so prominently in the annals of English commercial policy). The greatest single source of all these articles, together with iron, was the Baltic, and the persistently unfavourable balance of trade with that area was regarded as a serious flaw in England's economic position. The need to pay for so many Baltic imports in hard cash may help to explain the English greed for bullion which was to be so much ridiculed in a later age.

Away from the few commercial centres, and from the rural areas where manufacture for export was important, one entered a very different England. For many countrymen the contents of the pedlar's pack afforded their only glimpse of high-grade manufactures and the riches of the East, and, dependent upon occasional slow-moving wagons for passenger transport, countless simple Englishmen lived and died within walking distance of the place where they were born. The stage coach, slow and uncomfortable though it might be, was for the well-to-do rather than the poor, and real wealth was necessary to support the expenses of travel by private coach. Away from areas such as north-east Norfolk where the proximity of water-borne transport made large-scale commercial farming possible, production was largely for subsistence and only small surpluses were brought to the local market towns for sale. Yet these small surpluses, converted into rent and tithe, formed the economic basis of the ruling class and the support of the Established Church.

At the apex of rural society was the great titled landowner. Though socially aloof from his lesser neighbours and a citizen of the cosmopolitan world, he was forced, whatever his inclinations, into the tangled and petty rivalries of local affairs. On the national stage his consequence would be reckoned largely by the extent of his local authority, and this was something which could not be secured without effort. Next below the magnate and his natural rival for local power was the country gentleman, who might sometimes in his property and breeding compare with the great nobleman, or might be the simple and ignorant owner of a few acres. However inconsiderable on the national scene, the country gentleman was of supreme importance to his humbler neighbours; as the economic overlord of a village, distinguished with His Majesty's commission as a justice of the peace, and treated as squire with traditional deference, he exercised a local authority which was almost unchecked and usually unchallengeable. The decisions of a magistrate had to conform to the Common Law, and appeals could be made against them in the courts; but where most of the accused were ignorant and subservient, justice was often natural rather than exact. His travels would seldom take him out of the county and the limit of his ambitions was usually to stand well with his equals and to hand on his landed heritage undiminished if not increased to his heirs; yet even these modest desires usually involved him in the struggle for local power. Beneath the owners of the soil came those who cultivated it: freeholders, copyholders, tenants at will and landless labourers who together formed a large majority of the population of England. In the social hierarchy the freeholders occupied a special position; though they normally paid a customary rent for their land, they could not be dispossessed and might leave it to whomever they chose, and their independence not only ensured them comparative social distinction but also earned them the right to vote in county elections.

In this rural environment, with its well-recognised social gradations and social obligations, the ruling class learned a code of behaviour and first lessons in public life. As landlords and magistrates they accepted responsibilities, while their complete conviction of their natural right to rule gave a bland assurance to their occasional acts of ruthlessness. They knew from their cradles the facts of life in the English countryside, but time was to show them singularly blind to problems of industrial England or colonial America. Active in dispensing simple justice and in settling the problems of local administration, a member of the ruling class was normally impelled also to be active in the economic sphere. The apparent changelessness of rural custom often concealed the forces of rapid social change. The landowner had to exert himself if he was to advance his family or even to avoid decline, and many old families, dragged down by debt, inefficiency or indiscretion, sold out or contracted marriage alliances with the daughters of moneyed men. Many old estates passed into the great accretions of landed property which provided the economic support for the rising aristocracy; others were acquired by men from the city, from the Indies or even from the local market town. Though the quick cut and thrust of commerce were absent, competition was nevertheless intense, and stimulated both the adaptation of traditional agriculture to commercial farming and the fight for local political power. Improved agriculture was already practised by a few enterprising landlords before the end of the seventeenth century, and as the eighteenth century advanced an increasing number of gentry sought the means by which their land might yield a commercial profit, and looked with reforming zeal upon untidy and uneconomical strip acres in open fields and commons grazed at will by the undersized livestock of the villagers. The political struggle was always complicated by rivalries between the rising magnates and by the continuing influence of older and less wealthy aristocratic families. Yet over the years a dominant theme emerges as the greater landowners are seen on the offensive, gathering dependents among the lesser gentry, driving the more important squires out of the parliamentary boroughs, and by the middle of the century pressing hard upon the county seats which had always been considered the special preserve of the gentry; while their greater capital resources and often their superior intelligence enabled them to win the battle for agricultural profits.

The key to the political struggle lay in the boroughs of England and Wales which returned three-quarters of the members of parliament, and in most boroughs the immediate control lay with a small urban oligarchy of attorneys, bankers, merchants and brewers entrenched in a self-electing corporation which had by royal charter exclusive control over the town's property and not infrequently determined how the traditional qualification for electoral franchise should be bestowed. A landowner might establish an 'interest' in a borough by the purchase of urban property, and in a few instances he could obtain absolute control by doing so, but his usual concern would be to win over a majority of the corporation by occasional threats, frequent promises, and the bestowal of what favours he could command. If successful, he might be recognised as the patron of the borough with the right to nominate one or both members, and was expected in return to secure petty patronage for members of the corporation, care for the interests of the town, and foot the bill for anything from municipal buildings to celebrations on national holidays. The patron might speak of 'my borough', but it was a possession not easily secured, nor retained without constant attention. A few boroughs only could be purchased outright as property and these fetched a price which was often within the reach only of the richest city merchants and returned 'nabobs' from India. The reward for success in controlling the representation of a borough was greater influence at Westminster and increased local authority, and the struggle itself was an integral part of the process by which the fittest survived in English eighteenth-century society.

Closely entwined with this social structure was the Church of England. Though much parochial work was carried out by curates and clergy of humble origin, the leaders of the Church, the higher clergy and the incumbents of rich benefices, belonged to the same social class and shared the same interests and responsibilities as the landed gentry. Bound to the splendid liturgy of the Church and spiritually subservient to his bishop the clergyman was no innovator; though life tenure might give him a certain independence, the whole tradition of the Church was against religious idiosyncrasy. Religion supplemented the law in sustaining a social fabric in which the notion of ordered hierarchy was implicit, and in which children were taught to submit themselves to their masters and order themselves lowly and reverently to their betters. The union of religious and social order was often epitomised in the dual function of a wealthy clergyman as spiritual pastor and justice of the peace. Though often obscured by personal quarrels the alliance of squire and parson was a keystone of national life, and the gentry clung to the Church with an affection which transcended political principles.

Very different was the position in society of the dissenting congregation, for the historic association of dissent with rebellion was still a living reality in the rural community. Not only did the Dissenters worship apart but their religious organisation was also a standing criticism of a hierarchical society. With a separate and often superior educational system, with a trained and diligent ministry, and with an appeal from authority to conscience and the Bible, the Dissenters contrasted sharply with the establishment. Moreover, though the Test and Corporation Acts branded the Dissenters as second-class citizens, they retained the right to vote if otherwise qualified, and, with their strength concentrated in towns and among small property owners, they commanded an electoral influence out of proportion to their numbers. It was this fact which made the Dissenters peculiarly attractive as political allies for greater landowners in their struggle with the lesser gentry; by 1714 this curious alliance between seemingly incompatible groups was of outstanding importance, for it formed the backbone of the Whig party.

In 1714 the distinction between Whig and Tory still represented a real division of interest and opinion between groups competing for national power. Nourished in part by memories of the past and constantly fed by the struggle for local power, the party conflict had risen to a height of bitterness during the reign of Queen Anne. The Whigs formed a party of new men and new interests; their leaders were drawn from the greater landed families who gathered territory and influence with each turn of the political wheel during the seventeenth century and few of their titles could be traced to an earlier period. From such aristocrats those other beneficiaries of seventeenth-century expansion, the moneyed men, found a greater measure of social recognition and political understanding than from the squires who cherished a long lineage and thought of national policy only in terms of advantage to the landed interest. As new men the Whigs appropriated the new ideas of the age. They stood for limited monarchy and the supremacy of parliament, for the Petition of Right and the Bill of Rights, for the Toleration Act and the Protestant succession, for hostility to France, the enlargement of commerce and the security of property whether in land or funds. Against these new men the party of Church and King stood on the defensive, counter-attacked during the closing years of Anne's reign, and then went down to irretrievable defeat in 1714. Their failure was largely a failure in leadership. The landed gentry who formed the nucleus of every conservative party until the late nineteenth century did not produce political leaders from their own ranks and were usually led by men from outside their own class, and in 1714 such men were not to be found. The bishops provided no Tory leader, the old royalist aristocracy was weakened by poverty and the extinction of ancient lines, Bolingbroke had gambled and lost, Harley was an old and broken man, and no other careerist politician was likely to be attracted by the prospect of rallying a divided and discredited party. New leaders might have emerged had not the Tories suffered from split minds; some, the 'Hanoverian' Tories, were content to accept a welcome from the Whigs and endure the stigma of desertion from their own party; others were fascinated by the idea of a legitimate king who would recognise his friends but unable to resist the force of the constitutional slogans which the Whigs had appropriated; they could drink to the king over the water but could not forget his Roman Catholicism, they could cry that the Church was in danger but doubt the wisdom of associating it with a rebellious cause. It all ended in grumbling acquiescence and, when the opportunity was offered to strike a blow for the Stuart heir, all but a few zealots watched events from their own manors. Tories continued to sit in Parliament, but a Tory government was no longer a possibility, and deprived of the chance to exercise national power Toryism sank into the quagmire of local politics where it provided a name and a tradition for country gentlemen who continued to contest the strength of Whig magnates and to reprobate the influence of the Crown which had once been their special care.

The Hanoverian succession was not only a triumph for the Whigs but also an opportunity to exploit their success. They might now expect to add to their own influence that of the Crown, and they were plentifully supplied with men of experience and ability such as the Tories lacked. Yet the completeness of their success looked like producing its own antidote in factional divisions within the party. Whig knowledge that their own future lay in the security of the dynasty was offset by the ambitions of various Whigs to monopolise power. George I chose his advisers from the group led by Townshend and his brother-in-law Robert Walpole because he was not sure of the reliability of Marlborough and his son-in-law Sunderland, who headed the other main faction; but for the time being all Whigs co-operated to win an election, crush a rebellion, and save their non-conformist allies from the consequences of recent Tory policy.

Electoral victory was achieved in January 1715 when a general election gave the Government a majority of 150, but in the autumn came the expected appeal of the Jacobites to arms. The earl of Mar raised the Stuart standard in the Highlands, Ormonde was probing at the coast of Devonshire, and English Jacobites in the north-west were under arms. But the leadership and strategy of the Jacobites were weak and the death of Louis XIV deprived them of their best friend. Mar failed to dislodge Argyle, principal Scottish representative of the Hanoverian cause, at Sheriffmuir, and his forces disintegrated before the determined pursuit of General Cadogan. A decisive defeat at Preston ended the hopes of the English Jacobites, and Ormonde failed to rouse the Tories of the south-west. By contemporary standards the Government was lenient in its revenge, and could afford to be so, for it had gained permanent advantages. The revolt made it possible to brand Tories as potential disturbers of the peace, and its failure proved that desire for peace was stronger in England than any sentimental attachment to the old dynasty. The disturbances gave the Whigs an excellent excuse for avoiding the election which would have been due in 1718. The Septennial Act, defended both as an emergency measure and as a permanent relief from the expenses and tumults of frequent elections, was to contribute a good deal to the success of the Whig magnates who could now husband their resources for an overwhelming attack once in seven years.

If the Protestant succession was a party victory for the Whigs, it was a deliverance for the Dissenters. Acquiescent in, though unreconciled to, the restrictions imposed upon them by the Test and Corporation Acts, they had been driven to desperate alarm by the Occasional Conformity and Schism Acts. The latter became a dead letter upon the accession of George I and both were repealed in 1717; but an attempt to modify the Test and Corporation Acts had to be dropped, and the Dissenters had to be content with an Act of 1718 enabling their members who had been duly elected to Corporations to retain their seats if unchallenged within six months. From 1727 the annual Indemnity Act enabled them to take the Anglican sacrament after instead of before election. These measures relieved the Dissenters from threats to the existence of their societies as organised religions, but did not give them all that they might have desired, and the retention of the Test and Corporation Acts had a permanent influence upon English society. Many conscientious Dissenters found it difficult to qualify themselves for office by deliberate fraud, and the law still allowed Anglicans to prevent the election of Dissenters, though not to unseat them once six months had elapsed. The most important result of the Whig concessions was to enable the Dissenters to play a part in the public life of towns where their numbers were considerable; they were not relieved of the stigma of being second-class citizens, and the evasions by which they might occupy seats on petty corporations did not open to them the road to important public duties. A great number of the best educated and most sincere men in the country continued to live a life apart; the country was deprived of their services and they narrowed their interests to those of a single social group. If a man wished to get on in the world, he had to be an Anglican; religious divisions came more and more to correspond with social divisions, and in this way the Whig leaders served the interests of the Church to which they belonged. Dissenters might, however, compare their lot favourably with that of the Roman Catholics who were treated in England as resident aliens and in Ireland as enemies of the State.

The High Church party offered a challenge to Whig hegemony at the very heart of English society, but it was tamed by the appointment of Whig bishops (an unusual number of vacancies occurred soon after 1714) and by putting an end to meetings of Convocation. In 1717 the Lower House of Convocation prepared an attack upon Hoadley, bishop of Bangor, and the Government intervened to save its favourite episcopal representative by proroguing Convocation. Save for one occasion, in 1741, it was not permitted to transact business until 1855 and the lower clergy were reduced, like their allies the squires, to grumbling and impotent criticism of their superiors. With Convocation silenced, several genuine attempts at Church reform died: the agenda for the prorogued Convocation of 1717 had included proposals to check clandestine marriages, improve the qualifications of ordinands, establish charity schools, and extend foreign missions. Though the most obstinate critics of the new Government were silenced, this did not necessarily contribute to the well-being of the nation.

The circumvention of immediate dangers released dissension among the Whigs. Townshend offended the king by differing with him over foreign policy and criticising his Hanoverian advisers, and the star of Sunderland rose when he accompanied the king to Hanover in 1716. In 1717 Townshend was dismissed and took Walpole with him into opposition; committed to support of the dynasty, they found a convenient means of combining loyalty with opposition by attaching themselves to the prince of Wales who was on the worst possible terms with his father. In this there was considerable constitutional significance, for it was a first step toward removing from opposition the tang of treason. The new ministry was notable for an unprecedented use of Crown patronage to maintain a slender majority, for an attempt to alter the fundamental law of the peerage, for the foreign policy of Stanhope, and for the financial policy of Sunderland. The Government feared that their majority in the House of Lords might be overturned if George I died and his successor created new peers, and by the Peerage Bill of 1719 it was proposed to limit the size of the Upper House to six beyond its number in that year and to substitute twenty-five hereditary peers for the sixteen representative peers of Scotland. The bill was defended upon the abstract grounds that the Upper House ought to be immune from passing changes in political fashion, but it was very unpopular in Scotland and killed in the Commons by Walpole who appealed to the country gentry not to close the door upon the legitimate ambitions of their families.

It was the notable achievement of Stanhope to unite Great Britain with France and the Dutch in an alliance to maintain the Peace of Utrecht. This alliance secured the conditions of external security which were so essential to the Hanoverian dynasty, and though its only direct result was to check the Mediterranean ambitions of Spain, it was the cornerstone of British policy for some years to come. As First Lord of the Treasury Sunderland tackled the urgent problem of the National Debt which was complex, expensive, and offered remote chances of repayment. Following a suggestion made by Walpole Sunderland introduced a sinking fund for debt redemption and initiated a conversion scheme to reduce the interest charge to an uniform 4 per cent by 1727. Unfortunately this well-conceived policy was an immediate cause of the South Sea Bubble.

Among the economic fallacies of the age was an exaggerated belief in the possibilities of credit. The National Debt itself was looked upon as a 'fund of credit' which might be used to finance commercial projects, and the South Sea Company, formed in 1711 to exploit trade with South America, was capitalised by taking over a substantial part of the Government's short-term debt. When Sunderland put forward his conversion scheme the company sought to strengthen its position by offering to take over the whole debt at a diminishing rate of interest, to pay off private holders of government securities with issue of South Sea stock, and to pay a premium of seven and a half million pounds. Not trusting to the merits of the offer to persuade those in authority, the Company added the inducement of lavish bribes to ministers. The Company's advantage would lie in its increased prestige (it would command almost a monopoly in the limited stock market of the day) and in fixing the rate at which it would exchange South Sea for government stock (the higher the price of its own stock the more it could acquire of government securities whose eventual repayment at face value was guaranteed). But at home and abroad an outbreak of speculative activity was probable in 1720, for confidence had been gradually reviving since the depression year of 1710 and opportunities of productive investment were too few to absorb the disposable wealth of England, France and Holland. Extensive speculation in the stocks of several new or revived joint-stock companies began early in 1720 and this changed to speculative mania when parliament approved the South Sea scheme. Shares of the Company rose to ten times their face value by June, and parliament passed the Bubble Act which forbade the issue of transferable shares by companies forming since 1718 or misusing old charters. The South Sea Company welcomed the Bubble Act as a weapon to use in the stock market against its competitors, but the legal proceedings which it initiated against them shook confidence all round; prudent men had already begun surreptitious selling in the summer and by the autumn confidence had collapsed and the whole financial structure of the country seemed to be in danger.

The damage to the nation was not quite so great as might have been inferred from the frequent and pathetic examples of individual failure. The Bank of England and the East India Company stood firm, the speculative crisis did not induce a general depression, and apart from the South Sea venture the country's trading position was still sound. Walpole, recalled to the Government in 1720, was able to restore confidence by dividing two-thirds of the South Sea Company's holding of the National Debt equally between the Bank and the East India Company, and by turning criticisms against stock-jobbers rather than against the Government. The most serious consequence was a suspicion of joint-stock finance, which hampered for many years the flow of capital into productive projects, and a decided set-back to the development of a national investment market. Means were found of evading the provisions of the Bubble Act by various forms of unincorporated partnerships, but the legal position of those who wished to invest remained precarious; later in the century canals were to be financed by legitimate joint-stock investment, but the major part of industrial development had to be financed by the savings of men on the spot and not through the machinery of a national stock market.

The political consequence of the Bubble was to break the Sunderland faction and to clear the way for the Townshend-Walpole group. The young duke of Newcastle, who united the extensive influence of the Pelham and Holles families, transferred his support from the old to the new ministers and thus created an alliance of political talents and territorial influence which was to dominate politics for many years to come. Carteret, the pupil of Stanhope, was forced out of office in 1724, Townshend himself was forced to resign in 1730, and Walpole was left in sole command of men with first-rate influence and second-rate abilities. Walpole reached his political prime in 1733, but the defeat of his enlightened excise scheme in that year seems to have damped down his initiative and for the next seven years he seemed content to hold what he had won. By the end of the decade his position was beginning to crumble, he was forced into war against his better judgment in 1739 and even allowed himself to be overruled in the cabinet. Even so he held on until 1742 and resigned only when it seemed that his hold upon the House of Commons was irretrievably damaged.

A man with the training of a country gentleman, the over-bearing manners and expensive tastes of a great aristocrat, and the talents of a first-rate man of business was well fitted to rule over Hanoverian England. In debate he never achieved great oratory, but he was powerful and persuasive. His mastery of political tactics was displayed both in parliament, where he had to weld together a stable majority, and at court where he had to counter intrigues designed to rob him of the king's confidence. His record for positive legislation was meagre, but an eighteenth-century government was not expected to legislate overmuch, and the imprint left upon a whole generation by his dominant personality was strong and abiding. He realised that the security of the dynasty—always the main object of his policy—could best be achieved by conciliating the landed gentry, fostering commerce, keeping the Church quiescent, and avoiding war. He aimed to lighten the burden of taxation, especially that of the land tax, which was the most burdensome to the landed gentry; he refrained from pressing central control upon local authority and permitted the passage of savage penal laws for offences against property; he refused to risk a revival of High Church fanaticism by an attack upon the Test and Corporation Acts; and he maintained good relations with France as long as he was allowed to do so. The corollary to his gentleness in political matters towards the gentry was the active encouragement, by an adroit use of Crown influence, of the territorial power of his allies among the landed magnates. The strength which accumulated in the hands of the Whig aristocracy made it appear almost as an independent power within the State, but the slow growth of loyalty to the dynasty, which Walpole fostered among the country gentry, was to be an instrument ready to the hand of George III in his struggle with the magnates.

Finance and commerce gained most from the rule of Walpole. If he did not innovate, at least he brought out the elements of strength in a system which he had inherited and which was fundamentally sound. By 1727 he had paid off eight and a half millions of the National Debt from the Sinking Fund, reduced the interest to a uniform 4 per cent, and negotiated a new loan at 3 per cent; he had thus somewhat exceeded the expectations of Sunderland in spite of the South Sea Bubble. In his later years his finance grew more careless and the Sinking Fund was used as a general reserve to meet deficits and extraordinary expenses, so that the country was spared additional taxation at the expense of debt redemption. The cheap money and confidence which he was able to exploit resulted in part from his own commercial policy. He made fiscal policy play a rational part in commercial regulation instead of being a haphazard scramble for revenue. Trade and industry were aided by the abolition of export duties and the institution of some export bounties, by the abolition of duties upon some raw materials used in home production, and by placing heavy duties upon imports which competed with domestic manufactures. The re-export trade was helped by an extension of the warehouse system, which permitted certain colonial imports to remain in bond without the payment of customs duty and to pay an excise duty if released for home consumption. An attempt to apply the same system to wine and tobacco was represented by an unscrupulous opposition as a prelude to further taxation enforced by an army of excisemen; in the face of widespread popular clamour Walpole had to drop this scheme in 1733 and with it his favourite project of abolishing the land tax. He left the country with increased trade and increased revenue, with the fiscal system greatly simplified, and with a testimony to financial soundness in the growing volume of foreign investment in the National Debt.

The defeat of the Excise Bill was the most notable success of the opposition to Walpole. The permanent Tory opposition was supplemented by Whigs whom he had excluded from office, and behind the various opposition groups Bolingbroke, permitted to return to England in 1723 but excluded from the House of Lords, employed his great talents in a vain effort to regain power. Against the Government were ranged the most formidable parliamentarians of the age—Carteret, Pulteney, and the rising Temple-Grenville connection led by Lord Cobham and including William Pitt—the press was dominated by opposition pens, and though Walpole was able to survive and even to profit by the succession of George II, Frederick, the new prince of Wales, formed an opposition court. The long-continued impotence of so powerful a combination requires some deeper explanation than Walpole's ascendancy over two kings, his friendship with Queen Caroline until her death in 1737, and the territorial influence of the Pelhams. His safe and often silent majority was a testimony not only to the influence of the Crown but also to Walpole's success in quieting the clamours of the past and in giving England an era of prosperity such as she had not known before. Until the question of peace or war was presented in 1739 the opposition could find no great principle with which to rouse the nation or unite their members. The Whig opposition was formed by a number of groups each wanting office for itself, and no more than a temporary *entente* was possible between them and the hard core of honest but unambitious Tories. The stock slogans of opposition—no corruption, no Hanoverian influences in foreign policy, lower taxes and less expenditure—had an unreal flavour so long as opposition Whigs wanted not a change of system but a share of power. Bolingbroke, who attempted to provide the opposition with a theory of government, never got to the heart of the problem of English politics. Willing to accept the revolution of 1688 as 'a new magna carta, from whence new interests, new principles of government, new measures of submission, and new obligations arise'[1], he looked back to the reign of William III in which a non-party monarch was supposed to have ruled with the advice of the best men in the kingdom, and parliament was not the instrument of royal policy but its enlightened critic. The fault of the present age lay in the corrupt abuse of power by ministers who had usurped the authority of the Crown; but he did not explain how the precarious balance of William's reign could be preserved indefinitely or how any government could be assured of the necessary stability for effective rule. Even Pitt, who was in substantial agreement with Bolingbroke, later found it impossible to fight a war without the support of a disciplined majority in parliament, and so long as no great differences divided the people this discipline could be obtained only by using the influence of the Crown.

The Walpole system was in fact a logical solution to the constitutional dilemma of the age, and this helps to explain why the system survived the man. His resignation in 1742 did not produce a political revolution; the addition of Carteret to the cabinet and the distribution of some minor offices for his friends was the sum total of political change. During Walpole's long rule the men whom the duke of Newcastle termed the 'old

[1] Henry St John, Viscount Bolingbroke, *A Dissertation upon Parties*, Letter I (1771 edition), p. 12.

corps of Whigs' had made themselves indispensable to any government, and political combinations revolved around them. Carteret, who treated his colleagues with scant courtesy, relied upon the favour of the king, ignored the arts of political management, and hoped that a vigorous foreign policy would establish his influence in the country, found that he had sadly miscalculated political realities. In 1744 he was forced out by the 'old corps' and Henry Pelham, brother of Newcastle, became principal minister as First Lord of the Treasury. On the other hand, influence could not win all the tricks and even the most negative of governments had to find some principles upon which to stand; that chosen by the Pelhams was a 'broad bottom' or conciliation of all those who showed genuine attachment to the dynasty. Places were found for two of the Grenville-Temple connection, though the king accepted Pitt only after a sharp tussle with the ministers in 1745, and even a Tory, Sir John Hynde Cotton of Cambridgeshire, was included in the Government. At a lower level the Government issued instructions that magistrates should be chosen from 'gentlemen of Figure and Fortune, well affected to His Majesty's government, without distinction of parties'.[1]

Probably the defeat of a new Jacobite rising did more than political readjustment to consolidate the power of the new Government. In July 1745 the Young Pretender landed in Scotland, raised the Highlanders, scattered a loyalist army at Prestonpans, and occupied Edinburgh. In the autumn he invaded England and reached Derby by December; here, only a few days' march from London, his luck turned. His small army had not been increased by many English recruits and he had left much opposition in his rear. As George II was preparing to leave his capital, the Pretender reluctantly abandoned the idea of a dash upon London, and returned to Scotland; though he was able to win one more victory at Falkirk he suffered a crushing defeat at Culloden in April 1746 which ended the Jacobite menace not only in this campaign but for all time. In Scotland a consequence of the rebellion was the subjugation of the Highlands; in England it demonstrated that loyalty to the Hanoverians had taken root.

Henry Pelham, though not a spectacular figure, was a good House of Commons man and an able financier of the school of Walpole. After the European peace in 1748 he cut expenditure, reduced the land tax, and carried out a great conversion scheme by which the interest on the debt was brought down to 3 per cent. His death in 1754 left Newcastle in sole command, but with little notion how to use his power. Moving himself to the Treasury he appointed a well-meaning diplomat, Sir Thomas Robinson, as Secretary of State, thus provoking two junior ministers, William Pitt and Henry Fox, to show the bitterness of their frustrated ambition by attacking the new Secretary in the Commons. Newcastle then made a deal with Fox which resulted in the latter's appointment to the

[1] British Museum, Add. MSS. 32,993, fo. 308.

secretaryship and a furious and denunciatory attack from Pitt, whose conduct led to his somewhat overdue dismissal from office. Britain drifted into war in 1756 amid a welter of abortive German alliances and awoke to find Minorca lost and the country threatened by French invasion. The foreign situation increased the tempo of opposition at home, and Newcastle was compelled to seek the support of Pitt on any terms; but Pitt would accept no terms whatever. Conscious of his own power in parliament and in the country he would have nothing less than the first place and in November 1756 George II was compelled to entrust his Government to the man whose attacks upon Hanover he bitterly resented and of whose rhetorical appeal to popular emotion he had the most profound distrust. Hitherto Pitt, commanding immense prestige and confident in his own pre-eminent ability, had appeared irresistible. In office, with a hostile king and without consistent support from the old corps of Whigs, he proved all too weak, and inexperienced colleagues did not contribute towards the Government's strength. In April 1757 the king abruptly dismissed Pitt and after three months of crisis a sensible compromise was found in an alliance between Pitt and Newcastle with the former in sole charge of the war and the latter as First Lord of the Treasury. During the temporary restoration of political stability which followed England was able to win her triumphs of the Seven Years War.

The death of George II in 1760 opened a new period of political manœuvre. The king had had all the faults of narrow and obstinate men, but as a constitutional monarch his actions had risen superior to his character; though often influenced by personal prejudice, he had made it his business to see that the country was given effective government, and he had done something to establish a new code of conduct for a limited monarch as an arbiter rather than as a leader in politics. His grandson and successor professed with sincerity his attachment to the Constitution, but it was to the Constitution of William III rather than to that of George II. George III envisaged a truly separate executive, supported by a truly loyal legislature, and directed by an active king and by non-party ministers whom he would select. His condemnation of corruption and his resentment of the power wielded by the landed aristocracy were laudable and popular, and only time would reveal the patriot king compelled to use the methods which he had condemned; yet the tactics which he employed at his succession to the throne roused the suspicion that national interests might be subordinated to political advantage. It was his first object to break the loveless marriage between Pitt and the Newcastle Whigs. The strength of the ministry was the popularity of Pitt, and Pitt could hardly be dismissed in the midst of the war which he directed with such success. Peace therefore became the king's first aim and his friend and adviser Bute, a man without parliamentary influence or experience, was appointed as Secretary of State expressly for this object. An opportunity presented itself when Bute persuaded Newcastle to support him in opposing Pitt's desire for an immediate declaration of war against Spain; Pitt then resigned with the magnificent though legally indefensible claim that 'being responsible I will direct and will be responsible for nothing that I do not direct'.

Newcastle soon became uneasy at the ascendancy in the cabinet of Bute, at his own exclusion from the confidence of the king, and at the overt intention of making peace without securing favourable terms for Prussia. Loath to surrender the Treasury, yet old and unhappy, he finally resigned in May 1762. Save for a six months' interlude in 1756–7 he had held cabinet office for forty-five years, thirty-two as Secretary of State and eight as First Lord of the Treasury; though he had established no claim to distinguished statesmanship he was by no means the contemptible figure which some contemporaries believed him to be. Perpetually anxious about the minutiae of politics and immersed in trivial but delicate matters of patronage, he had nevertheless been the principal support of that alliance between executive authority and the power of the landed aristocracy which had been the outstanding characteristic of early Hanoverian England. A less scrupulous man possessed of his influence might have sown discord in the country, but Newcastle provided stability at the cost of some debasement of political principle. Hardwicke, his constant friend and able mentor resigned with him, most younger members of the 'old corps' went into opposition, the balance of power which had dominated the political scene was at end, and a chapter in British politics was closed.

The long period of relatively stable government had fostered pride and confidence in the Constitution. In England, it was affirmed, the major problems of politics had been solved, and the task of the present was not to improve but to preserve. The men of the eighteenth century linked change with decay rather than improvement, and they did not realise that the spirit and purpose of institutions might alter without formal amendment. Nowhere did this limitation of the eighteenth-century mind do more to obscure political debate than in the attitude towards the relationship of executive and legislature. Since 1702 no additional restrictions had been placed upon the power of the king, and his executive authority had been strengthened by an improved revenue system and by the political management which normally secured a parliamentary majority for his Government. But the limitations placed upon royal authority during the seventeenth century meant that the king could not exploit this new strength without the willing co-operation of his more influential subjects. If the power of the Crown increased, it was because there were enough subjects of the Crown who wished it to increase.

The royal command became, for many, not a burdensome directive but a warrant for the exercise of autonomous power; an earlier age had seen this happen in the courts of law and during the eighteenth century it became characteristic of many administrative processes. At the periphery the tendency was strikingly illustrated in the justices of the peace whose administration was neither supervised nor directed. At the centre departments tended to fortify themselves against interference of all kinds by the erection of procedural barriers which incidentally multiplied the fees and thus the value of public office. It has long been a problem to ascertain how far this centrifugal tendency operated at the very heart of government in the relations between the king and his ministers. By law, in the public view, and to a large degree in practice the king was the active ruler of the country; his legislative power had been whittled away to an unused veto, but his executive power was still great. When political decisions had to be made the king was the only person known to the law who could make them, and even if the decision was forced upon him it was still his decision. He had an unchallengeable right to consult with whom he would and to choose those to whom he would delegate executive authority. In practice, however, this wide freedom was limited by the political fact that no government could function without a majority in parliament, and the king could choose his principal servants only from the comparatively small number of men who held the key to parliamentary power.

In earlier periods the overmighty subject had been shorn of power when his rank and formal responsibility no longer entitled him to share in the active business of government. In the early eighteenth century the magnates were once more placed near the source of authority, and when, at some time after 1714, an inner cabinet of 'efficient ministers' makes its appearance they are to be found in this innermost citadel of power. Their claim to be there rested upon their command of electoral influence; however humbly they might kiss hands after appointment, they did not owe their power to the king alone and it required no theory of ministerial responsibility to convince them that their influence in parliament was one asset which must not be sacrificed. Final decisions might lie with the king, but the ministers were brokers of political power who claimed the right to tell the king what was possible. It was no care for the rights of subjects but the plain requirements of political management which led ministers to object when the king consulted with men who had no ministerial responsibility, to assert that the king and his ministers must appear to be of one mind, and on one occasion at least, in February 1745–6, to insist that they could not be responsible for the king's government unless the king's decisions were entirely to their liking. If it was a part of their business to respect the wishes of the king, they also knew that the mechanics of eighteenth-century politics made it imperative that the house of government should not be divided against itself. It was this link between executive authority and electoral influence which threatened to submerge the personal wishes of the king and to lead the country along the road to modern cabinet government. The inner cabinet of 1760 lacked definition of its responsibilities, the true balance of power was obscured by language inherited from the past, and when ministers forced the hand of the king they would not acknowledge that they were doing so; but it would be foolish to assert that nothing had happened since 1688.

No one minister automatically took the lead in the cabinet, but the direction of national finances, combined with control of a great volume of patronage, made the First Lord of the Treasury a person of importance in any government. A combination of this power, an unrivalled talent for managing royal personages, and his own dominant character enabled Walpole to anticipate the behaviour of a modern Prime Minister in forcing the resignation or dismissal of dissident colleagues, acting as the sole channel of communication between king and ministers, and preventing the king from seeking advice elsewhere. Walpole set a pattern which could not be ignored—in future men would expect to speak of one minister as *the* minister—but only the loosest of precedents had been set. Future First Lords could not claim the same position by right nor establish it save by force of character. Newcastle spent much time in worrying about the real or supposed attempts of ministerial colleagues to gain the confidence of the king, and the popular cant of the day regarded it as reprehensible when one minister usurped all power. The logic of a situation in which the king ceased to be concerned with day to day decisions on detail meant that someone else had to take the lead in the cabinet, but the modern premiership was not to appear until leadership of a party gave to one person an independent source of power and a special standing in the cabinet.

The inner cabinets of the eighteenth century were smaller than modern cabinets and the scope of their discussions was more limited. A normal inner cabinet consisted of three officers with ancient titles and few duties (the Lord President of the Council, the Lord Privy Seal, and the Lord Chamberlain), the Lord Chancellor, the two Secretaries of State, and the First Lords of the two boards which performed the duties of the Lord Treasurer and the Lord High Admiral. The chancellorship of the Exchequer might carry with it membership of the inner cabinet, but this office was frequently held by the First Lord of the Treasury. Cabinet discussions were concerned mainly with foreign policy, and hardly at all in normal times with domestic affairs which were left to the departmental heads. Parliamentary tactics would probably be decided informally by the ministers most directly concerned. The navy had a comparatively simple administration under the Board of Admiralty but the army had evolved a system of divided responsibility and overlapping commands which was remarkable even in an age of administrative incoherence. War policy and the disposition of troops were directed by the Secretary of State, of the Northern or Southern Department according to the geographical location of the fighting, and he was also through the Lords Lieutenant responsible for the militia. Orders for troop movements were addressed to the Secretary at War, who was also directly responsible to the King in Council for estimates, recruitment and commissions, and to the commander-in-chief for discipline and service details. The king in person was the commander of all guards and garrisons, and the Master General of Ordnance was directly responsible to him for the supply of arms and ammunition both to the army and to the navy.

The secretaryship of State might well have emerged as the leading office—and was so while Pitt held it—but for its curious geographical division, its limited patronage, and its lack of concern with finance. The two secretaries had identical powers as executants of the king's will and for domestic and colonial affairs there was no formal division of the work; for foreign affairs their duties were divided into Northern and Southern Departments. The Board of Trade was responsible for maintaining the laws of trade and navigation and for the detailed supervision of colonial affairs; it usually advised the secretaries on the instructions which were to be issued to colonial governors and made recommendations to the King in Council on the allowance or disallowance of acts passed by colonial legislatures. For many of the activities of which a modern government takes cognizance, including the Poor Law, highways and education, there was no central responsibility whatever.

While an Act of 1705 prevented members of parliament from accepting offices created since that date, there was nothing to prevent an old office from becoming a sinecure or from allowing its duties to be performed by deputy. Hard pressed to find suitable rewards for its 'friends' in parliament, the Government allowed more and more administrative offices to be treated in this way, and in several departments a dual system came into being consisting of those who did the work and of those who did so only in name. In general the public spirit of the deputies and clerks was higher than that of their masters, and where the administrative machine functioned well the explanation was usually to be found in the devotion of obscure and hard-working civil servants. Initial appointments to these lower offices were usually made as political favours to some more important person who wished to find employment for a protégé or dependant, but promotion was largely by seniority and merit, and dismissals were rare. Inefficient men might drift along undisturbed, but efficient men enjoyed the same security of tenure. Rigid adherence to rule was often a greater danger to efficiency than professional laxity; this danger was increased by the fact that salaries were low while fees were good (thus giving numerous officials a vested interest in procedural exactitude) and by the habit of receiving gifts as a kind of retaining fee from men who wished to ensure that their business with the Government did not suffer from poor knowledge of complex procedures. Meanwhile the responsibility of government departments as custodians of public money was being secured by a silent revolution which established Treasury control over government spending. The Admiralty acknowledged no control over its finances, but the army, always regarded with suspicion by parliament, had to submit to a growing control over its estimates; the minor departments were rigidly controlled and even the Civil List could not evade the Treasury when its expenses began to outrun its income. Thus there came into being the modern distinction between the spending departments and the Treasury, acting as the trustee of public money.

Away from Westminster the task of carrying on the king's business devolved mainly upon local magistrates. Theirs was the first responsibility for the maintenance of law and order and they could expect the assistance of regular troops only in the greatest emergencies. Even in a matter so vital to good government as the assessment and collection of direct taxes—the Land Tax and the 'assessed taxes' of which the most important was the window tax—the burden of the work was carried out by county commissions composed of local magistrates. This was indeed one of the weakest links in a government not conspicuous for administrative strength, but attempts to improve it by the appointment of salaried officials to check the work of the county commissioners were successful only in part. A study of executive authority away from the centre of government illustrates the essential formula of eighteenth-century politics: that government worked as well and as far as a sufficient number of influential men wished it to work.

King, Lords and Commons composed the national legislature, but the royal veto was not used after the reign of Anne and the king in person had no power to initiate legislation. The House of Lords was some 220 strong, of whom twenty-six were bishops, sixteen representative peers of Scotland, and the remainder English hereditary peers; the number increased very little during the period, though the extinction of old lines allowed for the introduction of some new blood. Containing a majority of the important men in the kingdom, the House was regarded as the guardian of law and property against encroachments by king or people, and within the accepted framework of eighteenth-century ideas it fulfilled this duty with dignity and with a sense of responsibility to the nation. Much of business was purely legal for, as well as being the supreme court of appeal in civil cases, the Lords considered in detail bills of divorce and private bills affecting property, and even in political debates a judicial atmosphere prevailed.

Very different was the House of Commons where important debates were hectic, personal invective not always restrained by the Rules of the House or by the conventions of polite society and partisanship so intense that even legal business, such as an election petition, could be decided by a majority in the face of the evidence. Most of the speeches were made by a comparatively small number of men, but questions were decided by the votes of silent members and among the most respected of these were usually to be found the members for English counties. Though very few county elections were contested during the first half of the century and though most county members owed their seats to an understanding between local factions, the theoretical freedom of election by freeholders whose land was valued at 40s. or more a year gave them independence and prestige. Borough members arrived in the House for a variety of reasons and the electoral system of each borough was a study in itself. Franchise might be restricted by a logical tax-paying qualification or by the wholly illogical vesting of the right to vote in the occupants of certain burgage properties. The statement that all freemen in a borough could vote often concealed the fact that the corporation might make freemen with a sparing or a liberal hand according to the political situation. In some boroughs residence was necessary, and in others non-residents outnumbered the resident voters; some were entirely under the influence of a patron, some could be won by the longest purse, and some could be bought in the market like any other piece of property. There were large trading towns in which the contests were real and tiny villages which retained the privileges of a corporate borough though trade and population had long since vanished. Though sometimes criticised, the electoral system survived the rare proposals for reform; change would not only disturb carefully tended electoral interests but also raise the difficult problem of substituting a rational for an irrational definition of the right to vote. With all its deficiencies the Commons claimed to represent the people of Great Britain, though in a way alien to modern ideas. The eighteenth century did not stop at the idea that a man with a stake in the country was the man qualified to share in government; they believed that he also had a stake in liberty. Men of property were regarded as the natural defenders of popular freedom because they would be the first to feel any encroachment upon it. The House also represented the property interests of the country in a way which corresponded roughly to their economic and social importance: it represented the dominant influence of landowners, the great trading interests never lacked spokesmen, the universities were directly represented, and the professions indirectly by the many lawyers in the House. Thus the Commons rose superior to the means by which they were elected and until late in the century few men failed to respect these representatives of great landowners, corrupt corporations, and moneyed wealth.

At one time historians were prone to speak as though the influence of the Crown formed an irresistible force in eighteenth-century politics; a more modern view will realise that this influence was small in comparison to the aggregate of that possessed by the great landowners. It did, however, play an important part, for where competing interests were nearly balanced,

Crown influence might well turn the scales. Many members had no wish for government employment, but they and their patrons did wish to increase their own local authority by controlling the flow of Crown patronage. Among the favours with which a member might oblige his constituents were recommendations to appointments in the forest and revenue services, to colonial appointments and posts in the government departments, and to Church livings of which the Crown was patron. A 'friend' of the government would expect the ministers to attend to these recommendations, and it was the business of a government 'manager' to meet these demands, make promises when he could not deliver goods, and offer alternatives when he could not fulfil promises. A judicious attention to these difficult problems would secure a stable majority, but there was never enough patronage to satisfy everyone or to make parliamentary management a purely mechanical affair. The damage lay less in the use of political influence than in its constant extension. More and more positions of responsibility and trust were brought within the political net, and from the top corruption spread to meet the demand from below; the Church, the universities, the law and the armed forces were all made in varying degrees to serve the exigencies of political management. Behind the easy spread of corrupt influences lies the important fact that the king's government had to go on, that it could not be carried on without a secure majority in parliament, and that so long as the ruling classes were not divided upon fundamental matters there was no incentive other than self-interest to support one government rather than another. Party discipline could not replace the discipline of patronage until men were confronted with real issues to which they attached an importance which transcended personal convenience. This does not excuse eighteenth-century politicians, but it helps to explain why decent men did not regard their methods as wholly subversive of national well-being. There was also the fact that public opinion never ceased to influence parliament. If successful public agitation was rare, the frequency of sporadic rioting kept upper-class Englishmen aware that in the final analysis the people might be their masters.

The House of Lords was a court of law as well as being a part of the legislature; justices of the peace combined executive and judicial functions; but, in spite of this fusion of powers at the top and the bottom of the judicial hierarchy, there could be no real doubt that the judicature was separate and distinct. The judges, under whose control came the whole Common Law jurisdiction, could be removed for grave misconduct by addresses from both Houses of Parliament and until 1760 their commissions expired with the demise of the Crown, but otherwise they enjoyed independent tenure for life. The Common Law judges divided the year between Westminster and travel on circuit to hold Assize courts in the county towns. No part of the criminal law escaped judicial control, for any decision of the justices of the peace could be questioned in a higher court by use of the writ *certiorari*, and during the eighteenth century it became usual to send all capital offences for trial at the Assizes. Grand Juries were guided though not controlled by the judges, but they confined themselves to deciding whether evidence produced warranted criminal prosecution and never decided upon guilt. Two forms of court which had formerly administered an international law—the Ecclesiastical Courts and the Court of Admiralty—had had their jurisdiction narrowed down by the jealousy of common lawyers: the one to non-criminal offences by the clergy, cases affecting the validity of marriages and grants of probate and administration of wills; the other to strictly maritime cases. There remained one great court, which had increased rather than lost power, and which was not a Common Law court: this was the Court of Chancery. Indeed, the decline of the Ecclesiastical and Admiralty Courts had benefited Chancery by allowing it to extend its jurisdiction in testamentary cases and by giving it a wide range of mercantile jurisdiction. In the eighteenth century, however, the equitable jurisdiction of Chancery was coming to be the supplement rather than the rival of Common Law.

The independence of the judges and their increasing hold upon the legal system of the country opened other dangers. Freed from control by the executive the law might become a thing apart from the general life of the nation or it might reflect too strongly the prejudices of the judges and of the class to which they belonged. In the eighteenth century both these dangers were apparent. The customs and procedure of the law had so hardened that they presented insuperable barriers to any man who was not a trained lawyer. Blackstone was to restore the study of the law to the general education of an English gentleman, but in the early eighteenth century it was the exclusive concern of a professional body which had a vested interest in innumerable difficult procedures. The delays, expenses and technicalities of the law increased yearly in notoriety, and at the very centre dignified confusion prevailed in the overlapping jurisdictions of the three great Common Law courts of King's Bench, Common Pleas and Exchequer. Judges demanded an exact compliance with technical forms, and a curious sort of justice was executed when a man accused of a minor capital offence might be excused not only from a barbarous penalty but also from all punishment whatsoever if the slightest flaw could be shown in the indictment.

Though judges could make no law, the right to interpret, where both Statute and Common Law were silent, amounted almost to the power of legislation. The increasing complexity of commercial practices, the desire to safeguard newly acquired estates against sale or dispersion by improvident heirs, new forms of trust for property, and new forms of property in government funds and transferable stock for which the ancient law provided no means of conveyancing, all presented problems which called for legal innovation. In meeting this challenge Hardwicke proved himself one of the greatest of Lord Chancellors; he made free use of the equitable jurisdiction of Chancery to solve the many problems presented, and the rules which he formulated were later grafted upon the Common Law by Lord Mansfield. Not the least important change which took place during the eighteenth century was that the Law Merchant ceased to be a separate law administered by separate courts, and this took place through judicial decision without any legislative enactment.

While the Constitution was a vague concept all were agreed that its main justification was individual liberty, and men looked to this liberty as the peculiar blessing of the English race won by the wisdom and sacrifices of earlier generations. An Englishman was free from arbitrary arrest, imprisonment or punishment; he could not be taxed unless his chosen representatives consented; he might meet with his fellows and say what he thought provided that he did not provoke a breach of the peace; he might write what he liked provided that it was not obscene, or a seditious, blasphemous or defamatory libel. More realistically, since parliament made the law, his liberty consisted in doing anything which parliament considered respectable, or, as the execution of the law was in the hands of local authorities, in observing the law as they interpreted it. If a dispute was likely to become serious the Riot Act of 1715 gave to magistrates the virtual right to define a riot, and having defined it to disperse it with force. The critic of government had to beware of the law of libel, for if the written page could be shown to have been written with malicious intent to cause a breach of the peace it was a criminal libel; if likely to bring into hatred or contempt the king, government, parliament, any legal authority or the law of the land, it was a seditious libel; while any criticism of religion might be a blasphemous libel. Moreover, the jury was asked to determine only the fact of publication and the interpretation of innuendos and not the nature of the libel. Libels on peers were summarily punished by the House of Lords, and this was extended to mean publication of anything written of a peer, alive or dead, without his or his heirs' consent. Even with their limited powers juries sometimes helped those accused of libels, but the Special Juries Act of 1730 enabled judges in such cases to swear in a jury with a higher property qualification. In 1729 a prosecution against the printer of Bolingbroke's 'Craftsman' failed, but he was later convicted by a special jury. These were serious limitations upon the freedom of the Press, but while there was an eager market for political publications hundreds of printers were prepared to risk prosecution.

To prosecutions for seditious libel there still clung some remnant of the idea that it was immoral to attack the powers that be, but the justification for restraints upon liberty were grounded mainly upon the need for social order and the protection of private property. If divinity no longer hedged the king, reverence for property had largely taken the place of religion as the cement of society. Upon the need to preserve property Locke had based the justification for civil power and men of the eighteenth century accepted without question the particular status and privileges which property entailed. To protect private property men were driven to extravagances which they otherwise eschewed, and the reckless multiplication of capital offences was a disgrace to the age. The so-called Waltham Black Act of 1722, passed to meet a temporary outbreak of lawlessness in Waltham Forest and several times renewed until it became part of the permanent law of the land in 1758, is said to have added no less than 350 capital offences to the Statute Book. On the other hand, there was little attempt to match the severity of these deterrents by improving the police force; the lessons of the seventeenth century had been too recently learnt for men not to regard servants of government as the potential instruments of despotism, so that England presented the contradictory picture of a barbarous severity in her criminal law and such weakness in the detection of crime that lawlessness actually increased. This was a part of the price which Englishmen paid for their extraordinary freedom from government regulation.

A country in which property counted for so much was unlikely to be egalitarian in spirit, yet when property competes with birth for social distinction there are likely to be some careers open to talents. The self-made men of the eighteenth century are too numerous to ignore; among the most distinguished were Hardwicke, son of a country attorney; Bishop Butler, author of the *Analogy*, son of a Presbyterian draper; Archbishop Secker, son of a small non-conformist freeholder; Pitt, the son of a 'nabob', and Clive rising from the ranks of the poor gentry. Bankers, attorneys and corn merchants took over estates from the ancient country gentry whose sons went into trade, the law, or the service of the East India Company. The great social revolution of the period by which, particularly in the north, great conglomerations of landed property replaced small estates, sent large numbers of young men in search of salaried positions; the official papers of eighteenth-century statesmen teem with their applications for employment, and those who were refused had to enter the more humble professions or fend for themselves in the trading world. One fortunate by-product was that they brought into their new occupations traditional standards of honesty and upright conduct, and the growth of professional codes of conduct is one of the most important and least noticed legacies of the eighteenth century. This, together with new demands for men of business and professional skill, was forcing up the social status of attorneys, grown rich by conveyancing real estate, and apothecaries, gradually improving their medical competence. The British merchant was certainly not behindhand either in accepting professional standards or advancing up the social ladder.

These social changes were facilitated by an educational system which offered fair opportunities for a boy born above the line which separated the propertied from the propertyless. The gap between grammar schools and public schools was less wide than it is today, and the son of the yeoman or shopkeeper might be educated side by side with the sons of local gentry; the universities contained many poor students working their way towards professional qualifications; and apprenticeships in numerous walks of life demanded but modest premiums. Below the 'property line' opportunities were far less good, and the great majority of Englishmen (but not Scotsmen) went unlettered to their graves; there were a considerable number of Charity Schools, but most of them aimed no higher than fitting a child for the station in life to which he had been born.

Above a certain line there was thus a relatively fluid, below it a comparatively static, society, and the gap tended to widen as new wealth enriched the propertied classes. The overall trade of the country increased to a remarkable extent and the favourable balance of trade (for what that is worth) showed a marked improvement. The standard of living in the upper and middle classes undoubtedly rose, for not only had they more money but increased trade gave them a wider range of goods to buy. How far this improvement was passed on, if at all, to the poor, is still a matter of doubt and controversy. The old view of the early eighteenth century as a golden age must be abandoned in view of modern studies of the London poor and artisan wages. In London all the evidence points to a rapid increase in over-crowding, bad health, crime and prostitution in the lower strata of the population; private philanthropic efforts such as those of Thomas Coram, General Oglethorpe, and Jonas Hanway did no more than scratch the surface, and not until the middle of the century are there signs that these public misfortunes might one day be accepted as public responsibilities. In 1751 came the first effective Act to check the sale of cheap gin which had spread such havoc among the London poor and this may well mark the turning point, for after it conditions steadily improved. Over the country as a whole it is impossible to generalise; not only are the data scanty but insufficient allowance has been made for local variations in a country where so many still lived in economic isolation. Artisan wages, for instance, show some improvement in London, a very marked improvement in the north, and stagnation or retrogression in the west. Published price data are taken almost entirely from London and the home counties; it is, however, sufficient to show a period of steady prices with a downward trend early in the period and an upward trend towards its end. Over the whole period prices were lower than those which prevailed during the War of the Spanish Succession or the War of American Independence. There is, therefore, some reason to believe that the living standards of the majority of the English poor did not decline and may have improved slightly.

What is more certain is that there was a considerable movement of population from the countryside to the towns and to centres of rural industry. This movement was accelerated by agricultural improvement, which inevitably displaced some people, while the growing consumer markets in the towns helped to stimulate changes in the ancient methods of farming and to increase the expected profit from the consolidation of holdings. There is no need to dramatise the decline of the yeomen; a principal factor was that over long periods there was always someone ready to give a good price for good land, and though some who sold out may have become landless labourers it is unlikely that many did so. The former yeomen are to be found in the rising class of tenant farmers, in the growing body of industrial craftsmen, in recruits for the commercial world, and in the steady stream of emigrants to the New World. The fruits of agricultural change were better and more abundant, though not necessarily cheaper, food, and this, combined with cleaner living conditions, better medical care, and reduced infant mortality, fostered an increase in the population which was accelerated to a marked degree about the middle of the century.

In industry increased demand at home and abroad, increased capital available for merchant entrepreneurs, and an increased labour force led to greater production, but this was, for the most part, within the familiar organisation of merchant and craftsman and without the exploitation of new inventions. Kay's flying shuttle, invented in 1733, was just coming into use at the end of the period, but it had not yet revolutionised weaving. A cotton spinning machine was in operation in 1742, but by 1760 mechanical spinning was still extremely rare. Of more immediate importance was Abraham Darby's discovery, early in the century, of a way to smelt iron with coke in place of charcoal, thus freeing the languishing iron industry from dependence upon native timber, and preparing the way for a great period of expansion; but even this major innovation was little known by the middle of the century. For most capitalists it was still easier to exploit cheap labour than to install expensive experimental machinery; but the most formidable barrier to industrial development remained the inadequacy of internal communications. This could be remedied only when men could be induced to invest money in long-term projects of improvement. Cheap money, facilitated by Walpole and Pelham, prepared the ground for long-term investment, but incentives were often lacking. In 1759 the duke of Bridgewater began work upon a seven-mile canal to carry coal from his colliery at Worsley to the people of Manchester; the success of this venture opened a new phase in British economic history, for it demonstrated both the returns which could be expected from such investment and the means by which the economic unification of the country could be completed.

In retrospect the early eighteenth century does not appear, as is still occasionally believed, as an age of stagnation, but as one of the creative periods in English history. Behind the façade of a tiny 'polite' society it was a rough age in which the weakest went to the wall, but in every field the rewards were substantial for those who could aspire to them. The achievements of countless individuals were written large in trade expansion, agricultural improvement, great fortunes, splendid country houses and solid urban residences, the winning of an Indian empire and the triumphs of the Seven Years War. All this was done under a government which did little more than hold the balance of social power and accepted little responsibility for the welfare of its subjects. Yet the achievements were indissolubly linked with a political system under which, whatever qualifications the modern student may wish to make, Englishmen felt that they were free. This sense of freedom was the fruit of seventeenth-century conflicts, but it could hardly have ripened save in the security of Hanoverian England.

CHAPTER XII

THE WESTERN MEDITERRANEAN
AND ITALY

I N the early eighteenth century the western Mediterranean and Italy
were dominated by Spain, where the new Bourbon dynasty, galvanised
into activity by the ambition of Elizabeth Farnese, achieved a remarkable revival. From 1714, when she arrived in Spain as the second wife of
Philip V, till 1746, when the death of her husband removed her from the
centre of Spanish political life, Elizabeth and a series of able advisers
acted with an energy and daring that gave Spain the initiative in the diplomatic negotiations affecting the Mediterranean region. Because of her
family connections with Parma, Piacenza and Tuscany Elizabeth's ambitions were focused on those territories, and Italy was thus affected by the
newly revived Spanish diplomacy. Portugal, on the contrary, though it
gave a queen to the second effective Bourbon king of Spain, was little
concerned in the Mediterranean diplomacy of the period. Portugal was
satisfied to have regained her independence. Her colony of Brazil was
providing her with a very large income and until 1750 she was content to
enjoy independence and prosperity, taking very little part in European
diplomacy and making very little contribution to European civilisation.
After that date, with the advent of Pombal, Portugal suddenly outstripped
Spain in reforming activity.

It was a very remarkable achievement by Elizabeth Farnese and her
husband's chief ministers to gain the diplomatic initiative for Spain in
the early eighteenth century, for at the end of the reign of Charles II
Spain's economic resources had been in a state of almost total ruin. In
1692 the Crown had for the third time declared itself bankrupt although
during the seventeenth century the weight of taxation had been increased
considerably. The *alcabala* tax on all sales had been increased to 11 per
cent in 1639 and to 14 per cent in 1663. New taxes had been imposed on
saltwort in 1621, on stamped paper in 1637, on oil, wine and vinegar in
1642 and on soap and even on ice in 1649, but all these expedients had
failed to meet the needs of the Crown and had only added to the ruin of
the country. By the second half of the seventeenth century there were
many unmistakable signs that the Spanish economy was gravely sick.
The volume of Spanish shipping plying between Spain and the Indies was
75 per cent lower at the end of the seventeenth century than it had been
a hundred years earlier. As early as 1655 many cities which in the early
sixteenth century had been famous for their manufactures, were complaining bitterly of impoverishment. Toledo, Seville, Granada and

Valencia, which had previously been renowned for their silk fabrics, and Córdoba whose leather had become proverbial, were all appealing for help. Many guilds which had previously been flourishing had by 1655 almost completely disappeared. Martinez Mata mentioned thirty. The woollen manufacture of Toledo had declined by about three-quarters in the first two-thirds of the seventeenth century. The population of the towns had also declined, and Toledo and Segovia were supposed to have lost more than half their inhabitants between 1594 and 1694. In 1687 the marquis de los Vellos spoke of emigration to America as a national scourge, and in 1681 the French ambassador spoke of people emigrating in thousands. Internal trade had dwindled almost to nothing and foreign trade dwindled so much that in the eighteenth century it was commonly said that of all the merchandise sent to the Indies in the great annual fleets the only things supplied by Spain herself were 'some sweetmeats that are liked in the Indies'.[1] Agriculture had shown signs of stagnation even earlier than industry, as is suggested by complaints from the *Cortes* from 1523 onwards and by writers commenting on the economic condition of Spain in 1578, 1600, 1608 and 1619. A *consulta* of the *Consejo de Castilla* dated 1619 referred to houses falling into ruin and peasants running away.

The causes of this economic collapse were several, and they would not have been easy to remove even if the Bourbons had clearly understood them. One of the chief causes seems to have been that the large sums of bullion from Spanish America caused inflation in the period between 1550 and 1600. The abundance of bullion encouraged the Spaniards to indulge a taste for great luxury and made Spaniards increasingly reluctant to work. As late as 1782 many trades were still considered 'vile' and Spaniards looked on manual work as a disgrace. The presence of bullion in the New World attracted men overseas, which reduced the working population in Spain. Men also left the countryside and inland towns and congregated in the ports. Depopulation of the countryside and inland towns was intensified by the number of men and women who went into religious orders, and of men who became civil servants. In 1700 the population of Spain was estimated at 5,700,000: in the time of Charles V it was said to have been eight millions. Antiquated guild regulations hampered industry and a great many minute regulations crushed initiative as effectively as the large sum of money which every goldsmith in Toledo was expected to deposit before he could open a shop. Industry was further hampered by the changes in the value of the Spanish coinage, in particular the inflation caused first by the influx of bullion between 1550 and 1600 and then by the debasement of the coinage from 1600–50. In other countries the price revolution stimulated trade and industry but in Spain wages rose even more rapidly than prices so that manufacturers were unable to profit by the inflation. But perhaps the most serious burden on

[1] J. Lamphill, *A Concise History of Spanish America* (1741), p. 300.

Spanish trade, as on agriculture, was the tax on all sales instituted in the time of Ferdinand and Isabella, increased from the original 10 per cent to 14 per cent during the seventeenth century and augmented by other taxes on all kinds of commodities. Bad communications also strangled trade. Until the eighteenth century the only effective roads were those between Madrid and various royal palaces. Such a good port as Vigo had no passable communication with the interior. So costly was it to transport commodities by land inside Spain that at Cadiz wheat from Palencia, which was only 40 leagues from the port of Santander, cost twice as much as wheat shipped from France, and in Asturias wine, which in its native Castile had cost 20 *reals* the *arroba*, sold at 46 *reals*.

The depopulation, the increasingly heavy taxes and the bad communications hampered agriculture as they did industry, but there were also special reasons why Spanish agriculture was impoverished by the time of the accession of the Bourbon kings. The soil and climate of Spain certainly produce excellent wheat, but Spain is by no means a fertile country. As much as 45 per cent of the land is infertile or very poor, and during the sixteenth and seventeenth centuries the productivity of even the good land had been reduced by reckless deforestation. Peasants cut wood for charcoal and the shepherds of the migrating flocks of the *Mesta* burned trees to make better pasture for next spring. Even what fertile land there was was not fully exploited. Considerable tracts in the centre and south of Spain were uncultivated because these were the sheep walks along which about 2½ million sheep, in flocks of roughly 1000, migrated from Soria, Segovia, Cuenca and Leon each autumn and returned each spring. The system of landholding also discouraged agriculture. Great noblemen sometimes held enormous territories, especially in Andalucia, where the reconquest had been rapid. These were only partly cultivated by gangs of workmen who were moved from one district to another. Even in the earlier-settled Aragon two-thirds of the land was uncultivated. Farmers had been expected to billet troops and had found it increasingly difficult to raise any loans. When to these sources of economic weakness are added the expulsion of the Moriscos and a fanatical preoccupation with the affairs of the next world rather than with prosperity in this, it is not difficult to realise the economic prostration of the country which confronted Philip V at the end of the long war that decided his claim to the Spanish throne.

The problems of restoring the prosperity of Spain were immensely complex and they were not made any less difficult by the social structure of the country in 1713. The most important part of Spanish society in the eighteenth century was the Church. At the end of the century, out of a total population of 10½ million, 191,101 people were professionally connected with the Church. 70,170 were secular clergy, though only about half of these had actually any care of souls, 37,550 men and 24,348 women were professed members of religious orders; the balance was made up of lay brethren, convent servants, sacristans, employees of the Inquisition and the *Cruzada* and those pious but ignorant or stupid people who could never hope to qualify for ordination as priests and who instead took minor orders or lived in a convent as persons dedicated to God. Moreover, the Church exercised an influence on Spanish life much greater than might have been expected from the proportion of people who could be classified as professed ecclesiastics. In the smallest village there was a church, and in even a small town such as Olmedo with a population of 2000 there were seven churches and seven convents. Valladolid, with a population of 21,000, had forty-six monasteries and fourteen parish churches, while monks, nuns and priests made up more than one-twentieth of the town's total population. Throughout Spain there were *cofradías*, or religious associations, made up of members of a trade or inhabitants of a district. In Castile alone at the end of the eighteenth century there were 19,024 of these associations, which still exist throughout Spain, meeting for worship, performing charitable tasks throughout the year and in Holy Week parading through the streets dressed in long cloaks and high pointed caps, attending the sacred image to which their association owes particular devotion. Some of these images, which were normally kept in a parish church, were decorated with immensely valuable clothes and jewellery. Indeed, the whole setting of the services in the Spanish churches was of great luxury. Money which might otherwise have been used productively in industry or agriculture or have been put to some charitable purpose was locked up in altar furniture, in vestments, reliquaries and jewels for shrines and sacred images. When church plate was sacrificed for national purposes it was often found that the resources of the churches had not been so great as had been popularly supposed, but even so the value of the gold, silver, jewellery and vestments, to say nothing of pictures and statues, was considerable. The income of the Spanish Church during the eighteenth century was large. From land the Church derived an income of 359,806,251 *reals* at a time when 10 *reals* made a *peso* and a *peso* was valued at 4s. 4d. in contemporary English money. From tithes the Church obtained 418,000,400 *reals* and from first fruits 230,000,000 *reals*. Dues paid for masses amounted to 53,732,744 *reals*, for christenings 15,000,000 *reals*, for marriages 7,500,000 *reals* and for funerals 60,000,000 *reals*. In addition 3,630,000 *reals* were made by selling Franciscan habits, since many pious Spaniards liked to die in the habit of a friar. Very considerable sums were collected by begging (one estimate suggested about 53,000,000 *reals* a year) and in addition there were special local collections such as a tax on wheat, which went to St James's Compostella, or a tax on sheep going through the province of Salamanca, which went to one chapel. In addition certain localities made gifts, sometimes in kind, to local religious houses. At Tolosa the local authorities supplied the monks with wood and, in return, the monks provided the town with a preacher in Lent. The clergy were exempt from the *alcabala* and paid *millones* only at a reduced rate. Many ambitious priests left country livings as soon as they could and hung about cathedral towns or in Madrid hoping for preferment. The greatest prize was a canon's stall in some cathedral for, as their critics alleged, the canons did not baptise or marry, confess, bury, teach or administer. Their only duty was to appear regularly in the cathedral for divine service and even here they often left the actual intoning to paid choral singers. Among those priests who did not manage to get a canon's stall many were content to live comfortably on their tithes, leaving the administration of the parish to a curate and the preaching to a friar. Many of the priests were ignorant, for not every diocese in Spain had by the eighteenth century complied with the requirements laid down at the Council of Trent by setting up a seminary. The selection of a priest for a country parish was often a farce. The Council of Trent had laid down that there was to be a competition. In eighteenth-century Spain the candidates were often chosen before the contest 'as though they had been fore-ordained by God'.[1] Yet many of the members of the Society of Jesus were learned, and the Spanish bishops were by no means so aristocratic or so worldly as those of France. Philip V, for example, appointed the son of a charcoal-burner to be archbishop of Toledo, and many of the other prelates were of relatively humble birth. The preaching friars were much beloved and in the eighteenth century there does not seem to have been the strange mixture of religious fanaticism and political anti-clericalism which was later to be the characteristic of Spain. In the eighteenth century the influence of the pulpit and confessional was very powerful in Spain, and although there were saintly and philanthropic prelates interested in promoting economic reform, who set up model farms and popularised up-to-date agricultural machinery, the more usual role of the churchmen was symbolised by the monk, whose horizon was bounded by the walls of his cloister and who recoiled in horror from any contact with the secular world. Churchmen who had not renounced the world were concerned to build magnificent and costly churches such as the cathedrals at Cadiz, at Lerida and at Vich, the convent of San Francisco el Grande in Madrid or the church of St Mary in San Sebastian. They organised magnificent spectacles and led imposing processions to mark Holy Week or Corpus Christi Day. But they also tended to encourage the laity in conservatism and superstition; to the reforming energy of the new French dynasty the clergy throughout Spain gave very little help and were for the most part nothing but an impediment.

The same apathy, if not actual hostility, to reform was as characteristic of most of the Spanish nobility as of most of the men of religion. Even

---

[1] A statement made in 1776, quoted by Desdevises du Dezert, 'La Societé espagnole au 18ème siècle', in *Revue hispanique*, vol. LXIV, p. 328.

at the end of the eighteenth century the nobility amounted to almost 5 per cent of the whole population, being 500,000 as compared with 191,101 religious. In the provinces of Biscay and Guipuzcoa everyone claimed to be of noble descent. There were 'gentlemen' whose nobility was recognised only in their own village. There were others whose title to gentility was that they had begotten seven male children in succession, but however poor these *hidalgos* might be they were exempt from conscription for military service; they were not expected to have troops billeted on them; they could not be arrested for debt; they might have a coat of arms carved over their door and they expected to be addressed by the title of 'Don'. Various lucrative posts were also open to them by reason of their birth. The ordinary *hidalgos*, no less than the 500 titled nobility of Castile and the 119 grandees of Spain, were eligible for office in one of the military orders. The Order of St James had eighty-seven *comanderias*, one of which was worth 206,971 *reals* a year and five of which were worth more than 100,000 *reals* each. The Order of Calatrava had fifty-five such posts, six of which were worth more than 100,000 *reals* a year. The Order of Alcantara had thirty-seven, of which the best was worth 178,096 *reals*. Even the less wealthy Aragonese Order of Montesa had thirteen *comanderias* of which the poorest was worth 12,348 *reals*. The king could distribute these offices as he chose and by the eighteenth century they involved no inconvenient vows of chastity or indeed any serious obligations on the noble who was fortunate enough to become entitled to the income (or to part of the income, for the king sometimes granted part of the income of one of these offices to one man and part to another). The nobility could also hope for some place at court; a formal, ostentatious and oppressively dull world in which the chief excitements were a royal birthday, when the nobility filed past the king and queen to kiss hands, or a royal wedding when there might be illuminations and fireworks. The reports of travellers all confirm the tedium of court society in eighteenth-century Spain. There were plays and occasionally operas or concerts and there was also hunting, but there was very little conversation. French visitors were struck by the ignorance of the Spanish noblemen. The grandees talked about the battles fought by their ancestors, but it was very improbable that they had any idea where these battles had taken place. Of the seventy-six grandees described by the abbé de Vayrac most were remarkable only for their names, their titles and their riches. These men offered no resistance to the establishment of an effective absolutist government in Spain, but hardly any of them did anything to assist in the regeneration of their country. Indeed, the system of landholding, by which part, at least, of a noble estate had to pass by a system of entail to the eldest male child, has been criticised, by Jovellanos among others, as one of the principal causes of the decay of Spanish agriculture. The heir who inherited land under an entail could not sell it. He could not even

THE WESTERN MEDITERRANEAN AND ITALY

pledge it to raise money to carry out urgent improvements. That entails did not always sap the enterprise of rural proprietors can be seen in England, but in Spain the rural nobility was as completely apathetic as the nobility of the court was solemnly preoccupied with questions of precedence and punctilio.

The townspeople, the professional men, merchants and officials were those who, by the end of the eighteenth century, had benefited most from the rule of the Bourbons, but in 1713 these classes offered little sign of vitality. The towns were small and for the most part poor except for churches, convents and charitable institutions run by the Church. Houses were poor, bare and, by the standards of other parts of western Europe, uncomfortable. The fashions of the seventeenth century persisted longer in Spain than elsewhere in western Europe and garments were usually dark in colour and severe in cut. Food was very simple and, by French standards, barbarously cooked. The chief occupation of the women was to go to church; that of the men was to attend to their business and to spend a great deal of time meeting, talking and smoking. A sympathetic observer might stress the tranquillity,

the landed proprietors lived comfortably enough, the artisan had work, the beggar found relief at the door of the convents, taxes were in proportion to one's resources. The priest was respected, the ecclesiastical hierarchy was more brilliant than ever, the throne was bravely defended. Public authority, without being tyrannical, protected...the man of property by punishing what deserved to be punished. The will of the king made itself felt everywhere; a single authority commanded and all obeyed....We lived happily and at peace...respecting in human things the authority of the King and in spiritual things the august power of God.[1]

A more critical observer might well have applied to the Spaniard of the early eighteenth century what was written of the Guatemalan in 1797,

this man...who says little and thinks less, or perhaps it were truer to say does not think at all, who is satisfied to follow what others have thought out before him and what experience has shown to be true. His way of life is uniform, regular, unchanging; he will never change; you will never make him discuss anything which might induce him to change. When the advantages or rather the necessity of change becomes inescapable his only guide is custom and his only rule of conduct is habit.[2]

Such was the attitude of mind usual in the towns of Spain from Bilbao to Cadiz. The ideas of the country people were even less favourable to reform of any kind.

That reforms were carried through in spite of all these obstacles while the Bourbon kings were ruling Spain in the eighteenth century is, however, certain. When Charles II died in 1700, Spain had an army of 20,000, her fleet consisted of twenty ships and her finances were in ruin. By 1800 she had an army of 100,000, a fleet of 300 ships and a treasure of 650 million *reals*. Her population had increased during the century from

---

[1] M. Fernández, *La Hacienda de nuestros abuelos*, p. 2.
[2] *Gazeta de Guatemala*, 20 February 1797.

5,700,000 to 10,541,000 At intervals she had been able to pursue a vigorous foreign policy which had enabled her to recover for Spanish princes, if not for the Crown of Spain, some of the Italian territories lost at the Treaty of Utrecht. Most of the conspicuous reforms were made in the latter part of the century during the reign of Charles III, but some important steps had been taken before 1759, and this is remarkable because neither Philip V nor Ferdinand VI was in any sense a reformer. The problem of Spanish regeneration during the first half of the eighteenth century is: how was it initiated and continued when the throne was occupied first by a hypochrondriac and then by a nonentity? It may even be said that the first reforming autocrat of Spain was Louis XIV. In his instructions to the French ambassador Marsin in 1701 Louis wrote: 'It would appear as if the monarchs of Spain since Charles V had tried by their bad conduct to destroy their realm rather than to preserve it.'[1] Philip V came to Spain with French experts in his train and thenceforward there were at court men who knew how things were done in France. Sometimes the chief office of State might be held by a Spaniard such as Portocarero, but in the background were officials trained in the traditions of Colbert. For the next six years, though interrupted by brief palace revolutions, the Frenchman Orry did much to enable Spain to finance the long war fought to resist the claim of the Austrian archduke to the throne. One of the first reforms was to abolish many of the extravagant offices, concessions, pensions and grants which had been made in previous reigns. In 1703 there were further attempts at economy and simplification. Orry was never in a position to inaugurate a comprehensive scheme of reform. All he could do was to make the ramshackle administrative and financial system of Spain work more efficiently. There were now no favourites to squander the country's resources. Orry saw that the taxes were collected more efficiently and honestly. Somehow as a result of his reforms the Crown managed to raise enough money to pay the troops until the campaign of 1710–11 decided Philip's hold on Spain. The war was expensive and destructive, especially in Catalonia, but in some ways it did much to encourage reforms in Spain. The fact that the country had been able to fight a war, to eject a foreign invader, and to make good her claim to choose her own king had a considerable effect in rousing the Spaniards from their lethargy and fatalism. The energy and bravery shown by the king when he went to his possessions in Italy, his courage and constancy in face of serious military reverses, the energy, good sense and courage of the young queen, Marie Louise of Savoy, all increased Spanish self-respect. In later life Philip might for long periods degenerate into a hypochondriac imbecile who refused to be washed or to have clean linen on his bed and who lay gazing into vacancy with a finger in his mouth, but

---

[1] *Recueil des Instructions données aux Ambassadeurs...de France*, XII, *Espagne*, ed. A. Morel et H. Léonardon (Fatio, 1898), p. 6.

even this could not quench what his courage and enterprise had aroused in Spaniards before 1714; after 1714 he had already passed under the control of his second wife, the dominating Elizabeth Farnese whose ambition for the next thirty-two years supplied the driving energy that forced further reforms in Spain.

Elizabeth Farnese was in no sense a reformer, but she had immense energy and indefatigable ambition. She never left the side of her uxorious husband and favoured those advisers who could produce from Spain the resources which were needed to establish Don Carlos and Don Philip in Italy. Alberoni was more than an adventurous diplomat.[1] His energy was prodigious and, as he said himself, it made the Spaniards shudder. He came to power when Spain's revenue had been increased by almost a third by the more effective control of Aragon, Valencia and Catalonia, and her expenditure reduced by a half by the loss of costly possessions in Flanders and Italy.[2] He realised how much Spanish administration could be improved by a process of centralisation. It was he who effectively reduced the power of the councils in the government of Spain. In his time the post of Counsellor of State became purely honorific. In an attempt to increase the royal revenue he not only continued Orry's policy of cutting down pensions and getting rid of abuses in the collection of taxes, but he did what he could to encourage trade. He began to reform the tariff system so as to keep out foreign manufacturers. At the same time he did a little to encourage manufacturers in Spain. In 1718 he set up a printing press and at Guadalajara he established a cloth works. He also continued the policy, begun by Orry, of attracting foreign craftsmen to Spain. Alberoni exempted them from taxes on food. In 1718 he also experimented with the idea of sending single register ships to the Indies instead of waiting for the annual fleet. But his chief achievement was to build up a new Spanish fleet. He set up a naval college at Cadiz, made special arrangements for recruiting sailors and established two shipyards, one in Galicia and another in Catalonia. He did something to enable goods to circulate more freely inside Spain, and it was during his brief period of power that an experiment was made to reform the system of taxation. In Valencia revenue had hitherto been raised by a 5 per cent tax on retail sales, by a 5 per cent duty on all merchandise or produce entering the country, and by another 5 per cent tax on certain specified goods. In 1717 all these taxes were abolished except for the customs duties to be levied at the sea ports. A single tax on salt was substituted. This had a very beneficial effect on Valencian production and the number of looms rose from 300 in 1717 to 2000 in 1722.

[1] E. Bourgeois, *Lettres intimes adressées au Comte I. Rocca* (1892), gives useful material for correcting the common interpretation of Alberoni as the initiator of an aggressive policy.
[2] Bubb to Stanhope, 19 Feb. 1716. Brit. Museum Egerton MSS. 2171, fol. 136. B. J. Roud has provided this information.

Ripperda's contribution to the recovery of Spain was largely by his diplomatic effrontery, which enabled her for a time to ally with her old enemy the Emperor and set the chanceries of Europe in a turmoil. But he had some very interesting schemes for restoring Spanish prosperity. Perhaps it was because he had been born and educated in the United Provinces that Ripperda was so interested in trade. On the fall of Alberoni in 1719 he was put in charge of the royal manufactures and he favoured the establishment of cloth works in Segovia and the introduction of foreign craftsmen. He is supposed to have had a scheme for developing Spain's trade with the Indies, and he is said to have suggested ways of reducing English smuggling and even of getting the English to relinquish their newly acquired right under the *Asiento* to supply negro slaves to the Spanish colonies. He hoped that the king of Spain would introduce a policy of economic protection to revive Spanish industry which, he thought, might be still further promoted by the establishment of a Bank of Spain. He is supposed to have claimed that by these measures the king of Spain would be able to maintain an army of 130,000 men, a fleet of 100 ships and to enjoy a revenue of two million *écus*.

In 1727 Ripperda fell before he could attempt to put his economic projects into practice, but he was soon followed by a man who was able to foster Spanish economic life so well that, whereas the royal revenue had been 142 million *reals* in 1700, by 1737 it was 211 millions. Don José Patiño was born in the duchy of Milan of a Spanish family which had been connected with army finance and provisioning. He had studied theology and thought of becoming a Jesuit. He later studied law. A temporary administrative post in his native State during the War of the Spanish Succession brought him to the notice of the French allies of Philip V, and in 1707 the king of Spain appointed him a member of the *Consejo de Ordenes Militares*. He did not hold the post for long, however, for he was sent off as *intendant* of Estremadura. Here Patiño began to gain a reputation. The province was drained even of its normally very poor resources by the war with Portugal, yet the new *intendant* managed to restore order among the troops and even to pay them by improving the system of taxation. Patiño was transferred to Catalonia, where his rigorous economies and his efficiency materially contributed to the military successes of Philip V. While he was there Patiño mastered the technicalities of naval construction. In 1717 he was sent to Cadiz as a military and naval *intendant* and president of the *Casa de Contratacion* to revive the fleet. There Patiño achieved considerable success. He found the ships rotting at anchor and not a cauldron of tar to caulk their seams; after three months the ships for the trade with Buenos Ayres, Havana and Vera Cruz were at sea. Patiño had also established an arsenal really capable of producing ordnance. He had also enlarged his experience of finance, for he had been appointed by Alberoni the head of a commission of Spanish and English merchants which had been set up under the Treaty of Utrecht to discuss tariff reforms. The work of the commission was interrupted by war, but Patiño may have gained some insight into Anglo-Spanish trade which would later be most useful. Patiño moved from Cadiz to Barcelona, fitted out the *Principe de Asturias* in a fortnight and it was largely thanks to his work that in 1717 a fleet of thirteen ships was able to sail for Sardinia. A year later Spain was able to dispatch twenty-two ships of the line, three armed merchantmen and 300 transports to attack Sicily. Patiño, *intendant* in Sicily, had to ruin the fleet which Patiño, *intendant* at Cadiz, had created. He obeyed Alberoni only under protest, but after the failure of the Sicilian venture Patiño for some years was under a cloud. He was restored to his intendancy at Cadiz, but two successive Ministers of Marine distrusted and disliked him. Ripperda also disliked him and Patiño was threatened with what he looked on as exile in a foreign embassy.

While Patiño was in Madrid waiting for instructions Ripperda fell. Patiño's friends used their influence and in 1727 he became Minister for Marine and the Indies. Three months later he was put in charge of the finances of the kingdom. During the crisis of 1729–32 he was given the additional burden of Chief Secretary of State, for their Catholic Majesties thought him abler than La Paz. During his tenure of office Patiño managed to build up another navy to replace the one lost off Sicily. The measure of his success is that in 1732 a fleet of 600 ships sailed from Alicante and conquered Oran. The arsenals and dockyards at Cadiz and at Havana were able to fit out ships. The sailors were paid. The college set up to train officers had, before the end of the reign, produced two eminent men: Don Jorge Juan and Don Bernardo Ulloa. Patiño also managed to collect far greater sums from Spanish America than had been found possible by his predecessors. He insisted that the colonial governors should send a regular contribution every year, and South Sea Company factors later reported that one excuse offered for not paying debts owing to the Company was the necessity of sending a sum annually to Spain. Patiño also extracted as much money as possible from each annual trading fleet. In 1728, by altering the value of the coinage, he was able to get one-third of the galleons' treasure instead of the usual quarter. In 1729 he imposed an extra 4 per cent duty on cargoes brought from the Indies and at least 2 per cent of this was expected to go to the Crown. 'By all the little tricks that a thorough knowledge of the whole detail could suggest to him (he) got His Catholic Majesty as great a share of these effects as he possibly could'.[1] In 1731 the Cadiz merchants agreed to lend the king 200,000 pieces of eight. In the same year Patiño prevailed on the merchants to agree that the tax on goods from the Indies should be raised from 5 per cent to 8 per cent. He did not raise the duty again but contented himself

[1] Cayley to Newcastle, 25 August 1729. P.R.O., S.P.F., Sp. 219.

with forcing the merchants to send fleets regularly to the Indies. Patiño was not interested in whether the merchants could expect a good market for their commodities: he wanted cargoes brought to Spain so that he could collect the tax for the royal treasury. He was never in a position to put through comprehensive reforms. He was always trying to find the money needed to satisfy Elizabeth Farnese's political ambitions or Philip V's grandiose schemes for building a second Versailles at San Ildefonso. Certainly the royal revenue increased from 142 million *reals* under Charles II to 211 million *reals* in 1737. The chief merit of Patiño was that he, like Orry and Alberoni, managed to ensure that the ambitions of Elizabeth Farnese and Philip V were never thwarted by lack of ships or lack of money.

The country which was the focus of Elizabeth Farnese's ambition was Italy. To observers in the early eighteenth century Italy seemed an extraordinarily attractive place. 'All who have been led by curiosity or by business to Italy are unanimously agreed' that no more just description of the country can be given 'than to call it by the name of garden'.[1] To the traveller in the early eighteenth century the passage over the Alps was both alarming and unattractive. After trembling to see the road bordered by a precipice, after struggling to climb what seemed inaccessible heights, after freezing among eternal snows and having been mortally bored by seeing nothing but desolation and 'des objets hideux'[2] the traveller found Italy a terrestrial paradise. The air was mild, the climate was reputed to be the best in Europe, the countryside—at least in the north—was extremely fertile. The country seemed a 'garden planted with orange trees'.[3] The number of towns and the magnificence of their buildings made the traveller think Italy incomparable. To a sober, well-informed traveller in the mid-eighteenth century like the German Bielfeld, Italy appeared both prosperous and progressive, and it is easy to understand why, even apart from family pride and maternal ambition, Elizabeth Farnese was prepared to struggle tenaciously to obtain Italian possessions for her sons. To Bielfeld and other travellers the industry of the Italians completed what nature had begun. The wines of Italy were famous throughout Europe. Oranges, lemons and other fruits were sure of a market in the north. Italian olive oil, then as now, was highly esteemed. Fish was abundant and the Italians knew how to preserve it. Quarries produced fine marbles which were used not only to add to the magnificence of Italian buildings but which were in demand among kings and nobles all over Europe. Italy produced the finest silk in the world. Her velvets,

[1] Bielfeld, *Institutions Politiques*, vol. III (1774), p. 269.
[2] *Ibid.* p. 269.
[3] *Ibid.* pp. 269–70. Bielfeld is said to have drafted the work in 1757 though the last volume only appeared posthumously.

stockings, gauzes and a hundred other things were of excellent workmanship and foreigners thronged to buy them. The only economic weakness noticed by Bielfeld was that Italy could not produce enough corn to supply her needs, but this was made up by imports from Sicily, from the Greek archipelago and from Africa. He also observed that the Italians were indifferent sailors and that they left commerce to more maritime nations. But as against these weaknesses he recorded their flourishing cultural life. In the mid-eighteenth century the fine arts still made Italy their capital. Painting, sculpture, architecture, music, had all achieved the highest degree of perfection in Italy. Science and letters were no less cultivated than the arts. The eighteenth-century traveller perceived numerous universities, academies and scholars of distinction dispersed among a large number of towns. These eulogies of Italy and particularly of Rome were echoed by Goethe, but they did not take into account the miserable condition of the peasants, the prevalence of crime even in such cities as Venice and Rome, the brutalities and complications of the Law, or the superstition and intolerance of the Church.

Italy in the eighteenth century was a land of violent contrasts, of great wealth and great poverty, and this contrast was made to appear more brutal because, in spite of the apparently large number of towns, there was not a very considerable middle class. In the south, most of which was covered by the kingdom of Naples, conditions were very different from the terrestrial paradise which greeted travellers who crossed the Alps into the Lombard Plain. The south, and more particularly the provinces now known as Apulia, Lucania and Calabria, was very largely rural. The little towns such as Lecce or Brindisi were sleepy and poor, the soil was infertile, the climate could be harshly, parchingly hot, water was scarce, trees were few. Malaria was endemic and had sapped all energy from the peasants. Even today it is a proverb in Lucania that Christ never got any farther south than Eboli, and in the early eighteenth century the condition of the peasants in the kingdom of Naples was even more miserable. Peasants had to sell their produce to their lord. They were tried in their lord's courts. Conditions in the papal states, which stretched from south of Rome to just south of Venice, were not much better. In nearly every State in Italy the Church presented a peculiarly difficult problem. The kingdom of Naples is a particularly striking example: there the Church owned something like one-third of all land. In a country with a population of about 5,000,000 there were 50,000 monks and nuns, 50,000 priests, 165 bishops and twenty-one archbishops. The annual income of the Church was about 12,000,000 *ducats*, and in a country where the squalor was unsurpassed in Europe the great ecclesiastics lived in ostentatious luxury and paid no taxes. In Tuscany the Grand Duke Cosimo III, who died in 1723, had regarded it as a point of honour to have in his dominions at least one convent for every existing religious order. In Piedmont the activity of the Inquisition enforced a rigid orthodoxy, so that writers such as Baretti or Alfieri left the country. Habits in many parts of Italy were barbarous. The nobles in the kingdom of Naples maintained armed bands which could be used equally well to cow the peasantry or overawe representatives of the central authority. In the papal States in the one decade between 1759 and 1769 there were 13,000 homicides. In elegant and fashionable Milan crimes of violence were frequent. In Venice between 1741 and 1762 73,000 people were either executed or sent to the galleys for life. Legal punishments were brutal, and torture was a usual part of criminal procedure. And yet in spite of poverty, oppression and ecclesiastical censorship there was a stirring in the intellectual life of Italy after 1713 which was caused perhaps by the removal of Spanish control over Naples and the Milanese. Vico, Beccaria, Alexandro and Pietro Verri, Genevesi (one of the earliest professors of political economy in Europe), Filangieri (who wrote a history of legislation), Pagano, Delfico, Galanti and Galiani all showed that intellectual activity in Italy was not dead.

This world of the Italian States was very considerably modified during the eighteenth century: partly by the Peace of Utrecht, which removed Naples and Milan from Spain and put them under the government of the Habsburg emperor, and still further as a result of the activities of Elizabeth Farnese. By 1748 she had established Don Carlos as king of Naples and Sicily, and Don Philip as duke of Parma. By way of compensation for the loss of Naples the Habsburgs had been given the right of succession in Tuscany. Piedmont was compensated for the loss of Sicily by being given Sardinia. These changes, which were complete by 1748, had been brought about by thirty-five years of tortuous diplomacy and five wars. At the end of the War of the Spanish Succession in 1713, the Great Powers agreed to recognise Philip of Anjou as Philip V of Spain and the Indies, but they refused to recognise him as the ruler of Milan, Naples, Sardinia and Sicily which since the sixteenth century had belonged to the Spanish Crown. Milan, Naples and Sardinia went to compensate the Emperor for not having been recognised as king of Spain. Sicily went to the duke of Savoy in return for his services to the allied cause during the war, though his adherence to the cause had been extremely wavering. It is characteristic of opinion among the Italian princes at this time that they preferred to see the aggrandisement of the Habsburgs rather than of Savoy, and this jealousy among the Italians favoured the Habsburgs throughout the eighteenth century. In 1717 Elizabeth Farnese launched an armed raid on Sardinia, and in 1718 another against Sicily. The Great Powers of England, France and the Emperor acted together and Spain was defeated, but it was then decided that the Emperor should cede Sardinia to Savoy in exchange for Sicily.

The next change in the political map of the Italian states took place when Elizabeth Farnese pressed the claims of her eldest son, Don Carlos, to the Farnese lands of Parma and Piacenza and to the Grand Duchy of Tuscany when the last of the Medici, who had no male heir, should die. This scheme Elizabeth pursued through the international Congress of Cambrai. It inspired the Diplomatic Revolution of 1725, when Spain electrified the courts of Europe by concluding an alliance with her erstwhile enemy the Emperor. When the Emperor showed that he would not risk a general war to realise Elizabeth's plan, she discredited Ripperda, who had negotiated the alliance, and concluded the Treaty of Seville in 1729 with England and France. In 1731, on the death of the last Farnese duke of Parma, these two countries supported the introduction of Don Carlos into the Duchy. In 1733 a general war broke out over the Polish Succession, and Elizabeth Farnese used this as a pretext for Don Carlos to attack Austrian forces and establish himself on the throne of Naples. This conquest was confirmed by the Treaty of Vienna in 1735, by which the Habsburgs, in compensation for Naples and Sicily, were given the reversion of Tuscany which was promised to Francis of Lorraine, the husband of Maria Theresa. The War of the Austrian Succession[1] gave Elizabeth Farnese another opportunity to acquire territory for her sons, and by the Peace of Aix-la-Chapelle in 1748 Parma and Piacenza were ceded to Don Philip.

The effect on Italy of these changes in government were on the whole beneficial. Milan, which in 1713 exchanged Spanish rule for Austrian, was on the whole better governed. Long-stifled ideas of freedom began to stir once more in the *salons* of Milan and in the University of Pavia. Gradually feudal privileges and exemptions were reduced. Local government was simplified, and the finances were reformed: in 1757 a single, uniform tax on land was introduced which encouraged intensive cultivation and increased the prosperity of Lombardy. Under the future Joseph II some attempt was made to reform the Church, and as many as a hundred convents and monasteries were suppressed. The Concordats of 1757 and 1784 allowed ecclesiastical property acquired since the sixteenth century to become liable to taxation. Milan in the eighteenth century provided the society in which Beccaria and other reformers could meet and discuss their projects. Tuscany, under Joseph's brother Leopold, became one of the best-ruled States in Europe. Serfdom was abolished, the criminal code was revised, torture and secret trials were prohibited, internal customs barriers were removed, and guilds were abolished. The Inquisition was suppressed and ecclesiastical jurisdiction was limited to spiritual matters. Naples and Sicily presented a more difficult problem, for there the Church and the nobility were very powerful, but Charles, with the help of the enthusiastic reforming lawyer Bernardo Tanucci, achieved considerable successes. By a Concordat of 1741 he remedied the worst ecclesiastical

---

[1] For the Anglo-Spanish friction which led up to a declaration of war between these two powers in 1739 see ch. IX.

abuses. Ecclesiastics were made liable to taxation though at only half the rate paid by the laity. Gradually the number of ecclesiastics was reduced from 100,000 to 81,000. In the field of law Tanucci achieved considerable progress. Procedure was made less brutal, and the feudal jurisdiction of the nobility was restricted, but even Tanucci could not produce a complete new code and the Neapolitans continued to be ruled under a mixture of eleven different systems. In finance Charles managed to buy back some of the taxes which had been collected by farmers. He also introduced a uniform tax on property and made a beginning in the task of fostering foreign trade. In Parma and Piacenza after 1748 the court became a centre of French culture, and the Bourbon duke showed considerable spirit in resisting papal claims of suzerainty. Don Philip was even able to abolish clerical immunities.

In the rest of Italy, where there had been no change of government, things went on as they had during the seventeenth century. Venice drowsed beside her lagoons, waking to celebrate the carnival or admire the latest comedy of Goldoni, but with no effective interest in politics. Genoa remembered that her safety depended on a strict observance of her neutrality. In Rome Clement XI did pioneer work as a penal reformer of the Roman prison of San Michele. Benedict XIII, a man of great personal piety, prohibited gambling and wigs, but left the conduct of politics to Coscia because he had himself a total lack of experience in secular affairs. Clement XII was old and infirm and for the last eight years of his pontificate from 1732 he was blind. Benedict XIV, who occupied the papal throne from 1740 to 1758, was genial and witty and a great patron of the arts. Horace Walpole described him as 'loved by Papists, esteemed by Protestants, a priest without insolence or interest, a Prince without favourites, a Pope without nephews'.[1] He concluded a series of concordats which convinced the anti-clerical reformers that the Papacy was powerless. Clement XIII, who succeeded Benedict in 1758 and reigned till 1769, had neither the skill to avoid nor the ability to control the storm which was beginning to threaten the Society of Jesus. Rome remained one of the most honourable courts at which to be accredited ambassador, but the popes of the eighteenth century cut no figure in international diplomacy and they did hardly anything to improve conditions within their own States. In the north of Italy, Savoy, or the kingdom of Sardinia as it was called after 1720, remained rather isolated from the main stream of Italian developments. The rulers of the house of Savoy had played a dangerous diplomatic game for very high stakes. They had emerged in 1713 with greatly increased territories to which in 1720 they added the title of king. Victor Amadeus had no desire to curb the power of his nobles or restrict the oppressive activities of the Holy Church and the Holy Inquisition.

The garden with its orange groves and its balmy air so admired by

[1] Quoted in the *Cambridge Modern History* (1934 ed.), vol. VI, p. 589.

German travellers was indeed a delightful place and many of its inhabitants were beginning to revive under the rule of the Austrian Habsburgs and the Bourbons. But those States which did not pass under their control still contained, during most of the eighteenth century, horrible examples of squalor, superstition, and feudal oppression.

With the death of Philip V of Spain in 1746, Elizabeth Farnese ceased to direct Spanish policy and Spain ceased to have any further designs on territories in Italy. A spectacular change came over Spain's foreign policy. The melancholy Ferdinand VI had not even his father's interest in military affairs; still less had his asthmatic and childless wife, Barbara of Braganza, the energy and ambition of Elizabeth Farnese. The new monarchs were not much interested in foreign affairs or indeed in domestic reform. Their only genuine interest was in music, and they made Farinelli, whose songs had beguiled the melancholia of Philip V, superintendent of the court theatres. Ferdinand was much under the influence of his Jesuit confessor, Father Ravajo, who regularly conveyed to him the advice of a small committee of the Society of Jesus. In matters of foreign policy Ferdinand was generally pacific, and after the conclusion of the Peace of Aix-la-Chapelle in 1748 he was content to follow the system worked out by his minister Don José de Carvajal y Lancaster. Carvajal has left a key to his policy in two political testaments written respectively in 1745, before he had been given office, and in 1753, the year before he died. For Carvajal the fundamental consideration was that Spain was at once a European and a colonial power. Like Patiño he hoped to be able to develop the resources of Spanish America, and he hoped that wealth from this source might be used to realise his pet project of reviving Spanish industry. In Carvajal's opinion any power suitable as an ally must have maritime strength and must be prepared to keep other nations from smuggling in Spanish America. Like most of his contemporaries Carvajal visualised the Continent of Europe as a balance in which swung France and Austria, and he thought that the object of all policy should be to hold the balance steady and so prevent war. This he hoped to do by increasing the strength of Spain to such an extent that she could hold the balance steady. He was convinced that the best way to achieve this recovery of Spanish power would be by industrial reform at home: the conclusion of foreign alliances was only a supplementary measure. Among the European powers Carvajal favoured an alliance with Portugal, since a good understanding with that country would leave Spain with only one frontier to guard. France had betrayed Spain too often, and the two kings were rivals for the domination of Christendom. Moreover, Carvajal believed that because of the close family ties between the two royal houses it would be possible for the two Crowns to remain on good terms without concluding an alliance. The Emperor was often the object of attack and had no navy, so that an alliance with him offered no attraction. Holland was too weak for her help to counterbalance the enormous illicit trade in the Indies that must be tolerated if she became Spain's ally. Prussia was still, in the opinion of Carvajal, the satellite of France and she had no fleet. Russia again could be no help in the West Indies. Denmark had possessions in the West Indies, and Campillo, the predecessor of Carvajal, had thought fit to conclude an alliance with that Power, but Carvajal thought Denmark too weak and soon repudiated the alliance. The Italian States, Poland and Sweden were all too weak to be of any use as allies. There remained one Power which was wealthy enough to be formidable in Europe and commercially vigorous in the New World, whose king did not covet any Spanish possessions in the Indies. This Power was England and, in spite of religious differences and a tradition of hostility that had extended from 1588 to 1667 and had continued throughout most of the first half of the eighteenth century, this country seemed to Carvajal the most attractive ally. While Carvajal held office and even after his death in 1754, when Spanish foreign policy was controlled by Richard Wall, Spain pursued a conciliatory policy towards England. A commercial treaty was concluded in 1750 and never had English complaints about seizures in the West Indies been more sympathetically treated. When Ferdinand VI was succeeded by his more energetic half-brother Charles in 1759 this friendly attitude towards England began to change, and disputes over logwood cutters in Honduras and the prizing of Spanish ships by Britain combined with pressure from France to induce Spain to declare war on England. But in the interval between 1748 and 1761 there had been an opportunity for further progress in the revival of the economy of Spain.

Carvajal's desire to revive Spanish industry caused some amusing incidents. No sooner was peace concluded with England than Carvajal sent orders to the Spanish ambassador in London to decoy skilled British artisans to Spain. Men and machinery were sometimes smuggled out of England, though sometimes the ships were interrupted by the British and sometimes the men deserted their new masters and went home. One woollen weaver who did go to Spain was said to be the best man at the work in Europe. But the work of collecting these artisans and shipping them out of England was one that caused the Spanish ambassador acute anxiety. In 1750 the Spanish admiral, Don Jorge Juan, came to London to suborn shipwrights. The English authorities became suspicious and Don Jorge had to escape disguised as a common sailor pulling an oar in the captain's boat to join a Biscayan ship which happened most opportunely to be leaving the Thames. This ended Carvajal's attempts to recruit British workmen through the Spanish embassy. The advantages to Spanish industry were few and the risks were disproportionately great. After 1750 skilled foreign workmen were obtained privately for the most part through Irishmen already in the service of the king of Spain. At each of the great naval bases at Cadiz, Cartagena and Ferrol, there grew up an Irish faction. Mullins at Cadiz even went so far as to fit out a fleet to carry immigrant Irishmen as well as legitimate cargoes.

More serious and more far-reaching than Carvajal's efforts to get new blood for Spanish industry were the reforms of the marquis de la Ensenada. Recalled to Spain from Italy on the death of the reforming minister Campillo in 1743, Ensenada was made Minister of Finance, War, Marine and the Indies. Up till this time his chief experience had been of naval affairs. His first post, at the age of 18, had been in the Ministry of Marine. In 1730 he had been appointed Contador Mayor of Cartegena. In 1733 he had sailed with the fleet that helped to conquer Naples, and it was in return for these services that he had been created marquis by Charles of Naples in 1736. On his return to Spain Ensenada did much to improve the arsenals at Cartagena and Caracca, and to make Cadiz a first-class naval base. He also did something to improve the methods of obtaining volunteers to serve in the navy, and he wrote a famous memoir in 1751 explaining how the decay of maritime trade and of fisheries had caused the collapse of the Spanish navy. Ensenada was interested in many other sides of Spanish life. He was the first minister to devote serious attention to the roads, and he built one over the Guadarama to link the two Castiles. In 1749 he did much to get rid of abuses in the customs service when he forbade customs officials to purloin a share of various cargoes of foodstuffs carried in Spanish vessels. Undoubtedly Ensenada did much to revive the economic life of Spain. But he was also much given to writing long reports and to drawing up schemes which were never put into effect. He had a project for producing a unified code of law. He did a great deal of work to prepare the way for a single tax which should replace all the complexities of Spanish imports. A commission was appointed to investigate the facts, but before the investigations were complete Ensenada issued a decree in 1749 to put this single tax into effect. The scheme was not understood and the decree remained one of those annotated by Spanish officials 'obeyed but not carried into effect'. In 1754 Ensenada fell from power, and though he returned on the accession of Charles III he was soon once more dismissed. Many of his grandiose schemes remained on paper, but he had continued the reforms of Orry, Patiño and Campillo, and his numerous reports prepared the way for much more penetrating examinations by the ministers of Charles III.

But with the accession of Charles III in 1759, and more particularly after the restoration of peace in 1763, a new phase begins in the Bourbon reforms. Under Philip V and Ferdinand VI reforms had been attempted largely under the pressure of diplomatic and naval necessity. Neither of the early Bourbons had been in any sense an enlightened despot. But Charles III was a king really interested in reform and with twenty years' experience in Naples behind him. His achievements and those of his ministers are deservedly famous,[1] and might have put Spain back among the Great Powers of Europe, if he had had an heir as able as himself, if the country had not become engulfed first in the Napoleonic War and then in civil wars, and if Spain had also possessed the material resources which enabled the countries of northern Europe to take a leap forward in prosperity and power in an industrial revolution.

In the first half of the eighteenth century when Spain, inspired by a new dynasty, by the queen's ambition and by the vision and hard work of a series of able ministers, was reviving: when some, at least, of the Italian States, encouraged by the reforming rule of Bourbon and Habsburg princes, were stirring from their long sleep, Portugal, rich with the wealth of Brazil, concentrated on devotional exercises and the production of port. She did not experience reforms until the advent to power of Pombal in 1750.

Portugal was not infertile, but in the eighteenth century she was not able to produce enough grain to meet her own requirements. Some contemporary observers such as Bielfeld were sharply critical of the condition of Portugal. It was asserted by some contemporary travellers that out of a population of about 3,000,000 an extraordinarily high percentage were ecclesiastics. It was certain that a large number were gentlemen and, as such, completely idle. Some were employed overseas, others in long voyages to the Indies or to Brazil. Religious intolerance made Portugal unattractive to foreigners. It was said that the climate was unfavourable to begetting children and that Portuguese women were not long fit for childbearing, so it was hardly to be wondered at that the number of men available for agriculture, industry, trade or learning was very small. In the middle of the century Portuguese industry hardly existed. Some dried fruits and sweets were manufactured, some artificial flowers and other fancy goods were made in convents, but otherwise Portugal manufactured very little. Yet because of her port 'which had become almost a necessity to the English',[2] her imports from her empire and especially the gold which flowed steadily in from Brazil during the eighteenth century, Portugal was wealthy. Part of this wealth was spend on building Mafra, and part John V used to obtain privileges from the pope. In 1716 he obtained the right to convert his court chapel into a patriarchate. In 1739 the pope agreed that the new patriarchate should always enjoy the rank of cardinal and that the office should be filled by a member of the Portuguese royal family. A special church was built in Lisbon and canons were created and given as their endowment one-quarter of all the benefices of Portugal. Further donations by the king to Rome secured the concession that the new canons should all be cardinals and the patriarch should enjoy

[1] For details of his foreign policy 1759–63 see ch. IX.
[2] Bielfeld, *Institutions Politiques*, vol. III (1774), p. 7.

almost the status of the sovereign Pontiff himself. In 1749 the king of Portugal sought an additional title comparable to 'His Most Christian Majesty', 'His Catholic Majesty' or 'the Defender of the Faith'. After a good deal of negotiating and further costly gifts he obtained the right to be addressed as 'His Most Faithful Majesty'. Portugal at this time was richer in ecclesiastic establishments than perhaps any country in Europe. It was said that there were nearly 900 religious houses, that the Church not only accounted for nearly half the population but owned something like two-thirds of the land. The three orders of chivalry, the Order of Christ, that of St James and that of Aviz were, like those of Spain, ecclesiastical in character. The first had 454 commanderies, the second 150 and the third forty-nine. The power of the Papacy in Portugal was exceptionally great. The universities of Coimbra, Lisbon and Evora were part of the ecclesiastical order, and the Inquisition was very effective.

The government of Portugal was essentially monarchical, but the Braganzas did not instil any new energy into this country as the Bourbons did in Spain. When Portugal had revolted against Spain in 1640 the movement had been to some extent anti-authoritarian, for one of the Portuguese grievances was that the Spanish king had imposed taxes without the consent of the *Cortes*; but gradually the power of the Portuguese king became almost as great as that of the king of Spain had been. The *Cortes* was dissolved because it had claimed the control of expenditure, and the regent refused the Crown because the *Cortes* had claimed its bestowal. In theory it remained true that the *Cortes* had to be consulted if the Braganza line should fail or if the king wished to impose a new tax. But in fact the Braganzas were blessed with healthy children and while Brazil continued to supply huge sums of gold there was no need to impose any new tax. By the middle of the eighteenth century there had been no meeting of the *Cortes* since 1697. The governmental machinery was comparable with that of any other absolutist monarchy of the early eighteenth century and dated back to the restoration of Portuguese independence. At first the most pressing needs of the new State had been to wage war against Spain. There had been no time for comprehensive reforms of the administration; what reforms were made were done piecemeal. In 1643 a law made clear that the machinery which had worked before the national revolt was to remain in operation. The king had the advice of a Council of State composed of four men. As a matter of urgency a Council of War was created. By decrees of 1641 and 1642 the number of Vedores da Fazenda, who were the financial experts, was increased to three. In 1642 a *Counselho Ultramarino* was set up to deal with most of the business of Portugal's overseas possessions though some of the economic questions were dealt with by the Vedore da Fazenda and religious affairs were the concern of the old-established Mesa de Consciencia, which had been in operation since 1532. All these bodies were purely advisory. All major decisions had to be taken by the king, and in his executive capacity he had the help of Secretaries of State. Originally in the seventeenth century there had only been one of these officials called an *Escrivao da Puridada*, but the work was so enormous that he was soon given a second colleague. Sometimes there was one chief official with secretaries under him, sometimes a powerful man could still combine all the offices in his own person, but in general the tendency in Portugal, as elsewhere, was in the direction of specialisation.

It was as Secretary of State that Pombal put through a series of reforms which in twenty-seven years achieved more spectacular results than had been achieved in half a century in Spain, In 1750 John V died after eight years of imbecility, during which the Government had been carried on by a regency. On the king's death the queen regent summoned Sebastian Joseph de Carvalho e Mello, later marquis de Pombal, to become Secretary of State and direct foreign affairs. The new minister managed to acquire a complete ascendancy over the new king and till the death of Joseph I in 1777 Pombal exercised absolute power in Portugal. Pombal had been ambassador in Vienna and in London and he perceived that by contrast with England Portugal, in spite of her colonial riches, was stagnant and feeble. Pombal was a man of great courage and he did not hesitate at once to attack the Church which had a stranglehold on the intellectual life of the country, was swallowing a large part of the riches from Brazil and was in a position to exercise very strong pressure on Portugal's foreign policy. In 1751 he opened his campaign. In future the Inquisition was not to carry out any *auto da fe* or execution without the approval of the Government. He next attacked the Jesuits. In 1754–5 Jesuits had offered armed resistance to the Spanish decision to cede seven of their missions in exchange for the territory of Nova Colonia which had long been claimed by Spain. The Jesuits had also been very hostile to the company created by Pombal in 1755 to trade to Maranhiao and Pará. Pombal wasted little time. The king's Jesuit confessor was dismissed and Jesuits were forbidden to approach the court. The Portuguese court, which under John V had paid the pope to grant ecclesiastical privileges, now made representations to the Holy Father pointing out the misdoings of the Jesuits in America. In 1758 the pope appointed Cardinal Saldanda as visitor and reformer of the Society of Jesus in the dominions of His Most Faithful Majesty. A month later Saldanda ordered the Jesuits to stop trading and suspended them from preaching and confessing. In January 1759, on evidence brought to light by investigations into an alleged conspiracy to kill the king, all property in Portugal belonging to the Jesuits was sequestrated, and in September the Order was expelled. The Jesuit College at Lisbon was turned into a secular College of Nobles, and Pombal introduced into the University of Coimbra faculties for the study of natural science.

While in process of achieving this astoundingly rapid victory over the

Church Pombal turned against the nobility. In September 1758 an attempt had been made to shoot the king. In December some of the nobles most conspicuous in their opposition to Pombal were arrested. They were found guilty of having instigated the crime and were executed, and it was papers found during this trial that provided Pombal with evidence for his expulsion of the Jesuits. Having broken the power of the only two institutions in Portugal capable of offering effective resistance, Pombal carried through an extensive policy of reform. In 1761 he reformed the system of internal administration, abolishing many useless and expensive offices. He simplified the judicial system. He promoted trade, partly by setting up a company to deal with Marantrao and Para, partly by creating in 1756 an Oporto wine company with the exclusive right to buy all the wine at a fixed price. That this much annoyed the English and excited formidable riots in Oporto in 1757 did not deflect Pombal from his policy of encouraging native Portuguese trade. He built up the navy so that it numbered thirteen ships of war and six frigates. He repaired fortresses and reorganised the army. In his energy and ruthlessness, in his immediate and uncompromising attack on the Church, Pombal has much in common with the Habsburg Joseph II. He is an even better example than Don Carlos, king of Naples, of the reformer who by the middle of the eighteenth century had begun to reorganise every department of life until administration, law, economic life, even the Church, felt the bracing wind of a new age. Portugal, which at the beginning of the eighteenth century had been more stagnant than any country in the western Mediterranean, with the possible exception of Naples, had by 1763 outstripped them all on the road to the efficient absolutism characteristic of the later *ancien régime* of the enlightened despots.

CHAPTER XIII

THE ORGANISATION AND RISE OF PRUSSIA

ETWEEN 1640 and 1786 four generations of Hohenzollern rulers transformed Prussia from a collection of scattered and loosely combined provinces into a European Power. The labours of Ranke, and of the German scholars who continued his work in the Prussian State archives, particularly Schmoller, Hintze and Hartung, have left us in little doubt as to 'how things really were' in the field of internal administration in this century and a half, and the evidence can readily be checked in the well-edited volumes of the *Acta Borussica*. About the personalities of the Great Elector, King Frederick William I and Frederick the Great, and their claims to the admiration and imitation of later generations, the views expressed by historians have naturally been as various as their political backgrounds and ethical convictions, but it is generally agreed that among the presuppositions governing the actions of these monarchs three were never questioned: that kingship is a sacred trust, that authoritarianism is the only rational form of government and that its primary aim is the increase of the power of the State. 'The happiness of the king's subjects does indeed appear alongside power [in the political testament of Frederick the Great], but the spirit which governs the whole system is that of power politics, not welfare legislation.'[1]

To appreciate the achievements of the Prussian rulers we must remember what they started from in 1713. Brandenburg-Prussia was then one of the many composite 'territories' which, along with many smaller and some very small States, went to make up the ramshackle Holy Roman Empire. It was only in the language of diplomacy that the State as a whole was called 'la Prusse'. For the ordinary official the 'Kingdom of Prussia' meant East Prussia, which lay outside the boundaries of the Empire, and the 'King of Prussia' was for Brandenburg 'the Elector', for Pomerania, Magdeburg and Cleve 'the Duke', for Mark and Ravensburg 'the Count' and for Halberstadt and Minden 'the Prince'. These differences in title reflected the history of the gradual growth of the State, through inherited accessions of land rather than by military or diplomatic action. It was normal for a German ruler's authority to be based in this way on a number of different legal titles to scattered possessions, but the more important dynasties had long been striving to imitate the great national States and establish a strong central government in their lands. So in Brandenburg the Great Elector had vigorously asserted his authority over the provincial

---

[1] O. Hintze, *Das politische Testament Friedrichs des Grossen von 1752*, reprinted in *Gesammelte Abhandlungen*, Bd. III, ed. F. Hartung, Leipzig (1943).

'Estates', the lesser nobility and the city corporations which had become so independent of their former feudal superiors during the period of transition to the money-system. Through improvements in the administration of the domain lands and the introduction of a system of indirect taxation (the 'Excise'), as well as by the acceptance of French subsidies, he had made the central power virtually independent financially of the Estates. These innovations had led to the beginnings of a new centralised bureaucracy, side by side with the old officials of the various provinces, and through it much had been done by central direction to strengthen the economic position of the country. All these measures had been co-ordinated with the establishment for the first time of a useful standing army and the pursuit of an ambitious foreign policy, so that in the opinion of Frederick the Great it was the Great Elector who had laid the foundations of Prussian greatness.

But before Prussia could really count as an independent Power in Europe, serious difficulties had to be overcome which resulted from the geographical disposition of its provinces, their low economic development and their lack of manpower. The central block straddling Elbe and Oder, Brandenburg, East Pomerania, Magdeburg and Halberstadt, had no natural boundaries, and no good port until, in 1720, part of West Pomerania was acquired, with Stettin. East Prussia, beyond the Vistula, was widely separated from it and indefensible in time of war, as were also the small provinces on the Rhine and Weser. Silesia, the seizure and holding of which cost Frederick so much, was clearly a valuable addition to the central block. Saxony would have been still better, and was always desired. West Prussia and the neighbouring districts brought to Prussia by the First Partition of Poland at last linked up East Prussia with the central mass, but not until 1772.

Prussia remained a mainly agrarian country until well into the nineteenth century. In 1713 the poor soil of a sandy plain was cultivated by methods which had hardly changed at all for a thousand years. The system of land-tenure was as unfavourable to progress as in any of the other German States and more and more oppressive to the peasantry the further one went to the east. Even on the large estates the primary aim was to provide for home requirements, communications being too bad and markets usually too distant to encourage more than a subsistence economy, even when it was technically possible to produce a surplus. There were few towns and those very small, and practically no foreign trade except of a passive kind, consisting mainly in the import of luxuries from France for the aristocracy. Home industries produced only the most necessary articles for the local market, hampered by a guild organisation which no longer worked smoothly and feared nothing so much as free enterprise.

To a backward economy we must add the devastating effects of the Thirty Years War in Brandenburg, Pomerania and East Prussia, and of the Swedish-Polish War, the Tartar attack and finally the plague of 1709 in the last-named province. One-third of the population of the province is estimated to have died of plague and famine, which the Government had no reserves to prevent; in 1709–10, 18,000 died in Königsberg alone in one year. It is not surprising to learn that the density of the population of East Prussia was about a quarter of that of France, and less than a third of that of Württemberg, Saxony, or England and Wales, while that of Brandenburg was only slightly higher, and that of Pomerania considerably lower.

Before the end of the Thirty Years War the Great Elector had arrived at the view that the interests of the dynasty could not be maintained unless he had an army entirely at his own disposal, which could serve him in the scattered provinces without interference from their ruling classes, the Estates. During the war the outlying provinces had fended for themselves, led by their diets. The co-operation in a common policy of all the provinces which happened to have been inherited by the elector offered as yet no obvious advantages except to the dynasty itself, and it could only be brought about if the elector could compel the assent of the unwilling, if necessary by force. A standing army was set up for the first time in 1644 and maintained, at reduced strength, in peace-time. A series of bitter struggles between the central Government and the provincial Estates followed, as in all similarly constituted German States with ambitions towards absolutism. The Estates did not see the necessity for a standing army, they particularly objected to paying taxes for its maintenance and they did not wish to be involved in ambitious policies, but rather to stand aside from the disputes of major Powers in peaceful resignation to the will of God. The elector had least difficulty with Brandenburg, the oldest possession of his house. The Estates agreed in 1653 to the levying of a direct tax, the 'Contribution', provided that the nobility was exempted from payment and confirmed in its rights over the peasantry. In the outlying provinces it proved necessary to arrest leaders and to threaten the use of armed force, but here too the Elector eventually had his way. The provincial Diets were not formally abolished, but as the Estates had agreed to what was in effect a permanent tax, they had lost their main function, and even in the Rhenish provinces, the most independent because of their remoteness, they only concerned themselves from now on with matters of local government. By 1713 their administrative functions had been almost entirely taken over everywhere by the new permanent officials of the central government.

Frederick William I had even less respect for the traditional rights and privileges of corporations and deliberately pursued a totalitarian policy, in order to build up a strong centralised monarchy. But he too was content with establishing his own undisputed authority, and carefully refrained from interfering with the individual privileges of the nobility, above all with their exemption from taxation. In the central provinces, however, the king reasserted feudal rights which had long been thought to have lapsed, and against much opposition compelled his 'vassals' to make an annual payment as commutation for the services formerly exacted in return for their holdings. In the same spirit, but much more important in its consequences, was his demand that the sons of the nobility should regard it as a duty they owed to their rank to serve as 'Junker' or ensigns in the army and in the 'Tables of vassals' their activities were systematically recorded and checked. There was strong opposition here too at first, but the establishment of a corps of cadets for the education of young noblemen, and the social distinction that came to be associated with service, as a consequence of the king's personal interest and example—he was one of the first European monarchs regularly to wear uniform—gradually fostered the growth of a strong *esprit de corps* and a sense of corporate obligation. It had long been a jealously guarded privilege of the nobility to occupy the principal offices in their native province. They were now shuffled around in other provinces in the interests of impartiality and the formation of a wider patriotism. There is a close parallel to many of these measures in Peter the Great's Russia, but in Russia the discipline had to be even more draconic, and for a number of reasons the nobility remained there a much more amorphous and unreliable body than the 'honoured and faithful nobility', praised by Frederick in 1752 as having constantly given evidence of its attachment to the throne.

It is not surprising if the aristocracy did not at first regard it as an honour to serve in the kind of Prussian army which existed in 1713. It was a mercenary army, recruited both inside and outside Prussia, with a liberal use of force, by colonels, contractors in manpower who received a lump sum for keeping their regiments up to a specified strength. There were many foreigners and adventurers among the officers, as there had been since the Thirty Years War, and these were now gradually replaced by Prussians, mainly, though not exclusively, from the nobility. Forcible recruiting was officially discountenanced because of the opposition which was encountered to an expansion of the army, especially from landowners thus deprived of labour, but it continued all the same and earned Prussia a bad name. From 1721 compulsion was confined to the lower classes, chiefly the sons of peasants bound to the soil. Sometimes their own masters were their officers, and after a year or two they were sent on leave to work on the estate again, being recalled only for the two months of the autumn manœuvres. But more and more recruits were obtained from outside Prussia by up to a thousand professional recruiting officers, well provided with money and not scrupulous in their methods. The king was willing to pay high prices in particular for 'tall fellows' for his own regiment at Potsdam. Sometimes up to two-thirds of the army consisted of foreigners. Finally in 1733 the cantonal system was introduced for home recruiting, by which the whole country was divided into 'cantons' of 5000 households.

Each canton had to provide the replacements for a particular regiment, stationed in or near the district, and still from the lower classes only, the sons of peasants and craftsmen. This system, with its very obvious class discrimination, reflecting the social structure of the country, continued in force throughout the century, and prepared the way for universal military service. Though discipline was still extremely harsh, as it had to be to prevent so many pressed men from deserting, the men received a rudimentary education too, and were conditioned to habits of order and obedience which left their mark on the nation, especially as the lower ranks of the civil service were recruited almost exclusively from ex-soldiers.

In this way what had been a kind of private industry was gradually nationalised, one may say, with very important consequences for the whole national economy. The troops were stationed in a number of garrison towns, almost entirely in private billets, and as they constituted a high proportion of the town's population, often half or more, and received comparatively little of their stores and equipment from central depots, their presence meant a great deal to local trade, and much of the State control of prices which was a feature of economic life was exercised in their interest and enforced partly by their garrison commanders. The national and civic administrative system was in fact devised with military needs in view and filled with the military spirit. The king gave his personal attention to every detail, for he was a born organiser, with a passion for order and economy. He would spend hours at his desk adding up figures, wearing linen sleeves to protect his uniform, and he found relaxation in drilling his regiment of giants at Potsdam in the more efficient methods devised by Leopold of Dessau. He would have liked, no doubt, to drill the whole population, and went far towards doing so.

The main problem of the Government was to find the means of meeting the heavy cost of a constantly expanding army. It was this which led to the important financial and administrative reforms, the vigorous efforts to increase production of every kind and the internal colonisation policy, for which Frederick William's reign is remarkable. On his accession, the revenues of the State were derived from two principal sources, the income from the royal domains and the proceeds from taxation in its two forms, the 'Contribution' paid by the country districts and the 'Excise' raised in the towns. By the further exploitation of these sources and strict economy the income of the State was more than doubled in the course of the reign, and at the same time a war treasure was accumulated.

The domain lands were surprisingly extensive. It was estimated by a contemporary in 1710 that between one-third and a quarter of all the peasants were domain peasants. Frederick William I reversed the policy which had been tried and found wanting in his father's reign, of selling the buildings and stock and farming out the domain lands at a yearly rent on an indefinitely long 'hereditary' lease. There had been good points about the scheme, but it had been mismanaged and the proceeds largely wasted on court extravagances. Frederick William introduced instead the system of short leases which persisted with few changes well into the nineteenth century. Under this system a whole 'Amt', an estate of considerable size, was let for a fixed annual rent, with its home farm, the outlying farms and peasant villages and all appurtenances, to one man, who could sublet any portions. For the six years of the lease the Crown Bailiff (*Beamte*) acquired virtually the same authority and the same rights as one of the landed gentry. It was part of his duty to maintain the peace and administer justice, but in return he could claim the fines and customary dues, any monopoly rights of the lord of the manor over mill or brewery and above all the peasants' feudal services. As he took all risks, the Government could count on a fixed cash return from domain lands and could budget accordingly, insolvent or inefficient farmers being readily removable. The system encouraged the growth of a rural middle class who were in the van of agricultural progress, and at least an attempt was made to protect the peasants from exploitation by regular inspections, and by the fixing and gradual lightening of *corvées*. A further consequence was that lavish gifts in kind could no longer be made, as in earlier days, to officials and courtiers. Some traditional perquisites persisted for some time, but the general tendency was to put everything on an impersonal money basis, for which the treasury was strictly accountable.

At the end of Frederick William's reign the income from the domains was roughly equal to the revenue from taxation. Both 'Contribution' and 'Excise' were well established by 1713. The country tax, the Contribution, a complicated property and income tax rather than a real land tax, had first been levied in Brandenburg about a century earlier, always for military purposes. It was only after the establishment of a standing army that the Estates in the various provinces agreed to it as a permanent institution, but though their officials, who had at first been responsible for its collection, were gradually replaced by civil servants under the so-called War Commissariat, the nobility were able successfully to resist the extension of the tax to their own lands, except in East Prussia. It was based on surveys long out of date, in Brandenburg on one of 1624, and the rate of taxation varied greatly from one district to another, but it was only in East Prussia again that even Frederick William I ventured to insist on a revision and the introduction of the much fairer 'Generalhufenschoss'. Similar measures were introduced by Frederick II in the newly won provinces (in Silesia in 1742 and West Prussia in 1772), but elsewhere the Contribution remained practically unchanged until 1861. It was a heavy burden on the peasantry, amounting on the average according to Hintze to about 40 per cent of the net yield of a peasant's holding. In addition, we must remember, the peasant had to pay in many cases quite as much to his landlord also.

The Contribution had originally been levied in town and country alike, but when it had become clear that the towns were under-taxed the Great Elector had introduced the Excise into Brandenburg, first as an alternative open to the towns at choice and finally as the uniform system of taxation for them. It involved a small ground, occupation and poll tax, but was in the main an indirect tax, from which few goods were exempted, on food and drink and merchandise of all kinds. It was collected partly through the producer or the seller of goods, partly on their introduction into a town. Frederick William I extended the Excise from the three provinces where it was in force on his accession to all, and made it into a method of economic control which soon became indispensable. Even in the reign of his successor, it remained a tax on the middle class, confined to the towns, where trade and industry were carefully nursed so that the fiscal yield might be greater. A further burden on the towns was 'Service Money', a levy on individual households to provide a common billeting fund.

A similar type of excise was tried in many other German States in the seventeenth century. Holland had led the way, and theorists generally favoured indirect taxation. But collection did not always prove as simple as it seemed, as it called for reliable officials under strict control. In Prussia, says Schmoller, 'a capable, conscientious civil service came into existence mainly because of the demands of the excise and developed under its influence'. The twofold importance of the Excise, as a source of revenue and as a means of economic control, becomes quite clear when we look into the duties of the local Commissaries (*Steuerräte*) responsible for its collection, the representatives in the towns of the provincial War Commissariat, which was controlled in its turn, in the early years of Frederick William I's reign, by the 'General War Commissariat' in Berlin. To understand their functions we must look at the reform of civic administration undertaken in Frederick William's reign, a particularly revealing episode in the emergence of the Power-State, jealous of the authority of corporations within the State, concerned for the economic welfare of its citizens but determined above all to make every class contribute to the building up of military strength.

The military function allotted to the towns was to provide quarters for a large standing army and to pay a large share of its cost through the Excise. First the infantry and then the cavalry had been moved to the towns, the latter only in 1718, because it was easier there to control their behaviour and in particular to see that they paid for what they received, for the peasantry had been constantly exploited by them. But the towns, governed by oligarchies often corrupt and inefficient, were too easy-going and traditional, and above all too independent, for the taste of an authoritarian government. Government commissions were set up to examine them, singly or in groups according to their size, and to reform their constitution, their administration and their system of finance. The process took a considerable time, but it was for the most part completed by 1740. It was the duty of the Local Commissary to maintain the new order and to see that everything functioned well.

The spirit of progressive minds now was that of the Enlightenment, delighting in the orderly, the rational, the practical, and little disposed to respect the traditional privileges of individuals, or any other survivals from the past. The commissions made a clean sweep of the old town councils and replaced them by smaller bodies of paid officials, appointed for life and strictly responsible to the Government. By the time of Frederick II, when they could be trusted, they were allowed to exercise rights of co-option which had been at first merely nominal, but they remained local organs of the central Government, entirely under its thumb. The three burgomasters were responsible for police, judicial and economic matters respectively, assisted by six or more councillors, drawn from business or the professions. The council appointed a town clerk, treasurer and secretary. If it called together representatives of the citizens, it was only to give publicity to some act such as the auditing by the Local Commissary of the annual accounts. It was his business, not that of the citizens, to keep a check on the town council, particularly on the administration of its funds. The State had made itself responsible for any existing debts at the time of the reforms, but it left the councils with no power to levy rates. All towns owned land outside, in the shape of estates, woods, commons, often considerable areas, though probably scattered. These were farmed out on short lease like the royal domains to bring in a fixed income, and current expenses of administration, salaries, the cost of construction and upkeep of streets, public buildings and the like had to be met out of these sums, supplemented if necessary by a grant from excise proceeds.

The Local Commissary had not only to watch over everything in the Government interest and to co-operate with the garrison commander, but also to initiate most schemes for the improvement of the town. His district might consist of one large town, or half a dozen or more small ones. He lived in the district, visited every part of it regularly and was always ready to receive complaints and suggestions. In his day-to-day work he was mainly concerned with questions of police, in the wide sense assigned to the word in that age by paternal governments, not only in Prussia. He inspected weights and measures, sampled the quality of food, helped to fix bread, beer and meat prices, and granted licences for the sale of liquor. He saw to it that beggars, if able-bodied, were made to work, and if sick were sent to hospital, and he even kept on eye on unsocial behaviour, drunkenness, idleness and disaffection. He was the local agent by whom the Government's control of industry and trade was exercised, for in the latter half of Frederick William's reign the craft guilds were deprived of most of their functions, and it was the Government which made itself responsible for industrial discipline, for the regulation of competition and for the maintenance of the quality of industrial wares.

The most important of all the Commissary's duties, however, was to see that the maximum was raised from the Excise and that it was honestly and economically collected. He nominated the collector and the gate-clerk, inspected their books, which were made up daily, and sent in their monthly statistics to his superiors. Customs duties could not easily be levied at the frontier in a State made up of so many odd portions, so the mercantilist policy characteristic of that age, particularly vigorously pursued by Frederick William I and his successor, had to be put into effect chiefly through the Excise. Mercantilism, as Schmoller has shown, is not to be judged by its theories about the increase of money or the balance of trade. What was really behind it was the attempt to arrive at a higher integration of economic and political power than had been achieved by the city or (in Germany) the territorial State, and to this end to re-organise society and the institutions of government. Frederick William's intention certainly was, by regulating the flow of trade through excise duties, to foster home production of every kind and as far as possible to keep out foreign luxury goods, or to take a heavy toll of those for which there was nevertheless a demand, all in the interests of his treasury and ultimately of the army. It was in the same spirit that a duty was put on corn in 1721, directed against imports of Polish grain, which were finally completely forbidden in 1732, or that the export of raw wool was prohibited in 1718, a ban which remained in force for ninety years. Complementary measures were the banning of imports of foreign cloth and cotton, the setting up of wool depots in small towns, and of the 'Lagerhaus' in Berlin for the manufacture of fine cloth for officers' uniforms, an enterprise later taken over for a time by the State. In spite of all these measures and the encouragement offered to manufacturers and skilled workers, especially foreigners, the trade balance remained adverse, for Prussia's industries were still in their infancy.

They were hampered particularly, in the view of the Government, by the traditionalism and inefficiency of the guild system. Here too the time had come, it was thought, for forms which had been well adapted to their purpose when a town with the country around was an almost self-sufficient unit, to be re-cast, now that a central Government existed which felt itself called upon to organise everything in the interests of the country as a whole. There is plenty of evidence that reforms were necessary, but it is also clear that the Government forced the pace in its totalitarian zeal, being intolerant of any organisation which claimed autonomy, as the guilds did in their limited sphere.

The most obvious defect of the guild system at this time was the incapacity of the masters to maintain due discipline among their journeymen and apprentices, but there were many complaints too about skilled men being prevented by out-of-date guild regulations from becoming independent masters, and about endless quarrels, between one guild and another, as to their competence, and between the town masters and so-called blacklegs practising their craft in the villages. The journeymen, craftsmen who had served their time as apprentices but were not yet established as masters, had for long been well organised in unions of their own, the local centres of which, in each trade, were linked up with other centres all over Germany. These 'brotherhoods', as they were called from the time of their origin in the fifteenth century, had served a useful purpose in a country where so much importance was attached to a man's gaining experience in many different centres before settling down. The young journeyman arriving in a strange town immediately found advice, companionship and often pecuniary assistance, if he needed it, in the inn where his trade met, and in particular he was helped to find employment. But it was hard to prevent a body of high-spirited young men from occasionally overstepping the mark, when they had given no hostages to fortune and could easily escape, if in trouble, to a centre of their craft in another town or even another State. Various German States had for long been trying to deal with the strikes and general disorderliness of the journeymen, and had even made a move to have an imperial law passed in 1672, but without success. But in the 1720's the problem of the journeymen became acute for Prussia, because their strikes were interfering with the temporarily flourishing cloth trade with Russia—Russia too needed uniforms, though very soon English competition proved too strong for the Prussians. On Frederick William's initiative, after eight years of negotiation between the States, that minor miracle, an agreed measure, was actually passed by the Imperial Diet in 1731, though it could only be made effective by the action of individual States. In Prussia all guild charters were revised as soon as possible and a new Prussian industrial code was drawn up between 1732 and 1735, bringing the guilds under strict State supervision and turning them, in effect, into instruments of the Government's industrial policy, corporations which existed only on sufferance.

The journeymen, the chief source of trouble, were subjected to strict discipline. Their unions were abolished and all their papers confiscated, but each trade was allowed to have its meeting place as before in an inn, which still served as employment bureau, and to retain its sickness insurance fund, but under supervision. The men went on their travels as before, but only within Prussian territory. The old ceremonies and time-hallowed phraseology, which had served as a kind of shibboleth, were done away with and the journeyman was supplied instead with a certificate made out by the guild officials and the master by whom he was last employed, establishing his identity and testifying to his good character. No one might employ him unless he could produce this document.

Together with a copy of his birth and apprenticeship certificates, it had to be deposited with his guild in his new place of employment and replaced by one from his next master before he could take another post. The system came into general use in Germany and proved a very effective form of control.

Even after this reform, more survived of the medieval guild system in Prussia than in England, where capitalism was so much further advanced, but the old forms were adapted to the purposes of the well-policed State and everything became more bureaucratic, impersonal and prosaic than in the rest of Germany. Private enterprise was in some respects given more scope, but always under State supervision, while the working man was more closely controlled than ever before. Skilled workers were not allowed out of the country, but foreign workers were made welcome as immigrants. Journeymen, like peasants, were liable to be compelled to serve in the army, but master-craftsmen and others in established positions in the towns were exempted, because of the State's need of their all-important contribution through the excise to the revenue.

The shortage of manpower was more acutely felt the more the Government strove to develop the country's resources to the uttermost and to increase its military strength. The army, we have seen, was largely re-cruited abroad. It is estimated to have brought in three to four hundred thousand men in the eighteenth century, most of whom married and settled down in Prussia. From the Great Elector's time onwards the Government actively encouraged immigration, both from other parts of Germany and from abroad. The fact that the ruling house belonged to the Reformed or Calvinistic branch of protestantism, and the bulk of their subjects to the Lutheran, had made official policy unusually tolerant even before the Enlightenment took firm hold of Prussia in the days of the philosopher-king. The Great Elector welcomed Huguenot refugees from France after the Revocation of the Edict of Nantes. Many of them were men of substance, with a knowledge of crafts not yet developed in Prussia, others professional men of distinction. Altogether some 20,000 of the best of France's bourgeoisie settled in Prussia between 1672 and 1700, forming an important element in Berlin and exerting a lasting influence on intellectual and economic life. About the same number came as Protestant refugees evicted from the Bishopric of Salzburg in 1732, simple peasants, who were settled, with infinite trouble, mostly in East Prussia. These were much the largest single groups, but there was a steady trickle of immigrants from all the countries of Europe, but particularly from the rest of Germany latterly, down to the end of Frederick the Great's reign. There were Prussian agents in various centres looking out for likely people, special organisations to receive them, and even Frederick himself, we know from his letters, if there was a fire in a Saxon town, for instance, told one of his officials to look out for useful people who might now be willing to emigrate.

More than propaganda was needed, of course, to attract people, so they were offered travelling expenses, some initial support and, if they were peasants, land and perhaps cattle and equipment, if craftsmen, the right to practise their trade without fees or formalities, as well as exemption from taxes for a period and, of course, from military service. Manufacturers made their own terms and were eagerly sought after. Schmoller states that on a conservative estimate about 16 to 20 per cent of the whole population of Prussia in 1786 were immigrants since 1640 or their descendants, and according to Dieterici's figures, the density of the population of Brandenburg, for example, was more than trebled in the course of the eighteenth century (rising from 636 per square 'Meile' to 1930), a rate of increase not paralleled in any German State outside Prussia or in any of the many European States also mentioned by him. In England and Wales, for instance, it was in 1809 one and four-fifths of what it had been in 1700, and in France one and one-sixth.

The aims and the results of Frederick William's home policy have been outlined, but the changes made during his reign in the machinery of government, his reorganisation of the civil service and his method of retaining personal control have still to be considered. Here, as in the army which he created, he provided his son with an instrument which was equal, with few adjustments, to all the exacting demands which Frederick made upon it.

We have seen what a variety of tasks were performed by the representative of the central Government in the towns, the Local Commissary. He had developed out of the regimental commissary who watched over the king's interests when the army was still raised and officered by colonels, for whom this was a private and profitable enterprise. His military origin was reflected in his full title, 'War and Tax Commissary', and his primary function still was to collect taxes for military purposes.

In the central provinces first and later in all, a parallel set of officials exercised similar functions in those parts of the countryside which were not domain land. They were called Rural Commissioners (*Landräte*). Each took charge of a particular district, supervising the collection of the country tax, the Contribution, and making himself responsible for the 'policing' of the peasantry in the widest sense, for directing them, that is, in the way in which the central Government thought they should go. These Rural Commissioners had originally been the representatives of the Estates on the provincial tax boards, and were still always country gentlemen, resident in the district and elected by the local gentry, except when Frederick William, mistrustful of their class, raised objections. They received only a small salary. Unlike our justices of the peace they had no judicial functions, except on their own estates. The Crown Bailiffs who leased the royal domain lands were themselves responsible, as we have seen, for the 'policing' of the areas assigned to them and as no

Contribution was raised there, a fixed revenue being already guaranteed to the Crown by the lessees, the Rural Commissioners had no authority over them or their peasants.

The provincial authority to which both the Local Commissaries (in the towns) and the Rural Commissioners (in the country) were responsible was called the War Commissariat. It was a board of permanent officials with collective responsibility, and every War Commissariat was in its turn directed by the General War Commissariat in Berlin, also a 'collegial' body, one, that is, in which decisions were reached by vote in committee. All this array of officials was a comparatively recent growth, evoked by the financial needs of a State which maintained an increasingly expensive standing army. Their duties demanded that they should have some conception of the interests of a unified monarchy of Prussia, as an incipient Great Power rather than as a collection of small provinces.

But the old kings of Prussia were, as Seeley puts it, 'compounded of the General and the Landowner'. They were concerned not only with war but also with the efficient management of the royal estates. Side by side with the General War Commissariat there was therefore an older financial authority, the General Finance Directory, with Chambers (*Amtskammern*) under it, one in each province, to administer the royal domains through the Crown Bailiffs scattered over the province, each in an area of domain land, an 'Amt'. The officials of these Chambers tended to be more provincial and circumscribed in their outlook than the War Commissariats. They were interested in rural economics and the exploitation of other sources of Crown revenues beside the domains, the salt monopoly, for instance, and the beer tax. At all events the two sets of officials were found to be constantly at loggerheads, to the disadvantage of the common purpose they served. They were therefore combined, in 1723, into one administrative system. The central authority in Berlin was called the General (Finance and Domains) Directory. In the provinces the War Commissariats and the Chambers were fused into provincial War and Domains Chambers, and these were served by the same local officials as before, combined into one service, Local Commissaries in the towns, Rural Commissioners in the country, Crown Bailiffs on the domains.

This hierarchy persisted with few changes throughout the rest of the century. The General Directory was responsible for the general administration of the whole of Brandenburg-Prussia, for the management of its finances, with military needs as a primary concern, and for the supervision of trade and industry in the interests of general economic prosperity and the consequent augmentation of the revenues of the State. It consisted in Frederick William's day of four ministers and a constantly growing number of Privy Financial Councillors, at first three or four, finally a score. Each minister was responsible for a particular province or group of provinces, but also for certain affairs concerning the country as a whole.

One was postmaster and master of the Mint, another looked after army supplies, a third dealt with land utilisation policy and State boundaries. Two principles were followed simultaneously, it will be seen, in the division of the ministers' labours, each being responsible both for a whole complex of affairs in an assigned area, and for a particular type of affairs in all areas. There was a similar confusion of purpose in the local Chambers, with the added complication that they had important judicial as well as administrative functions. The friction which resulted, intensified later by Frederick's creation of functional ministries alongside the General Directory, made Stein's drastic reform of the system of administration urgently necessary in 1808.

The responsibility of even the ministerial members of the General Directory was still severely limited. Each merely prepared business concerning his own department as a preliminary to the discussion of everything in plenary sessions, where a decision was reached by vote. Later he supervised the execution of the board's collective decision if it received the royal assent. The real initiative usually came from the king, a chairman who, on principle, never attended the meetings of the board but issued his instructions in the form of Cabinet Orders, after reading his ministers' written reports. It is true that in any matter covered by an explicit administrative law the General Directory could itself issue a decree marked 'par ordre exprès du roi', without consulting him further, but it was chary of doing this and left all important decisions to him. This autocratic system of 'cabinet rule' (totally distinct of course from cabinet government as understood in England) was not invented by Frederick the Great. He took it over from his father, the only difference being that before coming to his decision he seldom asked his subordinates for more than information, whereas his father had often been glad to seek their advice and to act upon it.

Such were the principle military, financial, economic and administrative reforms through which, in bursts of fierce energy, Frederick William reorganised the whole State of Prussia in a quarter of a century and prepared for its meteoric rise under his son. The whole government machine was in excellent working order, revenues amounting to about seven million *thalers* could be counted upon, and of this sum five millions could be devoted to military purposes. From the rest it was possible not only to pay the whole cost of the civil service and the court, but also to set aside each year a contribution towards a State Treasure for use in war. By 1740 nearly eight million *thalers* were available, packed away in casks in the cellars of the royal Schloss. Above all, Frederick William's care for his army had extended far beyond the regiment of tall guards who were his special joy. In a country with little over two million inhabitants he had built up a well-trained and well-equipped field army, that is not including garrison forces, to the peace-time strength of 72,000, twice as big a force as his father had been able to muster in war, comparable with France's estimated strength of 160,000, Russia's 130,000 and Austria's 80–100,000 regular troops.

These achievements, without which Prussia could not have developed subsequently in the direction and at the rate she did, were the results of a choice which involved the comparative neglect of certain aspects of life which until then had been the principal concern of patriarchal governments in the small Lutheran States of Germany. The maintenance of justice here below and the preparation for the life to come by the fostering of pure doctrine had been subordinated by Frederick William to the pursuit of power. Yet he was deeply religious in an undogmatic, pietistic way. It was the king's aim in his religious policy to discourage religious controversy among Protestants—it was expressly forbidden in the pulpit—and to bring together as good citizens both the Lutherans, who formed the great majority of his subjects, and the Reformed minority, which included the royal family. He even allowed Catholics among his troops to have their own chaplains, though he would have nothing to do with Jesuits, especially after their treatment of the Protestants at Thorn (in Poland) in 1724, when he tried in vain to save leading citizens condemned to death.

Outlining his policy in his political testament of 1722, the king warned his successor against allowing ministers of any religion to interfere in lay matters, in which they all aspired to be little popes. Elementary education, still in the hands of the Church, was as much neglected in Prussia as everywhere else, and made little advance even under Frederick the Great. There were hardly any village schools, and no teachers but old soldiers or perhaps sedentary craftsmen like tailors, who taught as they sewed. Frederick William had little regard for institutions of higher culture either, unless, like a medical institution serving military needs, or a chair of economics, for the practical training of civil servants, they had some obvious practical value.

As to the law, the king said in 1722 that he had spared no pains to reduce its delays and injustices, but to little effect, and he did not seriously press for its reform later. His aim was to make it possible for a civil suit to be finally settled in a year, even if there were an appeal to two higher courts. There had long been a demand for the codification of Prussian law, and in East Prussia at least Samuel von Cocceji published a modernised form of the Provincial Code and brought order into the administration of justice. When he was made Chief Justice in the last years of Frederick William's reign his reforming zeal made no progress against his obstructive opponents, chiefly for lack of firm support from the king, whose view of lawyers in general was so low that he compelled advocates to wear ridiculously short cloaks, 'that the public might know with whom they were dealing'. Minor reforms were made in criminal procedure, beginning in Brandenburg early in the reign and extended later to other provinces. Their effect was to introduce some measure of central control over manorial and civic courts. After the preliminary examination of the accused, proceedings were still secret and conducted entirely in writing.

In spite of the progress of Enlightenment some penalties were made more severe than ever, though restrictions were imposed on the use of torture. Thieves were still commonly hanged and infanticides drowned in a sack.

As Frederick, the Crown Prince, grew to manhood, the temperamental opposition between father and son, increased by the father's handling of the boy's education, by family differences and political intrigue, led to the dramatic clash of wills so frequently described by German historians, novelists and dramatists, a crisis of the first magnitude for a State where an uncontrolled system of autocracy made so much depend on the personality and ability of the ruler. 'If Frederick William had really carried out what according to the old reports he intended, and ordered the execution of his son, the State, which it was his aim to maintain, would on the contrary have been in danger of immediate collapse.'[1] Fortunately for Prussia, the Crown Prince bowed to the inevitable, with bitter resentment in his heart at first, after seeing his friend Katte beheaded before his eyes on the king's orders, a living sacrifice for the one who was alone responsible for the attempted flight, Frederick himself. But it is evident from his later acts that he began to see behind his father's grim fanaticism a motive not foreign to his own nature, and one which became more and more important for him as he learned to understand local administration, at Küstrin, and the spirit of the Prussian army, on being given his regiment. He caught by infection the sense of duty to something greater than himself, and when this was combined with the love of power, the same self-assertiveness which had prompted his revolt became the desire for glory and for the reality of power which inspired his first decisive action as king, the invasion of Silesia.

In November 1737 the Crown Prince was already writing to Grumbkow: 'The king seems to have been destined by Heaven to make all the preparations which wisdom and prudence demand before the beginning of a war. Who knows whether Providence has not reserved for me the task of making glorious use of these preparations, to bring about the fulfilment of those aims which the king's foresight had meant them to further?' Frederick already recognised it as his task to continue in essentials the work of his father, but in so doing to give expression to his own dynamic personality.

In the father [as Ranke says] autocracy still took the form of self-willed obstinacy, with all the seventeenth century's trust in naked force, combined with religious feeling that had a Pietistic strain in it and led him to accept, even when it was against his own interests, the idea that a general order must prevail in the German Reich. In the son, on the other hand, there is manifest from his earliest years a lively impulse towards the development of his own personality; he absorbs the knowledge of his time with the double zeal of a self-taught man; in religion he holds firm only to the most general principles; he recognises the Reich when it confers a right on him, but not when it demands a duty.[2]

[1] L. v. Ranke, *Zwölf Bücher preussischer Geschichte* (Gesamtausgabe der deutschen Akademie, München, 1930), vol. III, p. 341.　　　[2] *Ibid.* p. 341.

It is beyond the range of this chapter to attempt any study of the character of this most remarkable of modern kings, whose gifts in many respects amounted to genius, though they manifested themselves in nine-tenths of his activity as an infinite capacity for taking pains and enduring the unendurable. Our subject is his peculiar contribution to the organisation and rise of Prussia, as a continuation of the work of his father in slowly building up army, administration and finances. In his will he justly claimed that he had worked according to his lights, as it is every man's duty to do, for the good of the society of which he was a part. Among his achievements he singled out his maintenance of the law and his reform of justice, his management of State finance and his creation, through wise discipline, of the finest army in Europe. In these aims, as he freely acknowledged, he had been following out Frederick William's tradition of dutiful devotion to the State, strict economy of time and money, and military efficiency at all costs. He had added to them a new concern for the administration of justice, as a prerequisite of economic progress. Above all, he had risked all these gains in two wars of his own contriving, by the fortunate issue of which Prussia became for the first time a Power in Europe, and its king a legendary figure.

Here again the main facts are clear, but the interpretation of them, the lessons for future action drawn from them, the emphasis laid on different aspects, have varied enormously, according to the nationality, political views and general philosophy of the historian. Frederick's contribution towards moulding the character of Prussia has been more obvious, even if perhaps not more far-reaching, than that of his father. Group patterns of behaviour resulting from Frederick William's organisation of his country have persisted for two centuries and spread from Prussia to Germany as a whole, but Frederick, hailed as 'Great' after his first war, seized the imagination even of contemporaries opposed to his political aims, making them, like the young Goethe, 'Fritzian' if not 'Prussian' in their senti-ments, while for succeeding rulers of Prussia and the military and ruling class he became the inimitable model of perfection.

Frederick William died content to know that the destiny of Prussia was in safe hands, but for contemporaries, unaware of the full extent of the reconciliation between father and son, it was astonishing to see a young prince, surrounded at Rheinsberg by French wits and apparently absorbed in the culture of the French Enlightenment, the correspondent of Voltaire and author not only of French verses in the style of the age, but of the *Anti-Machiavel*, with its contempt for conquerors and its laudation of true humanity, transformed almost overnight into a wily and disillusioned diplomat, a daring and determined general and a ruthlessly efficient administrator. Yet the *Anti-Machiavel* is far less opposed to Frederick's form of Machiavellianism than it might seem, being chiefly directed against confessionalism in religion and against the inefficient autocratic rule of his lesser fellow-princes, their ignoble contentment with the mere trappings of power. Frederick's expressed ideal was a king who should be the foremost civil servant of the realm, restlessly active in promoting the prosperity of his people by fostering trade and industry—as a means, he might have added, to the attainment of real power.

Even on the throne, Frederick in his poems often made the claim, which some of his biographers have taken seriously, that his deepest desire was to escape from war and the cares of a monarch to 'repose in the arms of philosophy', but the tension between the Sans Souci side of his life and the other was more apparent than real. 'Philosophy' meant in the main the literary life, as practised in France by anti-clerical men of wit, cultivated and sceptical, free as they thought from the illusions of the vulgar. Frederick did find real pleasure and relaxation in turning verses in a style and with a background of feeling which he had absorbed with the French language, but in which he could never be completely at home. In the same way, in these degenerate days, a statesman may unbend over a cross-word puzzle. He had the ambition to combine with his real kingship the role of a prince of wits, but his kingship was his life. He tried hard to take life's evils philosophically too, in the spirit now of Epicurus, now (especially in later life) of the Stoics. Some of his late letters to d'Alembert seem to express genuine wisdom inspired by these sources and tested in a hard life. But in general Frederick had none of the detachment of the philosopher. His fundamental conviction was that 'man is made to act', and that what he thinks about the world is not of any great account. In his confident youth he had hoped to 'compel fate itself by careful calculation', but as the years went by he became ever more fully aware of something greater than himself which lived through him and his sense of duty, accomplishing a purpose which he did not understand but firmly believed to exist, for he remained a convinced Deist for all his scepticism. Some such feeling was perhaps at the back of his unquestioning acceptance of his inherited authority and the duties it brought, though he was more fully conscious of a desire for the power and fame which might be his.

In the organisation of the State for power, so much that we think of as typically Prussian had already been accomplished by Frederick William that it might seem there was little left for Frederick to do in this field. As Hartung says: 'For the most part the construction of the Prussian State was completed by 1740. Frederick the Great made no changes in its essential features.'[1] He continued to develop the system in the direction of an intensified autocracy, but he was not primarily, like his father, an organiser, but a man of action, more ambitious and capable of a more sustained effort. His outstanding intellectual gifts were matched by immense self-confidence and audacity, so that from the first his conception

---

[1] *Deutsche Verfassungsgeschichte vom 15. Jahrhundert bis zur Gegenwart*, 2. Auflage (Leipzig and Berlin, 1922), p. 74.

of his political aims and his consequent attitude to the leading States of Europe, and in particular to Austria, were very different from his father's, as is brought out in Ranke's contrast of the two. Frederick William was violently irascible, constantly tempted to use his fists on those who annoyed him—the affront of being struck by him in public at the age of eighteen was Frederick's grievance before his flight—but as a ruler he was peace-loving, content to husband potential power. His army was too beautiful a thing to be lightly used. Frederick had none of his respect for the imperial tradition, and an even stronger feeling for his own and his dynasty's dignity, so that Prussia seemed to him to have played a humiliating role in his father's reign in its relations with Austria. When the death of the Emperor Charles VI left the Habsburgs without a male heir, Frederick decided immediately on a policy of audacious aggression. A short, sharp war would, he thought, put him in possession of the next objective he needed for the extension of the power of the State. 'There were hardly any grounds, we must admit,' says Hintze, 'for a clear, unambiguous legal claim to Silesia.'[1] Frederick would not even hear of negotiations. Against all advice he insisted on facing Maria Theresa, whose spirit and quality he underestimated, with a *fait accompli*, by invading Silesia without warning. He left it to the lawyers to trump up a claim. That was their business. In the same spirit he twice in the course of this war planned, and on the second occasion brought off, a separate peace, the kind of thing that the *Anti-Machiavel* had expressly condemned.

The relevance of these facts for the understanding of later German policy does not need to be underlined. It should be remembered, however, that Frederick could justly claim to be paying back his rivals in their own coin, that in international politics, as he said in the *Political Testament* of 1768, he was dealing with 'fourbes et fripons'. The tortuous history of the diplomacy which accompanied every step in the war reveals France and the other Powers as equally regardless of ordinary morality. In the preface to *The history of my times* (1743) Frederick declared roundly that private morality was not applicable to (international) politics, where the interests of one's own State were alone decisive, and a ruler must be prepared if necessary to break his word. The passage is moderated in 1746, but 'the good of the people' is still regarded as the paramount consideration. In the final edition of 1775 there is an attempt to limit the dangerous free-dom thus accorded to a monarch, non-observance of a treaty obligation being approved only when the ally has been the first offender or when it is physically impossible for a State to keep its word. Morality is confused with law, when Frederick claims that it is inapplicable to relations between States because here there is no higher court, supported by sanctions, to appeal to. That he realised he had been playing a dangerous game, and that Prussia had acquired a reputation for strength and determination, but

[1] O. Hintze, *Die Hohenzollern und ihr Werk* (Berlin, 1915), p. 324.

also for ruthlessness and unreliability, is clear from the first version of the *Political Testament* (1752), where he warns his successor against breaking his word more than once or possibly twice. In the second version (1768) he argues that even on grounds of expediency it is unwise to be, like Mazarin, a rogue in things both great and small, whom nobody can trust. He has learnt, in the Seven Years War, that no State can rely merely on its own strength, and he now needs the support of Russia. The whole discussion illustrates the anarchical condition of international relations in Europe which forms the background, for instance, to Kant's essay *On Perpetual Peace*. One of the preliminary conditions for the establishment of his League of Nations is that peace treaties shall no longer be regarded as preparations for the next war, and he holds it impossible to establish a lasting peace while diplomacy acts on such maxims as 'Fac et excusa' (Act first and excuse yourself later) or 'Si fecisti, nega' (If you have done something that shocks people, say that you haven't).

The system of Frederick's government in peace-time can best be studied in the ten years 1746 to 1756, the period between the wars, when all his principal achievements were initiated. After the Seven Years War his task was to restore the country and to develop the projects already begun. All the time, as his *Political Testament* shows, he was conscious that as king of Prussia he must constantly be prepared for war, 'toujours en vedette', and direct his whole policy towards this preparedness. He was doubly committed, by the tradition of his house and by his own first act as king, in which Hintze sees a tragic quality, in that 'out of this free act grew the fate that was to shape his life', an interpretation on which Gooch makes what German historians regard as a typically British moral comment: 'More detached observers might prefer the formula that he reaped what he had sown.'

Frederick continued his father's system of 'government from the king's cabinet', with still more confidence in himself and less in others. His fundamental distrust of the character and contempt for the intelligence of the mass of his subjects led him to look upon even his ministers of State as mere instruments, to be treated with offensive rudeness. But his own energy and efficiency were beyond all praise. He rose early, after only five or six hours of sleep, read his ambassadors' despatches and any letters from the nobility before breakfast, and before dinner at midday he had answered these and scribbled or dictated enough to indicate how all the petitions, reports from government departments and other State documents, sorted and prepared by his cabinet secretaries for his final decision, were to be dealt with. These pithy marginal comments, written in pencil on the documents themselves, were still being imitated, with a difference, by the Emperor William II.

Everything found a place in the activity of this tireless worker, who was always ready to concentrate on the task in hand in a common-sense spirit, and bore his immense burden of routine with a certain grim humour. He had no family to distract him—his poor queen, though well provided for and treated with outward respect, saw nothing of him after the Silesian War—and he proved amazingly tough. A calendar on his desk reminded him of the duties of the day and week, of the dates when outstanding reports were due, and so forth, and the year too was mapped out to enable him to inspect his kingdom methodically between May and August, and the army in autumn. Wherever he went his secretaries accompanied him and the day's business proceeded as at home.

But a system of government so centralised that it pivoted on one man had not only the defect that in a hereditary monarchy the succession of supermen it called for could not be guaranteed. It did not work perfectly even with a Frederick at its head, when its tasks were as complex as they had become by now in Prussia. As W. L. Dorn[1] has shown, 'Harmonious co-ordination of the central agencies of administration was notoriously lacking', for Frederick was attempting too much. He depended for his information almost entirely on written documents, which had to be made as succinct as possible so that he could cope with the mass of papers brought before him. He had no personal contacts with most of his officials, made little use of their experience and judgment, for they were allowed no initiative, and was therefore bound to make mistakes by over-hasty decisions in highly technical matters, though on principle he never admitted them. Though he used every form of check and countercheck that his ever-suspicious ingenuity could devise, setting officials spying on each other and agents called 'Fiscals' to spy on all, corresponding directly with subordinates to verify statements of their superiors, obtaining secret conduct-reports on all officials annually, and inspecting personally everything he possibly could on his yearly rounds, a minister as astute as Hoym in Silesia certainly contrived to save himself much trouble by concealment and deception,[2] and according to Benckendorf, Herr von Fuchs, another minister, kept a box by his bedside which, when opened after his death, was found to contain nothing more precious than edicts, with a note which read: 'None of these carried out to my knowledge.'[3] Though actual corruption was rare, many naturally aimed at pleasing the king, perhaps with a little window-dressing, rather than report unpopular truths. The same still happened under Hitler.

The General Directory soon lost favour with the king because its wheels moved so slowly. In the revised instructions he drew up for it in 1748, he is outspoken about the shortcomings of its officials and inclined to put them in the wrong in the event of a dispute with either the nobility or the peasantry. He warns them against attempts to exploit either of these

[1] *Political Science Quarterly*, vol. XLVII (1932), p. 75.
[2] W. L. Dorn, in *Political Science Quarterly*, vol. XLVI (1931), p. 417.
[3] *Acta Borussica, Getreidehandelspolitik*, vol. III, p. 40.

classes in the interests of the revenue. Because he needed a sound peasantry for his army, the peasants' burdens were not to be increased—though he could not free them, as he would have liked to do, for he needed the loyal support of the nobility—and for the same reason he did not want the Government to buy up nobles' estates for domain land, as Frederick William had done. In the economic policy which he prescribes he is a mercantilist, like his father, but he bases his views on a clear-cut theory. 'Two things', he tells his officials, 'are conducive to the welfare of the country: (1) To bring money in from foreign countries. This is the function of commerce. (2) To prevent money from leaving the country unnecessarily. This is the function of manufactures.'[1] In the second year of his reign he had already found the General Directory unequal to the task of promoting trade and industry and had created his first functional ministry for this purpose. Two other separate ministries followed before the Seven Years War, one for the newly acquired Silesia in 1742, and one for military administration in 1746, following the lessons of the war, when the commissariat had often failed him.

It was in the difficult years following the Seven Years War that Frederick gave his General Directory the unkindest cut of all, and by the establishment of the 'Regie', in 1766, brought a number of his leading officials as near to open opposition as they ever dared to come. He showed how little he thought of the efficiency and even the honesty of the excise officials by taking the quite extraordinary step of setting up a new form of excise under a French tax farmer, de Launay, and a staff of about 200 French officials, who brought in French methods of collection and received a percentage of what they could extract from the king's subjects in excess of the yield of 1765. He would have farmed out the taxes entirely as the French did if the agents selected had been able to raise the required guarantee. The post too was put under French management for a time (1766–9). This is nationalism with a difference, very typical of the Age of Reason. Further separate ministries were Mining (1768) and Forestry (1770), and several other branches of the administration were placed under officials responsible only to Frederick himself, namely the Mint (1751), the government bank and the tobacco monopoly (1766) and the coffee monopoly (1781). The Foreign Office (the 'Cabinetsministerium') and the Department of Justice had been separate from the General Directory even under Frederick William.

Being freed from the cumbrous procedure of the General Directory, these specialised departments functioned much more rapidly, and to the same end, various ministers in the General Directory itself were told by Frederick to act without reference to the rest, and he corresponded with them and often with their colleagues individually, so that the principle of

[1] Marginal note to the revised instructions, quoted by F. Hartung, *Studien zur Geschichte der preussischen Verwaltung* (Berlin, 1942), p. 23.

collective responsibility was progressively undermined. In one respect the king's burden was thus lightened, for when he had given a new branch of the administration its marching orders, as he always did, in the form of a detailed 'Reglement', they had full control of all routine business, and usually conducted it most efficiently, though on anxiously stereotyped lines. But the grave disadvantage was the absence of any provision for the discussion of common problems, as in normal cabinet government. Instead they had to correspond about them, thus adding to their mountains of paper, and no one but the king could see any branch in relation to the whole administration. The provincial chambers, however, continued to control a whole complex of affairs for their particular provinces, still retaining collective responsibility, and in the organisation of the economic life of these very different regions, where co-operation between different branches was essential, the king entrusted more and more to these bodies, by-passing the General Directory which was supposed to control them. The presidents of these chambers, always noblemen, came to be some of the most influential people in the country, constantly in close touch with the king. Under them the rural commissioners, also members of the nobility, exercised 'police' powers in the widest sense over all country districts outside domain land, not only in the central provinces now, but everywhere except in the remote Gelderland and East Friesland, while the local commissaries continued, as before, virtually to rule the towns. When Silesia was occupied, its administration was organised on the same lines as that of the other provinces, but under a minister responsible, as we have seen, only to the king.

Frederick's attempts to foster the economic life of the nation, always one of his chief concerns, were made, like those of his father, not in the interests of the individual citizen, but in those of the State and its military power. He continued vigorously the policy of internal colonisation, with results already described. To provide for the settlement of these colonists was the most exacting task of the provincial chambers. Every acre of land had to be utilised, even sandy wastes, moorland and swamps being laboriously reclaimed. In this way nearly 300 new villages were created between the wars in Pomerania, Brandenburg and the Oder marshes, mostly on reclaimed land, and still more after the Seven Years War, when over 40,000,000 *thalers* were spent on improvement schemes, mainly for agriculture. Great efforts were made in this period to introduce the latest English methods of agriculture and new crops, the most important of these being of course the potato, though sugar-beet too was already in cultivation in the later years. The peasants resisted these, like all other changes, tenaciously, and though the potato was introduced in the 1740's, it was not eaten to any great extent until 1770–2, when there would have been a danger of famine without it. In the end it was far more effective than all the elaborate measures for the control of the corn trade. Attempts to consolidate holdings met with little success, and peasant land was protected against enclosure by the landlords, in the interest of the cantonal recruiting system. The country remained feudally organised, the peasants being still, on most private estates, especially in the east, quasi-serfs, bound to the soil, often with unlimited services. The sharp differentiation between town and country was maintained, on the traditional principle that each class had its own contribution to make to the military strength of the State, the peasantry supplying the bulk of the men, the nobility the officers and chief officials and the trading and industrial classes the sinews of war.

Frederick looked to industry above all to increase the revenue of the State and to convert the passive trade balance of his father's day into an active one. From this point of view craft industry was of no great importance, providing as it did ordinary consumer goods for home consumption by the mass of the population and these in comparatively small quantities, for so much that is now bought in shops was still made at home. The guilds were already, after Frederick William's reforms, state-supervised organs for the control of the craft worker and craft industry, and they were left as they were. Frederick's attention was concentrated on 'manufactures', in which Prussia, when compared with Saxony and some districts on the lower Rhine, or still more with England, Holland, France or Switzerland, was still very backward. The age of coal and iron had not yet dawned, machinery played only a small part in the development of this early capitalism, and it still depended in the main on the old handicraft techniques, the workers being organised, however, in domestic industries or in 'factories' in the old sense. Handloom weavers, for instance, would weave yarn supplied by an entrepreneur, working either in their own homes or in his workshop. They were paid by him for their labour and he marketed the product. Some manufactures were set up under special licence from the Government and freed from guild regulations. Frederick William's attempts to encourage the manufacture of woollens on these lines were actively continued, but Frederick was still more interested in silk, because it took more money out of the country. He even tried to get country parsons and schoolmasters near Berlin to grow mulberry trees for silk-worms, without much success. Good results were obtained from the manufacture from imported raw material of silk fabrics and velvet, luxury goods in great demand with the upper classes. Immigrants with skill or capital were specially sought after, as we have seen, and given every inducement to settle in the towns, especially in Berlin and Potsdam. Individual enterprise was what Frederick wanted, not State factories, though he took over a porcelain factory which was in difficulties, but he directed the plans for industrialisation like a campaign, acting as his own Minister of Commerce after 1749. He was in touch with all concerned and used the Prussian representatives abroad as commercial agents. Quantitatively the results were meagre, compared with those of

nineteenth-century industry, but they were important in the conditions o
that day, and Prussia, particularly Berlin, was well started on the path
towards industrialisation. Silk and woollen goods were the largest items
in the list of Prussian exports at the close of Frederick's reign, 650,000
thalers worth of silk and 620,000 *thalers* worth of wool going from Brandenburg to foreign countries (including of course other German States), and
silk and wool to the value of 470,000 and 500,000 *thalers* respectively to
other Prussian provinces. Cotton goods did not amount to half the value
of either of these. There was now a favourable trade balance of three to
four million *thalers*, and the total industrial production was estimated at
about 30,000,000 *thalers*.

From 1747 Frederick regularly made use of trade statistics in planning
economic developments, regulating the excise rates to control the flow of
goods. Barriers to internal trade were reduced to a minimum in the
central provinces and Silesia. Canals were constructed between Elbe and
Oder, Elbe and Havel, Havel and Oder, bringing water-borne trade to
Berlin, and towns like Frankfurt-am-Oder and Stettin were forced to
give up their staple rights. At the same time, every obstacle was put in the
way of imports, and to protect the new industries a tariff war was waged,
particularly with Hamburg, Saxony (Leipzig) and Austria. Some modest
attempts at overseas trade came to nothing. The corn trade (mainly in rye,
wheat bread being eaten only by the well-to-do) continued to be controlled
through the State depots, the number of which grew from twenty-one to
thirty-two, the aim being to be ready at all times for the needs of a campaign, to guard against the danger of famine and to keep corn prices steady,
again mainly for the benefit of the troops, who in peace-time had to buy
their own rations. In the larger towns they constituted at least a third of
the adult male population, in Potsdam and Berlin considerably more. It
was in fact in its military effectiveness above all that this economic system
justified itself. Prussia was able to keep going without additional taxation
in the Seven Years War, meeting an increased expenditure of about
150 millions. Of course, British subsidies (4,000,000 *thalers* a year from
1758), war levies raised in occupied territories (in Saxony a sum varying
between 5,000,000 and 10,000,000 *thalers* a year) and wholesale deprecia-
tion of the currency also played a very important part in financing the war.
In the course of his reign Frederick more than doubled his army, increasing it from 72,000 to 195,000 men, until it constituted 4 per cent of
the population, and required nearly two-thirds of the State revenue for
its upkeep. At the same time the war treasure was increased from
8,000,000 to 50,000,000 *thalers*. Nearly half of the revenue was still
derived from the domains and the rest from taxation. The 'Contribution'
from the country districts remained at the old fixed rate, but the 'Excise'
increased with the taxable capacity of the middle classes.

It is not necessary to speak here of Frederick's ceaseless efforts in peace-time to improve his army and the country's defences in every possible way. He built new fortifications, especially in Silesia, improved the system of grain depots on strategic lines, drilled and inspected all arms regularly, wrote a manual on generalship as well as a striking poem on the art of war, and kept an eye on everything in the annual manœuvres.

The one feature in which Frederick's organisation of the country had, to begin with, almost no help from his father was the administration of justice. The driving force behind his reforms here too was an economic and military need. Justice, too, had to be nationalised to complete the process of consolidating the power of the State, and Cocceji was enabled as soon as the Silesian wars were over to continue the work interrupted near the end of the preceding reign. In an audience with the king in 1746 he put forward a plan with three main aims: to establish a single centralised judicial system throughout Prussian territory, with new uniform procedure that would reduce delay to a minimum; to weed out and improve the personnel; and to codify the law for the whole monarchy. The first two objects were attained in about five years' work, but the legal code was only planned in the last years of the reign, and not completed until 1795 by Carmer. As a result of the reforms, every province was left with only one central court, the 'Regierung', from a majority decision of whose judges a litigant could appeal only to the High Court in Berlin. Judges were reduced in number and adequately paid, but prohibited from taking dues and fines, as hitherto, for themselves, and from sending the dossiers to university law faculties for an opinion. Landowners had to provide State-approved, properly trained 'justiciaries' to conduct their manorial courts—the other courts of first instance, in the towns, had already been reformed. Procedure everywhere was simplified and greatly speeded up under pressure from above, 3000 outstanding actions being settled in the first year in Pomerania, where the worst delay had occurred. The advocates were examined and doubtful ones were combed out of the profession; under protest, they continued to wear the hated short cloak, which Frederick urged them to look upon as a toga.

Even Cocceji was unsuccessful in his attempt to abolish administrative justice. The provincial chambers retained very considerable powers of jurisdiction in anything affecting the 'public interest', particularly of course the revenue of the State. The king himself agreed, however, in principle not to interfere with the normal course of justice in civil cases, in response to petitions, for instance, though he often did so in criminal cases, and freely removed or punished judges who seemed to him unsatisfactory, as in the famous case of the miller of Sans Souci, in which it is now fairly clear that Frederick was in the wrong. On the whole, the reforms gave the ordinary citizen greatly increased security in his civil rights, especially in regard to property, and a firm basis was laid for capitalistic development.

CHAPTER XIV

RUSSIA

IN Russia, a new phase began with the defeat of Sweden at Poltava in 1709. The changes made by Peter the Great before that battle had been tentative and makeshift, dictated mostly by the immediate needs of war. When his victory at Poltava had freed Russia from the threat of invasion, he launched a programme of premeditated and consistent reforms, from which all his most enduring achievements emerged.

In the days of Peter the Great the chief source of Russia's wealth was her forests. The fertile steppe land of the south had not yet been brought under the plough. The spearhead of the southward colonisation movement was formed by the Don Cossacks, most of them deserters from the army, dissenters escaping persecution, or runaway peasants, all of whom despised the plough and lived a life of plunder along the rivers. In central Muscovy, which was the main agricultural area of Russia, some peasants continued the practice of burning tracts of forest, sowing their crops on the ashen soil for thirty to forty years and then moving off to repeat the process elsewhere. Even where the population was more permanent the peasants were reluctant to enrich the soil because their strips of land were redistributed every seven to twelve years. Most peasants used a light wooden plough with an iron share, but some still preferred a primitive hook plough that had been used in Russia for 700 years. Crops were harvested with the sickle in spite of Peter's efforts to introduce the scythe. Rye was the main crop in central Russia, but Peter induced the Baltic landowners to produce flax and hemp for export. North of a line stretching from St Petersburg to Kazan there was hardly any agriculture, the inhabitants being mostly lumbermen, trappers and fishermen. But this northern forest area with its sable, marten, fox and squirrel furs, its salt, and above all its timber, still provided most of Russia's wealth.

Russia's output of iron increased so much under Peter that she became self-supporting in munitions. The iron works at Tula founded in 1632 by Vinnius, a Dutch engineer, were enlarged to provide cannon and ships' tackle for use in Peter's first campaign against the Turks in 1695. When the war with Sweden began, foundries were established at Olonets and St Petersburg to exploit fresh sources of iron which had been discovered on the western shores of Lake Ladoga. But prospectors had already found better quality ore in the Urals, where there was an abundance of timber for smelting. In 1699 Demidov, a foreman at Tula, was sent to establish a foundry at Nevyansk, and before Peter died ten more foundries were in operation in the Urals. Soon after Poltava Russia ceased to import iron and by 1716 she had a surplus for export. By 1725 her annual output had reached 20,000 tons, more than half of it from the Urals.

Peter had also hoped to see his whole army uniformed in cloth of Russian manufacture, but he never achieved this ambition, though fifteen new textile factories were set up in the Moscow district during his reign. By 1725 the number of industrial undertakings of all types in Russia had risen to more than 200, many of them having several hundreds of workers. As an emergency measure Peter financed some of these undertakings by direct State investment, but he did not favour this as a permanent practice. From 1712 he insisted that merchants should employ in industry part of the profits derived from trade, and after the end of the Great Northern War he issued a general instruction for the transfer of State factories to private ownership.

The provision of labour for the new enterprises presented few difficulties. In the cities private owners employed the local poor, while the State conscripted thieves, prostitutes, drunkards and orphans for work in its factories. Iron foundries and other undertakings in less populated districts were manned by huge drafts of peasants 'ascribed' from State lands. More than 12,000 peasants were drafted to Olonets and about 25,000 to mines and foundries in the Urals. From 1721 merchant factory owners were permitted to buy peasants. To avoid an infringement of the rights of the nobility, these peasants were attached in perpetuity not to the factory owner but to the factory. If labour was plentiful, skilled craftsmen were few. Some Russians were trained by foreign craftsmen working in Russia and after 1711 factory managers were required to establish training schools for apprentices between the ages of 15 and 20, but in spite of these efforts industrial technique made no advance under Peter.

Communications improved under the stimulus of war, but many obstacles to the development of internal trade remained. Before Peter, paved roads had been made by laying planed logs side by side across earthern tracks. Peter considered the possibility of building a network of stone-paved roads, but abandoned the idea in favour of improving water transport. In 1708 he opened a canal linking the Volga and the Neva, which enabled shipwrights in the Baltic to obtain oak from the middle Volga, and work on another canal to by-pass Lake Ladoga was begun in 1718. But transport costs remained high. The movement of grain from Kursk to St Petersburg, for instance, increased the price 1600 per cent. Private trade was further hampered by customs dues exacted at the boundaries of cities and between Russia and the Ukraine. In addition each merchant had to pay an annual tax amounting to 5 per cent of his turnover, though nobles, peasants and clergy were permitted to engage in commerce free of tax. Credit facilities were as yet little developed. The merchants themselves operated a private system of letters of exchange which was used also for transactions by the State. In European Russia and in western Siberia small payments were made in cash but in eastern Siberia the local inhabitants still preferred barter.

The volume of Russia's exports to the West doubled and redoubled itself year by year after Peter had established a foothold on the Baltic. When he captured Ingria the foreign merchants who controlled most of the trade with the West were asked to transfer their depots from Archangel to the site of St Petersburg. During the 1690's only fifty to sixty foreign ships had visited Archangel annually. In 1720 more than 100 ships put in at the Baltic ports and in 1725 more than 650. Peter was not consciously a disciple of Colbert, but his urgent need for specie made him pursue an essentially mercantilist policy. In 1715 Russian consulates were opened in western Europe to promote the sale of Russian goods. Russian merchants were sent abroad at State expense to learn salesmanship. In 1724 Peter imposed import duties of 25 to 75 per cent on all luxury goods and on commodities of which adequate quantities were produced in Russia. At Peter's death Russian exports were valued at 4,200,000 *roubles* per annum and imports at only 2,100,000. As these figures include trade with the Middle East and Asia where Russia bought cotton, silk and tea and could sell little in exchange, the success of Peter's commercial policy in the West is particularly striking.

Though Peter developed industry and expanded foreign commerce, he found great difficulty in obtaining enough money to meet his military expenses. In 1701 he sequestered the revenues of the Church. He debased the coinage in 1710, but this provoked great discontent in the cities. The State extended its monopolies to include tobacco and salt, indirect taxes were imposed on beards, windows, baths and many other things and in 1718 Peter revised the system of direct taxation. Previously a tax had been levied on each household, but peasants had been evading tax by grouping themselves into large households. After his visit to Paris Peter adopted the French system of a direct tax on each individual. He ordered a census to be taken of all male peasants and the cost of the army and navy to be shared equally among them. In the first census of 1718 members of the priest and merchant classes without any obvious employment were counted as peasants. Slaves, who had hitherto paid no tax, were declared free but liable to tax. The number of male peasants was established at 5,500,000 and the new tax fixed at 74 *kopecks* per annum. This nearly trebled the amount of tax demanded of each peasant, and, as all male peasants were liable, an adult male had to earn enough to pay the tax for his male children and perhaps for his disabled father. But the new tax stimulated agriculture, for the peasants cultivated more land to pay it. By these fiscal reforms Peter increased the State revenue two-and-a-half times in fifteen years. In 1724 it amounted to 8,500,000 *roubles*, 4,600,000 being provided by the poll tax.

The total population of the Russian empire in 1725 was slightly over fourteen millions of which by far the most numerous group was that of the Russians themselves. Of the other groups the German landowners in Esthonia and Livonia were generously treated to gain their allegiance after the acquisition of the provinces in 1721. The Ukrainians on the other hand were subjected to political and economic assimilation especially after the betrayal of Peter by Mazepa in 1708, when a Russian resident and two Russian regiments were installed at the Ukrainian capital and land in the Ukraine was granted to Russian noblemen. After 1722 there was no hetman for nearly thirty years and the Ukraine was governed by a board in St Petersburg. A Ukrainian, Cyril Razumovsky, was made hetman in 1750 but he had close connections with the St Petersburg court and continued the russification of his people. The policy of russification was even more evident among the Tartar and Finnish peoples of the middle Volga and among the Bashkirs of the Urals. Many Bashkirs were ascribed to work in the Ural mines and the right to own peasants was denied to anyone who refused to embrace the Orthodox faith.

Among the Russian section of the population Peter did not radically change the social structure, but he considerably simplified it during the last fifteen years of his reign. He set clearly defined tasks for the four major classes, and smaller social groups were merged with one or other of these. The fiscal reform of 1718 enlarged the peasant class which by 1725 comprised more than 90 per cent of the population. The nobility accounted for 2 per cent, the merchants for 3 per cent and the priests for 2 per cent. The merchants were especially favoured by Peter. Besides breaking down the barriers which had separated them from the rest of society, he introduced a considerable degree of municipal autonomy in 1721. Inspired by the example of Riga and Reval he divided the residents of each city into two guilds, one for the wealthier merchants and industrialists, the other for small tradesmen and artisans. Members of both guilds elected the mayor and the aldermen who collected taxes and administered justice in the cities. But though the merchants were a most important instrument in Peter's reforms they retained their traditional dress and customs. Many were Old Believers and most of them deplored Peter's cultural innovations.

Unlike the merchants the peasants reaped no benefits from Peter's reforms. Indeed, they had now to provide additional taxes for the State as well as work or money for their immediate landlord. More than 60 per cent of the peasants, most of them living in the central provinces and the western lands which had been conquered from Poland-Lithuania, were serfs attached to private owners. In the fertile country south of Moscow they performed services (*barshchina*) for their landlord two or three days a week. Where the land was poor and the peasants earned their living by shoemaking, pottery, ikon painting and other types of cottage industry, they paid an annual levy (*obrok*) varying from 50 *kopecks* to 2 *roubles*. The amount of money or work exacted was fixed by the landlord who might also determine the size of his serfs' allotments, redistribute the land within the peasant communes, control the economic relations of serfs with persons outside the estate, command or prevent a serf's marriage or sell a serf with or without his land and even apart from his family. A serf was forbidden to leave his village without a passport issued by the landlord, and soon after Peter's death landlords were empowered to collect the poll tax. About 15 per cent of the peasants lived on lands belonging to the Church. As monks were usually more exacting landlords than laymen, agrarian disturbances were frequent on Church lands and many Church peasants fled to Siberia or to join the Cossacks on the Don. Among the 13 per cent of the peasantry who lived in Siberia and on the northern fringes of European Russia serfdom was almost unknown. But Peter was determined to make these peasants bear their proper share of the taxes and when he imposed the poll tax he exacted from them an additional 40 *kopecks* per annum as *obrok* to the State. Life was better for State peasants than for private serfs, though they were Peter's main source of mobile labour and might be employed digging canals, building St Petersburg or on work in the mines. Other small categories of peasants included the Crown peasants and the *odnodvortsy*, men who held small estates on a service tenure on the south-eastern frontier. These might well have been classed as serving nobility, but they were counted as peasants in the census of 1718 and by the end of the century had become merged with the State peasants.

It was the class of the serving nobility which was altered by Peter more than any other. In the sixteenth century there had been an important distinction between the nobles who held land in perpetuity (*votchiny*) and the 'serving people' who held estates by service (*pomestiya*). During the seventeenth century this distinction had disappeared, for all estates had become hereditary. In 1714 Peter gave legal recognition to what was already happening in practice by declaring all estates to be *votchiny*. In other ways the composition of the class was radically changed. Peter swelled the ranks of the nobility by recruiting men from other social classes and made provision that this source of recruitment should continue even after his death. In 1722 all posts in the army, navy and civil administration were classified into fourteen parallel grades. Peter insisted that every one should start at the bottom: those who reached the eighth grade from the top were granted the privileges of nobility. The nobles were also forced to adopt a new style of living. Russian dress and beards were banned and Peter introduced a compulsory system of hospitality by which each noble in turn had to entertain his fellows and the emperor. This hospitality was contrary to Muscovite tradition and proved economically disastrous to the nobles who had not the resources to afford the burgundy and champagne, French brocades and English furniture that were considered indispensable. Within a few decades many nobles were ruined by extravagant efforts to ape the dress and entertainments of western Europe. In addition to revolutionising the social habits of the nobility Peter reasserted the principle, enunciated in the sixteenth century but disregarded for some time before his accession, that a noble must serve the State for the best part of his life. He even tried to create a landless group of nobles who would be forced by economic necessity into State service. This was the object of the Entail Law of 1714 which, contrary to the Muscovite custom of inheritance, declared that estates might not be divided but must be left in their entirety to a single son or relative chosen by the owners. In 1725 a Russian noble began service at the age of 10 when he was compelled to go to school. At 15 he had to leave school whether he wished or not, for to remain at school after 15 was regarded as tantamount to evading State service. Most young nobles of 15 applied for posts in the civil service, but two out of three were usually drafted into the army where they served as privates in one of the three regiments of the Imperial Guard for five years before being posted to other units as officers. Few noblemen volunteered to serve in the navy. Those who failed their examinations at the age of 15 were sent to sea compulsorily, but even compulsion did not provide enough recruits for the navy and Peter had to employ Danes and Dutchmen as ships' captains. If a young noble began his service in the administration, he might start in the chancellery of the Senate or of one of the colleges, in the office of a provincial governor or in one of the Russian missions abroad.

The army, in which the majority of young nobles served, was another institution to be completely reorganised by Peter. Under his predecessors it had consisted partly of foreign mercenaries and partly of peasant levies raised by noblemen. After Narva, Peter replaced this force by a standing army, uniform in organisation and raised by conscription. In 1705 he conscripted one man from every twenty peasant households. The number of conscripts varied in subsequent years, but the total strength of the army in 1724 was more than 200,000 not including about 100,000 Cossacks and other semi-regulars. The troops were paid by the State, but billets, food and forage for all units stationed in the empire had to be supplied by the peasants. The term of service for all ranks was for life.

The administrative system Peter reformed as fundamentally as he did the army. When he set off on the Pruth campaign in 1711 he left the government in the hands of a Senate of nine members. On his return he retained the Senate to advise him in the preparation of legislation, to direct the work of provincial administration and to act as supreme court of justice. Attached to the Senate was a chancellery for the conduct of clerical business. Peter supervised the work of the senators closely. From 1711 their sessions were attended by an officer of the Imperial Guard who had orders to arrest and report any senator who behaved improperly. In 1722 the Guards officer was withdrawn and replaced by a permanent official, the *general prokuror*. The system of supervision was completed by the appointment of an *oberfiskal* to see that State funds were not mis-applied.

From 1715 Peter felt that the Senate was overburdened with work. After consulting foreign experts such as Fick of Holstein and even the philosopher Leibniz he published a general regulation in 1718 abolishing the fifty Muscovite *prikazy* and organising each branch of the administra-tion in one of nine colleges, which were to act as intermediate links be-tween the Senate and the provincial administration. One college was to deal with tax collection, another with expenditure, while a third supervised and co-ordinated the work of these two. Two more colleges controlled commerce and industry respectively. The remaining four handled foreign affairs, war, admiralty and justice. Each college consisted of a president, vice-president and four members. Each college had its own chancellery and each worked under the supervision of a *prokuror*. The collegiate system was copied from Denmark and Sweden, and at first all colleges had foreigners as vice-presidents.

In his reform of the provincial administration Peter made a number of experiments, none of them entirely successful. After social disturbances among the Don Cossacks in 1708 the whole of Russia was divided into eight provinces each under the control of a governor who had full powers to use the military forces at his disposal should any future disturbance break out. In 1713 Peter developed this security measure into a compre-hensive scheme of local administration by setting up in each province a board of counsellors (*landraty*) to collect taxes and to help the governor with other non-military business. The *landraty* were in theory to be elected by the local nobility, but in fact most of them were appointed by the Senate. In 1715 each province was subdivided, with a *landrat* to administer each division. This system was scrapped in 1719 when Russia was divided into fifty provinces each administered by a *voevoda* appointed by the Senate. The *voevoda* was to be assisted by a tax collector, a forestry official, and another official responsible for collecting grain to supply the army. The tax collector was appointed by the college responsible for State revenue: the rest by the Senate. This new arrangement proved too costly, however, and three years after Peter's death it was abandoned. Even during Peter's lifetime it had been made largely redundant since by 1722 the bulk of the army was quartered in European Russia and regimental commanders had been ordered to collect taxes and supplies of grain.

The provincial officials were not even required to administer justice, for it had been one of Peter's aims to keep administration and justice separate. In 1725 there were ten judicial circuits in Russia, each with its own assize court. Legal procedure was slow and complicated, however, for there was no code of law later than 1649. Peter had intended to co-ordinate laws promulgated since 1649, but the only field in which he introduced any clarification was criminal law. A code of military law was prepared in 1715 and in the following year Peter decreed that the section dealing with criminal law should apply to the entire population. The death penalty, by hanging, shooting, beheading, burning alive, impalement or breaking on the wheel, was prescribed for over 100 offences. Lesser crimes were punished by penal servitude in the galleys or in mines, by social degradation and by imprisonment. The State made no provision for the maintenance of ordinary prisoners who were led through the streets in chains to beg. Under a regulation of 1698 a court was required only to consider written depositions, but Peter issued a fresh instruction in 1723 permitting judges to hear witnesses and accused in person. The validity of evidence depended on the social status of the witness. The law held that a priest was a better witness than a layman, a nobleman than a peasant, a man than a woman. But the evidence most highly valued was a confession by the accused.

In his treatment of the Church Peter won the final victory in a struggle which had lasted for more than two centuries by abolishing the Patriarchate and making the Church subordinate to himself. In 1721 the Ukrainian prelate Feofan Prokopovich justified this action by pointing to the political inconveniences created by the Patriarch's claims to be 'equal in power to the tsar himself or even more exalted'. Later Prokopovich affirmed that though the monarch derived his supreme and uncontested power from God himself the autocracy existed also with the consent and for the good of the entire people. The second of these arguments was advanced by Peter's foreign administrative advisers to justify the existence of the State to which Peter himself took an oath of loyalty in 1721. After abolition of the Patriarchate the Church was administered by a Synod, created in 1721. This was similar in composition to the colleges but consisted at first exclusively of churchmen. However, after the death of its first clerical president this post was abolished and the Synod was directed by a lay *ober-prokuror*. Peter's reform in Church administration had little effect on the secular clergy, though he ordered the Synod to raise the standard of their discipline and education. The monks and nuns on the other hand, of whom there were about 14,000 and 10,000 respectively, were regarded by Peter as social parasites, and to prevent any increase in their numbers small monasteries were closed and entry into the remainder was strictly limited. As for the Old Believers, Peter would not admit them to the State service and he exacted from them twice the normal amount of taxes. But as a religious sect they were tolerated and only those who expressed political criticism were tortured or imprisoned.

Peter met with little co-operation in his efforts to create a secular system of education. At the end of the seventeenth century there was one printing press in Russia and one educational establishment, the Slavonic-Greek-Latin Academy in Moscow. Both were in the hands of the clergy.

Between 1701 and 1715 Peter opened a naval academy, an engineering school, an artillery school and a medical school. Attendance was so poor that in 1714 it was made compulsory for sons of the nobility. The naval academy provided instructors for the first elementary schools opened in the provinces in 1715 for 'young persons of every class'. The cost of the elementary schools was borne by the admiralty and by 1722 there were forty-two of them with about 2000 pupils. By 1725, however, the number had dropped to twenty-eight with 500 pupils, primarily because priests had been advised by their bishops not to allow their sons to attend secular schools. In 1721 the bishops themselves had started to open schools in their dioceses. By 1725 there were forty-six diocesan schools, teachers being provided from the Slavonic-Greek-Latin Academy. A few months after Peter's death the admiralty proposed that the secular elementary schools should be merged with the Church schools. When the Synod refused, most of the remaining secular schools were closed.

Peter's attempts to educate nobles, merchants and civil servants by providing suitable books were hardly more successful. He personally selected many of the books printed by the Synod Press in Moscow, while another press in St Petersburg and two in Holland worked exclusively to his orders producing text-books on arithmetic, navigation and astronomy, including the first work in Russian on the Copernican system. Though copies of lives of the saints were bought in thousands, few of the books printed to Peter's orders were sold. Those of the laity who could read preferred novels describing the amorous adventures of young nobles abroad, but none of these novels was printed in Russia until 1750.

When Peter died, in 1725, there was no change in the formal character of the autocratic power, but no one after him exercised that power so personally and directly as Peter had done. Most of his immediate successors were women. Lovers of comfort and distraction, with little taste for the wearisome routine of government business, they were pleased to find someone who would undertake their duties for them.

At the moment of Peter's death no one knew who was to succeed him. His only son, Aleksey, had been put away for alleged complicity in a plot to overthrow Peter in 1719. Three years later the emperor had revised the succession law to permit the reigning monarch to choose his own successor, but he had failed to nominate an heir for himself. The only male descendant to survive him was his grandson Peter, son of the unfortunate Aleksey. Peter Alekseyevich's claims to the throne were supported by the Golitsyns, the Dolgorukys and other leading families of the Muscovite aristocracy. With a ten-year-old boy as emperor, they hoped to purge the nobility of the new elements introduced by Peter, to revive the Boyars' Duma and to lead Russia back into the path from which Peter had diverted her. Of the other claimants to the succession Field-Marshal Menshikov in particular favoured the Empress Catherine, whose transformation from

Livonian peasant girl into crowned empress had been as remarkable as his own and who shared his interest in self-preservation.

Menshikov was in a very strong position to press the claims of Catherine. As President of the College of War, he had the Imperial Guard under his command: and, having distributed largesse in advance to the personnel of the Preobrazhensky regiment, he ordered them to surround the palace in St Petersburg while the succession was being discussed. Under these circumstances the Dolgorukys and their associates had no choice but to yield. Catherine was proclaimed empress in her own right, with Menshikov as virtual dictator. It was clear even to Menshikov that the choice of Catherine was only a temporary solution, for the health of the new empress was poor and it was not improved by the manner of her living. In the event of her death Menshikov had no second candidate to support, and he was forced to propose a compromise with the league of Boyars. He would accept Peter Alekseyevich as Catherine's successor, provided that his opponents would agree to a marriage between Peter and one of Menshikov's daughters. A bargain was struck and, in pursuance of the terms of the 1722 succession law, Catherine drew up a testament naming Peter Alekseyevich as first in the line of succession, and after him her two daughters Elizabeth and Anna Petrovna.

As their part of the bargain, the Dolgorukys asked for some share of the power which Catherine had delegated to Menshikov, and the compromise was sealed by the creation of a Supreme Privy Council, which contained members of both factions. It was intended that the new Council should sit under the presidency of the empress herself. But after a few sessions Catherine lost interest in the Council's work, and permitted it to legislate in her absence. By 1727 the Council had taken over the more important functions of the Senate and the Colleges, and the administrative system designed by Peter the Great ceased to exist.

When Catherine died in May 1727, Menshikov honoured his promise and took the oath to Peter Alekseyevich. But nothing could alter the fact that Peter was the candidate of the Dolgorukys, and from the beginning of the new reign Menshikov was disturbed by the insecurity of his position. In the late summer of 1727 the Field-Marshal became seriously ill. Convinced that he was about to die, he wrote a valedictory letter commending his family to the emperor's favour. After six weeks he recovered, but when he returned to his duties he found that the Dolgorukys had not been idle in his absence. In the Supreme Privy Council, they had won the allegiance of the solitary neutral member, the Vice-Chancellor Ostermann. They had placed a member of their family in the imperial household as tutor to the emperor. Most serious of all, they had gained control of the Preobrazhensky and the Semenovsky regiments. Menshikov tried to reassert his authority, but without the support of the Guard there was no hope for him. He was arrested, tried and sent into exile with his whole family. On his departure the Dolgorukys were quick to consolidate their position. Menshikov's supporters were excluded from the Supreme Privy Council. The emperor was betrothed to Catherine, daughter of Aleksey Dolgoruky. The seat of government was returned to Moscow. The Secret Chancellery was abolished. Peter the Great's complex system of local government was abandoned on grounds of economy, and the provincial *voevody* were given what amounted to complete autonomy. For two and a half years the emperor spent the entire spring and summer on hunting expeditions in the country round Moscow; and, as the members of the Supreme Privy Council were ordered to accompany him, the internal government of the country virtually came to a standstill.

Had Peter lived to manhood, it is improbable that any of his grand-father's work would have survived at all. But in January 1730, on the day appointed for his wedding to Catherine Dolgoruky, he died of smallpox. Faced by the necessity of choosing a new candidate, the members of the Supreme Privy Council became divided against themselves. Aleksey Dolgoruky forged the signature of Peter to a document naming Catherine as his successor, but a majority in the Council gave its support to an alternative project put forward by another member, Dmitry Golitsyn. Golitsyn, remembering how the powers of the Swedish monarchy had been restricted after the death of Charles XII, believed that the moment was opportune for a similar attack upon the autocracy in Russia. His candidate for the succession was one of Peter the Great's nieces, the widowed Duchess Anna Ivanovna of Courland. He proposed that the crown be offered to Anna provided that she agreed in advance to accept a number of 'conditions' formulated by Golitsyn himself. The 'conditions' obliged the empress to ask for the assent of the Supreme Privy Council before marrying, choosing an heir, declaring war, concluding peace, making appointments above the rank of colonel or sentencing a nobleman to death. The Council also was to have command of the army and the Imperial Guard.

A message containing these proposals having been sent to Anna at Mitava, she accepted the 'conditions' and set out for Moscow. But before she arrived in the capital, the Supreme Privy Council had encountered opposition from an unexpected quarter. In January 1730 Moscow was crowded with members of the nobility who had assembled for Peter's wedding but found themselves called upon to decide the fate of the monarchy. They were dismayed to discover that Anna had agreed to divide her authority with the Supreme Privy Council. Some of them felt that, if there was to be any division of the imperial power, then it should be shared with the nobility as a whole. Others argued that the interests of the nobility would best be served by a restoration of the autocracy.

On 25 February, a fortnight after her arrival in Moscow, Anna received delegations of the nobility in the Kremlin. One of them, led by the poet and diplomat Antioch Kantemir, begged the empress to resume the title and the powers of an autocratic monarch. Other projects were presented for the empress' consideration, but when the attendant officers of the Guard had made it clear by literally rattling their sabres that they desired a restoration of the autocracy, Anna took the copy of the 'conditions' which she had signed in Mitava and tore it into pieces. The Supreme Privy Council was dissolved. Its members (Ostermann excepted) were arrested and executed or sent into banishment. Some of them lived long enough to benefit from an amnesty in a later reign: but the league of Boyar families never appeared on the political scene again. Anna promised to follow in the footsteps of Peter the Great and as a symbol of this intention the court returned to St Petersburg.

Golitsyn, regretting the failure of his plan, prophesied that 'those who cause me to weep now will weep more bitterly themselves'. His forecast proved to be true, for the nobility, having rescued the monarchy from the designs of the Supreme Privy Council, found themselves faced with a new enemy in the person of the empress's favourite, Ernst Johann Bühren. Bühren came from a family of Westphalian origin which had settled in Courland and received the title of nobility during the seventeenth century. Anna had befriended him in 1718, and on her accession he followed her to Moscow. In Russia he never held any official appointment beyond that of head of the imperial stables (he shared the empress's passion for riding), but his influence was immense and his reputation sinister. At his suggestion Anna revived the Secret Chancellery, and in the ten years of her reign more than 10,000 of her subjects were arrested on the suspicion of conspiring against her. In the eyes of the Russian nobility Bühren personified the German element which was predominant at court and in the administration throughout the 1730's. Senior appointments in the imperial household were given to friends of Bühren who had accompanied him from Courland. Münnich, a soldier of fortune who had entered the service of Peter the Great in 1716, was made commander-in-chief of the army, and new responsibilities were entrusted to the Vice-Chancellor Ostermann.

When she dissolved the Supreme Privy Council, Anna promised to restore to the Senate all the prerogatives which it had enjoyed under Peter the Great, but it was not long before the Senate was degraded for a second time. From March 1730 the empress was assisted by a small personal chancellery consisting of Ostermann and two Russian members. In the following year this chancellery was renamed the 'Cabinet of Ministers' and given official status as an intermediary between the empress and the higher branches of the administration. In time Anna, following Catherine's example, permitted the cabinet to govern for her. She announced in 1735 that the decisions of the cabinet were to have the same force as imperial *ukazy*: and since the two Russian members of the cabinet were political nonentities, control of the entire administration was placed in the hands of Ostermann.

Ostermann himself was not in the beginning hostile to the Russian nobility. It was he who, on Anna's arrival from Mitava, had advised her that it would be prudent to grant the nobility some concessions. Following his advice Anna had rescinded Peter the Great's Entail Law in 1730, and in the following year an arrangement was made which permitted the nobility to enter the services with officer's rank. At the age of 15 young noblemen were invited to enter a new establishment, the Cadet Corps of the Nobility. Right of entry into the corps was a privilege of the class; and when a nobleman left the corps at the age of 20, he was posted direct to a regiment with the rank of ensign without the necessity of serving as a private soldier for a period of probation. In 1736 the empress went a step further to meet the demands of the nobility by limiting the term of service to twenty-five years, and allowing one son in each family to remain at home and manage the family estate. It was unfortunate for the nobility that this concession was made soon after the outbreak of hostilities with Turkey. The operation of the 1736 *ukaz* was suspended for the duration of the war, and when peace came in 1739 the concession was still withheld on the instructions of Bühren.

By 1739 a nationalist group of the nobility was in open revolt against the German element at court. The nobles were led by Artemy Petrovich Volynsky, one of the most brilliant and unscrupulous of Peter the Great's younger administrators. In 1729 Volynsky had been governor of the province of Astrakhan, but on the accession of Anna he returned to the capital, insinuated himself into the favour of Bühren and eventually secured a seat in the Cabinet of Ministers. Once in the cabinet he felt strong enough to dissociate himself from Bühren, and gathered round him all the malcontents in the capital—members of the Church as well as the nobility. Bühren was aware of the conspiracy against him, but he took no action until Volynsky pleaded with Anna herself to dismiss her favourite. Volynsky was arrested at once and after torture in the Secret Chancellery he confessed that he had tried to poison the empress and seize the throne himself. Bühren secured Volynsky's execution, but he could not feel safe from attack by the nobility as long as the Imperial Guard remained in the capital. As early as 1730 he had tried to assure himself of support within the Guard by forming a new regiment, the Izmailovsky, which was commanded by one of his German friends and recruited from Esthonians, Livonians and other sections of the population which had no connection with the Russian nobility. After the Volynsky affair, he confided to a friend his intention of removing the Guard from St Petersburg altogether and replacing it with ordinary regiments.

As it turned out Bühren owed his downfall not to the national feeling of the Russian nobility but to the jealousy of his German associates.

During Anna's lifetime it was impossible for them to persuade her to part company with Bühren, but when she died in October 1740 they could no longer reconcile themselves to playing a subordinate role. Anna was succeeded by Ivan Antonovich, son of her niece Anna Leopoldovna and Prince Anton Ulrich of Brunswick. As the emperor was still an infant, Bühren assumed the regency: but Ivan's mother was an ambitious woman and, believing that she had prior claims to the regency, she enlisted the support of Münnich in removing Bühren from office. After a night raid on Bühren's palace by a detachment of the Preobrazhensky under the command of Münnich himself, Anna Leopoldovna was established as regent and for three weeks Münnich governed in her name. Then Ostermann, who had been content to play a waiting game for sixteen years since the death of Peter the Great, felt that his chance had come at last and persuaded Anna Leopoldovna to displace Münnich in favour of himself. But his triumph too was short-lived, for in November 1741 the intervention of a foreign power precipitated yet another palace revolution.

Since the death of Peter the Great the Russian army had diminished in efficiency, but the legend of Poltava was still alive in Europe. At different times Austria, France and Britain sought the assistance of Russia as a military ally. Ostermann had concluded an alliance with Austria in 1726 but since then the French Government had made more than one attempt to lure Russia into their camp. During the War of the Polish Succession Cardinal Fleury had sent an emissary to St Petersburg offering an alliance on terms which even Ostermann thought worthy of consideration. As the war progressed diplomatic relations between the two countries were severed, but when ambassadors were exchanged again in 1739 Fleury sent the marquis de la Chétardie to St Petersburg with express orders to undermine the Austro-Russian alliance. To this end he was authorised, if necessary, to engineer a palace revolution and secure the dismissal of Ostermann. Soon after his arrival in Russia la Chétardie had entered into negotiations with the sole surviving daughter of Peter the Great, the Tsarevna Elizabeth. Elizabeth herself had no political ambitions, but she was popular with the soldiers of the Preobrazhensky (her palace in St Petersburg adjoined the regimental barracks) and she was regarded as a possible candidate by the nationalist group of the nobility.

In his efforts to persuade Elizabeth to seize the throne la Chétardie was joined by the Swedish ambassador and the tsarevna's private physician Dr Lestocq, who was in receipt of a considerable annuity from the French Government. After some months of vacillation Elizabeth agreed to the following plan. Sweden was to declare war on Russia, the avowed object of the Swedish army being to deliver the Russians from the German yoke and to place Elizabeth on the throne.

With the Swedish army on the march Elizabeth was still hesitant, but her hand was forced in November 1741 when the Guard received orders to leave the capital and proceed to the front. Lestocq persuaded the tsarevna that, if she did not act before the Guard left, her chance would be lost for ever. On the night of 24 November she was enthusiastically acclaimed at the barracks of the Preobrazhensky, and with a company of the regiment she set out for the Imperial Palace. By 3 o'clock on the following morning the emperor, his mother the regent, his father, Münnich and Ostermann were all under arrest, and Elizabeth issued a manifesto proclaiming her accession. She justified the step which she had taken by recalling the testament of her mother, Catherine I, who had named Elizabeth and Anna Petrovna as next after Peter Alekseyevich in the line of succession. Anna had died in 1728, but her son the duke of Holstein was nominated as Elizabeth's heir. As a gesture of thanksgiving Elizabeth promised that none of her subjects would be condemned to death during her lifetime. Ostermann and Münnich were subjected to mock execution and then exiled. The Cabinet of Ministers was dissolved and the Senate once again had its former prerogatives restored.

From the point of view of France the revolution was a failure. After Ostermann's arrest the direction of Russian diplomacy was entrusted to Alexander Bestuzhev-Ryumin, who failed to observe Elizabeth's undertakings either to Sweden or to France. The Swedish troops in the north, so far from being welcomed as deliverers, were put to flight across the swamps of Finland. Russia honoured her obligations to Austria as scrupulously as ever. In a last effort to sever relations with Vienna, Lestocq fabricated evidence to discredit the Austrian ambassador in St Petersburg, the marquis de Botta. De Botta, it was alleged, was involved in a conspiracy to overthrow Elizabeth, his accomplices being Natalia Lopukhina, a lady of the court, and members of the Bestuzhev family. After a long inquiry Lopukhina and one of the Bestuzhevs were publicly flogged and mutilated. De Botta was withdrawn from St Petersburg, but the Austrian Government refused to take seriously the charges levelled against him.

More than ten years later a genuine attempt to interfere with Elizabeth's provision for the succession was made by Sir Charles Hanbury Williams, the British representative in St Petersburg. At the beginning of the 1750's the British Government were alarmed by the possibility of a Prussian attack on Hanover, and they instructed Williams to approach Elizabeth with an offer of substantial subsidies if she would order Russian troops to enter Prussia. Elizabeth was at first unwilling to commit Russian troops in the defence of Hanover but Bestuzhev, who had been in the pay of the British since 1746, presented the offer in a favourable light, and a convention between the two countries was signed in 1755. Before Elizabeth had ratified it, however, the convention was rendered null and void by the conclusion of the Treaty of Westminster. The sudden alliance of Britain with Prussia gave rise to consternation in St Petersburg. For the first time since her accession Elizabeth followed the example of her predecessors and delegated her powers to a 'Conference attached to the Imperial Court'. The conference assumed supreme control of diplomatic and military policy, and a majority of its members was in favour of a *rapprochement* between Russia and France. This was a development which Bestuzhev and Hanbury Williams were determined at all costs to prevent. Since the empress was known to sympathise with the francophile group, they sought the co-operation of the 'Young Court'. Hanbury Williams had no confidence in the duke of Holstein, for he was a feckless young man, frail in body, undeveloped in mind and little versed in Russian politics. But in 1745 he had married Princess Sophia Augusta of Anhalt-Zerbst, who was rechristened Catherine on her reception into the Orthodox Church. The marriage had not been a happy one, and Catherine spent her hours of solitude studying the life and interests of the country of her adoption. She was determined and intelligent, and Williams felt that she would make an admirable accomplice. Having discovered from her lover, Stanislas Poniatowski, that she was financially embarrassed, the British ambassador offered her a gift of £10,000 and outlined his proposals to her. As the empress was subject to frequent attacks of apoplexy, it was generally believed that her death was imminent. When the duke of Holstein succeeded her, Catherine was to be proclaimed Empress Consort, equal in rank and power to her husband, and was to ensure that the conference broke off negotiations with France. Catherine was prudent enough not to decline the proposal, but she did not commit herself.

The fulfilment of Williams's plan was overtaken by the outbreak of the Seven Years War. In December 1756 Russia had acceded to the Treaty of Versailles and in May 1757 the Russian army, commanded in the field by Field-Marshal Apraksin but subject to the instructions of the conference in St Petersburg, crossed the Prussian frontier. Bestuzhev and Hanbury Williams believed that their cause was lost, but new hope came in September 1757. After Apraksin's victory at Gross Jägersdorf the empress fell ill again. Were she to die, then Catherine would seize power, suspend military operations against Prussia and withdraw from the alliance with France. But the empress recovered, and at the prompting of the new French ambassador, de l'Hôpital, Bestuzhev was arrested. Apraksin too was recalled to the capital and placed under arrest, for it was alleged (without foundation) that his decision to withdraw to Memel after Gross Jägersdorf was made at Bestuzhev's request. Against Catherine there was no evidence, Bestuzhev having burnt his papers. But she was not free from suspicion, because during the summer of 1757 she had been in correspondence with Apraksin. She received a reprimand from the empress and, having once had her fingers burnt, she never raised a hand against Elizabeth again. She withdrew from court altogether and formed a liaison with Grigory Orlov, an officer of the Izmailovsky regiment.

In the beginning the affair provided Catherine simply with distraction, but she knew enough of the history of past years to understand the political advantages of such an attachment.

When Elizabeth died in December 1761, the provisions of her testament were carried out without incident, the duke of Holstein being proclaimed emperor with the title of Peter III. On the morrow of his accession hostilities with Prussia were suspended. The emperor was a personal admirer of Frederick and he intended to depart for Pomerania to place the Russian army and himself at Frederick's disposal. But before he could leave the country, his unpopularity with the nobility had cost him the throne.

Throughout Elizabeth's reign the nobility had continued their struggle for emancipation. On her accession Elizabeth had confirmed the 1736 *ukaz* limiting the period of service to twenty-five years, and more concessions were to follow. During the 1730's the nobles had devised a new method of evading service. Male children were inscribed on the rolls of the Guards regiments at birth: in infancy they were promoted to the rank of sergeant: by the age of 10, before they had left home, they were commissioned officers: and at 25 many of them had reached the rank of general and, under the terms of 1736 *ukaz*, were eligible for retirement. Bühren had tried to suppress this practice: Elizabeth gave it legal sanction. By the 1750's some noblemen were pressing for the complete abolition of compulsory service. Elizabeth was prepared to grant this final concession, but the conference advised her to wait at least until the conclusion of the war with Prussia. When fighting was suspended in 1761, the nobility appealed to the new emperor to release them from their obligations. Peter, apparently ignorant of what this would entail, acceded to the request, and in February 1762 he issued the 'Manifesto on the Release of the Nobility', permitting noblemen to leave the service at any time, except in war, and to travel abroad as they wished, provided that they returned home at the summons of the emperor. There was only one drawback for those who took advantage of the manifesto. Noblemen who resigned from service were banned for life from appearing at court.

The manifesto of 1762 completed the emancipation of the nobility, but it did not win gratitude for the emperor. For this he had only himself to blame. He took delight in ridiculing the ceremonies of the Orthodox Church. He insulted priests and vilified his own wife in public. The Grenadier Company of the Preobrazhensky, which had been granted the title of Personal Bodyguard to Elizabeth for the part it had played in the revolution of November 1742, was dismissed from the capital and replaced with a detachment of troops from Holstein. A prince of Holstein was appointed commander-in-chief of the Russian army.

The nobles were unable to tolerate any further affronts, and in February 1762 Grigory Orlov and his brothers began canvassing support for Catherine in the Izmailovsky and Semenovsky regiments. By June preparations for the emperor's overthrow were complete. In the middle of the month the emperor left the capital for a holiday in the country before joining the army in Pomerania. During his absence one of Orlov's accomplices was arrested. Orlov decided to act before the conspiracy was compromised, and on the night of 29 June he summoned Catherine to the barracks of the Izmailovsky, where the soldiers were roused from their bunks to take the oath to a new empress. There were some skirmishes between the Izmailovsky and Peter's supporters, but, when morning came, Catherine was conducted to the Cathedral of Our Lady of Kazan to give thanks for her accession.

The Church played no part in the palace revolutions of the eighteenth century. Feofan Prokopovich intervened on his own initiative to safeguard the autocracy during the crisis of 1730, but the Synod as a body gave its blessing indiscriminately to each new occupant of the throne. The economic insecurity of the official Church discouraged its leaders from attempting a re-entry into politics.

For eight years the court of Anna Ivanovna treated the Church with polite indifference, but in 1738 the cabinet complained that the arrears of poll tax due from the Church peasants had reached an unreasonable figure, and the Senate was authorised to take over the management of Church estates from the Synod. Elizabeth was by nature more devout than her prececessor, and one of her first acts was to restore the Church lands to the Synod's control. But on the outbreak of the Seven Years War the domains of the bishops and the monasteries were lost to the Synod once again, and this time for ever. In 1757 they were placed under the management of temporary lay officials, who allotted a small portion of the revenues to the Synod and handed over the rest to the treasury. When the war was over a special board was created to administer the Church lands on the treasury's behalf in perpetuity.

In spite of the financial difficulties of the Church, the diocesan schools founded in 1721 were still the mainstay of the educational system in the 1760's. In 1737 the Synod instructed the bishops to convert the diocesan schools into seminaries, offering at least something more than a primary education. The conversion was impeded by lack of funds, but by 1762 there were twenty-six seminaries with about 6000 pupils. The standard of education was not high, but the seminaries provided many of the students for the St Petersburg Academy of Sciences and for the University of Moscow.

The St Petersburg Academy was an institution wider in scope than its name suggests. It comprised not only an academy in the proper sense of the word, but a university and a 'gymnasium' as well. The academy flourished from its foundation in 1726. Before he died, Peter the Great had sent invitations to the first academicians, who included the historian

Gerhard Müller from Leipzig, the geographer Joseph Delisle from Paris, the naturalist Johann Gmelin from Tübingen, the mathematicians Nicolas and Daniel Bernouilli from Basle and other savants of genuine distinction from all over Europe. By the time of Elizabeth's accession some of the chairs at the academy were already held by Russians, and the political conflict between the nationalist and the German elements at court was reflected in an attempt by the Russian professors to purge the academy of foreign influences. In 1745 two German professors were dismissed for asserting the Scandinavian origin of the Varangians. Others left in protest, and by 1750 Müller was the only foreigner of ability who remained.

The university and the 'gymnasium' were slower to develop than the academy, for the number of pupils who attended was small. Students from the diocesan seminaries and from the Slavonic-Greek-Latin Academy in Moscow were sent to the university at State expense from 1730 onwards, but even this form of inducement had little success. The professors at the academy argued that the cost of living in the capital was too high for students and that it was impossible for a university to flourish in a city where there were educational establishments of a purely utilitarian character. Another university was opened in the old capital in 1755, with faculties of law, history, natural science and the humanities. Here too the number of voluntary students was small, but Elizabeth induced members of the nobility to attend by promising that university attendance would be deemed equivalent to service for the same period.

Even after this concession had been made the University of Moscow attracted fewer noblemen than the Cadet Corps. In addition to their military training the cadets received instructions in deportment, singing, dancing, and foreign languages: and by the end of Elizabeth's reign the corps had become the centre of literary and artistic life in the capital. One of the cadets, Sumarokov, translated the tragedies of Corneille and Racine for the first theatrical performances at the Russian court, and himself wrote the first original tragedy in Russian. When these plays were acted before the empress, the corps provided the players. The first literary periodical founded by the academician Müller contained articles on moral themes translated by the cadets from English, French and German: and they co-operated in the publication of the first printed novels (nearly all of them translated) during the 1750's. At the same time French had become the fashionable, if not yet the official, language of the court, and the wealthier nobility ordered their books direct from Paris. Before her accession Catherine had already become acquainted with Montesquieu's *De l'esprit des lois* and Voltaire's *Essai sur les mœurs et l'esprit des nations*.

As the field of their interests widened, the nobility found it increasingly difficult to remain solvent. During Anna Ivanovna's reign the sums spent on entertainment by the members of her court had risen so high that legislation was introduced to restrict expenditure on building, furniture and clothes. On Elizabeth's accession the competition in extravagance began again and, following the example of the empress herself, the nobility strove to reproduce in St Petersburg every detail of the court of Louis XV. Before Elizabeth's death not a few of the families raised to the nobility by Peter the Great were ruined. Of the rest, some made use of the facilities offered by the Bank of the Nobility. Founded in 1754 with capital provided from the treasury, the bank offered loans at 6 per cent on the security of noblemen's estates. Those who accepted assistance from the bank did not realise at the time that they were placing themselves in bondage to the State. Eighty years after the bank's foundation more than two-thirds of all the estates of the nobility were mortgaged without prospect of redemption.

The more provident of the nobility invested such capital as they had in industry, and the percentage of industrial undertakings owned or managed by noblemen at the end of the 1760's (sixty-eight out of 325, according to one estimate) was higher than at any other time during the century. Bühren drew a substantial portion of his income from a group of ironworks in the Urals leased from the State on his behalf by a friend. Noblemen of more modest means particularly in the *obrok* regions opened distilleries, tanneries and linen and cloth mills on their estates, the labour being provided by the serfs.

For the great majority of the nobility, however, the only means of obtaining increased income was a more intensive exploitation of their land. On many estates operated on the *obrok* system, the dues exacted from each peasant were raised to 4 *roubles*. In the more fertile provinces peasants were forced to work as many as six days a week for the landowner. They were allotted no land at all for their own use, but received a fixed ration of grain from the landowner for their subsistence. Revolt and desertion became more frequent in consequence and, as the central Government wished to be relieved of the responsibility of maintaining order on the land, the landowners were given powers to deal with recalcitrant peasants. By the time of Catherine's accession they were permitted to sentence their serfs to deportation or penal servitude without reference to the public courts.

The administration of the national finances after the death of Peter the Great was chaotic. For years on end no accounts were kept of revenue or expenditure. In peace-time the peasants were allowed considerable latitude in the payment of the poll tax: and then, on the outbreak of war, they would be forced to pay off all their arrears at once. Sufficient funds were provided by these haphazard methods to meet the costs of the army and the administration during the 1730's, but from the time of Elizabeth's accession the State was continually on the verge of bankruptcy. In 1749 Elizabeth entrusted the task of restoring financial equilibrium to a member of the Senate, Peter Shuvalov, who showed the same kind of resourceful-ness as the 'profit-seekers' of Peter the Great. His first step was to raise the prices of all commodities marketed by the State under its monopoly rights. The capital for the Bank of the Nobility was furnished from the profits of the State *vodka* monopoly, and Shuvalov raised more than half a million *roubles* in one year by trebling the price of salt. At the beginning of the Seven Years War he followed the example of Peter the Great by diverting a large part of the Church revenues into the treasury. Later, when there was an urgent need for ready money, Shuvalov farmed out the collection of individual items of indirect taxation to merchants, who were required to pay handsomely in advance for the concessions.

Shuvalov's advice on economic affairs was not confined to the budget. In 1753 he proposed that all customs barriers within the empire be abolished, and the recommendation was put into effect in the following year. To compensate for the lost income from internal customs dues, the duties on goods imported from abroad were raised. Import duties on luxury goods had been reduced in 1731 as a concession to the nobility, but Shuvalov drafted a new tariff law in 1757, imposing duties as high as 100 per cent. Between 1725 and 1762 the volume of Russia's foreign trade had increased more than threefold, but with exports amounting to 11 million *roubles* and imports to nearly 8½ million *roubles* per annum, the credit balance had become proportionately smaller. The most valuable export was iron from the Urals, and the best customer was Britain. During the 1730's British merchants were granted preferential concessions in St Petersburg, and even during the Seven Years War, when Britain was numbered among the enemies of Russia, trade between the two countries was not seriously interrupted.

CHAPTER XV

SCANDINAVIA AND THE BALTIC

W ITH the end of the Great Northern War the Scandinavian countries entered upon a period of much-needed peace after more than a century and a half of bitter though spasmodic inter-Scandinavian warfare. This struggle had fundamentally been one between the two more powerful nations, Denmark and Sweden, for political and economic control of the Sound and the Baltic, but the other Scandinavian countries had also been vitally affected by it: Norway because of its dynastic union with Denmark, Finland because that duchy formed part of the kingdom of Sweden. In its last phase, during the Great Northern War (1700–21), this inter-Scandinavian rivalry had become inextricably intermingled with the wider struggle of many Powers against the Baltic empire conquered by Sweden; Denmark-Norway's allies in the war had at one time or other included Saxony, Russia, Poland, Prussia and Hanover.

As far as the long inter-Scandinavian conflict was concerned, the Great Northern War imposed a settlement which lasted in its entirety for nearly a century, while the specific Dano-Swedish-Norwegian borders established have survived to the present day. Denmark gave up all hopes of reconquering the provinces Scania, Halland and Blekinge, lost to Sweden in the seventeenth century, while Norway similarly reconciled herself to the loss of Härjedalen, Jämtland and Bohuslän. The Swedish attempt to conquer Norway was abandoned immediately after the death of Charles XII in 1718, and the project of a Swedish acquisition of Norway was not revived till the very end of the century (and then along lines which excluded plans for direct conquest).

While within the northern equilibrium the Dano-Swedish warfare resulted in a balance of power between the two Scandinavian units which proved lasting until the upheavals of the Napoleonic period, in terms of the European balance of power their long conflict had as its most significant outcome the establishment of Russia and Prussia as strong States on the shores of the Baltic with the reduction of the Scandinavian countries to Powers of lesser rank. From 1720 onwards Sweden and Denmark are no longer principal participants in European power-politics, and their history is for the rest of the century to a great extent moulded by the policies of greater Powers, of Russia, Great Britain and France in particular.

The problems which faced the Scandinavian countries after the war were in many respects similar. Their immediate need was peace and time to restore the ravages which the Great Northern War had wrought in the finances and the economic life of both Denmark-Norway and Sweden-Finland. The two units faced their post-war problems with strikingly similar resources in manpower, some 1½ millions each, and in many respects they attempted to solve their problems of recuperation and reconstruction along broadly similar lines. Land in the possession of the Crown was sold to provide revenue; agriculture was fostered to maintain a growing population; industry, commerce and shipping were encouraged according to the mercantilist principles which were current in Europe at the time. Both countries were anxious to retrieve their European position by alliances and subsidy-treaties with richer and higher-ranking Powers; both attempted by skulful use of the diplomatic situation and of their own naval, military and commercial assets to achieve such treaties and alliances. Finally, being of the comity of European nations, both shared a European climate of opinion. The mercantilist theories which held sway in Copenhagen and in Stockholm, as in the other capitals of Europe, began as the century wore on to be tempered by the freer economic doctrines which reached the north from England, France and Germany. The interest shown in western Europe in scientific and technological research was strongly evident in Scandinavia, while the ideas of the physiocrats found immediate response in both States. The religious, artistic and cultural impulses of the age were also quickly transplanted to the north, the pietistic movement being strong in the early part of the century and the cult of rationalism and enlightenment gaining ascendancy after 1750.

In spite, however, of the similarities of the problems facing Denmark-Norway and Sweden-Finland after the war, and in spite of the similarities of ideas which all the Scandinavian countries shared, the two States reacted variously to their problems and to the influences from abroad. Out of a different national past and the different social structure each stressed different aspects of the problems and worked within different social and constitutional frameworks. A very long tradition of past enmity tended to obscure what common interests each possessed, while theoretically opposed forms of government served to set the countries apart. For Denmark-Norway the century was characterised by a continued belief in absolutism, benevolent and enlightened absolutism, but autocracy none the less, as the best form of government. For Sweden the century was one in which the chief characteristic was, until 1772, intense reaction against absolutism, the nation conducting that experiment in parliamentary government known as *Frihetstiden*, 'the Age of Liberty', i.e. freedom from absolutism.

Throughout the eighteenth century most subjects of the Danish Crown showed a complete satisfaction with absolutism, introduced as their form of government by the *coup d'état* of 1660 and destined to last until 1848. They congratulated themselves that the Twin-Kingdoms (a term commonly used to denote Denmark-Norway in the period 1660–1814) were not victims of party-strife, such as played itself out in Sweden from 1718–72, and they compared their lot favourably with that of other monarchies where absolutism was less benevolent and enlightened than under the Oldenburgs. The Oldenburg dynasty remained, however, suspicious of the old nobility at whose expense the *coup* of 1660 had been made; when Frederick IV's will was opened in 1730 it contained warnings to his successor against attempts by the old nobility to resume political power, through force or through infiltration into the administration. Such fears were largely ungrounded, for the old nobility, shorn of its privileges and hit by a period of agricultural depression, was by the eighteenth century in no position to challenge absolutism. It was declining in numbers and was both socially and economically overshadowed by the new nobility created by the Oldenburgs and by the rising burgher class. The Oldenburg fears help to explain, however, that distrust and even morbid suspicion which successive Danish kings had of members of the old nobility, and even of many non-nobles who made their way into high office. A preference for non-Danes in the administration is therefore very marked throughout the period until 1776. Geographical proximity and dynastic ties alike encouraged a steady influx of ambitious men from the German States; men from Norway and from the duchies Slesvig and Holstein (the former fully and the latter partly in the possession of the Crown of Denmark) often made their mark in the administration and in the armed forces. The Oldenburgs of the eighteenth century knew how to choose intelligent and capable men to help absolutism function; the well-known names of Schulin, Moltke and the two Bernstorffs, uncle and nephew, can be supplemented with those of a great many lesser but competent servants of the State. Following absolutist tradition the kings tried to keep control of foreign and military affairs in their own hands, but the dynasty's capacity for personal initiative deteriorated markedly for two generations after 1746 and policy in these matters also became, until 1784, the province of ministers.

The critical and rational spirit of the Enlightenment in Denmark was not directed against constitutional issues, though it attacked strongly the social and economic old regime. This positive criticism was on the whole encouraged by the Crown, so that contemporaries felt that rational change was rendered more likely and more practical by absolutist paternalism. The personal absolutism of the individual monarch was in any case tempered by the continuity which the different *Kollegier*, or administrative boards, provided in spite of changing ministers and changing rulers. Of the three Oldenburgs who ruled before 1766 Frederick IV (1699–1730) is usually reckoned the most successful: an able and energetic monarch who applied himself with zeal to the post-war problems of his country. His son, Christian VI (1730–46), was a less impressive king, but his strong sense of duty and his religious piety made him anxious to further the education and welfare of his subjects. Even the weak-willed and dissolute Frederick V (1746–66) showed an ability to pick good advisers and to stick to them, though he had no desire to play an independent part in the government of the country. During his reign the *Kollegier* took more and more power unto themselves and the king's councillors, members of his *Geheimeraad* or council (who were generally styled ministers), became so influential that a form of council-government, *Raadsstyre*, developed, not at all compatible with absolutist theory. The system worked well enough during Frederick V's lifetime; but when his son, Christian VII, began to govern, a conflict developed between the council-government of ministers inherited from his father and the young king who desired to follow the precepts laid down by Frederick III in 1660 for an absolutist monarch: a conflict which in conjunction with Christian VII's mental illness paved the way for the Struensee experiment of 1770–2.

The most absorbing domestic problem of Denmark in the eighteenth century lay in the relationship of the Danish peasant to the agricultural development and prosperity of the country. The position of the Danish peasant differed greatly from that of the Norwegian farmer in that very few yeomen farmers had survived in Denmark while in Norway the majority of farmers owned their own land: the native nobility having died out and the tenants of the Crown having been able to buy their land when it was offered for sale in the seventeenth and early eighteenth century. In Denmark Crown land had similarly been offered for sale, but here the tenants were in no position to buy their farms, which were sold either to the well-to-do new nobility or to the burghers, both classes as a rule absentee landlords. The last freeholders, those of Jutland, were ruined by the cattle-plague of the 1740's which stopped their hitherto profitable export-trade of cattle to Germany and Holland. The Crown attempted to alleviate their lot by calling in agricultural experts from Germany to begin reclamation of the Jutland heath and the cultivation of the potato, but progress was necessarily slow. For the great masses of the Danish peasant, the tenant farmers of the islands, the Crown could do little. Frederick IV had wanted to rescue the tenant farmer from his utter dependency on the estate owner and had in 1702 abolished the *Vornedskab* (which tied the peasant for life to the estate where he was born), decreeing that except during his six years of military service the peasant should be free to move after giving due notice to the landlord. The war and the agricultural depression, however, impoverished both landlord and tenant: the latter became in arrears with his rent and the former tried to compensate himself by increasing the amount of labour due from the tenant farmer on the estate. A flight from the land began, the younger peasants making their way to the towns or joining the beggar population recruited from dissatisfied peasants and army deserters; a development which made the estate owners put pressure on the king to have the *Vornedskab* restored.

The Crown refused to adopt such a retrograde step, but in 1733 Christian VI, in order to ensure enough labour for the land and enough soldiers for the army, consented to a compromise solution, the *Stavnsbaand*, which tied the peasant to the estate for as long as his liability for military service lasted, i.e. from his fourteenth to his thirty-sixth year. The landlords used this decree to tie the peasants ever closer to the estate and conditions not markedly different from the *Vornedskab* developed when the soldiers who had completed their military service were by law obliged to return to the estates where they were born.

The pietist and the rationalist alike attacked the *Stavnsbaand* on moral grounds, while the political economists urged the need for improvement of agriculture, the mainstay of Danish economy. The example of Norway was cited, where the Crown, by offering prizes for the growing of root crops and for improved strains of cattle, had been able to promote better husbandry. In Denmark such encouragement had little or no effect owing to the indifference of the peasant and the customary practice of *Fællesdrift* (cultivation in common). The Crown did what it could to educate the nation towards change, as did progressive estate owners and many of the rural clergy who were interested in the new ideas in agriculture. In the Academy at Sorø, founded for the education of young noblemen wanting to enter State service, agricultural reform was advocated. In 1755, on the occasion of the king's birthday, Frederick V's subjects were invited to send in proposals for the general economic improvement of the Twin-Kingdoms, publication at the Crown's expense being promised for all useful suggestions. As a result eight volumes of *Dansk-Norsk Økonomisk Magasin* were published (1757–64), and much of its space was given over to advice on improved agricultural methods and to plans for improving the lot of the Danish peasant. The *Stavnsbaand* was criticised as being equivalent to serfdom, *Fællesdrift* was condemned; proposals were made that the tenant farmer's children should be allowed to inherit the farm, since this might encourage the farmer not only to bring up a family, but also to improve his land once common cultivation had been abandoned and a fixed rent substituted for the natural rent and labour of the old system. The Crown was implored to force these and other changes through, but the king, relying on the estate owners both for the Crown's income through taxation of the land and for recruits for the army, had to move slowly. A committee examining ways and means for getting rid of *Fællesdrift* was appointed in 1757; and though no enforced reform followed, ordinances were promulgated which facilitated change. The work of the committee did much to publicise the new ideas, while the example of individual landlords, in improving both methods of agriculture and the lot of the tenant farmers, did even more. The period under review became therefore one of transition, preparing for the great land reforms and the freeing of the peasant which came before the end of the century.

The general economic policy of Oldenburg absolutism was to make the Twin-Kingdoms complementary. For this reason the whole of southern Norway was in 1735 declared closed to foreign corn. The economic unification was carried further when Norwegian iron, glass and other manufactures were given monopolies in the Danish market, Danish goods receiving reciprocal privileges in Norway. It should be noted, however, that the system was tempered at all times by smuggling on a large scale, particularly in Norway where the traditional trade connections with England and Scotland were valued, and where English textiles were found to be better in quality and cheaper (even at smuggler's prices) than the Copenhagen products. The mercantilist system put high duties on goods from abroad allowed into Denmark-Norway, and ordinances completely prohibiting various imports multiplied from 1735 onwards as native industrial undertakings got under way. A Danish bank was set up in 1736 to help industry by providing reasonable loans, but while the bank proved successful many of the newly established industries remained artificial. The foreign experts called in were sometimes adventurers who had failed to make good in their own countries, the kings and statesmen were often gullible where manufactures and factories were concerned and good money was poured after bad. In retrospect it can be seen that it was only the natural products of the Twin-Kingdoms or of their colonies which could be processed and marketed with profit, but it should be remembered that the purposes of mercantilist policy were to some extent fulfilled even where the new industries failed to take root: work being provided and the drain of gold and silver from the kingdoms stemmed. The heavy expenditure of the court, on magnificent building projects and on luxury, must also be looked at in the light of mercantilist ideas as to the usefulness of such expenditure on the national economy.

Trade and shipping were similarly encouraged. The royal family invested heavily in the trading companies, such as the West India Company, the Africa Company, and the General Trading Company to keep them going and advised or even forced (by such stratagems as percentage deductions from the salaries of government officials) their subjects to do the same. The most successful was the Asiatic Company, its eastern goods finding ready markets in Europe. Between 1746 and 1756 the Crown negotiated commercial treaties with most Mediterranean States, treaties which facilitated the expansion of Dano-Norwegian trade and freight-service in that sea during the Seven Years War, the war years bringing great prosperity for Scandinavian shipping generally.

The monopolistic doctrines of mercantilism were but slightly modified in the period under review. Copenhagen's many privileges were much resented by other towns in the Twin-Kingdom, and criticism brought the Crown to rescind the capital's exclusive right of importation of salt, tobacco, wine and grape-brandy (the valuable 'four species'). Though

Copenhagen's position as the economic nerve-centre of the State could not be challenged, in Norway the rising young townships gained some share in the privileges of the older ports. For Norway the century was one of material and cultural progress and Norwegians began to experience that the centralised system of government was less suited to the life of their country than formerly. Petitions were made for a specifically Norwegian *Kollegium*, high court, bank and university, all of which were refused since they ran counter to the very spirit of the *Helstat* (the unitary State) which demanded that local interests should be put aside for the combined welfare of the monarchy as a whole. The petitioners did not at this stage visualise any separation from Denmark, nor was any criticism of Oldenburg absolutism implied. Absolutism had indeed brought about a great improvement in Norway's position *vis-à-vis* Denmark—the idea of equality within the Twin-Kingdoms having replaced the pre-1660 tendency to treat Norway as a vassal under Denmark—and absolutism was therefore popular with the Norwegians until the strains and stresses of the Revolutionary and Napoleonic periods brought forth a separatist nationalist movement.[1]

The Crown's vigilance for the economic recovery of the Twin-Kingdoms was matched by its efforts to improve Denmark's position in Europe. Technically Denmark-Norway belonged to the victors in the Great Northern War, but in reality the gains were small compared to those of the other partners in the anti-Swedish coalition and disappointing when measured against expectations. The most obvious gains were financial: the money paid by Sweden for the return of her Danish-held German provinces and by Hanover for Bremen, and the relinquishing by Sweden of that exemption from Sound dues which she had enjoyed since 1613. The most significant victory won by Denmark lay, however, in Sweden's renunciation of her traditional alliance with the duke of Holstein-Gottorp and her consent to the Danish Crown's acquisition of the ducal parts of Slesvig. By incorporating the scattered ducal parts of Slesvig with the royal parts of the duchy, Frederick IV was at last able to begin the reversal of that process of splitting the two duchies, Slesvig and Holstein, into ducal and royal parts which had begun in the mid-sixteenth century by Christian III's providing for his brothers out of land from the duchies. The potential dangers of this arrangement had become clear in the seventeenth century when a dynastic and political alliance was formed between Sweden and the duke of Holstein-Gottorp, now sole possessor of the non-royal parts of both duchies. Through this alliance Sweden obtained a backdoor into the king of Denmark's dominions in time of war and Danish attempts to reabsorb the ducal parts of Slesvig-Holstein

---

[1] Traces can still be found at times in the work of Norwegian historians of the anti-Danish attitude prevalent in the nineteenth century, echoes of J. E. Sars' view, but on the whole it is becoming accepted that Oldenburg absolutism genuinely intended and attempted the happiness and prosperity of both countries.

by force had been frustrated. The peace of 1720 marked the first stage of success for Danish policy of regaining effective royal control over the duchies. It was realised in Denmark, however, that this reversal of Sweden's traditional policy might not last long. The peace treaty had been negotiated by Sweden's newly elected king, Frederick of Hesse, who had personal reasons for abandoning the Holstein-Gottorp cause: his closest rival for the Swedish Crown having been the young Duke Charles Frederick of Holstein-Gottorp (see pp. 332, 351–2). There was a strong possibility that the duke, if Frederick remained childless, would in time be chosen king of Sweden: in which case he would certainly repudiate those articles of the 1720 treaty which were contrary to his interests in Slesvig. To guard against this eventuality Frederick IV secured the guarantees of France and Great Britain, the mediators in the peace between Denmark and Sweden, of his rights to the whole of Slesvig.

For the rest of the century Danish foreign policy had two main objectives: to get other Powers besides England and France to recognise the right of the Danish Crown to the whole of Slesvig and, secondly, to get the Danish Crown recognised also as the lawful owner of the scattered ducal parts of Holstein. During the Great Northern War Danish troops had occupied most of these territories; but the occupation had not been recognised by any Power, and because of objections voiced by the Emperor Charles VI as the overlord both of Frederick IV (in his capacity as duke of the royal parts of Holstein) and of the duke of Holstein-Gottorp some of them had to be returned.

Though these two objectives governed Danish foreign policy until 1773, when success was finally achieved, the duchies remained possessions of the Crown of Denmark rather than parts of the kingdom of Denmark. Frederick IV released his new subjects in Slesvig from their oaths of loyalty to the duke of Holstein-Gottorp; but the administration of the duchies remained separate in the German part of the Danish chancery as opposed to the Danish part which dealt with the Twin-Kingdoms. The old customs barrier between the duchies and Denmark proper remained; and the ancient tradition whereby Holstein formed part of the Holy Roman Empire of the German nation, while the more northerly Slesvig, though not part of the Empire, was by the declaration of 1460 eternally joined to Holstein, created difficulties which prevented that administrative incorporation which Frederick IV desired. The wording of the oath of loyalty which Frederick IV's new subjects took to the Crown of Denmark in 1721 has indeed been variously interpreted by historians,[1] though not until the era of nineteenth-century nationalism did this part of the problem possess any practical significance.

[1] See Kristian Erslev's three essays of 1901, 1902 and 1913 reprinted in *Historiske Afhandlinger* (1937), and Holger Hjelholt, *Inkorporationen af den Gottorpske Del af Sønderjylland, i Kronen 1721* (1945).

The first post-war crisis involving Slesvig-Holstein came in the years 1723–7 and was caused by Russian support for the duke of Holstein-Gottorp. Tsar Peter was annoyed with Frederick IV, who had refused to marry his son to the tsar's daughter, Anna, and had even refused him the title of tsar. A project was therefore set on foot in Russia for marrying Anna to the sworn enemy of the Danish king, Charles Frederick of Holstein-Gottorp, who was accordingly invited to St Petersburg and given a guarantee for his ducal possessions both in Slesvig and Holstein. Anxiety grew in Denmark lest Russia might begin a war to recover the young duke's heritage, a preoccupation which served to draw Frederick IV close to George I of England since that monarch, as elector of Hanover, feared for Bremen and Verden if a new war should break out in the north. Tension was highest in the years 1723–6 when the Holstein party in Sweden (see p. 355) had great influence, and plans were made for proclaiming Charles Frederick Swedish heir-apparent so that he, with a combined Russo-Swedish force, could invade Denmark, recover his ducal possessions and then proceed to reconquer Bremen and Verden for Sweden. The fall of the Holstein party at the Swedish Diet of 1726-7, however, made any such combined attack unlikely, and the death of Catherine I in May 1727 changed the situation in Denmark's favour. The old-Russia party, now powerful in St Petersburg, gave up the cause of Charles Frederick and he and his wife had to flee Russia. Count Horn, in control of Sweden's foreign policy from 1727 to 1738, was anxious to keep the peace; and when Christian VI became king of Denmark in 1730 there was also a change of system in Copenhagen, the new king setting aside the advisers of his father and beginning to work for better relations with Sweden. The Hanover alliance of Britain, France and Prussia of 1725 had already to some extent drawn both Sweden and Denmark into its orbit, since Sweden had joined that alliance as a full member in March 1727, while Denmark (sponsored by George I) had by a convention of April 1727 promised military support to the alliance.

The break in the Anglo-French alliance which came in 1731 posed problems for Christian VI, since from that time onwards London and Paris became once more (after fourteen years of co-operation) rivals for the support of the two northern Crowns. The final Danish choice was influenced by the friendlier relations established between Denmark and Sweden and by the hope which Christian VI conceived of a future dynastic union between Denmark-Norway and Sweden-Finland. Since the Holstein party had lost favour in Sweden, Charles Frederick was (temporarily at least) out of the running and Christian VI convinced himself that his son, the Danish crown prince Frederick, might be elected Swedish heir apparent. To increase his son's chances when the succession issue was debated in Sweden, Christian in 1742 chose the French alliance to the exclusion of the English to please the pro-French Hat party in power in

Sweden. France thus became victorious in the protracted diplomatic struggle for Denmark, and from 1742 until 1762 the Twin-Kingdoms remained within the French grouping of Powers. The alliance with France brought Denmark useful subsidies and in return very little was exacted, Christian VI managing to keep his country out of the War of the Austrian Succession and Frederick V's ministers maintaining a policy of neutrality during the Seven Years War.

In the Swedish succession issue, however, Christian VI was destined to disappointment. The Swedish peasants showed enthusiasm for the Danish candidate, but the lavish hospitality and considerable sums of money that were used to gain members of the other Estates were wasted, the Estate of Peasants alone favouring the royalism implied in the choice of a prince reared in the tradition of absolutism. When in 1743, as the price of a cheap Russian peace after the war of 1741–3, Sweden elected Prince Adolphus Frederick of Holstein-Gottorp-Eutin heir apparent, Danish disappointment was bitter and the old fear of combined Russo-Swedish support for Denmark's enemy revived. Tsaritsa Elizabeth, who had become ruler of Russia by a *coup* in 1741, had not only become reconciled to the house of Holstein-Gottorp, but had declared the head of that family since 1739, Duke Charles Peter Ulrik (son of Charles Frederick and Anna), her heir. With the prospect of the duke as future tsar, and his cousin and heir (since he had as yet no children) as future king of Sweden, the position of Denmark seemed precarious. Christian VI was tempted to start immediate war on Sweden when Adolphus Frederick refused to give up any claims on Slesvig-Holstein which he might inherit; mobilisation of the Danish and Norwegian armies began, but Christian refrained from attack when it became clear that Denmark would receive no foreign support while Sweden could count on Russian help. A pacific policy was indeed the only possible one in the light of Denmark-Norway's position and resources at the time; a policy which was continued also under Frederick V. Bernstorff, the Hanoverian-born diplomat who took over leadership of Danish foreign policy in 1751, was hopeful that the Crown could achieve its objective, the full possession of Slesvig and Holstein, by diplomatic skill; and though in 1762 only circumstances outside Danish control averted war, Bernstorff lived to see this goal all but achieved along lines laid down by himself in 1763–7. Bernstorff was forced to resign in 1770; he died in 1772; the *Mageskifte* was carried out in 1773 by his nephew A. P. Bernstorff (see p. 350). Some progress had been made in the Slesvig-Holstein question before Bernstorff's term of office. As the price of Denmark's guarantee of the Pragmatic Sanction, Charles VI had in 1732 recognised Danish possession of all Slesvig by a treaty made jointly with Tsaritsa Anna at a time when the cause of the Holstein-Gottorps had been temporarily abandoned by Russia. When Adolphus Frederick became unpopular with Tsaritsa Elizabeth by refusing to be subservient to her, the

Danes in 1746 secured a Russian promise for a friendly settlement of the problem of the duchies. More important was the understanding which developed between Sweden and Denmark once the danger of war receded after 1743; the Hat party in power agreeing in 1749 that Adolphus Frederick should give up all claims he might inherit in Slesvig-Holstein in exchange for the Danish principalities of Oldenburg, Delmenhorst and a sum of money. A seal was set on this bargain in 1751 when Bernstorff and the Hats arranged a future marriage between Frederick V's daughter Sophia Magdalena and Adolphus Frederick's son Gustavus.

These welcome arrangements lost their value, however, when Duke Charles Peter Ulrik became the father of a son (the future Tsar Paul) in 1754. All overtures from Denmark to the duke for an amicable settlement over Slesvig-Holstein had been refused, and the duke had repeatedly declared his intention, once he were tsar, to chase the royal Danish family not only from the duchies but from Denmark itself. A moment of great crisis came therefore for the Oldenburg dynasty and for Denmark when the duke in January 1762 became Tsar Peter III, determined to restore the inheritance of his line by the use of all Russia's military might.

Up to this moment Denmark-Norway had managed to keep out of the Seven Years War. Bernstorff had attempted to make his policy palatable to both England and France, and the armed neutrality arranged with Sweden in 1756 had not been used too pointedly against either side. The trade and shipping of the Twin-Kingdoms had benefited greatly from the war, but the prospect of the accession to the Russian throne of the duke of Holstein-Gottorp had caused increasing anxiety during the last year of Tsaritsa Elizabeth's life. When that accession became a fact, war between Russia and Denmark seemed unavoidable. Tsar Peter made immediate peace with Frederick II of Prussia in order to free his hands to attack Denmark; Frederick V's ministers were determined to resist by force any attempt to wrest from the Danish Crown the former ducal parts of Slesvig, the full possession of the whole duchy having been guaranteed to Denmark by the majority of European Great Powers, to whom appeals for assistance were now sent. The moment seemed also opportune for Frederick V's acquiring indisputably by a military decision the ducal parts of Holstein for which no guarantee had ever been obtained. The Danish army had been put on a war footing during the previous year and some 30,000 men now marched to meet the approaching Russian army. The Danish fleet was in better state than the Russian, and court circles in Copenhagen felt reasonably confident of the outcome of the naval struggle which would undoubtedly follow a clash of the armies. On land, however, the position was doubtful, the Russians having the advantage of a fully mobilised and battle-trained army. It was also disquieting that neither England nor France responded to the Danish demands for assistance; and the alliance with France, though it did not expire till 1763, became noticeably cooler through Danish disappointment with French behaviour in 1762.

The issue between Denmark and Russia was not put to the test. Peter III's sudden deposition and death and the accession of his wife Catherine, who immediately signified her friendly attitude to Frederick V, conjured away the danger at the last moment, the two armies having already taken up battle positions.

Catherine II's attitude to northern problems brought about a re-orientation of Danish foreign policy. The opportunity to arrive at a settlement with Russia on behalf of young Duke Paul was too good to miss, and Bernstorff was willing to sacrifice the friendship of Sweden and France in order to achieve a final solution of the Slesvig-Holstein problem. Negotiations were begun at once and by 1763 the tsaritsa had promised to make an amicable settlement when her son should reach his majority. By 1767 a treaty was signed whereby an exchange, the *Mageskifte*, was arranged to take place as soon as Duke Paul was declared of age, Catherine agreeing that he would then exchange the ducal parts of Holstein and renounce his claim to those of Slesvig in return for Oldenburg, Delmenhorst and a sum of money. For his part Christian VII promised to continue the policy which Bernstorff had inaugurated to please Catherine in 1762: to uphold with Russia the Swedish Constitution, that is to prevent a return to Swedish absolutism which the tsaritsa feared as synonymous with an aggressive, anti-Russian foreign policy. In 1773 on Duke Paul attaining his majority the *Mageskifte* was carried into effect, and the Crown of Denmark had at last full and undisputed possession of both Slesvig and Holstein. The Swedish constitutional regime which Denmark and Russia had bound themselves to uphold had by this time, however, been practically undone by the *coup d'état* of Gustavus III in 1772, which neither partner in the *Mageskifte* had attempted to prevent: Russia being preoccupied with Turkish and Polish affairs, Denmark with the domestic turmoil of the immediate post-Struensee period and disinclined in any case to intervene unless Russia kept her to the bargain.

In the period of *Frihetstiden* in Sweden,[1] which began with the death of

---

[1] Judgments on *Frihetstiden* have varied very much. The nineteenth-century historians G. Geijer and N. Tengberg continued the critical line of S. Lagerbring, the first historian of the period, who was anxious to justify the *coup* of Gustavus III and therefore stressed the bitter party-struggles and the opportunities which these offered to foreign powers to interfere in Sweden, endangering Sweden to the point of a possible partition, such as happened in Poland. The only nineteenth-century exception to the critical view was that of A. Fryxell who proclaimed *Frihetstiden* the golden age when Sweden's kings were effectively muzzled. The first large-scale modern study was that of C. G. Malmström, *Sveriges politiska historia från konung Karl XII:s död till statshvälfningen 1772*, 6 vols. (1855–77), which appeared in a revised edition 1893–1901; a work which is still valuable though mainly concerned with political and diplomatic history and still critical of the party struggle. The great challenge to the accepted view of the period came with F. Lagerroth, *Frihetstidens författning* (1915). As a con-

Charles XII in 1718 and came to an end with Gustavus's *coup* in 1772, political power lay in the hands of the Four Estates of the Realm. The explanation of, and the justification for, the victory of the anti-absolutist forces in 1718–19 lies in the circumstances that an opposition had secretly been preparing for such an opportunity as the shot at Frederikshald offered; its leaders were thus capable of taking the initiative in a situation of some danger for Sweden. Charles XII left no direct heir and had not settled the question of the succession. The two claimants to the throne, his younger sister Ulrika Eleonora, and the son of his elder sister, Duke Charles Frederick of Holstein-Gottorp, were used to checkmate each other; the former receiving the support of the opposition party only at the cost of foreswearing absolutism. At the Diet (*Riksdag*) of the Four Estates which met in January 1719 the anti-absolutist party, a loose grouping of influential landowners, officers of the armed forces and administrators, also won the day. To emphasise its break with absolutism the Diet proceeded, even before the succession issue was debated, to bring the late king's adviser, the Holstein-born Baron Goertz, to trial. He was accused of sowing suspicion between Charles XII and his people and, more significantly, of depriving the Council and the administration of their lawful share of control in the affairs of Sweden; for this crime he suffered the death penalty. Goertz's connection with Holstein had damaged the position of those in the Diet who favoured the duke of Holstein-Gottorp as king, and Ulrika Eleonora's husband, Frederick of Hesse, cleverly co-operated with the anti-absolutist party to get his wife chosen queen. In May 1719 Ulrika was crowned, having first declared herself willing to sign and keep a constitution to be formulated by the Estates. While the work on this constitution was still in progress, however, the council and the colleges of the administration began to despair at the wilfulness of the queen, whose behaviour gave evidence of the absolutism in which she had been reared. Count Horn, one of the leaders of the anti-absolutist party, therefore prevailed on Ulrika to abdicate in favour of her husband who, it was hoped, would prove more amenable to the wishes of the Estates since he had no shadow of hereditary claim to the throne. It was arranged that Ulrika should resume the crown if her husband died in her lifetime, but the duke of Holstein-Gottorp's followers were once more disappointed, their desire to have him nominated next in succession being defeated in

stitutional historian he emphasises in this and in later works the importance of *Frihetstiden* as the vital bridge connecting Sweden's distant democratic past with the democratic developments of the late nineteenth and early twentieth centuries. Recent attempts at synthesis are: L. Stavenow, *Frihetstiden 1718-1722*, vol. 9 of *Sveriges historia till våra dagar*, 1922 (revised edition of vol. 7 of *Sveriges historia intill tjugonde seklet*); C. Hallendorff, *Frihetstiden*, vol. 4 of *Svenska folkets historia* (1928); E. Hjärne, *Från Vasatiden till frihetstiden* (1929); *Svensk Historia genem Tiderna*, ed. H. Mailander, vol. III (1949), relevant chapters by Walfrid Holst. A great many monographs have appeared in recent years on various aspects of the period, interest being concentrated on social, economic, constitutional and biographical topics.

order that the bargaining power of the Estates might be kept high in the event of Frederick and Ulrika dying without issue. Charles Frederick now left Sweden to accept asylum in Russia with Tsar Peter, remarking bitterly that the Swedes had been in too much of a hurry to move the clock 'from XII to I', exchanging the old Vasa and Caroline tradition for the new and untried house of Hesse.

The most striking feature of the Constitution of 1720, which Frederick I duly signed, was the reduction in the Crown's power. Within the Council (*Råd*) majority decisions should prevail, and as the king was given only two votes this meant that the Crown could be outvoted. The Crown's right to ennoble families was greatly restricted, and its customary privilege of bestowing office was rendered almost null and void. Since the Council was no longer the king's council, but the Council of the Estates, the Diet and not the king should propose councillors, the king being allowed choice from a list submitted by the Estates. It was stressed that the councillors themselves were to be no more than the plenipotentiaries of the Estates, charged with taking care of the interests of the Estates when no Diet was sitting, responsible to the Estates for all steps taken. It was finally decreed that Diets should meet at no longer interval than three years, and that all persons in the service of the State should take an oath to uphold the Constitution.

The way in which the constitutional machinery set up in 1719–20 would work was by no means a foregone conclusion. A strong king might have set aside the Constitution, but neither Frederick I (1720–51) nor his successor, Adolphus Frederick (1751–71), was in a position to do so; they were both foreign-born and elected on the express condition of foreswearing absolutism; neither had that feeling of belonging in the country which helped Gustavus III, the first Swedish-born king since Charles XII, so immeasurably in 1772.

With the Crown thus for a long time reduced to a position of little influence, freer play was given to the Council and the Estates. A certain conflict between the two came to the fore once their victory over the Crown was accomplished, a struggle ending in the ascendancy of the Estates. This victory was no more a foregone conclusion than the defeat of royalism. The *Råd* had in earlier periods of Sweden's history known how to control the Estates, and during the early years of *Frihetstiden*, particularly from 1727 to 1738 when Count Horn was powerful in the Council, it seemed as if Sweden was once more governed by an oligarchic council in the interests of the landed nobility, the higher bureaucracy and the higher clergy. A significant change had, however, taken place in 1720 in the composition of the *Råd*. The fully developed Council of the seventeenth century had consisted of the heads of the colleges *ex officio* as well as of the king's personal advisers, and all councillors had held their seats for life (as was customary in all posts of the Swedish administration). In 1720, however, the connection between the Council and the colleges was broken (with one exception: the chairman of the *Råd* was, as hitherto, to be the President of the Chancery); and this innovation paved the way for a type of 'cabinet' development since the conception of councillorship for life was weakened through the loss of the *ex-officio* members from the colleges. As the party-system developed, demands were raised that councillors should be changed according to the success or failure of the parties as expressed in the composition of the Four Estates whenever a new Diet met. The pre-1720 conception of councillors as State servants holding office for life died slowly, however, and made necessary processes of impeachment for treason and malfeasance to remove those who were not willing to resign voluntarily. The parliamentary principle of change in the composition of the Council according to change in the relative standing of the parties in the Diet did, all the same, gain ground throughout *Frihetstiden*, and it was indeed this development which put an end to the period of council government and secured the supremacy of the Estates in the constitutional struggle. On the other hand, the jealousy with which the Estates guarded their supremacy prevented the Council in its function as the 'cabinet' of the Estates from developing into a strong executive. The important 'Secret Committee' (*sekreta utskottet*)—the most influential of all the committees of the Estates—took over much of the initiative which had formerly belonged to the Council, but even here the Estates were reluctant to hand over real power, and the problem of how to forge a strong executive which would not arouse the jealousy of the Estates was still unsolved in 1772.

Within the Estates there was also tension and conflict. The First Estate, not elected for each Diet as were the other Estates but representing every noble family of Sweden and Finland by its head (or the head's delegate), had before 1720 been divided into three classes according to rank and had voted by class; so that the two higher classes, though numerically inferior, had been able to outvote the lower nobility. The ennobled civil servants and officers of the armed forces who made up the bulk of the lower nobility won an important victory in 1720 when it was laid down that voting should be by hand and not by class, and a further undermining of the influence of the high nobility took place in 1734 when it was arranged that election of members of the Estate for committees and deputations should be by secret ballot. This democratisation of the House of Nobility was the result partly of the impoverishment of the higher nobility which had taken place during the reigns of Charles XI and Charles XII, and partly of the increase in the power of the bureaucracy (i.e. the lower nobility) so typical of *Frihetstiden*.

The clergy formed the Second Estate. The archbishop was its chairman, the bishops sat *ex officio* and about fifty delegates, elected by and from the parish clergy, usually attended the Diet. A certain 'anti-noble' attitude can be noticed in this Estate and in the Third Estate, that of the burghers, whose membership generally amounted to some 120. These delegates were often mayors or other town dignitaries, and nearly always men of wealth, intent on the promotion of trade, industry and shipping. The Fourth Estate, that of the peasants, was elected by and from the free landowning farmers, and some 100 delegates were usually returned. The peasants were distrusted by the other Estates for their royalist sympathies, an attitude dictated on the part of the peasants not by their fondness for absolutism as a constitutional theory, but by their desire for a strong king who could curb the many petty lords of the bureaucracy, for, as a common country saying had it, 'everyone who wears a wig thinks himself a king these days'. To restrain the Fourth Estate the nobility, the clergy and the burghers, though allowing it to choose its own chairman, insisted on its secretary being nominated by the chairmen of the three other Estates, and commonly a man capable of controlling the royalism of the peasants was found. The Fourth Estate was at a further disadvantage in that peasant representation on the important Secret Committee was not allowed as of right, though in times of crisis twenty-five peasants were invited to join the fifty nobles, twenty-five clergy and twenty-five burghers who made up that body.

While there was friction inside the First Estate between high and low nobility, the House of Nobility tended to represent a united front against the attack of the other Estates on the privileges claimed by the nobility: exclusive right to noble soil, so that non-nobles who had come into possession of such soil could be forced to sell it; enforcement of the ancient prohibition of marriage between noble and non-noble; confirmation of various economic privileges and judicial rights, giving a fair amount of immunity from taxation and some legal power over tenants on noble estates; and finally the important exclusive right to high office in the administration (including councillorship) and in the armed forces, with preferential right to all other office. The non-noble Estates refused to admit these demands, and by 1723 Count Horn, pleading the need for unity in the face of a difficult foreign situation, managed to arrange a compromise settlement whereby the nobility gave up its claim for preferential right to lower office, agreed that non-noble might marry noble and possess, in certain cases, noble soil; in return the nobility received confirmation of its exclusive right to high office in the administration, in the armed forces and as a prerequisite for membership of the Council. The struggle between the First Estate and the non-noble Estates continued, however, throughout the century, the commoners demanding that the nobility's exclusive right to high office should be modified: their ultimate aim being the right of non-noble to have equal access, on consideration of merit only, with the nobility to all posts, a demand which was not granted till 1809.

The political parties which developed during *Frihetstiden* cut across the conflicting interests of estate and class. All parties agreed on the importance of constitutional government as opposed to absolutism, on the desirability of rebuilding Sweden's prestige abroad, as well as on the need to speed economic recovery at home. Where they differed was, first of all, on the issue of the Swedish succession; secondly, on the paths to be followed in foreign policy and, thirdly, on the methods by which prosperity was to be restored.

The first clearly defined, though shortlived, party was the 'Hessian' one, built round Frederick I and the foreign policy advocated by him: alliance with George I of Hanover-England, at the cost of great concessions to Hanover, Prussia and Denmark, for the purpose of gaining British naval support in the Baltic against Russia. The grandly conceived plan for a European offensive against Tsar Peter came to nought, however, as the South Sea Bubble and Law's crash diverted the attention of England and France to domestic affairs. Sweden was left at the mercy of Russia who imposed the harsh terms of Nystad of 1721; Frederick I was discredited and the Hessian party ruined.

The next party to gain influence was the 'Holstein' one, whose hopes centered on Duke Charles Frederick of Holstein-Gottorp. The Russian support given to the duke gave the party a programme of friendship with Russia as a means of regaining some of the lost Baltic empire. If Charles Frederick were proclaimed heir-apparent in Sweden, it was argued, Tsar Peter might be willing to restore some of the provinces lost to Russia, or, alternatively, he might support Sweden with his armed forces so that land ceded to Prussia and Hanover might be reconquered. When the Diet of 1723 met, the Holstein party proved strong enough to secure a large present of money for Charles Frederick and the title of Royal Highness (as a sign that he was not excluded from the Swedish succession); the next year the party forced through the Diet an alliance with Russia. The prospect of a war against Denmark, with probable European repercussions through the Anglo-French guarantees of Slesvig, which this alliance implied, brought about a *rapprochement* between Count Horn (President of the Chancery since 1721 and therefore chairman of the Council), who was anxious to preserve peace, and Frederick I, who did not desire a war which would benefit the duke of Holstein-Gottorp. The Hanoverian George I of England, concerned for the safety of Bremen and Verden if the peace of the north should be disturbed, helped to bring about this understanding. Count Horn thereupon broke with the Holstein party at the Diet of 1726 and proceeded to bring Sweden into the Hanover alliance of England, France and Prussia in 1727, a move which was forced through the Council only with the help of the king's double vote.

Round Horn was built up the third party of *Frihetstiden*, a party made up of the Hessians, of the traditionally pro-French families who approved of the Hanover alliance, and of the moderate Holsteiners who did not want to risk war by following the more extreme wing of their party. Russia continued to support this extreme wing even after Peter the Great's death and tried alternatively with offers of subsidies and threats of force to draw Sweden closer to Russia. The death of Catherine I in 1727, however, brought with it the abrupt loss of support in St Petersburg for Charles Frederick, and, as a result, the Holstein party in Sweden began to lose influence and break up. Those who had composed its more extreme wing remained all the same in opposition to Count Horn, forming one of the nuclei of the Hat party, and lived to see him caught, as they had prophesied, in the shifting sands of renewed Anglo-French rivalry and friction.

The disintegration of the Hanover alliance weakened Horn's position considerably, and his general policy came in for much criticism. In economic affairs he soon found himself unable to defy the opposition and was driven to adopt stronger mercantilist measures than he desired, such as the formation of the Swedish East India Company (1731) which led to trouble with England. In foreign affairs Horn's caution also came under fire. His attempt to pursue a conciliatory policy towards both Britain and Russia (once that country had given up its support for the duke of Holstein-Gottorp) was sharply criticised by the opposition, which advocated a patriotic policy. A new generation had grown to manhood who but dimly remembered the privations and disasters of the war, who extolled Charles XII as the defender of the north against Russia and who clamoured for the recovery by arms of Sweden's Baltic empire. The War of the Polish Succession inflamed the opposition. Many Swedish volunteers fought in support of Charles XII's old candidate for the Polish crown, Stanislas Leszczyński, in the belief that Sweden and Poland would have to make common cause against Russia; and Horn, who in 1735 renewed the 1724 treaty with Russia, was branded as a traitor.

During the elections for the Diet of 1738 the opposition emerged as a fully organised party, proudly calling themselves the 'Hats', hinting at the glory of military headgear. Their opponents they labelled the 'Nightcaps' or 'Caps', implying that Horn and his followers were sleepy cowards, old men in nightcaps. This election campaign showed clearly the party organisation which became so typical of *Frihetstiden*: coffee-house meetings were held, party slogans were much used, emblems were widely worn, pamphlets were published and votes were bought not only by the Caps and Hats themselves, but also by representatives of foreign Powers. Diplomats entertained delegates to the Diet lavishly, paid travelling and other election expenses, and presents were distributed in money or kind before an important vote in the Estates. Towards the end of *Frihetstiden* some patriots began to rebel against the more extreme forms of foreign buying of votes, but generally it was held throughout the period that the influx of gold and silver from abroad was beneficial to Sweden's economy and that the subsidising of delegates had a political advantage in that it enabled Diets to sit for longer periods than would otherwise have been possible, thus strengthening the Estates against any revival of despotism.

In the elections of 1738 the Hat party won a decisive victory and entered upon a period of power which lasted till 1765. Count Horn resigned of his own free will, and, after an impeachment process, sentence was pronounced on those of Horn's colleagues in the Council who refused to follow his example. All were found guilty and deemed to have lost their seats as councillors, and the empty places in the *Råd* were filled with Hat party members. This removal of the recalcitrant councillors, the so-called *licentiering*, has by Swedish historians been judged the most vital stage in the parliamentary development of *Frihetstiden*. Horn himself, during his years of power, had been anxious to keep the Council strong in relation to the Estates and had not attempted to interfere with the dignity or position of those councillors who were his political opponents. The more moderate Hats wanted, for similar reasons, to avoid a forced resignation of Horn's followers, but the more extreme Hats were in a majority and argued that they would be unable to carry Hat policy through the Council if their opponents continued to be members of that body. The majority view won, but not without a precedent having been established which was later to be used against the Hats.

The moderate Hats were also closer to Horn in their views on economic and foreign policy than to the extremist majority of their own party. They wanted to continue his moderate mercantilism; and though they wanted to regain the Swedish Baltic empire, they hoped to do so by negotiation and by the use of skilful diplomacy, by isolating Russia before presenting a demand for the modification of the Peace of Nystad. The hands of the moderates were forced, however, in these respects also. The strict mercantilism of the Holstein party of the 1720's (exemplified by *Produkt-plakatet* of 1724 which, modelled on the English navigation acts, hit hard at Dutch and English shipping in the Baltic, and by the importation ordinances of 1726) was therefore revived, the Hats intensifying support for Sweden's industrial undertakings and accompanying it with an ever stronger protection against foreign competition. In retrospect it can easily be seen that only the profits deriving from Sweden's and Finland's well-established exports, above all from the Swedish iron, allowed the Hats for so long to continue mercantilist experiments with new manufactures, but until the crisis of 1762–3 (brought about partly by Sweden's participation in the Seven Years War and partly by the effects of an international financial crisis) the Caps raised no strong protests against the theory of Hat economic policy, though they continually urged moderation on the party in power. Similarly the two parties were in some measure of agreement on agricultural policy. The resumption of Crown lands from the nobility which had been carried out by Charles XI and Charles XII had in Sweden stopped that development of a peasant-class subservient to the estate-owners which was so typical of Denmark, and by 1700 the land was held in roughly equal proportions by the Crown, the nobility and the peasants. During *Frihetstiden* the tenants of the Crown were encouraged to change their position, by the payment of a sum of money (the *skatteköp*), into that of free tax-paying farmers, a change which brought them little economic gain but increased social prestige and political power. In 1757 the Estates decreed that farmers could, if they so wished, put a stop to the customary common cultivation of land by the village. This reform, *Storskiftet* (so called because of its emphasis on the exchange of strips of land and consequent consolidation of holdings), did not produce immediate results since the conservative attitude of the farmers changed but slowly in its favour, but it was of immense future importance. It is worth noting that both parties had encouraged *Storskiftet*, both being conscious of the need to increase the yield of Sweden's soil after the loss of the corn-granary of Livonia. The Academy of Sciences (*Vetenskapsakademien*), founded in 1739, had the support of both Hats and Caps when it commissioned Linnaeus to undertake a tour of all Sweden's provinces to suggest improvements in methods of cultivation and when it encouraged Wargentin to begin his work on population statistics. The Swedish Government statistical office, the first in modern Europe, was founded in 1749.

Where the two parties differed violently was over foreign policy, the Hats allying Sweden to France as soon as they got into power, an alliance detested by the Caps. The War of the Austrian Succession, with French diplomacy encouraging a Swedish attack on Russia to prevent that country coming to the aid of Maria Theresa, precipitated Sweden's entry into a war before proper military preparations had been made. The Hat leaders chose to believe that it was not necessary to lay out large sums of money on the army, arguing that Sweden did not intend to act against Russia alone. The European situation after 1740 gave them hopes of regaining the eastern Baltic provinces through Swedish support for Peter the Great's daughter Elizabeth in her bid to oust Tsar Ivan IV. With French mediation it was secretly arranged that the Swedish army should attack Russia while proclaiming its intention to withdraw as soon as Elizabeth had been made tsaritsa; the new empress would in return for such help hand over the lost Baltic lands to Sweden. The Caps were against this venture, but it was not difficult to awaken popular enthusiasm for a war against Russia and in July 1741 the Swedes began hostilities.

Sweden's high expectations were soon bitterly disappointed. A strong attack in the early days of the war, when Russia was still unprepared, might have brought results, but tied by the arrangement with Elizabeth, the Swedish army showed initial restraint. From Elizabeth's point of view the plan worked well; the presence of Swedish forces inside the Russian border, threatening St Petersburg in the autumn of 1741, proved an important factor in the success of her *coup*. As tsaritsa, however, she refused, or was unable to carry out, the fulfilment of her part of the bargain. The Swedes, having withdrawn into Finland as soon as news of Elizabeth's proclamation reached them, lost their opportunity; and when the Russians began to take the initiative, the war went from bad to worse for the Swedes. Their navy, stronger at this time than that of Russia, was incapacitated by epidemics among the sailors; their army suffered from lack of leadership, the party struggles of Hats and Caps having been carried on to the battle-field with paralysing effects. With the capitulation of Helsingfors in August 1742 Finland was given up to a repetition of the Russian occupation during the later years of the Great Northern War.

For Finland the war of 1741–3 meant a serious interruption in the recovery programme begun after Nystad, planned by a special government commission of 1725–7. After 1721 the people who had fled to Sweden returned; some prisoners-of-war found their way back; the Åland Islands and Østerbotten, both systematically razed by the Russians to provide a neutral zone between Russia and Sweden, were resettled; the towns (such as Åbo, which had lost its stone houses, torn down to provide building-material for St Petersburg) were rebuilt. The war of 1741–3, coming after a run of bad harvests from 1738 to 1741, put a temporary stop to the improved position of the Duchy; but Russian agents who toured Finland after the capitulation to tempt the population to cast off their ties with Sweden, offering them autonomy under Russia, met with no response.

The failure to defend Finland raised serious difficulties for the Hat party. In the elections for the 1742 Diet the Caps obtained majorities in all the Estates except in that of the burghers. The Secret Committee, following the example of Horn in 1727 and of the Hats in 1738, was filled with Caps and the fall of the Hats was confidently predicted. That they managed to weather the storm of 1742–3 they owed to their unprincipled but clever concentration of the attention of the country on the issue of the succession. Ulrika Eleonora had died during the war (November 1741), and there had been at the time a suggestion that the duke of Holstein-Gottorp, the 14-year-old Charles Peter Ulrik (son of Charles Frederick and Anna Petrovna) should be declared heir to the Swedish throne in order that Elizabeth might be prevailed on, through a skilful playing on the young duke's descent from Peter the Great, to keep her bargain with the Hat leaders. Tsaritsa Elizabeth had, however, forestalled the plan by inviting her nephew to stay with her in St Petersburg, an invitation which had been readily accepted. At the Diet of 1742 there was no constitutional need to broach the succession problem, the Estates having decided in 1720 that such a discussion should not take place till the throne became vacant, but the Hats opened the debate in the Diet from a conscious desire to turn the nation's thoughts away from the defeat in Finland. The question aroused tremendous interest all over Sweden, became inextricably inter-woven with the peace negotiations with Russia and caused intense dip-lomatic activity among all the Powers interested in the north. In Sweden there was a general feeling that the obvious choice would be the young duke of Holstein-Gottorp, who, as his first name proclaimed, was not only a grandson of Peter the Great but also a grand-nephew of Charles XII. The Peasants' Estate led the way by choosing him heir to the throne in October 1742, the other Estates followed suit and a deputation was sent to St Petersburg to make him the offer of the Swedish succession upon the death of Frederick I and to invite him to live in Sweden. The deputation arrived too late, for Tsaritsa Elizabeth, well informed of what was happening in Sweden, had already prevailed upon the duke to become her own heir. As an earnest of his prospects in Russia he received the title of Grand Duke, and he for his part embraced the Orthodox faith just a few days before the Swedish deputation arrived in the Russian capital. The tsaritsa could now take a firm line with the Swedes and informed them that only if the Estates would elect an heir-apparent of her own choosing would she agree to restore Finland. The candidate she had in mind was the prince-bishop of Lübeck, Adolphus Frederick of Holstein-Gottorp-Eutin, the cousin and heir presumptive of Charles Peter Ulrik.

Discussion now had to start afresh in Stockholm. The Danish crown prince Frederick was much talked of and the Fourth Estate came out in his favour in March 1743. The Hats tended to support the candidate preferred by France, the Count Palatine of Zweibrücken (related to the house of Vasa), while the Caps, on England's advice, backed Prince William of Hesse, the brother of Frederick I. Denmark promised, if her crown prince were chosen, to aid Sweden's reconquest of Finland with her fleet and army, but the three higher Estates were reluctant to consider the Danish candidature seriously since they feared that such a choice would inevitably lead to future attempts to increase the power of the Crown. The question of peace terms with Russia loomed large, and once preliminary negotiations started in Åbo the name of the Russian candidate came increasingly to the fore. The Hat leaders soon became prepared to accept Adolphus Frederick if Russia would restore all, or nearly all, Finland. The Russians, on their side, showed themselves anxious to keep as much of southern Finland as possible to secure the approaches to St Petersburg. The ferment in Sweden continued to grow during the spring and early summer of 1743, the Fourth Estate gaining temporary admission to the Secret Committee, a sure sign of the seriousness of the crisis. The peasants all over the country, exasperated by the incompetence shown in the war, by the high-handedness of officials and by the lack of support outside their own Estate for the Danish crown prince, marched in protest from the valley of Dalarne, and from other districts, to the capital. Five thousand peasants were already streaming into Stockholm when news arrived of peace preliminaries signed at Åbo: a strip of Finnish territory would have to be sacrificed, all the rest would be restored as soon as Adolphus Frederick was chosen heir-apparent. These terms, rowed across the Åland Sea with all possible speed, changed the situation. The Hats gained the upper hand once more, since the peasants had nothing as positive to offer as the return of practically all Finland. Adolphus Frederick was now chosen heir to the Swedish Crown with right of succession for any male children that might be born to him, a provision which seriously impaired that future bargaining power *vis-à-vis* the Crown which the Estates had envisaged in 1720. In early August the Peace of Åbo was signed; at the end of the month Adolphus arrived in Sweden, followed in October by 12,000 Russian troops which were to be stationed in Sweden to prevent Denmark undoing the succession settlement by force.

The immediate effect of the Peace of Åbo was to make Sweden dependent on Russia. The heir-apparent was grateful to the tsaritsa for having improved his prospects in the world, and his pro-Russian attitude could be expressed in the Council where he was given a vote with permission to use the king's double vote if Frederick I were absent from the meeting. The presence of Russian troops on Swedish soil and the addition of a Russian squadron to the Swedish navy further emphasised Russian power over Sweden. In the long run, however, this state of affairs had a sobering effect on the Hat party. A moderate Hat, Count Tessin, took over leadership of the party until 1754, intending firmly but cautiously to rid Sweden of Russian interference and control. By co-operation with the Caps he managed (in spite of Adolphus Frederick's refusal to renounce any claims he might inherit in Slesvig-Holstein) to reach a temporary understanding with Denmark by the exchange of declarations to the effect that the two countries would stop their mobilisations and act according to the treaties of friendships which existed between them. With the ratifications of these declarations Russia had no longer any excuse to keep her troops in Sweden and by July 1744 the last Russian soldier had left. Tessin would have liked to cement good relations with Denmark by a marriage between Adolphus Frederick and a Danish princess, but this plan was counteracted by England, who (as during the succession crisis of 1742–3) was determined to prevent a possible future Scandinavian union, being convinced that a strong bloc controlling the entrance to the Baltic would not be in her interests. A bride was therefore found for the heir-apparent at the court of Prussia, Tessin himself escorting Frederick the Great's sister Louisa Ulrika to Sweden in the summer of 1744 after her marriage by proxy to Adolphus. A friendship grew up between the Prussian princess, keenly interested in art and literature, and Count Tessin, representative of the cosmopolitan culture of the Hat party, and through this friendship Adolphus Frederick was weaned from his dependence on Russia. His wife, dominating him, brought him for some years into the Hat camp, both of them hoping that through their co-operation with the Hat leaders the power of the Crown might be increased. In this hope they were disappointed though the help they gave the Hats proved valuable, particularly in the field of Swedish-Danish relations. As soon as Tsaritsa Elizabeth realised that Adolphus Frederick had escaped her tutelage, she attempted to make Denmark join herself and England, in the party struggles of Sweden, to support the Caps against the Hats, who in their turn received help from France and sometimes from Prussia. Tempted by promises of an amicable settlement of the Slesvig-Holstein difficulties, the Danes responded to these Russian overtures, and there were occasions during the years 1746–8 when Denmark actively co-operated with Russia and England in the Swedish party struggles. To conjure the danger represented by this increased support for the Caps, the Hat leaders used their influence with Louisa Ulrika to persuade her husband to give up the claims he might inherit from the duke of Holstein-Gottorp, a renunciation which paved the way for a treaty of friendship between Sweden and Denmark in 1749 and for the betrothal in 1751 of Gustavus (the son born to Adolphus and Louisa in 1746) and a Danish princess. These arrangements made possible a period of co-operation between the Hats and Bernstorff: and not until the reign of Catherine II did Russia obtain that solid Danish support for the Caps which Elizabeth had attempted to secure.

Throughout the 1740's the organisation of both Hats and Caps became more fully developed. Both parties now possessed a central committee, consisting of the chief party leaders, in which policy was decided; each party divided its members into small groups (*rotar*) to facilitate discipline and each had party whips (*aktörer*) whose duty it was to keep members of the party together and convey to them the orders of the leaders. From the middle of the 1740's the two parties nearly balanced each other in the Estates, but the Hats managed to keep in power, partly through clever political manœuvring and partly because the Caps were less firmly united than the Hats, the moderate Caps disliking and distrusting their party's dependence on Russia.

With the death of Frederick I in 1751 a new factor was added to the party struggle. Louisa Ulrika as queen was less willing than before to acquiesce in the limitations on the power of the Crown which the Estates had decreed. Intellectually she remained within the circle of the Hats, politically she decided to break with them when Tessin proved unwilling to further her plans. She began to collect round her the beginnings of a court party composed of some few genuine royalists and a good many disappointed renegades from either of the two major parties. This emergence of a court party led to a measure of reconciliation between Hats and Caps, both parties co-operating in counteracting any move which the king, urged by his queen, made to interpret the Constitution of 1720 in favour of the Crown. In a series of bitter struggles, over the king's right to influence administrative and military appointments and over the king's duty to accept majority decisions in council, the Crown was decisively defeated. To make sure of robbing the king of all influence in matters of promotion it was decided that seniority should be the only criterion for promotion, a change which had detrimental effects on the civil service as well as on the armed forces; and to overcome the awkwardness of the king's refusal to sign majority decisions with which he disagreed, such decisions were legalised by the use of a facsimile of the king's signature. When the queen, in revulsion at these counter moves on the part of the Hats and Caps, connived at a revolutionary attempt of her followers to seize power by force in the summer of 1756, great humiliation was heaped upon the royal family. Eight of their chief supporters were executed; the education of Gustavus was taken away from their control; the proud queen was forced to listen to a deputation from the clergy who lectured her on the evil of her ways; the king was made to announce that the Estates would be justified in breaking their oath of allegiance to him if he allowed any further attempts to increase the power of the Crown contrary to the Constitution. A medal commemorating the victory of the Estates was joyfully struck.

Sweden's entry into the Seven Years War on the side of Prussia's enemies can in part be interpreted as a continuation of this policy of teaching the Prussian queen a lesson; though the main reason was the temptation to regain from Prussia territory lost to the Hohenzollerns during the Great Northern War. The Hats were convinced that Frederick II had no chance against the great coalition ranged against him and thought that Pomerania could be retrieved by the mere fact of Sweden's entering the war on the side of Prussia's enemies. They were, however, as in 1741, guilty of unfounded optimism, and the war, known in Sweden as the Pomeranian War, proved no more successful than the war against Russia. The nation, so enthusiastic in 1741, was now on the whole indifferent, and there was a good deal of sympathy for Frederick II, whose gallant fight was compared to that of Charles XII. The position of the Hat party became steadily worse as the war produced no startling successes. The financial extravagance inherent, but hitherto not obviously apparent, in the ultra-mercantilism of the Hats was now brought into the open by the strain which the war expenditure imposed on the nation. Misfortune also tended to produce dissension within the ranks of the Hats; and the queen, who at the beginning of the war had worked for patriotic co-operation between Hats and Caps, began to move towards the Caps. Instinctively she sensed the coming defeat of the Hats and hoped to make terms with the Caps to the advantage of the court. When Russia on Peter III's accession left the anti-Prussian coalition, Frederick II turned his forces strongly against the Swedes in Pomerania: to avoid military defeat the Hats had to beg the queen to negotiate a separate peace for Sweden with her brother.

This peace of 1762 brought neither gain nor loss to Sweden, the *status quo* being restored, but it cost the Hats their last vestiges of prestige. In the election campaign for the first post-war Diet, due to meet in February 1765, the Hats tried to keep the nation faithful by emphasising the many advantages which they had brought to Sweden's economic life: their impetus to industry, their control of prices, their industrial tribunals, the enlarged fishing and merchant fleets, the success of the Swedish East India Company. The opposition knew, however, how to exploit the reverse side of this general picture of prosperity: many of the loans to industry had not been repaid and more paper-money had been issued to cover loans and prizes and bonuses than the country could readily absorb; no solution had been found for the difficult problem of how to restrain the peasants from home distilling of spirits from grain (both for consumption and for sale as an easily transported cash crop) so that the import of corn was necessary even when the harvests were good. The opposition called itself the Caps, stressing of its own accord its descent from the Cap party of Count Horn's days, but history knows its members as the 'Younger Caps', thus emphasising also the new ideas which the party wanted to put into practice. The party had inherited much of the caution of the older Caps. It was anxious to avoid an adventurous foreign policy and proclaimed its intention to give up the French alliance of the Hats and tie the bonds with Russia and Great Britain closer, the two Powers which were concerned to keep the peace in the north. The Younger Caps prided themselves on their specifically Swedish outlook as opposed to the more cosmopolitan attitude of the Hats, and there was much talk during the campaign of a return to simple Swedish manners and life to combat the extravagance of the Hat regime. The reforms which the Younger Caps advocated, however, were those of the late eighteenth-century opposition everywhere in Europe: relaxation of mercantilism, a more positive agricultural policy, administrative reform to encourage initiative, attack on the privileged position of the nobility, freedom of the press to promote political discussion.

In the election campaign of 1764–5 the Younger Caps were successful; they obtained a majority in all four Estates, filled the Secret Committee with their nominees and forced the resignation of those Hat councillors who refused to go willingly after the now familiar pattern of impeachment. The change of party, that fall of the old regime which the Younger Caps thus accomplished peacefully, was in itself the result of that parliamentary development which Hat, Cap, and Younger Cap regarded as the chief gain of *Frihetstiden*.

CHAPTER XVI

POLAND UNDER THE SAXON KINGS

THE so-called Saxon period of Polish history, from 1697 to 1763, was after 1717 one of uneasy peace, illusory prosperity and bad leadership, an era of decline during which Poland degenerated into Sarmatia—an earthly paradise for a minority of its inhabitants and a wild benighted squirearchy in the eyes of the outside world. The term 'Gentry Democracy' (*demokracja szlachecka*), sometimes used to describe Poland's Constitution between 1572 and the second half of the eighteenth century, is a complacent and self-contradictory misnomer, especially when applied to the years 1697–1763. This system at the best of times had never been a democracy but an aristocracy disguised as an elective monarchy which, in the second half of the seventeenth century, assumed the form of oligarchy and, in the first half of the eighteenth century, sank to the level of anarchy.

One of the principal defects and a distinctive feature of the Saxon period was the constant and fruitless attempt on the part of the leading families in the land to seize power for themselves. Their failure and the Crown's inability to subdue its enemies and enforce its own authority prolonged the struggle, absorbed the energy of the parties and finally brought the machinery of government to a standstill.

In the initial stages of the development of the Polish Republic, in the fifteenth and sixteenth centuries, the *szlachta*, although an aristocracy in relation to the country as a whole, enjoyed equality within their own class. By the beginning of the Saxon period, however, the *szlachta* were freer than ever but no longer equal. The chief source of wealth was the land and of this an overwhelming proportion was in the hands of the ruling body of nobles—the magnates, the aristocracy proper. Theirs were the latifundia in Lithuania and Ruthenia, theirs the high offices of Church and State with their revenues, and theirs, consequently, was the power. The lucrative civil and military appointments as well as the leases of land, all much sought-after by the gentry, were directly or indirectly in their gift. The landless *szlachta*, who in 1690 lost the right to participate in the election of a deputy, depended for their livelihood as bailiffs, stewards, retainers and small farmers on the aristocracy as well as on the gentry. Both haves and have-nots paid for the magnates' favours by voting for their candidates at the regional diets (*sejmiki*). This reciprocity turned the gentry and the minor *szlachta* into the aristocracy's clients and cat's-paws, liable to be pitted against another party in alliance with the Crown for the price of further benefits bestowed on their leaders, or against the king as an instrument of extortion. Under these conditions the right of each deputy to veto a decision of the Diet, hitherto virtually in abeyance and regarded not so much as a legitimate part of parliamentary practice as the theoretical evidence of unanimity, was revived in the middle of the seventeenth century to be abused as a means of wrecking the work of a whole *Sejm* by a single deputy, almost invariably in the interest of a native magnate or, after 1680, of a foreign Power. The new contractual relationship between the two or three dozen magnates and the million *szlachta* on the one hand and the Crown and the magnates on the other, paradoxically brought the structure of Polish society closer to feudalism than it had ever been in the Middle Ages. This analogy is enhanced by the wide autonomy which the regional diets, usually dominated by an aristocratic faction, had acquired in military and financial matters. In the seventeenth century they assumed responsibility for raising and maintaining the military contingents due from their palatinates from taxes which they imposed on the lower orders. Their authority far exceeded that of the *starosta* (*capitaneus*), once the king's arm in each district, now the representative of his diminished power. His administrative duties, consisting in the promulgation of royal ordinances, the collection of tax arrears and the preservation of order in the town where he resided, were light; his judicial ones were more onerous but could be and often were delegated to substitutes. The palatine (*voevoda*, *comes palatinus*), also nominated by the king, formerly in charge of the now obsolete *levée en masse*, was still a dignitary with a seat in the Senate but hardly any longer a functionary. His duties as judge in lawsuits between Jews and Gentiles and his power to impose economic controls mostly devolved upon his deputy, appointed and paid by himself, as in the case of the *starosta*. Revenue was collected and, in the case of local needs, managed, by publicans and stewards elected from among the *szlachta* at the general and regional diets. In the towns the municipality was responsible for gathering the current taxes, in the country, the landlord or, if so privileged, the village community. It was this state of affairs—government of the *szlachta* by the *szlachta* for the magnates—that prompted a contemporary foreign traveller to remark that the vast republic of Poland had fewer civil servants than the petty principality of Lucca.

The functions and organisation of the central Government had undergone no change since the late Middle Ages. The chancellor, as a rule in orders, fulfilled the function of prime minister, the vice-chancellor that of foreign secretary, the grand marshal was, as it were, the constable and the marshal of the court—the chamberlain. The two treasurers were in charge of State and court finances respectively, the grand hetman was commander-in-chief. Each Polish minister had a Lithuanian counterpart. The king of Poland and grand duke of Lithuania was an elective constitutional monarch. In addition to appointing his ministers he chose from among the 150 senators—the archbishops, bishops, *voevoda* and castellans—a body of twenty-eight advisers known as the senators resident, of whom seven attended upon the king in half-yearly rotation. But the king with his Government and counsellors, as well as the full Senate, constituting the Upper House, were subordinate to the will of the biennial Diet without whose sanction no major decision of policy might be taken. One ancient right the king still retained, that of appointing all the officials in the land. But even here his authority was only partial, for they were irremovable and could only be dismissed for felony. Another royal prerogative was the distribution of *panis bene merentium*, in other words the allocation for life of estates from the royal demesne to those who were deemed to deserve them. A further part of the *bona regalia* served to endow the various State offices, few of whose holders were consequently salaried.

As regards the legal administration there was no uniform system of law for the whole realm or even a complete code of Polish law. The peasants fell under seignorial jurisdiction, the lord of the manor acting as both legislator and judge, except in villages where the original settlers had been granted the privileges laid down by German municipal law (*Magdeburger Weichbild*). Here their descendants enjoyed a measure of legal autonomy. Similarly the towns had their own courts dispensing justice according to German law. The *szlachta* were tried and judged according to Polish law, written and traditional (*ius commune terrestre*), in the first instance by the *starosta* in criminal cases, while civil ones went before the *podkomorzy* (*subcamerarius*) or the *sędzia ziemski* (*iudex terrestris*). From their sentence the parties could appeal to the elective *trybunał*, one of the several high courts of somewhat conflicting competence. A parliamentary court composed of the king, the Senate and a number of deputies tried infractions of the common law, criminal cases and offences against officials; the chancellor together with assessors appointed by the king from among Church and State dignitaries heard appeals from the sentences of municipal courts and tried cases brought against them; the referendary's court took cognizance of the appeals of peasants on the royal demesne against officials or tenants. Any conflict of laws resulting from the different social origin of the parties was automatically resolved in favour of Polish law. There was no corporate body of judges, there was no Bench just as there was no Bar, but merely professional pleaders, trained through apprenticeship and recognised by the several courts. Theoretically the king was still *iudex supremus*, so that during an interregnum all judicial proceedings ceased and temporary law courts were set up, but in fact so complete was the legislature's disregard of the executive and the judiciary that the Diet acted as a supreme court and often quashed sentences imposed by the *trybunał*, and acting on the same principle, the regional diets often annulled judgments pronounced by the *starosta*, the *sędzia ziemski* or the *podkomorzy*. When all the organs of the State were judged to be failing in their functions, as happened only too frequently under the Saxon kings, the *szlachta*, in genuine or alleged self-defence, formed a confederacy (*konfederacja*), a free association for the achievement of a common political aim, theoretically deriving its authority from the Crown—in practice mostly directed against it.

If Poland's institutions were anachronistic, her economy was backward. It is no wonder that the Diet of 1719 should have refused to wage any more wars. Out of the seventy years between 1648 and 1717 fifty-five were years of war, hunger, fire and pestilence. Pillage by native and foreign armies had caused more damage than actual military operations. Property had been destroyed or looted, money had been stolen and grew scarce. The population shrank by roughly one-third, and with it the area of land under cultivation. The production of grain naturally dropped, all the more so as before about 1750 the lack of capital forbade technical improvement. The output of serf labour fell as the *corvée* was heaped on until it reached an average of three days a week. The peasant's other economic obligations to the landlord—services and taxes in money and kind—also culminated in the first half of the eighteenth century. His legal status remained unaltered, he was still tied to the soil and the landlord kept the *ius vitae ac necis* over him until 1768. In every sense the seven to eight million serfs were losing ground to the *szlachta*. In the upheaval of the second half of the seventeenth century a large proportion of the peasantry had lost their hereditary rights to the farmsteads in their possession. The landlord would now arbitrarily reduce a serf's holding or compel him to sell part of it. Hence the fall in the proportion of medium-sized estates from 25 per cent in the seventeenth century to 11 per cent of the total in the eighteenth century, accompanied by the first appearance of the agricultural labourer, full-time if he was landless, part-time if merely short of land. Stratification, incidentally, was not confined to the peasantry: the equality between the magnates, the middle *szlachta* constituting nearly half the total, and their petty landless brethren had long been purely nominal. But in some parts of the country the reconstruction of the old-fashioned manor founded on serfage was considered too costly and was abandoned in favour of a contract by which the peasant held his farm in return for a quit-rent. Such a conversion was carried out on some estates of the royal demesne in Lithuania and in villages belonging to the municipality of Poznan. The condition of Poland's agriculture in the Saxon period is best reflected in the grain exports, carried by foreign ships. The average for 1700–19 was 20,000 *lasts* (the Danzig *last* was about 3107 *litres*), in the period 1720–62 it rose to 31,000, about one-third of the record average for the first half of the previous century. Poland's successful competitors in European markets were England, Brandenburg, Livonia and, especially in the middle years of the century, Russia.

The towns, with their aggregate of about 500,000 inhabitants, fared even worse than the country. Apart from Warsaw with over 100,000 inhabitants in 1772, Danzig, Cracow, Vilno, Lvov with over 20,000, Poznan with about 5000 in 1773, and Thorn and Lublin with about 10,000 in 1772, there were scores of small towns numbering between a few hundred and a few thousand inhabitants. But small and large alike showed no signs of recovery from the ravages of war and were going to rack and ruin; trade and industry were on the point of extinction. The causes of this state of affairs have yet to be fully investigated, but it is certain that in the smaller towns at any rate the landlord's exploitation and unfair competition ruined the craftsman and turned the town into an agricultural estate. Having first subordinated the town council to his own authority, he would arbitrarily impose heavy dues and taxes on the craft guilds and finally put them out of business by establishing his own workshops manned by serfs in a part of the town (*jurydyka*) exempt from the municipal jurisdiction. At the same time he ruined the local traders by importing foreign goods over their heads. In order to support themselves, most of them as well as the majority of the artisans were obliged to take to agriculture in the suburbs and leave the Jews, whom the law of the land forbade to till the soil, to play the part of the middle class as small-scale traders and craftsmen but principally as farmers of the landlord's economic monopolies and privileges such as the sale of alcohol, tar and hay, dues from cornmills, etc. A similar process could be observed in the royal boroughs, squeezed dry by the unscrupulous *starostas*. The wool industry organised on capitalist lines, flourishing since the middle years of the century in the towns of Greater Poland and paralleled only in Polish Prussia, Warsaw and Cracow, was an exception to this dismal rule. But elsewhere the absence of protective tariffs and the lack of capital discouraged the townsman from becoming a pioneer of industry; the first industrialists were for the most part *szlachta*. The all too few ironworks and the modest factories of carpets, screens, mirrors, etc., founded in the latter part of the reign of Augustus III all owed their existence to the initiative of a few enlightened magnates. Useful as this was, however, it still fell short of bridging the yawning gap between the country's production and consumption of manufactured goods. Although they were not allowed to engage in trade under pain of derogation, the *szlachta* were, in addition to paying virtually no taxes, exempt from export duty and allowed to import goods for their own use equally free of duty. These privileges alone go a long way towards explaining the indigence and paucity of Poland's middle class. As far as external trade was concerned the *szlachta* were, in effect, a clandestine *noblesse commerçante*. The merchant's inevitably higher prices debarred him from competition and reduced him to a position of agent. Economic controls, too, favoured the *szlachta*. The prices of home manufactured goods were kept low in relation to agricultural prices; consequently the landowners' profits mounted as those of the artisans declined, making investment impossible. The depression was aggravated by the monetary crisis inherited from the preceding period. There was a surplus of copper coins, the new silver coinage was debased and only gold coins retained their value. Banking was still in its infancy and in the hands of a few foreigners.

It is plain that Poland's economy, just as her social and political structure, was unsound because it was top-heavy. A great part of her material weakness was due to the absence of a constructive fiscal and financial policy whose object should have been to divert to the coffers of the State a far greater share of the income from the wealth concentrated in the hands of the favoured few.

In this unproductive and isolated agricultural society there was no place for the urban and cosmopolitan culture of western Europe. Education no longer flourished. The Calvinist schools, like the Arian ones before them, had been forcibly closed down in the second half of the seventeenth century and with them disappeared an important link with the West. The Lutheran ones were German and exercised no influence; the academy of Zamość was moribund, that of Vilno was no more than a Jesuit college; the university of Cracow was a nursery for schoolmen and had spent its last three million *zlotys*[1] on the beatification of John Cantius; the *szlachta's* education was almost entirely in the hands of the Jesuits. Each country in each period has the Jesuits it deserves; the Polish ones, having eliminated all competition from the dissenters, now regarded their mission as accomplished and did not even trouble to follow the precepts of the *Ratio Studiorum*. They taught Latin grammar by rote, Latin poetry reduced to the level of metrical exercises, formal, mostly panegyrical Latin rhetoric and macaronic Polish; their moral education inculcated veneration of the *liberum veto*, belief in the natural superiority of the *szlachta*, ritualism, religious intolerance and unquestioning devotion to the Church.

Learning was extinct; the most valuable scholarly work of the period is K. Niesiecki's armorial (*Korona Polska...*); the most characteristic, B. Chmielowski's encyclopedia 'The New Athens' (*Nowe Ateny...*) described by S. Pigoń as a monstrous example of ignorance about which it is difficult to decide what is to be more admired: whether the compiler's ingenuousness or his industry or perhaps his accuracy in quoting imaginary sources. Before 1750, when the Piarists ventured to publish a few extracts from Copernicus, no written reference was made to the earth moving round the sun. A shaft of light was let into this realm of darkness when A. S. Załuski, bishop of Cracow and chancellor of Poland, put his private library at the disposal of the public (1747). The collection eventually grew to the size, then unique in Europe, of 300,000 books and 10,000 manuscripts. The literature of the period consisted mainly of aids to devotion—lives of the saints, hymn-books, legends and verse paraphrases of the Bible.

[1] I *ducat*=3·42 grammes of pure gold=36 *zlotys*.

The favourite secular genre was the versified romance, but hardly any-one who could read French for pleasure read Polish. The half dozen or so political writers before the turn of the century succeeded neither in determining the causes of Polish anarchy nor in recommending an ade-quate programme of reform. None of their work was stirring or persuasive enough to rival the conceited optimism of the *Domina Palatii Regina Libertas* which since its appearance in manuscript about 1670—the three printed editions are characteristically dated 1727, 1736 and 1745—coloured the political outlook of the average *szlachcic*. 'The purgatory of freedom', wrote the unknown author, 'is better than the hell of despotism. Thanks to the protection of Providence we keep falling and yet we shine, we keep perishing and yet we live.... With this anarchy of ours we succeed as well as others with the most subtle distillations of government.' The principal cause of anarchy, the free *veto*, was largely glossed over until Stanislas Leszczyński first denounced it, however obliquely, in his 'Free Voice to make Freedom safe....' (*Głos wolny...* 1749). More than another decade went by before Stanislav Konarski, a protégé of the Czartoryskis, ad-ministered the antidote to the poisonous doctrine of the *Domina Palatii...* with his 'On the Effective Conduct of Debates' (*O skutecznym rad sposobie*, 1761–3), wherein he calls for a government responsible to a two-chamber parliament abiding by the decisions of the majority. This project of reform was not realised until a generation later, but the immediate effect of the book was nevertheless important: since the appearance of its third volume in 1762 no single Diet was disrupted. Konarski's other great public service was the reform, in 1753, of the schools run by the Piarist Order to which he belonged, on the model of the *Collegium Nobilium* established by himself in Warsaw (1740). From then onwards the Piarist schools taught critical thinking, clarity of expression, citizenship, the rudiments of science and modern, in addition to classical, languages. The Jesuits, in order to compete with their rivals, had to follow suit. Thus were two of the country's most crying needs—a scheme of political reform and a new system of education—met by a single man. Konarski's activities, however, foreshadow the subsequent period in which their full impact was felt, rather than the age of Augustus III.

In 1717 Frederick Augustus, elector of Saxony, came to an agreement with his rebellious Polish subjects after twenty years of almost continual crisis both at home and abroad. For two years after his election in 1697 Augustus was confronted with a party favouring a rival king of Poland. In June 1697 François Louis, prince de Conti had been acclaimed by a vast multitude while a smaller crowd had chosen Frederick Augustus, elector of Saxony. Both set out for Poland, but the Frenchman arrived in Danzig at the end of September only to meet with a hostile reception and to find that Augustus had been crowned a fortnight earlier. His attempt, in concert with Peter the Great and the king of Denmark to attack

Sweden's possessions on the shore of the Baltic led to a crushing defeat of Augustus in July 1701 which the Swedes followed up by overrunning Vilno, Warsaw and Cracow and by making use of those Poles who had been opposed to Augustus in 1697–9 to elect an anti-king of Poland in 1704 in the person of Stanislas Leszczyński. In 1706 Augustus had actually been compelled to renounce the crown, and though, after the defeat of Sweden by Russia at Poltava in 1709, he was able to return to Poland his position was insecure. Leszczyński's supporters attacked from the north in 1711 and again in 1712, while in 1714 there were signs of unrest in Poland itself and demands for the evacuation of Saxon troops assumed dangerous dimensions by 1715. From the trial of strength between the king and the *szlachta* (the confederacy of Tarnogród) it was the Russian ambassador who emerged as *tertius gaudens* and the most powerful political factor in Poland. In November, under the auspices of the Russian envoy, the king and the confederates' leaders signed the Treaty of Warsaw which received the silent assent of an ephemeral Diet on 1 February 1717. The settlement of 1717, the only legislative achievement of the whole Saxon period, wrought no profound changes in Poland's Constitution. Most of its provisions, doomed to become a dead letter, merely saved the faces of the reconciled parties: all the king's decisions were to be subject to the approval of the majority of the senators-resident, he would not be allowed to keep in Poland more than 1200 Saxon guards and six Saxon officials; others did not reach far enough to become beneficial: the hetman's power as financial administrator of the army was considerably reduced, he was prohibited from standing as a candidate in a royal election but was still appointed for life: one was pernicious; the army establishment was fixed at 24,000 but sufficient credits were not provided even for that small number.

The economic aspect of the settlement was more encouraging. The establishment of the army, composed as before of native and foreign volunteer mercenaries, if small, was at least permanent and would no longer be fixed according to circumstances by successive Diets. More important still, for the first time in history, Poland's finances were to be managed according to something resembling a budget. The revenue was defined as consisting of the *kwarta* which in fact was not one-fourth but two-fifths of the income accruing to tenants on the royal demesne—officials and recipients of *panis bene merentium*—indulgently assessed according to an obsolete cadastral survey; customs duties farmed out for 350,000 *zlotys* p.a., the tax on wines farmed out for 58,000 and, lastly, the lump sum of 220,000 imposed upon and collected by the Jewish community. Thus between 1717 and 1764 the annual income of the State was about 900,000 *zlotys*; for which the Treasurer had to account at each Diet. More than half the budget was earmarked for the army, which, in addition, made its own arrangements for the collection firstly of the poll tax worth nearly four million *zlotys*, exacted from the whole Christian population but weighing most heavily upon the peasantry and levied on the basis of an out-dated census, and secondly of provender money, the so-called *hiberna*, due to the army from royal and ecclesiastical estates, worth about one million. The palatine Diets lost the right to raise taxes for military purposes but were allowed to impose *czopowe* (literally 'tap money'), a former State tax, on the retail sale of alcohol and spend the proceeds on local needs.

The price which the mediator exacted for this compromise was exorbitant. The tsar not only did not withdraw his troops but proceeded to squeeze Poland out of the Baltic seaboard by occupying Courland (May 1718) which, legally, should have reverted to Poland on the extinction of the ducal Kettler dynasty, and refusing to hand over Livonia, contrary to his earlier agreement with Augustus. In addition, he plotted a reversal of alliances with Charles XII's minister, Goertz. The *szlachta*, realizing only now whose game they had been playing, cried shame upon Peter. The king, encouraged by this reaction and by the tsar's growing unpopularity with western European courts, undertook a policy of emancipation from his tutelage. The Diet of Grodno (late in 1718) successfully resisted Russian and Prussian attempts to disrupt it with a hired *veto* and allowed the king to resort to the unusual expedient of proroguing the Diet 'as if', in the words of the astounded Russian envoy, 'he were an autocrat'. This stiffening of the Polish attitude and the need for reinforcements on the Swedish front, but not the conclusion of the Treaty of Vienna (see below), caused the tsar to withdraw his troops.[1]

In his efforts to emancipate himself from Russian tutelage after the settlement of 1717 Augustus drew nearer to Vienna. In 1718 Flemming, the Saxon Kabinetts Minister, succeeded in arranging the marriage between Prince Frederick Augustus, the future Augustus III, and Maria Josepha, a niece of Charles VI. This private alliance found its counterpart in the Treaty of Vienna concluded between Austria, George I and Saxony in January 1719. The parties agreed to compel Russia to evacuate Mecklenburg and Poland, guaranteed Poland's frontiers and her rights in her dependencies (Courland) and undertook to guard Augustus II against foreign intrigue so as to enable him to carry out constitutional reform. The attitude of Sweden, still formally at war with Saxony (until December 1719), was none the less friendly and the possibility of an Austrian, Swedish Polish and Saxon alliance against Russia could be envisaged. It now remained for the Diet, recalled late in 1719, to ratify the treaty and usher in an era of military glory and, as Augustus secretly hoped, of authoritarian reform. His hopes were soon disappointed. The deputies not only did not approve the treaty but protested against any policy that might embroil the country in another war which, they considered, would complete the ruin

[1] J. F. Chance, *George I and the Northern War* (1909), p. 292, note 3.

of the *szlachta's* estates. In 1720 the king once more fruitlessly attempted to persuade the Diet to take part in the formation of an anti-Russian bloc. After this fiasco, Augustus II and the Poles went their separate ways, he promoting the interests of the house of Wettin, the *szlachta*, lulled by a false sense of security, eating, drinking, making merry and cultivating their garden of anarchy, ignorance and religious intolerance.

In a country where the Catholics wished that 'in one catholic kingdom there were one faith and with it one heart and one soul for its citizens', the dissenters not unnaturally found '*patria non patria sed theatrum miseriae et ergastulum oppresionis facta*'. The plight of Poland's 200,000 Protestants, consisting mostly of German Lutheran townsmen and colonists in Royal Prussia and Greater Poland, but including also about 1000 gentle Polish families, had been deteriorating steadily since the earliest days of Augustus's reign. During the brief Swedish occupation they had naturally fared better. Charles XII had restored the long-forgotten freedom of worship and would have equalised the Protestants' religious rights with those of the Catholics, had not Leszczyński convinced him that they could not allow their sympathies to offend the *szlachta's* religious sentiments. After the restoration of Augustus the Protestants' enemies made capital out of their collaboration with the Swedes. The king's protection availed them little and at the first opportunity they were put back in their place with a vengeance. Article IV of the Warsaw Treaty forbade the restoration of old Protestant churches and ordered the destruction of those erected between 1704 and 1709. All worship in the latter was prohibited under pain of a fine in the first instance, imprisonment in the second and banishment in the last. All things being equal, civil offices and military rank were to be granted to Catholics in preference to Protestants. The Catholic zealots interpreted the loosely worded article as a legal basis for depriving the dissenters of all religious and the majority of civil rights until they returned to the fold of the Roman Church. Actions against Protestants were now brought before ordinary courts composed exclusively of Catholics instead of mixed ones appointed by the king or delegated by the Diet. As to the churches it was argued that they were either old, therefore originally Catholic, and must be rehabilitated, or new and must be destroyed. In 1717 the *trybunał* of Lithuania excluded on religious grounds its four Protestant members and thenceforth no heretic was allowed to sit on a Lithuanian *trybunał*. In the same year the Diet excluded one out of the seven Protestant deputies, in 1718 this procedure was applied to all Protestants and became customary. In the remaining years of the reign of Augustus II no addition was made to Protestant disabilities, but the extremists' animosity did not die down. In 1733 they prevailed upon the Convocation Diet to declare that 'in this realm *exoticos detestamur cultus*' and to debar non-Catholics from all civil offices, '*salvis modernibus possessoribus*'. Augustus III, the first king since 1572 not required to keep the peace between the various Christian denominations, confirmed this law in 1736. The destruction of Protestant churches and the closing down of Protestant schools continued, condoned rather than approved by the majority of the *szlachta*, until the death in 1748 of their bitterest enemy, Archbishop K. A. Szembek. It is estimated that between 1718 and 1754 in Greater Poland alone the Protestants lost thirty churches; in Little Poland they suffered no less; in Lithuania the original number of fifty-one was reduced by more than half.

Poland's neighbours were quick to seize upon the religious question as an opportunity for intervention. The dissenters became the subject of clauses in treaties between States (Prussia and Sweden; 1703, 1705, 1707) even before they themselves had begun to lay their grievances before the Protestant Powers and to appeal to them to protect their rights (1713). Russia and Prussia first pledged themselves jointly to defend the rights of the Protestant and Orthodox communities in 1730 (see below), but until 1724 Peter the Great's interest in Poland's religious minorities was confined to the at least 600,000 strong Orthodox community. Orthodoxy at that time was a declining spiritual force in eastern Poland and in Lithuania. By 1702 the Uniate rite had engulfed all the eastern bishoprics except that of Mohilev; in 1708 the main stronghold of Polish orthodoxy, the stauropigial[1] confraternity of Lvov, fell to the Basilians. Only Russian help could save the Orthodox community from further disintegration, but it was not afforded until Peter I grasped its potentiality as an instrument of secular policy. Article nine of the 'perpetual peace' treaty of 1686 guaranteed civil and religious rights to the Orthodox but only in 1720, when his influence in Poland was waning, did Peter, assuming the function of protector of the Orthodox community in Poland, energetically remonstrate with the king. Augustus II obliged him with a manifesto assuring the welfare of the see of Mohilev and confirming all Orthodox rights and privileges. Such a personal statement, however, made behind the back of the Diet, had no legal validity. The tsar registered his protest and, pending further action, sent a commissary to Mohilev instructing him to report on the position of the Orthodox in Poland (1722). But the tumult of Thorn which occurred two years later did not provoke his return to the attack.

Thorn was a manufacturing town inhabited by an almost equal number of Poles and Germans but governed by the latter owing to their predominance in the craft guilds. The Catholics' bulwark and a constant irritation to the Protestants was the local Jesuit college. The feud between the two communities reached its climax on 16 July 1724, when a Protestant mob provoked by a Jesuit student burst into the college grounds and desecrated the chapel. When the matter was brought before the Senate, the king, himself an indifferentist and not, as a rule, unsympathetic to the

[1] A religious institution subject directly to the Patriarch (or to the metropolitan).

dissenters but anxious to ingratiate himself with Catholic opinion, instead of having the case tried before his own court or that of the Diet, in October referred it to the jurisdiction of the chancellor. The court, composed exclusively of Catholics, sentenced to death the twelve principal rioters as well as the mayor and his deputy for not checking their violence, ordered the 'rehabilitation' of a Catholic church and allotted half the seats on the town council to the Catholics. The Protestants thereupon sent out an appeal to their co-religionists in the West. Co-ordinated protest by the Protestant Powers followed,[1] but was not supported by Russia: Peter I did not repeat his earlier demand for justice for the Protestants as well as the orthodox minority. Augustus officially rejected the protests but hinted privately that until he was allowed to rationalise Poland's Constitution he could not accept responsibility for such regrettable occurrences. Russia's non-committal attitude and Prussia's fear of embroilment brought the crisis to a gradual if inconclusive end. But the Roman Catholic hierarchy would not relent until not only the last Protestant but also the last Orthodox subject of His Polish Majesty was reclaimed for the pope and the rivalry between the two Churches, pregnant with dire consequences for Poland, lost nothing of its fierceness in the forty years to come. Time and time again the Orthodox clergy would appeal to St Petersburg through the Russian ambassador in Warsaw to stop the forced conversions of churches, flocks and monasteries. St Petersburg would instruct the ambassador to make a formal protest to which he would receive a more or less evasive reply and there the matter would rest. Any further action was bound to ruffle those border magnates who were also the pillars of the Russian party and was naturally considered inexpedient. Moreover, the protests were sometimes groundless as the conversions were by no means always forced. The bishop of Mohilev, Volchansky, in a letter addressed to the Russian ambassador in 1753, ascribes the transition of congregations to the Union to the clergy's 'inconstancy in their faith'.

The refusal of the Diet of 1720 to accede to the Treaty of Vienna prevented its realisation and encouraged Russia and Prussia to carry out the terms of their secret agreement concluded at Potsdam in February of the same year. The two Powers had pledged themselves to safeguard Poland's political institutions—in other words, to promote Polish anarchy—to protect the rights of the dissenters and to impede a Saxon succession to the throne, thus creating a prototype for the subsequent treaties of 1726, 1729, 1730, 1732, 1740, 1743, 1762. Unaware of this conspiracy but exasperated by the *szlachta's* rejection of his national policy, Augustus performed a rapid volte-face and approached Russia and Prussia with a new plan of dismemberment. The tsar, still playing the part of Poland's

---

[1] There is no evidence to support J. Feldman's statement that reprisals were made against the Catholics in Prussia, Scotland, Ireland, Gibraltar and Minorca. See his 'Sprawa dysydencka za Augusta II', *Reformacja w Polsce*, vol. III (1924), p. 115.

protector, acted in character and revealed the project to the *szlachta*, creating an excellent impression. Russia's acquisition of Livonia by the Treaty of Nystadt, concluded in the next year (1721) without Poland's participation and merely providing for her accession, was less popular. The Treaty of Constantinople with Turkey in 1720 virtually released Peter from his obligation of non-interference in Polish affairs and expressly allowed Russia to step in, should any foreign State violate the principle of the free royal election.

After 1720 Augustus concentrated all his efforts on winning the support of his subjects and of his fellow-rulers for a Saxon succession in Poland, but met with a natural and stubborn opposition on both fronts. So unpopular were the Wettiners with the *szlachta* that, when in 1726 the gentry of Courland offered the duchy to Prince Maurice of Saxony, an illegitimate son of Augustus II, the Diet refused to recognise or assist him and demanded Courland's incorporation in the Republic but did not instruct the hetmans to forestall the Russians, who drove out the Saxon and restored the *status quo ante*. Augustus himself was powerless. Most of his former supporters had abandoned him for the tsar; his own creatures had nearly all died without leaving him the legacy of a powerful court party. The mass of the *szlachta*, including the magnates, were dissatisfied with the Saxon king, wished for a change of dynasty and approved the one-point programme elaborated by their leaders, the Potockis (Teodor, the primate, and Josef, palatine of Ruthenia) to secure the ultimate election to the throne of Stanislas Leszczyński, since 1725 father-in-law of the king of France. Such was the object of their agreement with the French ambassador, the marquis de Monti (1729), and to this end they sought the support of Austria and Russia. If they succeeded and Leszczyński received the Crown from their hands, the Potockis, in addition to owning vaster latifundia, holding more ecclesiastical and secular offices and consuming more *panis bene merentium* than any other noble family, would wield the royal power. The neighbouring States, too, did their utmost to frustrate Augustus's efforts to secure the Polish throne for his son, Frederick Augustus. Although the king had recognized the Pragmatic Sanction in 1713, the Emperor feared his or his son's participation in the general scramble for the Austrian succession. In 1726, in order to avert such a possibility, he concluded an alliance with Russia, in order to prevent the establishment of the Saxon dynasty in Poland. Isolated and, since 1728, a sick man, Augustus sought the private and political friendship of Frederick William I, only to be once more outwitted by the Russians. In 1732 Russia and Prussia signed a secret treaty, drafted by the Russian ambassador in Berlin, C. Loewen-wolde, excluding both Frederick Augustus and Leszczyński from the Polish succession. Should the king in the meantime attempt a *coup d'état*, Russian and Prussian troops would march in to restrain him. It was to his 'good friend's' minister, Grumbkow, that, on the brink of the grave in

February 1733, Augustus confided his 'grand design' for the partition of Poland between Russia, Prussia and the house of Wettin.

At home Augustus could rely to a limited extent on the nearest approximation to a court party, the ancient but hitherto undistinguished Lithuanian princely house of Czartoryski, led to the fore by Stanislas Poniatowski, formerly an adherent of Leszczyński, now palatine of Masovia, related to the Czartoryskis by marriage and acting as intermediary between them and the court. Through A. A. Czartoryski's marriage (1731) to Poland's richest heiress they became one of the wealthiest families in the land. Less numerous and therefore more united, better educated and more public-spirited than the Potockis, as anti-Russian but not as Francophile as they, the Czartoryskis did not lack ambition but aimed higher than the mere acquisition of power, regarding their country not as a happy hunting-ground for careerists but as a sick political organism which they would cure. Their probity earned them the hostility of the magnates and the sympathy of the middle *szlachta*. They did not support the court constantly and on principle but from time to time and from expediency. The undertaking which they gave the king (1726) to cast their votes in favour of his son at the next election was accordingly vague and could not be regarded as binding. Augustus none the less thought it politic to nominate Stanislas Poniatowski commander-in-chief of the Polish army as a preliminary step to appointing him grand hetman of Poland. As, however, the appointment could only be made before a properly constituted diet, the Potockis, who looked upon the hetman's baton as part of the family monopoly, disrupted every parliament from 1729 onwards at its inception, including that of 1732, the last in Augustus II's reign. The court and the Czartoryskis could only console themselves with the knowledge that in each one they would have commanded a majority. The number of diets disrupted under the first Saxon king was nine out of a total of thirteen.

The words 'My whole life was one ceaseless sin', reported to have been spoken by Augustus the Strong on his deathbed, characterise to perfection his scandalous private life, but must not be extended to his career as sovereign. On this head tradition has it that he protested before God never to have intended any harm to Poland and, indeed, to have worked for the public good and the maintenance of peace. However that may be, the first statement does not damn him any more than the second exculpates him. The fact remains that he shirked the responsibility of constitutional reform even before he had realised the impossibility of personal government and that he conducted a foreign policy which was as often as not against the national interest. The consequences of the northern adventure into which he plunged so recklessly proved as disastrous for Poland as they were advantageous for her neighbours. Territories that Poland might have recovered or gained—Courland and Livonia in the east, Swedish Pomerania in the west—became bridgeheads for the fatal expansion of Russia and Prussia. To go as far, on the other hand, as to accuse him of having invented the idea of partition and suggested it to Poland's enemies is unjust.[1] In the disruptive atmosphere of the Great Northern War the idea, first conceived in 1656, obtruded itself, and not only to Augustus but also to Leszczyński, always ready to carve up the Republic with his friends or his enemies, provided he remained king in his own part, and to the Lithuanian separatists, gravitating towards Russia in 1705 and again in 1714.

On the eve of the death of Augustus II the French ambassador in Warsaw, the marquis de Monti, informed his king that although profound peace reigned in the country it was disturbed beneath the surface by the intrigues and animosities of the foremost families. In the interregnum that followed, however, Monti used his powers of persuasion and the large funds at his disposal with such skill that he succeeded in reconciling the Potockis with the Czartoryskis and in prevailing upon them to adopt Leszczyński as their joint candidate. The unfortunate episode of his puppet reign had by now been forgiven or forgotten, and during the intervening years his idealised person had, in the minds of the *szlachta*, become the symbol of Polish liberty, greatness and national tradition.

The primate, Teodor Potocki, bent on making the result of the election a foregone conclusion, morally compelled the Convocation Diet to pass a resolution excluding all foreign candidates, in other words, all Leszczyński's possible rivals. The act of exclusion, signed and sworn by all the deputies, would have constituted a violation of the principle of a free royal election, had not the more slippery signatories qualified their assent with the reservation '*salvis omnis constitutionibus de libera electione*'. Meanwhile Saxon diplomacy had prevailed on Austria and Russia to abandon their plan for keeping out Frederick Augustus as well as Leszczyński and planting in Poland the Infante of Portugal. It was clear that, in the circumstances, only Frederick Augustus of Saxony could compete with the *Piast*. In July 1733 he came to an understanding with the two imperial courts. In return for their backing he renounced in advance Poland's claim to Livonia, promised Courland to Anna Ivanovna's favourite, Bühren, and pledged himself to respect Polish liberty. The Holy See helped by declaring that the oath taken on the resolution excluding foreign candidates was not binding. Warsaw was again teeming with Saxon agents offering a good price for votes, but genuine sellers were hard to find. When Stanislas appeared in the capital out of the blue, having, on the orders of Cardinal Fleury, travelled by land and incognito, he was greeted with almost unanimous enthusiasm. In September some 12,000 voters proclaimed Stanislas king. Voltaire wrote: *Stanislas à l'instant vint, parut et fut roi*...—but not for long: the time was no more when a royal election

[1] Cf. W. Konopczyński in *The Cambridge History of Poland* (1941), vol. II, p. 24.

was decided by the will of the *szlachta* alone. A Russian army, 30,000 strong, was marching to protect the pro-Saxon minority assembled at Praga, on the opposite bank of the Vistula. The waverers took fright, turned their coats and crossed the river, all the more easily as many had taken bribes from both sides, 'If this is liberty which one sees here,' wrote the British envoy, George Woodward, 'the Lord preserve us from such liberty. Here are what they call great and little nobility which are slaves to one another by turns. All goes in confusion and disorder. The character of the nation is mighty haughty in prosperity and as humble in adversity.'[1] As soon as the Russians arrived, some 3000 voters, mostly clients of the Lithuanian magnates who had estates and privileges to lose by the election of a *persona non grata* to the Empress Anna, acclaimed Augustus III king of Poland.

Leszczyński fled before the approaching Russians and sought refuge in Danzig where he awaited Swedish and French help. Louis XV felt himself obliged to declare war: 'His Majesty was married to a commoner and so the queen', as d'Argenson puts it, 'had to be made the daughter of the king.'[2] The War of the Polish Succession was not fought on Polish soil and in the end benefited only France. The French attack in Lombardy successfully tied down the Austrian army, but French diplomacy, in spite of earnest endeavours, did not succeed in spurring Turkey and Sweden to military action. The Swedes were afraid of repeating their mistake of twenty years before; the Turks might have intervened in view of the Empress Anna's breach of the treaties of 1711 and 1713 but were engaged in a war with Persia and unwilling to fight on two fronts. Leszczyński and his adherents, therefore, were left to face the Saxons and Russians alone. In January the Russians laid siege to Danzig. The Lutheran inhabitants, in the hope of improving their commercial relations with France and in order to keep a tolerant king on the throne, afforded Leszczyński every help. Their army of mercenaries held the town in the teeth of blockade, assault and bombardment until all hope of relief from sea or land had to be abandoned. Two thousand Frenchmen arrived in June, but this was not enough to tip the scales in favour of the defenders. A small force of loyalists tried to fight its way through to Danzig, but was defeated. The French ambassador reported that the Poles had neither army nor guns nor ammunition nor money; since the relief of Vienna (1683) there had been no Polish army, it was only fit to fill the columns of newspapers. Disheartened and fearing for his safety, Leszczyński, at the end of June 1734, slipped out of the city to seek refuge with Frederick William I at Königsberg. In July the town surrendered. The dignitaries, including the principal members of the Family—as the Czartoryskis had come to be called—who had accompanied Leszczynski on his flight, were allowed to swear an oath of

[1] Public Record Office, S.P. 88/42, ff. 8, 9, 1735.
[2] *Histoire de la diplomatie*, ed. M. Potiemkine, vol. I (Paris, 1947), p. 247

allegiance to Augustus. In August Stanislas received sufficient encouragement from Versailles and had high enough hopes of Swedish and Turkish intervention to call upon his followers to continue the fight and even to contemplate an invasion of Saxony. In November a confederacy was formed at Dzików (near Sandomierz) under the leadership of A. Tarlo. The confederates concluded a purely formal treaty of friendship with France through their special envoy, Ożarowski, September 1735, while Leszczyński attempted in vain to effect a Franco-Prussian *rapprochement* designed to draw Prussia into the war. Fleury, impatient to bring hostilities to an end, made a last misplaced effort on Stanislas's behalf and tried to persuade Russia that he would be a far more convenient neighbour than Augustus but, finding no response, made peace with Austria. The final peace treaty stipulated for Leszczyński's abdication (1736), but allowed him to keep his royal title and awarded him as a consolation prize the duchy of Lorraine, won by France in the war.

In Poland the differences between the king and the confederates were composed at the Pacification Diet of June–July 1736. It empowered Augustus to give Courland as a fief to a prince chosen by the local diet and acceptable to Russia, Prussia and Poland, a periphrasis for the post-dated appointment of Bühren. Leszczyński's second exile was an advantage to Lorraine, where he did much good work in a private capacity without being a great loss to Poland. In 1733 he cut as sorry a figure as he had done in 1705. Twenty years of exile may have taught him a good deal of political philosophy, but did not make him a soldier or a statesman. His interest in his own welfare had grown rather than diminished, he was more than ever prepared to exchange the heavy burden of his crown for a handsome indemnity. Far from being a *roi philosophe* he was a philosopher turned king against his better judgment. Augustus III had even less to recommend him as man or ruler. He was a pious Catholic, having renounced protestantism on his father's orders in 1712, but he neither spoke Polish nor liked Poland. Apart from the period 1733–6 and his unwilling stay in Warsaw during the Seven Years War he spent in Poland altogether about two years. A dullard, with no interests outside the fine arts and only one passion—hunting, he entrusted his conscience to Jesuit confessors and delegated his power to favourites—J. A. Sułkowski, the Master of the Hunt until 1738, and afterwards the all-powerful H. von Brühl, prime minister of Saxony, a third-rate 'Richelieu, Medici and Rothschild of his times'. Polish interests he subordinated to Saxon ones and the latter to his dynastic ambitions.

Everyone admits [wrote Leszczyński in 1734 in the macaronic style of his day] that this splendid fabric of our Republic *mole propria ruit*, that it must be succoured, that, indeed, it cannot subsist much longer without a miracle.... Are our walls secure? The gates are open on all sides, the enemy enters and scours the innermost reaches of our land, sprawls across the country, imposes contributions, starts fires and takes prisoners. How can a country subsist without justice in its law courts, without concord in its councils, without military discipline in the army, without money in the treasury and without order *in politie*?[1]

During the next thirty years this appalling state of affairs grew steadily worse. Under Augustus III the precarious balance between the *Libertas* of the Diet and the *Majestas* of the Crown was completely upset: out of fifteen Diets only one ran its full course. The only constitutional remedy that might have checked the paralysis creeping over the body politic, that of a confederacy, was often mixed but never applied. The king, in exercising his prerogatives, did not go beyond appointing officials and controlling foreign policy. The only real power in the country was vested in the wealth and the offices of the magnates. United for a common end, it might have been effective, but the Branickis, Sapiehas, Sanguszkos, Radziwiłłs, Rzewuskis, Wiśniowieckis, Lubomirskis, Tarłos and a score of others, split into factions, chose rather to fight among themselves under the leadership of the Potockis and the Czartoryskis. It is now that, on closer examination, Polish history 'turns out to be that of a handful of families and their quarrels.[2] Neither the Family nor the Potockis being strong enough to overpower the other party—to outvote it was useless since the *liberum veto* made nonsense of majorities—both resorted to what they seemed to regard as pursuing a foreign policy, but what was in fact gratuitous or mercenary but invariably treacherous collaboration with a foreign Power.

The Potockis' aim was a confederacy to dethrone the king and make war on Russia; the price of French or Russian help was immaterial. Their favourite method of action between 1740 and 1756 was to hinder the court or the Czartoryskis by bribing a deputy with Prussian or French money and, for a handsome commission, to disrupt the Diet. The wiser and more honest of these self-styled 'republicans' or 'patriots' and guardians of *aurea libertas* secretly desired the establishment of a constitutional monarchy under Prince Charles Edward Stuart, a grandson of John Sobieski. The Czartoryskis after 1736, bitterly disappointed in France, continued to aim at supremacy and reform. They looked for patronage to the imperial courts and, after 1756, to Russia alone.

The only matter in which most of the rival magnates and the court appeared to see eye to eye was that of army expansion. But if all desired it, they did so from different motives. The Potockis wished Augustus to put the new regiments, under the command of Josef Potocki, grand hetman of Poland (1736–51), at the disposal of the Franco-Prussians, the Czartoryskis wanted him to lead them into the camp of the Austro-Russians. Appropriate projects in various forms were consistently brought up by the Czartoryskis at every Diet between 1736 and 1752, but for lack

[1] S. Leszczyński, *Głos wolny, wolność ubezpieczający*. Published 1749, dated 1733.
[2] A. Brückner, *Dzieje kultury polskiej*, vol. III (1931), p. 12.

of confidence between the parties, statesmanship in the leaders and public spirit in the deputies, were never approved. Army expansion postulates credits, credits require taxation, but no Diet would agree even to abolish the reductions granted earlier to certain distressed provinces, let alone vote new impositions. The irreconcilable attitudes of the two parties first made themselves felt at the time of the Russo-Turkish war. While J. Potocki was organising a confederacy and seeking Swedish, Turkish and Prussian support, the Czartoryskis were trying to persuade the Russian ambassador to back their scheme for army expansion. The Russian victory of 1739 dashed the hopes of both parties. The year 1741 saw another attempt by the Potockis to form a confederacy with the professed aim of achieving an expansion of the army, proposals for which they had opposed at the recent Diet, and the secret one of dethroning the king. Towards the end of the same year Sweden, again at war with Russia, sent emissaries who attempted to create a diversion of Polish malcontents in the Russian rear. On both occasions the trouble-makers took their cue from Prussia. Against the background of the diplomatic and military events of 1742–4 the Potockis, with their passion for confederacy and their Prussian leanings, appeared as the natural enemies of the court: the Czartoryskis, on the other hand, with their Russian and Austrian sympathies, as its natural allies. In this capacity, in 1744, they once more laid their proposals for rearmament before the Diet. The situation was analogous to that of 1719 and even more favourable: Russia's sanction of genuine reform could be traded for the privilege of participating in a coalition against another deadly enemy, Prussia. The Czartoryskis obtained the tsaritsa's promise not to interfere, the king succeeded in winning over the Potockis by agreeing to J. Potocki's retaining the command of an augmented army. Brühl, too, was determined to leave nothing to chance. Aware of Prussian sappings designed to disrupt the Diet, he made use of *agents provocateurs*, one of whom, during a crucial debate, flung a purse filled with Prussian gold on the floor of the House and accused ten deputies of bribe-taking. The Diet was saved, but only to become the scene of angry recrimination and reached its term without taking any measures or even punishing the traitors. Poland had lost a unique opportunity, Frederick II had extricated himself from his predicament for the bargain price of 15,000 *ducats*, 4000 out of which went to his principal agent, A. Potocki. Two years later the Czartoryskis once more came to an understanding with the Potockis for the sake of realising the reform which they had been advocating for over a decade and again the Potockis broke up the session. In 1748, as if to conjure away the evil disruptive powers, the Czartoryskis prematurely advertised the coming Diet as *boni ordinis*. It lasted barely long enough to allow the Family to propose the creation of a Committee of Ways and Means before it was broken up by a hireling of the 'republicans' financed by France and Prussia.

In spite of their reverses in the Diet, the Czartoryskis were now in the ascendant, but Brühl, the very man who brought them to the height of power, was soon to be the cause of their downfall. In 1748 they succeeded, to the indignation of the *szlachta*, jealous of their privileges, in inducing the *trybunał* to confirm, on false evidence, Brühl's descent from a Polish noble family. The Potockis exploited this mood. At the inauguration of the court's next session their adherents forcibly prevented the newly elected president, a member of the Family, from taking office and questioned the mandate of each judge-elect belonging to the rival party to participate in the proceedings. The Czartoryskis resorted to the same tactics, the court was not constituted and the administration of justice in Poland (but not in Lithuania) came to a standstill until the Potockis mastered the next *trybunał*. For the time being the powerless legislature and executive were matched by a powerless judiciary. The Diet of 1750 which should have dealt with judicial reform was disrupted by the Potockis. The only remaining constitutional way out of the deadlock could not be used, for the tsaritsa refused to support a confederacy and the Prussians hinted that if one were formed under Russian patronage they would be in Warsaw first. The resourceful Czartoryskis called for administrative measures to end the crisis. Let the king, they suggested, bestow rank and office regardless of tradition, precedence and influence, upon loyal men of worth, ready to co-operate with his government. The Potockis jibbed at the very suggestion of such a reform that would turn the magnates into an aristocracy of service and Brühl, for his part reluctant to stake everything on the Family, made the appointments in the customary way. Despairing of reform, he and the king now transferred their attention to the question of the succession. The Czartoryskis, in an effort to maintain their waning influence, assured Brühl that they would support his plan for the permanent establishment of the Wettiner dynasty in Poland at the coming Diet and in return obtained the vice-chancellorship of Lithuania for one of their Sapieha kinsmen. The Potockis, however, intending, in the event of the king's death, to favour the candidature of the prince de Conti, were sure to uphold the principle of a free election. Realising that its abolition would be impossible without the help of foreign gold and troops, Brühl applied for both to Austria and Prussia but met with a refusal. The Diet of 1752, before which the plan, in any case doomed to failure, was to have been laid, was disrupted by the Potockis at its inception. Brühl now abandoned the Wettiners' interests and, dispensing with the co-operation of the Czartoryskis, promoted his own. Ably seconded by J. Mniszech, an ambitious intriguer who had done him the favour, refused by a Poniatowski, of marrying his daughter (1748), he sold influence at court to the 'republicans'. Together with Brühl the Czartoryskis lost another ally, J. K. Branicki, grand hetman of Poland since 1751, who went over to the 'patriots'. The Czartoryskis decided that the only way to check their fall from power was to divide their opponents. In 1753 they endeavoured to lure to their side some of the 'republicans' with shares in the entail of Ostróg whose illegal parcelling they had obtained for the purpose. Contrary to the Family's expectations and to their extreme embarrassment, the transaction, instead of being hushed up and connived at, was exposed and criticised in the Diet. The Czartoryskis, for the first time, felt themselves obliged to resort to disruption. The king thereupon entrusted the administration of the estate to his commissioners and bestowed his favours on the jubilant 'republicans' through the agency of Brühl and Mniszech. The Potockis' political opinions and affiliations, however, remained unchanged and this made them unacceptable to Brühl as a substitute for the Family.

The one permanent feature of Poland's internal situation during the Seven Years War was the constant presence of foreign troops on Polish territory. Only when this fact is taken into account is it possible to gauge the astounding inertia and shortsightedness of all parties. The beginning of hostilities in the spring of 1757 brought the Russians to Lithuania for the rest of the war. Early in 1758 Russian garrisons were quartered in the principal towns of Royal Prussia including Elbing and Thorn but not Danzig. From Prussia they moved south into Greater Poland where they stayed four years, and between 1758 and 1761 their operations against Prussia were based on that area. The presence of one belligerent naturally attracted the other. In 1758 the Prussians raided Russian supply depots; the Senate felt obliged to admit that they were within their rights since Poland had, by letting in the Russians, failed to safeguard her neutrality; in 1761 they made another foray, in 1762 they returned to compel the landowners to sell them grain at nominal prices, in 1763 they organised a forced repatriation of Prussian colonists and extorted indemnities for their land.

Augustus III's defeat at Pirna at the very outset of the war (1756) presented the Czartoryskis with a chance of regaining their predominance at court and in the country. In the previous year the British ambassador and the Family's fairy godfather, Sir Charles Hanbury Williams, had taken the young Stanislas Poniatowski to St Petersburg where the future king tried to charm the court, in the person of the Grand Duchess Catherine, into advising Augustus to favour the Czartoryskis. Now the king was sending him to the Russian capital as Saxon envoy with instructions to request the prompt expedition of Russian troops to East Prussia. In Lithuania, where the Family had been steadily losing ground to Mniszech and his allies, the imminent arrival of the Russians won them the mastery of the *trybunał* (1756). In 1758 J. K. Branicki, blamed by public opinion for the violation of Poland's frontiers, marked out Brühl as the scapegoat and accused him before the king of unconstitutional and maleficent interference in Polish affairs. The king ignored the charges and Brühl took his revenge by suppressing the royal administration of the Ostróg entail. If the Czartory-skis did not return to power it was mainly because they preferred rivalry to co-operation with the court. When in the same year the king wished to secure the Duchy of Courland, formally vacant since 1741, for his son, Prince Charles, the Senate approved his temporary investiture not owing to, but in spite of, the Czartoryskis, who were determined to prejudice the chances of a Saxon succession to the throne which they coveted for one of themselves. The Family had burnt their boats and from this moment their relations with the court bore all the features of a feud. Mniszech, marshal of the court since 1742, ruled supreme and was at last able to give full scope to his policy of temporisation and paid preferment. Against him were ranged the Family and Branicki (who in the meantime had once more sided and then quarrelled with Brühl) with the remnants of the Franco-Prussian party scattered by the Reversal of Alliances. The Family offered their services to the French and at the same time angled for English and Russian assistance, waiting the while for the accession of the Grand Duchess Catherine. On several occasions did the Czartoryskis, smitten with anglomania since their acquaintance with Sir Charles Hanbury Williams and their visits to London, offer their services to England. In 1759 they wished to earn the right to style themselves the English party; in 1761 they declared their readiness to organise an uprising on the Russian lines of communication; in the spring of 1763 they applied to George III for a subsidy of £20,000. The indifference of the cabinet of St James's to these advances is best explained by George III's retrospective formulation of the principle underlying England's attitude to Poland since the accession of the Hanoverian dynasty: he wrote in 1763, 'my kingdoms are interested in Poland's affairs only in so far as they concern my allies'.[1]

The extraordinary Diet, called in 1761 to deal with the reform of the currency, was disrupted. The Government could do no more than issue four consecutive decrees reducing from nominal to real the value of the debased coinage. The culprit was Frederick II. In addition to looting Greater Poland he contrived between 1757 and 1762, with the help of dies seized from the Saxon mint and a network of Jewish agents, to drain the whole country of its good money and replace it with counterfeits worth 50 per cent less. His gain was equivalent to the twenty million *thaler* which he received as a subsidy from Pitt. Inflation raged and discontent was rife; at the judicial elections the *szlachta* expressed their feelings by voting for the Family. Catherine II's seizure of power in 1762 was the signal for their final offensive against the court. At the Diet of that year they provoked disruption by questioning the validity of Brühl's son's naturalisation; in the Senate they vigorously criticised the Government's incompetence and defended Catherine's right to expel Prince Charles

[1] Quoted by W. F. Reddaway, 'Great Britain and Poland, 1762–1772', *Camb. Hist. Jour.* vol. IV, no. 3 (1934), p. 224.

from Courland and reinstate Bühren. In the summer of 1763, having obtained Catherine's promise of money, arms and, if need be, military intervention, the Czartoryskis began to organise a confederacy. As soon as the Peace of Hubertusburg was signed, the king, accompanied by Brühl and Mniszech, returned to the hunting and opera-going of his beloved Dresden (April 1763). The Czartoryskis' warlike preparations were in full swing. Eight thousand Russians under Saltykov were marching on Vilno when suddenly Catherine, prompted by N. Panin, seizing the initiative and reserving the decisive voice in Polish affairs for herself, ordered Saltykov to withdraw and deferred all aid until the interregnum. This unexpected development confused and disconcerted the Family's adherents, but emboldened their foes. The 'republican' magnates led by J. K. Branicki threatened to use force against the Czartoryskis at the resumption of the *trybunał*. The king's sudden death in June 1763 saved the Family and inspired Stanislas Poniatowski to comment with a line from Voltaire's *Mahomet*: 'Chaque peuple à son tour a regné sur la terre, Le temps de l'Arabie est à la fin venu.'

In the reign of Augustus III Poland's relations with other European Powers were maintained mostly by Saxon diplomats, and Polish envoys seldom appeared at foreign courts. This practice reflected the character of Augustus's foreign policy which served Saxon interests first, the House of Wettin next and Poland only occasionally. Its fundamental principle, dictated by the disloyalty of the 'republicans' and the geographical position of his dominions, was a somewhat one-sided friendship with his eastern neighbour.

The Russians skilfully exploited his weakness. For their encroachment on neutral Polish territory during the Russo-Turkish war Poland received no satisfaction beyond an assurance that it would not happen again. In consequence of her non-committal attitude during the war the Turks, on Fleury's advice, did not insist on a renewal of the guarantee of Poland's territorial integrity at the peace settlement of Belgrade (1739), nor were the hamstrung Polish diplomats allowed to press the point by arguing that Poland had shown her good will towards Turkey by refusing Austria's invitation to join in the war on her side. In 1740 the new king of Prussia, Frederick II, aroused Polish and Saxon suspicion by hastening to pay homage to Poland before the arrival of the king's representatives, but in 1741 the Saxons could not resist Frederick's generous though vicarious offer of Moravia as well as a corridor between Poland and Saxony through Silesia and, with Russia's leave, threw in their lot with Prussia against Austria. They suffered heavy military losses, but when Frederick, after secret negotiations, made peace with the Emperor (1742), reaped none of the promised rewards. The Prussians were now in possession of the whole of Silesia; Greater Poland and Royal Prussia were all but encircled and Cracow could be reached from the new frontier in two marches. Brühl, swearing vengeance, abandoned Frederick and allied himself to Austria in December 1745 and Russia in February 1744. The territorial union between Poland and Saxony would be accomplished at Prussia's expense. The members of the anti-Prussian coalition looked forward to Augustus's bringing in Poland, but their hopes were disappointed by the disruption of the Diet of Grodno in November 1744. Austria, England, Holland and Saxony, however, still optimistic, signed in January 1745 the Warsaw treaty of alliance, comprising among others a secret obligation to support Augustus's, i.e. the Family's, programme of reform. But before the year was out, the Silesian wars ended in the defeat of the Saxons and their allies at the Peace of Dresden, December 1745. The king's subsidy treaty with France in April 1746 bolstered up the Saxon army and the marriage of his daughter Maria Josepha to the dauphin added to the prestige of the dynasty. He did not, nor could he, as king of Poland, repay Louis XV by preventing the march of Russian troops across the Republic to the western battlefields and back (1747–8). If Augustus was a useless ally, Louis was a double-faced friend: the beginning of his intrigue to place Prince Louis François de Conti on the Polish throne dates from this time. After the expiry of the French subsidy treaty Brühl negotiated a similar one with England in 1751, represented by Sir Charles Hanbury Williams, and used the ambassador's good offices to sound St Petersburg as to an international agreement guaranteeing the Saxon succession in Poland. If Russia, he suggested, were willing to give such a guarantee she might persuade Austria to join her. But by now neither Power felt interested in strengthening Poland's government; on the contrary, both disapproved of the Family's attempts at political reform. Already in 1748 the Russian envoy had made arrangements to disrupt the Diet in case no other party did so, and Maria Theresa had declared that she would regard the abolition of the *liberum veto* as harmful. Encouraged by Russia's coolness, the French ambassador, the comte de Broglie, spared no efforts in trying to draw the king into a league with France and the Potockis. Having failed, he offered, in 1755, to pay $1\frac{1}{2}$ million *livres* for an anti-Russian confederacy. The reaction of the sabre-rattling 'republicans' was disappointing in the extreme, but the Reversal of Alliances fully although unexpectedly justified their reserve. During the Seven Years War Russia not only used Poland as a military base, but, availing herself of her alliance with France and taking advantage of the military situation, between 1759 and 1761 twice pressed for France's approval of a revision of Poland's eastern frontier. Choiseul, in whose opinion French interests could suffer solely through a curtailment of *aurea libertas*, was prepared to co-operate, but was restrained by the directors of the *Secret du Roi*—to whom the Family had appealed through a special envoy—and instructed to mitigate the zeal of the Russian expansionists through the more moderate chancellor, Vorontsov, as intermediary. Peter III, in his brief reign, withdrew from the war and revived the by now traditional Russo-Prussian under-standing concerning Poland. The secret clause of the treaty of mutual assistance concluded between Peter III and Frederick II in June 1762 provided for a common policy in Poland. The next king was to be a Pole, placed and kept on the throne by the contracting parties. Three weeks later Catherine II usurped the Crown. In the spring of 1764 she and Frederick filled the blank in the secret clause with the name of Catherine's former lover, Stanislas Poniatowski.

The most characteristic feature of the 'Saxon' epoch is the failure of the legislature or of the executive to carry out political reform. So com-plete was the paralysis of the body politic that it led to the atrophy of Poland's internal and external sovereignty. In international politics she had ceased to count as a partner or adversary and was reduced to the status of a prize, since Augustus II sank from the position of Peter's ally to that of his satellite (1709). After the Diet's refusal to accede to the Treaty of Vienna (1719) Augustus adapted Poland's foreign relations to his own dynastic plans. Augustus III was practically a tributary of Russia and used Poland's strategic position to further the interests of Saxony. Twice, in 1720 and in 1744, the lack of essential national unity prevented the execution of a policy that might have restored Poland's position as a Great Power and checked the expansion of at least one of her dangerous neighbours. Foreign intrigues there were in abundance, but national foreign policy there was none. At home no individual or party even attempted to decide any important issue without foreign influence. Out of the twenty-eight Diets held under the Saxon kings, twenty-three were wrecked. Prussia and France, frequently her partner, were each implicated in seven disruptions, Russia was involved in eleven. Only six Diets were wrecked by the Poles themselves. During sixty years of Saxon rule Poland suffered virtually no territorial losses, but her growing weakness was creating a vacuum which only regeneration or foreign occupation could fill. Both Russia and Prussia violated her frontiers with impunity and treated her land as though it were a 'wayside inn'. Hand in hand with political disintegration went economic backwardness and intellectual stagnation. The signs of renais-sance were few, but the idea of dismemberment, as has been seen, was already current. The preservation of Polish anarchy was an axiom of Prussian as well as of Russian policy. In his *Instructions* (1722) Frederick William I recommended his successor to live in good friendship with the Republic of Poland, to show it his confidence continuously and always to form a party for Prussia in the Diet so that it might be disrupted when thought fit. He must work with all his might to see that Poland remained a free Republic and that there should be no sovereign king. Frederick II, as Crown Prince, declared the conquest of Polish Pomerania by Prussia to be 'necessary', and before finally executing this idea repeated it in his political testaments of 1752 and 1758. His interest, he declared elsewhere, demanded that Polish affairs should remain in a state of perpetual confusion and that no Diet should last. The might of the House of Brandenburg and the 'freedom' of the Polish Republic he regarded as a concomitant. Russia set herself up as the patron of the Polish benefice. Peter the Great helped Augustus II to establish his rule, Anna actually enthroned his son. Her First Cabinet Minister, Ostermann, continued Peter's policy of weakening Poland until the time came for decisive action. In the reign of Elizabeth Russia's safety was considered to depend on her allies, namely the Maritime Powers, Maria Theresa and, as a protection against Prussia and Sweden, the king of Poland, provided he was also elector of Saxony. So long as Russia and Prussia were potential or actual enemies, Poland's quasi-independence, however precarious, was assured. Russian ambassadors were instructed to behave loyally towards the king and not to side with any of the political parties, not even the Czartoryskis. But the Russo-Prussian alliance and the death of Augustus III spelled Poland's ruin: her role as a contestable but inviolable sphere of influence had come to an end. Prussia's territorial claims had already been defined, Russia's were formulated in 1763 in Z. Chernyshev's project for the extension of the empire's western frontier for the sake of 'completeness and security'. In the event of Augustus's death Russian troops were to occupy roughly the same territories as those which she annexed at the first partition. The ministerial conference summoned as soon as the news of the king's demise was received, approved the scheme but agreed wistfully that, in view of certain circumstances, the great benefits which the State would derive from its realisation were more to be desired than expected. At the close of the Saxon period the partial dismemberment of Poland by Russia was, short of a miracle, a foregone conclusion.

CHAPTER XVII

THE HABSBURG DOMINIONS

AFTER the conclusion of the Peace of Utrecht, Charles VI carried on the war against France single-handed for some months; but on 7 March 1714, Prince Eugene signed, in Charles's name, the Peace of Rastatt, under which Charles held his Italian possessions and the Spanish Netherlands, subject to agreement with Holland on a Barrier Treaty. The treaty with France was ratified for the Empire in the following year and the Barrier Treaty concluded at Antwerp on 15 March 1715. No agreement was yet reached with Spain.

Meanwhile, Charles had to regulate the position in his own dominions. His election to the imperial throne had at least been unanimous, even though the Perpetual Capitulation which he was required to sign left him with powers more limited than those of his father or brother. In the Austrian and Bohemian Lands,[1] the Estates possessed neither the power nor, in most cases, the wish to query either his succession or the continuation of the now established system of government, which not only left the determination of central policy to the monarch's free discretion but also abandoned the main administrative functions to his Statthalters in the different lands. It was only in Hungary that the position was still unregulated. Joseph I had lived long enough to see the negotiation of the Peace of Szatmár in 1712, which put an end to the long and bitter fighting led by Ferenc Rákóczi, but the Peace was actually signed only after Joseph's death, and still awaited ratification. It was, moreover, rather an armistice than a true treaty of peace: it provided for the cessation of hostilities, and for a general amnesty, and it continued in general terms the rights and liberties of Hungary (including Croatia) and of Transylvania; but it reserved discussion of all specific points for a Diet to be convoked in 1712.

There were elements on both sides opposed to agreement. Charles's military advisers, Prince Eugene in particular, were ineradicably suspicious of the Hungarians, whom, like Leopold II, they considered 'a hard and rebellious race which can be subdued only by savage torments'; while in Hungary, the *kurucz* spirit[2] was not dead. But all in all, there was, again on both sides, a more widely spread and sincere desire to reach a lasting settlement than had existed for many decades. Charles himself was pro-

---

[1] The Austrian Lands consisted of Upper and Lower Austria, Styria, Carinthia, Carniola, Tyrol, Breisgau and Burgau. The Bohemian Lands were Bohemia, Moravia and Silesia.

[2] *Kurucz* (lit. 'Crusader') and *labanc* (lit. 'footsoldier', in the imperial army) were the names currently applied in Hungary to the anti-Habsburg and pro-Habsburg parties respectively.

foundly convinced of the need, in his own interests, of pacifying Hungary. 'It is very important', he noted once, 'that quiet should prevail in this country'; and he saw that he did not possess the force to achieve this otherwise than by conciliation. 'The Hungarians', he wrote again, 'must be relieved of the belief that they are under German domination.' He had, moreover, none of the personal antipathy to Hungary which was not uncommon in his family. As for the Hungarians, they were tired and dispirited, and most of them were only too glad to seize the chance offered by the not ungenerous terms of Szatmár to save their persons and their estates from the wreck. Thus when Charles, after ratifying the Peace, duly convoked the Diet at Pozsony, the Hungarians met him half way, the most difficult parties to the negotiations being, indeed, the Hungarian *labanc* nobles, who feared lest a too generous interpretation of the amnesty might result in their losing the estates confiscated from their *kurucz* rivals which they had acquired or marked down for themselves.

The proceedings were protracted, since the Diet had to go into prolonged recess owing to an outbreak of plague. Yet agreement was reached easily enough on the main points. Charles was crowned and took the coronation oath, and signed the inaugural Diploma in each case in the form used by Joseph I. Charles thus swore to respect the rights of the Estates and to defend the integrity of the country, undertaking in particular not to detach parts of Hungary and incorporate them in others of his dominions, and he gave a solemn promise to rule Hungary only according to her own laws, existing or to be legally enacted in the future and not 'according to the pattern of other provinces'. In particular, the Hungarian court chancellery in Vienna was to keep its full independence and not to be subordinated to any court authority; similarly the Hungarian *camera* was to be independent of the *Hofkammer*. Many of the questions of detail were entrusted to commissions, one of which evolved a plan for the modernisation of Hungary more radical and more imaginative than anything else of its kind produced before 1942. But this was deferred for further consideration, as was the religious question, on which Catholics and Protestants could not agree. Decisions were reached only on two other important points, those decisions being in each case detrimental ultimately to the Hungarian national cause, but at the time partly justified by the real difficulties under which the Hungarian nobles were labouring owing to the frightful reduction both of their own numbers—only some 32,000 families were left in the country—and those of the peasants. Comprehensive provisions were enacted to prevent peasants from leaving their masters' land, and the whole basis of the national defence system was altered. The old institution of the '*noble levée*' was left in being, but the Diet itself recognised that the force which the *levée* could provide could not assure the defence of the country, and therefore voted for the establishment of 'a strong standing army', which at first was to have consisted of two-thirds Hungarians and one-third 'foreigners', the proportions being afterwards reversed at the Hungarians' own wish. The Diet agreed that it must pay for this force, but successfully defending the 'noble' privilege of exemption from direct taxation, consented only to vote annual sums for the purpose; only in emergency the king could agree the sum with a special *konkurszusz* or representative committee of the Estates. The money was to be raised from the traditional taxpayers, the socage peasants, on whose bowed shoulders yet another burden was thus laid. It was proposed at the time to set up a special Hungarian War Council, but that promise was never fulfilled, and Hungarians were not even often admitted to membership of the central *Hofkriegsrat*. The standing army thus remained a purely central institution and a powerful instrument in the hands of the Crown, the more effective since in times of peace the bulk of it was, partly for reasons of economy and partly as a precaution against renewal of unrest, stationed in Hungary, where its commanders made their own arrangements without reference to the local authorities. Here, again, the national independence lost what the nobles' pockets had gained.

During these negotiations, question arose for the first time of that theme which was to be the guiding *motif* of Charles's whole reign: of the Austrian succession. His brother's death had left Charles the last male to bear the name of Habsburg and his own marriage, concluded in 1708, had not yet proved fruitful. All too many distant collaterals through the female line existed, but the only remaining direct members of the line were Joseph I's two young daughters. Under the *Pactum Mutuae Successionis* of 1703 (a purely family agreement) Charles had succeeded before his nieces, and his son, if he had one, would follow him, but if he died childless, or left only daughters, Joseph's daughters should have succeeded him. In the Austrian and Bohemian Lands the monarch's right to determine the succession was admitted, and nothing excluded succession through the female line. In Hungary, on the other hand, as matters then stood, this was not the case: if the male line died out, the nation, under the existing capitulation, recovered its right to elect its king.

Since a female could not in any case wear the imperial crown, it was especially important for Charles to establish a strong *Hausmacht*; and he was also firmly resolved, if he had a daughter, that the succession to the family dominions should be hers, and not his nieces'.

The point was raised at Pozsony unexpectedly and, so far as the evidence goes, spontaneously, by the Croatian Diet, which instructed its delegates to the Hungarian Diet to declare its readiness, if the nation recovered its elective right, to elect that female member of the house of Habsburg who should be ruler of Styria, Carinthia and Carniola—those provinces of Austria which had formerly been associated for defence purposes with the old Croatia. A committee of Hungarian councillors suggested that

Hungary, too, should agree to elect an Austrian archduchess, and in support of this proposal not only admitted but urged the advantage, in the interests of Hungary's defence, of her being united *indivisibiliter et inseparabiliter* with the Austrian and Bohemian Lands; but it suggested also making the consent part of a settlement which should include fairly extensive concessions, especially in the economic field, in favour of Hungary. Charles was not anxious to set a precedent for bargaining with the Estates of all his dominions. For the time, he confirmed the Hungarian Diet's right of election, should the male line die out; but on 19 April 1713 he solemnly promulgated, in the presence of his privy councillors, a unilateral declaration to the effect that on his death all his hereditary kingdoms and lands should pass undivided to the male legitimate heirs of his body, according to the rule of primogeniture. If the male line died out the territories were to pass to his legitimate daughters and their issue, again according to primogeniture. If the female line died out, the succession passed to the collaterals. There the matter rested for the time. The war with France had still to be wound up, and that with Spain continued. The latter was in this last phase carried on with diplomatic rather than military weapons; but the next years saw a more serious military campaign, the only really fruitful one waged by Charles during all his long reign. In 1714 the Porte declared war on Venice, and quickly overran many of the Venetian possessions in Crete and the Morea. In 1716 Charles renewed his alliance with Venice and summoned the Porte to abandon its gains in the Balkans. The Porte refused, declared war on Austria and sent an army 150,000 strong across the Hungarian frontier. Prince Eugene, although his force was only 62,000 strong, met the Turks at Petrovaradin and on 7 August inflicted on them a defeat so crushing that they only reassembled at Belgrade. On 13 October Temesvár, which had been in Turkish hands for 165 years, was taken, and the whole of south-east Hungary cleared. Operations were now suspended for the year, but in 1717 a greatly reinforced army, supported by river craft brought from the Netherlands, assembled in south Hungary, and after a fortnight's siege, Belgrade fell on 17 August. This was the end of the military operations. Protracted negotiations set in, and on 31 July 1718 Austria and Turkey concluded the Peace of Passarowitz, under which the Porte ceded to Charles not only the Bánát (whereby the whole of historic Hungary was thus reunited under the Habsburgs), but also Little Wallachia, Northern Serbia with Belgrade, and a strip of Northern Bosnia.

While this was going on, Charles had, on 29 May 1716, allied himself with England. On 2 August 1718 he joined the alliance concluded the previous year by England, France, and later Holland, against Spain. Charles now renounced his claim to the Spanish succession, recognised the succession of the Spanish Infante, Don Carlos, to Tuscany, Parma and Piacenza, and abandoned Sardinia to Victor Amadeus of Savoy, receiving

Sicily in exchange. Fighting went on in Sicily until the fall of Alberoni led, on 17 February 1720, to the Hague Peace with Spain, which confirmed the provisions of Charles's treaty with the western Powers.

For Charles, the question of the succession had now become all important. A son was born to him in 1716, but died in the same year. He was left with two daughters, Maria Theresa, born in 1717, and Marianne, a year her junior. It seemed certain that Charles would now have no male heir of his body, and he turned seriously to securing his daughter's succession.

In 1720 he sent copies of the relevant documents, including in particular his Declaration of 1713, to the Diets of all his dominions, requesting their formal confirmation of them, in order that 'the lasting, indissoluble union of the kingdoms and Lands' should be assured. As regards most of the Diets, this was meant only as a precaution, for when the Estates of the Tirol—the only Land outside Hungary to show so much independence—objected that the document should have been submitted to them 'consultando' before promulgation, they were told that 'no Land had the right to determine the succession contrary to the will of the monarch'; what was being required of the Diet was not assent but 'pure obedience'. In fact, the Estates of all the German Austrian Lands, as also of Bohemia and Moravia, the Italian possessions and the Netherlands, ended by receiving the expression of the monarch's will with 'seemly thanks' and unconditionally, although one or two of them added riders voicing this or that special wish. Thus the transaction brought no change in the constitutional relationship of any of these Lands to the Crown.

In Hungary, on the other hand, the Diet clearly had the right to be consulted, and Charles was particularly anxious to gain its free consent. Fortunately for him, the Diet of 1722–3, before which the documents were laid, was in a sober mood. Its members were well aware that it was the imperial forces alone which had driven the Turks across the Danube. There was no desire to witness another Turkish invasion, nor was the *labanc* party anxious to see recently-settled questions reopened by a return to power of their *kurucz* rivals. Meanwhile, the situation seemed favourable for a final general settlement of the relationship between king and nation. On 30 June 1722 the Diet agreed unanimously to accept the female succession—'for', as one speaker said, 'one can't, after all, elect the Muscovite or some other Power', and as a result of this decision, and of accompanying bargaining, a great constitutional settlement, which remained basic up to 1848, and indeed up to 1918, was reached. Under Laws I and II of 1723 Hungary accepted the female succession, stating that it was following the order laid down by the monarch in his other dominions. There were nevertheless certain differences between the Hungarian law and the Austrian succession: the former not only specifically confined its scope to the descendants, male or female, of Leopold II

—if his line died out, the nation recovered the right of free election; while it was arguable that under the Austrian succession a claim might be advanced based on a more remote collateral relationship—but also enumerated, as condition of eligibility, not only legitimacy and membership of the Catholic Church, but also archducal rank; thus excluding children of a morganatic marriage. This point might have become important had the Archduke Franz Ferdinand lived to succeed Franz Josef in the twentieth century.

So long as the succession, thus defined, remained, Hungary regarded herself as united 'indivisibly and inseparably' with the other dominions of the king-emperor, this union being valid 'for all events and also against external enemies', but the king repeated his undertaking of 1715 to rule Hungary according to her own laws, and not after the pattern of other provinces, and to maintain her integrity. He promised that every sovereign, by his coronation oath and in the accompanying Diploma, should confirm this promise and, in general, the promise to respect the freedoms and rights of Hungary. Among these, Charles confirmed the 'noble' privilege of exemption from arrest except after previous citation, and recognised the noble's right of exemption from taxation as 'the fundamental privilege of the nobility of the kingdom'. He also promised to convoke the Diet regularly.

The full independence of the Hungarian court chancellery in Vienna was confirmed; it was answerable only to the king and independent of any court instance, including the Privy Council. For the conduct of current affairs, a *Consilium regium locumtenentiale*, modelled on the Bohemian *Landesregierung*, was established. This was to sit in Pozsony and to consist of the Palatine, as president, and twenty-two members of the Estates. It had to carry out the laws enacted by the Diet, in whose name it could also make representations to the king, and to see to the execution in Hungary of decisions relating to the common army. It corresponded with the king through the Hungarian court chancellery in Vienna.

The standing army became more important still, since the nobles' obligation to serve was now confined to exceptional cases, when Hungary was attacked by a foreign enemy. The king could, on the other hand, employ the standing army according to his discretion, inside or outside the country, for offensive or defensive purposes. A committee of the Diet, presided over by the Palatine, allocated the proportion of 'war tax' to be paid by each county, town, etc., the 'porta' or socage peasant holding being taken as the unit. On a lower level, the king was to appoint the *föispán*, or chief administrative official of each county, the organisation of which was otherwise left unchanged. The *föispán* had to convoke the county Diet at least once every three years and to preside over the election of his executive deputy, the *alispán*, who, with the other county officials, was elected as before, by the nobles of the county. A Supreme Court of Justice, sitting permanently in Pest, was established, with four other courts in different parts of Hungary and one in Croatia. Once this settlement was reached, Charles's position was clear; and on 6 December 1724 he solemnly and publicly re-enacted his declaration of 1713, with the assents given thereto by his various dominions, the sum of these constituting the real 'Pragmatic Sanction'.

A main objective of Charles's life, from this moment on, was to secure international recognition of, and guarantees for, the Pragmatic Sanction, in order that Maria Theresa, who now seemed certain to be his heir, should inherit all his dominions intact, without dispute. It was true that both the elector of Saxony, when he married Joseph I's elder daughter, Maria Josepha, in 1720, and the elector of Bavaria, when he espoused her younger sister, Maria Amalia, in 1722, had solemnly sworn to recognise the Pragmatic Sanction as taking precedence over the *Pactum mutuae successionis*. Yet Charles could not feel confident that these claims, or, indeed, others to various of his dominions, might not be revived. Prince Eugene advised him rather to put his trust in a strong and efficient army and to take steps to create the same, but the largest army in Europe could hardly have made diplomacy unnecessary; Charles's insistence on the succession only added one more thread to the tangle of the international situation, for Charles a guiding thread, but intertwined with the conflicting ambitions and interests of a dozen Powers. Its absence would hardly have altered the character of the ensuing period, which has been well called that 'of barren congresses and rotten alliances'.

At first Charles was at odds simultaneously with England, Holland, France and Spain, all of which felt their commercial interests threatened by his foundation of the East and West Indian Trading Company mentioned below. Rivalry between France and Spain enabled Charles to detach the latter Power and to gain, by instruments dated 30 April and 1 May 1725, both Spanish recognition for the Pragmatic Sanction and privileges for the Company in Spanish ports. England, France and Holland answered with the alliance of Herrenhausen (3 September 1725), which also included Prussia. Charles was able to counter this on 6 August 1726 with an alliance with Russia bringing the desired guarantee from that country. In order to avoid an irreparable breach with the Maritime Powers, he suspended the operations of the Company for seven years. Prince Eugene also succeeded in getting from the king of Prussia his guarantee of the Pragmatic Sanction and a promise to support the candidature of Maria Theresa's husband, provided she married a German, for the imperial crown. Spain replied by concluding the Treaty of Seville (November 1729) with England, Holland and France, but that alignment could not be maintained. England approached Austria, and under the Treaty of Vienna (16 March 1731) Charles gave up the Ostend Company, agreed to Spain's occupying Parma and Piacenza, and received in return guarantees of the Pragmatic Sanction from England, Flanders and Holland. The Reich followed in 1732, Bavaria, Saxony and the three Palatinate houses dissenting. The elector of Saxony was, however, brought round next year, when Austria joined Russia and Prussia in supporting Augustus III's candidature to the Polish throne, against France's candidate, Stanislas Leszczyński.

In the next three years Charles was fighting against a new combination, headed by France, with which Spain and Sardinia were associated in Italy, and in Germany, the Wittelsbach prince of Bavaria, the Palatinate and Cologne; while Russia took the field in Poland, as Austria's ally, against Stanislas Leszczyński. A preliminary peace was signed in Vienna on 3 October 1735, and in connection therewith provision was made for a further factor. Francis Stephen, duke of Lorraine and Bar, had been brought up at Charles's court and was one of the persons designated by Charles as possible husband for his elder daughter and heiress. He delayed finally settling the question in deference to the possibilty of a union with Spain, but the matter was really decided by Maria Theresa's own wishes, for she would hear of no other husband but Francis. The marriage was celebrated on 12 February 1736, and in the definitive peace of 8 November 1738, which in the main confirmed the arrangements concluded at Vienna, the Italian succession was settled by allotting Parma and Piacenza to the Emperor, Novara and Vigevano to Sardinia, Naples, Sicily and Elba to Spain, and Tuscany to Francis Stephen, who relinquished Lorraine in favour of Stanislas Leszczyński, after whose death it was to revert to France. Sardinia adhered to the Peace on 5 February and Spain on 31 April 1739. All contracting Powers recognised the validity of the Pragmatic Sanction.

The judgments passed by later historians on the aspects of Charles's reign other than the diplomatic or military (to which most of them, following Charles's own example, have devoted their chief attention) have been singularly various. Some have looked back with nostalgia to the years when Vienna was 'the real political, philosophical, architectural and poetic centre of the world', and when the 'Austrian' spirit reached its most perfect synthesis and its fullest power. Others have seen in those same years a period of intellectual obscurantism and social and political stagnation, during which the real interests of the peoples were sacrificed to barren dynastic ambitions. There is something in both views.

The *Hochbarock* culture of the age—that outward and visible sign of the inward union between a high-aristocratic society dedicated to every form of devotion and a Church no less hierarchic and very little less worldly—found at Charles's court an expression surpassed nowhere in Europe either for splendour or for delicate and curious grace: for that court was not only the seat of what was already the most august dynasty of Europe, but also a unique meeting-point where influences from Germany, Italy, Spain and the Netherlands met and mingled with those of the Danubian peoples to produce results which were not only magnificent but also at once local and universal. The dominant note was the Italian: two Italians, Apostolo Zeno and the more famous Metastasio, successively held the post of court poet, in which capacity their chief duty was to compose libretti for the operas which were the fashionable form of entertainment; but characteristically while Italian opera comprised half the repertoire at Vienna's new theatre at the Kärntnerthor, it alternated with broad popular farces in the Viennese dialect.

The heart of this life was in the court itself; Charles personally composed an opera, which was performed, his daughters dancing in the ballet, amid applause. The radiance of the court illuminated Vienna, which only half a century earlier had watched the Turkish bashibazouks cantering round its walls, but now blossomed like a rose. Not only the Hofburg itself was enlarged and modernised, but all round it the great noblemen, whose tastes and ambitions, even more than their duties, kept them in the closest possible proximity to the fount of honour, built their sumptuous palaces, and these alternated with churches equally splendid and equally numerous. The art of Fischer von Erlach, Donner and their fellow-workers adorned streets and squares with fountains and statues, and craftsmen and merchants found their way or were brought by the Emperor's order from Germany and Switzerland, to Vienna, to supply the needs of a brilliant and luxurious society.

But Vienna was a special case: its glory developed at the expense both of the provincial centres and of the countryside. The great nobles, a comparatively small number of whom owned between them a large part of the country, particularly in the Bohemian Lands, visited their country estates only to hunt and to relax, and the revenues which they drew from their peasants' labour were spent in the capital; they hardly went near the provincial centres at all. Lady Mary Wortley Montagu, who visited Prague in 1716, wrote of it that while retaining 'some remains of its former splendour', it was 'old built and thinly inhabited'. The ladies were dressed after Vienna fashions 'after the manner that the people of Exeter imitate those of London'. As to the rest of Bohemia, she found it 'the most desert of any I have seen in Germany; the villages are so poor and the post houses so miserable, clean straw and fair water are blessings not always to be found, and better accommodation not to be hoped'.

The nobles competed between themselves for the high offices of State, for most of which they alone were eligible, and took no interest in local affairs. The Bohemian Diet which assented to the Pragmatic Sanction consisted of eighteen lords and twenty-two knights, and that was an exceptionally large attendance. The smaller nobles and gentry were equally apathetic, nor would they have ventured to assert their wills against strong opposition from the centre. It was rather the apathy of the Estates themselves than any systematic pressure from Vienna that was responsible for the steady further decline in local independence which marked Charles's reign, for although Charles showed himself despotic and in certain respects obdurate, this was by environmental influence rather than by temperament. His nature and his tastes alike inclined him far rather to the aristocratic than to the bureaucratic form of government. Thus such innovations as were introduced during his reign in the machinery of government (outside Hungary) consisted for the most part of relatively minor adaptations of the existing central institutions. High policy was determined, under Charles himself, by the Privy Council: strictly speaking, since the title of Councillor had been so widely broadcast as to become merely honorific, by a small 'Privy Conference'. In the Emperor's absence, the *Obersthofmeister* presided over the meetings; the other officials whose portfolios covered all Charles's dominions were the presidents of the *Hofkriegsrat* and the *Hofkammer*, dealing respectively with defence and with the management of those financial resources directly under the control of the Crown, and the First Austrian Chancellor who dealt with the affairs of the imperial house. The Second Austrian Chancellor was the administrative head of German-Austrian affairs, so far as they came within the competence of the Crown at all, and similar chancelleries dealt with Bohemian, Hungarian and Transylvanian affairs. To these Charles added two new chancelleries, for the Netherlands and the Italian possessions respectively. It is true that in the conflict of ill-defined competences, the chancelleries tended increasingly to have the last word, as against the Estates or the municipalities, but this was rather the effect of the spirit of the age, than of intention. Bartenstein, the Secretary or *Referendar* to the Privy Council, who was the real head of the administrative machine, and incidentally the only non-aristocrat in the circle of Charles's influential advisers, made no special effort either to centralise or to make more uniform the institutions of the multifarious lands of the monarchy, or to increase either the number or the influence of the institutions common to them all. Thus although the Pragmatic Sanction laid, in a sense, the foundations of the Austrian empire, they were foundations on which little was built during Charles's reign.

There were two fields of which this remark was not wholly true. Prince Eugene did what he could to improve and expand the standing army, but the *débâcles* which followed his death showed that his reforms had not penetrated deeply enough: they lacked the essential political and financial background. In finance, too, Charles and his advisers, painfully conscious of the shortage of money which handicapped all their policy, sought pertinaciously for remedies, but knew not how to find them. Austria's central finances could have been set on a firm footing only by a radical political reform, and this was not attempted. A pertinacious search went on for means to support the credit of the State, and since each experiment was usually begun before the others were liquidated, a most complex financial system was evolved, little of which survived; the Wiener Stadt-bank, little regarded when founded, proved an exception. Attempts were made to foster industry by State organisation, and textile, porcelain and other factories were founded on the Crown domains, but most of the products were inferior, and by ill-fortune, the most flourishing of the enterprises were founded in Silesia, so soon to be lost. These attempts, incidentally, were stubbornly resisted by the guilds.

Precisely Charles's reign saw, indeed, a number of very ambitious projects to expand Austria's international trade. An Oriental Company was founded to conduct trade with the Orient and the port of Coblon on the Coromandel Coast acquired from the Great Mogul: the consent of Venice was extracted to freedom of trade in the Adriatic, and Trieste and Fiume were declared free ports. A merchant marine and a small navy were built at Trieste, and in 1722 the Emperor confirmed the Charter of the East India Company, granting it the right to trade in the East and West Indies and in Africa as an independent body, empowered to conclude its own commercial treaties with foreign Powers, subject only to payment to the government of a 6 per cent tax on its net profits. But this enterprise, hopefully begun, only incurred the jealousy of the Maritime Powers, and Charles sacrificed it in the end to the dearer objective of his daughter's succession. The fleet was sold to Venice in 1736. Based as it was essentially on Charles's possessions in the Netherlands, the project left little mark on the Austrian provinces, except for the expansion of Trieste and Fiume and the construction of improved communications to those ports, including the famous road over the Semmering Pass and the 'Karlstrasse' through Croatia.

The real rulers of the Austrian and Bohemian provinces were the ecclesiastics, and especially the Jesuits. The Church's glories were not confined to the capital, although even there many of the great new build-ings, including the huge Karlskirche, were ecclesiastical; it was in these days, too, that Vienna first became an archiepiscopal see. But while many big non-ecclesiastical buildings of Austria, outside Vienna, are either of earlier or of later date than Charles's reign, it produced the great monasteries of Melk, Klosterneuburg and Dürnstein, and some of the most impressive ecclesiastical baroque of Prague (as the same age did in Salzburg, then a mediatised city, and other cities of the Reich). But the activity even of the Jesuits was mainly negative. The canonisation of St John of Nepomuk, which was celebrated in Prague with great pomp in 1729 was, by exception, a positive act. Otherwise the Jesuits themselves were now adding little to the world's culture or learning, and their record in the period was chiefly one of repression. In Bohemia in particular, which was visited by many secret preachers and missionaries from over the frontier, the persecution of the Protestants went on with vigour: there was a long tale of imprisonments, torturings and condemnations to the galleys. Following the widespread expulsion of Protestants from Salzburg in 1722–3, to assist which the Emperor lent his authority and even his troops, similar expulsions took place from Carinthia, Styria and Upper Austria, in 1723–5. Protestant literature and learning were stamped out, and little took their place. The expulsions were a large contributory factor in the continued decline of trade and manufacture, in both of which the Protestants had led the way.

It was incidentally rather than of set purpose that Czech nationalism reached its lowest ebb during the period. It suffered, not because of any national rivalry between Czechs and Germans but because of its association with protestantism; moreover, the old Czech aristocracy had almost perished in the persecutions of previous decades, and the day was not yet come when the Bohemian aristocracy would find political advantage in an alliance with Czech nationalism. Of Bohemia at this time the chief modern historian writes that 'never had life been flatter, apathy more universal, the intellectual and moral level lower'.[1] Austrian local historians of the Tirol, Styria and Carinthia pass very similar judgments on conditions in their own provinces.

The position in Hungary remained materially different from that in Austria or Bohemia. Hungarian historians are reluctant to credit Charles with any genuine intention of keeping his promises towards the nation, and although they may do him a measure of personal wrong, it is certainly true that many of his chief advisers, Prince Eugene at their head, were filled with an ineradicable mistrust towards the rebellious nation, and regularly counselled the most restrictive interpretation of those promises. In several important respects they had their way, notably in respect of the country's territorial integrity. Transylvania was kept as a separate unit; the disputed 'Partium' was divided between Transylvania and Hungary. The Bánát, when recovered under the Peace of Passarowitz was, on Prince Eugene's advice, kept as a *neoacquistica* and placed under a military governor, Count Mercy, who took his orders direct from Vienna. The recovery of the Bánát made the two newly established Military Frontier Districts of the Maros and the Tisza strategically superfluous, but they were kept in being, and the existing Districts west of them even slightly enlarged, so that a complete line ran from the borders of Transylvania to the Adriatic.

After 1727 Charles convoked the Diet once again for a relatively unimportant session in 1728–9, but never thereafter. Even when the Palatine, Pálffy, died in 1732, and the Estates should have met to elect his successors, Charles left them unconvoked and, while assuring the Hungarians that the step was only 'provisional', appointed Maria Theresa's prospective husband, Francis Stephen, to preside as his representative over the Con-

[1] E. Denis, *La Bohème depuis la Montagne Blanche* (1906), p. 379.

silium; a step which proved the more unpopular because Francis Stephen seldom visited the country and, when there, treated its high society with conspicuous incivility. The Hungarian Court Chancellery found itself *de facto* subordinate to the *Konferenz* in Vienna, to which its proposals were submitted for decision, and to the First Austrian Chancellor. Neither a Hungarian *Hofkriegsrat* nor a Hungarian *Hofkammer* was established, and in the fields controlled by both these institutions, Hungary found herself as strictly subordinated to Vienna as any province.

Finally—after the Hungarian Catholics and Protestants had themselves repeatedly failed to agree—Charles, by the so-called 'Carolina Resolutio' of 1731 imposed on the Protestants, of Hungary many of the disabilities under which their co-religionists suffered elsewhere in his dominions. The Roman Catholic religion became the religion of State. Outside the places authorised in 1681, Protestants could hold divine service only in private, and then only for members of the family. They had to observe Catholic feastdays and holidays, and if they used the services of Protestant clergy, had also to pay the Catholic *stola*. The text of the official oath administered to public servants excluded them from such service.

Yet with all those qualifications Hungary kept a considerable measure of internal independence, and her Estates a degree of power over their own affairs and their nation's greater than that possessed by any equivalent class on the Continent at that time except in Sweden. They kept the greater part of the control of local affairs entirely in their own hands and gave way only very partially on central issues. It was perhaps unfortunate for the nation's future that the one point for which the nobles fought with a desperate tenacity which won them victory on each occasion was that of their own immunity from taxation. Charles repeatedly demanded that the war tax should be levied on all lands, whether 'urbarial' (i.e. cultivated by the socage peasant) or 'dominical' (directly farmed by the noble) and as regularly the nobles refused to sacrifice their cardinal privilege. A strengthening of the royal authority, such as Maria Theresa was able to carry through, would certainly have benefited the nation and mitigated the social injustice to which the nobles' defence of their legal rights opened the way. It is true that they themselves argued at more than one *konkurszusz* that the peasants could not bear increased taxation, and carried their point. But even this proved in the long run no unmixed blessing. The consequent disproportion between Hungary's contribution to the exchequer and that of other lands aroused the jealousy of the Lands and the resentment of the central authorities. The parsimony of the nobles also deprived Hungary of that strong national army of which she was later to stand so sadly in need.

The Hungarian nobles defended their cause so stubbornly and so successfully because they remained Hungarian; and that in spite of far-reaching changes which took place in the social composition of their own class during Charles's reign. A high proportion of the old families had died out or had been ruined, and the amnesty did not really restore the fortunes of the losers. The *neoacquistica* Commission was allowed to fall into desuetude after 1715, when the verification of title-deeds was entrusted to a Hungarian Commission; but even where the good-will was present, the documents were not. In the county of Baranya, where there had been 540 noble landowners in the fifteenth century, only six large estates now existed, and eighteen small ones. Six claims were put forward, all unsuccessful. The estates which remained unclaimed passed to the Crown, and were usually bestowed by Charles on his military or civilian servants in lieu of arrears of pay. It was the same process that had taken place in Bohemia eighty years earlier, and like his predecessors in Bohemia, Charles bestowed his donations largely on foreigners: in 1715 over 250 non-Hungarian noble familes were granted '*indigenat*' on this basis. But the German, Spanish or Italian recipients, unlike their counterparts in Bohemia, could make nothing of their new property, which too often consisted of square miles of swamp or sand, tucked away in some remote, inaccessible and unappetising region, among an alien and formidable people. In most cases they sold them. The purchaser was sometimes an immigrant Greek, Serb or Armenian, but much more commonly a Hungarian: either one of the existing *labanc* landowning familes, or not infrequently a man of quite humble birth, since fortunes were easily made by adroit buying and selling. As most of the *labanc* families were themselves quite new, the 'magnate' class which now became so powerful in Hungary was composed very largely of new men. Owing alike the acquisition and the prospect of retention of their estates to court favour, this aristocracy established an 'aulic' class, and the Habsburg rule in Hungary rested largely on it (its other chief pillar being the Roman Catholic Church). But it was still native-born, and, even in politics, remained Hungarian where the Bohemian nobility had largely ceased to be Czech.

Charles's reign also saw the rapid continuance in Hungary, although neither the beginning nor the completion, of a process which had extraordinarily important immediate social and economic effects, while the political results which developed from it a century later were more far-reaching still. This was the repopulation of the country.

It is estimated that in the days of Matthias Corvinus Hungary had contained four million souls, and the generally accepted calculation puts the total population in 1715 at only 1,700,000 in Hungary proper and 800,000 in Transylvania. Recent investigators have argued that this estimate is half a million, or perhaps even a million, too low, but it is certain in any case that the Turkish occupation and the subsequent wars had devastatingly reduced Hungary's numbers. They had, moreover, transformed the geographical distribution of the population. In the Middle Ages large areas of the mountains in the north and east had been practically un-inhabited, whereas the central plain had been studded with villages and market towns. Now it was the sheltered areas (in the north and north-west) which harboured a relatively dense population, while the centre and south had relapsed into swamp or prairie, its villages wiped out and its few survivors clustered for safety in the big 'village towns' such as Szeged or Debrecen. In the county of Nyitra 125,000 inhabitants were counted in 1715; in Pozsony, 80,000; in Sopron, 85,000; in Vas, 118,000, against only 5000 in Arad; 2500 in Csanad; 9700 in Csongrad and 12,000 in Bács-Bodrog, a county which had already seen a considerable immigration. In these areas it was possible, as travellers testified, to journey literally for days without seeing a human habitation.

A corollary of this was a big change in the proportions of the various ethnic elements, compared with the Middle Ages. The Slovak and Ruthene areas had escaped the chief brunt of the wars, while the Serbs had been strongly reinforced by the immigration under Leopold. The most purely Magyar areas, on the other hand, had lain full in the path of the armies, and although many Magyars had taken refuge behind the Habsburg lines, yet their proportion, which, according to some calculations, had in the fifteenth century reached 90 per cent of the total, was now little over 40 per cent: the minimum calculation quoted above puts their numbers in 1720 at only 1,160,000; the higher estimate at 1·25–1·75 millions.

In the more sheltered parts of Hungary, the population had probably already begun to rise again before 1715; but it was only after the Peace of Szatmár, and still more, after the Peace of Passarowitz, that the process could extend to the whole country. It now went on with extraordinary rapidity. By 1787—the date for which the next figures are available—the population, taking the country as a whole, has trebled; Charles's reign must have seen its full share of this increase. The different parts of the country were, of course, affected in very different measure, for the process was a complex one. There was a general increase, due to the cessation of fighting in all parts of Hungary, and owing to this, the population, even of the sheltered areas, doubled. At the same time, there was a general down-ward and outward flow of the Hungarian population, of all nationalities, from those areas towards the empty spaces of the centre and the south; this flow being partly spontaneous and indeed, in defiance of every attempt by the local landlords to check it, partly organised by the new landowners of the areas of reception. The wealthier of these landlords, including the Crown, also brought in large numbers of colonists from outside Hungary, most of these being Germans from Austria and Southern Germany (whence their generic name of 'Swabians'). These the military authorities controlling the Bánát and the Military Frontier reinforced by inviting in further contingents of Serbs; and there were also substantial uncontrolled immigrations of Roumanians from the Danubian provinces. Naturally, by the end of Charles's reign and even by long after that, Hungary was still far short of an optimum population, or of optimum distribution of what population she had. While parts of the northwest would already be regarded—given the then methods of cultivation—as congested, the south held space to spare for many decades further, and considerable areas remained entirely empty up to the twentieth century. Nevertheless, the processes both of repopulation and of redistribution of population made large strides in the first half of the eighteenth century and the country began to recover something of a European aspect.

The repopulation made little change in Hungary's occupational structure. Count Mercy, in the Bánát, tried to introduce industry, and many of the settlers brought by him from the west were artisans. Some of the big landowners in West Hungary experimented along the same lines. But communications were still too primitive to allow any important growth of trade or industry; moreover, in their competition for the scanty available labour, the landowners ruthlessly exercised what pressure they could to prevent the growth of the towns. Hungary remained to an overwhelming extent agricultural, the biggest social differentiation between its various parts being that in the north and the west and in Transylvania the land was mainly cultivated by socage peasants, while in the big new estates it was more largely farmed directly by the landlords, an economic form preferred by most landlords, as their land then remained 'dominical' and not subject to taxation. The labourers, moreover, enjoyed less security of tenure than the socage peasants, and the landlord's profit from their labour was usually larger than that which he derived from the *corvée* unwillingly performed—however ruthlessly it was exacted—by the socage peasants. The Bánát, and some of the areas retained by the Crown in its own hands, were settled with free peasants, while in the Military Frontier the peasants discharged their obligations by military service.

An important effect of the *impopulatio* was to carry further, to the continued detriment of the Magyar element, the changes in the ethnic composition begun by the Turkish wars. This was partly, but only partly, due to policy. A largely spontaneous movement by which the Magyars moved down into the plain, while the Slovaks and Ruthenes followed on their heels, carried the ethnic frontiers in the north between Magyar and Slovak, Magyar and Ruthene, many miles south. In the east the Roumanians not only increased their numbers in Transylvania, but appeared in the Partium and the Bánát, where they had been unknown a century before. Central Hungary was still chiefly Magyar, but here the landowners filled up many vacant places, sometimes with Slovaks but chiefly with 'Swabians'. In the south the policy was deliberate. The military authorities distrusted the Magyars politically and militarily and sought consciously to strengthen other elements against them. Their favourites were the Germans, as being generally reliable, and the Serbs. Magyars were deliberately excluded from the Bánát, which contained at one time settlers of seventeen different nationalities, including Catalans, Frenchmen and Cossacks, with the Germans as the largest element; its population, under 45,000 in 1720, numbered over 700,000 fifty years later. The Serbs were an especial stumbling block to the Hungarians, who were, of course, well aware of the designs of Vienna; moreover, they alone of all the nationalities claimed— and could quote promises supporting their claim—a separate 'national' status within the Hungarian State. The Diet made repeated efforts to get the unwelcome guests repatriated to Serbia (now under Austrian rule) or alternatively, placed under its own direct control; but always in vain. It is true that the situation was equally unsatisfactory to the Serbs, who had hoped to be settled in a single area, under their own leaders, temporal as well as ecclesiastical, owing allegiance to the Emperor only. Instead, they were dispersed along the frontier, under Austrian military commanders. After the death of Brankovics they were once allowed to elect a vice-*voevoda*, Jovan Monosterlije, but he was placed under Austrian control, and the only Diet which he convoked was dispersed by the military. After his death the post was not filled again and the only 'national' authority left to the Serbs was their Patriarch, whose authority was, indeed, large; in 1731 it was extended to cover Belgrade and *neoacquista* Serbia, and the orthodox Roumanians also came under it. Even without the desired organisation, however, the Serbs remained a truculent element, and in 1734-5 took the lead in a serious rising in the Tisza-Maros district, the reasons for which were, however, social, or even Hungarian political, rather than Serb national; the rebels included Roumanians, peasants of various nationalities, and even Hungarian partisans of the exiled Rákóczi.

The end of Charles's reign was unhappy. His many wars had cost Austria dear, not so much in blood, military or civilian—it was their redeeming point that they were not fought on Austrian home soil—but in a scarcer commodity still, money. It was symptomatic that Prince Eugene was invariably the first to propose any reasonable settlement. On 1 April 1736 the veteran soldier died, leaving the Austrian army, so far as events showed, without a single commander of even average talent; and that at a moment when both his genius and his special experience were particularly needed. Russia had attacked the Crimean Tartars, eliciting a declaration of war from Turkey. Russia then called on Austria for help under the Treaty of 1726. At the Congress of Nimirov, brought about in August 1737 through British and Dutch mediation, Charles asked for himself only minor frontier rectifications in Moldavia and Serbia, with the fortress of Vidin, but Russia's demands were so extensive that the Porte broke off the negotiations. The Austrian armies, led by Feldmarschall Seckendorf, had advanced into Serbia during the Congress and taken Nish, but when the Porte turned seriously to resistance, the imperial armies were driven back so decisively that Seckendorf, after being recalled, was arrested. The Turks advanced, while from behind their lines György Rákóczi, Ferencz's elder son, proclaimed himself prince of Transylvania.

Rákóczi's appeal was quite ineffectual and he himself died next year; but Count Königsegg, who commanded the Austrian forces in 1738, was no more successful than his predecessor, and Wallis, who followed him in 1739, was defeated at Kroszka, near Belgrade, and besieged in the fortress. Count Neipperg was sent down as negotiator, and on 1 September he and Wallis, both of whom were afterwards imprisoned, concluded the extraordinarily unfavourable Peace of Belgrade, under which Austria lost all she had gained under the Peace of Passarowitz, except the Bánát.

The mortification felt by him over this treaty hastened Charles's end. He died on 29 October 1740, leaving Maria Theresa, only 23 years old, to face the world with a disorganised and demoralised army, an empty treasury and a barely concealed disaffection not only in the perennially discontented Hungary, but in the German provinces and in Bohemia also; while beyond her frontiers the indefatigable Fleury was busy encouraging Austria's enemies, and the outlines of a new coalition, including Bavaria, Saxony, Prussia and Spain, were taking shape.

The results showed themselves very quickly. When Maria Theresa circularised the courts of Europe, demanding recognition of her succession, the elector of Bavaria at once invoked an old document (the marriage contract between Albrecht V of Bavaria and Anne, daughter of Ferdinand I) to claim the succession for himself. Immediately after, Frederick II of Prussia demanded the cession of the greater part of Silesia (a claim for which he only later put forward a legal basis) offering Maria Theresa, if she would cede him that province, to support her against Bavaria and to secure Francis Stephen's election to the imperial crown. Maria Theresa rejected this proposal with spirit; whereupon, in December 1740, Frederick suddenly invaded Silesia and easily captured Breslau. The elector of Saxony now repudiated his recognition of the Pragmatic Sanction and revived his wife's claims under the *Pactum Mutuae Successionis*. Spain demanded Hungary and Bohemia, and Sardinia, Lombardy. In May 1741 France and Bavaria concluded the Treaty of Nymphenburg, to which Spain, Prussia and Saxony afterwards adhered, Prussia, Saxony and Bavaria agreeing between themselves on the partition of the Bohemian Lands. Maria Theresa was to be left only with the eastern provinces of Austria, and Hungary.

At first it seemed a question whether she would keep so much. A strong party in Vienna openly favoured the Bavarian cause, and in Hungary the position was highly uncertain. When Charles died the Hungarian Diet had been of necessity convoked, after an interval of twelve years, to consider the formalities of the coronation. The succession itself was not seriously disputed, but the Estates, who could justly complain that Charles had failed to fulfil many promises towards them, wished to extract from their new sovereign a much more stringent coronation oath and inaugural Diploma. Hard bargaining went on behind the scenes, skilfully conducted for the queen by the new palatine, Count János Pálffy (son of the mediator of the Peace of Szatmár) and the *personalis*, or Chief Justice, Grassalkovich, who eventually persuaded the Diet to accept the old oath and Diploma, with the single addition that the exemption from taxation of 'noble land' was to be enacted a fundamental and unalterable law.

This point settled, the coronation took place in form on 25 June 1741; but meanwhile the international situation had steadily deteriorated. On 31 July a Franco-Bavarian army entered Austria. Charles Albert took Linz, where the Estates recognised him as their king, then turned north and entered Prague, where he was received in the same fashion. Maria Theresa's position was almost hopeless. Most of her inadequate army was tied down in Silesia. The only possible source of large-scale reinforcements was Hungary, and there the Diet was stubbornly arguing one 'gravamen' after the other. Maria Theresa made a long series of concessions. She promised to reside in Buda and to build a palace there; to fill the higher offices in Hungary, lay and ecclesiastical, exclusively with Hungarians; to respect the independence of Hungarian offices and to re-incorporate those parts of the kingdom then differently governed. Each concession evoked a new demand.

On 11 September Maria Theresa called members of both Houses to her, put the situation to them, and in a dignified speech declared that she entrusted the fate of herself, her children and her crown, to their valour and their loyalty. The assembled Hungarians, affected by her youth, her beauty and her distress, at last acceded to the demand in the customary formula *vitam et sanguinem*. Nine days later Francis Stephen, whom the Diet had accepted as co-regent, took the oath in that capacity. Maria Theresa exhibited her son and heir to the assembled Estates, who greeted the spectacle with shouts of enthusiasm which Joseph II's later attitude towards them was destined to prove singularly ill-judged.

From the immediate military point of view, the Diet's gesture was largely a token one. The Diet promised 25,000 men to be raised by '*noble levée*' and 30,000 *portás*, i.e. peasant-soldiers from Hungary proper, which with the contingents from Transylvania, the Frontier and the Bánát, would have brought the military contribution from Hungary, in the widest sense of the term, to 100,000 men. But the *levée* and *portás* troops took time to raise and their numbers never reached the promised figure. The first contingent to take the field, in the event the largest—came from the Frontier, under Austrian command. But besides the fact that some of the Hungarian troops proper, when they did arrive, did brilliant service, the political effect of the Diet's gesture was very large, both in inducing the Austrian Crownlands to follow the example set, and in raising Maria Theresa's international prestige and strengthening her position. It was largely because she no longer seemed helpless that those changes took place in the international situation which in their turn eased the military position. On 9 October 1741 she perforce surrendered Lower Silesia to Frederick, but next year her armies cleared the enemy from Austria and occupied Bavaria. The long struggle which followed saw many shifts of fortune and many changes of alliances, but the existence of the Austrian monarchy was never again imperilled as it had been in the summer of 1741. At last, after Maria Theresa had grudgingly signed peace with Frederick at Dresden on 25 December 1745, the longer struggle was concluded by the Peace of Aix-la-Chapelle, of October–November 1748. Under this, Frederick retained his gains of Dresden, i.e. all Silesia except Teschen, Troppau-Jägerndorf and Glaz, but Maria Theresa kept the rest of her father's heritage, except for Parma, Piacenza and Guastalla, ceded to Spain. Meanwhile, Francis Stephen had been elected Emperor on 4 October 1745.

The nine years which separate the Peace of Aix-la-Chapelle from the opening of the Seven Years War constitute Maria Theresa's 'first reform period'. They saw, indeed, many changes of vital importance for the inner structure of the Austrian monarchy; and yet the period was essentially one of transition rather than quiet fulfilment, and of preparation for particular purposes. Maria Theresa holds, of course, an honourable place in the gallery of Europe's benevolent despots, and her general philosophy was of her kind. She believed it to be her unquestionable right to exercise her supreme will, under God, throughout her dominions, subject only to her duty to God, rather than to her subjects, though she also thought she ought to exercise her power for her subjects' welfare. She sought her ends by the usual methods of centralisation and of the substitution of a centralised bureaucracy for the old power of the Estates. Yet her measures were essentially particular and not general. She had seen herself attacked by greedy neighbours, her whole position endangered and Silesia lost to Frederick of Prussia. She could not get over this loss and it was her fixed determination to repair it and to revenge herself on Frederick, whom she detested most bitterly. The measures which she now initiated were empirical ones, designed to achieve this end and the form which they took was determined by the empirical deductions drawn by her and her advisers from the events of the preceding eight years (and also, of the last years of her father's reign, of which she had been an impatient observer). The central conclusion (apart from those directly relative to the international situation) was that the army was not equal to its task even of defending Austria, much less of recovering Silesia. Always willing to learn from an enemy, Maria Theresa had taken greatly to heart the lesson of Frederick's superior military efficiency, and many of the measures to which she devoted her closest personal attention were directly aimed at increasing the technical efficiency of the army. Among such measures were the foundation of the Military Academy in Wiener Neustadt, the establishment of regular camps, the introduction of manœuvres, the improvement of the conditions both of officers and of other ranks. But the deeper cause of the army's weakness, of which she had had dismal experience, lay in the political system: the power still retained by the Estates to grant or withhold supplies, and the inadequacy of these when they came. The ultimate need was to increase the sources of revenue, which meant raising her people's whole standard of paying-power; but before this could be attacked such sources as already existed must be made available to the Crown, and this again involved simplifying and centralising the governmental machinery. As she wrote in a memorandum which she afterwards composed for the instruction of her children, she saw as early as the Peace of Dresden that she must concentrate on the internal affairs of her dominions, and that the chief evil was: 'that at the same time various *ministri* only regarded each his own land. It was also a great abuse, which weakened the service, that the Capi and Presidents were paid by the Estates and remunerated by them at their pleasure', thus falling into 'permanent dependence' on the Estates.

Maria Theresa's practical sense included a recognition of her limitations, and she did not attempt to introduce the same measure of reorganisation throughout all her dominions. The Italian and Netherlands chancelleries continued to work to all intents and purposes quite independently, through viceroys in the territories concerned: Charles of Lorraine (Francis Stephen's brother and husband of Maria Theresa's sister Marianne) in the Netherlands and Count Ferdinand Harrach, who was followed by Count Lucas Pallavicini, in Lombardy. The Netherlands Constitution was left practically untouched, and Lombardy, too, was handled gently although some of the reforms afterwards introduced elsewhere—the compilation of an orderly land register, as preliminary to the settlement of the land tax, and the enforcement of the principle of the liability of Church property to taxation (achieved in 1757, after considerable negotiation with the Holy See)—were first introduced in Lombardy.

Hungary also was exempted. Maria Theresa was by no means blind to the narrow and oligarchic character of the Hungarian Constitution, nor did she think the Hungarian Estates at bottom more reliable than the Austrian or Bohemian, but apart from the fact that she had pledged her oath to the Hungarian Constitution and particularly to the exemption from taxation of 'noble' land, she felt a strong sense of obligation to the Hungarians for the last-minute aid rendered her at Pozsony. Her experiences, moreover, had led her to conclusions opposite from her grandfather's: the Hungarians were, she wrote, a good people at heart, from whom one could get much by kindness. The failure of her attempt to get by persuasion from the Diet of 1751 the regular supplies, the consent to which she was enforcing elsewhere by stronger methods, was a mortification to her; but when Haugwitz proposed extending his reforms to Hungary, she replied: 'I do not think it desirable to bring about any change in Hungary, for it would not be advisable to bring this about without a Diet, the less so because I should have had also to take into account the special conditions there, whence painful consequences might have arisen.'

The Diet was, accordingly, left unconvened, these precautions preventing the Hungarians, on their side, from raising fresh demands, but otherwise Maria Theresa abstained from crass infringement of the Constitution, preferring to work towards her end by gradually building up a party favourable to herself among the magnates. She even met some of the Hungarian wishes. The Military Frontier Districts of the Máros and the Tisza were liquidated and the county system introduced in Slavonia. Thereafter Serbian affairs were placed under a ' *Illyrische Hofdeputation* '. Transylvania was not reunited, but Maria Theresa admitted that she ruled there *qua* queen of Hungary. A palace was built in Pest (although never used for its original purpose) and several Hungarians appointed to high office.

Her early reforms were therefore confined to the Austrian and Bohemian Lands, and even here she did not begin immediately. She had come to the throne young and inexperienced, and her first years of rule were too full of immediate problems of war and diplomacy to allow her much time to look behind the weaknesses (which were not always apparent, since on certain occasions the old machine seemed to produce good results) to the underlying causes of them. She was, moreover, as she wrote, surrounded by councillors 'too prejudiced to give useful advice, and too respectable and meritorious to be dismissed'. In these years, accordingly, she made no important changes beyond liquidating Charles's complicated financial machinery, thus reinstating the *Hofkammer* as the sole central organ dealing with the national finances and transferring the affairs of the imperial house from the Austrian chancery to a new office, the *Geheime Haus- Hof- und Staatskanzlei*. The first holder of this office, Count Uhlefeld, proved, however, rather a tool of Bartenstein's than a useful executant of Maria Theresa's own wishes.

Bartenstein was now all-powerful, for 'Providence relieved' Maria Theresa, by death, of Starhemberg, Harrach and Kinsky, and the new members of the Privy Conference, Colloredo, Kevenhüller and Batthyány, were no match for the experienced *Referendar*. But at last 'Providence sent her' three men with and through whom she could work. The most famous of these, Kaunitz, was at first chiefly concerned with foreign affairs, although after he succeeded Uhlefeld as Chancellor in 1753 he exercised a general control over all policy. The two others were Count Ludwig Haugwitz and Count Rudolph Chotek.

Haugwitz was a Silesian nobleman who had been employed to reorganise the affairs of that part of Silesia retained by Austria. The success with which he achieved this led to his being invited to state his views on the larger issues raised by the loss of Austria's richest province—a situation with which Bartenstein was frankly unable to cope. Haugwitz at once produced a complete plan. Austria, he calculated, needed for her security a standing army of at least 108,000 men, the upkeep of which force would require an annual sum of 14 million *gulden*, being 5 million *gulden* more than the contribution usually voted by the Estates. To raise this additional sum Haugwitz proposed that taxation should be extended to cover all property, including that of the nobles, and to ensure continuity it should be voted for ten years in advance. This once granted, the 'loyal and obedient Estates' were to have 'nothing whatever to do with the militari' i.e. to be under no further expense in that connection, except that of supplying billets, and that only until barracks had been built.

The Estates were assured that the new arrangements would in no way diminish their rights, but there was much opposition to it, first in the Privy Council itself, where Count Harrach made himself spokesman of the nobility, then in the various diets, which had to be painfully talked over one by one. At last, however, all agreed (except Carinthia, where the reform had to be imposed by rescript) and the monarch's hold over the army became secure. Immediately, however, it became apparent that the new conditions called for something like a complete reorganisation of the internal machinery of the Austrian and Bohemian Lands, which the fact that the reform had been imposed on all of them alike, and on them alone of Maria Theresa's dominions, had at once welded into a closer unity and distinguished more sharply from the other dominions. Maria Theresa's next measures, which applied to these Lands alone, took account of this condition. On 15 January 1749 an imperial rescript enacted the fundamental principle of the separation of the judicial from the political administration; and on the following 1 May the Austrian and the Bohemian court chanceries, each of which had hitherto exercised both judicial and political functions, were abolished together with the surviving central offices in Graz and Innsbruck. In their place two new offices were created, the competence of each covering both the Austrian and the Bohemian Lands, the Supreme Judicature (*Oberste Justizstelle*) as Court of Appeal and highest authority in all matters of justice, and the *Directorium in Internis*, or *Directorium in Publicis et Cameralibus*, in supreme control of all administration, except foreign affairs, which remained the province of the *Haus- Hof-* und *Staatskanzlei*, and defence, for which the *Hofkriegsrat* remained competent.

Each of the two new offices in its turn found a large-scale reorganisation necessary. Work was begun on the preparation of new, unified codes, both of civil and criminal procedure. Neither of these was, however, completed till many years later. The new political administration came into being earlier. Each land was given, under the *Directorium*, a body, known at first as the *Deputation*, later, the *Repräsentation und Kammer*; later still, various names—*Gubernium, Regierung, Landeshauptmannschaft* —came to be used in the different lands. The original function of these bodies was to deal with those questions connected with the army—recruiting, pay, quartering, etc.—which the Estates had now relinquished, but as the Crown in the course of time assumed control of one question after another which had formerly been the province of the Estates, or entirely unregulated, each of these was assured, not to the Estates but to the *Gubernum*. Equally important was the extension of the powers and change in the character of the administration of second instance. Bohemia had long been divided into *Kreise*—units corresponding roughly to the English county—and most of the Austrian lands into analogous sub-units, and these had been administered by officials appointed and paid by, and receiving their instructions from, the Estates. These offices, which henceforward were called everywhere, except in Silesia, *Kreisämter*, were now systematised on a uniform plan. They were placed under a *Kreishauptmann*, who was an official of the Crown, and their staffs reinforced by other officials, also servants of the Crown. As their old functions were not abolished, the *Kreisämter* thus held a dual position, being responsible on some questions to the Estates and on others to the Crown. As, however, the activities of the Crown expanded, the latter aspect of their work came increasingly to overshadow the former and the offices themselves, which at first consisted only of the *Kreishauptmann* (usually a local nobleman), a couple of assistants and a few clerks and messengers, grew into one of the most important parts of the whole Austrian administrative system. It soon became customary to entrust to the 'political' administration, i.e. to the *Directorium* and under it to the *Deputationen* and *Kreisämter*, any work not falling specifically within the sphere of any other authority.

Even in the late 1740's and still more in the 1750's, a flood of orders poured out from the new officials, which ranged from the regulation of the university curricula to the prohibition of unnecessary popular festivals and to the enactment that sparrows must be kept down.

Parallel with these moves at home, an intense activity had been going on in the diplomatic field, primarily directed towards the same objective, the recovery of Silesia. This is particularly associated with the name of Count Kaunitz, for long years Maria Theresa's most faithful and most trusted adviser. Having carried out with success certain diplomatic negotiations, Kaunitz was admitted to the State Conference in 1748, and was its junior member when, after the Peace of Aix-la-Chapelle, Maria Theresa asked all its members to give their views on what policy of friendships and alliances Austria should pursue. All concerned were agreed on the aim, but while all the rest advocated maintaining, to this end, Austria's relations with the Maritime Powers and with Russia, Kaunitz alone, while agreeing that Austria's old allies were her 'natural friends', maintained that it was only with Prussia that peace, on terms acceptable to Austria, was impossible. The prime object of policy must be to isolate Prussia, and to achieve this, all prejudice must be laid aside. France in particular must, as she could, be won over.

Maria Theresa accepted Kaunitz's view, to achieve which he set himself patiently to work, first as ambassador to France, and after May 1753 as Court and State Chancellor. It was a difficult and delicate task: difficult owing to the intimacy of the Franco-Prussian connection, delicate because older friendships could not be safely jettisoned before new ones were assured and a false step might have left Austria isolated. The Franco-British dispute over the Netherlands gave Kaunitz his opportunity. In 1755 it led to the Anglo-Prussian Treaty of January 1756, but this made possible the Franco-Austrian Treaty of Versailles, concluded on 1 May following. In August Frederick made the opening move of the Seven Years War, when he marched not into Bohemia but into Saxony.

The details of this war belong rather to European than to Austrian history. Austria achieved early successes, both diplomatic and military, but could not follow them up. The army failed again; the generals were incompetent and the troops undisciplined. The Estates were disaffected almost everywhere, and Maria Theresa had such difficulty in obtaining from them the indispensable subsidies that she was obliged to reduce her forces at some of the most critical points of the campaign. On 15 February 1763 she had to ratify the Treaty of Hubertusburg, which in general confirmed the provisions of the Treaty of Berlin of 1745, thus again admitting the loss of Silesia in return for Frederick's promise to vote for the election of Josef as king of the Romans and recognition of Austria's claim to the succession of Modena. Once again the inner weakness of Austria had been laid bare, and Maria Theresa turned back to the task of internal reorganisation; this time with no immediate objective of war but in a more constructive spirit.

CHAPTER XVIII

THE WAR OF THE AUSTRIAN SUCCESSION

I T was not strange that the unexpected death of Charles VI in October 1740 led to a war. Though the Pragmatic Sanction had been guaranteed by most European Powers, respect for treaties seemed an inadequate safeguard of a State that was ill-prepared to resist aggression. Maria Theresa inherited an empty treasury and a weak and demoralised army. Her father's ministers, whom she continued in office, were old and incompetent. She herself had received no political training, and her husband Francis was an unpopular mediocrity. What made her position worse was that she could not count on the loyalty of her subjects. Many of the nobles in Austria and Bohemia were ready to submit to a rival claimant, Charles Albert, elector of Bavaria. The Magyar nobility appeared more likely to be eager to weaken Habsburg authority in Hungary than to defend Maria Theresa. Charles Albert, on his part, had made no secret of his intention to claim to be the heir of Charles VI; bad though that claim was, he genuinely believed in it. But by himself he could do nothing: he was in debt; his forces were weak; his generals and ministers incapable. His dependence was on French support, and of that he had good hope.

By a treaty made in 1727 France had pledged herself to support such just claims as the elector might have to any of the Habsburg dominions on the death of Charles VI without male heirs. In 1735, however, France had guaranteed the Pragmatic Sanction; but it could be contended that this guarantee was without prejudice to the right of a third party, and this should have been realised in Vienna, since during Charles's last years France had proffered, though without response, her good offices for a settlement of the Bavarian claim. On Charles VI's death the elector requested French support. Whether he would get it was uncertain. Fleury, who since 1726 had controlled French policy, was temperamentally cautious and disposed to pursue one objective at a time. Before the Emperor's death he had been preparing for French intervention on the side of Spain in the War of Jenkins' Ear. To support Charles Albert was likely to cause a war, not only with Maria Theresa, but also with the Dutch Republic and Britain, whose own security would be endangered if they allowed the destruction of the Habsburg State. Bound up, however, with France's attitude to Charles Albert's territorial claims was her attitude to the election of a new emperor. The treaty of 1727 had pledged France to support Charles Albert's candidature. But to support it without also seeking to augment his hereditary dominions was not practical politics.

An emperor needed large resources to maintain his dignity. Charles Albert could obtain them only by robbing Maria Theresa.

At this juncture, moreover, Fleury's position was weakened. For Louis XV began to listen to those who urged him to seize the opportunity to destroy the power of the Habsburgs. Fleury neither resigned nor was dismissed. But against his will France gradually became involved in an attempt to dismember the Habsburg State; however, he was able to use such power as he still retained to prevent the full extent of France's resources from being devoted to the support of that attempt and thereby to deprive it of its best chance of success. For a brief space, indeed, he was able to postpone any important French decision. It was the Prussian invasion of Silesia, in December 1740, that precipitated matters.

In so far as responsibility for the War of the Austrian Succession rests with any single individual, it rests with Frederick II. For he was in complete control of Prussian policy. Prussia, it is true, had claims, though bad ones, to parts of Silesia, but in Frederick's eyes these were useful merely to colour his action, which was motivated by desire to strengthen Prussia and acquire personal glory. Silesia was obviously a desirable acquisition, and Frederick thought he had a good chance of getting lower Silesia, if not the whole province. If necessary, he was prepared to fight for it, but he hoped to get it without serious fighting by striking quickly. The weak Austrian forces stationed there could do no more than try to hold a few fortified towns. After the invasion had begun Frederick made an offer to Maria Theresa: in return for the cession of Silesia Frederick was ready to pay her a sum of money, support her in the defence of her other dominions, and vote for her husband, Francis, the grand duke of Tuscany, at the imperial election. Rather to his surprise she refused. Indignant at his aggression, she put no trust in his offers and contended that she could not yield any part of her dominions without violating the Pragmatic Sanction and thereby weakening her title to the remainder. She also proposed to take vigorous action against Frederick. But some months elapsed before she could assemble even a small army to attack the Prussian forces in Silesia. She hoped that a quick success in the field would deter other potential aggressors and encourage some of the guarantors of the Pragmatic Sanction to support her. The value of the Prussian army, which had done little fighting for a quarter of a century, was unknown.

Early in 1741 Maria Theresa had high hopes of aid from George II. George was both elector of Hanover and king of Britain, and tended to put the interests of his German dominions first. Because of these he objected to Prussian aggrandisement. But British opinion was not particularly hostile to Frederick's ambitions. What did arouse concern in Britain was the possibility that France might ally with Spain against her; the best counter to that threat was to bring into play the traditional alliance of the Maritime Powers with Austria and Prussia. Britain's policy did not depend on the king alone. As elector, George was absolute; as king, he could not carry out a policy that had not the support of the Commons. Any policy not plainly contrary to British interests as then understood was likely to get such support, for the king was expected to give a lead; but even the appearance of an attempt to subordinate British to Hanoverian interests was certain to arouse a storm. Maria Theresa, however, never properly understood George's curious position. At first his utterances convinced her that she would have both British and Hanoverian support against Prussia. She hoped, too, that Saxony and Russia could also be induced to join in an anti-Prussian alliance.

Russian support was particularly important, for Frederick feared Russia as he feared no other Power, and Augustus the elector of Saxony, who was also king of Poland and owed his crown to Russian support, was likely to follow Russia's lead. In point of fact, Russian help could not then be had; unstable internal conditions and a war with Sweden (1741-3), largely due to French influence in Stockholm, prevented Russia from much concerning herself with events in central Europe for some time. The immediate result of Russia's inaction was that the elector was encouraged to play a waiting game. What he most wanted was an acquisition of territory that would make Saxony contiguous with Poland. Such an acquisition could be made only at the expense of Frederick or Maria Theresa. By inclination Augustus was pro-Austrian and anti-Prussian. But Maria Theresa refused to purchase his support by the cession of even a part of Silesia; all she was ready to offer was money and a share of such conquests as might be made from Prussia; she was most reluctant to agree to support, and to allow Francis to pledge himself to support, if elected emperor, the making of Augustus's hereditary dominions into a kingdom. To do so, she contended, was contrary to the imperial Constitution. Though an Austro-Saxon treaty of alliance was signed in April 1741, she put off ratification because it committed her to such support.

As early as March there were signs that George could not control British policy. Walpole had no desire to see Britain involved in hostilities with Prussia, and his influence so far prevailed that the British envoy in Vienna was instructed to urge Maria Theresa to come to terms with Frederick. She refused, but in spite of her refusal parliament granted her a subsidy at the end of April, and she was told that Britain would supply her quota of 12,000 troops, as required by the treaty of 1732, to defend the Pragmatic Sanction. To give this help did not necessarily entail war; Britain was preparing to act as Maria Theresa's auxiliary, not as a principal. Maria Theresa continued to hope that both British and Hanoverian aid would be actually given and that George would use his influence to gain Saxon support for her.

While these arrangements were being concerted the threat to Maria Theresa increased. In March 1741 a special French envoy, marshal de

Belleisle, was sent to those German electors who might be induced to support Charles Albert's candidature. He soon converted his mission into an attempt to organise a great coalition for the dismemberment of the Habsburg States. The support of the Elector Palatine was easily to be had; the ecclesiastical electors were so far responsive to French bribes and French threats as to promise their votes and to make it plain that they would not actively resist French intervention in support of Charles Albert's territorial claims. Frederick, however, whose army of 80,000 was now an important factor in central European politics, was slow to commit himself. When his troops won the first battle of the war, his bargaining position became even stronger. In April the Austrians at last took the offensive against the Prussian forces in Silesia. Frederick had dispersed them widely and only the slowness of the Austrian advance prevented them from being beaten in detail. The rival armies encountered each other at Mollwitz. The battle began with the rout of the Prussian cavalry by the Austrian cavalry, after which Frederick, believing all was lost, fled the field. But the Prussian foot remained steady and eventually drove back both the Austrian horse and the Austrian foot. The latter, consisting mainly of raw recruits, were no very formidable opponents. Still, the victory showed the value of the Prussian system of infantry training with its emphasis on fire power, and the Prussian foot continued to live up to the reputation they had won. Frederick, moreover, took prompt measures to improve his cavalry.

The battle of Mollwitz did not induce Maria Theresa to offer Frederick what he wanted, but it made it certain that France would attempt to carry out Belleisle's schemes, to which, indeed, she was already half-committed. But the arrangements between Charles Albert and France revealed that the elector was in no position to bargain. He could not get France to pledge herself by treaty to secure for him any part of Maria Theresa's dominions; all he obtained was a promise of a subsidy and a plan, drawn up by Belleisle, for joint Franco-Bavarian operations. According to this plan, after occupying the Bishopric of Passau and part of Upper Austria, Franco-Bavarian forces were to invade Bohemia and capture Prague. It was hoped that Prussia and Saxony would co-operate with these forces, and that hope was strengthened when, in June, Frederick, having failed to get Maria Theresa to accept his terms, at length made a treaty with France. Even then he did not commit himself very far. In return for a promise to give his vote to Charles Albert and a guarantee of French territory in Europe he got a guarantee of his own territories and also of Lower Silesia and a pledge that France would assist Charles Albert against Maria Theresa. But Frederick was left free to make peace with her. Whatever his real aims may then have been, he repeatedly urged both Charles Albert and France to strike hard and quickly.

The execution of Belleisle's plan proceeded too slowly for his and

Frederick's liking, but it proceeded, while Maria Theresa's hopes of military aid from other Powers were frustrated. In July George, seeing his electorate threatened with invasion by both a Prussian and a French army, refused to employ any of his 25,000 Hanoverian troops on her behalf and sought to secure Hanover by coming to an understanding with her enemies. Saxony, also, broke off negotiations with Maria Theresa and yielded to French advances. At the end of the month Charles Albert seized Passau. Shortly afterwards a powerful French force crossed the Rhine and marched to join him. Upper Austria was speedily overrun by the Franco-Bavarian forces, and Frederick urged them to march on Vienna, which was none too well defended. For the main Austrian army was in Upper Silesia, covering the strong fortress of Neisse which Frederick wanted to take, and it was plainly to his advantage that it be recalled to defend Vienna. Frederick's advice, however, though not disinterested, was perhaps strategically sound. But France refused to adopt it, and Charles Albert had to do what France wanted. The invasion of Bohemia began late in October.

The threat to Vienna combined with British pressure induced Maria Theresa to make a serious effort to come to terms with Frederick. She had previously tried to buy off France and Charles Albert by offers of territory in the Low Countries and Italy, only to meet with a rebuff. An offer of part of the Low Countries to Frederick had also met with a scornful rejection. In order to be able to use her army in Silesia against the Franco-Bavarian forces she once more turned to Frederick. The result was the conclusion of the Convention of Klein-Schnellendorf early in October. Nothing was signed by either an Austrian or a Prussian plenipotentiary, but a note of the terms agreed upon was drawn up by Lord Hyndford, the British envoy to Frederick. Frederick agreed to let the Austrian army march away; Maria Theresa agreed to let him capture Neisse after a sham siege and to leave him unmolested in the occupation of that fortress and of all Lower Silesia; negotiations for a definitive peace were to be begun before the end of the year; meanwhile the convention was to be kept secret; if news of it got abroad it was no longer to bind Frederick. This last condition can have been inserted only to give an excuse for the resumption of hostilities if one were desired; for secrecy was impossible. Frederick was not yet ready to commit himself to a final settlement, nor was it certain that Maria Theresa herself wanted one.

The immediate results of the convention were that Frederick got Neisse and that the Austrian army could be employed in the defence of Bohemia, when it had become plain that the Franco-Bavarian offensive was to be turned thither. The Franco-Bavarian army marched on Prague, before which city they were joined by a Saxon contingent. France had secured this support by promising Augustus Moravia and part of Lower Austria, which was to be turned into a kingdom. With the aid of the Saxons Prague was stormed. Shortly afterwards Frederick resumed hostilities against Maria Theresa.

In January 1742 Charles Albert was elected Emperor, whereafter he styled himself Charles VII. He received eight votes—all that were cast. He even got the Hanoverian vote; for in the previous September George, in order to safeguard his electorate, had promised to vote for Charles Albert and to remain neutral in his electoral capacity. It is, however, significant that the Bohemian vote was not admitted. The Electoral College would not concede Maria Theresa's right to exercise it through her husband whom she had appointed co-regent of Bohemia; nor would they recognise Charles as king of Bohemia, though he had proclaimed himself as such in Prague. To have decided in favour of either claimant would have implied a determination to back the decision with force, that is to commit the Empire to participate in the war. Charles never got the backing of the Empire for any specific territorial claim; French support had secured his election, but it could not do more.

Thus the election had no influence on the course of operations. Maria Theresa was able to act with vigour. The forces formerly assigned to the defence of Vienna and other units recalled from Italy were employed in an attack on the French and Bavarian troops in Upper Austria. That attack proved successful; Upper Austria was quickly liberated and an invasion of Bavaria followed, which soon resulted in the capture of Munich. The position of the French army in Bohemia became critical and was made worse by poor leadership. The command of the French troops had been conferred on marshal de Broglie, who was old, apoplectic, and disliked his task. He also distrusted Frederick and was disliked by him, which did not conduce to successful Franco-Prussian co-operation. Frederick would have liked the French to be powerfully reinforced and placed under the command of Belleisle. The former was not done, and, though Belleisle came to serve in Bohemia, Broglie, who was his senior, remained in command.

During the winter of 1741–2 Maria Theresa's forces steadily increased, and this increase was largely due to the contribution of Hungary. In the late summer of 1741 Maria Theresa had convoked a meeting of the Hungarian Diet and appealed to the Magyars for support; in order to get it she was compelled to make various political concessions. After hard bargaining as to their precise extent she got a small sum of money and the promise of a large force of troops for which Hungary was to pay. In fact the number of men who actually reached the front was far below expectation. Moreover, lack of discipline and love of loot seriously impaired the value of the Magyar cavalry; the Magyar infantry behaved better. But, though Maria Theresa failed to get as much as she hoped from Hungary, she got something appreciable and got it at a time when every little counted.

By the spring of 1742 Frederick showed signs of wanting to make peace with Maria Theresa. He had been annoyed by the failure of an offensive in Moravia early in the year, which he had conducted in reliance on promises of support from Saxon and French contingents. Rightly or wrongly, he believed the Saxons had behaved badly and the French had not done their part. He was also afraid that France would arrange a peace between Maria Theresa and Charles VII without consulting him or providing for his interests. He remembered that she had made peace behind the backs of her allies in the War of the Polish Succession and gave credence to rumours of Franco-Austrian negotiations. Frederick, too, had other reasons for wanting peace. Many units of the Prussian army had been actively engaged since December 1741 and badly needed a rest; the war chest, accumulated by his father, was becoming depleted and could not easily be replenished; it was not easy to raise a loan at home and impossible to raise one abroad, for, quite apart from his lack of credit, the British and Dutch money markets were closed to him while he was at war with Maria Theresa.

Britain was eager to bring about an Austro-Prussian peace. The neutrality of Hanover had been profoundly unpopular with British opinion and had contributed to the fall of Walpole, in February 1742. The British Prime Minister had to pay for the sins of the elector of Hanover. Vigorous action in support of Maria Theresa was expected of the reconstituted ministry, but action against France, not against Prussia. Carteret, the new secretary for the Northern Department, hoped to induce Frederick eventually to join an anti-French coalition; the first step towards this end was to renew pressure on Maria Theresa to buy off Frederick. In return she was offered further subsidies and the assistance of British troops. There was a plan to send a British force to the Netherlands, whence, in conjunction with such Austrian troops as were there and a Dutch force, it was to invade France. The plan looked attractive, since the French frontier was ill-defended. Its weakness was dependence on Dutch support, which was most unlikely to be given.

The Dutch Republic was far weaker than it had been a generation previously, when it had entered into the War of the Spanish Succession; moreover, the urban oligarchies who dominated it were by inclination strongly pacific. Though the Republic was pledged to guarantee the Pragmatic Sanction, it was averse to taking part in a war unless its security was endangered. The most obvious threat to that security would have come from a French occupation of the Netherlands. As a safeguard against that threat the Dutch had acquired the right to maintain garrisons in certain towns there—the barrier fortresses—and to receive an annual contribution towards the cost of those garrisons from the revenues of the Netherlands. But the Dutch knew that they could not defend their barrier without British support. Fear of forfeiting that support on more than one occasion caused the Republic to shape its foreign policy in accordance with British wishes, though it never became a client State. At this time, however, the Dutch were suspicious of George II. In 1741 they had seriously considered honouring their guarantee of the Pragmatic Sanction, when the announcement of the neutrality of Hanover had caused a reaction. British arguments in 1742 failed to induce them to involve themselves in a war with France, especially as there was no assurance of Hanoverian participation. In these circumstances the scheme for an invasion of France from the Netherlands could not be carried out. The Republic, however, did continue the policy of augmenting its forces that had been begun in 1741. That policy was due not merely to a determination to resist possible French aggression in the Netherlands and readiness to give military aid to Maria Theresa in Germany, if events made it a Dutch interest to do so, but it was also designed to demonstrate the patriotic foresight of the leading urban oligarchies to those sections of Dutch opinion that were hostile to them. William IV of Orange desired to secure the same position in the Republic that had been held by William III. His ambition had a good deal of support, especially among the masses, and it was plain that, if the oligarchies did not appear to be effectively defending Dutch honour and interests, William might be brought to power by an irresistible popular movement. Nor could the possibility be ignored that Britain might seek to foment such a movement, in the hope that William, who had married a daughter of George II, would be a useful tool. Thus the problems confronting the leaders of the Republic were of peculiar complexity.

In the spring of 1742, however, it was feared at Versailles and hoped in Vienna that the Dutch would assist in an invasion of France. This hope was one of the factors that disposed Maria Theresa towards making peace with Frederick. A Prussian victory over her forces in May was another. Frederick, on his part, was now ready to come to terms with her. He feared that the complete defeat of Broglie was imminent and wanted to get out of the war before it occurred. The Preliminaries of Breslau in June terminated the Austro-Prussian war; Frederick gained Lower Silesia, Glatz, and most of Upper Silesia. Unfortunately Maria Theresa had entrusted her interests at the negotiations to the British envoy to Prussia. Since British policy was to bring about a peace, he did not do his utmost for her. Had he struggled harder he could have saved her the whole of Upper Silesia except Neisse. Frederick's defection increased the threat to Broglie's army, whose position appeared almost desperate, when, a few weeks later, Saxony availed herself of a clause in the Preliminaries that enabled her to accede to the peace, though without any gains. Naturally the news of these events caused alarm at Versailles. The salvation of Broglie's army now became the first objective of French policy. The army under Maillebois that since 1741 had been quartered in Westphalia in order to threaten Hanover was ordered to march into Bohemia to cover Broglie's retreat. Since, however, it was feared that Maillebois might have to be recalled suddenly to defend France against invasion from the Netherlands, he was told not to run undue risks. Nor did he. He marched to Bavaria, forced the Austrians to evacuate certain parts of it that they had occupied, and then entered Bohemia, but, finding his communications were threatened and his supplies were running low, speedily withdrew to Bavaria. Broglie, however, leaving his army under the command of Belleisle, was able to make his way to Bavaria, where he took over the command from Maillebois. Attempts of a different kind to save the French army in Bohemia were equally unsuccessful. Fleury was ready to consent to the withdrawal of the French forces from Bavaria and the virtual abandonment at least for the time being of Charles VII, if Maria Theresa would agree to let the French army return safely home from Bohemia. Maria Theresa, however, rejected all overtures. Finally, Belleisle was able to avert the disaster of surrender; at the end of the year he and the greater part of his army evaded the rather loose Austrian blockade of Prague and retreated to Bavaria. The garrison he had left behind, by threatening to burn the city, obtained a capitulation that allowed them to return home. But the campaign in Bohemia had taken a heavy toll of the French and, what was equally important, had made service in central Europe unpopular with them.

Though the upshot of the Bohemian campaign was disappointing to Maria Theresa, she had good hopes of success in Germany in 1743. After Maillebois had been ordered to the relief of Broglie, George had thought it safe to allow his Hanoverian troops to be used outside his electorate; 16,000 of them had been taken into British pay and had joined the British forces in the Netherlands. Plans were discussed for the march of an Austro-British-Hanoverian army from the Netherlands into Germany, where it could act in concert with the Austrian army in Bavaria. Maria Theresa, however, could not concentrate all her forces in Germany, she had also to defend her Italian dominions against attack.

To Philip V of Spain the death of Charles VI appeared an opportunity to bring Italy under the domination of his family. As a result of the War of the Polish Succession he had already established Charles, one of his sons by his second wife, Elizabeth Farnese, on the throne of Naples. He now hoped to acquire for Philip, his second son by her, the whole or the major part of Maria Theresa's Italian dominions and, if possible, also Francis's Grand Duchy of Tuscany. King Philip, indeed, announced that he had a claim to the whole Habsburg inheritance, but this was a mere bargaining counter that enabled him to come to an agreement with Charles Albert. By the Hispano-Bavarian treaty of Nymphenburg of 1741 Charles Albert, in return for a promise of subsidies, recognised Philip's claims to the Habsburg lands in Italy. It remained for Philip to conquer what he could. To assemble an army strong enough to undertake operations in Italy took some time, and in the interval ways of conveying it thither were examined. In view of the opposition of the British Mediterranean fleet it was risky to try to carry the army by sea, and, in any case, whatever was done with the Spanish foot, most of the horse would have to go by land. Philip hoped that France would not merely permit Spanish forces to march through her territory, but would also actively support his Italian designs. At Versailles, however, those designs were looked upon as somewhat impracticable. It was obvious that the attitude of the king of Sardinia would have much influence on the course of events in Italy. Troops could not enter Italy from France without passing through his dominions; Charles Emmanuel, the then king of Sardinia, had an efficient army of 30,000 to 40,000 men and could take such advantage of the mountains of Piedmont as to make an invasion of Italy very difficult. By parity of reasoning his support in an attack on Maria Theresa would be invaluable. Whether that support could be obtained was doubtful; for his interest was to maintain a balance of power in Italy between Bourbon and Habsburg. The one chance of winning him to the side of the Bourbons was to offer him such an increase of territory that he would not regard the expulsion of the Habsburgs from Italy as a threat to Sardinian security. Spain, however, was not willing to sacrifice a large slice of the lands she hoped to gain for the Infant Philip, in order to purchase a Sardinian alliance. Fleury viewed the matter differently and urged Spain to come to terms with Sardinia, which she would not do. Spanish obduracy contributed to Charles Emmanuel's readiness to strike a bargain with Maria Theresa. He had never guaranteed the Pragmatic Sanction, and had put forward a claim to Milan on Charles VI's death, but he was prepared to give a limited support to Maria Theresa at a price. That price she was most unwilling to pay. He demanded not only a large part of the Milanese but also Finale, which Charles VI had sold to Genoa in 1713. Britain urged Maria Theresa to pay the price, for, like France, she realised the value of the Sardinian alliance and was equally ready to purchase it at the cost of a third party. Charles Emmanuel throughout the ensuing years was able to count on British support for most of his claims. It was, indeed, largely because he regarded British friendship as durable that he desired Finale, the possession of which would give Piedmont an outlet to the sea and make the support of a British fleet far more valuable. Thus, throughout the war the claims of Sardinia tended to be a cause of friction both between Britain and Austria and between France and Spain.

It was some time before Charles Emmanuel could get an alliance on the terms he wanted. But events soon forced him into co-operation with Maria Theresa. Late in 1741 and early in 1742 powerful Spanish forces were landed in Italy, some at Orbetello, one of the Tuscan ports belonging to the king of Naples, some at Spezia in Genoese territory. These landings were possible only because France permitted her Toulon fleet to support the Spanish fleet in covering the transports. The British Mediterranean fleet was then too weak to attack the combined French and Spanish fleets. After landing in Italy the Spanish troops marched into the Papal States—Benedict XIV had no power to stop them—where they were joined by a contingent of the Neapolitan army. The combined force, however, was still too weak to enable its commander, the Spaniard Montemar, to strike hard and quickly. Nevertheless, the threat it presented caused Charles Emmanuel and Maria Theresa to come to a peculiar agreement in February 1742. Charles Emmanuel promised to support Maria Theresa in the defence of her Italian lands, but reserved his own claim to the Milanese and stipulated that he could denounce the agreement on giving a month's notice.

This agreement was followed by vigorous joint action. Modena, whose duke had allied himself with Spain, was occupied before the Hispano-Neapolitan army could come to its defence. Shortly afterwards a British squadron, by threatening to bombard Naples, compelled King Charles to recall the Neapolitan contingent from Montemar's army. This threat was possible because Britain had strengthened her Mediterranean fleet. After January 1742 only single ships could carry troops or supplies from Spain to Italy. Most Spanish reinforcements had to go by land; that is to march through France and then attempt to force a passage through Sardinian territory.

No event of military importance occurred in Italy during the latter half of 1742. Montemar was not strong enough to attempt anything, and Charles Emmanuel would not join in an attack on him. Indeed, at the end of the year he diverted a large part of his forces to Savoy, which the Spanish army that was based on French territory had invaded. However, he was unable to expel the invaders and had to retreat before winter had made the Alps impassable. Early in 1743 Gages, who had superseded Montemar, was ordered to take the offensive, the result was a battle at Campo-Santo in the Papal States between the Spaniards and an Austro-Sardinian army. Both sides claimed a victory, but Gages retreated. Pursuit was impossible, since Charles Emmanuel refused to allow his troops to participate. Until he had made a definitive bargain with Maria Theresa he was determined not to assist her army further. Meanwhile he lent an ear to the overtures of France, which was increasingly eager to induce him to change sides.

French policy was now controlled, in so far as it was controlled at all, by Louis XV. Fleury had died in January 1743, and after his death the king had announced that he would do what Louis XIV had done after the death of Mazarin. But Louis XV was a very different man from his great-grandfather. Though intelligent, he was lazy and irresolute. To give France efficient leadership in a crisis was beyond his powers; but what he could not do he would not appoint a Prime Minister to do for him. Louis made a bad situation worse by his secretiveness; ministers were not always told what they should have known in order to do their jobs adequately. In such circumstances the king's policy was often unlikely to be satisfactorily executed. But there was, at times, an even more serious cause of inefficiency, the absence of any fixed policy. It is, however, pretty certain that Louis's first inclination after the death of Fleury was to seek to put an end to hostilities without too great a loss of prestige. Technically, indeed, France was not yet at war; she had been acting merely as the auxiliary of Charles VII. But a settlement was not easy to reach unless France would abandon Charles altogether, which Louis was not ready to do. He was, therefore, faced with the prospect of a continued struggle, about the outcome of which he felt by no means confident. There was a danger that France might have to face a great coalition without a single strong ally. Between France and Spain there was as yet no treaty. It was feared that Spain might come to a settlement with Britain and Austria, unless France bid high for her support, but such a bid meant entering into wide commitments. Thus the value of an alliance with Spain would largely depend on the prospects of receiving the aid of Sardinia.

In 1743 the efforts of British diplomacy were supported by the active intervention of British troops on the Continent. Early in the year the British force hitherto stationed in the Netherlands marched into Germany along with Hanoverian and Austrian contingents. Later George came over to take command of what was known as the Pragmatic Army. With him came Carteret as secretary in attendance; Carteret, however, claimed no strategic competence and, as far as is known, stood aloof from military matters. These were left to George, who had none of the qualities of a general except physical courage. His deficiencies had serious consequences. In June the Pragmatic Army blundered into a trap set for it by Noailles, who commanded an opposing French army, at Dettingen on the Main. Owing to the incompetence of one of Noailles's subordinates and the bad behaviour of some of the French infantry, the battle ended in a French defeat, which, although there was no pursuit, left French morale badly shaken. Nor was Dettingen the only French reverse. The other French army in Germany, that under Broglie, had already withdrawn from Bavaria before the Austrians under Charles of Lorraine, the brother of Francis. Without French support the Emperor's weak forces could do little. Those of them who did not surrender withdrew into Franconia, where, in virtue of a convention stipulating their neutrality, they were allowed by the Austrians to remain unmolested.

France could not do much for Charles VII, for she appeared to be threatened with an invasion, and the chances of repelling one were felt to be doubtful. The armies of Charles of Lorraine and George II constituted a formidable force; moreover, a Dutch contingent was about to be despatched to the Pragmatic Army and actually joined it before the campaigning season was over. Nevertheless, the threat to France was not translated into vigorous action. The Pragmatic Army did practically nothing after Dettingen; that of Charles of Lorraine by itself could do little. For the inactivity of the Pragmatic Army there was more than one reason. Britain was not yet at war with France—she was merely the auxiliary of Maria Theresa. An invasion of France might provoke a French declaration of war, and no British statesman wanted war with France unless Britain was assured of Dutch support. But the Dutch remained determined to avoid war with France if possible. Britain had also to take account of another factor—the attitude of Prussia. Frederick had steadily resisted British attempts to persuade him to fight France. On the other hand, he had from the first made plain his dislike of the intervention of the Pragmatic Army in Germany. It was not to Frederick's interest that France should be defeated, and Prussian intervention in her support was a possibility that could not be ignored.

While the Pragmatic Army remained virtually quiescent, British diplomacy was active. One of Carteret's aims was to persuade the Emperor to take part in an anti-French coalition. He hoped that if Charles were won over, he would be able to induce the Empire to declare war on France. The Emperor, on his part, had long been desirous of coming to an arrangement with Britain that would help him to procure some advantage for himself. Hitherto his hopes had been frustrated, largely because of his exorbitant pretensions and his refusal to break with France. Early in 1743 he had toyed with a suggestion, inspired by Frederick, that he might augment his hereditary dominions by secularising certain ecclesiastical principalities and annexing certain free cities. There were sixteenth- and seventeenth-century precedents for secularisation, but Catholic opinion was generally, though not unanimously, against it. When news of the project had leaked out, Maria Theresa had hastened to proclaim herself the champion of the Church, and Charles had hastily denied any connection with the scheme. After Dettingen Charles was so hard put to it that it seemed possible he might become a British puppet. Carteret came to an agreement—the so-called treaty of Hanau—with the Emperor's emissary, by which Charles promised to dismiss his French auxiliaries and to try to procure the co-operation of the Empire with the Maritime Powers to induce France to agree to a general settlement; Charles, moreover, agreed to renounce all claims to Maria Theresa's lands; in return, his hereditary dominions were to be restored to him and so augmented as to produce an increased revenue, while Bavaria was to be made into a kingdom; until these things had been done he was to receive a subsidy. This agreement, however, was never implemented. Charles's subsidy could come only from Britain, and, when they were informed of the terms, Carteret's cabinet colleagues in Britain refused to agree, and without their support there was no hope of getting the Commons to vote the money.

Their dislike of Carteret had a good deal to do with the attitude of his colleagues, but that was not the only thing that swayed them. The inactivity of the Pragmatic Army was unpopular with British opinion; a large proportion of the Hanoverian army was in British pay and seemed to be doing little to earn it; George, indeed, was suspected of pursuing purely Hanoverian ends. Though the ministers in Britain had not been told of a clause in the agreement with Charles that pledged him to favour George's electoral interests, they guessed that something of the kind existed.

It was some consolation to Carteret that, in September, a definitive alliance—the Treaty of Worms—was concluded between Austria, Sardinia and Britain. The treaty pledged Charles Emmanuel to support Austria and Britain until peace was made by common consent, in return for the promise of British subsidies and the cession by Maria Theresa of part of the Milanese, of Piacenza, and of her right of redemption of Finale. In point of fact she had no such right, as she candidly admitted. But it was assumed that Britain would provide the money and that Genoa would be forced to agree to the transaction. It was with the greatest reluctance that Maria Theresa agreed to these terms. But British pressure forced her to do so, when Charles Emmanuel threatened that, if they were refused, he would accept the advantageous offers that France and Spain had recently made him. However, the treaty afforded her the prospect of some compensation. It stipulated that, if possible, Naples and Sicily were to be conquered, in which event Maria Theresa was to have Naples and Sicily was to go to Charles Emmanuel. This stipulation did not conduce to Austrian-Sardinian co-operation; for Charles Emmanuel did not desire the expulsion of the Bourbons from Italy. On the other hand, the treaty led to Genoese support of the Bourbons and contributed to Prussia's re-entry into the war. By the end of 1743 Frederick was both angry and apprehensive. He believed, quite correctly, that Maria Theresa wanted to annex Bavaria or part of it, and he was determined to oppose Austrian expansion in Germany. He had attempted to strengthen himself by creating a league of German princes, of which the aim was to have been the defence of the imperial Constitution and the rights of the Emperor, but the scheme had collapsed for lack of support. When, early in 1744, he discovered that the Treaty of Worms embodied a guarantee of the Pragmatic Sanction without excepting the territory ceded to Prussia at Breslau, he read a sinister meaning into the omission and began to make plans for striking at Austria before she became too strong.

Louis XV, on his part, was convinced by the news of the Treaty of Worms that he must secure a Spanish alliance. In order to get it he pledged himself in October 1743 to aid King Philip to reconquer Gibraltar and Minorca and to secure Parma, Piacenza and Lombardy for the Infant Philip. These pledges, however, made in a moment of anxiety, Louis soon ceased to regard as binding.

In Britain itself the events of 1743 had important repercussions. George had failed to give the country the leadership it expected in time of war. He returned to Britain discredited and unpopular. One result of this was that it was impossible for him ever to take the field again. Another was the intensification of the opposition to his favourite minister, Carteret. George's support indeed, enabled Carteret to remain in office till November 1744, but his continuance did not mean that the king's policy was always adopted. Nor was his resignation followed by any marked change. George could not dominate his ministers; none of them could dominate both his colleagues and the king. Since the leading ministers were often at variance with each other, Britain's policy was marked by fluctuations and her war effort, considerable though it was, was deprived of much of its effect by lack of proper direction. At the end of 1743, indeed, there were signs of a growing demand that Britain should withdraw from participation in continental operations, and seek to bring about a settlement by diplomatic means, even if that settlement entailed further sacrifices by Maria Theresa. Early in 1744, however, the news of direct French threats to British security stimulated anti-French feeling.

France had made preparations to despatch a body of troops along with the Young Pretender from Dunkirk to England. British intelligence was good, and counter-measures were promptly taken. Only a storm prevented an encounter between the French ships and a superior British fleet. When the difficulties of an invasion became obvious, the French dropped the plan. But they went on with the execution of another scheme. Since 1741 a Spanish fleet had been sheltering in Toulon. In February 1744 it put out to sea along with the French Toulon fleet. The combined fleets were under orders to seek out the British fleet under Admiral Matthews that had been blockading the Spaniards in Toulon and to destroy it. In the event it was Matthews who attacked the combined fleets off Toulon. The result of the action was the flight of the French and Spanish fleets to Spanish ports, though they had suffered comparatively little damage; for Matthews had not been properly supported by his second-in-command and, on his own part, had abstained from vigorous pursuit. In Britain the battle was regarded as a national disgrace; the Spaniards, whose ships had borne the brunt of the fighting, looked upon it as a victory, but complained bitterly that their fleet had been ill-supported by the French. After this there was no serious attempt at collaboration between the French and Spanish fleets, and all hope of restoring sea communication between Spain and Italy was lost.

These events were followed by a French declaration of war on Britain and Hanover in March; in May came a French declaration of war on Maria Theresa and an invasion of the Netherlands. These declarations were in fulfilment of pledges to Spain. The Netherlands were invaded because they were the theatre of operations in which French success seemed most likely, and success was badly needed to restore French morale. Louis himself was at the head of the invading army; but the effective command rested with Maurice de Saxe, a bastard brother of the elector of Saxony. Saxe had long been in French service; because he was a foreigner and a Protestant Louis had been loth to put him at the head of a great army. But his abilities were so outstanding that he had eventually been promoted Marshal and picked out as the right man for the Nether- lands front. He justified his choice and served there till the end of the war. Louis, who was no general himself, had the sense seldom to overrule Saxe, who, indeed, could support his views with the threat to resign and seek employment elsewhere.

It was not surprising that the first stages of the campaign of 1744 in the Netherlands were favourable to France. Her best army under her best general was more than a match for the Austrian, Dutch, and British forces that opposed it. Inferior in numbers and without unity of command, the allies were unable to prevent the capture of Menin, Courtrai, and Ypres. Then events on another front gave them an opportunity; as had been planned, Charles of Lorraine crossed the Rhine at the head of a great Austrian army. The opposing armies were too weak to repel him. In order to save France from invasion, Louis marched to their support with a strong detachment and left Saxe to hold out as best he could against the allies, who now outnumbered him. Saxe, however, knew his own mind, while the generals of the allies were unable to agree. The result was that they achieved nothing.

It was not only in the Netherlands that opportunities were missed. When the Austrians invaded France they ran an appalling risk, for Frederick had committed himself once more to attack Maria Theresa. He had not only entered into the League of Frankfort with Hesse and the Palatinate, ostensibly to defend the rights of the Emperor, but he had also come to an agreement with Louis. Frederick was to invade Bohemia after the invasion of France had begun; when, as was expected, the Austrian army was recalled, the French should be able to maul if not destroy it during its retreat; further, the Emperor was to be enabled by French subsidies to raise a large army. The plan was promising; and Frederick's initial part was well performed. He duly invaded Bohemia and captured Prague. When, however, Charles of Lorraine was ordered to retreat, he was able to do so almost unmolested. Louis, while on his way to Alsace had fallen sick at Metz, and Noailles, the French commander, was languid in pursuit. When Louis recovered he decided that the chief French ob- jective was the capture of Freiberg, which was taken after a long siege. But that in no way helped Frederick. Nor was the Emperor able to do much. With such forces as he could raise and a small French contingent he entered Bavaria, which the Austrians were no longer able to defend, and there, in January 1745, he died. Frederick, however, had to face the main Austrian army, which by continually threatening his communications forced him to withdraw to Silesia before the end of 1744.

His prospects at the beginning of the next campaign appeared bleak. Maria Theresa's main war aim was now the recovery of Silesia; in order to further it she made peace with the new elector of Bavaria, Maximilian Joseph, in April 1745, on the basis of the *status quo ante bellum*. Frederick had no prospect of direct French military aid, and even his requests for a subsidy met with evasive replies. On the other hand Saxony had become the auxiliary of Austria, induced thereto by jealousy of Prussia and the promise of subsidies from the Maritime Powers, who could not afford to see Maria Theresa overwhelmed. Frederick hesitated to invade Saxony, which would have been to his immediate strategic advantage, because such a move might provoke Russia. Instead he awaited the attack of the combined Austro-Saxon army in Silesia. When opportunity served, he seized the initiative and won a great victory at Hohenfriedberg. The battle was a triumph not merely for the Prussian army, but for Frederick personally. He hoped it would enable him to make peace, which he was prepared to do on the terms he had accepted at Breslau. But these Maria Theresa would not yet concede, though the Maritime Powers urged her to do so. Frederick applied pressure by invading Bohemia again, but was manœuvred out of it. Though this retreat was followed by another Prussian victory at Soor in Silesia, Maria Theresa still remained obdurate, although warned by Britain that unless she made peace with Prussia she would receive no more British subsidies. Frederick, however, frustrated a further Austro-Saxon projected offensive by a rapid invasion of Saxony, made by two Prussian armies in December. The Saxons were defeated and Dresden was captured. There peace was concluded before the end of the year. In spite of his victories Frederick asked for no more than a return to the Breslau settlement. Fear of Russia and the exhaustion of his finances account for his moderation; Saxony had no option but to seek peace; Maria Theresa, however, agreed to come to terms with Frederick, only because her recent advances to France had been rebuffed. She had indicated readiness to make territorial cessions to France in the Netherlands and to the Infant Philip in Italy, if France would abandon her alliance with Prussia. But though France had done little to help Frederick in 1745, she still regarded Prussia as a valuable counterpoise to Austria. Maria Theresa had succeeded in procuring the election of Francis as Emperor in September, and France would not agree to anything that would strengthen Habsburg influence in the Empire.

In 1745 Saxe again scored successes in the Netherlands. At the outset of the campaign he besieged Tournai and when the allies, now commanded by the duke of Cumberland, George's younger son, tried to relieve it he defeated them at Fontenoy. The British and the Dutch blamed each other for their defeat. The Republic, which had not declared, and never did declare, war on France, made efforts to bring about a peace. In Britain, too, there was a peace party. But, while the Dutch were inclined to favour the embodiment of a clause in the settlement that would provide for the future neutrality of the Netherlands, such a clause found no favour in Britain. On the other hand, Britain was most reluctant to consider handing back Cape Breton, which was captured in June. It was certainly not a Dutch interest to go on fighting in order that the British might retain this conquest. Thus there was ample cause for disagreement. While discussions about peace terms continued, Saxe's army made further gains. His task was facilitated by the outbreak of a Jacobite rising in Scotland towards the end of the summer and the consequent recall of many British troops from the Netherlands. The 1745 rebellion, however, made it certain that Britain would not make peace until France was ready, not merely to desist from attempts to support the Pretender, but also to renew explicitly the guarantee of the Protestant Succession she had given in 1717. After the collapse of the rebellion she was ready to do so, but by that time events in Italy had taken more than one dramatic turn.

In 1744 Maria Theresa made an attempt to conquer Naples, where Austria still had many partisans. Gages' army, however, reinforced by a Neapolitan contingent, made a stand on the southern frontier of the Papal States. An indecisive battle at Velletri was followed by the retreat of the Austrians, who had to go to the assistance of Charles Emmanuel, whose dominions were attacked by a strong Franco-Spanish army. Owing, however, to the quarrels of the French and Spanish commanders the invasion achieved little before the advent of winter impeded operations. In 1745 the Bourbon armies fared better. Genoa agreed to allow them to march through her territory and to support them with an auxiliary force. Most of Maria Theresa's troops were then employed against Prussia, and the Sardinian army was too weak to hold its own. Gages was able to unite with the Franco-Spanish army that marched into Italy along the Genoese coast. But after the junction, differences between the French and Spanish generals gave Charles Albert a respite; Gages was under orders to seize as much as possible of the territories that were destined for the Infant and accordingly overran Parma and much of Lombardy. Maillebois, the French commander, who maintained that everything else should be subordinated to the breaking-down of Sardinian resistance, could control only the movements of his own army. He was able, however to besiege Alessandria and purposed after its fall to attack Turin. Charles Emmanuel, when he found himself faced with the prospect of military disaster, thought seriously of saving himself by coming to terms with France. Spanish hostility to him remained unabated, but France was still ready to bid high for a Sardinian alliance. D'Argenson, the French foreign minister, had a great scheme for Italy: the imperial authority was to be abolished therein; Austria was to lose her Italian possessions; ultimately there was to be a confederation of Italian States. Such a scheme was anathema to Spain and almost equally distasteful to Charles Emmanuel, who thought its execution would leave him at the mercy of the Bourbons. French pressure ultimately extorted Spain's consent to concessions for Sardinia. But Charles Emmanuel took a stiffer line after the Peace of Dresden made the advent of Austrian reinforcements probable and when, in February 1746, the French failed to agree to every detail of his terms for an armistice, he abruptly broke off negotiations and prosecuted a vigorous offensive along with the Austrians.

That offensive succeeded at first largely because the Bourbon armies were taken by surprise. Spain blamed France for their reverses. Louis, therefore, who feared Spain would seek a separate peace with Austria, sought to placate her by ordering Maillebois to obey the orders first of Gages and, later, of La Mina, who superseded Gages in July. Nominal unity of command did not produce harmony between the generals. The Bourbon armies, indeed, escaped destruction, but, mainly owing to Spanish insistence, they retreated to French soil and abandoned the Genoese to their fate. Louis then made a further effort to placate Spain by replacing Maillebois by Belleisle, who, however, was not successful in getting on with La Mina.

Relations between the Austrian general and Charles Emmanuel were equally bad. Charles Emmanuel had tried to conceal his negotiations with France from Austria, though he had kept Britain informed. Maria Theresa, however, discovered something about them after their breakdown and never trusted Charles Emmanuel again nor did she regard herself as any longer bound by the Treaty of Worms. Austrian suspicion of Sardinia did not conduce to successful military co-operation, especially when misfortune followed success.

Genoa, after the retreat of the Bourbon armies, sought terms. The Austrians insisted upon the occupation of gates into the city and the exaction of a heavy indemnity. Genoa's submission made possible the execution of a project advocated by Britain—an Austro-Sardinian invasion of Provence, supported by the Mediterranean fleet. The objective was the capture of Toulon. Early in 1747, however, the invaders retreated into Piedmont without having accomplished much. Their retreat was due, not only to the vigour shown by Belleisle, but also to the revolt of Genoa. In December the Genoese mob rose and turned out the few Austrians who were in the city. The Genoese Government then decided in favour of resistance; the Austrians laid siege to the city; France and Spain wished to relieve it; Belleisle and La Mina were ordered to do so if they could. Though their offensive made little headway in 1747, they nevertheless exerted sufficient pressure on the Austro-Sardinian armies to cause the siege to be raised. The signing of peace preliminaries in April 1748 prevented further major operations in Italy.

The sudden death of Philip V in July 1746 increased the chances of peace, for his successor, Ferdinand, had much more modest aims. He desired, it is true, a principality for his half-brother, the Infant Philip, but was content that it should be small. There were negotiations between Spain and Britain in 1746–7, but Spanish demands for Gibraltar and intransigence in commercial matters rendered them frustrate. Louis, however, heard of them, and felt even less sure of Spain than before. France, moreover, was feeling the strain of the war to an increasing extent. Funds became ever harder to raise. British naval superiority greatly curtailed French sea-borne trade; communication between France and her colonies became increasingly difficult. It was significant that in 1747 two French fleets convoying merchantmen to the colonies were attacked by the British with considerable success. These things were important; but they were not by themselves decisive. Louis sought peace not because he lacked the means, but because he no longer had the will, to go on fighting. Nor did French successes in the Netherlands abate his war weariness.

There Saxe continued to triumph. In 1746 he conquered a great deal more territory and defeated the Allies, who in this year were commanded by Charles of Lorraine, at Rocoux. Saxe would have liked to invade the United Provinces, in order to frighten them into withdrawing from the war, but was not allowed to do so until 1747. Then he opened the campaign by overrunning Dutch Flanders. This was the more mortifying for the allies because they had entered upon that campaign with high hopes. Plans had been made for assembling an army of unprecedented strength, and the command had been given to Cumberland, who now enjoyed the prestige of Culloden. But the actual strength of the allied army was below the estimates, and Cumberland had not become a match for Saxe. The conquest of Dutch Flanders had political consequences in the Republic. The masses, convinced that only the Prince of Orange could save their country, rose, and frightened the States of the five Provinces that had hitherto opposed the restoration of the Stadholderate into electing William who was already Stadholder of the other Provinces. William's elevation was welcomed in Britain, since it seemed a guarantee that the Republic would prove a vigorous ally. It could not, however, have any immediate effect on operations.

In July Saxe defeated Cumberland at Lauffeldt near Maastricht, but could not prevent him from effecting a retreat and covering that fortress. The French, however, were able to besiege and capture Bergen-op-Zoom, the great fortress in Dutch Brabant. Its fall exposed the Republic to the greatest peril in the following campaign, unless the allied army could be powerfully reinforced. The hiring of Russian troops seemed the best way of procuring such a reinforcement.

These could be obtained. Russia had men to spare and was willing to sell their services now that she had arrived at a settlement with Sweden which she regarded as tolerably satisfactory. She had, indeed, already agreed in return for a subsidy to maintain a force that would act against Frederick if he once more attacked Maria Theresa. She was also ready to agree, if she could get her price, to send 30,000 men to assist the allies in western Europe. The fall of Bergen-op-Zoom enabled her to make a good bargain, but the Russian corps had a long way to march, and before it could take part in operations peace preliminaries had been signed.

Early in 1748 William of Orange informed the British Government that only a large loan could enable the Republic to remain a belligerent. This move may have been due to war weariness rather than to the impossibility of raising funds, but it made peace inevitable. Parliament would not have sanctioned a loan to the Dutch, and without their aid it was impossible for Britain to fight on the Continent. Britain, moreover, had reason to believe that Louis would not seek to retain his conquests in the Netherlands. Negotiations at Breda in 1746–7 had broken down, not because France demanded large gains for herself, but because Britain wished to retain Cape Breton. But Britain was not prepared to continue waging a purely naval war with that end in view. The possibility, however, that she would do so, if France sought to annex a large part of the Netherlands, may have contributed towards Louis's continued moderation. Maria Theresa, indeed, at the Conference of Aix-la-Chapelle which opened early in 1748, offered to cede part of the Netherlands to France if Louis would not oppose an attempt to reconquer Silesia or would allow her to resume her cessions to Charles Emmanuel. The French plenipotentiary availed himself of these overtures to play off Austria against Britain in the hope of embittering relations between the two. But the decisive negotiations were between Britain and France. These countries agreed on preliminaries in April and upon the final treaty in October. The other belligerents had no option but to accept the terms presented to them.

The settlement was very nearly a return to the *status quo ante bellum*. The exceptions were few. The Duchies of Parma and Piacenza were given to the Infant Philip; Charles Emmanuel kept the lands, other than Piacenza, that Maria Theresa had ceded to him in virtue of the Treaty of Worms. The Dutch, though they were once more given the right to garrison the barrier fortresses, were unable to obtain a renewal of the annual contribution to their upkeep from the revenues of the Netherlands. Nor did the treaty provide for the neutrality of the Netherlands. Spain promised Britain a renewal of the *asiento* until 1752. Two further points require mention. The terms of the settlement were embodied in a single treaty, instead of in a series of separate treaties as in 1678, 1697, and 1713–14. Secondly, the Treaty of Aix-la-Chapelle contained a guarantee of Frederick's possession of Silesia, although Prussia was not a party to the treaty. The treaty, however, was so worded that it was doubtful if that guarantee was valid unless Frederick would agree to guarantee the treaty as a whole, which, he made plain, he would not do. But both France and Britain hoped by this apparently meaningless stipulation to court the favour of Frederick, whose support each hoped to get in the event of a future war. Nobody believed the treaty would inaugurate an era of perpetual peace.

The territorial changes to which it gave rise were by no means the only results of the War of the Austrian Succession. It was of the first importance that the Habsburg State, which had been menaced with destruction in 1741-2, had survived as a Great Power; indeed, in spite of some losses, it was in a sense stronger in 1748 that in 1740. Vigour had been imparted to its administration and policy; its army had increased in numbers and improved in morale; there was every prospect that a brief period of peace would enable Maria Theresa to effect reforms that would yet further increase the fighting power of her dominions. She had proved herself a great ruler, but the salvation of the Habsburg power had not been due to her alone; foreign help had contributed something; the inertia and mutual jealousies of her enemies had contributed even more. The conditions of warfare and the strategical theories of the time do not by themselves suffice to explain the weakness of the initial attack on Maria Theresa. What was more important was that in 1741-2 Fleury prevented France from making the maximum effort of which she was capable and that Frederick, whatever his wishes may have been, did not do his utmost to bring about the destruction of the Habsburg States. So favourable an opportunity never presented itself again. Though in 1744 Frederick devised a plan whose realisation would have eliminated the Habsburg State from the ranks of the Great Powers, French inertia combined with his own blunders and the vigour of Austrian resistance to frustrate it. After the failure of his campaign in that year, Frederick aimed only at a return to the *status quo ante bellum*. His victories in 1745 brought him great prestige; it was in consequence of them that his subjects began to call him 'the Great', but the Peace of Dresden did not make his tenure of Silesia secure, for it left Maria Theresa strong enough to contemplate a war for its reconquest with some prospect of success. Though the Habsburg power alone was scarcely a match for Prussia, Maria Theresa was not without hope of gaining allies in the near future. Frederick knew his danger and continued to augment his army as quickly as his finances permitted. His policy was one of watchful waiting; he had no desire to run further risks, and he coldly resisted French efforts to induce him to enter the war again before the Peace of Aix-la-Chapelle. The only thing that would have moved him was an imminent threat to Prussian security, and that did not come until some years later.

A by-product of Maria Theresa's hostility to Frederick was a period of tranquility for Italy. After the peace of 1748 Maria Theresa realised that, if she were to have any chance of implementing an anti-Prussian policy, she must sacrifice other ambitions and seek to put an end to the long rivalry between Bourbon and Habsburg in Italy. It was the easier for her to do so because her remaining possessions there were no longer threatened. Once Ferdinand VI had secured the installation of his half-brother Don Philip in a modest principality, he had no more wish to meddle in Italian affairs. He had no great love for Philip and had sought to establish him in Italy only because he would have found his presence in Spain troublesome. Philip, on his part, was by no means satisfied and, though he knew he could expect little from Ferdinand, hoped that his father-in-law, Louis XV, would some day secure a better provision for him. Louis, however, though benevolent, had no intention of starting another war for Philip's sake. The ruler of the other Bourbon State in Italy, King Charles of Naples, was content to wait for the day when he would succeed the frail and childless Ferdinand on the throne of Spain. Meanwhile Charles had an opportunity to consolidate his authority, hitherto none too firmly established, in Naples, where the pro-Austrian party withered away once it had become plain that Maria Theresa had given up the hope of affecting an Austrian reconquest. Thus after 1748 there was little risk that a conflict between the Bourbons and Maria Theresa would develop in Italy. For Charles Emmanuel of Sardinia this meant both an absence of opportunity and an absence of risk. If he had no prospect of conquering more territory, his dominions were safe from dismemberment. Moreover, his trimming policy in 1742–8, if it had not brought him all the gains he desired, had helped to avert what he most feared, the complete expulsion of either the Bourbons or the Habsburgs from Italy. Whether there was peace or war between them, he was not left at the mercy of either Maria Theresa or a combination of Bourbon Powers.

For France the immediate results of the war are harder to assess. The final settlement was certainly very different both from what had been hoped in 1741 and from what had been feared, after Dettingen, in 1743. France had not only succeeded in emerging without territorial loss from the crisis she had done so much to provoke, but she had also obtained what might be regarded as important, though intangible, indirect advantages. If it was a French interest—and many Frenchmen then thought it was—to weaken Habsburg power in Germany, the Prussian conquest of Silesia had certainly done so. Though France had not been able to prevent the election of Francis as Charles VII's successor on the imperial throne, it had proved impossible for Francis to bring about an imperial declaration of war on France, as Leopold I and Charles VI had done in earlier conflicts between Bourbon and Habsburg. From the Empire France had nothing to fear while Maria Theresa and Frederick remained unreconciled. Moreover, the course of the war seemed to have sharpened the divergencies of interest between France's opponents. For the Dutch the peace had come only just in time to save them from a further campaign of which the outcome promised to be disastrous. They certainly had no desire to take part in another struggle of the same nature and were much less inclined than before to follow Britain's lead in foreign policy. The weakening of the Anglo-Dutch alliance was patent to Versailles. So, too, was Maria Theresa's readiness to detach herself from Britain. The overtures she had made in 1745 and 1748 left no doubt of that. Ill-feeling between London and Vienna was plainly to France's advantage, and French diplomacy did something to stimulate it. It is true that these gains were somewhat counterbalanced by the fact that France had no ally upon whom she could count. She had done comparatively little to support Spain's interests at Aix-la-Chapelle, and Franco-Spanish relations were cool after the treaty. Upon Prussia no dependence could be placed. None the less, in view of the strength of her army and the state of relations between her former foes, France appeared formidable. That certainly was the view taken in Britain, where the peace was felt to be a lucky escape from a dangerous position, and the future was viewed with concern. It was believed that Britain could not stand alone and must take steps to secure allies in a future war. Though in the late war the old system of the co-operation of Britain with the Dutch Republic and the Habsburg State had not worked well, Britain's rulers retained their faith in it; they did not realise the strength of Maria Theresa's hostility to Prussia and were quite unwilling to commit their country to an anti-Prussian policy in order to ensure Maria Theresa's alliance. The country which they feared was France, and they assumed that the Habsburg State, in the future as in the past, would have good reason to fear her also. That assumption was wrong, but it could not be proved wrong until Louis XV had clearly indicated that France was ready to suspend her traditional hostility to the house of Habsburg. But neither in 1748 nor for some years later did he give any such indication. It did not follow that a diplomatic revolution was bound to occur because Maria Theresa wanted it.

CHAPTER XIX

THE DIPLOMATIC REVOLUTION

FROM the beginning of modern European history the antagonism of France and the house of Habsburg had been axiomatic. The reconciliation of these Powers is therefore usually regarded as the greatest of all diplomatic revolutions. Austria broke off her entente with Britain while France renounced her alliance with Prussia in 1756. During the War of the Austrian Succession the old alliances had not run smoothly. Britain and Austria had agreed that the Dutch had let them down, but had agreed in nothing else. Britain complained that the Austrians had demanded extortionate subsidies, had never kept their contingents up to the stipulated strength, and had concentrated on the war in Germany. Austria retorted that Britain had never given her adequate support, had forced her by threats to make territorial concessions to her enemies, had broken Carteret's promises to secure compensation for Austrian losses and had finally deserted her altogether. A new element had however appeared during the war which was to modify Anglo-Austrian relations. Prussia had emerged with startling suddenness as a Great Power and the era of 'dualism' had begun in Germany. This did not merely make Austria a less powerful and efficient ally, but gave Britain what she had not hitherto had—an alternative to the Austrian alliance against France. All through the war some British politicians had advocated the substitution of alliance with Prussia for alliance with Austria. Even those who did not go so far as this admitted the 'lameness' of the old system, caused by Prussian desertion, and made frantic and unavailing efforts to bring about a genuine reconciliation between the two German Great Powers. Ultimately, after a protracted struggle, the duke of Newcastle secured effective control of British foreign policy at the end of the war. In 1742 Newcastle had had 'the strongest prepossession that the house of Austria was not worth supporting', but he now decided that Austria was the essential corner-stone of the ambitious combination of Powers which he wished to bring together against France. He firmly rejected Frederick the Great's offer to take the place of Austria as Britain's continental partner and, to win the good graces of Maria Theresa, he set himself to secure the election of her eldest son as king of the Romans and by the conclusion of subsidy treaties with the venal princes of Germany to weaken the French party in the Empire. Even then when Frederick, prince of Wales, died in 1751, Maria Theresa deplored the increased influence at the court of London of the duke of Cumberland, whom she regarded as being more inclined towards Prussia.

Unfortunately for himself and his country, Newcastle's policy was based on a complete misunderstanding of Austrian intentions and ambitions. Though he did not become Chancellor until 1753, from as early as 1749 the decisive influence at Vienna on foreign policy was that of Kaunitz, who had, during the war, occupied important diplomatic missions at Turin and Brussels and had then represented Austria at the peace conference at Aix-la-Chapelle. His experience at Brussels convinced him that the Netherlands could not be defended successfully against a determined French attack and that, in any case, the restrictions imposed by the Maritime Powers upon Austrian sovereignty in the Netherlands made the province of little value. His subsequent experiences at Aix-la-Chapelle left him certain that Britain would do nothing to restore Silesia to Austria and he was already clear that this was a *sine qua non* if Austria was to recover her position as a leading Great Power. While at Aix he had discussed with the French representative the idea of French support for Austrian recovery of Silesia in exchange for cessions to France in the Netherlands. Although France had ultimately preferred to make a separate peace with the Maritime Powers and not with Austria, she had not decisively rejected the exchange project. Kaunitz, therefore, in the celebrated State Paper which he prepared for the empress-queen and the *Staatsconferenz* in March 1749, started from the assumption that the recovery of Silesia was vital to Austria. Therefore at the moment Austria's primary enemy was Prussia, not France under a weak king and a divided ministry. Austria should then try to convince France of her pacific views and seek to break off the Franco-Prussian alliance by persuading France that Prussia was a selfish and treacherous ally who had repeatedly betrayed France and on whom no reliance could be placed.

Maria Theresa accepted Kaunitz's plan. Henceforth, with one conspicuous exception late in her reign, she approved Kaunitz's objects in foreign policy and was content to leave the choice of means to him. But for his influence she might well have concentrated on internal reform, which interested her more and which she understood better, leaving to her successor the use of the increased resources bequeathed to him against the Prussian arch enemy. There may have been an inner conflict between her anxiety to keep her pledged word and her conviction that Silesia must be recovered sooner or later for Austria. Kaunitz showed her how to follow the dictates of her heart without doing violence to her conscience. By representing the struggle for supremacy in Germany—a question of power politics—as the defence of Empire, Law and Roman Catholicism against the unprincipled and heretic king of Prussia, he won the unfaltering support of his mistress. In the late autumn of 1750 she sent him to Paris to try and execute his own plan, but within a few months he had to admit his failure to shake the Franco-Prussian alliance. Quite apart from her suspicion that Austrian overtures were made in secret agreement with Britain, France could hardly be favourably impressed by an envoy who spoke with two voices insisting on the pacific intentions of his sovereign and at the same time hinting at the need for a European crusade to repress and render harmless the ambitious king of Prussia, the acknowledged leader of the Francophil party in the Empire. Conceal it as best he could, there was undoubtedly an offensive element in Kaunitz's proposals. His own summing up of the results of his mission was that he succeeded merely in persuading France not to hate Austria.

Meantime Maria Theresa at Vienna was carefully concealing from British and Dutch diplomatists her firm preference for the French alliance if it could be obtained. She denied with apparent sincerity the truth of the rumours that she was planning another war against Prussia for the recovery of Silesia: she waxed indignant over the stories that she had devoted English subsidies to the building of her favourite palace at Schönbrunn. She made it clear that she thought little of Newcastle's election project, which would merely whet the appetites of the German princes and make closer the union between the opponents of the election, France and Prussia, which it was her supreme ambition to disunite. Repeatedly she urged the British Government, if it had money to spend on the Continent, to spend it in subsidies to Russia and not squander it on petty German princes, whose military resources were insignificant and whose fidelity at best was doubtful. While pressing on with internal reforms, aided by Haugwitz, she resolutely refused to restore to the Maritime Powers the extensive military and commercial privileges they had previously enjoyed in the Netherlands to the detriment of Maria Theresa's own subjects there. Even when Kaunitz returned from Paris to Vienna as Chancellor in 1753, apparently cured of his French political prepossessions and resolved to maintain in the meantime the admittedly unsatisfactory alliance with the Maritime Powers, there was no real improvement in Austro-British relations.

Looking back, it is clear that the alliance of Austria and Britain, never really cordial, became less and less so in the 1740's and 1750's. Britain was becoming more and more preoccupied with colonial expansion and problems of world politics. Austria, less and less interested in western Europe, was becoming increasingly intent on the balance of power in central and eastern Europe in which Britain took little interest. While Britain persistently shut her eyes to the decline of the third partner in the alliance, the United Provinces, Maria Theresa took a much more realistic view and refused, by making concessions in regard to the barrier fortresses and Dutch commercial privileges in the Netherlands, to weaken herself for the advantage of an almost useless ally. Few contemporaries, however, realised what was happening. When war with France threatened in North America and on the Atlantic at the end of 1754, it was generally expected in Britain that Austria would take her share in the war on the Continent against France by contributing substantial forces to the defence of the

Netherlands which Newcastle regarded as a kind of common country in which we, the Dutch and the Austrians were all interested. If necessary, it was thought Austria would also help in Hanover. Nothing was further from the intentions of the empress-queen and her Chancellor. If the Franco-British sea war brought on a land war, they were determined not to divide Austria's forces, but to concentrate them against their most dangerous enemy, the king of Prussia.

On previous occasions Austria, in difficulties, had had to appeal to Britain and accept such help as Britain chose to offer. Now the relative positions of the two Powers were altered and Austria was resolved to drive a hard bargain, if indeed she would give help at any price. Britain must conclude subsidy treaties with Bavaria, Saxony, Hesse and other German States and combine these German troops with her own and those of Hanover and the Dutch to form a substantial army for use in Germany and the Netherlands. She must, at her own expense, win over the king of Sardinia to give effective protection to Austrian interests in Italy. Above all, she must immediately conclude a treaty of subsidy with Russia, which had hung fire for years, but was now essential not only for the defence of Hanover and the protection of Austria but to prevent France and Prussia from dominating the Empire. Britain agreed to make offers to Russia which would be sufficient to procure her co-operation, to hire 8000 Hessians for the defence of the Netherlands and to try to renew her subsidy treaties with Bavaria and Saxony. But she made these contributions to the common cause conditional upon the immediate dispatch of an additional 25,000 to 30,000 Austrian troops to the Netherlands and an undertaking by the empress-queen to send troops to participate in the defence of Hanover, if attacked, and to act by way of diversion if France attacked the British Isles. Kaunitz replied in June 1755 that what Britain would provide, considered in conjunction with the total inaction of the Dutch, was not enough to offer any prospect of successful resistance to France in the Netherlands. Yet in return for this inadequate British contribution Austria was expected to march to the help of Hanover if attacked and to operate as well by way of diversion against Prussia. Nevertheless Austria, in a last effort to save the old system, would supply 20,000 men in the summer of 1755 towards the defence of the Netherlands provided that Britain supplied at the same time an equal number of her own troops, or of her German mercenaries, and that the United Provinces and Hanover provided smaller contingents. In addition Britain must without further delay conclude the subsidy treaties with Russia and the German States and take effective steps to safeguard Austrian interests in Italy.

When no reply was received to his ultimatum, Kaunitz proposed to the *Staatsconferenz* a 'new plan', which turned out to be his old idea of an alliance with France directed against Prussia. French troops were already being collected on the frontiers of the Netherlands. Since Kaunitz did not believe it was possible to defend the Netherlands he must act quickly. Austria must offer to resign the greater part of the Netherlands to Louis XV's son-in-law Don Philip and recover the three Italian duchies assigned to Don Philip at Aix. France could take as a pledge Ostend and Nieuport. These proposals were to be communicated by the Austrian ambassador at Paris, Starhemberg, to Louis XV not in the normal manner through his ministers but by either Madame de Pompadour or the prince of Conti after a personal guarantee of inviolable secrecy had been obtained from the king. Starhemberg, to whom this difficult decision was left, decided to approach the king through his mistress and not through his confidential adviser on foreign affairs.

France had nothing to lose and much to gain by listening to the Austrian proposals. Bernis, one of the Pompadour's *protégés*, a penniless abbé with a long pedigree and a reputation as a wit, who had recently occupied the sinecure post of French ambassador to Venice, was selected by Louis XV to negotiate with Starhemberg. There seems to be no reason to doubt that the decisions which led step by step to the conclusion of the first Treaty of Versailles eight months later were taken by the king himself. Louis XV had long desired to secure an alliance with Austria, since this alone, he thought, would ensure a long period of peace and protect the Catholic Church. He had, reasonably enough in view of Frederick II's behaviour during the Austrian Succession war, no confidence in Prussia. More perhaps than Frederick's witticisms, Louis resented the Prussian assumption that a margrave of Brandenburg was an equal partner in the Franco-Prussian alliance. His bigotry had always been offended by the necessity of partnership with a heretic and an infidel whom on one occasion he compared with Julian the Apostate. Maria Theresa had been careful to emphasise the community of religious interests in her approach to the king. He may have been encouraged by his mistress and her friend the abbé for reasons of their own, but the *rapprochement* with Austria was fundamentally the work of Louis XV himself.

In his *Mémoires* Bernis later formulated the classical defence of the new system. Since the reign of the Emperor Charles V, Austria had lost numerous kingdoms and provinces and could no longer aspire to universal monarchy. She was, however, still a Great Power and therefore a valuable ally, especially as she had always hitherto been the nucleus of resistance round which the enemies of France had gathered. France had no need to fear invasion except from Germany; union with the dominant German power would protect this weak spot in the French frontiers and free her from the evils and misfortunes of war. Moreover, the alliance of France and Austria would benefit the other branches of the house of Bourbon and strengthen their position in Spain and Italy. Lastly, since Britain was the real enemy of France, and Austria had up till now been her most powerful ally, it was good policy to deprive Britain of Austria's support. Bernis dismissed summarily the main objection to the union of France and Austria, that it would make Austria too strong in the Empire, with the reply that his masterpiece, the first Treaty of Versailles, was based on the complete and absolute observance by Austria of the treaties of Westphalia: the moment Maria Theresa violated these treaties the Franco-Austrian alliance would be resolved into its original elements.

When Bernis received the actual Austrian proposals he believed that they offered real advantages to France. He was impressed also by the Austrian assertion that Britain and Prussia were already negotiating secretly with each other and it was partly for this reason that the duc de Nivernois was ordered to go to Berlin and discover the actual intentions of Frederick II. Had Nivernois discharged his duties promptly instead of dallying in France, it is quite likely that the Diplomatic Revolution would have been indefinitely postponed. Meantime Bernis procrastinated: Starhemberg was simply assured in September 1755 that the king of France desired fervently to maintain the Peace of Aix-la-Chapelle and would welcome Austria's co-operation for this salutary end. Austria, nettled by this reply, retorted that since her offers were apparently not agreeable to France, she would await French proposals of co-operation. Bernis then suggested a treaty of reciprocal guarantee by France and Austria to cover their possessions in Europe. To this treaty the allies of both Powers, Britain always excepted since she had already broken the Treaty of Aix-la-Chapelle, would be invited to accede.

At this stage Bernis, in December 1755, persuaded the king to name four of his ministers, Machault, Séchelles, Rouillé and Saint-Florentin, as a committee of the Council to superintend the conduct of the negotiation with Austria and, Bernis hoped, reduce the chance of his ending in the Bastille. Disappointed by the French reply to her first proposals, Maria Theresa had instructed Starhemberg to abandon the anti-Prussian aspect of the negotiation, but before the end of 1755 she had returned to the attack. He was told to try to do what Kaunitz had failed to do a few years earlier, namely to undermine the Franco-Prussian alliance by convincing France that it was unnatural. Once Prussia had attained her ends she would become France's most dangerous rival and, throwing off the mask of hypocrisy she had hitherto worn, would immediately change sides. In fact, France was to be regarded as a mere instrument cunningly used by Prussia to attain her ends, and the sooner she realised this the better it would be for her. As long as France trusted Prussia no lasting understanding was possible between Austria and France. The empress-queen concluded with the reflection that France might profitably await the full revelations of British and Prussian policy before reaching a decision on the Austrian offers.

In the years immediately following the War of the Austrian Succession the relations of Britain and Prussia had been at their worst. Britain had seized Prussian merchant ships during the war and refused to pay compensation. Prussia had then stopped payment both of capital and interest due to British holders of the Silesian Loan which Frederick had undertaken to pay off. Britain in 1750 had acceded to the treaty of the two empresses of 1746, though not to the fourth secret article, which Frederick, knew well was directed against himself. During the 1750's she was negotiating for a subsidy treaty with Russia which Frederick believed would, if concluded, be also directed against Prussia. Frederick retaliated by posing as the champion of the expiring Jacobite cause and leading the opposition to the king of the Romans scheme, to which George II and Newcastle attached so much importance.

That most of these quarrels were mere trifles is shown by the ease and rapidity with which they were settled once a common interest brought Britain and Prussia together. While it would be entirely wrong to regard Prussia after 1745 as a satiated State, Frederick II was well aware that further acquisitions would not be gained so easily. He already had his eye on Saxony and West Prussia as the most desirable additions to his territories, but the conquest of Silesia had put all his neighbours on their guard. In particular as long as Russia remained hostile and watchful on his eastern frontier and was likely to obtain British subsidies, any attempt to repeat his success would be not only futile but dangerous. Only if Bestuzhev was overthrown and his successor secured by bribes in the Prussian interest, if Britain was plunged by the death of George II into the difficulties inseparable from a minority, if the Ottoman empire was ruled by a worthy successor of Suleiman the Magnificent, and if France was controlled by an ambitious and omnipotent foreign minister would the omens be favourable for a war of aggression which would bring further advantages to Prussia. Such was the programme outlined by Frederick in his *Political Testament* of 1752. None of his conditions had been fulfilled by 1755 and in the closing months of this year fear rather than greed was the dominant motive in his mind.

Negotiations between Britain and Prussia began with the duke of Brunswick as a go-between in the summer of 1755. Britain at first asked for a unilateral declaration from the king of Prussia that he would not attack Hanover, as France indeed had previously suggested he might well do as a demonstration of his loyalty to the French alliance. Frederick asked nothing better than to be sought after by the two leading Powers of Europe. It flattered his vanity and he hoped to act as mediator between Britain and France. There was always the chance that some material advantage for Prussia might result, if he played his cards properly. He guessed correctly that the British approaches to him indicated a coldness, if not an actual breach, between Britain and Austria, caused by Austria's unwillingness to pull Britain's chestnuts out of the fire. He was more and more disgusted by the supine attitude of France and alarmed by her military unpreparedness. Her finances were in disorder, her ministers weak and divided and the court more concerned with the position of Madame de Pompadour and the long-standing quarrels between clergy and *parlements* than with the basic questions of foreign policy. He denounced the instructions drawn up for Nivernois as 'vague and wretched', and shared the general belief that France was anxious to avoid taking part in continental war, since this would lessen her chances of success in the naval war against Britain, which now could hardly be avoided.

In Frederick's view the weakness of his ally and her obvious intention to play as little part as possible in a continental war permitted, indeed compelled, him to take what action he could for his own security. Between 1749 and 1754 France had built thirty-eight ships of the line and in 1756 she had nearly seventy ships of the line ready for action. This naval strength might well enable her to reverse the decision of the previous war at sea, provided she did not require to play a major role on land. France would presumably not object to the neutralisation of Germany, and Frederick therefore suggested to the British Government the substitution of a convention of neutrality for the original unilateral declaration proposed by Britain. He suspected that France was negotiating with Austria for a promise that Austria would not support Britain if France abstained from attacking the Netherlands. What he was now suggesting to Britain would be parallel to such an agreement and, in his opinion, not incompatible with his alliance with France, which was purely defensive and moreover did not cover the present Franco-British war since it had originated beyond Europe.

At this stage Frederick received fresh reports of Russo-Austrian hostility to Prussia. There was nothing new in them, since such hostility had been evident and notorious at least since the conclusion in 1746 of the treaty of the two empresses. What was new was the conclusion by Britain in September 1755 of the convention of St Petersburg, which seemed to associate her much more closely than before with the hostility of the two empresses to Prussia. This treaty had been the central point of Anglo-Russian diplomatic relations for nearly ten years. Originally proposed by Bestuzhev to supplement Russia's obligation under the defensive Russo-British treaty of 1742 to send 12,000 men to defend Britain if attacked, it had been strongly advocated by Maria Theresa as essential to the strengthening of the old system. Russia would keep a substantial body of regular troops in her north-western provinces, i.e. on the frontiers of East Prussia. These troops would be maintained in a condition to operate at short notice and would be supported by galleys and warships in the Baltic. All this would cost money which must be supplied by the British Government.

The conditions on which Britain had acceded to the treaty of the two empresses bound Russia as well as Austria to defend Hanover if attacked *en haine de cet accession*, though George II as elector of Hanover had not acceded to the treaty. The Austrian Government had urged on Britain the conclusion of a subsidy treaty as a *quid pro quo*, but for long in vain. Newcastle preferred to push on the negotiation for the election of the archduke Joseph as king of the Romans, thus, as we have seen, embittering the relations between Britain and Prussia. Soon, however, he had reluctantly to admit that even the German princes he had bribed would hardly dare to give their votes for the archduke unless they were protected against Prussian resentment by a Russian army of observation on Prussia's exposed eastern frontier. This argument in favour of the Russo-British treaty lost force with the virtual abandonment by Britain of the election programme, but relations with Prussia did not improve. With the beginnings of Franco-British conflict in America the British Government had to face the possibility of a Prussian attack on Hanover, either on her own account, or, more probably, as the agent of France. No doubt George II's fears for his beloved electorate gave a fillip to the British ministers' activity, but it was their manifest duty to strengthen Britain's system on the Continent in every possible way.

Even if Russia regarded a Prussian attack on Hanover as included in the *casus fœderis* of 1742, it was clear that 12,000 Russian auxiliaries, who would take under the most favourable conditions months to reach the scene of the fighting, would avail little to protect Hanover directly. Much more effective would be a prompt and powerful Russian diversion against Prussia from the east. By April 1755 the British ministry decided that they must pay what they had hitherto regarded as the grossly exorbitant price demanded by Russia for this service. 'We can do nothing without the Dutch, the Dutch nothing without the Austrians, nor the Austrians anything without the Russians', wrote Sir Thomas Robinson. 'When we are masters of the latter we may take the part we please.' And even before the actual signature of the treaty the use Britain intended to make of it had fundamentally changed. The idea in London was now to hold it as a threat over Prussia's head and thereby, it was hoped, prevent a Prussian attack on Hanover and perhaps any war on the Continent. This was particularly attractive to Newcastle, since it would achieve the maximum result with the least possible expense.

Even before Frederick II knew that the Russo-British subsidy treaty had been signed, his lively imagination had conjured up visions of Prussia attacked from the east by the Russians, from the south by the Austrians and Saxons and from the west by Hanoverians, supported by other German troops hired by Britain, while combined British and Russian fleets blockaded and bombarded his Baltic coast-line. In such a struggle he was convinced he could expect little effective assistance from his only ally, France, intent as she was on winning the maritime and colonial war against Britain. Moreover, if France really wished to avoid entanglement in continental war, Frederick could argue that the neutralisation of Germany was a considerable contribution to the desired end. He hoped thus to escape from his dilemma. It had seemed he must run the terrible risk of a combined Anglo-Austrian-Russian attack as the ally of France in a war which offered little chance of gain for Prussia even if Prussia and France proved unexpectedly successful. The only alternative had seemed to be refusal to come to the help of France, which would probably mean the final breach of an alliance which had been of immense service to Prussia. The end of this alliance would undermine Prussia's whole position in the Empire and remove the one great obstacle which had up till now prevented the execution of Austria's and Russia's plans against him. These considerations explain why the reckless adventurer of the Austrian Succession war became now a fanatic for peace and why he found the British offers, which he had at first not taken very seriously, unexpectedly attractive.

Britain and Prussia had now a common interest—the maintenance of peace in Germany. During the debates on the Russo-British subsidy treaty in parliament in December 1755, the British ministers asserted loudly that it was purely defensive and would only be invoked if a European Power attacked the British Isles or Hanover. They sent Frederick a copy of the text of their treaty—as yet unratified—with Russia and then submitted to him a draft convention designed to keep the war out of Germany. Frederick accepted this with one important modification put forward by his minister Podewils, namely the exclusion of the Low Countries from the area to be neutralised. Frederick deliberately left France free to operate in the Netherlands if, contrary to his and her own expectations, she should subsequently wish to wage war against Britain by land as well as by sea. The draft, thus modified, was signed at Whitehall on 16 January 1756, but is customarily referred to as the convention of Westminster.

The preamble stated the desire of Britain and Prussia to secure the peace of Europe in general and of Germany in particular. By the first article they promised not to attack each other's territories and to do their best to prevent their respective allies from taking any hostile action against these territories. By the second article they agreed to combine their forces to resist the entry into, or passage through, Germany of the troops of any foreign Power and to maintain the peace in Germany. A separate and secret article attached to the convention expressly excluded the Netherlands from its scope on the ground that by the Treaty of Dresden (1745) Prussia had guaranteed only the German possessions of the empress-queen. Although it was in no sense a treaty of alliance but a mere *ad hoc* agreement to preserve the neutrality of Germany, it soon produced effects on the delicate diplomatic balance which were entirely unexpected by the two contracting parties.

Newcastle regarded the convention of Westminster as a first step to the inclusion of Prussia in the Anglo-Imperial alliance. Through his mouthpiece Holderness, Secretary of State for the Northern Department, he explained to the Austrians that the two Conventions of St Petersburg and Westminster gave them complete security against Prussia and would therefore enable them, without risk, to detach to the Netherlands the considerable reinforcements which they had hitherto declined to send on the ground that they were needed for the defence of Bohemia. So far as Russia was concerned, Newcastle and Holderness were even more cavalier. Their attitude was that he who pays the piper calls the tune. Frederick II was not quite so blind as Newcastle to the attitude and intentions of his ally, but he too had miscalculated. Not merely did he overrate British control over the court of St Petersburg, he underrated the effect of his bombshell on the haughty court of Versailles.

By January 1756 the Franco-Austrian negotiations begun in August 1755 had made little progress. France insisted that Austria should give her indirect but real assistance for an attack on Hanover; Austria refused categorically and offered instead a convention of neutrality to cover both Germany and the Low Countries. It was the news of the conclusion of the Convention of Westminster which broke the deadlock, and made possible Franco-Austrian agreement in the first Treaty of Versailles. Whereas Britain's allies objected to the substance of the Convention of Westminster, French objections were primarily to the method adopted by Frederick of negotiating, secretly and without consulting France, a convention with Louis XV's most bitter enemy. France's one important ally seemed to have basely deserted her on the eve of war and to be trying to deprive France of the rights, acquired in 1648, to take action in the Empire on behalf of oppressed German princes. What made appearances even worse was that the tardy French ambassador, the duc de Nivernois, appeared at Berlin with instructions to renew the Franco-Prussian alliance just in time to receive from Frederick the draft of his convention with Britain, accompanied by the information that it had probably already been signed at London. It is true that the French Foreign Minister, Rouillé, also argued that Prussia had no legal or moral right to sign such a convention while Britain was waging an offensive war against France, but fundamentally French resentment was directed at the indecency of Frederick's conduct and the ludicrous position in which he had placed Louis XV in the eyes of Europe.

Had Frederick been willing to repudiate the convention or perhaps even to disarm French *amour propre* by adopting a submissive attitude, the Franco-Prussian alliance might still have been saved. But Frederick resented French treatment of Prussia as an inferior Power: he said once that to be the ally of France was to be her slave. Indeed, Nivernois's instructions in November 1755 were explicitly based on the assumption that, while the Prussian alliance was useful to France, the French alliance was indispensable to Prussia. Therefore he met French reproaches with the blunt retort that what he had done was fully justified in international law, that it was done in any case to serve the interests of France and that if France did not like it, he would be compelled to transform his *entente* with Britain into an alliance. Finally, by comparing his action, designed to assist France to carry on the kind of war she preferred to wage, with the complete inactivity of France's closer ally, Spain, he touched what was undoubtedly a sore point with Louis XV and his ministers.

Before the news of the Convention of Westminster reached Versailles, Kaunitz was reluctantly postponing once again the execution of the offensive plans he had long entertained against Prussia. On 28 December 1755 France had definitely refused to co-operate in such schemes. She had offered to conclude instead with Austria a treaty of reciprocal guarantee of the existing possessions of France and Austria and their respective allies, with the solitary exclusion of Britain, which had broken the Treaty of Aix-la-Chapelle and was already waging war, without any formal declaration, on France. This treaty would be indistinguishable from a defensive alliance, since it would provide assistance in men or money to either contracting party if it was attacked in its European possessions. In addition, France proposed that Austria should undertake to remain neutral in the war between France and Britain, to exclude all British troops from the Netherlands and oppose the passage through the Empire of the Russian auxiliaries of Britain, to allow French troops to operate on Austrian territory if the Russian troops succeeded in approaching the French frontiers or attacked the allies of France in the Empire, and finally to take effective measures with the Bourbon courts to maintain peace in Italy. These proposals illustrate the depth and width of the gulf that still separated France and Austria after four months of confidential negotiations.

Maria Theresa and Kaunitz must have wondered whether it was worth while proceeding with them, but on 27 January 1756, still ignorant of the Convention of Westminster, they sent to Starhemberg a conditional acceptance of the French proposals. They objected particularly to giving an undertaking to oppose passage of Russian or other auxiliary troops through Germany and allowing French troops to operate against the Russian and other British auxiliaries on Austrian territory. Before this reply reached Starhemberg, the Convention of Westminster had become known at Versailles and the French negotiators made little attempt to conceal their indignation from the Austrian ambassador. Starhemberg did his best to exploit the new situation. He pointed out how right Austria had proved in warning France of the Prusso-British negotiations. He strove by rousing French wrath still further to secure the active support of France for the anti-Prussian coalition. Rouillé and Bernis were now ready to discuss the original Austrian plan which had been rejected by Louis XV in the autumn of 1755, but, as soon as they entered into details, serious differences emerged.

France had already decided not to renew the alliance with Prussia when it expired in June 1756, but she would still be bound to Prussia by the Franco-Prusso-Swedish defensive alliance of 1747 which did not expire until May 1757. She suggested, therefore, the postponement of Austria's anti-Prussian schemes until at least the summer of 1757. Moreover, even then, if France was to denounce her alliance with Prussia, Austria must unconditionally renounce her alliance with Britain. Since Austria did not intend to take any active part in the French war against her former ally, Britain, she could not, Bernis told Starhemberg, expect France to participate actively in Austria's plans against France's ally, Prussia. There must be absolute and entire reciprocity as the basis of Franco-Austrian accord.

When Starhemberg tried to argue that the true basis of the proposed alliance should be the securing of European peace by the destruction of the upstart king of Prussia, Bernis refused to listen to him. France would abandon Prussia and not raise a finger to protect her from Austria and Russia, but Prussia would be sufficiently punished for concluding the Convention of Westminster by the loss of Silesia. Austrian plans for the partition of the Prussian State amongst its neighbours went too far and, in any event, France would not join actively in the proposed attack on Prussia. Starhemberg himself commented that France would gladly see a sound balance of power re-established in the Empire, but had no intention of restoring Austrian supremacy. The Convention of Westminster had made possible a Franco-Austrian negotiation on the original Austrian proposal, but it obviously had not assured its successful conclusion.

Maria Theresa, therefore, on 6 March 1756 instructed Starhemberg to continue the negotiation on the French proposals of 28 December 1755 concurrently with discussion of the original Austrian plan, in the hope that the treaty of neutrality and guarantee would be used as the basis for Austria's offensive schemes. In Kaunitz's view his plan for the annihilation of Prussia was an indivisible whole and in particular he must have the co-operation of a 'third army' provided by France in addition to those of Austria and Russia to ensure the defeat of his arch-enemy, Frederick II. But patience was his strong suit. He was quite prepared to accept payment from France by instalments if this were preferred by Louis XV. At the end of the day, however, France must agree to supply an army of 60,000 or 70,000 men to be employed in Westphalia. This would prevent Hanover and the other Protestant States from giving help to Prussia and would facilitate Austro-Russian activities against Frederick. To his astonishment he learned that France had actually refused even to conclude the treaty of neutrality which Bernis had himself suggested at the end of 1755. France gave as her reason for the change of attitude that the making of such a treaty would now embarrass her. It would cause Frederick II to redouble his attempts to secure the prolongation of his alliance with France. Though Louis XV would not renew the alliance, there was still a powerful Prussian party at the French court headed by Belleisle and d'Argenson and supported vigorously from Berlin by Nivernois, the ambassador Frederick was accused of making the laughing-stock of Europe. Even Rouillé, who had been loudest in denunciation of Prussian misconduct in February 1756, unguardedly said to Starhemberg a month later that the Prussian alliance was a necessity to France. The more he and the other French ministers learned of the plans of the empress-queen, the more alarmed they became and the more doubtful of the advantages which an alliance with Austria had at first sight seemed to offer to France.

However, France had really gone too far to draw back. Louis XV was anxious to punish Prussia for her presumption in concluding the Convention of Westminster, and the best and most public way of doing this was to make a treaty with Austria. Even those ministers well disposed to Prussia were impressed by the Austrian threat that if France persisted in her refusal to sign the treaty of neutrality and guarantee, Austria would return to the old system. France, without an ally of importance in Europe, would then be faced by the combined resources of Austria, Russia, the Maritime Powers and perhaps even Prussia while Spain would at the best remain neutral. Therefore when Bernis recovered from a serious illness, certain ministers, d'Argenson being much the most important, who had hitherto been left in ignorance of the discussions with Austria were initiated into the secret on 19 April. The Council of Ministers authorised the signature of the two conventions of neutrality and defensive alliance which are together known as the first Treaty of Versailles (1 May 1756), though they were actually signed at Jouy, the country house of Rouillé. Rouillé and Bernis were the French plenipotentiaries; Starhemberg signed the treaty on behalf of Austria.

The convention of neutrality was modelled on the Convention of Westminster. Maria Theresa undertook to remain strictly neutral in the war already going on between Britain and France, while Louis XV promised not to attack or endanger the Austrian Netherlands or any other territories of the empress-queen. The second convention was a formal treaty of defensive alliance. The preamble asserted that the sole aim of the signatories was to ensure peace between their respective territories and to maintain as far as lay in their power the peace of Europe. If one of the contracting parties were threatened or attacked in its European possessions by any Power whatsoever, the other would at first employ its good offices to avert the threatened invasion and, if unsuccessful, undertook to send to the assistance of its ally a corps of 18,000 infantry and 6000 cavalry unless the party attacked preferred to accept instead a monthly subsidy at the rate of 8000 *florins* for every 1000 infantry and 24,000 *florins* for every 1000 cavalry. From the *casus fœderis* of this second convention the Franco-British war was expressly excepted. France took care to preserve her rights in the Empire by securing the confirmation of the Westphalian treaty, Austria secured anew French recognition of the validity of the famous Pragmatic Sanction of Charles VI, which preserved the Habsburg possessions in the new house of Habsburg-Lorraine.

Five secret articles were attached to this treaty, four of which are of importance. Article I provided that the *casus fœderis* would arise during the present war between Britain and France if one of Britain's allies, even acting as an auxiliary, attacked the European possessions of France or of Austria. This made it clear that the exclusion of the present war in the text of the main convention was conditional: an attack by Prussia, as the ally of Britain, upon Austria would compel France to assist Austria, while Prussian aid to Britain in resistance to a French attack on Hanover might well bring Austria into the war. The second secret article indicated as the Powers to be invited to accede to the treaty the Bourbon rulers of Spain, the two Sicilies and Parma and Maria Theresa's husband in his capacity of grand duke of Tuscany. Other States might be added to this list by mutual agreement. By the third article, in order to render permanent the good understanding between them, France and Austria agreed to continue negotiations for the completion of the work of the congress of Aix-la-Chapelle and to settle finally all territorial and other disputes which were dangerous to the peace of Europe and particularly of Italy. By Article IV France and Austria undertook, for the duration of the present war, not to make nor to renew any treaties with any other Power without the knowledge and participation of the other contracting party to the present treaty. This was obviously designed to prevent any attempt to renew the old system and indicates a certain lack of mutual confidence between the new allies.

None of these secret articles, however, supports the contention that France had yet been won over to connive at an attack by the imperial court on Prussia. Indeed, the third secret article indicates a clear divergence between France and Austria since the main feature of the Treaty of Aix, confirmed by this article, had been the European recognition of the incorporation of Silesia in Prussia, and the main territorial dispute which endangered the peace of Europe in 1756 was the desire of Austria to recover Silesia. The two parts of this clause were in fact plainly inconsistent with each other. Probably for France the real point of the article was the reference to Italy, which implied some sort of establishment in the Netherlands for Don Philip, the husband of Louis XV's favourite daughter.

Taken as a whole, the agreement reached by France and Austria on 1 May 1756, whatever its ultimate significance, registered for the time being the failure of Kaunitz to obtain the active participation of France in his anti-Prussian coalition. The idea of concluding a preliminary treaty between France and Austria, to regulate their relations during a Franco-British war, to be followed by a second treaty including Russia, the

Emperor and the junior branches of the house of Bourbon and intended to consolidate the Franco-Austrian alliance by removing causes of friction between them, especially in the Netherlands and Italy, had formed part of Bernis's original reply to Starhemberg's proposals. In September 1755 it had annoyed Maria Theresa and her Chancellor, though they were now glad to accept it.

More important than this, the treaty was based on a misunderstanding between the contracting parties. The leading French ministers, Madame de Pompadour and even Louis XV himself regarded the agreement as an end in itself. It would secure the peace of Europe and leave France free to devote herself to the maritime and colonial war. They were quite willing to consider Austria's offers for French neutrality in a war between Prussia and the two imperial courts, and if these offers proved high enough might very probably accept them. To Kaunitz and Maria Theresa, on the other hand, the first Treaty of Versailles was merely a milestone on the road to a general European war. After the hopes raised by the convention of Westminster it was indeed something of a disappointment to them, but they valued it because it displayed publicly the breach in the Franco-Prussian alliance and assured them of French support if Prussia attacked Austria. From this to the promise of French neutrality if Austria attacked Prussia did not seem a great step to Kaunitz, since a diplomatist of his ability need never fight an 'offensive' war. What he needed and intended to get was the promise of the active participation of France, by paying subsidies and sending auxiliaries, in his projected attack on Prussia. That this manifest divergence of views did not prove fatal to the Austro-French alliance was due rather to the folly of Kaunitz's antagonist, Frederick of Prussia, than to his own diplomatic skill. It is, however, to the credit of the Austrian negotiators that at the moment the first Treaty of Versailles was signed they had accurately estimated the king of Prussia's character and foresaw the probability of his mistakes.'We shall succeed', Starhemberg wrote, 'sooner or later in our great scheme and perhaps the king of Prussia himself will be our most effective helper.'

But these problems lay in the future. At the time of the signature of the treaty both courts, with the exception of a few oldfashioned or discontented *frondeurs* such as the marquis d'Argenson, were well pleased with their bargain. The reconciliation of the two leading Catholic Powers much pleased the pope, who raised Bernis to the cardinalate, but Kaunitz was anxious not to rouse religious passions and Benedict XIV warned his diplomatic agents never to speak of a 'war of religion'. Frederick II, on the contrary, did his best to pose as the protector of European protestantism, and in Britain this pose was to some extent believed, though even there it was usually realised that Frederick 'had cried out *religion*, as folks do *fire* when they want assistance'. The Protestant Dutch and Danes took no part in the war and the Lutheran Swedes joined France and Austria.

The publication of the first Treaty of Versailles after the exchange of ratifications caused a sensation in Europe. Its most immediate effect was probably felt in the United Provinces where the British envoy Colonel Yorke had been trying to persuade the States General to recognise the *casus fœderis* and to send to Britain the stipulated succours under ancient treaties. The French diplomatic representatives, on the other hand, had been urging the States General to proclaim their neutrality. The defection of Austria ended the internal struggle between the republican and stadtholderian parties over foreign policy, since without Austrian concurrence the defence of the Netherlands against France was plainly impossible. The States General accordingly announced their intention of maintaining a strict neutrality if France would assure them she had no hostile designs on the United Provinces or the barrier fortresses in the Netherlands. Louis XV graciously accepted these conditions on 14 June 1756. The diplomatic revolution had not merely split Britain and Austria: it had broken for a generation the even closer link between the Maritime Powers.

As immediate, and not less disastrous to Britain, was the effect on her relations with Russia. The controllers of Russian foreign policy were the Empress Elizabeth and her Chancellor Bestuzhev. Whereas Bestuzhev had shown himself a shrewd and consistent opponent of France throughout his career, Elizabeth had always had a sneaking fondness for France. Franco-Russian relations had been broken off since 1748, but in the autumn of 1755 a certain Chevalier Douglas as he called himself, though his real name was Mackenzie and he was a cadet of the noble house of Seaforth, arrived at St Petersburg as the agent of the French Government with a view to restoring normal relations between France and Russia. By this time there was an organised French party at the Russian court, headed by the reigning favourite Ivan Shuvalov and including some of his relatives and the timorous vice-chancellor Voronzov. Their intrigues secured the postponement for several weeks of the Russian ratification of the subsidy convention of September 1755 between Britain and Russia, but the Chancellor in the end extorted the consent of the Empress. She insisted, however, on making explicit what was not clearly stated in the treaty, that the diversion Russia promised to make in exchange for British subsidies would only be made in case of a Prussian attack upon Britain or one of her allies and that in no event would the Russian troops be sent to the Rhine, Hanover or the Netherlands.

Two days later news of the Convention of Westminster was received at St Petersburg. This placed the Chancellor in an extremely awkward situation since he had only been able to obtain the Empress's ratification of the treaty of September 1755 by emphasising the value of Britain as an ally against Prussia, but the Convention of Westminster proved that Britain was utterly useless as an ally against Prussia and thus destroyed the political basis of the Russo-British alliance. Russia had concluded the subsidy treaty to provide a convenient opportunity for an attack with combined forces on the king of Prussia: Britain had made use of it to reach an understanding with Prussia. This, while guaranteeing the neutrality of Germany, left Prussia free to display her aggressive tendencies outside Germany, perhaps against Russia. Indeed, since it protected her rear, it actually encouraged Prussia to do so.

The Empress Elizabeth at once established a special committee, or council, composed of her chief ministers and courtiers, and gave them instructions to recommend measures and take action designed to weaken the power of Prussia. The first recommendation made by the committee and approved with unusual decision by the Empress included an approach to the court of Vienna for collaboration in an immediate attack on Prussia. The committee also recommended winning the favour of France and, if possible, the obtaining of her undertaking not to hinder the joint operations against Prussia and to look upon the weakening of Prussia's power with equanimity (March 1756). It should be noted that Austria had been urged in earlier years by Russia to take immediate action against Prussia and had been assured of Russian support. The novelty was the formal decision to seek a reconciliation with France in view of the defection of Britain.

Kaunitz's diplomatic ability is shown as clearly in his handling of Russia as in his approach to France. His schemes always assumed Russian willingness to co-operate against Prussia, but he was deeply impressed by the unreliability of Russian policy. Since 1748 Elizabeth's attitude in foreign affairs had varied considerably, but had always been alarmingly aggressive. At first she had kept the chancelleries of Europe in continual disturbance by her demonstrations against Sweden. Then she had turned her activities against Prussia in 1753 and, in the following year, threatened to bring on a Russo-Turkish war. Rather than give Russia help in any of these aggressive plans, which contributed to maintain tension between Austria and France and to hold France and Prussia together, Kaunitz would have preferred to lose the friendship of Russia. Yet he concealed his natural annoyance with his impetuous and tactless ally and treated her with marked deference and consideration. This was all the more effective when contrasted with the condescending, almost contemptuous attitude of the British Government towards a Power which was trying to obtain British subsidies. Kaunitz, in fact, had made up his mind that Russia would assist him when the time came to settle accounts with Prussia, and he was determined that the choice of time should remain his. For one thing, he was determined not to attempt the recovery of Silesia with Russia as his only ally. Not only did he want a 'third army': he knew that subsidies were needed to give impetus to the cumbrous Russian military machine and Austria could not possibly supply subsidies from her own exchequer. It was not enough that France should stand aside. She must co-operate actively in the ruin of her former ally.

Kaunitz, therefore, informed Russia in good time of the breach between Britain and Austria and explained that it was due to the fact that Britain's sole enemy was France, whereas Prussia was the real enemy of the imperial courts. When the Convention of Westminster became known, he represented it as giving Russia and Austria a common grievance against Britain. He hinted that it might well lead to a change of system in France, advantageous to the imperial courts. Then, on 13 March 1756, Maria Theresa instructed her ambassador at St Petersburg to inform the tsaritsa, in confidence, of the secret negotiations between Austria and France and to propose, once they were assured of the concurrence of France, a joint attack on Frederick. Except that the tsaritsa was less convinced of the necessity of French co-operation, this exactly corresponded with the decisions previously taken at St Petersburg. It gave a fresh impetus to the military and diplomatic preparations already being taken to reduce the power of the king of Prussia. In April Russia offered, if Austria would do likewise, to attack Prussia during the year 1756 with 80,000 men and to undertake not to lay down her arms until Maria Theresa had recovered Silesia and Glatz.

Kaunitz had thus, before concluding the first Treaty of Versailles, taken Russia into his confidence and got the full approval of the tsaritsa. When the signature of the treaty was made known at St Petersburg it was warmly approved both by the partisans of Austria and by the influential clique of courtiers working for a Franco-Russian reconciliation. Douglas had reappeared in Russia and this time had no difficulty in arranging the resumption of normal diplomatic relations between the two courts. He was authorised also to try to purchase Russian neutrality in the war between Britain and France and to compensate Russia for denouncing her treaty of subsidies with Britain. Russia's reply to this overture was to try in a rather maladroit way to rouse French hostility to Prussia. Rouillé then retorted somewhat brusquely that the French Government was determined to preserve the peace of Europe and by implication, at least, rejected Russian plans to wage war on Prussia. Wide as the differences between Austria and France were in May 1756, they were even wider between France and Russia.

Nevertheless, it was clear by this time that Russia had thrown in her lot with Austria and would follow where Kaunitz led. This decision might conceivably have been reversed. Bestuzhev was still in office, but his position and prestige had been badly shaken. He himself, torn between hatred of France and detestation of Prussia, was probably incapable of formulating a clear line of policy even if he had been still strong enough to impose it on the Empress. So long as Elizabeth survived, Britain had lost her hold on Russia. But the health of the Empress was deteriorating in the summer of 1756 and this gave 'the young court', consisting of the heir apparent, the grand duke Peter, and his wife, the later Catherine II, a political importance it had not up till now enjoyed. While the grand duke was notoriously the admirer of Frederick II, his wife had now become the heavily bribed adherent and spy of the British Government. It may have been partly their influence which postponed the formal accession of Russia to the first Treaty of Versailles until 31 December 1756, though more important reasons for the delay are not difficult to discover. Russia demanded a subsidy of 5,000,000 *roubles*; France refused to give any subsidy directly to Russia and only a much smaller one to be paid through Austria. France insisted on preserving her alliance with Turkey and would not recognise a Russo-Turkish war as included in the *casus fœderis*. There were similar difficulties in regard to France's other allies, Sweden and Poland, over which Russia was intent on extending her domination. Kaunitz feared that the accession of Russia to the first Treaty of Versailles might enable Britain and Prussia to induce the Porte to attack the two empresses, especially if the anti-Russian Poles formed a confederation to resist the march of Russian troops across Poland and appealed for help to the Porte.

In the end a compromise was arranged. France, recognising, after Frederick's invasion of Saxony, the necessity for effective Russian co-operation against Prussia, abandoned her opposition to Russian troops operating on Polish territory. She received assurances from Russia, soon proved worthless, that this right would not be used to the detriment of Polish liberties. On the other hand, Russia reluctantly accepted the French contention that the subsidy she was to pay, to make possible Russian military aid on the desired scale, must pass through the hands of Austria. Even more unwillingly the Empress abandoned her attempts to break off the Franco-Turkish alliance or at least to get an undertaking that France, in the event of war between Russia and Turkey, would give no assistance to Turkey beyond the payment of subsidies. The union of the three Great Powers of continental Europe was now an accomplished fact. There was as yet, however, no offensive treaty against Prussia; and Russia, unlike Austria, maintained normal diplomatic relations with Britain throughout the Seven Years War.

Thus by concluding the subsidy treaty with Russia and trying in his innocence, not to say ignorance, to combine it with the Convention of Westminster, Newcastle had utterly destroyed the system of alliances which he and most of his contemporaries regarded as essential to Britain's security. He seems to have been entirely sincere in the hopes he expressed in March 1756 that Austria 'may now without running any risk of being attacked in Germany detach some considerable reinforcements into the Low Countries'. It did not occur to him that the court of Vienna might reasonably be annoyed that two electors, without previous consultation with the Emperor, should take it upon themselves to arrange for the peace of the Empire. Still less did he appreciate that Kaunitz, already deeply engaged in negotiations with France, would use this renewed approach from Britain as a weapon to overcome resistance at the French court to the first Treaty of Versailles.

The British envoy at Vienna, on 7 April 1756, presented a copy of the Convention of Westminster to Kaunitz, insisted that his court still had a solid preference for the Austrian alliance, and stated categorically that the British Government would decline to join in offensive schemes against Prussia 'which must carry ruin and inevitable destruction with them'. At the same time he demanded explanations of the negotiations being carried on between Austria and France. Kaunitz kept him waiting for an answer for a month. In a subsequent interview with the British envoy Maria Theresa asserted that Britain had abandoned her by concluding the Prussian treaty, 'the first intelligence of which struck me like a fit of apoplexy'. When asked whether she, an Austrian archduchess, would so far humble herself as to throw herself into the arms of France, she replied 'not into the arms but on the side of France'. Somewhat disingenuously she added that so far she had signed nothing with France and would never sign anything contrary to British interests. Both Maria Theresa and Kaunitz pointed out that the terms of the Convention of Westminster were particularly objectionable, since the exclusion of the Netherlands from the area to be neutralised invited France to attack this Austrian possession. This consideration no doubt increased their eagerness for a formal undertaking from France not to attack the Low Countries.

When the terms of the first Treaty of Versailles became known in London, Newcastle thought it imperative to try to form a counter-system and therefore redoubled his efforts to win over Russia. This was the more essential since without Russia even the loyalty of Prussia to the Convention of Westminster might well be suspect. As we have seen, however, his chances of success at St Petersburg were no greater than at Vienna. He was already, in June 1756, considering as an alternative the complete abandonment of the Continent to France and waging against her, single-handed, a maritime and colonial war in which Braddock's defeat in America and Byng's in the Mediterranean suggested ominous probabilities. Newcastle admitted sadly that his brilliant improvisation of January 1756 had recoiled on his own head. The idea that Britain and Prussia, who were being increasingly treated as outcasts by the other Great Powers, could combine effectively and successfully was grasped at Potsdam long before it began to appear at London.

Frederick had signed the Convention of Westminster with no more intention of changing his system of alliances than Newcastle, though he did envisage the separation of Britain and Austria as a result of it. He did his utmost to convince France that the convention was *une affaire momentanée*, the operation of which was limited to the present war and need not affect his permanent alliance with France. He convinced

Nivernois that there were no secret articles attached to the convention as Rouillé either believed or affected to believe. He instructed Knyphausen, his minister in Paris, to try to establish friendly relations with Madame de Pompadour, but she evaded his advances. When France showed how much she resented his conclusion of the Convention and objected above all to the renewal by it of the earlier Treaty of Westminster of 1742, Frederick went much further than he had at first meant to go with Britain. He solemnly warned France that the continuation of her present attitude might force him to consider an actual alliance with Britain. He knew of the Austro-French discussions, but was not at first greatly alarmed by them since he did not think France would so far misunderstand her true interests as to work for the aggrandisement of the new house of Habsburg-Lorraine.

When he knew that France did not mean to renew her defensive treaty with him, he invited the British Government in March 1756 to send a minister to Berlin, whereas a few months earlier he had explained that such a mission would rather embarrass him. He began to talk about a league of Protestant Powers, based on co-operation between Britain and Prussia. After the Convention of Westminster, he had believed that Austria was chiefly anxious to avoid becoming involved in a Franco-British conflict. By May 1756, however, he had formed the opinion, based largely on leakage of information from the French court as to the nature of the Austrian proposals to France, that the court of Vienna wanted nothing so much as a general war. If this were so, it was obviously urgent to ensure active and powerful support from Britain if Prussia were to be attacked because of the Convention of Westminster. Although a British minister, Andrew Mitchell, arrived at Berlin in May 1756 and at once won the confidence of Frederick, no effective steps were taken to draw Britain and Prussia into closer relations with each other in the summer of 1756.

It remains to consider the connection between the Diplomatic Revolution and the outbreak of the Seven Years War on the Continent of Europe. Some historians have argued that the reversal of alliances made a continental war inevitable. This view is based on the fallacy that the first Treaty of Versailles, though in form and appearance a defensive treaty intended to secure continental peace, was in reality the cornerstone of an offensive league against Prussia. Admittedly this was the vision which had throughout inspired Maria Theresa and Kaunitz, but they were well aware that they had a long and difficult road to travel before their designs were accomplished. They had succeeded in breaking off the Franco-Prussian alliance: now they must convince France that her interests lay in active participation in a crusade for the destruction of her former ally. The answer to the question, therefore, turns on the course and outcome of the negotiations which continued between Austria and France in the summer of 1756.

The relative positions of France and Austria were modified by the first Treaty of Versailles. Louis XV and Madame de Pompadour had made it in the hope of avoiding a continental war. Therefore when Starhemberg began to urge France into war against Prussia he no longer had the whole-hearted support of the king and his mistress. Madame de Pompadour's interest was to avoid war which might separate her from the king and prove as disastrous to her as the Austrian Succession war had to her predecessor. It would also increase the importance and influence of her enemy the count d'Argenson, Secretary of State for War and one of the leaders of the Prussophil party at court. Moreover, according to Bernis, the great advantage which Starhemberg had hitherto possessed was the threat that if France did not accept Austria's overtures, then Austria would join the enemies of France. Once the first Treaty of Versailles was signed, this threat could no longer be used. Austria had bound herself to remain neutral in the Franco-British war. If she tried the old threat under new conditions, she would awaken acute suspicions in her new ally and fling away substantial gains from the treaty. Finally, the most influential French ministers, notably d'Argenson but also Machault, Minister of Marine, and Rouillé, the Foreign Minister, were all, though for different reasons, dubious of the Austrian alliance if not actually hostile to it. They were little disposed to draw the connection closer. Starhemberg had already suffered from the ill will of d'Argenson and Rouillé and there was much less chance now of royal intervention to overcome their resistance. The Austrian negotiators still, in contrast to the drifting and divided counsels of France, possessed the great advantage of a clearly defined objective, but they no longer held the whip hand.

Hence although Bernis read to Starhemberg, on the very day on which the first Treaty of Versailles was signed, Louis XV's reply to the latest Austrian suggestions for co-operation against Prussia, for the next two months the continuance of the secret negotiation served only to emphasise the divergence between France and Austria. Louis XV wanted immediately the whole of the Netherlands for his son-in-law and himself in exchange for a promise not to aid Prussia and a cash payment. Austria required from France substantial subsidies and effective military co-operation against Prussia and would only promise to cede the Netherlands in whole or in part, conditionally on the recovery by herself of Silesia and Glatz after a successful war against Frederick. Moreover, she would never feel secure in their possession unless Prussia were partitioned and rendered powerless, whereas it was manifestly in the interests of France to keep dualism alive in Germany. France wanted to avert, with the least possible effort and expense on her part, any possibility of Austria becoming the effective sovereign of the Empire and directing against France the combined resources of Germany.

The contention that France had agreed, before the invasion of Saxony, to attack Prussia rests entirely on Starhemberg's report of a series of confidential and unofficial discussions between himself and Bernis, the leader of the Austrophil party, during the residence of the court at Compiègne in August 1756. Bernis, in his *Mémoires*, expressly denies this and contends that the obligations of the projected offensive alliance were intended by him to come into force only after Prussia had previously broken the Treaty of Aix-la-Chapelle. Thus the proposed accord between France and Austria would have been an exact parallel to the famous fourth secret article of the treaty of the two empresses of 1746. It is true that Bernis's statement was made years later and was by no means disinterested. Starhemberg certainly did not understand at the time that there was this preliminary condition to the execution of the arrangements Bernis and he elaborated together, but this misunderstanding might quite easily arise in informal talks. Even if Bernis's argument is entirely rejected as an *ex post facto* attempt to whitewash his own character and policy, there is no evidence that the measures agreed upon had the sanction of Louis XV. Moreover, Starhemberg's triumphant dispatch of 20 August in which he reported France's readiness to co-operate with Austria for the attainment of Kaunitz's ends makes it clear that there were still points of difference between the negotiators which would certainly have postponed and might ultimately have prevented agreement.

No less than seven different enclosures were required in the dispatch to explain exactly what these differences were. One of these papers, for example, listed six points on which no agreement had been reached: another mentioned eight points raised by the French negotiator which Starhemberg had promised to transmit to his court. Among the latter points was a suggestion that Austria should abandon the idea of partitioning Prussia and make use of cessions in the Low Countries to secure assistance from other Powers in her attack on Prussia. This gives some support to Bernis's representations in his *Mémoires*, since it implies that France had not yet agreed finally to Kaunitz's plans. At the most she had, with unfeigned reluctance, promised to consider means for the weakening of Prussia on condition that Austria gave active help to France in the war against Britain by allowing French occupation of the ports of Flanders and closing Trieste, Fiume and the Tuscan ports to British ships. In addition Austria must, at the end of the war, consent to a reduction of British and Hanoverian possessions equivalent to the weakening of Prussia desired by Austria. Even then Bernis was not willing to allow a French auxiliary corps to act against Prussia, although he would pay the empress-queen a substantial subsidy and place at her disposal 25,000 to 30,000 German mercenaries.

It is indeed unnecessary to enter into further detail, since by this time the plans for a projected attack on Prussia in 1757 were more and more clearly becoming an academic exercise in diplomatic bargaining. Both at

Versailles and Vienna reports of Prussian troop concentrations made it plain that the war was much more likely to result from a Prussian offensive in 1756. In spite of warnings from France and humble representations from Britain, Frederick walked blindfold into the trap set for him by Kaunitz. By his own reckless action he cemented the European coalition against him, which might otherwise never have been formed. The Seven Years War on the Continent was an early example of violent Prussian reaction against the dangers, real or supposed, of encirclement. Taking into account the character of Frederick II, it may have been a natural, but it was certainly not an inevitable, result of the Diplomatic Revolution.

CHAPTER XX

THE SEVEN YEARS WAR

THE Seven Years War in Europe, which began with the invasion of Saxony by Frederick the Great on 29 August 1756, was but one part of the world-wide struggle between Great Britain and France, which had commenced in the New World in 1754, though war between them was not officially declared until May 1756. Whilst the struggle of Prussia for existence was the main theme of the war in Europe, the operations on the Continent contributed to the larger struggle by influencing the energy and resources of the two contesting imperial Powers.

Prussia in 1756 was a new, half-finished country, composed of scattered fragments joined under one Crown, as a result of various marriages, by the chance of various deaths, and by conquest—a State without real frontiers, without geographical unity, inhabited by subjects who looked on the people of the next province as foreigners, and who owned a common allegiance to one thing alone, the person and the power of the sovereign. It lay scattered from the Niemen to the Rhine, divided into three principal groups: in the east was Prussia; in the centre the compact group of Brandenburg, Pomerania, Magdeburg, Halberstadt and Silesia; in the west the small territories of Minden and Ravensburg on the River Weser, Mark on the Ruhr, the Cleve duchies on the Rhine. On the borders of these possessions extended a fringe of contested lands, doubtful sovereignties, and potential legacies. Prussia had an artificial and precarious unity; its frontiers were one long law-suit; it had to win or lose, advance or retreat, extend or disintegrate—never satisfied since never secure. 'Everything in Prussia was tense, strained, keyed up to the limit and often beyond it; a sort of political face-lifting carried almost beyond bearing.'[1] Set a task almost beyond her strength, Prussia was always on the verge of a breakdown. Owing her existence partly to conquest, Prussia was all the more suited to become the conqueror of others.

These factors explain both Frederick's conduct in 1756 and the temptations offered to the European Powers who formed a coalition against him as a result of it. Austria's main aim was the recovery of Silesia, and the reduction of Prussia to the position of a minor German State. Russia, sharing this latter purpose, hoped to absorb East (Ducal) Prussia as a result of it. Sweden hoped to conquer Prussian Pomerania; France, the duchies of Wesel and Cleves on the Rhine. Antagonism against Austria had been a matter of habit in France, war against that Power a tradition, the securing of the Austrian Netherlands an obsession. As a result of the

[1] A. J. P. Taylor, *The Course of German History* (London, 1945), p. 28.

465

Diplomatic Revolution (ch. xix), and for the price of fighting an old friend, might not France obtain that compensation in the Austrian Netherlands which had been denied her by war in the past? France, however, had little to gain from the dismemberment of Prussia, with the resultant increase of Austrian and Russian power: for the French, European conquests, particularly that of Hanover from Great Britain, could be used at the peace treaty to set against colonial losses, whilst the defence of Hanover against French attack would engage British forces, otherwise available in the larger struggle between France and her vital enemy. The Diplomatic Revolution also explains the tentative opening of many of the campaigns of this war—an underlying, widespread conviction that the new grouping of Powers must soon give place to the old system.

Great Britain, allied to Prussia by the Treaty of Westminster, 16 January 1756, was faced with her customary dilemma. That treaty was wholly defensive in character: it stipulated the help of Prussia in case any Power (obviously France was intended) should invade Germany, the tranquillity of which the two Powers bound themselves to assure. By the inclusion of Prussia in their defensive system, the British Government hoped to stalemate France in Europe, and confine hostilities to North America. The main object of George II in Europe was the preservation of Hanover. Once war began, should Great Britain leave Hanover (and Prussia) to Providence, staunch ally of Great Britain in eighteenth-century warfare, concentrating all her effort against the real enemy, France, overseas—the 'blue water' theory? Or, while making the main effort in the colonies and at sea, should Great Britain draw French military and financial resources from overseas to continental campaigns, by continuing continental alliances—the 'old system'? The first alternative, in the event of a successful European coalition against Prussia, meant the loss of Hanover, with France left completely free to wage war elsewhere against Great Britain; the second meant mobilizing Britain's financial superiority to subsidise the armies of Hanover, Hesse and Brunswick, with a military alliance with Prussia to provide military leadership. Great Britain could not decisively attack France in Europe, but might weaken her efforts in the colonies, which remained in British opinion the main theatre of war. In any case, to allow Hanover to be completely overrun, as well as being anathema to George II, meant the sacrifice of colonial acquisitions at the making of peace. The eventual practical result in British policy was the customary, and most effective, compromise, illustrated by the changing attitude of William Pitt the elder (1708–78) to the conduct of the war.

Before he became Secretary of State for the Southern Department in 1757, and largely responsible for the prosecution of the war, Pitt had been strongly opposed to the sacrifice of British to Hanoverian interests, desirous of rigid concentration on colonial and maritime objects. 'Responsibility sobered the declamatory patriot until he saw the necessity of what he had denounced.... His greatness consisted in learning the lesson, not in having nothing to learn', as his hero-worshippers often claim;[1] as Basil Williams has said, Pitt rose on the stepping-stones of his dead self. Gradually, he admitted the value of continuing operations in Europe—which included subsidies to the Prussian army from April 1758 (p. 472), the provision of British troops to act with the troops of other German States in a separate Allied army, and combined naval and military attacks on the French coast, designed to alarm the French, and force them to keep troops disengaged from operations in Europe. These latter attacks, against Rochefort, September 1757, St Malo and Cherbourg 1758, and Belleisle 1761, have been criticised as expensive and useless; nevertheless, they were well-conceived campaigns, which alarmed the French, immobilised some part of their forces, and weakened their effort against Frederick and the allied army under Prince Ferdinand of Brunswick. Bute summed them up, writing to Pitt in 1758: 'the wisest plans may fail by timid execution, and the ablest counsels prove useless without willing instruments.'[2] That they were badly conducted on the whole is no criticism of their inherent value. In 1760, to obtain some decisive result in Europe, to strike at the one section of the French armed force that was still undominated, and so prevent a stalemate in the war, Pitt even placed his main emphasis on European operations—hence the criticism voiced in Israel Maudiut's *Considerations on the Present German War* of that year. This work argued that Pitt had allowed containing operations to become the main operations of the war, and it restated the naval and colonial theory. Maudiut assumed that there was only one way to fight France in Europe: a revival of the old Grand Alliance. The conflict between Austria and Prussia was a German civil war, which Great Britain only aggravated and prolonged by taking sides in it: her part should be that of mediation, so that peace might be restored as soon as possible, and both the rivals induced to direct their arms against France. Pitt's hope was to bring home to the French, by a decisive blow on the Continent, the futility of trying to regain in Hanover what had been lost beyond the seas, but he was not successful. By 1761, between Great Britain and France, there was strategic stalemate. The French forces were defeated at sea, French colonies taken, French trade ravished, but in Europe, France and her allies seemed on the verge of victory, with Prussia apparently outmatched. Only the providential death of the Tsaritsa Elizabeth, 5 January 1762, and the subsequent collapse of the anti-Prussian coalition, ended the deadlock.

From the beginning, the prospect for Prussia was bleak. Her population of four millions in 1756 was only one-third of that of Austria and one-fifth that of France. East Prussia was entirely isolated; Silesia was

---

[1] R. Pares, 'American versus Continental Warfare, 1739–1763', *English Historical Review*, vol. LI, p. 460.

[2] Brian Tunstall, *William Pitt, Earl of Chatham* (London, 1938), p. 209.

30-2

connected to the Mark Brandenburg by a corridor only seven miles wide; the Saxon border was only seven miles from Berlin. Engaged in a war on three fronts, with overwhelming groups of converging enemies, Frederick could only hope to manœuvre so as to deal with each particular enemy in turn, above all to prevent the Austrians and Russians from effecting a junction. Only thus could Frederick utilise his superior military skill. Separately, he was a match for any one of his opponents; together, they could overpower him. Utterly savage in his aims and methods, Frederick was educated to the highest degree in his capacity for organisation, and for concentrating his resources on a given object. The Seven Years War in Europe, particularly the conduct of the campaign of 1757, was a display of Frederick's military genius, his masterly defensive strategy, his swift and decisive offensives, and his endurance in adversity. There is no fixed system for winning battles: Frederick's merit was to adhere to simple principles, and to vary their application according to circumstances—in marked contrast to the stereotyped manœuvring of his opponents. His military assets, aided by the unity of command, by operations on interior lines, and by the disciplined strength of his State, Frederick exploited to the full. Even so, he was only saved on recurrent critical occasions by the inherent weakness of his adversaries—a coalition of courts with few common interests and many mutual suspicions, its members attempting to evade promises, or conclude separate peace treaties—and also by the mediocrity, or even inadequacy, of their military commanders. The offensive purpose of the anti-Prussian coalition is difficult to distinguish, veiled by constant defensive manœuvring tactics, and the avoidance wherever possible of major engagements—features common to all the wars of the eighteenth century down to those of the French Revolution (ch. VIII).

There are two points of view on Frederick's invasion of Saxony, which opened the war in Europe. The first holds that the Diplomatic Revolution was so closely associated with the Seven Years War in Europe that they may be regarded as cause and effect. Frederick later asserted that Austria and Russia had concluded an offensive alliance, and agreed on military action against him, which was only postponed in order to complete their preparations. In this view, the Seven Years War resulted from the purely defensive Treaty of Westminster, which Austria and Russia used as an excuse for hostile operations against Prussia. Frederick justified his action by likening himself to the quarry in a stag hunt organised by the kings and princes of Europe, who had issued invitations to their friends to be present at the kill. In this view, Frederick was provoked into a preventive war— by marching through Saxony to attack Austria in Bohemia. There is some support for this in Frederick's statement in his *Testament* of 1752 that a lightning stroke, such as the conquest of Silesia, was like a book, the original of which succeeds, while the imitations fall flat. The second view holds that Frederick deliberately provoked the war, hoping to repeat his successful gamble in Silesia in 1740 by conquering Saxony in 1756, as a preliminary to further acquisitions. 'Prudence is very suitable for preserving possessions,' he once wrote, 'but only boldness can acquire fresh ones.'[1] In either view, the avoidance or postponement of a continental war in 1756 clearly rested with Frederick, whose ultimate responsibility is beyond challenge. Frederick was aggressive and austere, because he felt himself threatened from all sides, and because he was determined to protect his new State. Whatever his motives, his action solidified the coalition against him which his invasion of Saxony was confessedly designed to prevent. The Second Treaty of Versailles was concluded between Austria and France, 1 May 1757, and the offensive alliance between Austria and Russia, 19 May 1757.

Frederick's invasion of Saxony began by investing the Saxon army, under the elector Augustus III, at Pirna, near Dresden, and by checking the attempt of an Austrian army, under Field-Marshal Browne, to relieve it, at Lobositz (1 October 1756), in Bohemian territory, not far from the Saxon frontier. The Saxon army capitulated on 16 October. The elector was allowed to retire to his kingdom of Poland, the troops were incorporated in the Prussian army, and Saxony was treated as a province of Prussia, both in exactions and devastation, until the end of the war. Austria retaliated by invoking her defensive treaty with France (the first Treaty of Versailles, 1 May 1756); in January 1757 Russia also accepted that treaty, and in February made a new treaty with Austria against Prussia. The entry of French and Russian armies into central Europe was now inevitable, whilst the delay in Saxony had compelled Frederick to postpone his invasion of Bohemia against the Austrians.

France opened her European operations by advancing her main army, 100,000 strong, under Marshal d'Estrées, against Hanover. Great Britain was unable to secure either the neutrality or the safety of that electorate, whilst Frederick, at war with the foremost military Powers of Europe, could offer no effective assistance. George II ordered the duke of Cumberland, with his army of Hanoverians, and mercenaries from the other German States (45,000 in all), the 'Army of Observation', to remain on the defensive: 'the position and operations of our army must be directed to our chief aim. This is: not to act offensively, neither against the empress-queen, nor any other Power, but merely protect our own dominions.'[2] After being defeated at Hastenbeck (26 July 1757), Cumberland fell back on Steede, on the North Sea, as his instructions ordered. There, hemmed in between the sea and the River Elbe, with no help forthcoming from England, and faced by a far stronger enemy, Cumberland signed the Convention of Kloster-Seven (8 September). As well as leaving Hanover

---

[1] P. Gaxotte, *Frederick the Great* (E.T.) (1941), p. 180.
[2] For the orders of George II, 30 March 1757, see Evan Charteris, *William Augustus, Duke of Cumberland* (1913), vol. II, pp. 252–5.

and Brunswick at the mercy of the French, this exposed to invasion the central provinces of Prussia. All auxiliary troops were to be returned to their respective countries. George II, who said that his son had ruined him and disgraced himself, conveniently forgot that on his authority Cumberland had been given full powers to do what he did; whilst the disastrous terms of the convention should not be forgotten, neither should the fact that from April, Cumberland's army had contained the whole power of France at a most critical period, and prevented it from moving against Frederick.

The Russians, under Apraksin, entered East Prussia on 11 August, took Memel, and defeated Lehwaldt at Gross Jaegersdorf, 30 August. Because of supply difficulties, their pronounced habit of counter-marching, and a false report of the death of the tsaritsa, they withdrew from East Prussia. The Prussians were not able to turn this good fortune to account, since they had to move their army to repulse the Swedes, who, operating from Stralsund, had invaded Pomerania in September; in January 1758, the Russians again took possession of East Prussia, which was not evacuated by them until the conclusion of peace.

In 1757 Frederick fought four major battles, three of which were decisive, and the last two the greatest of his victories. At the end of that year, his reputation was such that only the opposition of Maria Theresa prevented the French foreign minister, Bernis, from advocating an immediate peace before further victories made Frederick master of Germany, possibly of Europe. Estimating the Austrians, now under Prince Charles of Lorraine, as his most formidable assailant, Frederick began his campaign with the delayed attack on Bohemia, to which the invasion of Saxony had been the necessary preliminary. Seizure of the great Austrian magazines in northern Bohemia, the bases for an intended Austrian offensive against Saxony and Silesia, would effectively immobilize any Austrian effort. He failed to destroy the Austrian army at Prague (6 May), and was forced to besiege that city, into which the Austrians had retreated. An Austrian relieving army, under Daun, was attacked by Frederick at Kolin (18 June). Frederick here learned by bitter experience the difficulty of a frontal attack. He found the Austrian army in position on a range of hills parallel to and commanding the continuation of his line of march. He determined to march his army past it, with the object of wheeling into line to his right when his army should be overlapping the Austrian right flank. The Austrians, who could see what he was doing, understood what it meant. They were able to change their dispositions, and to strengthen their right. The fire of the guns against the flanks of Frederick's marching columns was so telling that the centre of the Prussian army, against Frederick's intentions, prematurely wheeled to the right into line, and attacked the Austrian front. Frederick's plan was wrecked, and he was defeated. His failure at Kolin impressed upon Frederick the necessity of surprise for success in the attack on an enemy's flank, and the impossibility of obtaining surprise against an enemy who could see what he was doing. This was the lesson by which he so brilliantly profited at Leuthen later the same year. Only the conditions of eighteenth-century warfare, the difficulties inherent in the pursuit of a routed army, saved Frederick's main army from complete destruction at Kolin. The Prussian defeat necessitated the raising of the siege of Prague, and the abandonment of Bohemia. Frederick's position was described by an English observer, on 28 August: 'The king of Prussia has now against him the Russian army and fleet, 20,000 Swedes, an army of the Empire supported by 30,000 French, and the great Austrian army of 100,000, and, as if he had not enemies enough, the convention to save Hanover from winter quarters will let loose 60 or 80 thousand more French.'[1]

The general advance by Frederick's opponents continued—the Austrians, who had regained most of Silesia, entered Berlin (16 October). At this critical period, Frederick marched against the army of the Empire, under Prince Joseph of Saxe-Hildburghausen, and the French under Soubise, in Thuringia. The Franco-German army was at first placed by Soubise in a position so good that Frederick would not risk an attack upon it. It was then moved at the suggestion of Soubise to another good position, which better covered its communications, and threatened those of the Prussians. But here the weakness of divided command was shown. Prince Joseph determined to prolong the march of the army in order to reach the Prussian rear. Frederick, who was watching this movement, immediately marched off his army behind a ridge which concealed it, so as to form his line across the head of the French advancing columns, which had no time to form line to meet him, were caught in disorder, and overwhelmed at Rossbach, 5 November—a 'genteel engagement', as Frederick described it.

He next turned against the Austrians, who had defeated Bevern at Breslau, 22 November; after a rapid march, Frederick routed them at Leuthen, 5 December, thus freeing Prussia from invasion, and recovering all Silesia except Schweidnitz. At Leuthen, the Austrian army was drawn up in two long lines. The Prussian army came up in columns perpendicular to the Austrian front. Frederick detached an advance-guard to show to the Austrians in their front, and to screen the march of his army, which moved to its right under cover towards a point in the prolongation of the left flank of the Austrian line. Here his columns wheeled into line and advanced obliquely until they were across the prolongation of the enemy's front. Then the Prussians advanced directly to the attack. The Austrians had no time to change front, except with a fragment of their army, and the portion attacked was crushed before the remainder could be brought into action.

[1] R. Lodge, *Great Britain and Prussia in the Eighteenth Century* (Oxford, 1923), p. 101.

Leuthen best exemplifies the value of the approach and battle order developed by Frederick in the Seven Years War—the oblique battle order, to cope with a numerically superior enemy. The oblique approach had been used indecisively at Prague; it was successful at Leuthen, Zorndorf (1758), and at Torgau (1760); only once, at Kunersdorf (1759), was it disastrously unsuccessful. The oblique battle order consisted of a flank attack by one wing of the Prussian army, giving it a local superiority. Cavalry and heavy artillery were concentrated on this wing, with an advance-guard of picked troops, such as the grenadier battalions. Conflict was refused with the other wing of the army, which was held in reserve, to be thrown into the front as required, or used to cover a retreat in case of a reverse. Instead of using the conventional parallel battle order, and frontal attack, responsible for the heavy casualties of eighteenth-century warfare, a flank of the enemy was attacked, and usually overwhelmed, before the mass of the enemy army had time to manœuvre to alter its front. An army of 70,000 infantry, conventionally formed three deep with 40,000 men in the first line, spread five miles from flank to flank. To change front or position must take a long time, for whatever the new position, the flank bodies were faced with a march of several miles before they could reach it. A decision was thus secured before the greater part of the enemy force came into action.

During the winter of 1757–8 Prussian operations secured the evacuation of the Swedes from Prussian Pomerania, and from Swedish Pomerania as far as Stralsund and the island of Rügen. The Prussians were only prevented from occupying these by lack of a fleet—hence the Prussian insistence on naval aid from Great Britain (p. 81). All the succeeding campaigns of the war resembled that of 1757. There were the same marches by the Prussian main army from one enemy to the next, from the Oder to the Elbe, from the Elbe to the Weser—an almost incessant movement. There was for the Prussian army little of the monotony and boredom which were a major unsolved problem of most eighteenth-century armies. As the years went by, Frederick might be strategically lost, but tactically he defied an inexorable fate, though becoming less and less able materially to carry on the struggle.

Meanwhile, a change in British policy recovered the position in western Germany. First the convention of Kloster-Seven was repudiated, 28 November, on the pretext that no term was fixed for the suspension of hostilities, and that the French interpretation of it was not justified by its terms. Next, a wider policy of support was developed. It was argued that any future collapse similar to that of Cumberland must be averted by coming to a fuller understanding with Prussia. This was finally achieved by the annual subsidy treaty (from 11 April 1758), granting a subsidy of £670,000 yearly, and whereby neither party was to carry on separate peace negotiations (p. 467). Moreover, the Army of Observation at Stade was strengthened—the British Parliament voting £1,200,000 for it for 1758 as against £164,000 in the previous year—and placed under the command of Prince Ferdinand of Brunswick. The subsidy secured the service of the best army in Germany; the Army of Observation, covering Frederick's western flank from French infiltration through Hanover, completed the whole British framework of containing operations. From then until the end of the war, Prince Ferdinand succeeded in neutralising ever-increasing French armies, leaving the main war in Europe to be fought by Prussia against Austria and Russia. Ferdinand thus enabled Frederick to give that dogged resistance to those two Powers, which would otherwise have been almost impossible. Without that aid, the burden on Prussia would have been unsupportable. Moreover, French attention and energies were distracted in exhausting and strategically unsound operations on the Continent, whilst Great Britain remained free to devote her main effort to the conquest of what, even after the bargaining away of colonial counters in the peace negotiations, remained an embarrassingly large empire.

Despite his grievous losses in 1757—400 officers killed, and 14,000 men killed or wounded at Prague; 400 officers killed and 13,000 men killed or wounded at Kolin; 540 men killed or wounded at Rossbach; 6000 men killed or wounded at Leuthen—Frederick was still able to put into the field in 1758 the same number of troops (150,000) as in the previous year. He began operations by once more moving against the Austrians, with the same unsuccessful result as in 1757. After clearing Silesia by retaking Schweidnitz (16 April), he invaded Moravia to besiege the fortress of Olmütz. This campaign illustrates another of the major factors of eighteenth-century warfare, the impossibility of operating far from magazines and bases in hostile country, because of the vulnerability of the baggage train (ch. VIII). The siege of Olmütz had to be raised in July, after Loudoun had cut off a convoy of four thousand waggons bringing supplies and ammunition to Frederick, and because of the inadequacy in either siege or campaign operations of the engineers—a marked cause of complaint to many eighteenth-century commanders. The convoy itself necessitated an escort of 13,000 men, whilst the complete baggage train of Frederick's army on the consequent withdrawal from Moravia into Bohemia comprised over four thousand waggons, necessitating the division of the army for its protection, and rendering it vulnerable to attack from decided opponents. The protection both of such baggage trains and of supplies between the base and forward units was a potent reason for the development in this century of light infantry and light cavalry formations.

As in 1757, the Russians produced the first real threat to Prussia. After their re-occupation of East Prussia, they moved forward, under Fermor, against Brandenburg, inspired by a request from Austria for more active participation in the war. There was also a threat of joint action by the

Russians and Swedes in Pomerania—Sweden having promised 30,000 men for such action. The Prussian army under Dohna, which had been blockading Stralsund, had to move to stop the Russian advance. Fermor besieged Cüstrin, at the confluence of the Oder with the Warthe, in Brandenburg, 15 August. Frederick, moving to relieve that town, defeated the Russians at Zorndorf, 25 August, in the bloodiest encounter of the war. Fermor withdrew by stages into Poland, and Brandenburg was saved. The Swedes, though deprived of Russian aid, and unable to retain Prussian Pomerania, held it long enough to deprive Frederick of its resources in this year—they withdrew to Swedish Pomerania only in December.

Frederick, for whom there was rarely rest in the campaigning seasons, had now to march rapidly to meet the Austrians, who had invaded Saxony; 'our infantry regiments', wrote Frederick to his brother, Prince Henry, 'are becoming postillions and couriers'; a significant tribute to their commander and their discipline that they continued to be able to meet the ceaseless calls upon them. Daun's objective in Saxony was the recapture of Dresden, and his attack was only diverted by the arrival of Frederick. Meanwhile, a second Austrian force entered Silesia, and laid siege to Neisse. Frederick left Dresden (26 September) to relieve Neisse, and was barred by Daun in an impregnable position. Annoyed by Daun's cautious tactics, and anxious to save Silesia, Frederick accepted battle at Hochkirch, 10 October. Here, once more, only Austrian failure to follow up victory saved Frederick, and enabled him to enter Silesia, compelling the Austrians to raise the siege of Neisse.

In the west, Ferdinand cleared Westphalia, Hanover, Brunswick, and Hesse from the French. He captured Minden (14 March), drove the French over the Rhine at Emmerich (27 March), and defeated the new French commander, Clermont, at Crefeld (23 June). He was not able to retain all these gains, nor was he able to invade the Austrian Netherlands, as he had intended. Faced by a French counter-attack under Soubise, which invaded Hesse and took Cassel, and by a force under Broglie which gained a small victory at Sonderhausen (23 July), Ferdinand nevertheless succeeded in holding Hanover and Westphalia, and in keeping the French fully engaged; so much so that the foreign minister, Bernis, again advocated peace, and had to be replaced in November by Choiseul.

In 1759 the strain on Frederick, and on his possessions, began to show. He could put only 100,000 men in the field, and was unable to seize the initiative by opening the offensive. But the Austrians, playing the eighteenth-century game of warfare, Seven Years War version, waited for the usual and expected Prussian attack. Being spared that, they next waited for the accustomed second move of the campaign, from the Russians. Daun, now Austrian commander-in-chief, was a master at waiting for his turn: the only offensive battle he ever planned, Liegnitz in 1760, was forced on him by the empress, and ended in a Prussian victory. The

Russians, under their new commander, Saltykov, advanced slowly from Poland, seemingly justifying Frederick's description of him to his brother, 'said to be more imbecile than anything in the clodhopper way which Russia has yet produced'. Saltykov methodically invaded Brandenburg, defeated the Prussian general, Wedell, at Züllichau, 23 July, and took Frankfurt-am-Oder. Reinforced by a small Austrian force, whose turn it now was to appear, Saltykov utterly defeated Frederick's main army at Kunersdorf, 13 August. A decisive combined thrust by the Russians and Austrians, such as Frederick himself in a similar situation would now have effected, might conceivably have finally overwhelmed the temporarily despairing king of Prussia, but once again, suspicion rather than real interest motivated Russian action. Believing Austria was not taking a vigorous part in the war, and determinined to maintain his own army, Saltykov retired whence he had come.

Meanwhile, in August, the imperial forces took Leipzig, Torgau, and Wittenberg; on 14 September, Daun took Dresden. Frederick, spared by the Russian withdrawal, moved to combat this threat, regaining all Saxony except Dresden. An army under Finck, sent by Frederick to cut Austrian communications between Dresden and Bohemia, was compelled by Daun to capitulate at Naxen, 21 November; the Austrians thus retained Dresden.

Operations in the west in 1759 began with the northern French army, based on Wesel, directed against Hanover and Westphalia, and with the southern army, based on Frankfort, aimed at Hesse. Ferdinand attempted to prevent the attack on Hanover by striking first in Hesse, but was defeated by Broglie at Bergen, 13 April, and pushed back into Westphalia. The French took Minden, and Münster, the great Westphalian fortress—a direct threat to Prussia, only retrieved by Ferdinand's rout of the French at Minden, 1 August, which, whilst also saving Hanover, secured the retreat of the French from Hesse. But French policy under Choiseul now changed to a concentration of force against Great Britain, leaving the Austrians and Russians to deal with Prussia. By the third Treaty of Versailles (March), Choiseul reduced French subsidies to Austria by half —six million *florins*; limited military support to 100,000 troops on the Rhine; refused to guarantee the return of Silesia to Austria as a war aim, and renounced the Austrian Netherlands on behalf of Don Philip, duke of Parma (arranged in exchange for the restoration of Parma to Austria by the second Treaty of Versailles). Believing that the war in Germany was only kept going by British financial support and supplies, and that only in western Germany could France secure the means of recovering territory lost overseas in the main struggle, Choiseul conceived a plan of invasion of England—a desperate blow at the financial heart of the enemy, not to conquer, but to cause panic and financial collapse. As Pitt had once said when describing the consternation that would spread through the city, 'when the noble, artificial, yet vulnerable fabric of public credit should crumble in their hands': 'Paper credit may be invaded in Kent.'[1] Choiseul's plan envisaged a *coup de main* upon London from the army in Flanders: 20,000 men from Ostend to land on the Essex coast, at Maldon, on the Blackwater estuary, two marches from London; 20,000 men from Brittany to land in the Clyde estuary, cross Scotland, and seize Edinburgh. A squadron, under the privateer Thurot, based on Dunkirk, was to draw off the British fleet by menacing the Irish coast, whilst the main French fleets, of Brest (under Conflans) and of Toulon (under La Clue), were to concentrate to cover the military blow. Pitt refused to be diverted from his policy by this threat. There was no calling out of the militia, no raising of volunteers, no issue of orders for clearing the threatened coastal areas. The defeat and disablement of the British main fleet was the sole expedient which could bring this enterprise within the limits of a sound military risk; Great Britain confidently placed reliance on a purely naval defence. Only the combined French battle fleet could force the way for such a coup—and the British blockade prevented that combination being effected. La Clue's fleet, attempting a junction, was dealt with at Lagos, 19 August, by Boscawen; the Brest fleet, when it came out, was defeated at Quiberon Bay, in November, by Hawke. These victories, as well as ruining the French navy (and therefore the invasion scheme), also influenced the new king of Spain, Charles III (Don Carlos of Naples), who retained bitter memories of British treatment of Naples in the War of the Austrian Succession, to continue Spanish neutrality.

The threatened invasion also brought to light one other vexed question, the rights of neutral maritime States in time of war, and the British right of search. Choiseul hoped to encourage the neutral maritime States to form an alliance against Great Britain, because of interference with their trade. By such an alliance, he hoped to secure the Dutch navy for use by France, and also support from the two Baltic countries, Sweden and Russia, with whom Great Britain was not at war. This would threaten British command of the Channel and the North Sea, at the crucial moment of invasion. Spain and the Mediterranean states of Naples, Tuscany, Sardinia and Genoa, were also involved in this problem, Spain having many other long-standing differences with Great Britain, particularly over logwood cutting in Spanish Honduras, and contraband trade between Spanish colonies and the British West Indies.

The main complaints of all neutrals were the actions of British privateers against their merchant shipping, and the British interpretation of 'neutral rights'. Privateers were ships owned and fitted out by private persons, acting under letters of marque, 'the merchant adventurers' marriage lines',[2] from the Government of a State, authorising them to capture enemy ships, and ships of neutral Powers carrying troops, arms and warlike supplies—

[1] R. Pares, 'American versus Continental Warfare', *English Historical Review*, vol. LI, p. 441.   [2] Michael Lewis, *The Navy of Britain* (London, 1948), p. 45.

'contraband of war'—to enemy ports. These captured vessels were dealt with by Admiralty courts, and if condemned as legal prizes, the profits from the sale of ship and cargo went to the privateer owner whose vessel had made the capture—a standing temptation to excesses by privateers. Great Britain further claimed that enemy goods were not protected from capture by being carried in neutral shipping, whereas the neutrals claimed their flag automatically protected all cargo except war contraband. The British interpretation not only implied that enemy goods so carried might be seized, but also that Great Britain had a right to stop and search neutral ships on the high seas. By the Rule of 1756, Great Britain also claimed that neutrals might not engage in any trade with a belligerent State which was closed to them in time of peace—thus, trade with French West Indian islands, closed in time of peace by the working of the French navigation laws, but released by the French in time of war to obtain general supplies and munitions, should not be carried on by neutrals. This trade could be effected either between French colonies and those of neutral Powers in the West Indies, or direct between French colonies and the neutral States in Europe. To lessen the exasperation of the neutrals, Pitt brought pressure on prize courts to release as many ships as possible, and he attempted to restrain the excesses of privateers by limiting commissions to the larger ships, of over 100 tons and ten guns. Maritime rights, however, were sacrosanct, whatever their reaction on the war in Europe.

For the last great year of the war, 1760, Frederick was still able to muster about 100,000 men against the 223,000 opposed to him—a marvel of organisation. The initiative again lay with his opponents. The Austrians began by invading Silesia, Loudoun defeating a Prussian force under Fouquet at Landshut, 23 June, and occupying Glatz, 26 July. Another Austrian force under Daun, and a Russian army under Czernitcheff moved to assist Loudoun, who, with these reinforcements all within reach (a force of 90,000 against the 30,000 of Frederick), attacked the Prussian army at Liegnitz, 15 August, and was defeated—a marked failure of co-ordination by the anti-Prussian coalition. Whilst Frederick was occupied in Silesia, the Austrians and Russians entered Brandenburg, and occupied Berlin (9–13 October). Frederick next moved to relieve that city, but was unable to check the retiring invader. Similarly, the Austrians were able to recover most of the electorate of Saxony, and although defeated at Torgau, 3 November, still maintained their hold of Dresden. Torgau was the last battle fought by Daun and Frederick, indeed, only once again in his life did Frederick take the field, and that without recourse to major fighting. Torgau again confirmed that, tactically, Frederick remained a master, in a now evident strategic stalemate.

Events in the west were equally indecisive. Broglie defeated Ferdinand's nephew, the hereditary prince of Brunswick, at Corbach (10 July). On Ferdinand's orders, the prince then made a diversion on the lower Rhine, but was defeated by Castries at Kloster-Camp (16 October). Only Ferdinand's victory at Warburg prevented the further progress of the French, and saved Westphalia and Hanover.

This military stalemate in Europe was confirmed by the events of 1761. Loudoun captured Schweidnitz in Silesia, 16 October, and the Austrians were able to take up winter quarters in Silesia and Western Saxony. The Russians, after entering Pomerania, occupied the maritime fortress of Kolberg in December, and remained in Pomerania for the winter. In the west, Ferdinand invaded Hesse in February, but, defeated by Broglie near Grünberg (21 March), was compelled to retire. But he, in his turn, checked a French invasion of Westphalia and Hanover at Villinghausen (15 July). Prussia remained unconquered, but in a desperate position—provinces which had hitherto supplied Frederick with recruits, money, and provisions, and which enabled him to carry on the unequal struggle, were now denied to him, whilst with the resignation of Pitt, 5 October, the steady support of Great Britain, and the continuation of the British subsidy, were already in doubt. At the close of 1761, Frederick thus summed up the position:

Every bundle of straw, every transport of recruits, every consignment of money, all that reaches me, is, or becomes a favour on the part of my enemies, or a proof of their negligence, for they could, as a matter of fact, take everything. Here in Silesia every fortress stands at the disposal of the enemy. Stettin, Cüstrin and Berlin itself are open to the Russians to deal with at their pleasure. In Saxony, Daun's first move, so to speak, throws my brother back over the Elbe....If fortune continues to treat me so mercilessly I shall undoubtedly succumb. Only she can deliver me from my present situation.[1]

Fortune relented, and favoured Frederick. By the death of the tsaritsa Elizabeth of Russia, 5 January 1762, the driving force behind the anti-Prussian combination since 1759 was removed. It was she who had stood out against suggestions of peace, determined on partitioning Frederick's territories, and reducing him to the rank of an elector, rendered harmless to his neighbours for the future. As Frederick was equally determined that not a single village under his rule should be lost, prolongation of the war was inevitable—which, saving a miracle, could only end by the complete collapse of the Prussian monarchy. Elizabeth was succeeded by her nephew, Peter III, who distrusted Austria, detested France, and almost worshipped the Prussian king, with whom he signed an immediate peace, 5 May, restoring all conquests, and securing Prussian support for a war against Denmark to assert the rights of his family in Slesvig-Holstein. East Prussia and eastern Pomerania were evacuated by the Russians; Sweden also followed the Russian example, and concluded peace, at

[1] E. Daniels, 'The Seven Years War', *Cambridge Modern History* (Cambridge, 1909), vol. VI, pp. 297–8.

Hamburg, 22 May. By a later agreement, of 16 June, part of the Russian army was placed at Frederick's disposal, who was now able to turn with renewed vigour against the isolated Austrians. Daun was defeated at Burkersdorf, 21 July, and when Schweidnitz was retaken, 9 October, Silesia was secured to Prussia. In Saxony, Prince Henry defeated the Austrians at Freiberg, the only great action of the Seven Years War in which Prussian troops were victorious when not personally commanded by their king. The assassination of Peter III, and his succession by Catherine II, in July, broke the alliance which had signally relieved Frederick—Catherine wanted no war against Austria for Prussian interests, still less a war against Denmark for Holstein—but equally she had no desire to renew the war with Prussia. It was impossible for Austria alone to defeat Prussia, and recover Silesia. As Silesia could not be regained, there was no hope for France of securing compensation in the Austrian Netherlands for herself. The death of Elizabeth thus opened the way for military stalemate to be solved by the conclusion of peace, hitherto prevented by the uncompromising attitude of Prussia and Russia.

The main course of the peace negotiations was, first, an attempt to make a separate peace between Great Britain and France, which failed, and resulted in the Family Compact between France and Spain, 15 August 1761. The defection of Russia and Sweden from the anti-Prussian coalition next left the continental war as a purely dynastic contest between the two German rulers of Prussia and Austria. There followed the renewed, ultimately successful, discussions between Great Britain and France. Austria, unable to achieve her aims alone, then made peace with Prussia. The making of peace reflected the dual character of the war, and recognised the fact that the nature of the objects which had caused the war between France and Great Britain were totally distinct from the quarrels of the other European Powers.

Frederick had suggested in 1759, and again in 1761, that France and Great Britain should open separate negotiations to settle their wider differences before a general conference undertook the settlement of Europe. He believed that if France once made peace with her real and original enemy, she would soon find a means of forcing Austria to follow her example. With the colonial struggle ended, the minor European conflict must quickly collapse. Frederick believed that

the separate peace between France and England could serve as the basis of the whole and that as soon as their differences were entirely settled, those two powers, concerting together, might agree upon the preliminary articles for a general peace, which the other belligerent powers must accept.

The obstacle to this proposal was Pitt, who refused to desert Frederick, or to consider any form of peace in which he was not included. Pitt further believed that much more should be taken from France before peace terms were considered; his plan for naval and commercial supremacy at the expense of France, based on a sound eighteenth-century conception of international relationship, was irrefutable. Even so, before his resignation, Pitt had advised Frederick to purchase peace by cession of territory: this became the main theme in the policy of Bute, 'resolved to take the principal part, but undetermined how to play it'.[1]

The usual accusation is that Bute and his colleagues alienated Frederick by withholding the British subsidy at a time of dire necessity—Frederick still spoke in 1773 of the infamous way in which he had been treated. But opportunity, not obligation, was the keynote of eighteenth-century diplomatic practice, and Frederick was the last man able to plead breach of treaty in foreign relations—he himself had made suggestions for a separate peace before Great Britain in this war. In fact, the subsidy was never absolutely refused by Great Britain until after Frederick repudiated it, because the conditions attached to it were unacceptable to him. In 1762 Frederick was far advanced in a secret and disloyal negotiation with Russia, the terms of which the British ministry would have disapproved if it had known them. Peter's change of front induced Frederick to prepare a scheme for the eventual partition of Austria's possessions. The secrecy maintained by Frederick as to his dealings with Russia was the main British cause of complaint as Bute wrote on 9 April 1762.

His Prussian Majesty has still continued to direct his ministers here...to press the payment of his former subsidy. But the condition upon which the King has declared ...was the employment of it towards the procurement of peace and not towards the continuation of war... to see the bounty of this nation converted to so pernicious a use as that of fomenting new troubles in Europe would be of all things the most disagreeable. The King must therefore receive further intelligence, and see more clearly what use is intended to be made of any subsidy which he might be induced to give, before he can determine to give any at all. And this pause is so much the more necessary as, in case H.P.M's treaty with Russia be actually concluded, and the might of that Empire taken consequently out of the opposite scale, he will then... have so little occasion for any assistance from England that he might even be ready to furnish a body of troops for H.M's defence.[2]

In short, the British declined to pay British money for a war in which Frederick and Peter contemplated the partition of the Austrian and Danish dominions.

Bute's blunder was Frederick's excuse rather than his reason. Bute's methods were clumsy and inconsiderate, but the subsidy had been given to preserve Frederick from ruin. In 1762, after his alliance with Russia, Frederick intended to use it to prolong the war. Bute was under no obligation to continue a subsidy originally granted for a totally different

[1] R. Pares, 'American versus Continental Warfare', *English Historical Review*, vol. LI, p. 463.
[2] J. H. Rose, 'Frederick the Great and England', Part II, *English Historical Review*, vol. XXIX, pp. 269–70.

purpose from that which Frederick now proposed to apply it. The breach between Great Britain and Prussia was inevitable: it occurred because of the fundamental divergence in the alliance from the beginning, well as that alliance had worked since 1758. 'Few alliances, having a beginning so sudden and almost fortuitous, were ever more loyally observed during the same length of time, and that, too, amidst conditions wholly different from those which brought about the original compact.'[1] Britain was at war with France and wanted Prussia to fight the French: to Prussia, Austria, not France, was the real enemy. Even before the Subsidy Treaty, Frederick had urged the sending of a British fleet to the Baltic to neutralise those of Sweden and Russia, with whom Great Britain was not at war. This was never possible—apart from the danger of cutting off supplies of naval stores from the Baltic, there were too many, and more pressing, claims on British naval strength in her main struggle. As the war progressed, British aims were largely achieved: not so those of Frederick, who wished the alliance to continue for what were increasingly Prussian, not British, interests. After 1760, with Prussia in a seemingly hopeless position, Britain was less and less interested in a war prolonged merely by Frederick's refusal to sacrifice territory to his enemies—she was prepared, as so often, to offer good advice rather than hard cash. Misreading the basic realities of eighteenth-century relations, overzealous for peace, completely out-manœuvred by Choiseul, disregarding completely the fact that military events were likely to tell in Great Britain's favour, Bute hoped for a permanent peace with France rather than the traditional uneasy truce. This explains his disregard of both British and Prussian interests during the making of peace. Operations in Germany in 1762 particularly gave him a valuable lever in the negotiations, which he rashly threw away at the outset. This disregard had serious consequences in the next decade—British isolation in the War of American Independence, the efforts of Frederick the Great in that war to obstruct British recruiting of troops in German principalities, and the refusal of passage through Prussian territory to any German soldiers in British service.

Choiseul countered Pitt's aim of continuing the war with France until she could agree to terms which ensured British supremacy by a threat to draw in Spain unless Pitt agreed to more moderate terms. After the British ultimatum, 29 July 1761, requiring 'a categorical answer and a final determination thereon', Choiseul prepared to continue the struggle with the help of Spain. He thus explained his motives in a memorandum drawn up in 1765:

I then proposed to Your Majesty two games to play together: one to keep up the negotiation with England in such a way that if it did not succeed this time it would serve from its simplicity as a base for the general negotiation which must take place

---

[1] J. H. Rose, 'Frederick the Great', *English Historical Review*, vol. XXIX, p. 275.

if Pitt fell before the influence of Bute. At the same time—and this was the second game which I thought essential—I entered into an exchange of views with Spain, so devised that if we were to make peace that Crown would find it to its interest to support us in the negotiation, and guarantee the stability of the treaty. If, on the contrary, we failed in this, my plan was that Spain should be drawn into the war, and that France would be able to profit by the events which this new complication might produce, and repair her losses. Finally, if the event proved unfortunate, I had in view that the losses of Spain would lighten those which France might suffer.[1]

The Family Compact, and its Secret Convention, stipulated that France was not to make peace until the many Spanish grievances against Great Britain were remedied, and that Spain was to declare war on Great Britain if peace was not concluded within eight months, by 1 May 1762. Spain on that date was to receive Minorca, taken from the British by the French in May 1756, and was to garrison it for the duration of the war. In the event of a successful outcome to the war, France was to make every effort to assure the cession of that island to Spain at the making of peace. Other maritime States wishing to join the convention should be permitted to do so. Portugal was to be invited to become a party to it, in order to close her ports and trade to Great Britain; in case of refusal, she was to be treated as a common enemy, and an ally of England. All military plans were to be concerted. The followers of the original Spanish plan were obsessed, like Napoleon later, with the idea that Great Britain's power rested entirely on her commerce, and they anticipated Napoleon in suggesting to France the formation of a continental system for the exclusion of British trade from European ports. Choiseul was to secure the adhesion of Russia to this scheme; Spain herself would deal with the Mediterranean Powers. The plan also proposed attacks on Gibraltar, Jamaica, and Ireland, and even suggested the invasion of the Austrian Netherlands by France, on the old concept of securing some indemnity against British conquests beyond the sea—a strange insurance policy against the probable failure of those grandiose projects. Choiseul preferred Spain to concentrate her effort on Portugal—who refused the offer to join against Britain, and was invaded in 1762. Assisted by a British force, she offered successful resistance. Only as a last counsel of despair in 1762 did Choiseul plan a joint French-Spanish counter-stroke at Great Britain, to rush her into accepting reasonable terms of peace—by an invasion over an uncommanded sea. Local temporary command for five to six weeks was to be secured by diversion to dissipate British naval defence—by operations in Portugal, and feints against Gibraltar and Jamaica. In order to avoid arousing suspicion by large troop concentrations, the operation was envisaged in successive waves, the troops (100,000 men) to act as a reserve to the Westphalian army between the Meuse and the Lower Rhine, only marching to the coast as and when required.

[1] J. S. Corbett, *England in the seven years war* (1907), vol. II, p. 185.

This secret alliance between the two Bourbon Powers was the occasion of Pitt's resignation, the cabinet refusing to accept his demand for immediate measures against threatened attack. Choiseul continued peace negotiations with Great Britain merely to gain time for the alliance to mature, and Great Britain ultimately had to face this new enemy. War was declared 2 January 1762; by the end of that year, Havana, Manila, and the Philippines were all in British hands, largely as a result of plans prepared by Pitt before his resignation.

For reasons shown above, all attempts at direct peace negotiations amongst the European Powers were unsuccessful before the death of Elizabeth. One example may be cited. On 22 January 1761, the French ambassador at St Petersburg notified the Russian Chancellor that peace was a necessity for France, because of her internal condition, and pointed out that Prussia, in her then desperate situation, would surely listen to reasonable propositions. A similar suggestion was made by Austria the following day. The tsaritsa replied by stipulating that there could be no public overtures until the 'essential and permanent crippling of the king of Prussia', original object of the alliance, had been accomplished. To this, she added terms which Frederick could never accept as long as the slightest possibility of fighting on existed—Austrian retention of actual conquests in Silesia, rectification of Sweden's Pomeranian frontier, and the ceding of Ducal Prussia to herself. A peace congress might be held, but the war should continue—a truce would only be advantageous to Frederick. Nothing resulted from the suggestion made by Galitzin, Russian ambassador at London, for a congress of all belligerents and their allies at Augsburg to adjust a general peace.

In 1762 direct negotiations between France and Great Britain were reopened, and preliminaries of peace, signed at Fontainebleau, 3 November, were confirmed by the Treaty of Paris, 10 February 1763. By the terms concerning the war in Europe, France agreed to restore the territory of all Great Britain's German allies, with the exception of Prussia: Hanover, Hesse, and Brunswick were evacuated and restored. Prussian territory (the Rhenish possessions of Cleves, Gelder and Mörs) was only to be evacuated with the knowledge and consent of Maria Theresa. Both sides agreed to render no further assistance to their European allies. Great Britain refused to make peace with France unless Spain also made peace at the same time. Choiseul induced Spain to agree to treat in August 1762, and Spain evacuated Portugal by the final treaty.

The settlement between Prussia, Austria and Saxony, concluded at Hubertusburg, 15 February 1763, reflected the military stalemate by restoring the *status quo ante bellum*. Frederick refused to allow Russia to participate in the negotiations for the peace that was to conclude a war from which she had already withdrawn. Frederick remained the undisputed owner of Silesia, Austria making no further armed attempt to recover that province. Even when negotiating peace with Russia in 1762, Frederick had been prepared to give up East Prussia in return for Saxony: now he had to relinquish that electorate, which he had hoped to retain in whole, or in part, to its elector, Augustus III, though refusing to pay any compensation for the damage inflicted on it. He also promised to vote for the archduke Joseph, eldest son of Maria Theresa, as king of the Romans.

British abandonment of West Indian islands and of French possessions in the East Indies answers the gibe as to the abandonment of Prussia. When a Power gives up part of its conquests in order to assure the *status quo ante bellum* to a hard-pressed partner, it is fair to assume some connection between the concessions of the victor and the restitutions made by the enemy to that partner. The action of the British Government in the Anglo-French negotiations assured to Prussia the recovery of her western possessions, which she had been unable to defend, and could not have recovered but for colonial sacrifices made by her ally to France.

Although the Seven Years War caused few territorial changes in Europe, it exercised an important influence on the position and future policies of the European powers. Fortune, and Frederick's military ability, had saved Prussia from extinction as a Great Power,

It could never be hoped that Prussia, a country vulnerable to an extreme degree on every frontier, could be effectively guarded against invasion. The only question was whether Frederick, the sovereign of this small, poor, ill-populated state, could keep an army in being against the united powers of two great empires, each able to bring into the field armies numerically superior to his own, and infinitely more elastic. That the answer to this question was favourable to Frederick was not only due to the military genius which enabled him again and again to attack and defeat the enemy, but also to the defective combination and mutual jealousies of his Russian and Austrian opponents, and to certain ingrained defects of temperament of which he was able to take full advantage.[1]

For seven years Frederick had held his own against the imperfectly co-ordinated force of Austria, Russia, Sweden, the South German States, and a great part of that of France, though at a terrible cost to his possessions. One in nine of the Prussian population perished in the war; the financial cost of which was only one-quarter to one-third covered by subsidies, and exactions on occupied territory. Frederick himself wrote:

Prussia's population had diminished by 500,000 during the Seven Years War. In a population of 4,500,000 that decrease was considerable. The nobility and the peasants had been pillaged and ransomed by so many armies that they had nothing left except the miserable rags which covered their nakedness. They had not credit enough to satisfy their daily needs. The towns possessed no longer a police. The spirit of fairness, and order had been replaced by anarchy and self-interest. The judges and the revenue authorities had given up their work owing to the frequency of invasions. In the

[1] H. A. L. Fisher, *A History of Europe*, one volume edition (London, 1936), pp. 759–60.

absence of laws a spirit of recklessness and of rapacity arose. The nobility and the merchants, the farmers, the working man and the manufacturers had raised the price of their labour and products to the utmost. All seemed intent upon ruining each other by their exactions. That was the terrible spectacle which the formerly so flourishing provinces offered after the conclusion of the war. The appearance of the provinces resembled that of Brandenburg after the end of the Thirty Years' War.[1]

It was estimated in the first year after the war that Pomerania had a right to 8766 head of livestock at 25 *thalers* each, and that 1246 burnt-down peasant houses required replacement. The Neumark had lost 68,866 sheep, and Cüstrin had been entirely destroyed by bombardment. In the open country of Silesia, 3723 houses, 2225 barns, and 3495 stables were required; in the towns, 2917 houses, 399 barns, 1380 stables. The Electoral Mark had lost 25,000 horses, 17,000 bullocks, 20,900 cows, 121,000 sheep, and 35,000 pigs.

By forcing Prussia into the ranks of the Great Powers, Frederick found himself almost completely isolated in Europe—on bad terms with Great Britain, without diplomatic relations with France, always the enemy of Austria and Saxony. In this situation, an alliance with Russia was compulsory. Russia, who gained little save prestige from participation in the war, found a common interest with Frederick in the fate of the kingdom of Poland.

France had played a subordinate role on the Continent, absorbed in unrewarding and exhausting operations. Still the foremost Power of Europe in population and military resources, she was no longer equal to her former reputation in war. With a still ostensible claim to be considered the first nation in Europe, but weakened by domestic controversies, France was profoundly shocked by the blow to her morale. A peace settlement which secured the maritime supremacy of Great Britain, and the military prestige of Prussia, could only be for France 'the disgraceful peace', to be remedied as soon as possible. Moreover, habit of mind and policy render difficult a reversal of alliances, such as had brought France into this war. Her great traditional hostility (to Austria) was sunk far too deep in the national consciousness to be uprooted by a generation of original diplomacy. The disastrous result of the Seven Years War, gravely shaking the monarchy, and preparing its downfall, was one reason why French governments after 1791 hurriedly returned to the known ways, to the tradition of war against Austria—the Austrian Netherlands were captured by Revolutionary France. France was no longer the arbiter of Europe. In the years which followed the Seven Years War, the balance of power shifted eastward. Austria, Russia, and Prussia dominated the affairs of the Continent, and French influence, particularly in Eastern Europe, was superseded. Great events, like the partition of Poland 1772,

[1] Fisher, *A History of Europe*, pp. 765–6.

and the dismemberment of Turkey 1774, took place without French participation.

Great Britain failed to make the best of either world, Old or New. That she was in a position to extract still harder terms than she did is certain. Pitt would have done so by crushing France beyond her power to retaliate, and reducing her to a second-rate Power. In his view, the peace was insecure, because it restored the enemy to her former greatness, and inadequate, because the places gained were no equivalent for those surrendered. Pitt's realism was opposed by those who believed that, even if France were crushed, she could not be kept indefinitely in that state. A vigorous people like the French would assuredly reassert themselves, and take revenge. Moreover, a virtual monopoly of the sources of naval power would produce a hostile grand alliance of exasperated maritime States. To do as she would be done to, and to rest content with a situation which would be endurable to a chivalrous enemy, Great Britain sacrificed much, to little purpose. She had already gone beyond what France could accept; to that age, concessions showed weakness, not strength, and revenge was already in Choiseul's mind. Besides, it was of no use to conclude what had been a war of intervention by an isolationist peace. The results of the Seven Years War meant that the wider struggle between Great Britain and France, the struggle for dominion rather than dominions, still had to be decided.

CHAPTER XXI

THE DEVELOPMENT OF THE AMERICAN COMMUNITIES

I. LATIN AMERICA

SPAIN in 1714 appeared to retain its American empire through the forbearance of the rest of Europe. At the end of the War of the Spanish Succession many outside observers thought that the Indies, or part of them, could easily be detached from Spain. Whether this opinion was right or wrong, however, the attempt was not made. Spain was supported politically by France, and the enemies of Spain wanted an extension of their trade rather than an extension of their colonial possessions. Spanish America remained Spanish; but the reputation of Spain, political, military and economic, had sunk very low, and throughout the first half of the eighteenth century a stream of books and pamphlets appeared, both in Spain and abroad, condemning Spanish policy and the feebleness and incompetence of Spanish administration in the Indies.

Most foreign writers on the subject were divided between their envy of the wealth, actual or potential, of the American kingdoms, and their contempt for Spanish mismanagement. This distinction appears very clearly, for example, in the *Spanish Empire in America*, by 'an English Merchant', [John Campbell], published in London in 1747. The author writes 'The weakness of the Spaniards is, properly speaking, the weakness of their Government. There wants not people, there wants not a capacity of defence, if the Governors and other Royal Officers were not so wanting in their duty, and did not thereby set so ill an example as corrupts and effeminates all who are subject to them.' The 'English merchant' proceeds to give a list of foreign attacks on Spanish colonial possessions, of which some succeeded, but more were beaten off by a spirited local defence; and he concludes: 'So it seems to be a thing out of dispute, that it is not so much the weakness of the Spaniards, as the weakness of their Councils, which have occasioned their losses in these parts.' These are, admittedly, the opinions of a man interested in a war against Spain for the sake of trade; but they are strikingly corroborated by Spanish writers. Jorge Juan and Antonio de Ulloa began the preface to their *Noticias Secretas de América* of 1749 with very similar words. 'The countries of the Indies, fertile, rich and flourishing...distant from their Prince and from his principal Ministers, governed by persons who often regard no interests but their own,...are now reduced to such a condition...that justice has

487

no authority, and reason no power, to make any stand against disorder and vice.'[1] The report which follows is one of the frankest and most detailed exposures of petty tyranny and administrative corruption ever written; it was, moreover, a secret report, written for the Crown by two naval officers who had been sent to South America on a scientific mission, and who had no motive for blackening the colonial Government. The glaring contrast between the wealth and potential power of the Indies, and the feebleness of the Spanish administration, was coupled by some writers with a sense of guilt concerning the manner in which the Indies had been acquired. This sense of remorse was not new—it had haunted Spanish theorists since the sixteenth century—but it was strongly reinforced by the political pessimism of the eighteenth century. Macanaz, in his bitter *Testament of Spain*, makes dying Spain bequeath to her successors '...some valuable possessions which a Genoese acquired for me, dethroning emperors and depriving of their liberty people over whom I had no better rights than they over me....I now declare that I possess such vast domains by usurpation and fraud....'[2] And later, 'It is true that I really control but little (of the Indies) besides the bare minimum on the coasts, together with a few islands; and a very small portion is owned by France and England; but the industry of those Powers has enabled them to develop the interior part of their Colonies by their activity and my negligence.'

How far was the pessimism of these accounts justified by the actual state of the empire as a whole? Spain itself was impoverished by the long and destructive Succession War which had followed the nerveless reign of Charles II and which had left the Bourbon Philip V upon the throne. In Charles II's reign the country had reached perhaps the nadir of decline; but throughout the seventeenth century sensitive Spaniards had been oppressed by a sense of decline, born of poverty, defeat and discontent. Their reaction to this sense of decline had been a withdrawal into defiant isolation, a stubborn clinging to ancient ways and a refusal to accept or recognise foreign ideas. The main stream of European thought in the seventeenth century, with its tremendous developments in philosophy, mathematics and natural science, had passed Spain by. Both Spain and Spanish America were intellectually, politically and economically backward by the standards of the time, and many thoughtful Spaniards felt this backwardness as a bitter humiliation.

The economic backwardness of Spain affected the Indies directly, since the growing European and *mestizo* population in the colonies could never obtain the slaves and manufactured goods they wanted from Spanish sources in sufficient quantity or at competitive prices; nor was Spain a very receptive market for any of their products, except gold and silver.

[1] A. P. Whitaker, ed., 'Jorge Juan and Antonio de Ulloa's prologue to their secret report of 1749 on Peru', *Hispanic American Historical Review*, vol. XVIII, p. 511.
[2] M. de Macanaz, *Testamento de España* [1740] (Mexico, 1821), p. 10.

Such prosperity as the Spanish Americans achieved was the result of their own efforts, and much—perhaps most—of their sea-borne trade was with smugglers. Traders from all the maritime nations of western Europe openly flouted the Seville-Cadiz monopoly and even goods carried in the official fleets often came from foreign sources.

If the Spaniards could not supply their colonies, still less could they defend them. There was no professional army in the Indies until the end of the Seven Years War; before that, provinces exposed to attack defended themselves as best they could by means of locally raised militias. As for the navy, it never recovered in the seventeenth century from the disasters which it had suffered in the later years of Philip II. The *Armada de Barlovento*, which was supposed to patrol the approaches to the Caribbean for the protection of trade, had a very intermittent existence; over and over again money appropriated to this service was diverted to other purposes. In war time, battle fleets were sent out from Spain, usually inadequately equipped, and too small for the tasks they had to perform. In peace-time, the colonists were left to defend themselves against pirates. Both in peace and in war the 'defence' of the smaller ports necessarily consisted, very often, in a hasty withdrawal inland with all portable property until the danger was over. This 'defence' was not always unsuccessful, for rum and yellow fever helped to weaken the attackers. Most of the larger ports, it is true, were fortified, and could put up a stubborn defence, as Vernon was to find at Cartagena in 1741; but by that time matters had improved. At the beginning of the eighteenth century the fortifications of most of the Caribbean ports were neglected and under-manned. The best defence of the colonies lay in the fact that their principal towns were all well inland.

The most serious symptoms of decline in the seventeenth century, however, appeared in the ordinary civil administration. The meticulous care in the selection of holders of responsible office, which had been a marked feature of the reigns of the Catholic monarchs, of Charles V and to a lesser extent of Philip II, gave way under the later Habsburgs to the haphazard promotion of favourites and ultimately to the general sale of offices to the highest bidder. The practice of sale had spread from minor offices—notaryships and seats in town councils—to non-judicial offices of all kinds. The Crown—usually against the advice of its counsellors— sold many highly responsible posts to persons who had little qualification for the work and who often acted through deputies. In Charles II's reign even seats in the Council of the Indies itself were sold. When membership of the chief policy-forming body of the colonial empire thus came to be regarded as a private investment, it was inevitable that a creeping paralysis should afflict the whole administration. The sale of offices was not a simple transaction between the Crown and its servants; it was a highly organised business in itself. Offices could not only be bought; like other forms of property they could be bequeathed, mortgaged, and seized for debt. Often they were bought as a speculation, with borrowed capital; sometimes they were given to court favourites, who sold them for their own profit. The money-lender and the dealer in offices thus came to play a considerable part in the business; many of the servants of the Crown in the Indies were perpetually in debt and looked to fees or less legal exactions to pay the interest. It is not surprising that, on the whole, the standard of honesty, initiative and diligence among seventeenth-century colonial officials was low, and the many admirable features of the Habsburg policy—its conscientious care for justice, its comparative tenderness towards native rights—were often forgotten.

The whole colonial administration, however, was so cumbrous, so clogged with paper-work and petty regulation, that any able and devoted officer must have worked with a perpetual sense of frustration. The Habsburg system was, on paper, highly centralised, in the sense that no decisions of more than trivial importance might be made, and no money spent, without reference to Madrid. This often meant that no decisions were made at all. The central organs of administration, moreover, even when ably directed, were inadequate for handling the volume of paper which they received with every fleet. The viceroys and *audiencia* judges always had to wait, sometimes for years, for answers even to quite minor questions. When decisions were received, they were difficult to enforce, for vital links were missing in the chain of command in the Indies. Each province was ruled by a governor, and the two major provinces by viceroys, each advised by a court of appeal which also served as a kind of executive council. There was no link between these responsible and highly paid functionaries and the *corregidores*—the district officers, as we should now call them. The *corregidores* were numerous and, with a few exceptions, poorly paid. Most of them governed comparatively small areas and had no training in law or administration. Being inadequately supervised, many of them governed badly. Some allowance must be made for the old Spanish literary convention of the *corregidor* as a figure of fun; but in general there can be no doubt that *corregimiento* was one of the weakest features of the Habsburg administrative system.

The untrustworthiness of the *corregidores* bore most hardly upon the Indians, who were moreover the people least able to avail themselves of the legal remedies offered by the appeal courts; for the *audiencias*, though specifically charged with the task of upholding Indian interests, were few in number, and their procedure was complicated and expensive. The *encomienda*—the old quasi-feudal bond between the *conquistadores* and the Indians established early in the sixteenth century—was dying out in most provinces in the early eighteenth century, and for most Indians the *corregidor*, the only Spaniard with whom they had regularly to deal, was the law. Many *corregidores* practised the most ingenious and rapacious local tyrannies with impunity. The *corregidores* assessed and exacted the tribute due to the Crown, and the forced labour for public purposes to which Indian villages were liable. In their capacity as magistrates they levied fines and court fees. All these duties offered endless opportunities for peculation and extortion. Moreover, the *corregidores* exercised, under the name of *repartimiento*, a commercial monopoly of certain classes of manufactured goods. This *repartimiento* had been intended as a means of making European tools and other useful articles more readily available to Indian cultivators. In the hands of an unscrupulous *corregidor* it became a means of forcing a variety of useless and highly priced articles upon the Indians to the private profit of the *corregidor*.

This gap within the colonial service between the high provincial officers —viceroys, treasury officials, judges—and the local officers such as the *corregidores*, though a serious administrative defect, was less serious than the growing social split between the two sections of white society in the Indies. While most of the 'career' officials, especially in the higher offices, were European born, wealth, social prestige and local influence were largely in the hands of the American-born aristocracy who filled the town councils and the municipal magistracies (*alcaldías ordinarias*). These American-born Spaniards displayed the leisured paternal arrogance of a colonial society accustomed to abundant native labour. Spanish-American white society in general had always despised trade and manual labour, and concentrated upon such activities as silver-mining and stock-farming, which involved the supervision of labour rather than actual personal effort. Great country estates and silver mines supplied the means to maintain elaborate town houses; and the numerous 'poor whites' shared the aristocratic pride of blood and dislike of work. In the eighteenth century the Creoles tended to draw further apart from the *mestizo* and Indian elements of colonial society—a tendency illustrated by a growing insistence on the exclusion of persons of mixed blood from the universities, and thus indirectly from the learned professions.

At the same time, the Creoles also drew further apart from the European-born Spaniards. A fiercely exclusive aristocracy, they regarded peninsular Spaniards, including the officials sent out to administer their affairs, with a mixture of envy and contempt—the provincial's envy of the metropolitan office-bearer, and the contempt of the descendants of the *conquistadores* for professional quill-drivers who rose from poverty to affluence by battening on the colonies. One of the problems confronting colonial reformers was whether to decentralise administration by making more use of Creole talent, or whether to centralise the system still further in the interests of efficiency and royal control. Many competent observers advised the Crown to pay more attention to Creole aspirations. The work of Juan and Ulloa is full of references to Creole jealousy, and the feuds which it caused. They urged the Government to make more use of the power and prestige of the elected *alcaldes*, local patricians whose orders, they said, would be more readily accepted by their Creole countrymen than were those of European officials. Campillo, one of the ministers of Philip V, wrote in the same spirit advocating the encouragement of inter-marriage between Creole and European families, and in particular a more general employment of Creoles, *mestizos* and Indians in the Spanish army. In spite of these repeated warnings, however, Spanish policy in the eighteenth century chose the second alternative, and generally ignored the demands of Creole ambition.

It was the function of the Spanish Bourbons to bring Spain back for a time into the main stream of European development and to reorganise the government of the empire on modern—which at that time meant French—lines. Their success was only partial, and at best slow by eight-eenth-century standards. The sale of offices, that ubiquitous hall-mark of slovenly administration, though reduced in extent and more carefully supervised in the eighteenth century, was not abolished until 1812. The most sweeping Bourbon changes—the supersession of the Council of the Indies as an administrative organ by a Colonial Ministry; the establish-ment of Intendancies as a link between the viceroys and the local officers; the abolition of the Seville-Cadiz trade monopoly, the lightening of the burdens upon commerce and the consequent great expansion of trade; the expulsion of the Jesuits—all these took place after the Seven Years War and have no place in the present chapter. The process of reform and administrative rationalisation began in the reign of Philip V and pro-ceeded continuously—though not always at the same speed—until nearly the end of the century.

One of the earliest symptoms of the new spirit in colonial administra-tion was a series of enactments aimed against the wealth of the Church. The large numbers of conventual clergy, the vast area of land held in mortmain, and the heavy burden of tithe and other ecclesiastical taxes, all these were familiar economic grievances in Spain and the Indies. A decree of 1717 rehearsed these complaints and forbade the foundation of new conventual establishments. In 1734 the Orders were forbidden to admit any novices for ten years; and in 1754 legislation was enacted prohibiting regular clergy from taking any part in the drafting of wills. This last enactment, several times repeated in later years, was clearly impossible to enforce. Humboldt, writing half a century later, is witness to the numbers and the wealth of the conventual clergy at the end of the colonial period. Except for such obvious measures as the restriction of rights of asylum, and a very necessary extension of the powers of the civil courts to try criminous clerks, the anti-clerical legislation of the early Spanish Bourbons was ineffective and half-hearted. Nevertheless, the influence of Galli-canism was already at work. The Bourbons, unlike their predecessors, always claimed the ecclesiastical *patronato* as a direct consequence of their own sovereignty and not by virtue of a papal concession. Throughout this whole period the Royalist sentiment in the government of the Church steadily increased. Eighteenth-century monarchy would tolerate no States within the State, and the power of the Crown over the Church was to find dramatic expression in the summary expulsion of the Jesuits from all the Spanish dominions in 1767.

Another highly characteristic Bourbon experiment, in a different field of Crown activity, was a radical reform of the coinage, carried out under ordinances issued by Philip V in 1728. The effect of these ordinances was to take the mints out of the hands of the private contractors who had formerly operated them. The Government was to purchase and coin all the output of the mines on its own account, and coinage on the individual account of miners or bullion merchants was no longer allowed. Elaborate regulations governed the design of the new coins, to discourage clipping and counterfeiting. The gold *escudo* was made of equal weight and fineness with the silver *real*; and when in 1750 a fixed gold-silver ratio of 16:1 was introduced, the *escudo* came to be worth two 'pieces of eight'. The new rules were put into practice almost immediately in New Spain (1732–3), but did not become effective in Peru until 1748. They did not entirely stop debasement and bullion smuggling—complaints continued throughout the century—but they apparently effected a considerable improvement and saving of expense. On the other hand, no solution was ever found for the chronic shortage of small change in the colonies. There was no copper currency, and Indians continued to use cacao beans for their petty transactions well into the eighteenth century.

The process of recoinage coincided with a great increase in bullion production, especially in Mexico, where the amount of silver coined at the mint doubled between 1700 and 1770. Most of this bullion, however, came from a few very rich mines. In a country where wealth was usually invested in land, the supply of liquid capital was insufficient to finance mining operations adequately, and to provide the machinery needed for the drainage and supporting of deep mines. There were three *bancos de plata*, banks which specialised in loans to miners, operating in Mexico City in the middle of the eighteenth century, but their resources were limited and their financial stability doubtful. Mining methods, moreover, were backward and slovenly. In consequence, only those mines where exceptionally rich veins lay near the surface could be sure of success. The industry as a whole was inefficient; the majority of mines were small and highly speculative enterprises, and financial disaster constantly overtook them. It was not until the reign of Charles III that government took steps to organise this very important industry, in order to ensure a better supply of capital for the mines and to provide proper technical training for those who operated them.

Although the early Bourbons did little to foster the mining industry in the colonies, they showed a lively concern over the channels through which the products of the mines reached Spain. The regulation of trade between Spain and the Indies claimed, as it had always done, a large share of the attention which government devoted to economic affairs. Foreign economic theories were not yet strong enough to break the Seville-Cadiz monopoly of the trans-Atlantic trade. The first care of government was to put down smuggling, and to revive the old system of convoyed fleets which had languished under Charles II and had disappeared altogether during the Succession War. The suppression of smuggling was entrusted mainly to the irregular force of *guarda-costas*, whose depredations caused such constant trouble with England. The fleets began sailings shortly after the Peace, and the *Projecto para Galeones y Flotas* of 1720 laid down rules for their regular despatch. Small fleets sailed to Vera Cruz at intervals of two or three years between 1715 and 1736; after that date sailings were suspended for twenty years because of wars or threats of war. During the same years only five fleets sailed to Portobello, and in 1740 the *galeones* were suspended. From 1740 ships were allowed to sail round Cape Horn to Peru, and were often granted permission to store and water at Buenos Aires, though this port remained officially closed to general traffic until 1778. Upon the abolition of the *galeones*, the Portobello fair disappeared, and with it the prosperity of the presidency of Panama. The New Spain *flotas* were restored in 1754, and sailed intermittently until 1789, when the convoy system was finally abandoned. It had long outlived its usefulness.

The breakdown of the convoy systems under the early Bourbons meant an increased freedom of trade, in the sense that an increasing share of the lawful trade was carried in 'register-ships', which sailed singly and achieved a more rapid and efficient turnover. These register-ships, however, might still legally be freighted only by members of the *Consulado*— the guild of privileged traders of Cadiz and Seville. The monopoly of the *Consulado* was curtailed only by the creation of other monopolies; for the Government sought a remedy for the prostration of trade in a foreign device—the joint-stock trading company. Limited groups of private capitalists received commercial, and sometimes administrative, privileges in particular regions of the Indies, in return for developing the resources of those regions and putting down smuggling. At first these privileges were granted in backward areas where goods from the fleets seldom penetrated, and where foreign smugglers had operated undisturbed. Thus in 1728 the Caracas Company was created, with a monopoly of trade with the Venezuelan coast. In 1734 the Galicia Company received the privilege of sending two ships a year to Campeche. The Havana Company was incorporated in 1740, and in 1755 the Barcelona Company for trade with Hispaniola and Porto Rico. Most of these ventures were started by syndicates in the north of Spain, an area whose merchants normally took no part in trade with the Indies. They were bitterly opposed by the Andalusian monopolists, and all except one proved, through bad management, ill-luck or government interference, to be financial failures. The exception was the Caracas Company, which lasted until 1785 and was eventually merged in the Philippine Company. The Caracas Company policed the Venezuelan coast and suppressed much of the foreign smuggling there. It doubled the shipments of cacao to Spain, and greatly reduced the price; it also developed a lucrative trade in tobacco, cotton, dye woods and indigo. The company was hated by the colonists, as monopolies usually are; but the prosperity of Venezuela began with the establishment of this monopoly.

The Creole merchants in the colonies gained nothing by these developments. The *Consulado* at Cadiz, despite the creation of the companies, or perhaps because of it, made strenuous efforts to confine the rest of the American trade more closely to its own membership. In 1729 it secured a decree confining the shipment of goods in *galeones* and *flotas* to active voting members of its own body. In the same year it issued regulations prohibiting merchant houses in America from acting as agents of the exporting firms. In 1735 the inhabitants of the Indies were forbidden to remit bullion to Spain for investment in goods for export to the Indies. Creole merchants might do business at Cadiz only through *Consulado* members; and although this rule was formally revoked in 1749, it remained in practical effect for thirty years after that date. Freedom of trade within the empire was not extended to Creoles until Charles III's reign. By that time the Creole merchant community had developed a sense of grievance and frustrated ambition too deep-seated to be appeased by a mere system of imperial preference.

In the realm of political administration the early Bourbons were equally conservative. They showed more care than their predecessors in the selection of high officials in the colonies, and this alone was enough to ensure a marked improvement in the quality of administration. Otherwise they made few changes of importance in administrative methods. They did, however, carry through a drastic re-grouping of the administrative units of the Indies. In South America the viceroy of Peru had been responsible for the government of Spanish territory throughout the continent including the remote, but growing, community on the Río de la Plata. In the eighteenth century the single viceroyalty was split into three. The vast area of the northern Andes was detached from Lima, temporarily in 1717 and permanently in 1739, by the creation of a new viceroyalty at Santa Fé, modern Bogotá. The Presidencies of Quito and Panama were left intact, though subject to the new viceroyalty; but Panama lasted as a separate jurisdiction only until 1751, when its *audiencia* was suppressed, and its judicial and administrative business transferred to Santa Fé. Venezuela, on the other hand, enjoying its new prosperity, was declared in 1742 to be a separate province, under its own governor, and independent of Santa Fé. Except for Bolívar's short-lived union, it has remained separate ever since. Chile similarly became a separate captaincy-general in 1778.

The story of the administration of the Río de la Plata area was complicated by disputes between Spain and Portugal over the possession of the east bank of the river. The Portuguese had maintained a small fort opposite Buenos Aires intermittently since 1680. The first formal Spanish settlement—Montevideo in the Banda Oriental—was founded in 1729. After much bickering and some actual fighting, a boundary treaty was signed in 1751 giving Brazil approximately the boundaries it possesses today. The treaty was based partly upon actual possession and partly upon geographical convenience; it involved the transfer to Portugal of a number of Jesuit missions, and the Indian inhabitants, encouraged by the missionaries, resisted the transfer by armed rebellion. Eventually, when Spain entered the Seven Years War in 1761, the treaty was abrogated; but its terms were repeated almost exactly in the Treaty of San Ildefonso in 1777, which closed the controversy. The creation of the viceroyalty of Buenos Aires in 1776 was dictated by military expediency, by the need to resist Portuguese claims on the east bank of the river. The upshot of the controversy was that the territory now known as Uruguay was colonised by Spaniards and not by Portuguese; and the tendency to rebellion displayed by the Jesuit missions contributed to the decision to expel the Society from all Spanish territories in 1767.

In North America, on the other hand, the viceroyalty of New Spain and the captaincy-general of Guatemala remained intact, and plans prepared in 1751 for the creation of a separate viceroyalty in northern Mexico were never put into effect. A separate military administration was set up there in 1776 to deal with Indian raids; but Gálvez, in making this change, rightly judged that the arid northern provinces could not support the expense of a separate viceregal establishment.

In all these changes, the ministers of Philip V, Ferdinand VI and Charles III showed their determination to consult geographical convenience and administrative efficiency, instead of accepting the old boundaries, based upon the accidents of conquest, which had so long endured under the Habsburgs. Most of the changes made in the middle decades of the eighteenth century proved remarkably permanent, and the chief administrative units of Charles III's day nearly all became separate independent republics in the next century.

The rearrangement of the old established governments of the Indies was accompanied by renewed expansion on the frontiers of the settled provinces. Most of this expansion was the work of missionaries who pushed into desert and forest far ahead of other explorers at this time.

The best known missions were the famous thirty villages established by Jesuits among the Guaranís in the Paraná–Uruguay basin; but industrious and orderly communities were also formed in the early eighteenth century among the Mojos and Chiquitos, to the east of the Andes, and among the fierce and recently subdued Araucanians of southern Chile. These were all Jesuit fields of activity. The Capuchins founded a number of successful missions from 1724 onwards in the lower Orinoco basin. At the northern extremity of Spanish territory, on the desert frontiers of northern New Spain, the Franciscans were similarly extending the area of their missions. New Mexico, which had been the scene of a bloodthirsty Indian revolt at the end of the seventeenth century, was slowly re-settled in the first half of the eighteenth by a series of missions strung along the Río Grande. Successful missionary work began in Texas in 1716 and in Nuevo Santander between the Pánuco and San Antonio rivers, in 1746. Meanwhile Jesuit missionaries pushed up from Sonora to Lower California and later in the century to Upper California. Most of these northern missions were protected by *presidios*—frontier block-houses— garrisoned by small parties of soldiers; unlike the Guaraní villages where the Jesuits, supported by the Crown, usually succeeded in excluding Spanish laymen from the mission area. Apart from this difference the missions throughout Spanish America were all organised on a somewhat similar plan. All practised communal agriculture and minor ancillary industries—weaving, tanning and the like—under the direction of the mission fathers. Many of the missionaries were enthusiastic innovators in agriculture; they introduced stock-rearing and fruit-growing in many districts where the people knew nothing of these arts, and in many ruined missions today the walls of derelict orchards can still be traced. Most of the missions depended for their success on the ability of the fathers to persuade semi-nomadic peoples to settle permanently in villages near the church and mission house, and to adopt settled agriculture. In a sense the mission of the eighteenth century was the successor of the *encomienda* of the sixteenth. Among primitive frontier peoples it was a far more efficient instrument of settlement. After the expulsion of the Jesuits, and with the decline of interest in missionary work in the later eighteenth century, many of the missions sank into neglect and ruin; but the work of settlement in many areas was continued by the ranchers and mining prospectors who followed the missionaries, and enjoyed the same military protection. The eighteenth century, therefore, was surpassed only by the sixteenth in the discovery of new mines and the founding of new towns. San Francisco, Albuquerque, San Antonio, Pensacola, Montevideo, Cúcuta, Copiapó, Rancagua, and many smaller places, all date from this period of active frontier expansion.

The extension of the frontiers of Spanish America was accompanied by an even more striking expansion in Brazil. In the seventeenth century the

Portuguese settlers had mostly been confined to the small towns and sugar plantations on the east and north-east coast. Nobody but slave-hunting *bandeirantes* penetrated far inland. The discovery of rich gold mines in Minas Geraes, Goiaz and Matto Grosso towards the end of the century, however, caused a rush to the west which, for a time, depopulated some of the maritime districts and opened the way to armed French landings at Río de Janeiro in 1710 and 1711. This vacuum was partly filled by a steadily increasing stream of immigrants from Europe. In the first half of the eighteenth century the boundary of Brazil was pushed forward to the eastern slopes of the Andes. The Spanish Government recognised this great advance beyond the old Tordesillas line, in the boundary treaty of 1750, negotiated chiefly on the principle of *uti possidetis*. The Portuguese Government had already organised the vast, newly explored, and almost empty forest tracts into new captaincies. The captaincy of São Paulo and Minas Geraes was created in 1709; from it were carved in succession the separate captaincies of Minas Geraes (1720), Goiaz (1744) and Matto Grosso (1748). In the far south, where the Spaniards were dangerous neighbours, the colonisation of the cattle province of Río Grande do Sul began in 1734, and in 1735 Santa Catarina was made a separate captaincy. So sprang into being a ranching and mining community in the south able to compete economically and politically with the older, sugar-planting slave-owning provinces of the north. The long decay of the northern settlements was already beginning. In 1751 a court of appeal was established at Río de Janeiro with jurisdiction over the southern captaincies, and in 1763 Pombal moved the capital of the whole country from Baía to Río.

Pombal, minister to Joseph I from 1750 to 1777, was the outstanding figure of his generation in Portugal, and did for Brazil much of what Ferdinand VI and Charles III did for Spanish America. The administration of the Portuguese settlements had always been looser, in some senses more feudal, than that of the Spanish colonies; but Pombal succeeded in introducing a degree of centralised absolutism remarkable in so vast and wild a country. More than any other administrator, he was responsible for giving Brazil the political unity which—unlike Spanish America—it was to retain. He abolished the numerous private captaincies which had survived—an obvious anachronism—to the middle of the eighteenth century, and greatly reduced the independent powers of local officials in the Crown captaincies. He abolished the old clumsy system of official annual fleets, and promoted commercial companies to take over the Portuguese monopoly of trade. He carried through a drastic reorganisation of the mining industry, involving a general adoption of up-to-date methods of extraction. Like Charles III, and for similar reasons, but eight years earlier, he expelled the Society of Jesus from the territories under his control, and caused thereby a serious loss to Brazilian society in terms of missionary work among the Indians, education among the colonists, and the general intellectual development of the territory. Pombal left Brazil a zealously guarded, methodically exploited colony, whose wealth and population already rivalled, and were soon to eclipse, those of the mother country.

Both in Spanish and Portuguese America the feeling that the colonies were beginning to outstrip the mother country was a contributory cause of dissatisfaction. One of the curious, yet understandable, Creole grievances seems to have been the disillusion which many Americans suffered on visiting Europe; Madrid was so much meaner than the American cities. The eighteenth century was a great period of building all over Latin America. Many fine baroque buildings in the Latin American cities survive from this time, and much of their 'churrigueresque' ornament reveals, in form and execution, the hand of the Indian craftsman. In the other visual arts, Latin America was less distinguished. Painting notably suffered a decline from the seventeenth century, in the colonies as in Spain. The eighteenth century was remarkable for the number and size of the paintings produced, rather than for their merit; but the demand for paintings in itself is evidence of growing wealth and of family or municipal pride.

In literary production the colonies still lagged far behind Europe. Most of the principal towns of Spanish America had printing presses by the middle of the eighteenth century, and three colonial periodicals were started in the first half of the century—the semi-official *Gacetas* of Mexico (1722), Guatemala (1729) and Lima (1743). All were monthly or bi-monthly—daily newspapers did not appear until nearly the end of the century. Scientific, literary and learned periodicals were entirely lacking in the first half of the century. Book production was hampered throughout by civil and ecclesiastical censorship, not particularly severe, but dilatory and obstructive. It was not until after the Seven Years War, when Latin America received the full force of French 'enlightenment', that the universities modernised their professional schools and dethroned Galen and Aristotle; that 'reading circles' sprang up in the principal towns; and that the passionate interest in political theory, so characteristic of the generation before Independence, became widespread.

The Seven Years War administered a severe shock to the Spanish empire. Spain in the New World was threatened with isolation in the face of a victorious and immensely powerful British navy. The fall of Havana, the strongest fortress in the Caribbean, revealed to Spanish Americans the weakness of the regular forces which Spain could send to their defence. With the exception of Cuba, however, the colonies suffered little actual loss from the war. It was Spain which suffered; and the Spanish Government naturally sought to recover its losses by making fuller and more efficient use of the resources of its colonies. The reign of Charles III was marked by closer relations with France, by more conscious imitation of French methods and ideas, and by a thorough overhaul of the administrative and military structure of the empire. Charles's aims and methods did not differ strikingly from those of his predecessors, but they were pursued more thoroughly and more ruthlessly. The supervision of local officials by central government became more continuous and more effective; and the subordination of American society to Spanish officialdom became more obvious and more consistent. At the same time Spain accepted a far heavier direct responsibility for the land defence of the colonies. The Seven Years War showed that local militias were not enough for the needs of the time, and from the end of the war, for the first time in the empire's history, a considerable force of regular troops was permanently stationed in the Indies. The senior officers were usually peninsular Spaniards, and Creole officers thought, rightly or wrongly, that their chances of promotion and their social standing in the mess suffered by reason of their American birth. On the other hand, the prosperity of the colonies mounted at a greatly accelerated speed, through the freeing of trade and the reduction of imposts as well as the natural increase of population and resources. The reforms of the Bourbons, therefore, helped to increase American wealth and self-confidence and at the same time to exacerbate the injured pride and sense of frustration of the Creole aristocracy. The traditional loyalty of that aristocracy was to the Crown rather than to Spain, and to the king rather than to the Crown. When the line of capable, masterful sovereigns came to an end, the Creoles could no longer be held to their allegiance by a masterless bureaucracy.

2. NORTH AMERICA

In 1714 the British settlements still adhered to a tiny coastal fringe stretching from Albemarle Sound to the river mouths of Maine, with isolated communities to the south on the Ashley and Cooper rivers and to the north in Nova Scotia; and there were still unsettled patches along the coast. The American communities were still centred on tide-water.

It had taken a century for settlement to reach the fall line of the rivers: but between the end of Queen Anne's War, in 1713, and the outbreak of the French and Indian War, in 1755, the occupied area more than doubled. Behind the fur traders, pursuing beaver and deer beyond the mountains, and the lumberjacks, attacking stands of white pine and oak in Maine, pioneers pushed inland, up the Susquehanna, the Mohawk and the Connecticut, along the high Appalachian valleys, and along the littoral into Maine and the Carolinas, intent on settling the land. This outward pressure of population was the basic determinant of the colonies' growth.

Between 1715 and 1750 the population grew from 400,000 to one and a quarter millions; by 1763 it was about two millions. Part of this was the result of natural increase in a rural society where land was abundant, food supplies assured and children an economic asset. But large families (Franklin speaks of eight children as normal), offset by a high death rate from disease, accidents and Indian war, only accounted for part of the phenomenal growth. More important were the immigrants who settled frontier and back country. From England, emigrant labourers and artisans joined the transient traffic of officials, merchants, clergy and schoolmasters across the Atlantic. Many were redemptioners, and a few felons provided Maryland with an alternative to slaves. But the English were a small proportion; by 1763 the first great wave of mixed migration, of Ulster-Scots, Highland Scots, Irish, French Huguenots, Germans and Swiss, had begun to transform America into a polyglot society.

The largest groups were Ulster-Scots and Germans. Between 1700 and 1776 about a quarter of a million Ulster-Scots settled in America. Driven by the decay of their textile industries, by rack-renting and by their inclusion, as Presbyterians, in the disabilities of the Test Act, they arrived in specially large numbers about 1718 and after the famines of 1728 and 1741. The first made for Boston; and thence, their fellow Calvinists proving inhospitable, inland to Worcester, Londonderry, New Hampshire, and eastern Maine. The later bulk of the Ulstermen, like the Germans, made for Philadelphia, attracted by the liberal Quaker institutions and the accessibility of Pennsylvania. Filtering through the settled townships they moved inland, into New Jersey, up the Susquehanna, and into the mountain valley of the Cumberland where they established a predominantly Scots-Irish frontier between 1730 and 1750. Thence they, or their children, moved south-west along high valleys like the Shenandoah into Virginia, and the Carolinas. The Ulster-Scots had a tradition of rebellion in religion and politics which submitted with ill grace to tide-water control, and was to lead them in great numbers into the Continental Army.

The Germans came largely from the Palatinate after its devastation in the War of the Spanish Succession. An early group came to rest in the Province of New York; but the refusal of the great landlords to grant satisfactory land titles led most of them to migrate down the Susquehanna to Pennsylvania where land was more plentiful, institutions more liberal, and many compatriots already settled. By 1776 there were probably about 110,000 Germans in that colony, about half the population. Most of these 'Pennsylvania Dutch' were Lutherans; they also included members of the more idiosyncratic sects who came to Pennsylvania following the lead of early Pietists whom Penn had pursuaded to join his Holy Experiment: Mennonites, Moravians, Dunkards, Swenkfelders. They, too, moved inland, to the fertile limestone lands of Lancaster County, and along the upland valleys into western Maryland, where Hagerstown was founded in 1762, and to back-country Virginia and North Carolina. The Germans shared with the Ulster-Scots the distinction of having broken most of the new ground, and of having borne the brunt of frontier hazards. Less mobile than the Scots, they were more determined to settle and farm. They chose the best soils, cleared the land with unique thoroughness, built solid barns and middens, bred better livestock, and quickly transformed mid-Pennsylvania into a rich farming country, which became the granary of the West Indies. Quietists, they wished to be left alone to practice their religion, husbandry and peasant culture; and they remained less prominent than the Ulstermen in politics. The only other important group of immigrants was made up of the negro slaves, imported into the plantation colonies, whose numbers increased from about 60,000 in 1715 to about 300,000 in 1760.

Colonists as well as immigrants played a part in filling up the back country.

The infertile farms of the New England coastal settlements proved inadequate to sustain her growing population and the less fortunate sought a better living further afield, filling up central Massachusetts, eastern Connecticut and Rhode Island. Some ventured north up the Connecticut River into New Hampshire and westward into upper New York. But hostile Indians and the barren hillsides of Vermont severely limited expansion in this direction. More and more New Englanders were turning to seafaring for a living. Ingenious Yankees turned their fish, timber, rum and fast-sailing schooners to good account to build up a prosperous trade network throughout the Atlantic basin. The trade contacts of Boston, Newport and New Haven with other Atlantic ports encouraged migration north-east to Maine and Nova Scotia and south-west to Long Island, New York, New Jersey and even as far as South Carolina. The settlement of Connecticut men on eastern Long Island exacerbated the hostility between New York and Connecticut over New Haven's commerce with that island. Congregationalists from Massachusetts continued to flow into East Jersey to give a Yankee stamp to parts of that province.

In the southern colonies the conditions of the plantation economy led to a spread of population. Bounties on forest products for naval stores supported a shiftless and poverty-stricken population of tar burners in the coastal pine barrens. Two new staple crops brought prosperity to South Carolina and rescued the infant colony of Georgia from inanition. By 1715 the cultivation of rice in the South Carolinian tide-water had become large-scale capitalist planting; and after 1730 when the home government allowed the export of rice, an enumerated article, to southern Europe, production rapidly increased. Even more profitable was indigo, introduced into South Carolina from the West Indies in 1742. This dye brought high prices in England, gave the planters profits from 33 per cent to 50 per cent and led to the cultivation of the upland interior of the colony. By contrast, the condition of the tobacco planters of Virginia and Maryland became increasingly difficult. While the price of tobacco remained level, the costs of production increased sharply and planting became increasingly unprofitable. The demands of rice and indigo planting increased the cost of slaves from about £25 in 1700 to between £40 and £60 in 1750. Meanwhile the fixed charges on the English selling price became so burdensome that in times of depression, such as the years 1720–34 and again from 1756–65, the planter took heavy losses and became ever more deeply mortgaged to his merchant. At the mercy of his merchant creditors the planter had no option but to continue to work his slaves and land year in year out at steadily decreasing returns. As a result the land in the tide-water counties became exhausted and the planters began to open up new lands in the back country which, although less accessible to navigable rivers, promised a better yield. This land hunger, which beset large planter and small farmer alike, led to a considerable migration westwards towards the Blue Ridge. Men with means and political pull made a policy of acquiring title to larger holdings of uncleared lands than they could ever hope to cultivate and, as their tobacco profits dwindled, looked more and more to profits from the speculative rent of land to would-be settlers. The result of this inexorable pressure upon the tobacco planter was that the advance guard of settlement in back-country Virginia and Maryland pushed up to the Appalachian foothills and clashed with the settlers streaming down the high valleys from Pennsylvania. The Virginian found his path crossed by the Ulster-Scot or German squatter, and the conflicts between these 'Tuckahoes' and 'Cohees' over land titles, political representation and religious establishment set up important tensions for the future.

The tendency of the plantation economy to expand in area and to concentrate in large capitalistic units is further illustrated by the early history of Georgia. This, the only new colony to be founded in the period, was designed to provide a bulwark against Spanish Florida, French Louisiana and the southern Indians; to exploit the profitable fur trade in that region; and to provide a haven for the unfortunates in England's debtor prisons. Its founder, James Oglethorpe, a soldier and philanthropist, conceived his colony as a frontier garrison manned by soldier-farmers who were to obtain a new start in life. For this period of initial settlement, control was vested in a group of London trustees who directed its affairs like a military operation. No large land grants were allowed and settlers were prohibited from alienating their holdings. Wages of freed servants were fixed. Although trade was in private hands, the Government operated saw and grist mills and encouraged the production of wine, silk and naval stores. Negro slaves and Catholics were prohibited since they were both considered a military liability in case of war with the Spaniards or the French. The fur trade was strictly regulated in order to foster relations with the Indians, the import of rum being prohibited. Oglethorpe himself established the first settlement of the Savannah River with military thoroughness in 1732. By 1740 some 900 English and 600 foreign Protestants had been transported to Georgia. But this long-range planning quickly proved misconceived. The land and labour policies prevented the suitable exploitation of this semi-tropical area, starving the colonists of capital and a proper labour force and limited them to wheat and cattle raising. Wine and silk experiments failed and without slaves rice production could not hope to compete with South Carolina. The fur traders were inhibited by the lack of servants and rum. Gradually the trust was forced into concessions. Land holdings were increased and alienation allowed. The import of rum and slaves was permitted. This relaxation of control allowed a more natural exploitation of the colony's resources. Large planters from South Carolina consolidated the cleared holdings into profitable rice plantations worked by a large force of imported slaves. These economic changes doomed the original experiment. In 1751 the trustees handed over their rights to the Crown which promptly organised Georgia as a royal colony with an elected assembly and a governor and council.

The increase in population provided more labour to make new land productive and the wealth of the colonies increased rapidly. The greater part of the increment from the hinterland fell to the hands of merchants and landowners; and the economic control they thus exercised was growingly irksome to the mass of small settlers and artisans.

The ownership of vast tracts of land by great landlords, preserved by entail and primogeniture, helped to crowd the settler westward in search of freehold. The estates of Lord Fairfax in Virginia, Lord Granville in North Carolina, Lord Baltimore in Maryland and the Penn family in Pennsylvania presented obstacles which the Ulster-Scots and the Germans had either to by-pass or, as squatters, to ignore. The great manors of the Hudson River helped deflect the flow of settlement southwards. But in addition to these existing holdings, men of means and political influence took advantage of the westward pressure of population to acquire title to western lands as a profitable speculation. Groups of Englishmen and colonists with the ear of government formed land companies like that of the London merchant Henry McCulloch which received nearly a million and a half acres in North Carolina during the 1730's or the Ohio Company of Virginia gentlemen which obtained from the Crown, in 1749, 200,000 acres between the Monongahela and Great Kanawha Rivers. But the speculative mania was not confined to the grandees. In New England townships, the heirs of the original proprietors kept tight rein on the undistributed land and refused to newcomers the rights of commons. The result was that with the growth of population a propertyless class was pushed out towards the frontier and the entrenched property owners reaped from the rise in land values a profitable increment ready for investment in the new land. After 1725 this led to a change in the traditional New England method of founding townships. Instead of being granted to bona fide settlers, the land was sold to speculators who became absentee landlords for frontier communities like those of the upper Connecticut River. In short, from New England to South Carolina restrictive land policies led to a growing cleavage of interest between the well-to-do and established of the older settlements and the poorer newcomers of the back country.

As with land, so with capital. The small farmer was comparatively self-sufficient; but he needed certain staples—from salt and molasses to implements—for which he must exchange his own produce. The surplus from the hinterland was not confined to farm products, for the colonial farmer kept a sharp eye open for trading opportunities to supplement the living he obtained from the soil. In the back country he was trapper, lumberman and land speculator; on the seaboard he might combine farming with fishing, shipbuilding or even domestic industry. The traffic in furs was augmented by the exploitation of new fur-bearing regions to the west and south of the Appalachians; forest products, from timber to tar and turpentine, provided ships' stores for Britain and laid the basis for a thriving shipbuilding industry in New England which constructed cheaper, lighter and faster ships than those of the home country. The fisheries continued to supply a profitable staple for New England's trading empire. The needs of the growing population for the basic minimum of consumers' goods continued to be catered for largely by the rural communities themselves: homespun and deerskin clothing, home-made footwear, furniture and household utensils and the products of the local blacksmith's smithy. But the rise of an urban population and the development of internal trade provided a more general market which resulted in an experimental growth of commercial manufacturing. The mining and production of crude iron went ahead rapidly with the return of peace, and blast furnaces and forges in Virginia and Maryland turned out pig iron which found a market in England as well as at home. But this incipient manufacturing fell foul of the interests of British manufacturers who were becoming aware of the importance of an expanding American market. The result was that the home government, by disallowing colonial measures of protection and by severely restricting overseas markets for colonial goods as in the Hat Act of 1732 and the Iron Act of 1750, inhibited any significant industrial growth.

The growing surplus from the rural communities found its way to the ports to provide the basis for the trading activities of a prosperous mercantile fraternity. The back-country farmer, chronically short of funds, was dependent for credit upon the merchant, and the balance of trade between back country and town was heavily in favour of the town. The merchant with capital behind him could take the initiative and earn high profits at the expense, it seemed, of the hard-earned bounty of the farmer's toil. The trade in provisions, furs, fish and timber products came increasingly into the hands of fewer and more powerful merchants and into the greater ports like Boston and Philadelphia at the expense of smaller ports like New Haven and New Castle. The growingly monopolistic practices of these groups called forth the resentment of the small man who found his outlets to market controlled. In Pennsylvania, for example, merchants and small producers kept up a running fight over such matters as the maintenance of free markets and auctions and the threat of Philadelphia's monopoly by the diversion of inland produce down the Susquehanna to the new port of Baltimore, whose rise dates from 1729.

The resentment of the back country farmers against the merchants was increased by problems of credit and the price level. The home government's prohibition against a colonial mint and the drain of specie abroad to balance the unfavourable trade account kept colonial currency in chaos. The unregulated circulation of mixed foreign coin was inadequate to meet the demands of trade in spite of the continued use of such devices as barter, commodity money, board and keep in lieu of wages, and the payment of government obligations in land. The colonies therefore continued to have recourse to paper money expedients. To pay contractors for supplies in Queen Anne's War the colonial governments had issued bills of credit in advance of the collection of taxes and these served as such a satisfactory currency substitute that with the return of peace and their prospective retirement a new method was sought to keep bills of credit in circulation. For the farmers had discovered that these bills raised prices and therefore lessened their burden of debt. The popular parties in the colonial assemblies began to advocate the issue of bills of credit on the security, not of taxes, but of the colony's greatest asset: land. 'Land banks' were launched to lend money in the form of bills of credit to the farmer on the security of his land. Since the farmer thus obtained much easier credit facilities than the merchants offered, the new device seemed a popular panacea to release the farmer from the merchant's grip. The merchants opposed such schemes for the same reason and, along with property owners generally, for the more important reason that since land was the security there was scarcely any limit to the amount of bills that could be issued and there was, therefore, no effective control over the inflation which was bound to follow. The result was that in colony after colony paper money schemes, forced through by the popular party and bitterly opposed by the oligarchy, effectively lightened the burden of debt and led creditors to hide from debtors demanding settlement in depreciated paper. In Massachusetts the inflation of paper reached such a point in 1733 that the home government instructed Governor Belcher to limit severely future issues and to redeem existing issues when they fell due. To avoid the consequences of this deflationary threat the farmers in 1740 organised a land bank to issue bills which depended entirely upon popular support for their effectiveness. In retaliation the merchants boycotted the land bank issues and organised a bank of their own with issues based on specie. The result was a minor insurrection of farmers who, in the governor's words, were 'grown so brassy and hardy' that they marched on Boston in 1741. Meanwhile the merchants appealed to the Crown, which promptly extended to the colonies the provisions of the Bubble Act and thereby declared the Land Bank illegal. As a result many of its subscribers, including Samuel Adams Senior, were bankrupted. In Rhode Island the farmers dominated the Assembly to such an extent that between 1710 and 1750 they created successively nine land banks, using the bills of a new bank to pay the charges on the old. In addition the Government continued to issue tax-supported bills greatly in excess of the tax yield, so that by 1750 Rhode Island bills had depreciated to an eighth of their face value. At this point the British Parliament took radical action by passing the Currency Act of 1751 which prohibited the creation of new land banks and the making of bills of credit legal tender. Only bills backed by taxes were to be permitted. This Act, which ended the heyday of debtor control, left a rankling grievance in the rural community.

The spread of settlement into the back country induced a quickening of the religious spirit. By 1714 the easier circumstances of the older settlements had resulted in a dampening of religious ardour. In New England, especially, the broadening horizons and prosperity of trade had softened the rigidities of seventeenth-century puritanism. In the Congregational Church mystical exhortation had given way to pulpit dissertation, and memory of the sorry orgy of witchcraft trials had discredited the old theocratic tradition. The prevailing temper was increasingly secular and rationalist. In the middle colonies such diverse denominations as the Congregationalist, Lutheran and Dutch Reformed churches, were characterized by a growing formalism and the Quakers were suffering from the same quiescence of the spirit as afflicted the English meetings. In the southern colonies, where the Anglican Church was established, the outlook was deist and the clergy as lax and venal as in the England whence, for the most part, they came. But the new immigrants, from German Pietists to Ulster-Scots Presbyterians, brought with them a more severely religious strain to sustain them in the wilderness and the demands of pioneering renewed the need for a personal and emotional religion. The result was a welling up of the religious spirit in a great evangelical movement which shook the orthodox churches to their foundations. This revival, which may be discerned from about 1725 onwards, placed a new emphasis on the mystical awareness of God, on the sense of sin, the personal relation of the individual to God and on the urgency of salvation through conversion. Whatever its denominational manifestation it was simple and unexacting in theology. Above all, in its emphasis on conversion and on salvation by faith it provided a release from old-line Calvinism with its total denial of the freedom of the will. Jonathan Edwards, the great Congregationalist minister of Northampton, Mass., provided the movement with its most formidable intellect and by the goad of his devastating preaching stimulated a great revival wave in the Connecticut River valley which spread its influence far and wide in the 1730's.[1] Theodore Frelinghuysen, a Dutch Reformed minister influenced by Pietism in Germany, co-operated with the Presbyterians in New Jersey in an evangelical crusade in the 1720's. Allied to the same strain were the Ulster-Scots Presbyterian minister William Tennent, who emigrated to Philadelphia in 1717 and devoted himself to the education of ministers for the Ulster-Scots on the frontier, and his son Gilbert who became a powerful revivalist preacher. As a result of these, and other, ministrations, revivals had begun to agitate colonial congregations in the 1730's, reaching a climax after 1739, when George Whitefield began his remarkable journeys from Georgia to New England which did most to spread the evangelical fervour throughout America. Revivalism led to conflict within the orthodox churches which were rent with schisms between 'old lights' and 'new lights'. But in spite of schisms and of much crudeness and falsity the revivals contributed a new vigour to American religious life. They were also responsible for an impulse to humanitarian endeavour, from anti-slavery sentiment and missions to Indians to the establishment of colleges like Princeton and Dartmouth. Although their influence was ubiquitous, it was especially marked in the back country. Here the simple, emotional religion with its abrupt contrast between sin and salvation provided a transient and sometimes a permanent solace against the loneliness and brutality of frontier life. The moral fervour of the 'new lights' lent strength to the rebellion of the up-country districts against the controls of orthodoxy, not only in religion but in politics.

Colonial society was in ferment. With the growth of population, settled area and wealth, seaboard and back-country communities were becoming more sharply differentiated. More and more colonists were leaving tidewater for the back country. As they joined the inland drift they turned their backs upon the ocean, cut their losses in the older communities and set their faces westwards towards forest and mountain. The long Appalachian corridors of migration tended to erase colony boundaries, and back-country areas in each colony found they had more in common than with their own tide-water. The mixture of races was beginning to produce an amalgam with distinct social characteristics. Meanwhile the established and the well-to-do remained in possession in the east, reaping

---

[1] Edwards's irresistible logic carried Calvinist theology to the extreme of positing a pitiless God against whose incomprehensible predestination man's moral striving was helpless. But in spite of this extravagantly orthodox standpoint his emphasis on conversion as evidence of a pre-destined salvation and his perceptive knowledge of the irrationalities of human psychology contributed great moral power to the new movement.

economic benefits from the filling hinterland, but fearing its effects for their own position and determined to maintain and strengthen their control. At the same time the growing ports bred a population of shop-keepers and artisans with divergent interests from those of the ruling oligarchy. As a result, tensions developed between the rich and established on the one hand and the poor and newly arrived on the other, between the parochial and the almost metropolitan, between the periphery and the centre, which were both sectional and class in character.

Between 1714 and 1763 the society of the seaboard became increasingly wealthy and diversified. The growing hinterland fostered the rapid expansion of the ports. Philadelphia grew from 10,000 in 1720 to be the first city in the colonies with a population of upwards of 20,000 in 1763. New York jumped from 7000 in 1720 to 13,000 in 1756, Charles Town from 3500 in 1720 to 8000 in 1763. In addition there were a score of smaller ports like Newport, New Haven or New Castle with a busy mercantile population. The more important of these towns were more than ports. Philadelphia, Boston, New York and Charles Town were provincial capitals sheltering not only government officials, merchants, professional men and travellers, but shopkeepers and artisans, with diverging class interests. Improved highways and taverns permitted carriage travel from Boston to Charles Town and inland some thirty or forty miles from the chief ports. From 1754 a stage line operated between New York and Philadelphia and the postal service, reorganised by Benjamin Franklin in 1753, cheapened and speeded correspondence. For the well-to-do and those with business to attend to, travel, for the first time, became customary. In the south the wealthy planters of South Carolina made a custom during the summer of visiting Charles Town which became a provincial centre of some distinction. As a result the great towns grew into important centres, not only for trade and shipping but for professional services and for social life. The profits of trade and the long-term credit of planting provided ready cash for a high rate of consumption and, with the growing amenities urban life began to ape, if not London and Bath, at any rate Tonbridge and York. New standards of display in houses, furnishings and clothes fostered colonial styles which, while derivative and provincial, were distinctively American and gave employment to the growing population of artisans and craftsmen. Increased leisure encouraged the pursuit of polite accomplishments from dancing, cards and music to reading and scholarship. Although the first American newspaper, the *Boston News-Letter*, dates from only 1704, between 1713 and 1745 no less than twenty-two new papers were published. Printing presses and libraries catered for a wider reading public and the growth of a common intellectual temper was signalised by the founding of an American academy in 1744 in Philadelphia which became in this period the cultural capital of America. The genius of Franklin with his omnivorous interest in all branches of 'natural philosophy' was thrown up by this new temper of mind in touch with the best thought of Europe.

The growing wealth and sophistication of the planting and mercantile oligarchy contrasted sharply with the simple poverty of the hinterland. Here there was coming into being a homespun society of men and women who had turned their back upon the customary society of seaboard and Europe. Westward-looking and preoccupied with the problems of forest, swamp and mountain, this society was becoming continental in outlook. Uprooted from custom, its restless movement made it semi-nomadic in character. Of mixed racial stock, it was becoming increasingly indifferent, if not antipathetic, to the English heritage. Steeled to frontier hardships it was self-reliant and outspokenly confident of its future. This society, founded on rebellion in economic, social and religious life, was becoming increasingly hostile to tide-water control, whether British or colonial. Looking to tide-water only for protection from hostile French and Indians, the time was to come when, with the French threat removed, back-country society would have no use whatever for external government.

The home government was too remote to appreciate the power of the forces released by the expansion of population and settled area. For Whitehall depended for its colonial administration upon the seaboard oligarchy which was only concerned to defend its control of colonial affairs against the demands of the growing population of small farmers and artisans whom it regarded as a rabble unfit for political power. In most colonies a narrow group of merchants and landowners held a monopoly of political power in their own interest. As in the home country, politics was a matter of influence and the economically powerful and socially elect were in a position to obtain favours which consolidated their power at the expense of the mass. A few families occupied the places of profit under the Crown and, especially in the matter of land grants, were not averse to feathering their own nests. It was to these families that a royal governor looked for his council and for leadership in putting royal policies into effect in the assembly. If the oligarchy was prepared to join forces with the popular party in asserting the rights of the assembly against the Crown, nevertheless they did not scruple to use the royal power to the full to resist popular pressures from below, even to the extent of appealing for parliamentary legislation as in the case of the extension of the Bubble Act to Massachusetts in 1741. The elected assembly was not always susceptible to control; but care was taken to see that its membership was heavily weighted in favour of property. The franchise was severely restricted although inflation extended the number of voters. Representation to newly settled areas was tardily granted and only on a differential basis so that in South Carolina the tide-water counties were granted six or eight representatives whereas the back-country counties, greater in area and population, received only one or two. In some of the tide-water counties of Virginia there were virtually 'pocket' constituencies controlled by a few large planters. In New England voting rights in the town meeting were limited to the heirs of the original descendants—a rapidly dwindling proportion of the town population—and in the upcountry settlements, founded as a result of grants to speculators, the voting rights remained with the Boston landlords. Similarly in the administration of justice, justices of the peace and sheriffs were appointed by governor in council and the vast size of western counties meant that the county court was often an impractical distance from the back-country litigant. As a result of this under-representation the back country was ham-strung in its attempts to secure policies in its interest. While the back country was taxed to support a colonial establishment and sometimes an established Church, it was difficult to obtain enough votes in the assemblies to impose taxes for urgent back-country purposes such as the construction of roads and bridges and the support of colonial militia for defence against Indian attack. The persistent refusal of assemblies to provide adequate defence against the Indians was the occasion of particularly bitter protests from the frontier. As a result of this political discrimination the back-country farmer felt victimised by the eastern oligarchy which so grossly neglected his interests; and, because that oligarchy sheltered under the protection of the royal governor's throne, it was only natural that the farmer should come to look upon the Royal Standard as the symbol of his oppressors.

Unlike their English neighbours, whom the Appalachian barrier had so long confined to the coastal settlement, the French were encouraged by the great corridor of the St Lawrence and the Great Lakes to disperse far into the interior in search of furs. That dispersal had, in 1714, resulted in a tenuous empire of forest and waterway reaching from the New Orleans levees by way of the intersecting arcs of the Mississippi River and the Great Lakes–St Lawrence system to the tide-scarred shores of the Bay of Fundy and the fog-bound Isle Royale. Apart from the struggling colony of New Orleans which, with some remote inland settlements in the Illinois country, constituted the Province of Louisiana, the French empire in North America was concentrated along the St Lawrence and constituted the Province of New France. New France emerged from Queen Anne's War shorn of Newfoundland and the isthmus of Nova Scotia but confident of her expanding power. That confidence was based upon the two staples which had made the colony: furs and fish. But any remaining hope that upon this basis there would grow a self-supporting community sending provisions to the French West Indies was doomed to disappointment. For the lure of furs and fish inhibited true settlement and there were few new French immigrants ready to shoulder the back-breaking work of tilling the unrewarding soil. At the outbreak of King George's War in 1744 a mere 50,000 French subjects in North America faced nearly a million British settlers. A mixture of Canadian environment and French character prevented Colbert's dream from coming true.

Unlike their New England neighbours to the south, the French settlements at the mouth of the St Lawrence failed to make fishing the basis for a flexible economy integrated with trade and farming. At vast expense the French Government erected the great new fortress of Louisbourg on the Isle Royal, and transported to that island the French fishing population of Newfoundland. It also hoped similarly to re-settle the Acadian peasants who now fed their cattle on salt marshes under British suzerainty; but most of the Acadians stubbornly chose to remain in the softer climate and more fertile land of the Bay of Fundy. The French fishery was still largely carried on by the big fishing vessels from Brittany and the resident fishing population of Cape Breton remained small and its trade unimportant. The town of Louisbourg had to depend on cattle from Acadia and flour, provisions and lumber brought by the Yankee trading ketches in exchange for French molasses.

To the west, the overriding demands of the fur trade prevented the growth of a healthily diverse economy. Along the shores of the St Lawrence from Quebec to Montreal the seigneuries languished. Receiving meagre dues and yet expected to perform the obligations of gentility, the seigneurial class had become impoverished and turned to shopkeeping, fur trading or a minor office for support. The *habitants* wrested a subsistence from their holdings; but their farming was slovenly and their more enterprising sons wandered away to a forest life. The distractions of war and furs kept farming at a low ebb.

The fur trade continued to attract the adventurous and those in revolt from the poor and church-ridden life of the St Lawrence Valley. Its *cadre* of *voyageurs*, although looked at askance by the clergy and the settled, maintained that tradition of reckless courage, insouciant good humour and forestcraft which was the genius of French Canada. The conditions of the trade were changing rapidly. To the south the Iroquois, who had been such excellent auxiliaries, had accepted the rule of the British in 1713 and their territory adjoining Lake Ontario was in hostile hands. Further west the problem of Indian allies was complicated by tribal wars. The French suffered increasing competition from the English whose manufacturers provided better trade goods—better kettles and woollens and rum which was a cheap and effective substitute for cognac. The French could not compete with these goods, and the Montreal merchants took to trading peltry for them with the English traders at Fort Albany. As a result, too, of this English advantage, the French began to feel competition in the Ohio Valley from Pennsylvanians and Virginians. Far to the north-west, also, the English were at work. The Hudson's Bay Company, which had received back its territories from the French at the Peace, used the better trade goods, cheapened by the economical sea transport into the heart of the beaver country, to attract Indian traders to the Bay posts. But until the journey of Anthony Henday in 1754–5 they made little effort to penetrate into the interior of the drainage basin. Instead, the French, led by La Vérendrye, thrust westwards and opened a series of posts in the 1730's which tapped the region between Lake Superior and Lake Winnipeg for their own trade. As a result of these new regions the supply of beaver was maintained and production stabilised. But prices rose with increased costs and the trade was decreasingly profitable. With trading posts a thousand miles from Montreal, inferior trade goods and the interruption of transport through Indian wars and Anglo-French hostilities, operating costs rose steeply. Although the wide dispersal meant that the traders were more independent of the Montreal merchants, the external trade continued to be handled as a monopoly, from 1717 onwards by the *Compagnie des Indes*. The decreasing profits of the Company embarrassed the colonial Government, which was financially dependent on the trade, and which at the same time incurred increasing expenses in the upkeep of defence posts.

New France was, in fact, ruled by two monopolies, of trade and government. The economy, centred on furs, failed to develop a network of trade in the Atlantic basin and depended on a single trunk-line between the St Lawrence and France. Similarly government, although flexible enough in the interior, concentrated authority rigidly at Quebec and Quebec in turn was severely subordinated to the French Ministry of Marine. The Government of New France kept to the end its centralised, authoritarian, paternalist character which served well the needs of the fur trade. But since that trade inhibited the growth of a populous colony of settlement the Government was finally overwhelmed by the problem of defence with which the governors-general of Quebec and the *intendants*, upon whom the entire government rested, were increasingly preoccupied. Around them a small class of French and colonial officials and merchants in Quebec and Montreal formed a society which was a pale imitation of Paris and which grew raffish and corrupt as the shadows of war and inflation deepened. The only counterpoise to this precariously balanced society was the Church. Under the authority of the archbishop of Quebec, the secular clergy and the orders continued to uphold the traditions of Laval, fostering a settled family life, prosecuting missions to the Indians and setting their face against the disintegrating influences of the fur trade. But even the Church became involved in politics and Jesuit missionaries, like Le Loutre, played an important part in stimulating the Indians against the British. The Church in Canada, faced by the peculiarly harsh conditions of colonial life, continued to draw its spiritual sustenance from the austere tradition of the seventeenth century and remained largely untouched by the newer winds of doctrine of the Age of Reason. In doing so it became truly Canadian in outlook and contributed forcefully to the growing sense of Canadian nationality which survived the collapse of New France.

CHAPTER XXII

RIVALRIES IN AMERICA

I. THE CARIBBEAN

THE settlements signed in Utrecht left Spanish America intact, but there were three main causes of dispute between the European Powers in the Caribbean. The first was between Spain and the rest, arising from the determination of the Spaniards to uphold a strict monopoly of the trade of their own possessions, and to take all necessary measures to defend the monopoly against other maritime traders. English, French, Dutch and Danes, on the other hand, were equally determined to break into the monopoly, either by extracting concessions from the Spanish Government, or by smuggling, or by a combination of the two. It is surprising that open conflict was not more frequent. The obvious inability of the Spaniards to maintain their monopoly in its entirety gave rise to the second dispute; that between the other Caribbean Powers over which of them should profit by Spain's commercial weakness. In this dispute England and France were the chief contenders, and their distrust of one another partly explains why neither of them quarrelled seriously with Spain for a generation. England and France were the principal rivals also in the third dispute, or group of disputes, over the possession of West Indian islands not occupied by Spaniards.

The immense importance attached to these disputes throughout the eighteenth century is at first sight hard to explain. The wealth of Spanish America was traditionally exaggerated, of course, and when buccaneering ceased to be a semi-respectable profession, trade seemed the only obvious way of securing a share of that wealth. In fact, the purchasing power of the Spanish colonial population—poor and primitive Indians for the most part—was small and the market easily glutted; but the high proportion of bullion in the products of the empire fired the mercantilist imagination.

A trade with Spanish America required bases in the Caribbean, where goods could be stored or transhipped and slaves refreshed, and where smugglers could find refuge. Islands such as Jamaica were valued largely for that purpose. Curaçao, indeed, had been seized deliberately as a smugglers' base. Most of the settled West Indian islands, moreover, were valuable in themselves. They produced large quantities of sugar and smaller quantities of other tropical products, indigo, coffee, ginger, cotton and the like, all of which were sold at considerable profit to the people who marketed them in Europe, though not always to the planters. To produce sugar, the West Indian planters, like the colonial Spaniards, imported slaves from West Africa in large numbers, so employing many ships and indirectly benefiting the manufacturers of the 'trade goods' with which the slaves were bought on the African coast. The planters also imported food and timber; the French islands got some of these supplies from France, but the English got almost all from North America; and since the North Americans preferred to buy their sugar and molasses from the French, who sold it cheaper, the food imports of the English islands had to be paid for in money. To obtain the necessary bullion the English islands were especially obliged to develop their smuggling trade with Spanish America. The illicit cutting of logwood in Campeche and later in the bay of Honduras was in part an answer—a quite inadequate answer— to this problem of the drain of money from the West Indies. All the problems and all the disputes in the Caribbean area were thus interconnected.

In competing for trade with Spanish America the English possessed one great advantage, or apparent advantage. The South Sea Company alone had a right to trade admitted, however grudgingly, by Spain. The peace settlement of Utrecht assigned the *Asiento* for the supply of slaves to the company for thirty years, together with land and facilities for the 'refreshment' of slaves on the Río de la Plata. At the same time the Company secured the novel privilege of sending a shipload of general merchandise to Spanish America every year. The size of the ship was limited, and the king of Spain was to have a quarter share in the cargo and five per cent of the profit on the rest; otherwise the Company's goods were admitted free of duty. These concessions, though less than had been asked, were on paper impressive enough to send the price of shares soaring.

In practice, however, the advantage possessed by England through the South Sea Company proved an illusion. In the first place, the cargo of the Annual Ship was to be sold at Portobello Fair, and not before the arrival of the galleons; the Company could not select the place and the time for selling at the best prices, as the smugglers could, so that its profits were necessarily moderate. Further, the Company specifically undertook, in return for its monopoly, to refrain from illicit trade. Admittedly this promise could be broken—was certain to be broken, either by the Company itself or by its agents trading privately; and admittedly no undertaking given by the Company could effectively bind interlopers; but the Spaniards lost no opportunity of recalling this part of the treaty, and the Company, by virtue of its official concession, its large stocks, and its expensive establishments in America, was vulnerable to Spanish resentment. The directors knew that any irregularity committed by an English ship might be punished by confiscation of the Company's property, and they sometimes dissuaded their government and the officers of the Royal navy from taking perfectly proper action against Spanish depredations, for that reason. The interests of unprivileged traders were sacrificed to those of the Company; and the Company incurred thereby a double unpopularity. The private traders of Jamaica hated it because of its obvious intention of superseding them. The sugar planters also hated it, on the grounds that it raised the price of slaves, and exported the best slaves to the Spanish colonies, leaving only the refuse for the English islands. Certainly the Company, having failed to secure an adequate supply of slaves from the Royal Africa Company, bought many of its slaves in Jamaica. It was also obliged by the terms of its *Asiento* to supply only slaves of a certain quality. This was in reality a serious handicap to the Company, for its cargoes were undersold by smugglers who shipped inferior slaves, of a quality which the Spanish colonists could afford not only to buy but to pay for; but this argument did not mollify the planters, or the private traders, or their Whig supporters in England.

While the activities of the South Sea Company were disliked in England and the English colonies, they were even more disliked in Spain. The Annual Ship in particular gave constant trouble. It was a new and—to Spaniards—an abhorrent departure from their normal trade policy. Only good faith and cordial relations could make such a concession work smoothly, and these were almost always lacking. Two outbreaks of war interrupted the trade, in 1718 and 1727; the Bubble crisis of 1720 brought discredit as well as interruption. Even in normal times sailings were irregular. The Spaniards suspected, reasonably enough, that the *Asiento* and the Annual Ship, instead of being accepted as substitutes for the old illicit trade, were used as a cover for smuggling. The Company's slave sloops from Jamaica carried other goods besides slaves: and the Annual Ship, while discharging its cargo off Portobello, was sometimes re-loaded by night from Jamaica. So the Spanish Government made endless difficulties over the grant of *cédulas* for the Annual Ships, and in fact only eight voyages took place in the whole life of the concession. The Company constantly complained that it made little profit by the Annual Ships and none by the *Asiento*; the king of Spain on his part suspected that the Company concealed its profits in order to defraud him of his share. The Company's steady refusal to produce its accounts for inspection lent some colour to this suspicion. Long before the expiry of the agreed thirty years, the Spanish Government wearied of the whole concession, and would have terminated it, had agreement been possible on the question of compensation.

If the Company, which negotiated directly with the Spanish Government and employed the British ambassador in Madrid as its agent, could not carry on a steady trade in amity, what of the interlopers? The colonial shipping of three or four foreign nations plied in the Caribbean, carrying lawful trade with their own colonies and unlawful trade with those of Spain. Law-abiding French traders, under orders from the Government, usually gave bond not to undertake illicit trade. The Dutch, on the other hand, went armed for an avowedly illicit trade; they were at least known for smugglers on sight. English colonial ships were far more numerons than either, but the English Government would never accept the suggestion that their shipping should give bond, as the French did. English shipping in the Caribbean included the South Sea Company's ships and slave sloops carrying a lawful, or ostensibly lawful, trade with Spanish America; ships engaged in normal traffic to England, North America or the islands; and smugglers to Latin American ports. In order to distinguish between fair traders and smugglers, the Spaniards claimed and exercised a right to stop and search foreign ships at sea anywhere in the Western Hemisphere. Against this the English loudly asserted the principle of the freedom of navigation on the High Seas.

The enforcement of the Spanish trade monopoly was entrusted to *guarda-costas*, fitted out in Spanish colonial ports and carrying commissions from the local governors. These ships were manned by ruffians trained in the long war against the buccaneers. They were fitted out privately and received their remuneration from the sale of the prizes they brought in. They cruised in the regular routes of colonial trade, stopping every English ship they met and searching for 'contraband'. The *guarda-costas* and the Spanish courts accepted the presence in a foreign ship of any Spanish colonial product—indigo, cocoa, logwood, or Spanish money—as evidence of unlawful trade. This was flimsy evidence indeed, for Jamaica produced indigo and logwood in small quantities, and had produced cocoa; and Spanish money was the commonest means of exchange throughout the West Indies. Moreover, a ship might be seized and condemned merely because its position at the time of encounter was—in the opinion of a Spanish court—off the direct course to a lawful destination. Colonial governors received a share of prize-money; no doubt there was much collusion between them and the captains of the *guarda-costas*. Ships approaching or leaving Jamaica had to pass close to the coasts of Florida, Cuba or Hispaniola, and many peaceful traders suffered unjust seizure and condemnation. The official process of appeal was long, expensive and usually fruitless; and even the intervention of the British ambassador at Madrid often failed to obtain redress.

As a result of these depredations, a long list of financial claims and a mounting wave of national indignation piled up in England against Spain. The merchants clamoured for redress and the Opposition supported them in Parliament. During the brief wars of 1718 and 1727, moreover, the property of the South Sea Company in Spanish territory was seized, and so another claim for compensation was added to the list. Against the bill, admittedly, had to be set the sums owed to the king of Spain by the South Sea Company—negro duties, share of trading profits, if any, and so forth—but the Company never allowed these to be ascertained, and estimates varied widely. Besides these financial disagreements, and the perennial dispute over free navigation, there was the problem of the log-wood cutters in Honduras, and a boundary difficulty—the question of the English claim to the territory of Georgia on the undefined frontiers of Carolina and Florida. None of these disputes was so grave as to lead inevitably to war. War was made unavoidable by the truculence and clamour of the 'trading part of the nation' in England, and in particular by the intransigence of the South Sea Company.

The special claims of the Company delayed the convention which ended the war of 1727. Throughout the 1730's a series of attempts to negotiate a settlement of differences failed for similar or connected reasons. In 1737 the company produced an ingenious plan for settling its financial quarrels with Spain, using the negro duties and Spanish share of profits to offset part of its claim for compensation. The plan was approved by the Spanish ambassador in London, but the negotiations in Madrid were interrupted by a sharp memorandum on depredations from Newcastle, in which he unwittingly offered an excuse for delay, by basing part of his argument on the irrelevant Anglo-Spanish treaty of 1667 instead of the more applicable 'American' treaty of 1670. The Spanish Government took advantage of this blunder to shelve both plan and memorandum. Meanwhile the depredations went on, and in March 1738 Captain Jenkins appeared with his famous tale of woe. The House of Commons promptly resolved that 'it was the undoubted right of British subjects to sail their ships in any part of the seas of America'. Letters of reprisal were offered to English merchants—an absurd gesture—and Admiral Haddock was sent on a minatory cruise in the Mediterranean. Finally, however, Walpole and the Spanish Ambassador between them produced a draft agreement, which was accepted in Madrid and actually ratified in January 1739 as the Convention of El Pardo. By its terms Spain was to pay £95,000—the estimated excess of Spanish over English depredations; but the South Sea Company refused to co-operate, because the Convention did not expressly recognise its rights of navigation, nor guarantee a renewal of its *Asiento*. The Company would accept no basis of negotiation but its own 1737 plan. The Opposition in England were by this time clamouring against any concession or agreement; Newcastle, impressed as always by popular clamour, and frightened by fresh reports of a Franco-Spanish family pact, kept Haddock cruising off the Spanish coast, despite the Convention; and the Spanish Government replied in May 1739 by suspending the *Asiento*. The £95,000 was never paid, and in October 1739 war was declared between England and Spain.

Both Ministry and people in England, in entering on a war over trade in the West Indies, must have been willing to fight France as well as Spain. France, besides being connected with Spain by dynastic ties, had long been England's chief rival for the trade of Spanish America; and in the mood of greedy and truculent imperialism in which the English entered the war, they were eager also to make permanent conquests of Spanish territory, which would certainly have led to war with France. The great preparations made for the departure of Lord Cathcart's expedition against Spanish America in fact prompted Fleury to send out a fleet under d'Antin, which might well have involved France in war; but d'Antin lay so long at St Domingue awaiting reinforcements and trying vainly to arrange a junction with the Spanish fleet, that his men fell sick, his stores ran out, and he was obliged to return to France without accomplishing anything. For three years the French did no more to support Spain. Fleury had no desire for war and no particular love for the Spain of Elizabeth Farnese. France and England kept the peace at sea, more or less, until 1744.

The war between England and Spain hung fire. Vernon's initial success in destroying the fortifications of Portobello was not repeated. He was obliged to spend part of 1740 looking for d'Antin's fleet. The great force sent out under Ogle and Cathcart to join him suffered from ambiguous orders and divided counsel. Havana was deemed too strong to be taken. Cartagena, where the galleons lay, was chosen as the first objective, but the combined naval and military attacks on Cartagena, and afterwards on Santiago de Cuba, were both failures. Indeed, the only other notable English naval operation in this war was Anson's voyage to the Pacific, which, magnificent achievement though it was, affected the course of the war very little. On the other hand, the English took many prizes and dislocated the normal lawful trade of Spanish America. Only one treasure fleet reached Spain, and no galleons or *flotas* sailed during the war. The Portobello galleons were never again restored. The trade had to be carried either by single casual 'register-ships'—which, though faster and cheaper than the convoys, were often taken—or by English or Dutch smugglers. The smugglers throve by the war, as their governments intended they should; and the English Government explicitly ordered Admiral Vernon to do all he could to protect and convoy English trade with the enemy's colonies.

The war between England and France in the West Indies, which broke out openly in 1744, was a very different affair. It was governed not by desire to acquire new territories or new trades, but by the bitter rivalry between two existing sets of sugar colonies. The French Caribbean islands—larger in area and with soil less exhausted—were competing more and more successfully with the English islands in the production of cheap sugar and in trade with Europe and English North America. Since England could not control the supply of sugar, none of the peaceful methods known to mercantilist economists could avail against this growing competition. The Molasses Act, which had been enacted in 1733 at the instigation of the West India interest in England to stop French West Indian trade with English North America, proved difficult to enforce, and naturally irritated the North Americans, whose interests it attacked. Fiscal concessions, such as the removal of sugar from the 'enumerated' list in 1739 to permit direct export to Europe, were of little help to the English planters, because they did not remove the basic cause of difficulty —high production costs. Depression in the English West Indies affected too many English interests to be tolerated; and in that time of truculent trade rivalry, if peaceful measures would not serve, war was welcomed as a possible solution of commercial problems.

War offered the English an opportunity to cripple the French sugar trade, which they could not defeat in open competition. Sugar planters on both sides disliked the acquisition of fresh sugar-producing territory; they feared that increased production would lower prices within their protected markets. Each side hoped not to acquire and exploit the enemy's colonies, but to destroy and depopulate them; in particular, to carry off the slaves, the most necessary, the most valuable and most movable part of the planters' capital. Failing the destruction of the enemy's colonies, the next best thing was to cut off their trade, starve them of provisions and slaves, and prevent them from selling their sugar. In this war naval activity was in practice almost confined to this second type of operation. By 1744 the energies of both combatants were taxed elsewhere, in Europe and North America. Forces were not available for major operations in the West Indies, and the fighting there was little more than a rehearsal for the much sterner struggle which was to break out in 1756. As a rehearsal, the war had lessons to offer. It revealed the disadvantage which the French suffered through having no permanent naval bases in the West Indies, and the great difficulty—as d'Antin discovered—of victualling a large fleet from the slender food resources of tropical islands. The English, with their established dockyards at Port Royal in Jamaica and English Harbour in Antigua, kept seasoned squadrons permanently on the station and subsisted them without much difficulty. On the other hand, the war also revealed the defects of the English trade system. The dependence of the French islands upon North America for grain and timber and upon Ireland for beef should have given the English an important tactical advantage; but war or no war, the shippers of New England continued shamelessly to trade with the enemy, either directly or through the neutral Dutch harbours in Curaçao or St Eustatius. The privateers which sailed from Martinique to prey upon English shipping were often stored with North American provisions; meanwhile the English islands went short, and sometimes had to be supplied with food from England.

The Treaty of Aix-la-Chapelle settled no important question between France and England in the West Indies. No territories changed hands. Four disputed islands in the Windward group—Dominica, St Lucia, St Vincent and Tobago—were declared 'neutral', and both parties agreed to evacuate them; but even had the colonial governments wished to carry out this agreement, it would have been difficult to round up the unorganised groups of squatters, mostly French, who drifted in from the older colonies. The islands remained an English grievance and a bone of contention for the next war; in this respect, as in others, the treaty between France and England was only a truce. The commercial treaty of 1750, which supplemented the general European settlement and wound up the maritime quarrel between Spain and England, was similarly inconclusive. It contained no reference to the freedom of navigation in whose name the war had begun. The irritating problem of the Honduras logwood camps remained unsolved. The South Sea Company had almost ceased to present a problem; it no longer traded; its last 'Annual Ship' had sailed in 1733 and its slave trade ended in 1739. Under the treaty it received £100,000 in return for the surrender of all claims under the *Asiento*. Thus the English gave up the long attempt to force or persuade the Spaniards to allow direct trade to their colonies. The illicit trade between the English islands and Spanish America went on, but it remained as illicit as ever, and could no longer be hidden by the *Asiento*. During the second half of the century the Spanish Government proved increasingly ready to reorganise its trade system, and increasingly able to protect its monopoly. While the English lost by the process, the French gained. They had stuck steadily to the old method of trade, consigning goods for Spanish America through Spanish merchants at Cadiz; and the greater part of this trade was in their hands by 1750. The French steadily enlarged their share of Spanish American trade at the expense of the English. Meanwhile their commercial competition in the West Indies and their strategic pressure in North America steadily increased.

In the mind of one leading statesman at least—Pitt—there was no doubt that the major purpose of the Seven Years War in the Americas was to safeguard English North America by seizing Canada. Nevertheless, the West Indies were again a centre of heavy fighting, and the forces employed there were far larger than in the previous war; far larger, incidentally, than those used in the simultaneous struggle for India. Great expeditions were sent out on both sides, and their commanders now had orders to annex the enemy's sugar colonies, not merely to pillage them. This change of policy, which was supported by the West India interest in London, was more apparent than real. At the outset of the war, England had lost Minorca to the French. The capture of this important naval base affected the West Indies directly, by releasing units of the French Mediterranean fleet for service in the West Indies. Subsequently the English took from the French Cape Breton Island with its great fortress, Louisbourg. Each side considered the possession of both places essential, and each hoped to recover its loss without surrendering its gain. It was to secure a bargaining counter, to avoid surrendering Cape Breton Island for Minorca, that Pitt was moved to attack Martinique, though later in the war, when victory exceeded his expectation, he began to favour the retention of some at least of England's West Indian gains for their own sake. Even the colonial governors and the planters in the West Indies supported this change of policy. The presence of full-scale naval war in the Caribbean reminded them of their small numbers and of their weakness against an enemy fleet or a slave mutiny, and forced upon them a more strategic, a less purely commercial appreciation of their position. The planters of Barbados and Antigua, weary of constant alarms, began to realise that their estates would be safer if Martinique, Guadeloupe and the neutral islands were in English hands, at least for the duration of the war. If it were decided at the peace to keep any islands captured from the French, then the danger of the admission of their sugars to the English market would have to be faced; but even that danger might be avoided by evicting the French inhabitants and by forbidding their English successors to plant sugar.[1]

Most of the serious fighting in the war was done by the line-of-battle fleets of the contending Powers. In 1757 the French launched an ingenious plan of co-ordination by three naval squadrons off North Africa, the West Indies and North America, which damaged English trade considerably and put Jamaica in fear of invasion for some weeks; but the necessity for going to the relief of Louisbourg prevented any of the French admirals from achieving much in the Caribbean. After 1757 the French gave up the attempt to maintain a constant relief of squadrons in West Indian waters. Theoretically the best English naval defence of the West Indies was therefore a thorough blockade of the Channel and Atlantic ports. Despite its superiority in numbers, the Royal navy could not watch all the ports at once, and strong French squadrons sometimes slipped through; most of them, however, were destined for North America, and after 1757 the initiative in the West Indies usually lay with the English.

Late in 1758 Pitt, now possessing in Louisbourg the key to Canada and confident of success in Europe, launched two attacks, one direct and one indirect, against the French West Indies. The indirect attack was against the French stations in West Africa, and culminated in the capture of Gorée by Keppel. This comparatively minor operation achieved economic results out of all proportion to the cost of the force employed. It crippled the French slave trade and seriously hampered the working of the sugar plantations in the French West Indies. Meanwhile a series of English naval victories in the Mediterranean and the Bay of Biscay destroyed or delayed French fleets intended for America, and created favourable opportunities for England in the Caribbean. The combined naval and military force under Moore and Barrington sent to attack the French West Indies found Martinique too strong for it, but seized, in the spring of

---

[1] This was sometimes suggested. 'Reflections on the true Interest of Great Britain with respect to the Caribee Islands' by a Planter of Barbados. Public Record Office, C.O. 28/50.

1759, the large and wealthy island of Guadeloupe, a French fleet under Admiral Bompar arriving just too late to raise the siege. The planters of Guadeloupe were allowed to capitulate on very favourable terms. They were to be neutral between France and England while the war lasted; their goods were to be admitted to English markets; their slaves were exempted from *corvée*; they retained French law under English military occupation, and were fully protected in possession of their property. English planters indeed were forbidden to settle, and nothing was done to alter the French character of the colony. After the initial damage of the fighting had been repaired, the island began to enjoy a new prosperity, for English and American merchants rushed in to supply the food, the timber and the slaves for which it starved. Feckless planters escaped from their debts to French *commissionnaires* and were allowed to run up new debts to English factors from Antigua. Best of all, they found at last a safe European and North American market for their sugar. The planters of Guadeloupe were envied alike by their compatriots in Martinique and by their English rivals. This was precisely the kind of conquest most disliked by the English planters; it struck directly at their profits without giving them any permanent promise of security. The flooding of the London market with Guadeloupe sugars was one reason for the drop in sugar prices in 1760, and explains the bitter complaints of the West India interest against the terms of the capitulation.

During the second half of 1759 and through 1760 Pitt's attention was occupied with Choiseul's threatened invasion of the British Isles, and with the last bitter struggle for the possession of Canada. During this time no major operation was attempted in the Caribbean, and in 1761 there followed the period of abortive and insincere haggling over peace, in which Choiseul, fortified by the prospect of a new compact with Spain, held out for terms which England would not accept, until Spain should be ready to enter the war.

Spain had concluded the Family Compact partly because the war between England and France had increased Spain's causes for complaint against England. In peace the English had done little to restrain their smugglers; in war they showed the arrogant disregard of the rights of neutral shipping, which belligerent naval Powers commonly display. The situation grew worse when the hard-pressed French threw open the trade of their starving Caribbean colonies to neutrals; for the invention and enforcement of the 'rule of the war of 1756' led to still further seizures. Worse still, as the tide of war turned in favour of England and against France, it seemed clear that Pitt intended, if he could, to seize all the French possessions in North America and the Caribbean, including the neutral islands in the Windward group, to which Spain made some shadowy claim. If England and France made peace upon such conditions, Spain would be left to negotiate alone with an England all-powerful in the West

Indies. In return for Spanish support, Choiseul promised to make the satisfaction of Spain's demands a condition of peace with England; but in the English view the very act of dragging Spain into the negotiations made peace with France impossible and war with Spain inevitable. The Compact in fact bound Spain to declare war before May 1762 if peace had not been made between France and England. Peace was not made, and the English Government anticipated events by declaring war on Spain in January.

The entry of Spain into the war brought no relief to France in the Caribbean. In the same month that war was declared, Rodney, fresh from England with a powerful fleet, took Martinique. Again a strong French squadron, this time under Blénac, was hurried out from France. Its departure was delayed, however, by repeated interceptions of the necessary stores on their way to Brest, and it arrived in the West Indies too late to save Martinique. Blénac's arrival at Saint Domingue in March 1762 caused the usual panic in Jamaica; but Rodney, with his great fleet well to windward, was able to detach a squadron large enough to deter Blénac from attacking Jamaica, and Blénac's expedition presently found itself blockaded and helpless at Saint Domingue. It might indeed have been destroyed before it got there, but for the short-sighted cowardice of the Governor and Council of Jamaica, who insisted on most of the available naval strength remaining in Kingston harbour to protect them.

To the annoyance of the English planting interest, the inhabitants of Martinique were granted a capitulation similar to that of Guadeloupe; though, since nobody expected Martinique to be kept at the peace, its capitulation was less likely to be of permanent importance. The neutral islands were less fortunate, no doubt because Rodney thought that his government might wish to retain them. Dominica had surrendered at discretion to a North American force in June 1761; Tobago was for all practical purposes English already; and Rodney reduced St Lucia, St Vincent and Grenada to submission shortly after the capture of Martinique. Of all the French possessions in the West Indies only St Domingue remained.

Meanwhile Spain, far from helping to save the French colonies, began to lose her own. The English Government at once prepared an attack on Havana; and profiting by former experience, the Admiralty planned the operation in detail and avoided the uncertainties and delays which had beset Cathcart's expedition in 1740. The chief difficulty was the presence in the West Indies of Blénac's fleet, which, having failed either to save Martinique or to join with the Spaniards to attack Jamaica, might at least have been expected to go to the help of Havana, especially as Rodney in the Leeward Islands had now no ships to spare; but Blénac, short of victuals and with his men falling sick, allowed himself to remain bottled up at Cap Français while the force commanded by Pocock and Albemarle sailed through the islands, picked up more ships and men from Jamaica, and proceeded undisturbed to reduce Havana. Havana had been thought by the Spaniards to be impregnable. Its fall in August 1762 made a great stir; the captors destroyed a considerable Spanish naval force and collected great sums in prize money, while the English politicians, when they heard of it, were encouraged to raise their peace terms still higher. Two other misfortunes befell Spain in the same year. An English fleet sailing from the East Indies captured Manila, and though the news of the capture did not reach Europe in time to affect the peace negotiations, the knowledge that the attack was being made had its effect. Finally, an invasion of Portugal, intended by Charles III as a diversion, proved an unexpected failure. Lisbon was never in serious danger, and the English, though they abandoned the war in Germany, did not allow themselves to be diverted from Havana. In October 1762 Charles III capitulated. The French had been pressing him for some months to make peace. After the fall of Havana Choiseul had to admit that France and Spain together were no match for England at sea. France could no longer face the strain of unsuccessful war, and her ally Austria was at last ready for peace.

The English ministers were almost as ready for peace as Choiseul, though for somewhat different reasons. George III was anxious to be rid of responsibility in Germany. Pitt, who would have fought till he deprived the Bourbons of every colony they possessed, had given place to the timorous and inexperienced Bute. Many English politicians felt nervous about the tremendous ascendancy achieved in the colonial field, and feared a future combination of all the other colonial Powers against England. The North American colonists were becoming restive; with Canada subdued, they saw no need of further fighting and such enthusiasm as they had shown for West Indian conquests had evaporated. They intended, after all, to go on trading to the French West Indian islands, whether those islands became British or remained French. For all these reasons, the Treaty of Paris was concluded in haste and embodied the concessions and compromises which haste entailed.

The numerous and valuable conquests made in the late stages of the war proved an embarrassment to the English ministers in their attempts to hasten the peace settlement. Something must be sacrificed, to have peace; but something beyond the original objects of the war must be kept, to satisfy popular clamour. The principal object of the war had been to safeguard the North American colonies, and to achieve this end there was little doubt that Canada, or part of it at least, would have to be retained; on the other hand, the trade and revenue of Canada was small, and the public reasonably expected the acquisitions at the peace to pay part of the cost of the war. The French West Indian islands would bring in an immediate revenue. They could more easily be settled with Englishmen than the vast spaces of Canada; and West Indian planters habitually returned to England to spend their money, while most settlers in North America stuck to their farms and businesses and kept their money, if they had any, in the colonies. These were plausible reasons for preferring West Indian to North American acquisitions. Guadeloupe in particular was a tempting prize. The slave traders naturally pressed for its retention. Even the West Indian interest was partly converted to a policy of annexation, for the planters and their advocates had learnt what dangerous neighbours Martinique and Guadeloupe could be, particularly as privateering bases. Many people in England thought that Guadeloupe should be kept, even in preference to Canada, and the question of Guadeloupe against Canada was made the subject of much pamphleteering and acrimonious debate. It is unlikely that the Government paid much serious attention to this debate so long as Guadeloupe alone was in question; but the conquest of Martinique in 1762 raised the problem of choosing between Canada on the one hand and all the French West Indies except Saint Domingue on the other. Rodney in particular attached great strategic importance to Martinique. If, as seemed likely, the French would not make peace without Martinique, then England might keep Guadeloupe in payment. Bute, however, apparently thought that France would not yield any settled colony, and decided in the end on a compromise. He agreed to restore Martinique and Guadeloupe, and, as a necessary adjunct, the French slaving stations in West Africa; but he demanded the cession of Grenada, all the neutral islands, and the whole continent of North America east of the Mississippi. These were all almost empty territories, open to English enterprise, and containing few Frenchmen to make trouble for the Government. With the cession of territory was to be included the right of navigating the Mississippi itself. In the final peace terms all these demands were agreed, except that France insisted on retaining St Lucia, on the ground that the island was essential to the defence of Martinique—a very good reason, as Pitt complained, for England to keep it; but the French had their way.

Bute's very moderate proposals were as good as the French could hope for, but they ignored the claim of Spain to be considered. Spain had been dragged into war in the interests of France, had suffered serious losses, and was now being urged to make a hasty peace, also in the interests of France. Charles III did not want the English on the shores of the Gulf of Mexico, where they could isolate Florida, run their smuggling trade under cover of the Mississippi navigation, and intercept the Mexican *flotas* with greater ease than before. Choiseul was obliged to recognise the force of the Spanish arguments, and decided eventually to buy Spanish acquiescence by ceding Louisiana to Spain.

The old disputes between Spain and England were settled without much difficulty. Spain gave up the claim to the Newfoundland fishery, and agreed to leave the prizes to the decision of the English courts. The log-wood settlements in Honduras received for the first time a precarious recognition. Spain agreed to tolerate the presence of the cutters and to respect their property; England agreed not to fortify the camps. Neither the boundaries of the settlements nor the rights of the cutters were defined, and the exact position of the English in Honduras continued to be disputed for the next twenty years. Finally, England restored Cuba to Spain and obtained Florida in exchange; and Spain renewed the treaties of commerce with England which were in force when the war began.

From the English point of view Bute's willingness to make colonial concessions in order—as he thought—to hasten a lasting peace was wasted, for a lasting peace with France was scarcely possible at that time. The long conflict of England, France and Spain in the Americas was by no means ended. Choiseul, far from being contented with England's moderation, began planning and organising for revenge almost as soon as the treaty was signed. Bute's desire for peace merely led him to accept terms less favourable than those he might have obtained; and Pitt, for all his factious ill-temper, was right in saying so. In the West Indies the concessions made were remarkable. Cuba commanded much of the American trade of Spain, Martinique and Guadeloupe much of the West Indian trade of France, and all these islands were also in close though illicit commercial contact with British North America—a contact which might have flourished the more if it had become open and lawful. There were good reasons, both strategic and economic, for England to retain some of these West Indian conquests; yet all were cheerfully restored, with little to show for their capture. No doubt the risk of prolonging a 'bloody and expensive war' had to be considered, and probably the English peace-makers assumed that English predominance at sea would always assure the mastery of the Caribbean, without the retention of the French and Spanish bases. Yet Pitt's forebodings were to be realised in his own life-time. The English naval command of the Caribbean, so glibly postulated in the 1760's, proved insufficient in the 1770's and 1780's to prevent the French from capturing many islands in the Leeward and Windward groups and threatening the safety of the whole of the British West Indies. The immense superiority achieved by England in the Caribbean during the Seven Years War had been thrown away at the peace, in return for continental gains which, though immense, were some of them very short-lived.

The English lost most of their mainland colonies within one generation, the Spaniards all of theirs within two. The West Indian islands, except for Haiti, remained loyal to their European masters; or at worst were unable to put disloyalty into effect. But the West Indies, though still a great source of wealth for European merchants and proprietors, were falling in the esteem of statesmen. Their importance as entrepôts for continental trade was already much diminished, and declined still further after 1763. They had only their exports of sugar to live by; with exhausted land, with expensive slave labour, with inefficient machinery, sugar was becoming more costly to produce; yet more and more was produced, and so it became more difficult to sell. To these difficulties was added the damage of repeated international wars. The older and smaller British islands showed signs of distress sooner than the French, but in all, absentee ownership and chronic indebtedness were becoming the rule. The West Indies suffered, and have suffered ever since, from being divided among four or five European colonial Powers, each group of islands producing sugar for a limited and protected market. The Peace of Paris was the last opportunity to unite the greater part of the West Indies under one flag, and that opportunity was missed.

2. THE NORTH AMERICAN CONTINENT

After the Treaty of Utrecht the British and French colonies in North America, though separated by a vast wilderness, became increasingly apprehensive of one another.

In the short term, the French colonies were in the stronger position. Their power was based on the riches of the wilderness itself, economically on furs, militarily on water communications and diplomatically on manipulating the Indian tribes. The conditions of the fur trade made it possible for the Governor-General, the Company and the Church, all operating from the St Lawrence valley, to control a vast and very sparsely populated hinterland. The weakness of the French colonies came, however, from this adaptation to the conditions of the wilderness and in the end was to outweigh the sources of strength. The French fur trade only required a very few men: the French did not settle in numbers large enough to develop agriculture or industry or even to provide enough soldiers. The exploitation of the forests soon reached a point of diminishing returns. Traders went even further into the hinterland and relations had to be established with even more distant Indian tribes. Concentration on the fur trade meant reliance on France for provisions, manufactures and weapons. The existence of New France depended on command of the sea and particularly the control of the approaches to the St Lawrence which was threatened by British occupation of Newfoundland and of Acadia. In the circumstances, the best hope for the French colonies was to pursue a boldly offensive policy, and by using the initiative which their centralised planning gave them they managed, between 1713 and 1754, to extend their power from the Mississippi and the Great Lakes to the Appalachians.

The strength of the British colonies was based on solidly settled communities, and in the long run it was to overwhelm the French empire in North America. It rested on a comparatively dense population whose frontier was resilient to infiltration. The French advance was by governmentally planned acquisition of strategic points; the British was like a creeping tide of trade and settlement whose movement was controlled by laws of private profit. Even the policy which restrained the colonists from competing against English products encouraged expansion, for the colonists, prevented from developing their own industries, were driven farther into the wilderness to get raw materials acceptable in exchange for English products. The colonists developed the forests of Maine and Nova Scotia for ships' timber, new lands in Pennsylvania which produced provisions for the West Indies, new plantations in the south which could grow more rice and tobacco. At the same time the excellence of English woollens and hardware gave the English colonists an advantage over French competitors for the Indian trade, and much of the capital needed to develop the western lands came from England. The chief weakness of the English colonies' position was that the easy-going temper of English politics encouraged a self-reliance which easily became narrowly provincial. Competition for Indian trade set Virginian against Pennsylvanian, Carolinian against Georgian. Colonial assemblies were reluctant to incur the expenses of adequate defence, and colonial militias would only serve on very limited terms. Even the mother country was reluctant to do more than maintain the British navy to defend the colonies. Not until 1749 was Nova Scotia founded at the expense of the mother country as a defensive bastion at the mouth of the St Lawrence.

So long as Anglo-French colonial conflict remained a matter of competition for the control of the fur trade, the French had great advantages to take the initiative and gain victories in informal fighting; but when the American dispute became part of a major conflict between great European Powers British sea power broke the tenuous threads that held the French colonies together. For the first half of the eighteenth century France and England isolated their American disputes; but after the reversal of alliances in 1756 these colonial conflcts were merged in a greater struggle which left England the dominant Power in North America.

After 1714 the French embarked on a systematic expansion more impressive than the haphazard drift of British traders and settlers into the wilderness.

To protect the all-important entrance to the St Lawrence, now threatened by British occupation of Acadia and Newfoundland, the great fortress of Louisbourg was built on Isle Royale and an attempt was made to minimise the British acquisition of Acadia by contesting the extent of its western boundary; by a drive, largely unsuccessful, to re-settle the French Acadians on Isle Royale and Isle St Jean and by more successful intrigues to keep the remaining Acadians neutral and to prevent them submitting to anything more than the highly-qualified oath of allegiance of 1727; by the efforts of the Church, in the person of the Abbé Le Loutre, to combine the loyalty of the Acadians to Catholicism with their loyalty to France, and of Jesuit missionaries, like Father Râle from his mission at Norridgewock, to incite the Abnaki Indians against the New England Protestants. Such efforts were the more encouraged by British tardiness in colonising Acadia and neglect of the tiny military establishment at Annapolis Royal. Only the New Englanders, pushing their settlements up into the Maine country, cutting timber for ships, and fishing off Newfoundland, showed signs of countering the French aggression.

Half a continent away the French set about exploiting their brilliant pioneering achievements down the Mississippi by opening up a secondary entrance to their dominion at New Orleans, founded in 1718 and in 1722 made the capital of the infant Province of Louisiana. Louisiana failed to fulfil the sanguine hopes of John Law and his fellow speculators. The climate, hostile Indians, the heavy capital required to start plantations and the dearth of suitable emigrants proved too formidable obstacles, and in spite of some success in the production of indigo the colony remained a continuing drain on French resources. But it had great strategic importance in controlling communications along the Mississippi and in extending the French sphere of influence and trade with the Indians of the Gulf hinterland. This clashed with the westward advance of Carolinians after deerskins. By the time of Queen Anne's War this remote wilderness had already become the scene of an obscure, but important, Anglo-French conflict for the Indian trade, the first round of the struggle for the control of the Mississippi Valley. The French could normally count on the Choctaw, the English on the Cherokee; influence with the rest, notably the Chickasaw and the Creeks, on the whole favoured the English who offered better trading terms. But the Carolina frontier was so insecure that after the Yamassee War of 1715 the British Government, apprehensive about the effects of French ascendancy over the southern Indians, took action in 1721 to protect it by building a fort on the Altamaha River which, within ten years, was to become part of the colony of Georgia.

The founding of Georgia in 1731, although primarily directed against the French also caused new friction with the Spaniards in Florida since the whole of the new colony lay within land claimed by Spain. The settlement on the Altamaha pushed the English seaboard frontier uncomfortably close to St Augustine. The Spanish forts there and at Pensacola and Apalache fostered intrigues with the Indians and provided a haven for Carolina's escaped slaves. General Oglethorpe's plans for the new colony included expeditions against the Spaniards and in 1738 he returned to Georgia at the head of a military force equipped for this purpose. The outbreak of hostilities between Britain and Spain in 1739 provided the excuse for forays against Florida. The results were inconclusive. In his final expedition in 1740 Oglethorpe penetrated within a few miles of

St Augustine before being forced to fall back through his own inept leadership and lack of co-operation from the naval force. The Spanish counter-offensive in 1742 against the Georgia coast was equally ineffective. The wilderness was still too formidable for either outpost to wield effective power far beyond the limits of its own palisades without full naval support.

In the vast area between the lower Mississippi and the Southern Appalachians the terrain was too difficult, the Indian problem too intractable, the distances too great and the hold of the three European Powers occupying its fringes too weak for them to come to grips with each other. The aspirations of Spain were to be determined by the more remote considerations of European diplomacy; those of France and Britain by a trial of strength on fields where each could mobilise in force against the other.

Four hundred miles and several months' canoe journey up the Mississippi the French were fostering a tiny settlement in the Illinois country in the heart of the continent between the Mississippi, Ohio and Wabash rivers. Here the fortified trading posts of Chartres (1718), Orleans (1720) and Vincennes (1732–3) sheltered a group of six villages where by 1750 a population of over a thousand Frenchmen and their Indian wives were engaged in trading and, with the aid of Indian slaves, in farming the fertile soil. The corn crops of Illinois provisioned the French forces operating in the Ohio valley, and, in time of dearth, helped to sustain posts on the Great Lakes like Detroit. For this reason and because of its strategic importance in linking the Great Lakes with Louisiana, the Illinois District became the key to French power in the interior and its protection from the incursions of the English a cardinal point in French policy. From the Illinois base French fur traders and agents operated along the Ohio, finding useful cohorts in the Piankaskaws, the Miami and the Shawnee Indians. But by the 1730's they were coming across the tracks of the English. Scores of Carolina, and then Pennsylvania traders, pushing west in search of furs, found the western Indians greedy for the cheaper Yankee rum and superior English kettles and woollens. The Iroquois, attempting to preserve their independence and their power on the Ohio, resisted this English penetration and by the beginning of King George's War in 1740 were negotiating with the French to drive the English traders from the area.

Farther north, also, along the Great Lakes, the French worked hard to strengthen their trading and strategic position. Here the great Iroquois Confederation of the Six Nations from its headquarters at Onondaga, south of Lake Ontario, controlled territory stretching from the Adirondacks to the Ohio (the original Five were joined in 1723 by the Tuscaroras emigrating from the seaboard). Although the Treaty of Utrecht recognised the friendly alliance of the Iroquois with the British, the Confederation continued to pursue its traditional policy of neutrality, attempting to play off white man against white man and successfully preserving itself as a strong buffer state between Canada and New York. The Iroquois were powerfully organised and, for an Indian Confederation, remarkably stable. Both British and French respected this neutrality, especially as it paid dividends in facilitating the collection and transmission of the all-important peltry. In this traffic the Six Nations played a vital role through their strategic position and their agency as collectors from tribes farther to the west. The French, whose main trade route passed along Lakes Ontario and Erie, were quick to rebuild their trading post on the Niagara River in 1719 and from this point of vantage they succeeded in controlling the bulk of the business. But the Dutch merchants of Albany, feeling the pinch of this competition, established a trading post farther along Lake Ontario at the mouth of the Onondaga River. This post, Oswego, established in 1725, was successful in drawing off the cream of the western trade from the Frenchmen at Niagara. Higher prices and the more attractive trade goods, especially the lavish provision of rum, were responsible. The year after Oswego was established the French re-built Fort Niagara of stone. The New Yorkers countered by erecting a strong stone fort at Oswego which Governor Burnet made clear to the French would be defended against any attack.

But the sachems of Onondaga, dependent on the fur trade for the European goods on which they had come to rely, were determined to prevent the Anglo-French competition from disrupting their economy by war. Equally pacific were the Albany Dutch who, in the interest of their lucrative trade, wished to continue the secret agreement made with the French in Queen Anne's War to prevent the region becoming an active war theatre. For the Dutch made good profits from a clandestine trade with Montreal, whereby English trade goods were exchanged for the superior French beaver. This neutrality policy was also supported by great land speculators like the Livingstons with holdings in the Mohawk valley. It was opposed by the Quebec authorities and, in the colony of New York, by those who advocated a more aggressive and less short-sighted policy towards the French, notably by the successive governors, Burnet and Clinton and by the great Indian trader and negotiator, William Johnson. But during King George's War the neutrality party controlled the New York assembly. Thus the power of the Iroquois and their policy of neutrality, together with the overriding exigency, for both the French and the New Yorkers, of maintaining the flow of furs kept the pressure of Anglo-French competition in the Lake Ontario region below the point of armed conflict. The end of the period of covert aggression came in 1739 with the outbreak of hostilities between Britain and Spain which merged with the more general war of the Austrian Succession. Thenceforward for a decade the inter-colonial rivalries of North America were exacerbated by war between their principals. But the tendency of the parent Powers to segregate the colonial conflict and to leave the initiative to their provincial authorities, providing only such naval support as could conveniently be spared from other theatres, left the character of those rivalries unchanged and prevented any major decision from being reached. The comparatively weak hold of France, Spain and Britain on the continent south of the Ohio prevented their coming to grips in this region, while the strength of the Iroquois Confederation kept the peace south-east of the Great Lakes. Only at two points were the French and British strong enough for active conflict. The control of the mouth of the St Lawrence and the headwaters of the Ohio was coming to be recognised as vital for the security of both systems, and in both places the war gave the signal for active conflict.

Characteristically, it was the French who took the first initiative. On news of hostilities, a squadron from Louisbourg promptly captured the little port of Canseau and harried Annapolis Royal. The British Government, preoccupied with the Jacobite invasion, were in no position to mount a land offensive against the French in North America. But a few of the king's New England subjects saw an opportunity to strike an unexpected blow at those French Papists whose pretensions at the mouth of the St Lawrence were threatening their fisheries, their timber, their trade, and their expanding frontier settlements in New Hampshire and Maine. This was nothing less than a colonial expedition against Louisbourg itself. The able governor of Massachusetts, William Shirley, persuaded the Commonwealth Legislature by one vote to agree to the scheme, to which Connecticut, Rhode Island and New Hampshire also contributed. As soon as the ice permitted in 1745, some 3000 militia set sail for the St Lawrence under the command of William Pepperrell, a Kittery merchant. This was all likely to prove summer madness without a naval force to wrest control of the ocean approaches from the French squadron at Louisbourg. Fortunately Shirley persuaded Newcastle to order Commodore Warren of the West Indies station to aid the expedition. It is to the credit of the speed, secrecy and daring of the New Englanders that the French were taken by surprise and had to abandon an important battery to the besiegers. Capitalising this initial advantage and ably partnered by Warren's squadron which prevented French reinforcements from getting through, the little army forced the surrender of the great fortress on 17 June. The capture of Louisbourg was the one signal achievement of British arms in North America during King George's War. For once a group of colonies were prepared to combine effectively to further their self-evident interests with the indispensable support of British sea power. The result was an overwhelming British victory which, had it been confirmed at the peace, would have ultimately rendered the French position in America untenable. Unfortunately for the New Englanders, Louisbourg was only one factor among many at Aix-la-Chapelle in 1748 and as a result of balancing many considerations, including the difficulty, in retaining Louisbourg, of adding to the already intractable problem of assimilating the Acadians, it was decided to hand back the fortress. Thus the golden moment for check-mating the French passed. It would not prove so easy again to find the occasion for an effective combination of British colonies against the French and when the time came it needed an expensive war and a British armament to bring it about.

No sooner had peace been signed than both sides took steps to con-solidate their positions at the mouth of the St Lawrence. The French set about re-building Louisbourg, and did all they could to protect its overland communications with Quebec by building Fort Beauséjour on the neck of Acadia itself and by keeping the Acadians to their French allegiance through the exhortations of the priest Le Loutre and the menaces of his mass-saying MicMac Indians. In 1749 the British Government at last moved to strengthen its position on the peninsula. Some 3000 British subjects were transported thither to found the port settlement of Halifax on the east coast bay of Chibuctou, under General Cornwallis who was made governor of the new colony of Nova Scotia. It was ultimately decided that on security grounds there was no alternative to removing the entire Acadian population to British territory less strategically exposed. At the outbreak of the French and Indian war some 10,000 French-speaking Catholics were ejected from their farms to begin an unhappy existence as 'displaced persons' as far afield as New Orleans and Brittany.

Meanwhile in the interior of the continent King George's War saw a less spectacular but equally important struggle for the control of that area between the Great Lakes and the Ohio which was so vital to the security of the French dominion. This struggle, hardly interrupted by the peace, led directly to the hostilities which inaugurated the French and Indian War.

The French plan, on the opening of hostilities, to drive the English traders from the Ohio did not materialise. The key to control was the manipulation of the Indians. The aim of the tribes was to preserve as much independence from the white men as was consonant with the continuing flow of those European supplies on which their economies had come to depend. Although wayward and treacherous, there was a certain hard-headed consistency in Indian diplomacy towards the whites. Neither French nor British could count on the degree of support necessary to enable them to establish a firm control of the region; but short of this the side which could offer the better trading terms could hope to achieve a temporary ascendancy. The circumstances of King George's War gave this advantage to the British. In 1741 the French played into their hands by handing over the interior trading posts to the Montreal monopolists on terms which resulted in extortionate prices easily undercut by the English traders, who also carried on a useful contraband trade with the French *coureurs de bois*. Further, as the war progressed the pressure of the British naval blockade was felt in the form of shortages of trading goods in the interior. These conditions resulted in a gradual cooling off of the tribes towards the French and in friendly approaches towards the British. In 1747 the French narrowly escaped disaster by the premature exposure of a far-reaching Indian conspiracy directed by Chief Nicholas of the Wyandots against Detroit. By the conclusion of overt hostilities the governments of Pennsylvania and Virginia were attempting to consolidate this tenuous ascendency in the Ohio region by negotiating with the Indians, and English fur traders, from such posts as Pickawillany on the Miami, were exploiting the opening they had made into the French monopoly of the Great Lakes beaver trade.

In 1749 the French governor-general, La Galissonière, determined to extinguish English influence west of the Alleghenies, sent an expedition of regulars and Canadians under Céléron de Bienville as far as the forks of the Ohio with the object of laying formal claim to the region and in the hope that a show of force would impress the dissident tribes now taking their cue from the Miami chief, La Demoiselle, on the Miami River.

The need to press home the French claims to the Ohio in full, even at the risk of alienating the Indians, was the more urgent because to the activities of English fur traders on the Ohio there were now joined those of English land agents. By 1750 the English tide of settlement had emerged in places on to the western slopes of the Alleghenies and magnates of the seaboard, with capital which could no longer be profitably employed in trade or planting, were seized with a mania for investment in the unoccupied and fertile lands of the Ohio valley. The resulting land companies were making plans, not only to trade but to settle, in the neighbourhood of the forks of the Ohio to which the French had already laid claim. Between 1750 and 1753 this area was the scene of repeated surveys; the Ohio Company built a trading house at Will's Creek on the Potomac, and in 1752 it obtained Indian agreement to the construction of a fort at the forks.

To forestall these designs the French took the offensive. In 1752 a French-led force of Chippewa and Ottawa Indians destroyed La Demoiselle and the English traders at Pickawillany, wiping out at a blow the English trading gains in central Ohio. The following year the new French governor-general, Duquesne, dispatched a further expedition which established a chain of three forts south from Lake Erie, at Presque Isle, Le Bœuf and Venango, in a line pointing straight at the forks of the Ohio. On hearing of this the governor of Virginia, Dinwiddie, sent the young George Washington to Fort le Bœuf to demand the French withdrawal and upon this being ignored, dispatched a small force to erect a fort at the forks. This the French expelled and in turn erected the stronger Fort Duquesne. Thereupon Washington was again sent, in 1754, with a small body of Virginian militia to drive the French from Duquesne. This force met and defeated some French troops in a skirmish at Great Meadows on the Monongahela, only to be defeated and captured in turn in July at the improvised Fort Necessity. Virginian and Canadian troops had clashed, and in the Ohio Valley the uneasy truce was at an end. The French and Indian War had begun.

For the moment the war remained an informal one between the Virginians and the French and Indians. The other British colonies were by no means prepared to back up the Virginians in their drive to the Ohio. The Carolinas were in no position to provide troops in view of their small white population and the alleged threat to internal security of negro slaves. The Pennsylvanians were jealous of the Virginia-backed Ohio Company and the Quaker-controlled Assembly covered its reluctance to grant taxes for defence behind a complacent pacifism. The New Yorkers were apprehensive about the effect of the conflict upon Indian relations. The advance of the French to the Ohio had driven a coach-and-four through the old neutrality policy. Impressed with French military power, the Iroquois were anxious at the threat to their independence and loud in their complaints at the lack of adequate British protection. In order to rally the Indians against the French, the Board of Trade called a conference with the Iroquois at Albany, in June 1754, which delegates from seven colonies attended. This propounded a statesmanlike Indian policy, but carried little weight with the colonial assemblies. The key Dominion of Virginia was not even represented although the Congress's policy threatened the interests of the Ohio Company. Franklin's Plan of Union, designed to provide a basis for common defence, although adopted by the Congress, found even less chance of acceptance. The Virginians were, therefore, left to defend their frontier alone although their resources in trained manpower and war-like stores were no match for the French regular troops and their Indian allies.

The British Government was, therefore, faced by an important decision. Two courses were open to it. The first was to adhere to the traditional policy of limited commitment. According to orthodox mercantilist doctrine the colonies were valuable first and foremost for their commerce and no investment in them would be worthwhile which would not bring a short-term dividend in trade. Apart from the protection afforded to their trade routes by the Royal navy, their defence from local attack was their own responsibility. The conflict on the Ohio was an American affair of commercial rivalry for furs and land. As the duke of Newcastle said: 'Let Americans fight Americans' and let Britain and France negotiate a peaceful solution to the dispute through the diplomatic machinery already established for this purpose in Paris.

The second course was to back the Virginians. To do so would mean conflict between British and French regular troops and ships and the grave risk of transforming a local into a general war. The choosing of the second alternative by the Newcastle cabinet, already implicit in the founding of Nova Scotia as a charge on the home government, marks a recognition that the mainland colonies had become of prime importance to the whole Colonial System. Their rapid growth in the previous forty years had made them the centre-piece of the old empire. Their value, both as markets and as producers, in the network of English overseas trade was such that their future could not be jeopardised by counting the cost of their defence. Moreover, they had ceased to be thought of as mere commercial plantations; instead, they had become populous British communities with the rights of British subjects, and their protection against the French aggression was regarded as a matter of national honour.

Having made its decision, the cabinet obtained the support of Parliament, in November 1754, for a limited campaign to which both Britain and the colonies would contribute. The purpose of this was the capture of Forts Duquesne, Niagara, Crown Point and Beauséjour: limited objectives which would drive the French back to their 1714 position without, it was hoped, a resort to open war between the two countries. Accordingly a small expeditionary force was dispatched to America early in 1755 under the command of General Braddock. This landed in Virginia instead of Pennsylvania, thereby being faced by a much longer march to the Ohio. The thoroughness of Braddock's plans for the campaign, which included the building of a road through the mountain wilderness capable of carrying heavy artillery, although well conceived to reduce Fort Duquesne, delayed and impeded his progress. He was also handicapped by the failure of Dinwiddie, largely through jealousy of his fellow Governor Glen's influence with the Indians, to provide more than a handful of Indian scouts. When on 9 July he at last arrived within seven miles of Duquesne a force of some 900 French and Indians succeeded in surprising him on line of march. In the ensuing confusion and as a result of serious errors of judgment on the part of Braddock's commanders, the engagement became a total defeat. Braddock was killed, the surviving remnants of his army fled, its supplies were lost and the entire campaign was abandoned. The Virginian-Pennsylvanian frontier was left defenceless before the pillaging Indians. Thus ended the British Government's essay in limited warfare against the French.

Meanwhile the French, although determined to defend their outlying positions, were equally anxious to limit hostilities to the American continent. French officials had for some time been conscious of the weakness of Canada in any open trial of strength with the British. Even in peace-time the chronic shortage of supplies with its attendant inflation, which plagued Intendant Bigot, gave rise to defeatist sentiment which was only overridden by the patriotic arguments of men like La Galissonière for whom capitulation to British expansion was unthinkable. In view of France's vulnerable sea communications and of the fact that her navy was not yet on a war footing, the French ministry was particularly concerned to avoid open hostilities with the British navy. They, therefore, employed fast naval vessels in 1755 to reinforce New France, successfully eluding British squadrons under orders to intercept them in American waters only. As a result the French used the summer of 1756 to capture Oswego, a stroke which won them the allegiance of the Western Indians. French power, based on her admirably designed chain of forts, now pressed the British back beyond the mountains to their seaboard bases. Only the capture of Fort Beauséjour on the Nova Scotia isthmus through the treachery of a French officer provided British consolation in this disastrous year.

It seems clear that by this time the British cabinet had become convinced that the campaign for limited objectives must be replaced by a full-scale assault on New France. Whether or not war on this scale could be kept limited and informal became quickly an academic question. For in the first months of 1756 occurred the Revolution in Alliances which heralded a new European war with France released, by her Austrian alliance, from extensive commitments on the Continent and free to pursue her overseas struggle with the British empire. From 18 May 1756 Britain and France were formally at war. The American conflict had at last merged with the power conflicts of the European system and the military might of both parent Powers could be mobilised to achieve a decision by force of arms on the American continent.

When Pitt took office in 1757 the British outlook in America was grim. New France had been reinforced and placed on an effective war footing. In that summer the French repulsed a large expedition against Louisbourg and captured Fort William Henry on Lake George. From their commanding position they could rely on Indian allies to harry the English settlements from Nova Scotia to Georgia. The provincials, demoralised by Braddock's defeat, were incapable of effective defence, and looked to the mother country for their safety. But Pitt's self confidence and organising ability quickly made themselves felt across the Atlantic. Having decided to make America the decisive theatre of the war, he made plans to strangle New France by a four-fold campaign by land and the effective use of naval power. The first fruits of this reorganised war effort were plucked in the summer of 1758. A naval force under Boscawen and troops under Wolfe made an effective amphibious force which succeeded in capturing Louisbourg on 26 July. The efforts of the new British commander-in-chief in America, Abercrombie, were not, however, successful against the French on Lake Champlain. The attack on Ticonderoga was a resounding defeat for the British and provincial regiments. Further west things went better. Bradstreet succeeded in capturing Fort Frontenac on Ontario and Forbes, after building a new road through the Pennsylvania mountains, managed at last, in November, to capture the site of Fort Duquesne, abandoned by the French.

These achievements marked the turning-point of the war. Although they had stoutly maintained their position on Lake Champlain, the French had lost the great outer bastion on the St Lawrence; the loss of Frontenac threatened communications between the St Lawrence and the Great Lakes and that of Duquesne meant the end to French ascendancy on the Ohio. Even more ominous was the pressure of superior British sea power. The fate of Louisbourg had been sealed in European waters the previous winter when the French navy was prevented by skilfully used British squadrons from sending a sufficient force for its defence. The capture of French supply ships by the British had induced severe food shortages in New France. The loss also of invaluable cargoes of Indian trade goods increased the French difficulties in holding the allegiance of the tribes whose guerilla activities had been such an important factor in the French success.

The plan for 1759 was an all-out assault on the St Lawrence valley from the newly-won bases. This called for a triple campaign. One expedition was to take Fort Niagara and thus completely sever the St Lawrence from the Great Lakes; the second was to proceed against Quebec by Lake Champlain, the third, by sea, up the St Lawrence from the east. The first expedition captured Niagara but could not advance down the St Lawrence; the second, under Amherst, took Ticonderoga and Crown Point but could not get beyond Lake Champlain before winter set in. All, therefore, hinged on Wolfe's advance up the St Lawrence. The capture of Quebec in September by Wolfe's amphibious force was a hazardous operation only brought to success by the superb seamanship of the naval commanders and the brilliant tactical leadership of the commanding general whose nice sense of the calculated risk was fully justified by the result. Even after the defeat of Montcalm and the occupation of the citadel, the British forces were still dangerously exposed to counter-attack from the strong French forces remaining at Montreal. All depended upon French reinforcements reaching the valley the following spring. Unfortunately for the French their naval power had been shattered by Hawke at Quiberon Bay the previous November; the relief convoy which set sail from Bordeaux in April was dispersed by the British and the first ships to reach Quebec up the St Lawrence in May 1760 proved to be those of the British navy. The British were in control of the entire lower St Lawrence and it was only a matter of time before Montreal surrendered in September.

Thus in two campaigning seasons the British, by reason of their command of the sea, the skilful use of their American positions, the effective deployment in the American wilderness of first-class European troops, and the mobilisation of the superior resources of their colonies, had succeeded in overwhelming the French who had threatened to drive them back on to the seaboard fringe of the continent. The laurels were won by the mother country rather than by the colonies. For although the colonies provided abundant supplies and some invaluable auxiliary troops like Rogers' Rangers, it needed the organising genius of Pitt, the professional competence of the regular army (especially when, under the direction of men like Howe and Bouquet, it had learned the techniques of forest warfare) and above all the superiority of the navy to defeat the powerfully organised forces of metropolitan France in the New World.

If the Anglo-French conflict in America was only finally resolved after the two parent Powers had pitted their resources against each other, the ultimate decision about the disposition of British and French power in the New World equally depended upon the course of the war elsewhere. The Seven Years War dragged on for over two years after the capture of Montreal. The accession of George III brought with it a change of ministry reflecting a war weariness at home which resulted in negotiations for a peace with France in 1761. But, in spite of their pacific intent, the Bute ministry were forced by the third Family Compact between France and Spain, signed in 1761, to declare war against Spain in 1762. Not until the following year was the Peace of Paris signed, and by this time further British naval victories against France, with the capture of Martinique, and against Spain, with the capture of Havana and Manila, increased the British bargaining power. In the peace negotiations the fate of New France was bound up with that of her other possessions, especially in the West Indies, held in pawn by the British. The question ultimately turned on whether the British should restore to France New France or the rich sugar islands of Martinique and Guadaloupe. The decision to retain New France and restore the West Indian islands represented a victory for British West Indian sugar planters who feared the admission of the richer French islands into the Colonial System, and for British merchants anxious to lay their hands on the lucrative Canadian fur trade. Above all it recognised the fact that the protection of the British mainland colonies demanded the elimination of the French threat to their expansion, even at the expense of restoring to France strategic positions in the West Indies which, as Pitt feared, might leave British communications dangerously exposed. Events were to prove that the unchecked expansion of the mainland colonies was to lead to a demand for independence which the mother country, handicapped by French interference, was unable to subdue by force. But meanwhile the British empire in America stretched from the seaboard to the Mississippi and from Hudson's Bay to the tip of Florida, for the Spaniards gave up Florida in exchange for the restoration of Havana and Manila and for acquiring from the French as compensation the seemingly unprofitable territory of Louisiana. Thus with Florida the pressure of British naval power half across the world succeeded where General Oglethorpe had failed.

CHAPTER XXIII

RIVALRIES IN INDIA

THE period between the death of Aurangzeb in 1707 and the end of the Seven Years War in 1763 witnessed the decline of Muslim rule in India and the growth of semi-independent 'country powers' owing little more than a vague allegiance to the enfeebled descendants of the Great Moguls at Delhi. The resultant anarchy enabled the French and English trading companies to intervene in Indian affairs. Their struggles for commercial and territorial supremacy ended in the victories of Clive by means of which the French were ousted from the Carnatic and the English East India Company became the *de facto* ruler of Bengal. It would, however, be incorrect to suppose that the disintegration of the Mogul Empire began with the death of Aurangzeb, for the anarchy that ensued was merely the acceleration of a decline that had been taking place for at least half a century. This cannot be fully appreciated without some knowledge of Akbar's policy.

The wise and necessary policy of the great Mogul Emperor Akbar was reversed by his immediate successors, Jahangir, Shah Jahan and Aurangzeb. He had deliberately accepted compromise as the basis of his empire, and by his policy of *sulh-i-kull* (universal toleration) and his abolition of the *jizya*, the detested poll-tax on non-Muslims, he had striven to conciliate the subject Hindu population and to secure their loyalty to his rule. It was his successors' gradual departure from the main principles of his rule, culminating in the religious and political intolerance of Aurangzeb, that eventually produced a far-reaching Hindu reaction and provoked the Marathas of the Deccan and the Rajputs, Jats and Sikhs of northern India to raise the standard of revolt, from the Maratha principality of Tanjore in the south to the plains of the Panjab in the distant north. A further basic principle of Akbar's administration had been to demand no more than one-third of the gross produce from the peasant, for, in Mogul India, the efficiency of the administration depended upon an equitable system of land revenue assessment and collection. Under his successors the pressure increased until by the reign of Aurangzeb, if not earlier, the revenue demand had risen to one-half of the gross produce. This is clear from Aurangzeb's revenue *farmans*.[1] Furthermore, no attempt was made to deal directly with the *ryots* as under Akbar, with the result that assignments of land revenue multiplied and farming of the revenues became more prevalent, especially as the Empire increased in

[1] For the Persian text and translation of these *farmans* see *Journal of the Asiatic Society of Bengal* (1906), pp. 223–55.

extent. The writings of contemporary European travellers corroborate the evidence afforded by the *farmans* and bear witness to the oppressive exactions of revenue farmers and other intermediaries of the central Government. Their frequent references to absconding peasants and untilled soil lead one to infer that the mass of the population must have lived dangerously near the subsistence level. The uncontrolled oppression of a selfish bureaucracy, for Mogul administration was bureaucratic not feudal, had led to a steady impoverishment of the agricultural classes, the most important revenue-producing part of the population.

It is true that, at the beginning of his reign, Shah Jahan did something to correct the inefficiency of his predecessor Jahangir, but his aggressive policy in central Asia, his expeditions beyond the Hindu Kush against Balkh and Badakhshan, and his efforts to recover Kandahar brought the Empire to the verge of bankruptcy. Then came Aurangzeb's hopeless attempt to conquer the Deccan, a political miscalculation and a military blunder of the first magnitude. Apart from the fact that disturbances created by the Rajputs and Jats in the north prevented him from concentrating all his forces in the south, Aurangzeb found it impossible to enforce an unpopular despotism over distant southern provinces where the physical features of the country favoured guerilla warfare at which the Marathas were peculiarly adept. Not only did the expansion of the Empire during the second half of his reign produce financial exhaustion, but it also proved fatal to its solidarity—consolidation had not kept pace with conquest. Gemelli-Careri, the learned Italian traveller who visited Aurangzeb's camp in the Deccan, records that the Mogul army, embarrassed as it was by the presence of harems and a huge camp-following, was far too unwieldy to operate over broken and hilly ground against mobile guerilla forces. All authorities agree as to the decay of the army as a fighting machine. Discipline there was none. Luxury and effeminacy were everywhere in evidence. Rarely, if ever, were fortresses taken by direct assault, and the history of Aurangzeb's attempts to crush the Marathas is one of prolonged sieges which, in the absence of defection within the walls, he was forced to raise. It must also be remembered that the Mogul Empire was an alien government. Drawing no strength from ancient tradition or popular support, it depended upon the efficiency of its military forces and the ability of the Emperor and his chief advisers. This probably led Irvine to ascribe the downfall of the Empire principally to the deterioration of the army. That it was a powerful factor cannot be denied, but here Irvine appears to confuse cause with effect. Large contingents of Rajputs had served in Akbar's armies, and it must not be forgotten that one of the reasons for the decay of Mogul military power was Aurangzeb's alienation of the Rajputs whom it had been Akbar's policy to conciliate.

Nothing is more noticeable in the age of the Indian Moguls than the corrupting effect of the possession of Hindustan upon its conquerors. The virile highlanders of central Asia had degenerated into sycophantic courtiers. From the middle of the seventeenth century there had been a marked deterioration in the character of the Mogul aristocracy. The younger sons of the nobility had grown effeminate in the harem where, surrounded by eunuchs and low-born favourites who pandered to their desires, they became familiar with degrading forms of vice from an early age. Internal decay resulting from the progressive deterioration of Akbar's administrative institutions was, therefore, the chief reason for the downfall of the Empire, a collapse which was facilitated by the revolt of the subject Hindu peoples suffering under the Muslim yoke and by the rebellion of the provincial governors fully conscious of the growing weakness of the central Government. This internal chaos was intensified by invasions and plundering incursions from the trans-Indus regions roughly corresponding to modern Persia and Afghanistan. Foreign invasion, however, was not so much a cause of the downfall of the Empire as symptomatic of a decline that had already taken place.

The Mogul conception of sovereignty was aggressive and, like the Hindu rulers who attempted to become the *chakravartins* or lords paramount of ancient India, the Moguls strove for paramountcy in the peninsula. There was no idea of a balance of power in the European sense, and, when the Empire disintegrated after 1707, the warring factions aimed, not at the just limitation but at the complete subversion of each other's power. The extent of the Empire combined with the absence of good communications defeated these efforts at paramountcy and nullified all attempts at centralisation. It is true that Akbar, in his wisdom, had laid down stringent rules aiming at centralisation and had instituted an elaborate system of checks upon the powers of the provincial governors, but, with the extension of the Empire after his day and the growing weakness of the central Government, supervision and control became increasingly difficult. It would appear, therefore, that the Moguls, in attempting to rivet their authority on the whole of India, had set themselves an impossible task, for it was not until after the development of communications in the second half of the nineteenth century that any real centralisation was achieved. At the beginning of the eighteenth century the Mogul Empire stretched from the Hindu Kush to the Coromandel Coast and was divided into twenty-one *subas* or provinces: Kabul, Kashmir, Lahore, Multan, Tatta (Sind), Ajmir, Delhi, Agra, Oudh, Allahabad, Bihar, Bengal, Orissa, Malwa, and Ahmadabad (Gujarat); together with the six Deccan provinces of Khandesh, Berar, Aurangabad, Bidar, Bijapur, and Hyderabad. But, when Aurangzeb's last illness came upon him in 1707, his authority was disputed throughout the length and breadth of these dominions.

One of the fundamental weaknesses of Muslim rule was the absence of any definite rule of succession. Although Muslim monarchs endeavoured to secure the succession of their favourite sons, in the interregnum between the death of one sovereign and the accession of another the nobility and the *ulema* were all powerful and usually exercised the right of election, even to the exclusion of the prince who had been declared heir-apparent in the lifetime of his father. This is certainly true of Muslim India, where the absence of any rule of primogeniture led to fratricidal conflicts attended by much economic dislocation. The death of Aurangzeb formed no exception to the general rule. An internecine struggle ensued between his three surviving sons, Muazzam, the eldest, who had charge of Kabul and the Panjab; Azam Shah who had recently been appointed viceroy of Malwa; and Kam Bakhsh who had been entrusted with the government of Bijapur. The contest for the throne was a race between Muazzam and Azam Shah for the possession of the imperial treasury at Agra, the contents of which have been estimated at 240 million rupees. Muazzam, when he heard of his father's death, immediately set out with all speed for Agra, proclaiming himself emperor with the title of Bahadur Shah. He was ably supported by his son, Azim-ush-shan, the viceroy of Bengal and Bihar, who took possession of the city of Agra. Azam Shah, who had proclaimed himself emperor at Ahmadnagar, was much more dilatory in his movements. Lack of funds and jealousy of his son, Bidar Bakht, whom he prohibited from making a rapid march on Agra, contributed to this delay. Eventually their combined forces were defeated by Bahadur Shah at Jajau near Agra, both Azam Shah and his son being numbered among the slain. All this took place in 1707. Bahadur Shah next moved against Ajit Singh, the Rajput ruler of Jodhpur who had neglected to acknowledge his accession, but the rebellion of his brother, Kam Bakhsh, who had crowned himself emperor at Bijapur, forced him to leave Rajputana for the Deccan. Kam Bakhsh was overwhelmed by superior numbers in January 1709. This accomplished, Bahadur Shah returned to Rajputana to deal with the recalcitrant rajas of Ajmir and Jodhpur, but a Sikh revolt in the Panjab compelled him to come to terms with the Rajputs.

Originally the Sikhs were a religious brotherhood who broke away from the fold of Hinduism and its caste restrictions in the time of Nanak (1469–1539), their first *guru* or religious leader. Nanak's gospel was one of peace, but his successors perceived that there could be no peace for the Sikhs within the Mogul Empire. Persecuted under Jahangir and Shah Jahan, they received no mercy from the bigoted Aurangzeb who cruelly put to death their ninth *guru*, Tegh Bahadur. Muslim persecution therefore transformed a sect of quietists into a brotherhood of fanatical soldiers. The real founder of the militant Sikh theocracy of the eighteenth century was Govind Singh (1675–1708), their tenth and last *guru*, the greater part of whose life was devoted to preparing his followers for a crusade against Muhammadan fanaticism. With the accession of Bahadur

Shah, Govind Singh entered the imperial service, a decision for which it is difficult to find any adequate explanation, especially when it is remembered that his father had been tortured to death by Aurangzeb. While serving with the Emperor in the Deccan he was assassinated. The Sikhs, embittered by years of persecution, now rallied round a pretender known as Banda who was not lacking in qualities of military leadership and overran large tracts of the Panjab, butchering the Muslims and violating their women-folk. It is significant that Banda struck coins in his own name. The three most important symbols of sovereignty in Muslim India were the *jalus* or the act of sitting on the throne; the right of the *sikka* or the striking of coins in the name of the new sovereign; and the reading of the Emperor's name in the *khutba*, or bidding prayer, on Fridays in the mosques. The striking of coins in the name of a rebel immediately converted what might have been regarded as a mere local disturbance into a direct threat to the central Government. Bahadur Shah therefore hurried northwards against Banda, who was defeated and forced to take refuge in the hills.

Bahadur Shah, an old man of sixty-four when he began to reign, possessed neither the ability nor the energy to restore the declining fortunes of the Empire and justly earned the sobriquet of *Shah-i-Bekhabr* or the 'Heedless King'. His most foolish act was an attempt to have the *khutba* recited after the fashion of the Shiahs. This religious innovation was repellent to the majority of his Muslim subjects, who were orthodox Sunnis, and led to riots in Gujarat and the Panjab which forced him to restore the old formula. It is impossible to postulate a succession of able despots, and the later Moguls, with the possible exception of Bahadur Shah, were miserable puppets controlled by court favourites and factions. Little was therefore done to check the centrifugal tendencies which were everywhere in evidence. Between the death of Bahadur Shah in 1712 and the accession of Muhammad Shah in 1719 five puppets were installed on the Mogul throne. To understand the reason for this rapid succession of pageant sovereigns some knowledge of the prevailing factions is essential.

The two principal parties struggling for power at the Mogul court were the Turanis and the Iranis. The Turani nobles, like the founders of the dynasty, were immigrants from the country to the north of the Oxus and had enjoyed great prestige in the palmy days of the Empire. The Irani nobles, who hailed from Persia, were less numerous but noted for their administrative ability. The Turanis formed a powerful body in the army and were orthodox Sunnis while their rivals were Shiahs. Thus, on the grounds of religion alone, there was always strong animosity between them. Opposing these two foreign factions were the Hindustanis, or Indian Muslims, either converts or descendants of former immigrants. Included in this group were many Rajput and Jat chiefs and all subordinate Hindu officials. The situation was still further complicated by the existence of court factions composed of favourites and adherents of either the

Emperor or his minister the *wazir*. These rivalries had been kept in check before 1707, but under the weak successors of Aurangzeb they grew in intensity and must be reckoned as one of the causes of the downfall of the Empire.

Bahadur Shah's death was the signal for civil warfare between his four sons, from which Jahandar Shah emerged as Emperor. A cruel and cowardly voluptuary, he was overthrown after a short reign of eleven months by his nephew, Farrukh-siyar, who owed his throne to the support of the famous Sayyid brothers, Abdulla and Husain Ali, the king-makers of this period. It was in Farrukh-siyar's reign that Banda, the Sikh leader, was forced to surrender and tortured to death in a revolting manner. Farrukh-siyar was an ingrate who plotted against his benefactors. His efforts came to naught and eventually, in the seventh year of his reign, he was deposed, blinded, and finally executed by the infuriated Sayyids. The two sickly youths who succeeded him need not detain us. Finally, in September 1719, the Sayyids, who were still powerful, crowned Muhammad Shah as Emperor. While this drama was being enacted in Hindustan the Maratha power in the Deccan had been steadily gaining strength.

The national hero who headed the Maratha revolt against Aurangzeb was Sivaji, whose descendants were the rajas of Satara. It is significant that, as the leader of a Hindu reaction, he revived the ancient Sanskrit designations and his council of eight ministers was known as the *ashta pradhan*. His administrative system was based both on Hindu political tradition and on Muslim practice. Much of his revenue was derived from the plunder of his neighbours from whom he levied a tax called *chauth*, a demand for a fourth of the land revenue assessment of a place. Sometimes an extra tenth known as *sardeshmukhi* was extorted. The levying of *chauth*, contrary to the assertions of patriotic Maratha historians, did not impose on Sivaji any corresponding obligation to protect a district from foreign invasion or against internal disorder, and, for this reason, should not be compared to the subsidiary alliance system of the British as developed by Warren Hastings and the Marquess Wellesley. The payment of *chauth* merely freed the inhabitants of the area where it was levied from any further plunder by Maratha troops, though, after Sivaji's death, Maratha officers often demanded in addition what was known as *ghas-dana* or fodder money for their horses. *Chauth* was based on force, and, as developed in the first half of the eighteenth century, could be levied from any part of India where the Marathas were powerful enough to enforce its collection. *Sardeshmukhi*, on the other hand, was confined in its application to the Deccan and was based on a legal fiction, Sivaji claiming to be the hereditary *sardeshmukh* of the Deccan.

After the death of Sivaji, his son and successor, Sambhuji, proved no match for the Moguls and was defeated and executed by Aurangzeb in 1689. Shahu, the son of Sambhuji, remained a prisoner at the Mogul court until his release on the death of Aurangzeb. This apparently conciliatory gesture was really an astute move calculated to weaken the Marathas and did in fact produce civil war in Maharashtra until Shahu's power was firmly established. Shahu's success was almost entirely due to the efforts of Balaji Visvanath, an able Chitpavan or Konkanasth Brahman whom he appointed as his peshwa, or chief minister, in 1714. The difficulties facing Shahu, the political confusion, in Majarashtra, and the weakness of Shahu's successors, were the chief factors underlying the growth of the power of the peshwas, who gradually supplanted the rajas of Satara as heads of the Maratha State. Balaji Visvanath, whose term of office extended to 1720, restored order in the Maratha country, came to terms with Angria, the hereditary admiral of the Maratha fleet who was in rebellion against Shahu, and in other ways consolidated Maratha power. By complicating the revenue accounts he increased Brahman control over the State finances. The chaotic condition of affairs at Delhi also favoured the consolidation of Maratha power. At first the Sayyid brothers at Delhi were intent on curbing Maratha pretensions and preventing their incursions into the strategically important province of Malwa, but, finding their lives in jeopardy because of the Emperor's plotting and recognising the inevitable, they came to terms. Shahu was to be confirmed in the possession of the original nucleus of Sivaji's dominions, his *swarajya* as it was termed. All recent conquests by the Marathas in Khandesh, Berar, Gondwana, Hyderabad and the Carnatic were to be recognised. The Marathas were to be allowed to collect the *chauth* and *sardeshmukhi* of the six Deccan provinces, in return for which they were to provide a contingent for the imperial army and to pay an annual tribute of ten lakhs of rupees. It was not, however, until the accession of Muhammad Shah in 1719 that imperial confirmation of these grants in the form of *sanads*, or charters, was obtained.

There is much controversy as to the exact aims of the Marathas. Sardesai contends that Sivaji did not desire political domination and that the later expansion of Maratha power was an indirect result of their zeal to preserve their religion, that their conception of *Hindu-pad padshahi* was not territorial aggrandisement but limited to the religious field. Referring to the policy of the first four peshwas, he asserts that 'in all their undertakings in the north, and their dealings with the Rajputs and other races, they steadily strove, not so much for empire or power, as for the release of the famous holy places of the Hindus' from Muslim control. It is difficult to follow the reasoning behind this statement. Not even a crusade is entirely a religious war, and the factors underlying the expansion of peoples and the growth of empires are many and complex. Of one thing we can be certain: the religious motive was not the sole reason behind Maratha incursions across the Narbada into Hindustan. In addition they were aggressive and predatory and continued to expand even after the immediate danger to the Deccan had been removed by the death of Aurangzeb. The peshwas appear to have realised that the Deccan was too poor to form the centre of an empire, and their incursions into Malwa and Gujarat were prompted by economic motives. At first leagued with their co-religionists the Rajputs, they advanced into northern India, but their aggressively selfish policy, their revolting cruelties, and their marauding proclivities, especially the levying of *chauth*, finally estranged the Rajputs and other Hindu powers with the result that they found themselves unsupported against the foreign invader in 1761.

It was under their second peshwa, Baji Rao I (1720–40), that the Marathas adopted a policy of territorial aggrandisement in northern India. In this they were encouraged by Nizam-ul-mulk, the Mogul governor, or viceroy, of the six Deccan provinces. On the accession of Muhammad Shah the administration of these provinces had been entrusted to Husain Ali, the younger Sayyid brother, but he was soon recalled to Delhi by his brother, Abdulla, whose position was being undermined by court conspiracies in which the Emperor was involved. It was at this juncture that Nizam-ul-mulk, leader of the Turani nobles and for this reason opposed to Sayyid predominance at Delhi, deemed it advisable to abandon Malwa, of which he was the governor, and establish himself in the Deccan. This naturally alarmed the Sayyids who took immediate steps to coerce him, but, before their forces had marched many miles beyond Agra, Husain Ali was assassinated and in a very short time Abdulla was overthrown by a powerful combination of Turani and Irani nobles at Delhi. For a time Nizam-ul-mulk was restored to favour. Leaving a deputy in charge of his Deccan provinces he proceeded to Delhi as chief minister of Muhammad Shah, but, disgusted with the incessant court intrigues which thwarted all his efforts at reforming the administration, he once more set out for the Deccan, defeating his deputy, who had been encouraged by the Emperor to resist his return, at the battle of Shakarkhelda in 1724. From this victory gained with Maratha assistance may be dated the establishment of the nizam's hereditary position in the Deccan with Hyderabad as his capital. But he still considered it advisable to recognise the Emperor and made no attempt to strike coins in his own name or to make use of the scarlet, or imperial, umbrella. The Emperor's name was also retained in the *khutba*. It was under this cloak of legitimacy that the provincial governors extended and consolidated their powers. Recognising the danger from the Marathas, the nizam agreed to pay them the *chauth* of the Deccan provinces provided he was allowed to make the collections himself, as it was obviously to his disadvantage to have Maratha officials interfering in his internal affairs. To this Shahu agreed, but his promises were written in water. To protect himself the nizam began to intrigue with certain discontented Maratha elements, especially Sambhuji the Maratha ruler of Kolhapur. This led to war in which the nizam, surrounded at

Palked by the more mobile Maratha forces, was compelled to sign the convention of Mungi-Shevgaon in March 1728. By this the nizam agreed to acknowledge the legality of the Maratha claims for *chauth* and *sardesh-mukhi*, to pay all arrears, and to reinstate the Maratha collectors whom he had ousted from his territories. The position of the Maratha central Government was further improved in 1731 when, by the Treaty of Warna, the Maratha ruler of Kolhapur accepted a position of subordinate alliance with Shahu. Finally, in the following year, the nizam entered into a secret agreement with the peshwa by which he offered to give the Marathas a free hand in northern India provided they neither attacked him in the Deccan nor molested his Khandesh possessions in the valley of the Tapti. This disgraceful compact not only facilitated the northward expansion of the Marathas but left the nizam free to assert his authority over the Carnatic.

Maratha raids into Malwa and Gujarat had begun towards the end of Aurangzeb's reign and from that time onwards central India was never secure from their depredations. To ensure the collection of *chauth* and to consolidate their hold over their rapidly expanding empire, Shahu and the peshwa, contrary to the practice of Sivaji who had favoured cash payments, granted *jagirs*, or assignments of land revenue, to the Maratha military leaders in these outlying areas. This practice, the *Saranjami* system as it was called, undoubtedly facilitated the growth of Maratha power, but, by encouraging a spirit of independence in these *jagirdars*, eventually led to the growth of independent Maratha States which was one of the chief weaknesses of the Maratha confederacy in the later struggles with the British for paramountcy in India. Prominent among the Maratha guerilla leaders at this time were Udaji Powar, Malhar Rao Holkar, Ranoji Sindhia, and Damaji Gaikwar, who laid the foundations of semi-independent States in Dhar, Indore, Gwalior, and Baroda. By the year 1734 the Marathas were firmly established in Malwa. This was a great strategic advantage, as Malwa lay athwart the main routes connecting the Deccan with Hindustan and formed an excellent *point d'appui* for their attacks on Gujarat and the ports of the western coast. By 1737 they had carried their depredations as far afield as Bundelkhand, Rajputana, and the Doab and had even defeated an imperial army outside the walls of Delhi. In desperation Muhammad Shah once more summoned his over-mighty subject from the Deccan. The nizam was received with great honour and was raised to the position of *wakil-i-mutlaq*, or chief minister of the Empire, with the title of Asaf Jah. He was entrusted with the task of expelling the Marathas from Bundelkhand but once more proved no match for Baji Rao, who surrounded his forces in Bhopal and compelled him to agree to the humiliating convention of Durai Sarai (16 January 1738), by which the Marathas were recognised as rulers of Malwa and granted the sovereignty of all territories between the rivers Narbada and Chambal.

While these operations had been taking place in central and northern India the Marathas had also been endeavouring to establish their power over the coastal strip between Bombay and Goa which had long been infested with pirates who preyed indiscriminately on European and Asiatic vessels plying in these waters. They first turned their attention to the piratical strongholds of the Siddis, or Abyssinians, of Janjira who had supported Aurangzeb in his struggle with Sivaji, in return for which they had been confirmed in the possession of Raigad and other fortresses captured from the Marathas. Thirty miles to the north of Janjira lay Kolaba, the headquarters of Angria, a Maratha in alliance with Shahu, who commanded a pirate fleet of *grabs* and *gallivats* often euphemistically referred to as the Maratha navy. Maratha vessels operating from Kolaba and other centres were menaced both by the Siddis and by the Portuguese of Bassein. In 1733 the English at Bombay entered into an offensive and defensive alliance with the Siddis which was directed against the piracies committed by Angria of Kolaba. As a result of this the Siddis ceased to molest the Company's ships in the general piracies they committed. The Maratha campaign against the Siddis was also intended to afford protection to Angria. In the operations that followed between 1733 and 1736 the Marathas failed to destroy the power of the Siddis, but did succeed in recapturing certain territories on the mainland including their former capital of Raigad, the Siddi possession of which had been peculiarly offensive to their national pride. Operations against the Portuguese were more successful. The Marathas had long cast covetous eyes on the commercially and strategically important Portuguese settlements on the island of Salsette and the adjacent mainland. Thana was taken in 1737 but it was not until 1739, and only after a desperate resistance, that the Portuguese of Bassein were forced to capitulate. The fall of Bassein brought the Marathas into dangerous proximity to Bombay and led to negotiations which ended in the Anglo-Maratha commercial treaty of 1739, which permitted the English to trade duty free in the Deccan. It was this campaign against the Portuguese which partly explains why the Marathas made no attempt to resist Nadir Shah's invasion of northern India.

Before the intrusion of European nations by sea, invasions from central Asia exerted a profound influence on the history of India. It was the possession of the strategic uplands of Kabul that facilitated the Mogul's conquest of Hindustan. Once established on the plains of India they experienced the greatest difficulty in controlling and retaining this outlying province of Kabul and the adjacent district of Kandahar. While the Empire was strong and the imperial forces had command of both the eastern and western extremities of the main mountain passes which gave access to the Panjab plains, India remained free from invasion. But it is significant that the decay of the Empire paved the way for Persian victories in the area corresponding to modern Afghanistan. There have been two types of invaders from central Asia: those who aimed at conquest and sought to consolidate their power in northern India; and raiders whose chief motive was the desire for plunder. To this latter class belonged Timur, Nadir Shah, and Ahmad Shah Durrani.

Nadir Quli Khan was a Khurasani general who rose to power on the ruins of Safavi rule in Persia. By 1736 he had secured Persia from foreign invasion and had consolidated his power sufficiently to enable him to dethrone the last Safavi puppet and assume the title of Shah. To protect his eastern frontiers he was forced to move against the turbulent Ghilzai tribes of western Afghanistan. At Delhi the ministers and advisers of Muhammad Shah failed to realise until it was too late the danger threatening on their north-western frontiers and hoped that Kandahar would prove impregnable. It is true that the Mogul governor of Kandahar was neglectful of his duties, but his failure must also be attributed to the inadequate support he received from Delhi, for no notice had been taken of his repeated requests for reinforcements. Anand Rao Mukhlis, the contemporary author of the *Tuz Kira*, bears witness to this neglect of the frontier provinces. The same is true of the Panjab. It must not be forgotten, however, that this neglect of the northern provinces was inevitable because of the growing Maratha menace on the southern frontiers. Much has been made by contemporary and later historians of the diplomatic rupture between India and Persia. As a cause of Nadir's invasion it has been magnified out of all proportion. It is true that Muhammad Shah had neglected to maintain friendly relations with Persia and had treated Nadir's envoys with studied neglect. He had also promised to prevent fugitives from Nadir's territory escaping into Afghanistan, in promising which he had set himself an impossible task. All this merely served as a convenient pretext for invasion. On the part played by Nizam-ul-mulk opinion is sharply divided. Modern Hindu historians denounce him as a traitor who actually invited Nadir to Delhi, while Muslim writers deny that there is any definite evidence to this effect and prefer to regard the role he adopted as that of a mediator. The accusation of treachery was current at an early date and occurs in Fraser's *History of Nadir Shah* published in 1741. In a Hindi poem, probably written between 1747 and 1757, Tilok Das assumes as common knowledge that Nadir was invited to Delhi by the Nizam.[1] The important point to remember is that Nadir Shah needed no invitation except that provided by the prevailing anarchy in India.

He experienced little difficulty in overrunning Afghanistan, for the year 1738 saw the fall of Kandahar, Ghazni and Kabul. Forcing the Khyber Pass, he debouched on to the plains at Jamrud and occupied Peshawar. Crossing the Indus at Attock towards the end of December, he took Lahore

---

[1] See *Journal of the Royal Asiatic Society of Bengal* (1897), where the poem is translated and edited by W. Irvine, pp. 24–62.

early in January. Even after news of the fall of Kabul reached Delhi no steps were taken to defend the Panjab by means of reinforcements, and it was only when Nadir's troops were sweeping across the Panjab that any preparations were made to resist his advance. With rare exceptions Muhammad Shah's nobles showed little inclination to lead their forces against the enemy. Not a single horseman came to his assistance from Bengal. The Rajputs, estranged beyond reconciliation, remained idle spectators of an empire's ruin. In desperation the Emperor appealed to the Marathas, but they were engaged in reducing the Portuguese stronghold of Bassein. It is sometimes asserted by Indian historians that prompt measures even at this late hour could have saved the Empire, but this seems to be a false appreciation of the situation and a misreading of history. Despite this lack of preparation Muhammad Shah, if the estimates of contemporary writers are reliable, was able to collect an army of 200,000 men, at least twice the size of the Persian forces. But once more history repeated itself and sheer numerical superiority proved of no avail against speed, mobility, shock tactics and enterprising generalship. When, on 24 February 1739, the rival armies met at Karnal, about twenty miles to the north of the historic field of Panipat, the forces of Muhammad Shah were completely routed. The greatness of Nadir's triumph has been over-estimated for, from a military standpoint, Karnal was a massacre, not a battle. Nadir now occupied Delhi where the *khutba* was read in his name. A false rumour of his death was the signal for a popular uprising in which several hundred Persian soldiers lost their lives. This was followed by an indiscriminate massacre of the inhabitants of Delhi, after which, in the words of a contemporary writer, 'the streets remained strewn with corpses, as the walks of a garden with dead flowers and leaves'.[1] Estimates of the slain vary between 8000 and 150,000.[2] The Persian account of the campaign, the *Jahan-kusha-i-Nadiri*, places the number at 30,000. It is equally impossible to compute the value of the booty acquired. At last Nadir was satisfied and, in May 1739, he set out on his return march to Persia, taking with him the famous Peacock Throne of Shah Jahan and the Koh-i-Nor diamond. Apart from the acquisition of vast booty and the annexation of all territories to the west of the Indus, the chief result of the expedition was to intensify the existing anarchy in India and to accelerate the decline of the Empire. It was a blow fatal to Mogul prestige, a blow from which there was no recovery.

Apart from the Persian invasion and ever-increasing Maratha expansion, the history of India during the reign of Muhammad Shah is that of the rise to power of able adventurers and provincial governors who laid the foundations of independent provincial dynasties. To the careful

---

[1] H. M. Elliott and J. Dowson, *The History of India told by its own Historians* (1877), vol. VIII, p. 89.
[2] L. Lockhart, *Nadir Shah* (1938), p. 149.

observer centrifugal tendencies are also apparent in the Maratha empire itself, although the increasing power and growing independence of the Maratha generals facilitated rather than restricted Maratha expansion. Another characteristic of this period was the steady growth of Anglo-French rivalry in southern India. To the reign of Muhammad Shah can be traced the origins of nearly all the important 'country powers' with whom the English were confronted when they first intervened in Indian politics. The State of Hyderabad was founded by Nizam-ul-mulk. From Ali Vardi Khan, a Muslim adventurer, descended the *nawab-nazims* of Bengal, while the kings of Oudh sprang from Saadat Ali Khan, the Mogul governor of that province. It was during this period of disintegration that the Rohillas became powerful in Rohilkhand, and the Bangash Pathans established themselves in Farrukhabad.

Saadat Ali Khan, Burhan-ul-mulk, the founder of the Oudh dynasty, was nawab of Oudh from 1722 to 1739. He not only maintained internal order but extended his territories so as to embrace Benares, Ghazipur, Jaunpur, and Chunar. His successor, Safdar Jang (1739–54), was appointed *wazir* of the Empire in the year 1748, and it was he who invited the Marathas to assist him against the Bangash Pathans of Farrukhabad, who on their side called in the Rohillas with disastrous results to these allies. The engagements entered into at this time formed the basis of later Maratha claims on Rohilkhand. Safdar Jang's son and successor, the *nawab-wazir* Shuja-ud-daulah, was the first ruler of Oudh to come into contact with the rising power of the English East India Company who, after defeating and then reinstating him, assisted him in the time of Warren Hastings to crush the power of the Rohillas.

With the establishment of Muslim rule in India bodies of Pathans or Afghans entered the country. After the death of Aurangzeb their settlements increased, until, in the words of the *Siyar-al-mutakhkharin*, 'they seemed to shoot out of the ground like so many blades of grass'. Those who settled in the country to the north-west of Oudh were termed Rohillas, or men of the hilly country, and the tract they occupied became known as Rohilkhand. The founder of Rohilla power in this area was an Afghan adventurer named Daud Khan who arrived in India after the death of Aurangzeb. His adopted son, a convert of obscure origin, received the name of Ali Muhammad Khan and succeeded him as leader of a band of mercenary troops. It was during his lifetime that the country, formerly known as Katehr, came to be called Rohilkhand. At first Ali Muhammad served as Mogul governor of this area, but, after a time, he felt himself powerful enough to withhold the payment of his revenues and to assert his independence of the Emperor. In this course he was encouraged by the anarchy consequent upon the invasion of Nadir Shah. The growth of Rohilla power was a menace to Safdar Jang of Oudh whose territories were exposed to their depredations. He therefore persuaded the Emperor to undertake a punitive expedition into Rohilkhand, with the result that Ali Muhammad surrendered to the imperial forces. But this was merely a temporary set-back, for, with the invasions of the Afghan ruler, Ahmad Shah Durrani, he was able to recover his former possessions. The chief cause of the growth of the Rohilla's power was the weakness of the central Government at Delhi. It was also made possible by the fact that they were able to take advantage of the internal struggles between the various Rajput chiefs and *zamindars* of Rohilkhand.

Reference has already been made to the Jat risings which formed part of the Hindu reaction against Aurangzeb's intolerance. It is usual to regard Churaman as the founder of Jat power, but he was merely a courageous guerilla leader who, rather than accept defeat, committed suicide in 1721. The real founders of the Jat State of Bharatpur were Badan Singh, who rose to power during the disturbances which followed Nadir Shah's invasion, and his adopted son, Suraj Mal, who similarly profited from the invasions of Ahmad Shah Durrani.

In Bengal for many years little attention had been paid to the orders of the central Government, and its governors were rapidly assuming an independent attitude. In 1740 Sarfaraz Khan, the viceroy of the three provinces of Bengal, Bihar and Orissa, was overthrown by Ali Vardi Khan, a subordinate official in charge of the administration of Bihar. From this usurpation can be traced the rise of the independent dynasty of the *nawab-nazims* of Bengal with whom Clive came into contact. There were many reasons prompting the Mogul Emperor to recognise Ali Vardi Khan's position. He was well aware of the fact that, while Nadir Shah had been in occupation of Delhi, Sarfaraz Khan had actually ordered coins to be struck and the *khutba* to be read in the name of the Persian monarch to whom he had transmitted the surplus revenues of Bengal. It seems, however, that the Emperor was bribed into acquiescence by the receipt of fifty-four lakhs of rupees, part of the plunder acquired by Ali Vardi Khan. Another important factor in Ali Vardi Khan's success was the financial backing he received from the famous Indian bankers, the Jagat Seths, who played such a decisive part in the later revolutions in Bengal. It must be admitted that he was a strong ruler, fully capable of restoring order to his troublesome charge. Unfortunately he was allowed but little time for consolidation and was almost immediately called upon to defend his recent acquisitions against Maratha incursions.

The wealth of Bengal was a powerful incentive to a predatory power based on the barren tracts of the Deccan, but, up to the year 1742, its isolation and Maratha preoccupations elsewhere had proved its salvation. With the extension of the Maratha's power in Berar under Raghuji Bhonsle the frontiers of Bengal became exposed to their depredations. In addition to continuous raiding, there were five separate invasions between 1742 and 1751. Taking advantage of the political confusion occasioned by Ali Vardi

Khan's *coup d'état*, they first invaded Bengal in 1742 under Bhaskar Pant, a general in the service of Raghuji Bhonsle. For a time Ali Vardi Khan was surrounded by Maratha forces, but, with the arrival of reinforcements, he extricated himself from his precarious position. Unfortunately, before this was accomplished the Marathas had plundered his capital of Murshidabad, captured Hugli, and committed terrible atrocities. Not only did they feed their horses on the standing crops and mulberry plantations, but they overran the province, plundering and burning the villages and violating the womenfolk. All authorities, both Indian and European, are agreed on this. A contemporary writer describes these human locusts as 'slayers of pregnant women and infants'. A modern Hindu historian has unearthed the evidence to prove that they indulged in the unspeakable practice of gang-rape.[1] Muhammadans sometimes assert that Sarkar's historical works have been written with a distinct Hindu bias. The impartial critic will certainly deny the truth of this assertion in the present connection, for his account of the horrors perpetrated by the Marathas on defenceless women, which forms part of a general condemnation of Indian atrocities at this time, cannot be construed into any attempt on his part to whitewash the sins of his co-religionists. In fact the atrocities committed by the Marathas in Bengal were only equalled by the later outrages of the Afghans around Delhi and Mathura. Eventually the Marathas were defeated by Ali Vardi Khan at Katwa, and, by the end of the year 1742, had been expelled from Bengal and Orissa.

The second invasion occurred in 1743 and was headed by Raghuji Bhonsle to whom Shahu had assigned his right to the *chauth* of these provinces. It was fortunate for Ali Vardi Khan that dissensions within the Maratha confederacy prompted the new peshwa, Balaji Baji Rao (1740–61), to go to his assistance. There were many reasons for this rivalry between Raghuji Bhonsle and the peshwa. Raghuji Bhonsle had disputed the peshwa's claim to the *chauth* of Bengal. Moreover, the old Gond kingdom of Garha-Mandla, which Raghuji considered within his sphere of activity, had been captured by the new peshwa. But there was a deeper cause than this, a cause rooted in the growing independence of the members of the Maratha confederacy and in Raghuji's desire to establish his power in Berar independent of the peshwa, whose policy was to bolster up the confederacy. With the help of this unexpected ally, Raghuji was driven out of Bengal, in return for which Ali Vardi Khan agreed to pay the peshwa the *chauth* for the province and an additional twenty-two lakhs of rupees. It is interesting to note that it was during this invasion that the English constructed the Maratha ditch to protect Calcutta. Ali Vardi Khan soon discovered that invaders cannot be bought off and that no reliance could be placed on the peshwa's promises, for he was once more forced to contend with a Maratha invasion in 1744. This third visitation

[1] J. Sarkar, *Fall of the Mughal Empire* (1922), vol. I, p. 87.

was the outcome of a reconciliation which Shahu had effected between the peshwa and Raghuji by which the peshwa was assigned as his sphere the provinces of Malwa, Agra, Ajmir, Allahabad and part of Bihar, while Raghuji received the rest of Bihar, together with the provinces of Oudh, Bengal and Orissa. Desperate at this recrudescence of the Maratha menace, Ali Vardi Khan had recourse to treachery and temporarily eased the situation by perfidiously massacring twenty-one Maratha generals at a conference. For a short time Bengal was freed from the Maratha pest, but Ali Vardi Khan was soon called upon to deal with mutinous Afghan generals who invited the Marathas into the province. This produced the fourth invasion of 1745. Raghuji was eventually driven out, but retained possession of Cuttack in Orissa. In 1746 the Emperor, hoping to save the provinces from further devastation, ordered Ali Vardi Khan to pay an annual sum to the Marathas for the *chauth* of Bengal and Bihar. This he refused to do, as he realised that the payment of *chauth* afforded no protection from further Maratha exactions. Nothing throws more light on the disintegration of the Empire than this pusillanimous policy on the part of the central Government and the fierce resistance of the provincial governors to the Marathas. Ali Vardi Khan bravely continued to defend his provinces against Maratha attacks and, by victories in 1746 and 1747, forced them to withdraw. But the Marathas persisted in their efforts and he was eventually compelled to come to terms with them in 1751, by which he agreed to pay their demands for *chauth*. He failed, however, to oust them from Orissa, and from this date Orissa, with the exception of a small area around Midnapore, the Orissa of the *diwani* grant of 1765, remained in Maratha hands and was incorporated in Raghuji's territory of Berar or Nagpur. The Marathas had not confined their activities to ravaging Bengal for, during these years, in addition to consolidating their power in Malwa and Bundelkhand, they had also overrun large areas in the Carnatic.

Dost Ali Khan, the nawab of the Carnatic, whose capital was at Arcot, was in theory dependent on the Mogul viceroy of the Deccan, but, in accordance with the tendencies of the time, he was striving to render himself independent of the nizam and to extend his authority over southern India. In pursuance of this policy his son-in-law, Chanda Sahib, had seized Trichinopoly and other places and was threatening the Maratha principality of Tanjore. At this stage Raghuji Bhonsle and other prominent Maratha leaders, who preferred the consolidation of Maratha power in southern India to the policy favoured by the peshwa of undermining Mogul power in northern India, persuaded Shahu to invade the Carnatic despite the fact that, by the Treaty of Warna, he had already ceded this sphere of expansion to his cousin Sambhaji, the ruler of Kolhapur. The threat to Tanjore therefore led to the invasion of the Carnatic by large Maratha armies under Raghuji who defeated and slew the dost at the Damalcherry Pass in 1740. This was followed by the capture of Arcot, Safdar Ali, the dost's successor, being forced to come to terms. In the following year Trichinopoly was taken and Chanda Sahib carried off prisoner to Satara. It was at this time that the Marathas unsuccessfully tried to force Dumas, the French governor of Pondicherry, to surrender Chanda Sahib's family to whom he had granted asylum. In 1742 Safdar was murdered by his cousin Murtaza Ali. The prevailing anarchy was intensified by the exploits of Morari Rao, the famous Maratha freebooter who had been left in charge of Trichinopoly. While the peshwa and Raghuji Bhonsle opposed each other in Bengal, the nizam, in 1743, entered the Carnatic to restore order and to re-establish his authority. Capturing Arcot and appointing his own nominee, Anwar-ud-din, to the nawabship, he proceeded to invest Trichinopoly, which surrendered after a five months' siege and was handed over to Anwar-ud-din's son, Muhammad Ali. This was the state of affairs when news reached India that England and France had been drawn into the War of the Austrian Succession. Up to this time the European trading companies in southern India had held aloof from these internecine struggles, apart from giving shelter to refugees at Madras and Pondicherry. Their policy had been to remain on the defensive and to confine their activities to the protection of their settlements. Southern India was now to become the scene of Anglo-French rivalry which eventually led to intervention in Indian affairs, an intervention which laid the foundations of European supremacy in India.

During the first half of the eighteenth century the trade of the various European countries had been at the mercy of the 'country powers'. With the exception of the English at Bombay they acknowledged the suzerainty of the Mogul Emperor, and their trading and other privileges were in the main based on Mogul *farmans*, which often proved valueless against the extortionate demands of semi-independent provincial governors and local officials. The necessity for obtaining imperial sanction for their commercial activities had prompted the Dutch to despatch Ketelaar's embassy to the court of Jahandar Shah, but, although important concessions were obtained, they were rendered nugatory by the murder of the Emperor in 1713. An English embassy under Surman which reached the court of Farrukh-siyar was more successful, and in 1717 obtained an imperial *farman* which confirmed and extended their trading privileges. Notwithstanding the disordered condition of India during this period the volume of her overseas trade, largely an export trade, increased enormously. The chief Indian exports were cotton and silk piece-goods, cotton yarns, and raw silk. An important change in her export trade had been the decline of the spice trade occasioned by the European demand for sweet in preference to spiced dishes, and the use of winter fodder for cattle which ensured a supply of fresh meat throughout the year. Bullion, particularly silver, was the principal import into India. Next in importance came broadcloth and other woollen goods, lead, copper, tin, and quicksilver. This, in brief, was the nature and direction of India's foreign trade in the first half of the eighteenth century.

By 1744 the chief European rivals for the trade of India were the English, Dutch, and French. The Portuguese, although they still held Goa, Diu, and Daman, had lost their position in the Indian trade in the first half of the seventeenth century. Compared with the English, Dutch and French, the other European companies, namely the Ostend company formally chartered in 1722, the Danish company re-established in 1729, and the Swedish company of 1731 cannot be regarded as serious rivals. For some time after the decline of Portuguese power the Dutch were the principal rivals of the English and remained so in Bengal until Clive's capture of Chinsura in 1759. The French were late-comers. Between 1666 and 1689 they had established factories at Surat, Pondicherry, Masulipatam, Chandernagore, Balasore and Kasimbazar. To these were added Calicut in 1701 and Mahé in 1721. The most important English settlements were Bombay, Madras and Calcutta. In addition there were establishments at Broach, Ahmadabad, Swally, Tellicherry, Calicut, Anjengo, Porta Novo, Masulipatam, Vizagapatam, Balasore, Kasimbazar, Dacca, Patne and Malda. It was fortunate for the English that the dispute between the London Company of Elizabeth and the English Company of 1698 had been settled by their amalgamation in the first decade of the eighteenth century into the United Company of Merchants of England trading to the East Indies. Unfortunately for the French, their company had become entangled in John Law's all-embracing System which collapsed in 1720. After this the French company was reorganised as the Perpetual Company of the Indies, and, by 1740, they were the most powerful rivals of the English in India.

News that war had broken out between England and France reached India in September 1744. At first Dupleix sought to protect French interests by means of a treaty of neutrality between the two companies in the east. As the English authorities in India had no power to enter into such an agreement his overtures were unsuccessful. Any hopes he might have entertained, and Dupleix was always an incurable optimist, were dashed to the ground by the arrival of Barnett with an English squadron which swept French shipping from the Indian seas and captured their China fleet. The next step of Dupleix was to summon La Bourdonnais from the French Islands. He arrived at an opportune moment for the French. Barnett had died and had been succeeded by the timorous and unenterprising Peyton who, after an indecisive conflict, eventually quitted the coast and sought refuge in the Hugli, thus giving the French command of the sea long enough to enable La Bourdonnais to capture Madras. This was followed by a sordid quarrel between Dupleix and La Bourdonnais over the disposal of the town. When an *impasse* had been reached, nature stepped in and a cyclonic storm which shattered part of the French fleet forced La Bourdonnais to repair to the Islands, leaving Dupleix to take over and plunder Madras. The departure of La Bourdonnais improved prospects for the English and, with the arrival of large naval reinforcements under Boscawen in April 1748, they regained complete command of the sea. The futile attempt of the English to capture Pondicherry need not detain us. By the Treaty of Aix-la-Chapelle, Madras was restored to the English in exchange for Louisbourg, the capital of Cape Breton Island. The mass of materials relating to these years, especially to the dispute between Dupleix and La Bourdonnais, has led historians to pay an attention to this war which is scarcely warranted by its importance, for it settled nothing. Aix-la-Chapelle was merely a breathing space. The war, however, did demonstrate the overwhelming importance of sea power.

The condition of India in 1748 was deplorable. It was in this year that Ahmad Shah Durrani, the Afghan ruler, made the first of a series of devastating raids and expeditions into northern India to which the 'country powers' were unable to offer any effective resistance. The death of the Emperor Muhammad Shah in the same year and the accession of a weak sensualist named Ahmad Shah were events of no political importance, for the authority of the central Government was confined to a small area around Delhi. The death of Shahu, the Maratha raja, in 1749 was likewise of little importance, for the consequent transfer of the Maratha central authority from Satara to the peshwa's capital at Poona was merely the logical outcome of a development which had already taken place. Of far greater consequence was the death of Nizam-ul-mulk, an event which produced chaos in the Deccan and, eventually, prompted the French to intervene in its affairs.

Anglo-French rivalry and the French bid for empire in India is a tale that has often been told. Intervention in Indian affairs had taken place before the days of Dupleix. As early as 1676 François Martin had seized the fort of Valdur in the neighbourhood of Pondicherry on behalf of a local chief. The Dutch had waged war against the zamorin of Calicut and taken certain forts in 1717. In 1725 a French force under Farelle re-captured Mahé from which they had been expelled by a local prince. As recently as 1739 Karikal had been occupied by the French governor Dumas. Reference has already been made to the steps taken by the English at Bombay to protect their commerce from the pirates who infested the coastal waters. In the main all these operations had aimed at the protection of European commerce. It is with Dupleix that large-scale intervention in the affairs of the 'country powers' first takes place. After 1748 there developed in southern India an unofficial war between the English and French companies. The English, by taking sides in a quarrel over the succession to Tanjore, were the first to intervene. This, however, was a minor episode compared with the grandiose schemes of Dupleix both in the Carnatic and in the Deccan. When Dupleix first intervened he probably did so for purely commercial reasons and for private gain. The idea of a French empire in India was of gradual growth, even to a man of his fertile imagination, and was probably prompted by Bussy's apparently successful policy in the Deccan. Of more importance than the details of the actual skirmishes and sieges is an assessment of the reasons for Dupleix's failure to achieve his aims. For this purpose a short résumé of the main events is essential.

On the death of Asaf Jah Nizam-ul-mulk in 1748 a struggle ensued amongst his descendants for the viceroyalty of the Deccan. While his eldest son, Ghazi-ud-din, was absent at Delhi, civil war broke out between his second son, Nasir Jang, and his grandson, Muzaffar Jang. A similar struggle took place in the Carnatic after the death of Anwar-ud-din between his illegitimate son, Muhammad Ali, and Chanda Sahib, the son-in-law of Dost Ali. While the French supported Muzaffar Jang for the viceroyalty of the Deccan and Chanda Sahib for the nawabship of the Carnatic, the English supported the claims of Nasir Jang and Muhammad Ali. To save their nominee Muhammad Ali, who was beleaguered in Trichinopoly, the English allowed Clive to attack Arcot and thus relieve the pressure on Trichinopoly. After taking Arcot Clive and his small garrison held out for fifty-three days against the troops of Chanda Sahib and his French allies. Stringer Lawrence's defeat of the French before Trichinopoly, the capitulation of the French forces under Law, and the failure of Dupleix's attempt to reverse this decision meant the ruin of his schemes for controlling the Carnatic. It is important to note that the English had been forced to resort to arms because Chanda Sahib had granted lands to the French which encircled the English position at Madras.

In the Deccan Nasir Jang, whom the Mogul Emperor had recognised as the successor of his father Asaf Jah, was assassinated in December 1750; whereupon the French championed the cause of Muzaffar Jang, who was escorted to Hyderabad and Aurangabad by a French army under Bussy. In return for this recognition and support Muzaffar Jang appointed Dupleix as his deputy over the provinces of southern India between the Krishna and Cape Comorin. On the assassination of Muzaffar Jang, Bussy promptly proclaimed Salabat Jang, third son of the late Asaf Jah, as viceroy, in return for which Salabat Jang, in October 1751, granted to Dupleix and after him to the French nation, free of all tribute, the provinces of Arcot, Trichinopoly and Madura. Bussy and Salabat Jang were now confronted by the Marathas who decided to raise their own puppet to the *masnad* in the person of Ghazi-ud-din. So seriously did Bussy regard this threat that he contemplated retiring from the Deccan. The situation was temporarily relieved when Ghazi-ud-din was poisoned, but Bussy was in desperate straits for money and for a time wished to abandon Salabat Jang because the financial resources of the Deccan were insufficient to support Dupleix's schemes. Recent research, however, has disclosed the fact that by July 1753 Bussy had been converted to Dupleix's way of thinking.[1] But his difficulties still continued, even after Salabat Jang had granted him an assignment of the revenues of the Northern Sarkars, for he was unable to compel the recalcitrant *zamindars* of that area to hand over their revenues. This was the situation when Dupleix was recalled in August 1754.

It is sometimes asserted that the resources of the French and English companies at the commencement of the struggle were practically equal. This erroneous assumption appears to be based on the resources available in the Carnatic, and fails to take into consideration the fact that the French settlements in India as a whole were much inferior to the English in every respect. It is obvious from Morellet's *Mémoire sur la situation actuelle de La Compagnie des Indes*, published in 1769 and based on documents no longer extant, that, when Dupleix intervened in the Carnatic and in the Deccan, the finances of the French Company were insufficient for his purpose. His optimism and lack of foresight led him to persuade the authorities in France that he could build up a territorial power in India the revenues of which would render it self-supporting and preclude the necessity of financial support from home. The wars that followed devastated the country and prevented the collection of the revenues upon which the success of his plan depended. In addition, the money intended for the Company's treasury often found its way into the pockets of the French officers who had come to India to shake the pagoda tree. Dupleix was well aware of this, for in 1751 we find him complaining of the immense fortunes made by Bussy and other officers in the Deccan. The result was that his debts increased year by year and eventually his credit was completely exhausted. It cannot therefore be contended that Dupleix was the victim of neglect. He asked for no money and he received none.

So far as the supply of troops from France was concerned he received, between 1750 and 1754, 4349 recruits, but they were the sweepings of the prisons and entirely untrained in the duties of their profession. With the exception of Bussy and possibly Mainville, his officers were lacking in powers of leadership and not eager for active service. In April 1750 thirteen officers deserted in the presence of the enemy, while those who arrived in 1752 were so young and inexperienced that the troops mocked at them. This failure to build up an efficient military force explains the numerous defeats his troops sustained and was one of the principal causes underlying the final failure in the Carnatic. On the other hand, the English troops and reinforcements were of better material, better paid, and, what was all-important, better led. There were no French officers in the Carnatic comparable to Clive and Stringer Lawrence. They were to the

[1] A. Martineau, *Bussy et l'Inde Française, 1720-1785* (1935), pp. 107–114.

English in the Carnatic what Bussy was to the French in the Deccan, but unfortunately for the success of Dupleix the Carnatic was the most vital theatre of operations. Bussy's expedition into the Deccan was a fatal division of forces and a dissipation of military strength. The history of India proves that empire builders require as a nucleus fertile areas of exploitation. Neither the Carnatic nor the Deccan fulfilled this purpose. A study of Dupleix's correspondence makes it clear that he was principally to blame for his own failure. Not only was he optimistic to the point of blindness, but he had one fatal defect in his character—that of under-estimating his opponents. The feeble resistance of the English at Madras and their subsequent futile siege of Pondicherry were to him conclusive evidence of their military impotence. What he failed to realise was that his schemes were bound to provoke English opposition, and that confronted with a resolute resistance he had not the military and financial resources necessary to accomplish his aims.

On the arrival of Godeheu to supersede Dupleix a provisional treaty was arranged which brought to an end the unofficial war between the two companies. It was by no means unfavourable to the French and did not extend to the Deccan, where Bussy continued to receive the support of Godeheu and his successor de Leyrit. The home authorities in London therefore proposed to ally with the Marathas in order to oust Bussy from his position, but the local officials at Bombay fortunately refused to co-operate; whereupon the troops under Clive intended for this campaign were diverted to a joint Anglo-Maratha attack upon Gheria, the pirate stronghold of Angria, which was reduced in 1756. Had Clive been entangled in the Deccan, he would not have been available for the Bengal expedition.

It was in 1756 that Ali Vardi Khan's successor, the nawab Siraj-ud-daulah, attacked and captured the English settlement at Calcutta and incarcerated the survivors in the notorious Black Hole, for which there is definite historical evidence which many Indian writers refuse to accept. It appears that the chief reason for Siraj-ud-daulah's attack was the fear of foreign aggression, a fear which had its origin in recent events in the Carnatic and the Deccan. There was also much truth in his contention that the English merchants in Bengal had fortified their settlements without his permission and had abused the trading privileges granted them by the imperial *farman* of 1717. Clive easily recaptured Calcutta and forced Siraj-ud-daulah to sign a treaty confirming all the privileges which the English had formerly enjoyed. It soon became obvious that Siraj-ud-daulah had no intention of abiding by the terms of this treaty, and that he was intriguing with the French with whom the English were once more at war. Supported by the powerful Hindu bankers, the Seths, whom Siraj-ud-daulah had insulted and estranged, Clive decided to replace him on the *masnad* by a puppet nawab, Mir Jafar, more favourably inclined to the English Company. The negotiations and operations leading up to Clive's easy victory at Plassey in 1757 are too well known to call for repetition. The results of this battle, however, were of supreme importance in the growth of British power in India, for by making the British the *de facto* rulers of Bengal, it placed at their disposal one of the wealthiest parts of India, the resources of which were used to destroy the French power in the Carnatic. It was an expedition sent by Clive from Bengal that captured Masulipatam and drove the French from the northern Sarkars, the revenues of which had been granted to Bussy. French power in Bengal came to an end with Clive's capture of Chandernagore, and all European opposition ceased with the repulse of a Dutch naval expedition to the Hugli and the capture of Chinsura in 1759. Thus before the arrival of the French general Lally at Pondicherry in April 1758, the English were firmly established in Bengal. One of Lally's first steps was to recall Bussy to the Carnatic which he correctly diagnosed to be the crucial centre of operations.

The Anglo-French struggle in the Carnatic during the Seven Years War was largely determined by naval operations. Although Lally took Fort St David he was forced to withdraw from his southern campaign in Tanjore by news of d'Aché's defeat off Karikal. This was followed by a vain attempt to capture Madras. It is significant that it was the arrival of English seaborne reinforcements from Bombay that forced Lally to raise the siege. The arrival of Sir Eyre Coote with a battalion of regular troops from England was symptomatic of the growing power of the English at sea and of their command of the long sea-route to India. Coote's defeat of Lally at Wandewash on 22 January 1760 was to the English in the Carnatic what Plassey had been to them in Bengal. Finally Pondicherry was forced to surrender to a combined land and sea attack in January 1761.

During this period of Anglo-French rivalry the Marathas had overrun almost the whole of northern India, from the Narbada to Peshawar in the vicinity of the Khyber Pass. It has been asserted that there is not a shred of evidence to support Grant Duff's statement that the Marathas watered their horses in the Indus, but the latest researches prove conclusively the truth of his contention.[1] From their advanced position on the north-west frontier the Marathas were gradually driven southwards by Ahmad Shah Durrani, the Abdali of contemporary chronicles, who was leader of the turbulent Afghan tribes of the area comprised by modern Afghanistan. Like Mahmud of Ghazni, Timur, and Nadir Shah, he was, so far as India was concerned, merely a raider; and, with the exception of Sind and the Panjab, made no attempt to annex any Indian territory to his central

[1] Grant Duff, *History of the Mahrattas* (1921), vol. I, p. 507; J. Sarkar, *Fall of the Mughal Empire* (1934), vol. II, p. 76. The evidence which corroborates Grant Duff is to be found in the manuscript Persian *Akhbarats* (news-letters) in the archives of the Bharat Itihasa Samahodhak Mandal and in the *Chandrachuda Daftar*, vol. I (1920), vol. II (1934). See also H. R. Gupta's valuable *Studies in Later Mughal History of the Punjab* (1944), pp. 175–6.

36-2

Asian empire. It was the barren nature of Afghanistan which compelled him to plunder the cities of northern India. In order to gain prestige and satisfy the marauding proclivities of his followers he was forced to adopt an aggressive policy. Between 1747 and 1769 he led ten invasions into Hindustan. In 1748 he reached Lahore and advanced to Delhi, but was defeated and forced to retreat. The invasion of the Panjab in the following year was merely a reconnaissance in force. In 1752 he conquered the Panjab and annexed Kashmir to his dominions. It was in 1757 that he captured Delhi and sacked the sacred city of Muttra. After indulging in terrible massacres he was forced to retreat owing to an outbreak of cholera in his army. The Maratha occupation of the Panjab in 1758 and the expulsion of his son Timur who had been left behind as viceroy, led to the Panipat campaign. The Marathas rapidly evacuated the province before the Afghan advance and fell back on Delhi, closely pursued by the Abdali's forces.

At the same time the Marathas had been engaged in a struggle with the nizam of Hyderabad whose powers of resistance had been weakened by Lally's withdrawal of Bussy to the Carnatic. At no time a match for the Marathas, the nizam's forces were overwhelmed by the peshwa's brother, Sadashiv Bhau, at the battle of Udgir in 1760. This was the apogee of Maratha power in the Deccan, for the nizam was forced to cede half of his dominions. Sadashiv Bhau was now entrusted by the peshwa with the formidable task of ousting the Afghans from northern India. The Marathas had not only to face a coalition of the northern Muslim chiefs, who joined forces with the invader, but they had to fight without the assistance of the Rajputs and other Hindu powers whom their extortionate demands for *chauth* and *sardeshmukhi* had estranged. The Marathas occupied Delhi without difficulty, but it was of little use as a base since food, fodder, and money were unprocurable. The situation, so far as supplies were concerned, was temporarily relieved by the capture of Kunjpura on the banks of the Jumna. But this advance proved disastrous as the more enterprising Abdali crossed the Jumna, cutting off Maratha communications with Delhi. The Bhau now decided to entrench his forces at Panipat. Deprived of all supplies by more mobile forces and faced with starvation, he was forced to leave his entrenchments and attack the Afghans. Although the Marathas fought desperately, they failed to withstand the fierce Afghan onslaught under the expert generalship of the Abdali and were routed with enormous losses at Panipat on 14 January 1761. The Abdali made no attempt to consolidate his position, and in March of the same year was once more on his way back to Afghanistan.

The Afghan victory at Panipat had far-reaching consequences. It enabled the nizam to recover from his defeat at Udgir and probably saved the State of Hyderabad from extinction. The preoccupation of the Marathas with the affairs of northern India also contributed in no small degree to the rise of an independent Muslim power in Mysore under an able adventurer named Haidar Ali. The Marathas lost prestige and it became apparent to the Indian world that neither the peshwa nor the Mogul Emperor could protect them from foreign aggression. Moreover, internal dissensions after 1761 seriously impaired the strength of the Maratha confederacy. Power now passed from the peshwa to the generals, Sindhia of Gwalior, Holkar of Indore, the raja of Berar, and the gaikwar of Baroda. Historians have tended to minimise the consequences of Panipat and to stress the fact that it was merely a temporary set-back from which the Marathas rapidly recovered. This view ignores the real importance of the victory, namely, that it granted the English the respite needed for the consolidation of their power in Bengal.

Clive's policy had been to strengthen the English position in Bengal and rule through a puppet nawab. His successor, Vansittart, after deposing Mir Jafar and replacing him by Mir Kasim, made the mistake of strengthening the power of the new nawab, who, from the beginning, asserted his authority and quarrelled with the English over the question of the abuses connected with the internal trade of the Company's servants. It cannot be denied that the Company's servants and their *gumashtas* (agents) had been guilty of gross abuses and oppression, to the truth of which the investigations of Warren Hastings at the time furnish ample evidence. For this reason many Indian writers have depicted Mir Kasim as a great patriot solicitous for the welfare of his subjects. It is, however, clear that he was aiming at complete independence and that his policy was to reverse the decision of Plassey. This the English could not allow. Exasperated by the attitude of Vansittart's colleagues, who were opposed to his conciliatory policy, Mir Kasim perpetrated the horrible massacre of Patna in 1763 when 150 Englishmen were put to death in cold blood, a far more deliberate crime than the Black Hole of Calcutta. The defeat and flight of Mir Kasim was followed by the restoration of the more pliant Mir Jafar. A final attempt to overthrow the English power in Bengal was made by the titular Mogul Emperor and his *nawab-wazir*, Shuja-ud-daulah of Oudh, but they were crushingly defeated by Munro at Buxar in 1764. This victory completed the work of Plassey. Henceforward the English were the unchallenged rulers of the province.

CHAPTER XXIV

ECONOMIC RELATIONS IN AFRICA AND THE FAR EAST

I. AFRICA

As the eighteenth century began, the white man's efforts at formal colonisation in Africa had come to a standstill. Indeed, some of these projects, the missionary kingdom in the Congo, the Portuguese holdings along the East Coast, the Jesuit beginnings in Ethiopia, had broken completely against the hard facts of Africa; the only surviving white settlers were the traders of Angola, and the farmers of the Cape, whose impact was as small as their prosperity. But if European flags or bibles made small headway, commercially a great connection was being built. The work of white traders, the play of the market, the needs of countries far away, were dragging West Africa into the world economy. This was not for the sake of its raw materials, for the gold and ivory of the West Coast would not by themselves have attracted much attention, had there not been a more fundamental commodity for sale.

The trade in African labour is very old, but the development of the New World in the seventeenth century had switched it from a northerly into a westward, transatlantic direction, and made slaving a more spectacular, as well as a more massive type of *Raubwirtschaft*. For the plantation economies of America a regular labour supply was vital, and only immigration could provide it, while the profitable geometry of the Triangular Trade benefited both African slave brokers and European traders. Herein lay the reason for the gigantic population transfers made by the slave trade.

The West Coast of Africa may be regarded as stretching between Senegal and Angola, through about 28 degrees of latitude and about 3500 miles of coastline, the whole region being known to the eighteenth century as the coast of Guinea. By African standards the region was well populated. The Gold Coast and the port of Whydah were favoured by the slavers as being densely peopled with those negro stocks appreciated in the West Indies, but the need for quick cargoes picked up as cheaply as might be drove them farther afield, to Bonny, to Old and New Calabar where they could tap the resources of the Niger delta. Contact with such crowded areas led the slavers into reckless guesswork that the population of Africa might be as high as 150,000,000, but they had no warrant for taking excuse from such large numbers. Neither were their critics justified in their sentimental attachment to 'Guinea's captive kings'. The tribes along the coast covered the widest variety of political and economic condition, from the strong monarchies of Ashanti and Dahomey, or the conciliar rule of the Akan chiefs to the small democracies of the Ibo; they might be miners, traders or farmers. It is difficult to generalise about them, but they were all affected by the hunger for white man's goods, and most of them came under the impact of his slave trade.

The spectacular growth of that trade in the eighteenth century followed the fortunes of sugar, so that a boom in the plantations would produce brisk trade for the Guineamen, unless the risks of war kept them in port. After 1740 prices rose satisfactorily till 1770 and production (at least in the British islands) followed suit. Accordingly, a larger labour force was called for, and the slavers redoubled their efforts.

The techniques of slaving varied a great deal, but they were all alike in relying on African middlemen, whose task it was to buy slaves in the inland markets and then to assemble them on the coast for the ships. The Guineamen usually sailed directly from Europe to the West Coast, were helped on their way round the shoulder of Africa by the currents, and then set out in search of a cargo. They might call at the forts maintained by their own national companies as depots for slaves awaiting shipment, but if they were private traders, there would be difficulties about this, and it would be more convenient to make landfalls here and there along the coast, buying slaves in small batches until the cargo was made up. But this coastal trade had the drawbacks of its piecemeal character: it was slow, it was uncertain, it lacked good supply points for water and stores. Consequently, the larger firms began to trade steadily at the same big markets, and thus set up a continuous contact with the local middlemen, who appreciated their custom; and it was in this way that the great slaving ports of Whydah and the Niger delta came to be established.

There was a considerable gain in convenience through this method, but it had difficulties of its own. At Whydah, for example, no ship might trade until it had paid the 'customs' in brandy, cloths and guns; and there must follow a host of miscellaneous payments in kind to the town officials, the canoemen, the hangers-on. Moreover, the negotiation for slaves was an esoteric affair. A slave was exchanged against trade goods, and these might have to be paid in advance, if a cargo had still to be bought inland. The unit of exchange was itself an almost metaphysical concept. Along the windward coast it was the iron bar; further to the east it might be cowries or cloth, copper bars or gold, but even when a slave had been priced in terms of these abstract units, it still remained to decide in what trade goods these units should be paid. Finally, there was the problem of assorting a cargo to please a fickle and specialised market. Brass muskets would sell well on the leeward coast, but elsewhere would find few takers; at one time all the beads sold on the Gold Coast had to be blue.

Voyages which might begin from England in July and only reach the West Indies in the following April meant a long wait between investment and return, but the efforts made to cut down the delay could lead to even worse troubles. A ship slaving at one port alone might gain a quicker turnround, but the ferocious rivalries of the slavers, their anxiety to get away from the pestilential rivers, the quarrels with the middlemen over credit, these might lead to gunplay or kidnapping, as in the affair of Old Calabar in 1767, when the English ships fired on the town's canoes, killing several hundred people, to encourage the others to resume trade.

Certainly the national companies were unable to check this lawlessness. It was these companies which had widened the trade in the seventeenth century, running it on notions mainly mercantilist, that one should supply one's own plantations with slaves, while denying them to one's rivals. Thus European governments backed their African companies as a means of integrating their own commercial empires, while hampering the companies of other nations; thus too the missionaries in the Congo would urge their flocks to sell slaves to only such traders as might be Portuguese and Catholic.

The wish of governments to keep a tight grip on the trade, allied to the need of a large amount of fixed capital in such a venture, had led to the setting up of the national companies, official enough, it was argued, to control it, strong enough, it was assumed, to keep it stable; these companies operated under charters granting whatever rights of monopoly their governments hoped to enforce along the African coastline. The forts they built in Senegal, the Gambia, the Gold Coast, and Whydah were the outward and visible sign of their power, and the base from which they laboured to engross as much as possible of the trade of the neighbourhood.

Such had been the theory of the trade; but by the eighteenth century its practice was changing, as the market opportunity began to widen. Thus the Dutch would sell slaves to all buyers, the Portuguese would buy from all sellers, the *Asiento* made the British the suppliers of the Spanish colonies until 1750. Moreover, the attractions of the trade enticed interlopers. The national companies, for all their mutual differences, were alike in their misfortunes. Forts had to be kept up, garrisons paid, trade plied, in bad years as in good. The interloper was spared these handicaps, he could afford to be more flexible and more enterprising, while his business methods, it may be, were more incisive. He disposed of more slaves than the chartered companies, and the planters could not do without him. The expansion of the African trade in the eighteenth century was due to the efforts of private merchants working in favourable conditions and selling in any market, while at the same time the national companies with their rigidities were forced on the defensive.

The Brandenburg Company was the first casualty, as it was the freshest recruit, in these new conditions. In 1682 the Great Elector had chartered a company to trade for slaves on the Gold Coast; from 1686 these slaves had been marketed in the Danish West Indies by agreement with

Copenhagen, and armed with this hopeful assurance the Prussians built two forts on the Gold Coast, Den Grossen Friederichsberg and Takoradi. There was much friction with the Danes, and the business did not prosper, so that by 1713 Frederick William I was pondering the 'abandonment of this business'. In 1717 the forts were sold to the Dutch, and Brandenburg was out of a bad investment.

The Danes for their part found that chartered companies had their weaknesses. The Danish forts on the Gold Coast, added to their West Indian island of St Thomas, seemed to offer the makings of a Danish triangle of trade, and from 1697 the Danish West Indian Company began to buy slaves on its own account in Africa. The result was disappointing, for the risks were too high, the returns too chancy, the Danish market in the Caribbean too small, and after 1733 the Company started to give up the trade to private merchants. These, in their turn, found the Danish market a poor speculation, and neither the size nor the prices of their shipments satisfied the planters. Accordingly, in 1755 and again in 1765, new companies were tried, and once again they were found wanting. The Danes found their slave trade an unprofitable affair, and it is not surprising that they were the first European nation to abolish it.

Yet these were merely the marginal enterprises of slaving, and the main work was done by other nations. Of these it is probable that the Portuguese share has been underestimated. They had large markets open for slaves, and with the growth of the Brazilian gold and diamond mining in Minas Geraes, labour was in great demand, and a variety of expedients was used to meet it. Several of the companies chartered by Portugal had come to a bad end through the difficulties of operating the *Asiento*, and there was need for a more flexible system. A new company was set up in 1724, and was granted a limited monopoly of slaving between Corisco and the River Gabun; but private traders from Bahia, Recife and Río de Janeiro were also allowed to operate elsewhere along the African coast. In the Niger delta and on the Gold Coast they traded cheek-by-jowl with other nations, often buying their slaves from the Dutch and the British; in Angola they naturally dominated, although they could not monopolise, the trade from that area; whilst to the north, around Sierra Leone and the Gambia, they were aided by the mulatto traders, usually of Portuguese stock, who lived there. The arrangement was admirably flexible and empirical. By buying slaves all along the coast, they could pick and choose, they could buy cheaply; by keeping on good terms with other Europeans, they could often purchase cargoes at the very forts whose upkeep was spoiling the balance sheets of their rivals; so that the English company could refer wistfully to 'the Portugueze who carry on the greatest trade with the coast of Africa without having any forts there'.[1] It was a sensible policy, and it has created the modern Brazil, but since this was

[1] *Journal of the Commissioners for Trade and Plantations*, 29 April 1726.

their only market, and since they lacked the capital for extensive speculation, they could not dominate the trade as a whole.

The Dutch were at once less restricted and better equipped. Their bases lay in the eleven forts which were maintained on the Gold Coast by their West Indian Company, but Dutch traders helped to pioneer slaving at Whydah and the Niger delta, indeed at any point offering a profit. In the New World they were equally free agents, for from their entrepôts at Curaçao and Saint Eustatius they would sell to any purchaser, thus exploiting the market demand to the full. Moreover, they were well fitted by their energy and their resources to handle a large share of the negroes on offer. They were dexterous traders and shrewd competitors, and it is a measure of their shrewdness that they would extend no credit to their African middlemen; it is no less characteristic that they should have studied with care the needs of the market, and sold at competitive prices, so that the English in 1729 were driven to gloomy speculations that 'most ships trading to Africa took in great part of their loading at Holland'.[1] But the growing capacity of English and Indian industry came to alter the cost ratios, and by 1750 the Dutch advantage had gone, and their competitors could cheerfully assert that 'the Dutch forts are worse supplied with goods than heretofore'.[2]

It would be misleading to follow the fortunes of the French and the British slavers in purely economic terms, for it was the wars of the eighteenth century which exerted the most formative influence upon them. In wartime, the slow and unhandy Guineamen of the enemy were an obvious prey, and the effect of war was to force up the price of slaves in the New World. British naval power drove the French slavers off the seas in the struggles of the 1740's and 1750's, just as the British slave trade was itself brought to a standstill during the American War. But apart from the effects of warfare, the organisation of the French trade to Africa called for serious inquiry and revision, for it satisfied neither the planters in the West Indies nor the Government in Paris. In 1716 the trade had been thrown open to all Frenchmen. Four years later John Law united the fragments of the French West Indian and West African companies into a new Company of the West, meant to redesign the triangle of trade, but the plan was ruined by financial weakness and Caribbean complaints. In the French case, as in the others, the slave trade passed more and more into the hands of private firms, which operated from Nantes, Bordeaux and St Malo, and which forced the chartered companies to give ground.

Yet once more the problem of the forts in Africa had to be met, for who but a chartered company would maintain them? The French holdings were divided into the Department of Senegal and the Department of

---

[1] *Journal of the Commissioners for Trade and Plantations*, 17 March 1729. *Acts of the Privy Council, Colonial Series*, 12 March 1730.
[2] *Journal of the Commissioners for Trade and Plantations*, 10 January 1750.

Guinea, and a great deal of effort had gone into the making of them. The Senegal region was reckoned to extend for 250 leagues south of Cape Blanco, and within it were the French headquarters at St Louis, and the outstations at Arguin, Portendick, Goree, and Albreda, with an inland post at Fort St Joseph in Galam. The trade in gold and gum was valuable, but the annual export of slaves did not average more than 100; in other words, it was not an area where private firms could usefully operate, for the gold trade demanded continuous contacts and depots. For this reason the forts had to be kept, and with them a chartered company. The company laboured to drive British trade out of the region, and under the energetic lead of André Brue it tried hard to penetrate inland. But after his departure in 1720 these schemes fell to pieces. The negroes were suspicious and hamstrung the trade, so that by the 1720's the department was running at a loss of 3,500,000 *livres* a year. Secondly, British sea power was too strong for the French. In 1758 Senegal was taken by the combined operations of William Pitt, and remained under British rule until 1783 as part of the new composite colony of Senegambia.

Nor were the private traders for their part much happier in war-time. Slaving was a risky business at the best of times, and for the French firms the war years between 1746 and 1748, and between 1756 and 1763, proved to be the worst of times, when capture or the fear of capture knocked the bottom out of their slave trade. Nevertheless, in peace-time it flourished. The private firms went farther and fared better than the chartered company. They operated in the Department of Guinea, trading along the Gold Coast and to Whydah, and then edging as far as the Gabun and points south, in their search for security and cheaper cargoes.

This movement to new slaving grounds is one of the most important trends in the history of the trade in the eighteenth century, and it was a change for which the British slavers were peculiarly well adapted through the looseness of their organisation and the large number of newcomers in their ranks. The Royal African Company remained until 1750 the official body entrusted with the African trade, but it had lost its monopoly since 1698, and after the Peace of Utrecht it fell on very hard times. The *Asiento* might have revived its fortunes, for the South Sea Company was anxious to buy its slaves, but its supplies were erratic and sparse, so that the South Sea Company, failing to get satisfaction, resolved to go trading in Africa on its own account. In 1729, when the *Asiento* was reaffirmed, the Company resolved to have done with the African trade, and to content itself with buying slaves landed in the West Indies. This was to ally itself with the private men, for the British trade was falling more and more into their hands. In 1725 Bristol ships carried 17,000 negroes, while the London firms may have handled more; by 1750 it was Bristol and Liverpool which were disputing the lion's share; a quarter of a century later, the prize had fallen to Liverpool, whose ships were bearing two-thirds of the British total.

Faced with competition so intense and so expert, the Royal African Company could do little but hope for aid from public funds. There were seven British forts on the Gold Coast, one at the Gambia, one at Whydah. They might represent a step towards formal colonisation, but could they compare in value with the informal empire of the private traders? In 1726 the Commissioners for Trade and Plantations addressed themselves to these questions. The Company could not dispute that the interlopers were carrying vastly more slaves to the plantations, but it blamed them for the higher prices that the planters were paying. Some of the planters agreed, but the commissioners did not, and they were not to be persuaded that the trade should revert to a monopoly.

Yet there was still a case for holding the forts, if only for the sake of the gold trade. Parliamentary voices might assert contemptuously that the company 'are now not worth a shilling',[1] but in 1730 parliament was induced to vote it a subsidy. Still, insolvency was not to be so easily avoided. The subsidy, it was complained, was too small, the Company's expenses were too high. In 1750 it was abolished, in spite of West Indian doubts, and the management of the forts was vested in a new and looser body, the Company of Merchants trading to Africa. Open to each and every African merchant, forbidden to trade corporately, the new Company was no more than a vestigial remnant of the old monopoly. The private traders had won.

The result of their victory was to bring to the British slave trade adaptability and enterprise at precisely the time when the British economy was becoming peculiarly well fitted to furnish it with the right exports for Africa at the right prices. After 1750 Lancashire textiles got their chance through the decline of Indian competition amid the confusion of Indian politics. The British slavers seized their opportunity, and in the quarter of a century after 1750 they came to dominate the whole of the African trade. In that period they raised the value of British exports (and re-exports) to Africa by 400 per cent, and before the American War they were carrying nearly 50,000 negroes a year. The unregulated nature of their trade helped in this prodigious expansion, for it was the firms which wandered away from the old slaving centres which picked up the big cargoes.

Yet, for all this, the private traders in their turn began to show signs of shrinking into an oligopoly. In 1752 there were 101 Liverpool slave merchants, all of them quite small men, but towards the end of the century the trade was falling into the hands of a few large firms. The French slave trade underwent a similar change, the small men gradually giving way to large combines such as the Angola Company, founded in 1749, operating a capital of 2,000,000 *livres* and a large fleet. In Holland, too, powerful concerns such as the Middelburg Company came to take a hand in the trade. This trend is readily explained by the nature of the commerce with

[1] *Historical Manuscripts Commission, Egmont*, I, 51.

West Africa. The slave trade was a risky trade. There was of necessity a long interval between investment and profit, if indeed there was to be a profit, which was always uncertain. It was a difficult task to find the right goods to fit the taste of the African consumer. Moreover, it might be necessary to offer him these goods on credit and sometimes they simply disappeared into the bush. In any case, the investor's troubles did not cease with the collection of a cargo. The middle passage had its own dangers, in the possibility of mutiny or the fear of capture; finally, in the New World the planters might force down the selling price or default on their debts to the slavers. The trade abounded in imponderables.

Heavy buying of slaves at the traditional markets along the Gold Coast and at Whydah led to fierce competition. In 1739, for example, a British ship languished on the Gold Coast for twenty-two months waiting for a cargo, and this in a trade where it was vital to sell in the West Indies at the beginning of the season. The negro middlemen, who were not slow in learning the tricks of the trade, saw their advantage and forced up the prices. There is plenty of evidence that negroes bought in the old slaving centres cost more and more. Davenant noted it in 1709, Atkins found Gold Coast prices rising in 1721, and forty-six years later it was calculated that prices had at least doubled of late.

It was a difficult matter to pass on these increases to the planters, so that the slavers' best hope lay in pioneering new African markets where the bidding would not be so fierce nor the sellers so sophisticated. Consequently, the more enterprising newcomers to the trade moved to the east and south. Some of them headed for the Congo and Angola; others began to deal with the Gabun; but the most important movement was to the bights of Benin and Biafra, and especially to the ports of the Niger delta, where prices were reported as being 60 per cent under those ruling on the Gold Coast. As early as 1729 it was feared that 'surely the Bite (*sic*) trade must be overdone',[1] but in fact it was upon their connection with this region that the British supremacy in the slave trade came to depend. In 1771 half the British slave cargoes came from the bights, and the trade with the Niger region came to be a peculiarly Liverpool trade. In 1784 and 1785 over 63 per cent of all the Guineamen of Liverpool were bound for the ports of the Niger delta.

It seems likely that the rising cost of slaves led to the use of bigger ships on which the congestion would not be so murderous. The port of Nantes appears to have bought 146,799 slaves between 1748 and 1782, and to have disposed of 127,133, which means an average loss of 13·4 per cent, and the mortality dropped as the trade became more rationalised.

Yet in spite of the difficulties, rewards could be high. The voyage of the Liverpool ship *Lively* in 1737 yielded a profit of 300 per cent;

[1] Bristol Public Library, Hobhouse Papers, Tyndall and Assheton to Isaac Hobhouse, 13 March 1729.

this was perhaps a great *coup*, but there is evidence that the French traders worked on an expectation of 25 or 30 per cent, and contemporaries regarded the value of the trade as self-evident, so that its early opponents had to criticise it on grounds of its injustice rather than of its inexpediency. But we stress the fortunes at the risk of forgetting the failures, such as the *Comte d'Hérouville*, which waited seven months for a cargo, and then crossed the Atlantic bearing precisely two slaves. All in all, the slave trade was not a simple success story, but a great and an unpredictable lottery. It is understandable that some African merchants should have preferred the sober business of dealing in gums or dyewoods to the hurly-burly of slaving.

The impact of the trade on Africa was only slightly a matter of white settlers, for although great things were one day to come from the European forts on the coast, their effect on African societies in the eighteenth century was small. On the Gold Coast, for example, the frontier was a ragged and weak affair, with the white men anxious to avoid trouble with their neighbours. Indeed, these neighbours held the whip hand, for it rested with them whether to open or shut the trade paths down to the coast, to permit or to deny a smooth flow of gold and slaves down to the forts. Hence the white men could be pinned on to the coast, and any inland penetration would have upset the trade. Farther to the north, however, where the Africans were not so strong, and where the Europeans were better led, there was more headway. André Brue in Senegal set himself to penetrate to the gold mines in Galam, built a fort there to dominate them, and even hoped to extend French power as far as Tourbat, 600 leagues to the east. Even after Brue had gone home, there was an expansionist school in Senegal, but the company ruled that 'the real mines for us lie in trading', and that the negroes should be left in peace. The British efforts in the Gambia did not even get as far as this. In 1720, 'in the bubbling time', great projects about African mines were canvassed by the duke of Chandos who induced the Royal African Company to send an expedition up the Gambia in search of gold: it ended badly, and so did the duke's fortune. Another journey in 1732 fared no better.

The only successful activity inland seems to have been the work of the Portuguese in Angola. Their political power on the coast was more firmly based than was that of the other Europeans farther to the north, so that they could edge their way inland with more confidence though the depth of their penetration is uncertain. The Portuguese were, in fact, the nation with the greatest direct contact with West Africa in the eighteenth century. The Dutch did not care for chaplains in their forts; the British sent out one missionary who made four converts; but the Portuguese encouraged Franciscans and Capuchins to work in Angola and to keep alive the remnants of Christianity to the north.

If European penetration was slight, there were good reasons for this.

Their dependence on middlemen, their dislike of the heat and the damp, left the white men without motive to go inland. But there was a more positive force confining them to the coast, and that was the growth of strong military kingdoms, themselves a result of the slave trade. The stronger was a tribe, the more slaves it could conquer to exchange for trade goods. The outcome of this was the rise of powerful military kingdoms, such as Ashanti or Dahomey, where able men formed confederacies of tribes to dominate the hinterland behind the ports, and to keep up the flow of slaves to the ships. After this it was a short step to wishing to trade with the white man directly on the coast, instead of staying dependent on the middlemen. Guadja Trudo, who became king of Dahomey in 1708, was impressed by the powers of European weapons. In 1727 this powder and shot helped him to fight his way down to the coast and to capture the great slaving port of Whydah. Similarly the Ashanti were busy at this time in organising their kingdom, and by 1768 news of them was beginning to worry the Europeans in their forts on the Gold Coast.

One of the gravest indictments of the Atlantic slave trade is that by stirring up wars between neighbouring peoples it exerted a ruinous effect upon African society. There can be no doubt that its impact was severe, but that is not to say that it shattered the peace of a continent. There is no warrant for supposing that Africa was a nest of singing birds before the coming of the white man. Moreover, not all wars produced slaves, and not all slaves were produced by war. For forty-five years after the capture of Whydah, the Dahomeans were at war with their neighbours; but the effect was to cut by 75 per cent the export of slaves from that port. In fact, warfare was only one of the many ways in which slaves could be acquired. The old institution of domestic slavery, designed to provide protection and to ease the chronic shortage of labour, might be the punishment of a crime, the payment of a debt, the guarantee of security for an otherwise masterless man. It was hereditary, and in some societies, such as Ashanti and Dahomey, practically universal, and the slave, once commended to his master, enjoyed carefully defined rights. But these rights might be disregarded by a master under the temptation of European goods, and some of the negroes who found their way to the New World had certainly been domestic slaves in the Old. For all this, the loss of so many people to Africa, however they had been enslaved, meant a serious loss to the labour force, and a narrowing of the margin of security, never very wide in African society.

How much of Africa was affected by these depredations, it is difficult to say. The humanitarians were to assert that almost the whole continent was laid waste, and they pictured long lines of slaves plodding vast distances across Africa down to the coast. There is some support for this view in the eighteenth-century records, but it is to be observed that this is all hearsay evidence, for no European seems to have accompanied a slave caravan before Mungo Park did so in 1797. Again, it should be remembered that in African terms lengthy journeys need not imply long distances. The slave captains would not have wished slaves to be fetched over large distances, for long marches would wear out their cargo, and would hold up the ships. It was for precisely this reason that the chief slaving centres grew up in densely peopled areas, such as Old Calabar, where slaves could be fetched in three days from the inland markets, and where the ships could expect a quick turnround. Perhaps this was an exceptionally favourable area, and many slaves were brought from 500 miles away, but these are not great distances by African standards, and do not amount to the ravaging of central Africa. Anthropological study of negroes in the New World has not found much trace of central African customs surviving among them.

While the merchants' frontier was forming on the West Coast of Africa, the Dutch farmers at the Cape of Good Hope were consolidating an area of formal white settlement. Founded in 1652 as a supply base for ships of the Dutch East India Company, the colony was a wholly dependent economy, directed by and for the Company, and subject to changes of fortune beyond the control of the settlers. But even at the beginning of the century, the colony was dividing into a Western region of the Cape peninsula and the Berg valley, and the Eastern farming settlements around Stellenbosch, which avoided as far as could be all contact with the seat of government at Cape Town. Yet they too were restricted by its policies. The internal market at the Cape was tiny, and there was little profit for the farmers in producing their wheat, wines and meat; but in any case the Company stood in their way, for they might sell their produce to authorised buyers alone, and they might not export, save through the Company. Such a system was heavy-handed, but it is likely that no system could have stimulated Cape farming at this period with so few at home to buy its produce, and with nothing to sell abroad which the world needed or wished to take. The Company, indeed, tried to help; efforts were made to diversify the crops with sugar, rice and indigo; wine and wheat were sent to the Netherlands East Indies; but none of these projects did well. It was only by accident and at intervals that the economy prospered, when the wars between 1740 and 1763 brought British and French fleets to Table Bay in search of provisions; but peace was bad for trade, fewer and fewer ships would call, and the Company sank into debt. In 1717 it had been decided to solve the labour difficulty by importing more slaves, of whom there were already nearly 2000 to almost the same number of free burghers. Importation went on steadily, and by the end of the century, the slave population of nearly 17,000 was larger than the free, and the western region had ceased to be a mainly white man's country.

But this atmosphere of stagnation was not to be found in the east.

Unlike the region of settlement, the east was driven by dynamic trends towards expansion and movement inland. Beyond the eastern frontier stretched lands with a good rainfall and offering no greater opposition than that of the Bushmen and the demoralised Hottentots. First the ivory hunters and then the cattlemen went through the mountain passes and found good country beyond, country moreover which was out of reach of the Company. The dispersal was swift, pushing the frontier north and east. In 1752 the pioneers were over the Kei River, in 1760 Jacobus Coetsee had crossed the Orange. The Company was opposed to this unregulated exodus, and in 1743 it offered the frontiersmen freehold land, so as to slow them down. But the flight of these fugitives from the eighteenth century could not be halted. The system of land tenure known as the loan farm added to the attractions of trekking. It allowed farmers to occupy land on indeterminate lease, ostensibly from the Company, on the payment of 12, or later 24, rix-dollars a year. This was to legalise squatting, and so to encourage trekking; moreover, since the squatter might not subdivide his land, his younger sons would soon be on the move again, pushing the trek still farther. Even the Company was forced to recognise the new frontiers in 1778.

In the following year the pioneers collided with the Xosa, the advance guard of the Bantu who were moving south, and from that date a new era in South African history began. Until 1779 the Boers had been confronted with native problems that were either easily solved or safely disregarded. Those Hottentots who lived in the colony had lost their tribal bonds and had merged into the general mass of coloured folks; those of them who kept their tribal solidarity had withdrawn to the south-west or to Griqualand or to the Orange, keeping on sufficiently friendly terms with the white men. The bushmen had stayed irreconcilable, and were hunted down by the newly developed commando system. But the Bantu were to prove more formidable.

There is a marked contrast between the fortunes of West and of East Africa during the eighteenth century. The East Coast was but dimly known to Europeans, and it was denied any but the smallest contact with them. It was denied too any but the smallest effect of the Atlantic slave trade, for it lacked the population density and the linkage with the Americas which set the Europeans to work in the west. What trade there was lay mainly in the hands of the Arabs, who also enjoyed the littoral supremacy, once they had ejected the Portuguese from most of their holdings. Still more striking is the absence in the east of strong, well-organised African kingdoms. The Bantu were on the move, it is true, but they were still small groups of wandering peasant farmers, and would not coalesce into large kingdoms until the end of the century, in the time of troubles. This was the case, for example, with the Zulu-Xosa people, who had settled in Natal since at least the sixteenth century, were still living as small communities, and were still unmolested by the white man. The authorities at the Cape had been mildly interested in Natal in 1689, but nothing had come of their interest; in 1719 a more definite step was taken when the Company set up a trading post at Delagoa Bay, but eleven years later it was withdrawn. Thenceforward for the next hundred years the occasional landfalls of slavers and shipwrecked sailors remained the only connection between Europe and Natal.

During the efflorescence of the Portuguese empire, the East African coast had risen from obscurity, for it was essential to their trading ventures in the Indian Ocean to hold bases along that coast, and these bases might also be used to win for Portugal the gold and ivory trades with the interior that the Arabs had enjoyed for centuries. Hence the power of Portugal had had its outward signs in the fortresses at Mombasa, Sofala, and Mozambique. But all this was altered by the series of blows through which the Dutch broke the trading empire of Portugal, and with its fall disappeared most of the point of the East African bases. At the same time these bases were menaced from Africa itself. An African rising in 1693 expelled the Portuguese from most of their estates between the Limpopo and the Zambesi, and then an Arab resurgence consummated their ruin. By 1698 they had lost everything north of Zanzibar, and even to the south the shadows were closing in. Sofala had to be sold, Mozambique to be disciplined by the Government of India. Nominally, the province of Mozambique still stood, but it was a province only on paper, with a few forts along the coast and a host of unreal claims inland. By the middle of the century it had become a phantom empire. Even the missionary impulse was spent, and but four churches remained to the Portuguese. What trade there was, they were content to leave to the Arabs and the Indians, except for the gold trade, since they kept in touch with the mines. Even this was to vanish towards the end of the century amid the Bantu upheavals, and the Portuguese turned to the slave trade, for it was sometimes worth while to ferry slaves from Mozambique to Angola. But this could never be more than a very marginal enterprise, and economically the Portuguese fragments in East Africa were a wasting asset until the reorganisation of the 1790's.

Three hundred miles to the east of Mozambique lay the island of Madagascar, which had possessed since the seventeenth century a stronger nuisance value than a commercial interest. Its strategic importance had been noted by the buccaneers, who made it their main base for commerce-raiding in the Indian Ocean, but the growing risks of piracy led the pirates to give up their trade, and to take to the more respectable life of slave traders. Once Madagascar ceased to be bedevilled by buccaneering, more formal colonising could be tried. The French attempt at a settlement had failed in 1675, and thereafter Paris had lost interest. But the new French colony of Île de France, which was begun in 1715, was vitally concerned with Madagascar, as a supplier of food, and in 1750 the French formally occupied the island of Sainte-Marie, whence they could dominate much of the east coast. Strategically, too, Madagascar was seen to be of use to the trade with India, and when French power vanished in the East, Choiseul perceived that the island would be a useful compensation. Accordingly it was annexed in 1768, and if this annexation meant little at the time, nonetheless it meant the staking out of a useful claim.

The Portuguese had been the spearhead of European influence on the East Coast, and as their power contracted, so did the empire of Ethiopia withdraw into itself. In 1633, after the death of their convert, the Emperor Susenyos, the Portuguese missionaries had been expelled from the empire, and fresh efforts in Gondar were violently blocked. Thenceforward, contacts with Europe were to be no more than tentative. Ethiopia sank into an isolation in which there were no more links with West Africa, no more missions to India. In 1699 Charles-Jacques Poncet noted that although natives with white ancestors still enjoyed some prestige, yet 'the horror which the Ethiopians have for the Mahometans and Europeans is almost equal'.[1] This sturdy xenophobia was shown in 1706 when a venture by a Franciscan caused a political *coup* to reassert the isolation and insulation of the country. But there was anarchy amid the isolation, and the political power of the emperors fell to pieces in a series of palace revolutions which made them mere *rois fainéants*, dominated by Ras Michael Sehul, the governor of Tigrai. It was this wreckage and solitude that James Bruce found in 1771 when he entered Ethiopia on what was to be the most elaborate of eighteenth-century explorations of Africa. He stayed for two years, journeying with Ras Michael and the Emperor Takla Haimanut II, enduring all things, observing all things. The trade of the empire, he found, was in the hands of the Arabs, who overlanded gold, ivory and slaves to the north. Indeed, the Europeans had no footing anywhere in north-east Africa save in Egypt; and over most of the continent to the south of the Mediterranean seaboard the white man was still unknown.

2. ASIA

The economic activity of Europe in the Far East (excluding India) in the eighteenth century was mainly concentrated in China, Indonesia, and the Philippines, where the European nations had established their trading centres. Japan had withdrawn herself into almost complete seclusion under the Tokugawa Shogans since the fourth decade of the preceding century and was to remain thus isolated until the appearance of Commodore Perry's squadron in 1853. Meanwhile her one eye on the external world was the settlement of Deshima, a tiny artificial island in

---

[1] C. J. Poncet, *Voyage to Ethiopia*, p. 124, in *Hakluyt Society Publications*, 2nd series, vol. c.

Nagasaki harbour, not more than 300 paces at its greatest extent, on which a few Dutch merchants lived a life of abject indignity, and which was the only channel of foreign trade. Therefore in this chapter it is in Canton, Batavia, Manila and their environs that our interest chiefly lies. One fact, at least, is common to these diverse areas of economic activity, and that is the independence of the natives of European manufactures and their indifference thereto at this period in their history.[1]

China

Swaying the wide world, I have one aim in view, to maintain a perfect governance and to fulfil the duties of my state: strange and costly objects do not interest me. If I have commanded that the tribute offerings sent by you, O king, are to be accepted, this was solely in consideration of the spirit which prompted you to despatch them from afar....As your ambassador can see for himself, we possess all things. I set no value on objects strange and ingenious, and have no use for your country's manufactures.

Although these words, from a mandate of the Emperor Ch'ien Lung on the occasion of his receiving the Macartney embassy from King George III in 1793, belong to a period considerably later than the one under consideration, they contain the key to the understanding of European relations with China for the whole of the eighteenth century. The 'Middle Kingdom' was self-sufficing, requiring nothing from the West in the material or, for that matter, the spiritual sphere. The emperor's statement, however, though true in essence, was somewhat in the nature of an oversimplification, for the trade with the West was permitted, and the court took its full share of the profits. The principal goods sought from China were manufactured silk, porcelain, lacquer, and tea, with some articles of luxury such as fans and screens, and for these the only payment the Chinese would accept was silver (and later, opium).

After 1723 intercourse between the Chinese and the foreigner was exclusively on a basis of material interest. The great opportunity for the conversion of China to Christianity (if it had ever really existed) had come in the seventeenth century, and by the second decade of the eighteenth it had definitely been lost. To begin with, the Catholic missionaries had been welcomed at court because of their scientific attainments, but their differences among themselves over the question of the ancestor worship and the translation of the word 'Heaven' into Chinese had discredited them with the Chinese, and the inferior reputation of the European merchants and adventurers—often mere pirates—had done further injury to the name of 'Christian'. The Emperor K'ang Hsi, in the earlier decades

---

[1] English woollens, for example, were a drug on the China market. Each of the company's ships was required by law to take one-tenth of its outward stock in English products; but lead found a better market than woollens.

of whose reign the missionaries had enjoyed high favour, died in 1723 and, a year later, under his successor, Yung Chêng (1723–36), Christianity was utterly prohibited throughout the empire.

Portuguese enmity had been successful in preventing the English from getting a footing in Canton until the very end of the seventeenth century. In 1689 a duty had been imposed in England on all imported tea, showing that the trade was already considered valuable enough to be taxable. In 1699 the Court of Directors of the East India Company had sent out a consul's commission to their chief supercargo, Allen Catchpoole, by which he was appointed king's minister, or consul, for the whole of the empire of China and the adjacent islands. Two years later, this official, in an attempt to open up trade, had been successful in obtaining permission for the Company to send ships to Chusan or Ningpo. Accordingly, the vessels arrived, carrying between them over a hundred thousand pounds in silver, but the exactions of the Chinese officials proved to be so unconscionable and the monopoly of the local Chinese merchants so complete that the venture was a dead loss and the ships were obliged to withdraw. Other ventures by the Company about this time, however, to Canton and Amoy, fared less ill. Catchpoole established a factory at Pulo Condore, an island off the coast of Cochinchina, but this came to a tragic end in 1705 when the Malays (said to have been instigated by the Cochinchinese) murdered every member of the foreign settlement. The risks and oppression suffered by the foreign merchants at this time were so great that it was only the large profits of the trade that induced them to continue.

The foreign trade at Canton was controlled by an official known to Europeans as the *Hoppo*, or 'Emperor's Merchant', who was the Imperial Commissioner of the Kwangtung Customs. The trade itself was conducted by four Chinese merchants who held the monopoly and had the right of farming out the trade piecemeal to others. This development was yet another handicap to the foreign traders in their endeavour to do business on competitive terms, but in spite of this and other disabilities, by 1720 the trade had so greatly expanded and the number and value of the commodities exported had so much increased that the Chinese attempted to establish a regular control. They introduced a uniform duty of 4 per cent on all goods in place of the various arbitrary amounts levied by the *Co-hong*, or body of merchants who held the exclusive privilege of trading with foreigners and who became responsible for their payment of duties and for their good behaviour. The Chinese authorities now proceeded to squeeze from the trade the maximum amount that it would yield—the duty was increased to about 16 per cent, and in addition to this the foreign merchants had to pay an extortionate fee to the ships' chandlers of the port before they would supply a ship with provisions, besides a heavy 'measurement duty' to the collector of customs.

It was now quite clear to the foreign merchants that there would be no end to these exactions unless they made a determined stand. In 1728 they made an appeal to the governor of Kwangtung and were successful temporarily in obtaining the suspension of the *Co-hong*. But the system had proved so convenient to the Chinese Government (relieving it of all the trouble of controlling the trade and of regulating the behaviour of the foreign merchants while ensuring that it received a due share of the profits) that the *Co-hong* was soon re-established and its monopoly confirmed. Indeed, an additional duty of 10 per cent on all exports was now imposed on top of the exactions already made and, in spite of the renewed and spirited protests of the foreign merchants, they were unable to get it removed until the reign of Ch'ien Lung, in 1736. Even then, the manner of making the concession brought home once more to the Europeans the insupportable terms on which they were permitted to trade, and, indeed, to exist in China.

The emperor, in taking off the duty of 10 per cent, required that the foreign merchants should hear the act of grace read *while on their knees*. This was too much to endure even for the long-suffering foreigners in search of a quick fortune and willing to put up with almost any injustice and indignity for a limited time. They met in a body and each one undertook on his honour not to assume this slavish posture nor to make any concession to the Chinese without acquainting the rest. Another demand of the emperor was that all arms on board the foreign ships should be handed over to the Chinese, but this demand was later waived in return for a payment of $10,000. Not long after this, the right of direct approach to the civil authorities by the foreign merchants was suspended, and the merchants of the *Co-hong* (the 'Hong Merchants' as they were afterwards known) became the only channel of communication with the Government. Thus in cases of complaint regarding the duties which they themselves imposed, the Hong Merchants were constituted judges in their own cause.

By this suicidal policy the Chinese authorities almost killed the foreign trade. In 1734 only one English ship came to Canton and one was sent to Amoy, but the extortions there were greater than those in any other port and the vessel withdrew. In 1736 the foreign ships at Canton comprised four English, two French, two Dutch, one Danish, and one Swedish. Before this date Portuguese ships had been restricted to Macao.

In 1742 the *Centurion*, the flagship of Commodore Anson and the only surviving vessel of his fleet, the first British man-of-war to sail in Chinese waters, arrived at Macao. The Commodore, engaged in circumnavigating the globe while making war on the Spaniards, was in no mood to submit to the arbitrary requirements of the Chinese, and he declined to leave the delta of the Pearl River until his ship had been furnished with provisions. His attitude, which combined decision with good manners, undoubtedly made a good, if fugitive, impression upon the Chinese, but the appearance of a European warship in Chinese waters with means, if necessary, to back up the requirements of its commander with force, was an isolated phenomenon in this part of the eighteenth century.

Throughout this period, among the nations of western Europe, it was left to the British to carry on the struggle for recognition of their rights as human beings. In 1664 the Dutch emissary, Van Hoorn, had been politely received when he appeared at the Chinese court, but his mission had been barren of practical results, and there was an interval of 130 years before the Dutch sent another embassy to China. The Russians, however, fared better than either the Dutch or the English. They, too, had sent earlier embassies to China without effective result, and in 1653 the tsar Alexis had sent his baliff, who refused to perform the kowtow and was consequently dismissed. There followed a series of trading missions to China, and in 1689 the Russians actually secured a treaty from Peking. There were frequent clashes between the two nations on the banks of the Amur, and, reinforced perhaps by the physical prowess of her outposts, the Empress Catherine in 1727 dispatched a mission which was to be the most successful of all. This was partly due, it is true, to the desire of the emperor Yung Chêng to counterbalance the intrigues of the Jesuits. The treaty of this year, in which the Russians were treated as equals, lasted until 1858 and is referred to by one authority as the 'longest-lived treaty on record'.

Because of the continued exactions of the *Co-hong* and its prevention of direct access to the local authorities, the English Company again attempted to trade with Amoy and Ningpo in preference to Canton. Samuel Harrison, Thomas FitzHugh and James Flint were sent to Ningpo to open up negotiations for trade and were well received, but when the Company's vessel arrived it was with the greatest difficulty that a cargo was obtained at all. In 1757 an imperial edict was issued restricting all foreign ships to Canton. Flint, who had acquired a fluent knowledge of Chinese (a unique accomplishment for a European merchant at this period), finding that his efforts to trade at Ningpo were fruitless, managed to secure a passage in a native vessel to Tientsin, and from there was able to make his case known to the emperor at the capital. This move was, surprisingly enough, productive of results, for the emperor not only took note of Flint's complaint, but appointed a commission to accompany him overland to Canton. On arrival there Flint proceeded to the English factory and shortly afterwards all the foreigners were summoned to appear before the commissioner who informed them that the *Hoppo* (the emperor's merchant) had been superseded and that all duties in excess of 6 per cent had been remitted as well as all enforced presents to officials and tonnage duties on foreign ships.

The sequel, however, proved that the success was illusory and events thenceforth assumed what was for many years to be a familiar pattern in Sino-European relations.

Some days after the commissioner's announcement, the governor of Kwangtung sent for Mr Flint in order to convey to him the emperor's orders. When he appeared the officials in attendance tried to make him do homage after the Chinese fashion. At the same time Flint was shown what purported to be an imperial edict, banishing him first to Macao and thence to England for having endeavoured to open up trade by way of Ningpo in defiance of the emperor's edict confining foreign shipping to Canton. The same day, the Chinese who had written the petition to the emperor on Flint's behalf was publicly beheaded for 'traitorously encouraging foreigners'. Flint himself was seized and taken to a place near Macao. Here he was imprisoned for two and a half years before he was released and allowed to sail for England. It appears that at any time he would have been released on payment of $1250, but the Company, arguing that it would encourage similar exactions, refused to pay the ransom and contented itself by petitioning for Flint's release. Thus it was that the first of the Company's servants to qualify himself adequately for his appointment by learning the Chinese language, and who moreover, at great personal risk took the initiative to further the Company's interests, obtained scant recognition from his employers.

The hardships of foreigners continued throughout this period without remission. The rule adopted by the Chinese was that 'the barbarians are like wild beasts, and are not to be ruled on the same principles as citizens'. They were to be 'ruled by misrule' according to the principles of the ancient emperors. Virtually the same principle in regard to foreign traders (remarks S. Wells Williams) was acted on in England under Henry VII, and the idea among the Chinese of their obligations towards foreigners was not unlike that which prevailed in Europe before the Reformation. One of the outstanding reasons for the contempt in which the Europeans were held with all classes was their complete ignorance of spoken and written Chinese. When all intercourse was carried on in a barbarous jargon ('pidgin' Portuguese and English) which both sides despised, the results were not unnaturally mutual misunderstanding and dislike often amounting to hatred. This feeling was accentuated by the disorderly behaviour of foreign sailors relaxing on shore after being cooped up on a long voyage and who were frequently drunk and quarrelsome. French and English seamen at Whampoa in the mid-eighteenth century could scarcely meet without coming to blows.

When a fracas of the above sort resulted in the death of one of the parties, the Chinese response was to stop the trade. It was not until 1780 that the Chinese intervened in a case in which foreigners solely were involved, but in that year they demanded the surrender of a Frenchman who had killed a Portuguese sailor in an affray, and when this demand was eventually acceded to, the delinquent was publicly strangled.

The case, however, that demonstrated with striking singularity the difference between the Chinese and the European conceptions of justice occurred in 1784. During the firing of a salute on an English ship, the *Lady Hughes*, a ball had inadvertently been left in the gun with the result that a Chinese was killed. According to the Chinese interpretation of the principle of responsibility, the man who fired the shot was answerable for the death of the victim. The conception of *mens rea* was one that had not as yet come within Chinese cognizance. Knowing that the English were not likely to surrender the gunner, the Chinese police seized Mr Smith, the supercargo of the vessel, and held him prisoner. Trusting too readily to assurances that all the gunner was required for was for 'questioning', the supercargo agreed to his being handed over to the Chinese authorities in exchange for himself, but after an interval of six weeks the unhappy gunner was strangled. This act was indeed contrary to the Chinese penal code, for by its provisions the man should have been allowed to ransom himself on a payment of $20.

This case, although it belongs to the last quarter of the century, highlights the disabilities under which foreigners had laboured for the previous sixty years or more. The latter complained of the delay in loading ships, the plunder of goods in transit to Canton, the injurious proclamations annually posted up by the authorities accusing foreigners of horrible crimes, the extortions of underlings of office, and the difficulty of access to the high authorities. The situation had within it most of the seeds of the conflict between China and Britain in the following century.

Indonesia

Jan Pieterzoon Coen is generally accorded the title of Founder of the Dutch empire in the Indies, but this title is better deserved by Nicolas Witsen. Of Coen's work nothing remains except the city of Batavia whose very name has now reverted to that which it bore as a Javanese village (Djkarta). When the commercial prosperity of the Netherlands East India Company had begun to fade, it was due largely to Witsen that it was able, as an agricultural enterprise, relying on tribute rather than profit, to obtain a new lease of life. Sugar and pepper were already grown, and in the first half of the eighteenth century coffee was of less importance than these crops, but it was the introduction of coffee which made large-scale agricultural enterprise a possibility and, in the latter half of the century, it became the chief source of revenue. Van Hoorn had experimented with the growing of coffee sent from India in his own garden, but the plant did not prosper in the foreign soil of Java. It was left for Witsen, the burgomaster of Amsterdam (whose other achievements included the sending of a painter to delineate the ruins of Persepolis, the mapping of Siberia, and advising Peter the Great), to carry this project to fruition. Through his initiative, coffee plants were in 1707 distributed among the district chiefs around Batavia and Cheribon. Unlike Hoorn's plants, these flourished and yielded beans, and four years later the first 100 lb. of coffee was delivered to the Company's warehouses by the Javanese regent of Tjandjur. Nine years after this the annual crop amounted to 100,000 lb. and by 1723 the amount was no less than 12 million lb.

This miracle of production, instead of stimulating the imaginations of the directors of the Netherlands East India Company (the 'Heeren XVII' as they were called), filled them with dismay. In the obsolescent system of the Company's trade, mass production and the selling at low prices in ever-expanding markets (the only policy suitable in the circumstances) could have no place. The reason was that a large-scale expansion of commerce would have necessitated a great increase in the Company's capital. The directors were unprepared for this. They wanted no prodigal output of coffee or other crops; they looked for a limited supply of East India products which they could sell at high prices, and in order to maintain their own monopoly they insisted on a strict control of production. One thing, however, the Company could not control and that was smuggling, and thousands of pounds of coffee found their way to the British settlement of Bencoolen in Sumatra.

The servants of the Company in the Indies understood the position quite well: it was the directors who were unable to take a broad view. Under the system of monopoly the native regents became rich, but the peasants did not. Fearing the power and self-confidence which this new wealth engendered among the Javanese regents, the Company took arbitrary action to control it and to draw off a larger proportion of the profits for its own advantage. It reduced the local price of coffee in Batavia from 50 to 12 *guilders* a *picul*, restricted the plantations, and further to force down the price, the officials at Batavia invented a distinction between a 'mountain *picul*' of 225 lb. and a 'Batavian *picul*' of 125 lb.—the first for weighing the produce on delivery, and second for calculating the payment due upon it—the difference being explained as compensation for loss of weight in drying. The effect of these measures was that coffee planting became hated by the mass of the people and for some years the Company could not even obtain the limited quantity it demanded. Thereupon it required the peasants to deliver the required quantity as tribute, nominally in place of the tribute of rice and other foodstuffs paid to the *Susuhunan* of Mataram whose sovereignty in the Preanger the Company now claimed. Coffee was destined to forge a close alliance of interest between the Dutch rulers and the regents of West Java.

The Company was now, under the influence of this policy, passing from a commercial into a territorial power (though the directors were the last to appreciate the fact). Had it not been for the initiative of Witsen, who had promoted the cultivation of coffee and prepared the way for the complete reorientation of the Company's political and economic system, the Dutch colonial empire might well have come to an end with the dissolution of the Company instead of prolonging its dominion into the middle of the twentieth century.

The tribute system of coffee plantation, while it bore heavily on the Javanese peasant and incurred their rather inarticulate resentment, was not without its incidental benefits. J. S. Furnivall, for example, points out that in the Preanger the people had been so overburdened with exactions from the native princes in the form of the tribute of rice and other food-stuffs that they had never really settled down and had continued to move from one mountain valley to another in the hope of shirking the tribute. They were thus semi-nomads engaged in wasteful agriculture, moving from place to place as the soil in their jungle clearings became exhausted. This hindered progress in welfare and civilisation. The coffee plantations tied the peasant down to permanent settlements in which they grew their rice on *sawah*, or wet-rice, plantations.

Dutch power had virtually been established all over the archipelago by about 1680 and most of the native chiefs were henceforth under obligation to dispose of their exports exclusively to the Dutch Company. Mataram had practically lost its independence, while Bantam continued to enjoy comparative immunity from Dutch interference for only a few years longer. These principalities, however, disintegrated rather from internal weakness than from any direct impact with outer forces. The Preanger districts had come under Dutch control in 1677 and Cheribon soon after. During the eighteenth century political control was extended slowly, and it was not until 1743 that the coastal districts of Java came under the Dutch. During the whole of the period under review and for long afterwards the Netherlands empire in Indonesia meant for most practical purposes Java alone.

Intermediate between the Dutch and the Javanese people were the Chinese. They were the retailers, the farmers of taxes, the money-lenders, and the general middlemen, as well as being the principal artisans of the country. They were, in spite of waves of suspicion engendered against them, regarded on the whole as quiet and industrious inhabitants and were favoured to some extent above the natives. Their numbers, however, were ever increasing and this fact led the Dutch to regard their presence with increasing apprehension. By 1740 there were estimated to be about 80,000 of them in Java. This was the result of a sudden great increase in clandestine immigration which the Dutch had failed to check. There was unemployment among them, and the Dutch decided to send as slaves to Ceylon any Chinese who could not prove that they were making an honest livelihood. This action brought to a head the rising discontent among the Chinese due to oppression by the Dutch police, and resulted in a rebellion followed by a massacre. The Government seems to have lost its head, and since it was unable to bring the situation under control, there ensued promiscuous slaughter in which over 10,000 Chinese were killed. Tem-minck, a Dutch authority on Java in the early nineteenth century, remarks, 'The impartial historian will agree with van Hoevell that this catastrophe must be imputed only to the ineptitude, the negligence, and the arbitrariness of the Governors-General who were invested with the power from 1725 to 1740, and without whose administration the elements of revolt would never have been formed.'[1]

After the rebellion (if it can fairly be so called) had been suppressed and the situation had become quiet again, the Chinese resumed and extended their operations as middlemen. Their numbers were soon made up again by further illicit immigration. The sugar industry, however, had been practically ruined during the troubles.

One of the principal causes of the Chinese penetration in Java was the farming out to them by the Dutch of the right to levy taxes. The method, however, above all others, by which the Chinese increased their hold over the people and the land was to obtain the lease of large territories (entire villages or districts) from the native rulers. The native princes and chiefs, on behalf of the entire population of the leased districts, contracted to deliver stated quantities of produce, to provide labour, and to pay land rent to the lessee either in money or in kind. The lessee usually maintained control as a kind of feudal lord. The system was responsible to a great extent for the disrepute in which the Chinese were held by the natives. By 1786 discontent had grown so strong that the people begged the Government of Batavia to depose the sultans and to establish direct Dutch rule over the whole territory. They believed that this would protect them from the extortions of the Chinese. But this request was refused.

Throughout the whole of this period the Dutch East India Company was in a state of decay. The reasons for this were to be found primarily in the bad administration of the Company in Holland, which gave rise to corruption and other abuses in the Indies. Yet of the many plans for reform submitted to the Board of Directors during the eighteenth century, not a single one touched on the main difficulty—the necessity of far-reaching reform in Amsterdam. The directors pursued a policy of parsi-mony with regard to their servants for which the latter compensated themselves by the acceptance of illegal gratifications, and they lived either in penury or in extreme affluence according to their opportunities, or lack of them, to obtain money by this means. Hence a governor-general receiving 700 *guilders* a month could bring home a fortune of 10 million *guilders*, whereas Zwaardecroon, the governor-general at the beginning of the eighteenth century, executed twenty-six lesser officials for trans-gressing the laws of the Company. Again, in 1731, the directors, in a sudden new drive against corruption, were successful for a while in

[1] This summing up is confirmed by a modern authority on the revolt, Johannes Theodorus Vermeulen, in *De Chineezen te Batavia en de Troebelen van 1740* (Leiden, 1938).

putting a stop to smuggling, but at the same time they deprived hundreds of Batavians of their main source of income. Owing to the maladministration of which the above-mentioned examples were symptomatic, the Company had been declining since 1693 when the net profit to date had been £48·3 million, and by 1724–5 operations showed a net loss. By 1779 this loss amounted to £84·9 million. These facts, however, were not discovered until the accounts were slowly unravelled at a later date; in the meantime no one knew the exact position. From the beginning the system of accountancy had been defective (Jan Pieterzoon Coen himself had introduced it, and it was never altered until the end of the Company); books were kept both in Java and in Europe, but the two sets were never compared or balanced. Yet towards the end of the century the Company was outwardly as prosperous as ever though inwardly it was rotten. Money was borrowed at high interest to pay the dividends to the share-holders and over the whole period of the Company's rule from 1602 to 1800 these dividends were maintained at an average rate of 18 per cent. The bankruptcy of the Dutch East India Company, however, belongs to a period long after the one here described.

The Philippines

When the Spanish colonised the Philippines, the native peoples were living in *barrios*, or villages, under a loose but fairly well crystallised form of government, the unit of which was a group of 150 families (*barangay*), and society was divided into serfs, freemen, and nobles. The Spanish erected their government on this native foundation, and created a system of administration which lasted until the Americans came in 1898, and which 'in its rigid centralisation set the style for the Commonwealth and the Republic that followed'.[1] The land system and the Church also bear the indelible marks of the stamp of Spain.

When the Spanish discovered that there was no wealth to be had in gold or spices, they turned to the possibilities of trade. They hoped to make Manila the emporium of the East, and cargoes of tea from Ceylon, teak from Siam, velvets, silks and brocades from China, and spieces from Indonesia were discharged in the port and piled in the warehouses to be loaded on the Annual Galleon for Mexico.

Because of the nature of the Philippines trade, the history of the economic relations of the islands in the eighteenth century turns greatly on the relations of the colonial power with the Chinese. The question as to whether the Chinese were a blessing or a menace to the Philippines had agitated the Spaniards throughout the seventeenth century, and the consensus of opinion was that they were the latter. What the critics of the

[1] Claude A. Buss, 'The Philippines', in Lennox Mills and associates, *The New World of Southeast Asia* (Minneapolis, University of Minnesota Press, 1949), p. 22.

Chinese particularly disliked was the silk trade. As far back as 1628 it had been argued that it was pernicious to allow the importation of the silk of China, both to the Indies and to Mexico, for although not more than 250,000 Mexican *pesos* or pieces of eight might be taken from Mexico to the Philippines annually, an incalculable sum was exported in addition. The Chinese would accept no other currency, nor would they exchange their silk for other merchandise. Consequently, they managed to carry away annually the greater part of these eight-*real* pieces that were coined in New Spain in exchange for 'grass, which is the substance of that coarse and hard silk which is so plentiful among the Chinese'.[1] 'Thus they weaken our strength and increase their own; and consequently, they can make war on us whenever they wish, without any cost to them as far as we are concerned.'[2]

The controversy continued into the eighteenth century. The people of Seville urged severe restrictions on the Manila-Acapulco trade on the ground that the wealth of Mexico was being drained off by the Chinese. In consequence of this agitation, the king, in 1718, decreed that the trade in Chinese silk goods be thenceforth prohibited. But the following year the viceroy of Mexico, de Valero, remonstrated against this prohibition on behalf not only of the Filipinos, but also of his own subjects, most of whom were too poor to purchase Spanish piece-goods from which to manufacture the clothes they wore, and who therefore depended on Chinese materials. Memorials issued from Manila and Cadiz respectively, each endeavouring to justify its own side in the controversy. At one stage Cadiz offered Manila the spice trade of Mexico as the equivalent of the latter's traffic in Chinese textiles. A decree of 27 October 1720 addressed to the marquis de Valero, viceroy of Mexico, laid down that two ships only should go annually from the Philippine Islands to Nueva España (Mexico), each of 500 *toneladas*. The value of the lading which the said ships were to carry to the port of Acapulco might be up to the amount of 300,000 *pesos* which must come invested strictly and solely in the following kinds of merchandise: gold, cinnamon, elephants, wax, porcelain, cloves, pepper, cambayas, and linens woven with colours (*lienzos pintados*), chitas, chintzes, gauzes, lampotes, Hilicos blankets, silk floss and raw spun, cordage, and like commodities. These ships were prohibited from carrying silken fabrics. Manila protested against the injury done to the islands by the decree, and eventually, on 8 April 1734, a new decree was promulgated increasing the amount of the trade permitted to Manila to 500,000 *pesos* of investment and 1 million in return.

---

[1] The reference (say Blair and Robertson) is probably to a plant called 'China grass' (*Boeheria nivea*), a shrub indigenous to India.

[2] Juan Velasquez Madr^{co}, *Economic Reasons for Suppressing the Silk Trade of China in Spain and its Colonies* (7 October 1628) in Blair and Robertson, *The Philippine Islands* (Cleveland, Ohio, 1903–12), vol. XXII, p. 279.

In the long run Manila interests had triumphed over those of Cadiz and Seville. Meanwhile, in 1709, many Chinese had been banished from Manila on the charge of carrying off the public wealth, and prosecutions of this kind led to their settling in smaller places in Luzon during the eighteenth century. In 1747 a royal order was received for the final expulsion of the Chinese, but its execution was suspended.

Spain was involved with England in the 'War of Jenkins' Ear' (1739–48) and again in the Seven Years War (1756–63). In the former the celebrated Lord Anson appeared in these waters in his circumnavigation of the globe and captured the Mexico-Manila treasure ship. His chaplain, Richard Walter, who became the historian of the voyage, remarks that the silks coming directly to Acapulco could be sold there considerably cheaper than any European commodities of equal goodness, and, he adds, 'the cotton from the Coromandel coast makes the European linens useless'.[1]

When a new archbishop of Manila, Don Fray de la Santissima Trinidad (Pedro Martinez de Arizala), arrived in the Philippines on 27 August 1747 he brought with him a decree expelling the Chinese from the islands. There had already been an order of expulsion, but this had not been executed owing to the personal interests of the governors, and for reasons of expedience the new decree was also held in suspense. In 1755 Governor Arandia received a new order from the king for the expulsion of the Chinese, excepting 5115 Christian Chinese and a thousand more 'who pretended to be studying Christian doctrine'. The Christian Chinese could remain so long as they confined themselves to agriculture, but actually most of them carried on trading notwithstanding.

A few years after this, when Spain was again involved in war in Europe, the English captured Manila in 1762 and held it for two years. At the time of the capture the Chinese who still remained in the Philippines took sides with the English, whereupon Simon de Anda, the lieutenant-governor, ordered that all Chinese in the islands should be hanged. This order was to a limited extent carried into effect in 1763. In the same year 6000 Chinese are said to have been massacred by the Spanish in Pangasinan for siding with the Filipinos in a conspiracy to oust the Spanish regime. In 1766 the survivors were rounded up and in 1769 the order for expulsion was as far as possible put into effect. Yet soon after Le Gentil is saying, 'I do not know any Spaniards who did not sincerely regret the departure of the Chinese, and who do not frankly admit that the Philippines would suffer for it, because the Indians were not capable of replacing the Chinese' (this was an echo of de Morga's lament after the massacre of the Chinese in 1603). In 1778 the order for the expulsion was revoked, but only Chinese workmen were encouraged as immigrants. A further decree

[1] Richard A. Walter, *A Voyage Round the World in the Years 1740–44 by Lord Anson*, 3rd ed. (London, Dent (Everyman's Library), 1930), p. 220.

of 1766 ordered that all Catholic Chinese who had committed excesses during the time when the British occupied Manila should be expelled from the Philippines, only true Christians being allowed to remain.

The order of expulsion of the Chinese was revoked in 1788.

While the trade of the Philippines was following the above pattern, land economy was shaped by the Spanish system of feudal tenure. All the land in the Philippines was in the king's name and he assigned huge estates to the nobles and the friars. The landlord might receive an estate of 25,000 acres with a thousand families in *encomienda* as serfs. He was the collector of rates and taxes, he paid wages according to his own notions of labour value, he was the judge of disputes among his vassals, and he had the virtual power of life and death over them subject only to his own conscience, the avaricious inspectors of the governor-general, and the prying eyes of the priest, who insisted upon the tithe to which the Church was entitled. The friars who had accompanied the explorers—Augustinians, Franciscans, Jesuits, Dominicans, Benedictines, and others—had also been given large land grants for their religious undertakings. The land system was modified, but not abolished, by the Americans and survived under the republic as a root cause of agrarian discontent.

INDEX

Abdali. *See* Ahmad Shah Durrani

Abercrombie, James, commander-in-chief in America, 538

Åbo, Sweden, 359, 360

Åbo, Treaty of (1743), 360–1

Acadia, 512, 529–30, 533–4
  deportation of inhabitants (1749), 534

Accaiuoli, papal nuncio in Portugal, 124

Aché, de, French naval commander, 563

Adam, Robert, architect, 69, 83

Adams, Samuel, senior, 507

Addison, Joseph, writer, 71–2, 80, 98

Administrative institutions and machinery, systems of:
  in Sweden, 144–5, 352–4
  in Russia, 145, 323–5
  in France, 145–6, 153–4, 215–21
  in Britain, 146, 160–2, 256–65
  in Spain, 147–8, 154–5, 487–8, 489
  in Prussia, 148–9, 155, 298–300, 303–5, 312–14
  in Austria, 149, 155–7, 399–400, 410–14
  in Hungary, 157, 391, 396–7
  in Brandenburg, 158–9, 294
  in Poland, 160, 365–8, 372–3
  in Portugal, 289–90
  in Denmark, 341–2
  in North America: British, 510–11; French, 513
  in the Mogul Empire, 542–4
  in the Maratha territories, 546
  see also Cameralists of the bureaus; Civil service; Justice, administration of; Taxation

Adolphus Frederick, king of Sweden, 16, 348–9, 352, 360–2

Afghanistan, 553–4, 563–4

Africa
  slave trade, 24–5; regions, 566–7; techniques and units of exchange, 567; trade controlled by national companies, 568; Prussian and Danish slavers, 568–9; Portuguese, 569–70; Dutch, 570; French, 570–1; British, 571–2; fierce competition and rising costs, 573; profit margin, 573–4; effect on African society, 575–6
  Portuguese territories, 25, 569–70, 574, 578–9
  European penetration limited, 574–5

Dutch settlements in South Africa, 576–7, 578; impact of pioneers on the Bantu, 577
  contrast between West and East Africa, 577–8

Africa Company, 344

Agriculture
  condition of labourers, 52–3
  botanical studies applied to, 90
  improved methods, 244–5, 267
  in England, 52–3, 243
  in Spain, 270, 271
  in Prussia, 293, 314–15; effects of the Seven Years War on, 484–5
  in Russia, 318
  in Denmark and Norway, 342–4
  in Sweden, 357–8
  in Poland, 368
  in Hungary, 406
  in the Jesuit missions in America, 497

Aguesseau, Henri de, chancellor of France, 225

Ahmad Shah, Mogul emperor, 559

Ahmad Shah Durrani, Afghan ruler, 24, 554, 559, 563–4

Aiguillon, Armand, duc de, governor of Brittany, 234

Aix-la-Chapelle, Treaty of (1748), 19, 23, 24, 210–11, 283, 410, 436–9, 520–1, 559

Ajit Singh, ruler of Jodhpur, 544

Akbar, Mogul emperor, 541–3

Åland Islands, 197, 198, 359

Albany, Dutch settlement in North America, 532

Albemarle, George Keppel, earl of, admiral, 522, 524–5

Alberoni, Giulio, Cardinal, Spanish statesman, 195, 197, 198, 278–9
  reforms, administrative, fiscal, naval, 277

Aleksey, son of Peter the Great, 326

Alembert, Jean le Rond d', philosopher and mathematician, 80, 89, 95, 309

Alfieri, Vittorio, poet, 282

Ali Khan, nawab of the Carnatic, 556–7

Ali Muhammad Khan, Rohilla leader, 553

Ali Vardi Khan, nawab of Bengal, 553, 554–6

Alliances, reversal of. *See* Diplomatic Revolution

Alva, duke of (quoted), 163

America, North
  Anglo-French colonial and commercial rivalry, 21–2, 512–13